D1535306

READINGS IN

BUSINESS CYCLES

Selected by a Committee of

THE AMERICAN ECONOMIC ASSOCIATION

1965

Published for the Association by

RICHARD D. IRWIN, INC.

HOMEWOOD, ILLINOIS

First Printing, May, 1965
Second Printing, November, 1966
Third Printing, January, 1969
Fourth Printing, July, 1969

PRINTED IN THE UNITED STATES OF AMERICA
Library of Congress Catalog Card No. 65–12418

Preface

Some twenty years ago, the second volume to appear in the American Economic Association's series of republished articles bore the title, *Readings in Business Cycle Theory.* The present volume, therefore, is the second collection of reprints in the business cycle field to appear in this series. As its title suggests, the first volume confined itself to business cycle theory. The title of this new compilation, *Readings in Business Cycles,* suggests the broader terms of reference that have guided the selection of articles for the present volume.

It is probably fair to say that two interrelated developments have strongly conditioned research in business cycles since the volume of readings edited by Gottfried Haberler appeared in 1944. One is the reformulation of business cycle theory in mathematical terms and the resulting proliferation of dynamic models which generate fluctuations or steady growth or some combination of instability and growth. The other development has to do with the application of econometric techniques to empirical research. Such econometric work has taken the form both of simultaneous estimation of complete models and the study of particular variables such as consumption, investment, or the level of wages. In part, these econometric studies have been put forward as critical tests of business cycle theories, and, in part, they have been carried out in a positive spirit to try to establish workable models of the economy.

The present collection of readings reflects this growing emphasis on mathematical formulation and econometric treatment. At the same time, the editors have sought to offer a fair sampling of work in the field that does not rest on mathematical treatment and elaborate regression analysis. We have not done as well in this respect as would otherwise have been possible because of one rule that we imposed on ourselves at the beginning—to exclude journal articles which had already been reprinted in another volume of the A.E.A. series or in other books of collected readings that are readily available.[1] Several excellent papers had to be excluded for this reason. We have, however, felt free to reprint papers which originally appeared as parts of books, particularly if the latter did not have a wide circulation.

There is yet another restriction that we imposed on our selections at the outset. We decided not to extend our coverage to include dynamic economics in general. More specifically, we decided to exclude the subject of economic growth. This does not reflect any valuation on our part of the relative importance of cycle and growth analysis, and it does not mean that we regard the

---

[1] Only when this volume was ready for the printer did we discover that two of the papers selected had been reprinted in other volumes. We have chosen to stand by our final selection, despite the modest inconsistency thus involved.

study of growth to be irrelevant to the study of cycles. We have included papers that consider both cyclical and growth phenomena; but, to be selected, a paper had to deal with problems of the cycle in addition to those of trends. Economic growth is, of course, a subject of the utmost importance, and it has commanded much scholarly attention that in former times might have been addressed to cyclical analysis. The subject of growth is now so important in its own right and has been the subject of so many recent investigations that it deserves a volume of readings of its own.

Moreover, we feel that cycles are still with us. They may appear to be different from the cycles before World War II, more so in some countries than in others, and stabilization policies may be more effective as a result of our improved understanding of the factors making for economic instability. But the (more or less) market economies of the postwar world are still subject to some measure of cumulative short-run instability. The subject of business cycles, therefore, remains an important subject, with its own large literature that is sampled in this volume.

With two exceptions, the present volume confines itself to the period since the end of World War II, when the first volume of business cycle readings appeared. These exceptions are Ragnar Frisch's famous essay, published in 1933 in the volume in honor of Gustav Cassel, and Lloyd Metzler's basic article on inventory cycles. Both, we felt, should be brought to the attention of students again.

There is one respect in which this volume breaks a precedent. It does not contain a detailed bibliography, as did previous books of readings in this series. With the recent publication of the comprehensive *Index of Economic Journals* by the American Economic Association, such a bibliography no longer seemed necessary. "Economic Fluctuations and Stabilization Policy" is one of the main headings in the new *Index*. Partly to compensate for the absence of a classified bibliography within the same covers as the papers reprinted here, we have prepared a brief introduction to each section broadly describing the body of literature from which each group of papers has been selected.

We should like to take this opportunity to thank the many economists who responded to our requests for suggestions. We also want to express our appreciation to Messrs. Ralph Abascal and C. S. Raman for their patience and help in preparing the manuscript for the printer.

May, 1965   R. A. GORDON
                                                            L. R. KLEIN

Table of Contents

I. THEORY

READING   PAGE

1. INTRODUCTION 3

2. A MODEL OF CYCLICAL GROWTH 6
   By R. M. GOODWIN
   From *The Business Cycle in the Post-War World*

3. MR. HARROD'S DYNAMIC THEORY 23
   By J. R. HICKS
   From *Economica*, 1949

4. ECONOMIC FLUCTUATIONS AND GROWTH 39
   By ARTHUR SMITHIES
   From *Econometrica*, 1957

5. A LINEAR MODEL OF CYCLICAL GROWTH 79
   By HYMAN P. MINSKY
   From *The Review of Economics and Statistics*, 1959

6. THE NATURE AND STABILITY OF INVENTORY CYCLES 100
   By LLOYD A. METZLER
   From *The Review of Economic Statistics*, 1941

7. MONETARY AND REAL FACTORS AFFECTING ECONOMIC STABILITY:
   A CRITIQUE OF CERTAIN TENDENCIES IN MODERN ECONOMIC
   THEORY 130
   By GOTTFRIED HABERLER
   From *Banca Nazionale del Lavoro Quarterly Review*, 1956

II. METHODOLOGY

8. INTRODUCTION 153

9. PROPAGATION PROBLEMS AND IMPULSE PROBLEMS IN DYNAMIC
   ECONOMICS 155
   By RAGNAR FRISCH
   From *Economic Essays in Honor of Gustav Cassel*, 1933

10. MEASUREMENT WITHOUT THEORY 186
    By TJALLING C. KOOPMANS
    From *The Review of Economic Statistics*, 1947

11. KOOPMANS ON THE CHOICE OF VARIABLES TO BE STUDIED AND
    OF METHODS OF MEASUREMENT 204
    By RUTLEDGE VINING
    From *The Review of Economics and Statistics*, 1949

READING   PAGE

12. A REPLY 218
      By TJALLING C. KOOPMANS
      From *The Review of Economics and Statistics*, 1949

13. A REJOINDER 226
      By RUTLEDGE VINING
      From *The Review of Economics and Statistics*, 1949

III. ECONOMETRIC MODELS

14. INTRODUCTION 235

15. A SIMULATION OF THE UNITED STATES ECONOMY IN
    RECESSION 237
      By JAMES S. DUESENBERRY, OTTO ECKSTEIN, and GARY FROMM
      From *Econometrica*, 1960

16. THE DYNAMIC PROPERTIES OF THE KLEIN-GOLDBERGER MODEL . . 278
      By IRMA ADELMAN and FRANK L. ADELMAN
      From *Econometrica*, 1959

17. AGGREGATE ECONOMETRIC MODELS 307
      By CARL F. CHRIST
      From *American Economic Review*, 1956

IV. STUDIES OF PARTICULAR VARIABLES

18. INTRODUCTION 337

19. PRIVATE INVESTMENT IN THE ELECTRIC POWER INDUSTRY
    AND THE ACCELERATION PRINCIPLE 340
      By AVRAM KISSELGOFF and FRANCO MODIGLIANI
      From *The Review of Economics and Statistics*, 1957

20. CAPITAL THEORY AND INVESTMENT BEHAVIOR 367
      By DALE W. JORGENSON
      From *American Economic Review: Papers and
      Proceedings*, 1963

21. THE NEW THEORIES OF THE CONSUMPTION FUNCTION 380
      By M. J. FARRELL
      From *Economic Journal*, 1959

22. THE "LIFE CYCLE" HYPOTHESIS OF SAVING: AGGREGATE
    IMPLICATIONS AND TESTS 399
      By ALBERT ANDO and FRANCO MODIGLIANI
      From *American Economic Review*, 1963

23. THE DEMAND FOR MONEY: SOME THEORETICAL AND EMPIRICAL
    RESULTS 428
      By MILTON FRIEDMAN
      From *Journal of Political Economy*, 1959

READING   PAGE

24. THE RELATION BETWEEN UNEMPLOYMENT AND THE RATE
    OF CHANGE OF MONEY WAGE RATES IN THE UNITED
    KINGDOM, 1862–1957 457
        By RICHARD G. LIPSEY
        From *Economica*, 1960

25. TESTED KNOWLEDGE OF BUSINESS CYCLES 489
        By GEOFFREY H. MOORE
        From National Bureau of Economic Research, Inc.,
        Forty-Second Annual Report, 1962

V. LONG CYCLES

26. INTRODUCTION 517

27. THE NATURE AND SIGNIFICANCE OF KUZNETS CYCLES 519
        By MOSES ABRAMOVITZ
        From *Economic Development and Cultural Change*, 1961

28. SECULAR SWINGS IN PRODUCTION AND TRADE, 1870–1913 546
        By P. J. O'LEARY and W. ARTHUR LEWIS
        From *The Manchester School*, 1955

VI. INTERNATIONAL ASPECTS

29. INTRODUCTION 575

30. ECONOMIC INSTABILITY IN AN INTERNATIONAL SETTING 576
        By JACQUES J. POLAK and RUDOLF R. RHOMBERG
        From *American Economic Review*, 1962

VII. FORECASTING

31. INTRODUCTION 595

32. FORECASTING AND ANALYSIS WITH AN ECONOMETRIC MODEL . . . 597
        By DANIEL B. SUITS
        From *American Economic Review*, 1962

33. RATE OF CHANGE APPROACHES TO FORECASTING—DIFFUSION INDEXES
    AND FIRST DIFFERENCES 626
        By SIDNEY S. ALEXANDER
        From *Economic Journal*, 1958

34. A SURVEY OF STUDIES IN THE ANALYSIS OF BUSINESS TEST DATA . . 641
        By H. THEIL and D. B. JOCHEMS
        From *IFO-Studien: Zeitschrift des Ifo-Instituts für
        Wirtschaftsforschung*, 1960

VIII. POLICY

35. INTRODUCTION 663

READING   PAGE

36. STABILISATION POLICY AND THE TIME-FORMS OF LAGGED
    RESPONSES 666
        By A. W. PHILLIPS
        From *Economic Journal,* 1957

37. TAXES, INCOME DETERMINATION, AND THE BALANCED
    BUDGET THEOREM 680
        By WILLIAM A. SALANT
        From *The Review of Economics and Statistics,* 1957

38. CED'S STABILIZING BUDGET POLICY AFTER TEN YEARS 696
        By WALTER W. HELLER
        From *American Economic Review,* 1957

39. MONETARY POLICY AND ITS CRITICS 713
        By JAMES R. SCHLESINGER
        From *Journal of Political Economy,* 1960

I. THEORY

1

Introduction

THERE HAVE been two main lines of theoretical development on the subject
of business cycles in recent years. On the one hand, there has been research
on nonlinear models and, on the other, there has been an attempted integration of cyclical and growth processes. Both approaches have been followed to
a large extent through the medium of mathematical models, and this is
surely the natural tool for the former approach.

Theorists have been seeking an explanation of *maintained* economic cycles,
that is, periodic swings that neither explode nor expire. Linear models,
except in very special cases, are not capable of doing this without the support
of external shocks. As early as 1940, Nicholas Kaldor developed a nonlinear
model that was capable of producing a "limit cycle."[1] An elegant mathematical formulation of the Kaldor model with incisive appraisals of the whole
field of nonlinear oscillations is given in a paper by Shinichi Ichimura.[2] One
important earlier theory of maintained oscillations was contained in Michal
Kalecki's model of the trade cycle, but nonlinearity was not the essence of his
approach.[3] The papers by Kaldor, Ichimura, and Kalecki have all been reproduced in other collections of essays or in books that are generally available,
and we did not include them in the present volume. The two representative
nonlinear models of recent origin included here are those of Richard Goodwin
and John Hicks. Goodwin's theory is presented directly in the paper reprinted
here, which builds on his earlier work. The paper by Hicks is a first draft of
the theory which he subsequently presented in *The Trade Cycle* and shows
how his formulation developed out of Harrod's theory of growth.

---

[1] N. Kaldor, "A Model of the Trade Cycle," *Economic Journal*, Vol. L (March, 1940),
pp. 78–92.

[2] S. Ichimura, "Toward a General Nonlinear Macrodynamic Theory of Economic
Fluctuations," in K. Kurihara (ed.), *Post Keynesian Economics* (New Brunswick: Rutgers
University Press, 1954), pp. 192–226.

[3] M. Kalecki, "A Macrodynamic Theory of Business Cycles," *Econometrica*, Vol. III
(1935), pp. 327–44.

Harrod's growth theory,[4] like that of Evsey Domar,[5] is excluded from explicit consideration in itself because we have decided to deal only with papers that have some business cycle content. The Harrod-Domar growth theories have inspired various extensions of multiplier-accelerator mechanisms that are capable of explaining both trend and cycles and do not merely take the trend as given. The paper by Arthur Smithies is a good illustration of a recent model in which heavy reliance is placed on ratchet effects and in which investment is made to depend on a flexible variant of the capital-stock adjustment process. In a different direction, Minsky elaborates upon the Hicksian model by exploring the implications, imposed by floors and ceilings, of changes in initial conditions, a topic which was also explored by Matthews at about the same time.[6]

Although Lloyd Metzler's paper is in the Keynesian vein and is a dynamic generalization of ideas that were being discussed just prior to World War II, it is now a classic contribution that is highly relevant to problems of today.[7] The subsequent contributions of Nurkse should also be mentioned.[8] Inventory movements have always been important in business cycles, but they have been of greater relative importance in the last two decades, for postwar cycles have generally been shorter than the textbook norm of 8–10 years and have had strong inventory components. Much practical research on inventory fluctuations is still based on Metzler's original contribution.

Most of the new theorizing on business cycles has emphasized real factors, and money is treated only secondarily, or, indeed, not at all. Monetary factors played a larger role in earlier theories of the cycle, and Gottfried Haberler properly reminds us in his essay to take appropriate account of monetary factors and of price and wage rigidities.

Haberler's judicious essay and his observation that "there can be hardly a doubt any more that so far the results of mathematical model-building] have been most disappointing" lead us to offer an additional comment. Except for Haberler's paper, the contributions in this section are all concerned with formal model building. This has been the dominant trend in the recent

---

[4] R. F. Harrod, "An Essay in Dynamic Theory," *Economic Journal*, Vol. IL (March, 1939), pp. 14–33, and *Towards a Dynamic Economics* (London: Macmillan, 1948).

[5] E. Domar, "Capital Expansion, Rate of Growth, and Employment," *Econometrica*, Vol. XIV (April, 1946), pp. 137–47, and "Expansion and Employment," *American Economic Review*, Vol. XXXVII (March, 1947), pp. 34–55. Both are reprinted in his *Essays in the Theory of Economic Growth* (New York: Oxford University Press, 1957).

[6] R. C. O. Matthews, "A Note on Crawling along the Ceiling," *Review of Economic Studies*, Vol. XXVII (October, 1959), pp. 10–15.

[7] See also his later papers: "Business Cycles and the Modern Theory of Employment," *American Economic Review*, Vol. XXXVI (June, 1946), pp. 278–91, and "Factors Governing the Length of Inventory Cycles," *Review of Economic Statistics*, Vol. XXIX (February, 1947), pp. 1–15.

[8] R. Nurkse, "Period Analysis and Inventory Cycles," *Oxford Economic Papers*, n.s., Vol. VI (September, 1954), pp. 203–25, and "The Cyclical Pattern of Inventory Investment," *Quarterly Journal of Economics*, Vol. LXVI (August, 1952), pp. 385–408.

literature. Nonmathematical formulations in the journal literature have been relatively few, and a number of the better ones have already been reprinted. One might cite several thoughtful review essays inspired by Hicks' *The Trade Cycle* and a few articles dealing with the instability of investment and the notion of changing investment opportunities.[9]

---

[9] See, for example, the following: A. F. Burns, "Hicks and the Real Cycle," *Journal of Political Economy*, Vol. LX (February, 1952), pp. 1-24; James Duesenberry, "Hicks on the Trade Cycle," *Quarterly Journal of Economics*, Vol. LXIV (August, 1950), pp. 464-76; Sidney Alexander, "Issues of Business Cycle Theory," *American Economic Review*, Vol. XLI (December, 1951), pp. 861-78; Nicholas Kaldor, "The Relation of Economic Growth and Cyclical Fluctuations," *Economic Journal*, Vol. LXIV (March, 1954), pp. 53-71; R. A. Gordon, "Investment Behavior and Business Cycles," *Review of Economics and Statistics*, Vol. XXXVII (February, 1955), pp. 23-34; A. D. Knox, "The Acceleration Principle and the Theory of Investment," *Economica*, n.s., Vol. XIX (August, 1952), pp. 269-97.

2

A Model of Cyclical Growth*

By R. M. GOODWIN†

I. INTER-RELATIONS OF GROWTH AND CYCLE

MY PRIMARY concern in this paper is with the simultaneous existence and mutual conditioning of economic growth and economic cycles. It is clearly desirable to have one theory that encompasses both or, at least, to have a more intimate union of the two analyses than is ordinarily effected. It may be argued that this is too ambitious an aim and, in the light of the difficulties that I have encountered, I am inclined to agree. It is better to isolate problems and attack them one by one. Yet, in this particular case, I feel that there are strong reasons to doubt the soundness of analysing on the one hand steady development and on the other stationary cycles. It may well be that many of the serious difficulties of each, considered separately, will yield to a combined attack. But to achieve an advance in this direction we must pay a price, and the price is the abandonment of all but the crudest elements of economic theory.

We all know of the nature and problems of the decomposition of time series into trend, cycles and residuals. The great pioneer work in this field has improved our understanding and has been crucial in establishing the existence of a "cycle" problem. At the same time, however, there is a danger that the "removal" of trend will give us a false picture of reality. Worse still, in terms of some of the models developed by Kalecki, Kaldor, Tinbergen, Hicks and myself, it is definitely not permissible. In the case of a linear system, by virtue of what is known as the superposition theorem, we may analyse all sorts of motions, *e.g.* trends, cycles, impulses, steady levels, etc., one at a time, and simply add the results to get the correct total behaviour. Or conversely we may "decompose," by spectrum analysis or any other method, the observed behaviour into its independent parts. For a non-linear system the theorem does not hold, and decomposition is invalid, how invalid depending, of course,

* Erik Lundberg (ed.), *The Business Cycle in the Post-War World* (London: Macmillan & Co., Ltd., 1955). Reprinted by courtesy of the International Economic Association, the editor, and the author.
† Peterhouse, University of Cambridge.

on the structure of the system. It remains to be established empirically that there are important non-linearities in the economy, but, for the time being, we must, I think, regard with grave misgiving the removal of trend, since this might remove much of the real problem.

The issue has been stated clearly by Mr. Harrod in his two articles in the *Economic Journal*[1] and in his *Dynamic Economics*.[2] He holds that the same theory must explain both growth and cycle, but it is, I think, fair to say that few have been convinced that he has provided such a theory. As Professor Tinbergen remarked in his review of Harrod's *Trade Cycle*[3] the multiplier-accelerator combination, considered simply, gives rise to an exponential trend, not a cycle. In effect, Mr. Harrod seems to have felt this too, for he has not, since then, attempted an explicit cycle theory. In Professor Hicks's *Trade Cycle*,[4] we see how difficult is the problem, for in elaborating the Harrod theory into a cycle model he loses the theory of the trend in all but a trivial sense. Professor Hicks gets a trend by putting in an exponential autonomous investment, but this trend is unrelated to required capital or indeed to anything except the necessity to get a trend. It is true that this meets Mr. Harrod's strictures against the models of the type of Kalecki or Hansen-Samuelson, but these can always be transformed into oscillations about a trend, by inserting a trend as a function of time. And this separation of trend and cycle is justified *if* reality is approximately linear. One should add, however, that the trend is not really explained if we merely apply a rising trend factor to our model. Evidently it is more difficult than Mr. Harrod concedes to construct a single theory which will explain both.

II. SCHUMPETER'S THEORY OF GROWTH AND CYCLE

In order to fuse growth and cycle unalterably we may make the following two assumptions: (*a*) economic progress is not steady but comes in spurts, these spurts occurring primarily in the booms; (*b*) the cycle is not a case of over- and under-shooting of a stationary level, but rather it is dominated by— and possibly would not exist without—economic growth. The source of these two assumptions is Schumpeter and, in my opinion, it is in his work that we shall find the most fruitful ideas for the analysis of the problem of trend and cycle. He was surely correct in saying that *the* essential element in the theory must be the occurrence of revolutionary advances in technique. It is not that Schumpeter is the only one to hold these views—one has only to think of Wicksell or Professor Robertson amongst others—but he has the most fully developed and integrated theory, and it is with his way of thinking that I am

---

[1] R. F. Harrod, "An Essay in Dynamic Theory," *Economic Journal*, 1939, and "Notes on Trade Cycle Theory," *ibid.*, 1951.
[2] *Towards a Dynamic Economics*, London, 1948.
[3] *Weltwirtschaftliches Archiv*, 1937.
[4] J. R. Hicks, *A Contribution to the Theory of the Trade Cycle*, Oxford, 1950.

most familiar. Also basic, but not quite so fundamental, is growth in the labour force. By itself, population increase will not suffice, as is amply illustrated, *e.g.* in Ireland or China, but in conjunction with (and in some very complex way caused by) technical improvement it is a powerful driving force.

Schumpeter's theory, as he often complained, is difficult to formulate in simple mathematical terms. Therefore such use as I shall make of it may seem rather a caricature, and definitely requires supplementing by reference to his own exposition and rich illustration of it. Beyond this I cannot follow him in his rejection of the Keynesian effective demand analysis. There seems no obvious reason why this important tool should not be used to strengthen his system, though he always rejected its assistance in forcible terms. By incorporating effective demand it is possible to lessen the excessive strain that is put on his special theory of the innovational process. Essentially he places *the* explanation of the cycle on the internal dynamics of successful innovation, subsequent imitation and consequent exhaustion of the new combinations. It may sometimes be so, but that it has always been so over more than one hundred and fifty years is difficult to accept. If, on the contrary, we emphasize the mutual conditioning of innovating and the state of trade, it becomes relatively plausible, indeed almost inevitable, that innovations will be carried. out in swarms.

Schumpeter's original, pure theory can be put simply: "The recurring periods of prosperity of the cyclical movement are the form progress takes in capitalist society."[5] Throughout his many vagaries in elaborating this schema in historical, statistical and theoretical directions he never abandoned this central part of his "vision" of capitalist reality. He thus fûsed into an organic whole the concepts of growth and cycle, and implied that the one could not exist without the other. The vital necessity of this view has been obscured in recent years because of the widespread preoccupation with the Keynesian system, but second thoughts, prompted both by Mr. Harrod's speculations and by the discovery of awkward statistical material, have brought us again face to face with a longer run reality in which Schumpeterian concepts are bound to play a central rôle. This is not to say, however, that we are back where we were before *The General Theory*. It has always seemed to me that the theories of effective demand and liquidity preference could be used to bring greatly enhanced usefulness to Schumpeter's theory, but it is plain that he would have none of it.

III. THE ESSENTIAL FEATURES OF A MODEL

To make quite sharp the essential point of the Schumpeterian theory, we may construct a simple model which, it should be emphasized, is not designed to do justice either to his schema or to economic reality. We assume

---

[5] *Economica*, 1927, p. 295.

a curve $p(k)$ of present value of all known capital projects as a function of the quantity of capital, k. Correspondingly, there is a curve, $s(\dot{k})$, giving the supply price of new capital as a function of the rate of net output of new capital, $\dot{k}$. Given competitive entrepreneurs, these two will be brought into equality, and the dynamic evolution of the system determined. The special feature of Schumpeter's thought can be represented by putting a hook in the curve $s(\dot{k})$, as shown in Fig. 1. There is a range of neutral equilibria between

FIG. 1

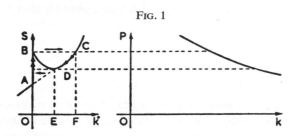

A and B, but the system is stable, for if the price and quantity were above or below this range they would tend to return to it. There is no oscillation. If we now introduce steady progress in the simplest form by assuming a regular rate of shift to the right in $p(k)$ we get a very different result. The profitable opportunities increase, but for all the reasons which Schumpeter has so vividly described nothing is done until they are potentially so high $(B - A)$ that an innovator successfully carries out a new combination. The path being opened, he is followed by many with a burst of investment at a rate F slowly declining to E. Then net investment ceases, and we again slowly accumulate investment possibilities as the present value rises slowly to B, at which point the barrier is again broken and we jump to C and so forth. If the steady advance is such as to require a rate of accumulation between O and E this process will continue indefinitely. In this case the growth is the explanation of the cycle, and the latter would not exist without the former. Here we see quite clearly that it would be totally inadmissible to draw a trend line through the resulting time series and "remove" it. The resulting cyclical appearance would correspond to no structural reality, and if we attempted to set up a model to explain it we would be talking nonsense.

In the physical sciences, whenever a steady source to an apparatus results in a fluctuating output, it has always been found that there is a non-linearity somewhere. This gives us a clue as to a technical requirement of the Schumpeterian theory, for we have a steady growth in ideas giving rise to bursts of investment and increases in output. In the preceding example the non-linearity is the hook in $s(\dot{k})$, and a somewhat different one will figure prominently in the model to be described below. It is not always necessary that there be growth to generate the oscillation. Thus a piece of chalk will only screech if moved across the blackboard, but an electric bell will ring about a stationary position; but both are non-linear oscillators and their difference is not fundamental.

The model to be presented below will be readily seen to be unsuitable for statistical testing. Rather is it analogous to the economy, and is meant to suggest the kind of development that goes on without, however, being able to take account of the rich complexities of what actually happens. There is general agreement that we need further investigation of hypotheses to be tested, and further testing of these, and that both activities are essential. I have endeavoured, in so far as possible, to keep to quantities that are potentially measurable.

IV. THE HISTORICAL VALIDITY OF THE MODEL

Once progress is admitted on the ground floor of a theory the awkward question arises about the historical validity of the system. The relevance and usefulness of economic theory to economic history has been small. If anything, business cycle theory has done better than some other branches. The situation becomes more serious the moment we restrict ourselves to a theory simple enough to be written down in a few equations. To imagine any connection between such a model and economic history seems grotesque, and yet, if there is no relation, there seems little use in constructing it.

To my mind there is no doubt that the special circumstances of each cycle and of each country seriously alter the character of the fluctuations. By seriously I mean gross distortion, so that a true cycle cannot really be said to exist, and can scarcely, if at all, be detected by screening the statistics. Some sort of alternation there is, but clearly there is no strict periodicity, and there may not be enough of a tendency to regular recurrence to allow us to speak of a cycle.

The fact that this tendency to alternation in levels of economic activity has appeared more or less uniformly in all advanced capitalist countries argues that there is some typical set of relations which would tend, in the absence of disturbance, to produce a regular cycle. The degree of uniformity, in the midst of all the tremendous changes of the past century, is as striking a fact as the lack of uniformity. There must be basic features of capitalism which will explain why these fluctuations have appeared in so many different countries over such long periods. It is these features which we must seek to isolate by ingenuity and perspicacity, even though they are hidden by the stormy history of capitalism. These elements must be capable by themselves of producing a cycle, and they will explain what uniformity there is in cycle after cycle. But any such theory must have many "open ends" through which we may insert the impact of historically given events, which will explain the enormous variability and irregularity of the cycle. Thus it is not that we can expect any simple, mathematical model to explain the wave-like character of economic history, but rather merely to explain the remarkable fact that there is some degree of uniformity in the otherwise unique course of development.

V. THE STRUCTURE AND FUNCTIONING
OF THE MODEL

First, we may go over in outline the structure and functioning of the model. The indispensable growth elements are improvements in techniques and the increase in the labour force, both of which are taken as given and more or less continuously growing. Innovational investment characteristically does not require increased output but, on the other hand, both greater employment and greater productivity mean larger output which will, with given techniques, call for more capital. The possibility of greater output is not the same as its realization, and for the answer to this we appeal to the Kahn-Keynes multiplier. The existence of a cycle means that aggregate demand is not always adequate to realize the full productive capacities of capitalism, and at first sight we might be tempted to wonder that they are ever realized. In general, new techniques require heavy investment outlays which swell demand, so that both the increased output per labourer and the increased number of labourers are absorbed. When the economy has achieved its new higher levels of output and capital it cannot hold them, because the great burst of investment (both innovational and accelerational) is necessary to create the effective demand, and, when it ceases, demand and output drop, thus creating unemployed capital and unemployed labour. Therefore we have a dynamic, but not a static, breakdown theory. Just as output rises each time to new heights, it also does not fall to its previous low, because the expansion generates fixed outlays which break the fall at higher levels on each swing. The revival awaits the accumulation of sufficient pressure for innovational investment. In the first approximation no lags are introduced, with the result that we have a two-phase cycle, full employment and deep depression. It is assumed throughout that the structural coefficients are such as to give explosive behaviour. Therefore investment, once begun, carries the economy to full employment, and this upper limit rises rapidly with the accumulation of capital, which allows the realization of the technological advance.

In simple terms the economy is strongly expansionist in both output and demand. It is always straining to get to the full employment limit, but, by the mere fact of being there for a time, it is projected downward again. To think of a mechanical analogy, we may picture a gas-filled balloon under-neath a stairway. A slight draught carries it steadily forward and it rises until it hits the ceiling, but then it bumps downward. After a time it begins to rise again, yet, having moved forward, it now passes the old level and rises until it hits the bottom of the next step. Thus it is essentially non-oscillatory, but is converted, by successive steps, into an intermittent upward drift. The central feature of the analogy is the parallelism between stair steps and full employment ceilings: it is these limits which control the character of the growth. It seems to me that full employment must, in some fairly intimate manner, guide the long-range behaviour of the model, otherwise it is difficult to see why we would not find that the model would predict, after a time, a cycle around a level of 50 or 150 percent of full employment, which is unrealistic. The concept of full employment I employ uncritically, and I do not think the many reservations required make any serious difficulties.

Throughout the argument capital stock will be taken as the central explanatory variable. Since the behaviour of capital is taken to be the main feature of the cycle this seems logical. The reason why I have not followed Professor Hicks and Mr. Harrod in taking income as the dependent variable, is that once we break the simple proportionality between capital and income, the behaviour of income no longer tells us anything conclusive about the behaviour of investment. To see this we must juxtapose actual stock to the desired stock of capital, and in view of this it seems preferable to work throughout with capital stock. Upon doing this we quickly realize how utterly hopeless it is to explain the lower turning point in terms of the necessity for replacement of a wasting capital stock.

There are more serious objections against the use of the quantity of capital than against the use of the quantity of output. Capital has never been satisfactorily defined quantitatively, and it is doubtful whether we can attach any useful meaning to the concept of variations in the stock of capital. However, at the cruder level of approach used here there is perhaps no very serious objection. Capital is taken to mean the stock of equipment, in the broadest sense, that is used in production, so that an increase in output calls for more capital, and a decrease for less. It is useful to pretend that capital stock is the sum of all past net investments, but since it is output and not capital that really matters, we need not worry if the resulting quantity of capital is partly fictitious. This problem arises sharply in the case of innovational investment which, in our system, means an unequivocal addition to capital stock. But our crude aggregative model ignores the fact that innovational investment also destroys capital, so that in fact we cannot be sure whether there has been an increase or a decrease.

Throughout I shall use the "flexible accelerator" as the explanatory principle for investment. I have described it in my contribution to *Income, Employment and Public Policy: Essays in Honor of Alvin H. Hansen*,[6] and more recently it has been discussed, with supporting evidence, by Dr. Chenery.[7]

---

[6] "Secular and Cyclical Aspects of the Multiplier and the Accelerator," *Income, Employment and Public Policy: Essays in Honor of Alvin H. Hansen*, New York, 1948.

[7] H. B. Chenery, "Overcapacity and the Acceleration Principle," *Econometrica*, January, 1952.

According to this principle, net investment will be undertaken as long as desired capital is greater than existing capital, and disinvestment in the contrary case. Desired capital, ξ, I shall assume to be determined by

$$\xi = vy + \beta(t), \tag{1}$$

where v is the acceleration coefficient, y is output, and $\beta(t)$ is a parameter to be associated primarily with changes in technique. Thus innovation means that more capital is desired with a given output, and the accelerator means more capital is desired only with increased output.

It is to be noted that, even if we ignore $\beta(t)$, this is not the acceleration principle, which assumes a perfect adjustment of capital to output at all times. On the contrary, it is assumed here that with a given stock of capital we can produce more (by overtime, etc.) than it was designed to produce, and, obviously, also less. Furthermore, in designed capacity, there is usually some stand-by or peak-load capacity which can be used. The point is that this high-level operation involves higher variable costs, strain on staff and equipment, delays, etc., all of which create a pressure to expand capital and capacity. Therefore the short-run is characterized by a failure to exemplify the acceleration principle, but it is also dominated by efforts to attain the accelerational quantity of capital. The assumption here is that entrepreneurs behave on homeostatic principles as exemplified by servo-mechanisms. We sidestep the question of expectations, although the rate at which investment proceeds in response to a given excess or deficiency of capital is a kind of measure of confidence in the continuation of current rates of output.

For the sake of simplicity, we assume that the pressure to expand is proportional to the difference between ξ and k, subject to two crucial non-linearities. The lower one is set by the rate of wastage of capital at zero gross investment, and the upper one by the maximum output of new capital goods

Fig. 2

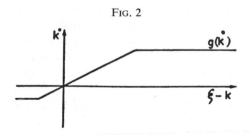

obtainable with given capital and labour supply. The picture is as drawn in Fig. 2, and we may write it for convenience as,

$$g(\dot{k}) = \xi - k. \tag{2}$$

Beyond this, I assume that full employment in the capital goods trades tends to coincide with full employment generally. A little reflection shows that it must be so, else we should either never attain full employment, or else have violent inflation in all booms. In general this result may come about in the following way: as the boom proceeds we may tend to hit capacity limits in the instrumental trades before general full employment; these trades, facing a backlog in any case, will divert some of their output to enlarging their own capacity; this process will continue so long as there is unemployed labour available. Thus we arrive, if not initially, finally, at simultaneous full capacity output in both producers' and consumers' goods industries. Beyond this point it is dangerous for the former to go, since it would mean sharply rising costs along with falling output in consumption goods. There is a tendency to moderate inflation in most booms, and it could be assumed that the maximum output in durable goods lies slightly above the general limit so that the investment trades often try to bid resources away from the others.

If this relation between capital goods output and general output is to be maintained it follows that, with full employment, further growth in output must be split between the two in the proportion given by the secular multiplier. Thus, if the multiplier is 5, a rise of 10 in total output will include a rise of 2 in the output of new capital. The assumption is clearly necessary to the proper functioning of the model, but it is bound to appear somewhat arbitrary unless we assume some equilibrating mechanism behind the scenes.

There remains the stimulating question whether or not innovations, which continually increase the amount of desired capital, raise the acceleration coefficient. My own inclination has always been to assume that the coefficient is increased, and I owe to the persuasive analysis of Mr. Harrod[8] and Mrs. Robinson[9] my present strong doubts on this score. The point is that new methods of production almost always require additions to capital stock, but they also destroy capital, sometimes by making it obsolete, sometimes by reducing the cost of replacing it. Therefore we may be continually adding to our capital autonomously but find that, after many years, a routine addition to output requires the same addition to capital stock as before.

In the absence of any information, or grounds for believing one effect or the other to predominate, it is simplest to assume that the acceleration coefficient v remains unchanged, and this I shall do. It seems much better not to lump this problem with the much more identifiable one of whether or not innovations are capital using or capital saving. Whereas Mr. Harrod defines capital using in terms of v,[10] I prefer to define it in terms of the increase or decrease of $\beta(t)$. The important point is "that major innovations and also many minor ones entail construction of New Plant (and equipment). . . ."[11] The fact that net investment with constant output need not

---

[8] *Dynamic Economics, op. cit., passim.*
[9] J. Robinson, *The Rate of Interest*, London, 1952, p. 42.
[10] *Op. cit.*, pp. 23 *et seq.*
[11] J. A. Schumpeter, *Business Cycles*, New York, 1939, vol. i, p. 93.

make industry "more capitalistic" is only paradoxical, because we are dealing with aggregates which suppress all structural interdependence.

To incorporate a theory of effective demand and the generation of income, we may follow well-established Keynesian lines and write

$$y = f(\dot{k} + \gamma(t)), \tag{3}$$

where $\gamma(t)$ is "public spending" suitably defined, and everything is in constant prices. I shall not discuss government anti-cyclical policy, and hence I shall suppress $\gamma(t)$, but the reader will find no difficulty in introducing it.

The slope of this function is the multiplier, and its inverse is the aggregate savings function (all lags are ignored and the equality of savings and investment is assumed). The uniqueness of this function has been one of the first central Keynesian doctrines to waver. Following Professor Duesenberry[12] we may represent the shape of this function as in Fig. 3. When going down we follow

FIG. 3

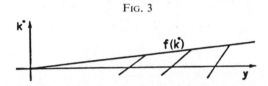

the steeper slope, and only when we venture again into new, higher ranges of income does saving again grow only slowly. The necessity for some such contrast between short- and long-run phenomena is clear, but the explanation of this anomalous savings function is not quite so well established.

Professor Duesenberry has advanced an ingenious explanation, and I should like to suggest some further considerations which also may help. Fundamentally, it may be an expression of the familiar Marshallian distinction between the long and the short period. The long period is much longer in the downward than in the upward direction. Thus, as the scale of output is expanded, all outlays go up easily, but a part of them "freeze" and become "fixed" and cease to be quickly reducible in the event of a fall in output. We can think not only of "fixed" interest but stable dividend policies, irreducible managerial, maintenance, sales and research staffs. Many workers also are not discharged, but many are and cease to be a cost to the firm. But to society they remain a fixed charge, and they continue to consume, though at a lower rate, whether through savings, charity, credit or public relief. Similarly, as Professor Duesenberry has shown, the consumer finds that his outlay is fairly easily variable in the upward direction, but is awkwardly rigid downward. In the long run, this would cease to be so. Finally, it is almost a law of political science, as well as a political slogan, that government outlays expand easily but resist contraction to an extraordinary degree.

---

[12] J. S. Duesenberry, *Income, Saving and the Theory of Consumer Behavior*, Cambridge (Mass.), 1949.

A related though distinct phenomenon is the fact, stressed by Mrs. Robinson,[13] that in the early stages of the boom there is a large increase in output before there is much increase in capacity, leading to large profits which are mostly saved. As the prosperity continues the accumulation of capital may lead to a fall in profits and hence in savings. This could generate the kind of savings function shown in Fig. 3, for in depression there is no significant decumulation, and hence the savings function will not be reversible. Here again aggregates conceal the real problem, for we must appeal to a classical competitive behaviour to explain why entrepreneurs undertake investment which *lowers* profits.

VI. THE COMPLETE MODEL

We are now in a position to assemble the various parts into a working model. Combining equations (1), (2) and (3) we get

$$\ddot{\xi} - k = vf(\dot{k}) + \beta(t) - k = g(\dot{k}),$$

or, rearranging,

$$k = vf(\dot{k}) - g(\dot{k}) + \beta(t). \tag{4}$$

The function $vf(\dot{k})$ is the same as $f(\dot{k})$ only much flatter, and therefore the situation at any point of time is as shown in Fig. 4.

Fig. 4

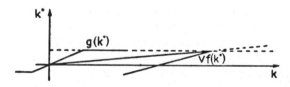

If we subtract $g(\dot{k})$ from $vf(\dot{k})$, call it $\phi(\dot{k})$, and add $\beta(t)$ to it, we get the result shown in Fig. 5. It is evident that an increase in $\beta(t)$ simply shifts the $\phi(\dot{k})$ curve to the right. All our relations are satisfied if we remain on the curve. All lags have been abstracted from in the interest of simplicity, and with the conviction that these are of secondary rather than of primary importance for the cycle.

To begin with, let us consider the case of a completely unprogressive economy with $\beta(t)$ constant, no increases in productivity and no growth in the labour force. If we begin at the upturn, we have capital k_1, and start accumulating at the peak rate. This means peak output, and a much larger amount of capital is desired than the existing stock. The capital goods fill this

---

[13] *Op. cit.*, p. 101.

backlog at the maximum attainable rate until we reach the amount k_3. At this point entrepreneurs would begin to slacken in their rate of new investment, but this proves impossible because the more they slacken the

FIG. 5

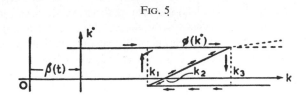

investment the lower is income and output, and hence the lower is desired capital by a multiple. There is no feasible position short of zero gross investment, below which point they cannot go and to which they instantaneously jump. This instantaneous jump from full boom to deep depression is a direct consequence of abstracting from lags, and we shall at a later point drop this assumption.

In consequence of zero gross investment output is now low, and the existing stock of capital, k_3, is greatly in excess of desired capital. Capital is now decumulated at the maximum possible rate until k_1 is reached, and then the process is begun all over again. If, as a result of a war or some such large disturbance, capital is slightly in excess of the equilibrium amount, k_2, combined with a low rate of net investment, we get an accelerated rise to k_3. This behaviour corresponds rather closely to the familiar "multiplier-accelerator process," but it is executed by this model only under exceptional circumstances.

The model is completely unrealistic in its depression behaviour. Even under favourable circumstances it would remain depressed much longer than in boom. The curve of Fig. 5 probably much over-estimates any actually achieved rate of physical wastage of capital assets. Our model identifies two things which are in fact not the same. Zero gross investment means the non-spending of depreciation allowances, and hence determines the lower level of income as represented. But unfortunately this does not represent actual disappearance of capital goods, especially since, following a boom, their age composition will be abnormal and actual disappearance quite small. Some reduction there will be, and also a general ageing which will be conducive to investment, but these effects will be weak. It should be admitted that this is a shortcoming both in this model and in that of Professor Hicks.

VII. THE SOURCES OF GROWTH

There are two sources of growth and these may be conveniently considered in turn. In the first place there is the rise in the full employment level, both because the size of the labour force increases and because the productivity of labour rises through innovation. The organic connection between cycle and trend will be most sharply emphasized if we assume that all growth in the full employment ceiling occurs only during booms. Thus, at the end of a depression there will have been some attrition in capital stock, but this may be roughly counterbalanced by the growth in the labour stock, so that we may plausibly assume that the full employment level is about the same at the end of the depression as it was at the beginning. In the ensuing boom full employment output may rise rapidly, because the capital is being accumulated to equip with newest techniques the expanded labour force. But this output rises above the previous peak and carries us into the range of the large secular multiplier. This time the acceleration coefficient gives us the large additions to desired capital which the rising output entails. The achieved rate of rise in full employment output, say of 4 percent or 5 percent per year, fixes the rate of growth of desired capital, and this, in combination with the slowly accelerating capital stock, determines the length of the boom.

If we continue along the top horizontal curve we eventually reach the termination of the boom. With secular progress the full employment limit rises, and the peak output of capital goods rises in a fixed proportion to it. This means that the flat top to $\phi(k)$ slowly rises, which raises the required capital and prolongs the boom. Therefore we move along a horizontal curve which is steadily rising, so that in fact we follow a slowly rising curve as is shown in Fig. 6. This postpones, but does not avoid, the final accumulation of sufficient capital to induce a slackening of investment and the consequent end to the boom. Whereas the boom is prolonged, the slump is shortened, because the "fixed" outlays which have become swollen during the boom now place a higher "floor" to output, and hence to desired capital. Therefore it is not necessary to carry out the absurdly unrealistic task of decumulating, by wear and tear, all of the capital accumulated during the preceding boom. It remains true, however, that realistic figures still give a depression that lasts longer than the boom.

The economy surges forward and plunges down, but it does not go back to its old low. There is no "progress" during depression; it all occurs during the boom, or at least it is all "realized" during the boom. Therefore there would be no meaning to drawing any smooth trend line through the time series of national income. Finally, it should be noted that secular growth takes place without any autonomous or innovational outlays.

Fig. 6

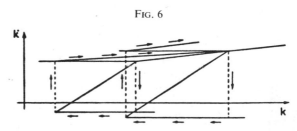

We have already taken account of the results of innovation in increasing productivity; it remains only to include the fact that they ordinarily mean additional investment outlay. We therefore allow $\beta(t)$ to rise, more or less smoothly, which implies that there has been in capitalism a continuous stream of ideas for new methods of production which have required additional capital outlays. These may occur slowly at some times and rapidly at others, but $\beta(t)$, being the resultant of many small events cumulated, is likely to be fairly continuous.

Making no more definite assumptions than this we get the Schumpeterian result that the steady accumulation of potential "new combinations" is converted into bursts of development which eventually exhaust themselves and relax into depressions. They may sometimes come as a result of his isolated, pioneer entrepreneur, but they need not. In this way we make a closer mutual conditioning between the state of trade and innovating activity.

The effect of a steadily rising $\beta(t)$ is a steady shifting of the $\phi(k)$ curve to the right. Thus it is not necessary to await the slow wasting of capital, for desired capital rises to overtake the existing stock. Therefore, depending on the given historical rapidity of growth of new methods of production, the depression may be so short as to amount only to a "crisis," or it may drag on for many years awaiting significant technological advance. Contrariwise, the advance of $\beta(t)$ postpones the end of the boom by increasing capital requirements, so that under favourable conditions the boom may be much lengthened. Since the model, like capitalism itself, is dominated by vigorous growth, we may use variations in $\beta(t)$ to account for, in part at least, the enormous variation from cycle to cycle and country to country. Thus we can account for snap depressions like 1907, or prolonged stagnation as in the 1870's or 1930's. Again, a long boom like the 1920's can be fitted in. The current post-war boom can be explained by the steady accumulation of possibilities during the great depression and the war, and by the length of time needed to accumulate the capital to exploit these as well as to equip the considerably increased labour force.

A questionable feature of this model lies in the fact that it lumps together the accelerational and the innovational demands for new capital. Yet this has much to recommend it, for new methods and forms of capital will be most readily installed when rising demand requires additional capital in any case. Probably most new types of capital are installed during booms, and so innovational investment is hopelessly mixed with accelerational investment. Also, while not necessary, a high and rising demand is favourable to innovational outlays.

VIII. THE LOWER TURNING POINT

Even allowing for the vigorously expansionist nature of capitalism, the lower turning point remains a difficulty for a model built solely on capital requirements. There are numerous factors which alleviate the problem and

I shall allude to three. Throughout we have taken no account of the distinction between working and fixed capital. As is well known there is no serious technical limit to the rate of disinvestment in the former, and hence the excessive stock of working capital may be quickly dissipated. As has been shown by Professors Lundberg[14] and Metzler[15] this leads to a rise in investment and output. The resultant increase in desired capital may well ignite a general boom much earlier than we would expect from the "fixed" capital model. Second, as has been pointed out by Mr. Harrod,[16] the aggregative model completely misses the vital fact of the heterogeneity of capital goods. Thus some capital wears out quickly and requires gross investment to maintain output. As the depression persists, there will be rising gross investment even though a vast amount of capital is still redundant. This means rising output and capital requirements, which rise to meet the declining stock. In fact, this dispersion in the durability of different capital goods must be a large part of the explanation of the failure of gross investment to fall to zero in deep depression. Finally, we should mention the possibility that government outlays for relief, war or public works may lift the economy enough to set off the boom. This point has been so completely discussed that it seems unnecessary to go into it.

IX. THE EFFECTS OF LAGS

The model has been presented in an extremely crude form, the better to bring out its essential features. One over-simplification must be softened, and this is the assumption of no lags. There are a bewildering variety of lags of which the most important is the time between the decision to produce and actual installation of new capital goods. In our model it is implicitly assumed that ordering a new capital good leads to immediate installation, and that the full effect of this on income also results immediately. The average lag, θ, due to fabrication time, is long, perhaps as long as a year or more. Taking account of the lags creates serious difficulties in our non-linear equations. One difficulty may be disposed of roughly, but perhaps fairly satisfactorily, as follows: There is a kind of average lag between the decision to invest and the outlays incident to the investment, and there is a further lag between the spending of money and its full multiplier effect; if we then take these two lags to add up to θ, we have the useful fact that a piece of capital goods and its income effect appear at the same time. The remaining difficulty may be evaded, for practical purposes, as follows: the function, $g(k)$, which regulates investment decisions, is linear except for its upper and lower limits; but these

14 E. Lundberg, *Studies in the Theory of Economic Expansion*, London, 1937.
15 L. A. Metzler, "The Nature and Stability of Inventory Cycles," *Review of Economic Statistics*, 1941. [Reprinted in the present volume.]
16 "Notes on Trade Cycle Theory," *Economic Journal*, 1951.

limitations determine completely the behaviour in their ranges; it is only in the rise from the lower limit to the upper limit and conversely that we are interested, and here we may without serious error assume simple linear relations. Therefore instead of $g(k_{t+\theta})$, we write $1/a[k_{t+\theta}]$, and instead of $f(k_t)$, we write mk_t, where m is the multiplier and a is a constant which tells the rate at which any deficiency of capital is being made up. To replace (4) we have

$$k_{t+\theta} - avmk_t + ak_t = a\beta(t),$$

or, if we expand $k_{t+\theta}$ in a Taylor series and keep only the first two terms,

$$0\ddot{k} + (1 - avm)\dot{k} + ak = a\beta(t). \tag{5}$$

This is a linear, second order differential equation, and it will ordinarily give rise to oscillations, which will be explosive if $avm > 1$. That this can ordinarily be expected to be so we see by considering the fact that v and m are both greater than unity and that though a may well be less than unity it is unlikely to be sufficiently less. Thus if $v = 2$ and $m = 2$, then a would have to be less than $\frac{1}{4}$, which would mean that the *annual* net output of capital goods would have to be less than $\frac{1}{4}$ of the deficiency in capital goods, which is not realistic. An explosive linear oscillation in the $\dot{k}k$ plane will be a somewhat distorted, unwinding, logarithmic spiral. Therefore, apart from the delicate point of transition, we have a cycle made up of two simple routines, the flat top and bottom, and the outward spiralling ends. The initial conditions for the two ends are specified by the horizontal slope of the phase line at the end of the depression and of the boom. Consequently, we get the kind of picture shown in Fig. 7. The harshness of transition from boom to depression and back

Fig. 7

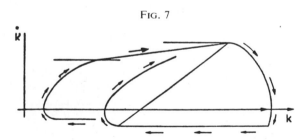

again is entirely softened. As gross investment begins after a slump, some time elapses before the multiplier-accelerator desire for more capital is fed back into the investment decisions. Therefore, in a process spread over time, investment rises, and the more entrepreneurs invest the more they want to invest, but they are eventually restrained by the amount that they are able to invest.

The model has a much shorter down-swing than up-swing, and in this it fits one of the most firmly established generalizations about business cycles. The actual down-swing (as distinguished from depression low levels) is shorter, because it is soon stopped by the limit on gross investment. It is shorter also because the shallower savings function holds for the whole of the down-swing, whereas it holds only for a part of the up-swing. Finally, it is shorter because of the shifting to the right of $\phi(k)$, although this is not shown in Fig. 7.

The curved portions of the diagram in Fig. 7 may be constructed to any desired degree of accuracy by the method of isoclines. We first measure in deviations from the equilibrium level as determined by $\beta(t)$. Writing b instead of $\dot{k}$ we have, from (5),

$$\dot{k} = \frac{dk}{dt} = b \; ;$$

$$\frac{db}{dt} = \ddot{k} = \left(\frac{avm - 1}{\theta}\right) b - \frac{a}{\theta} k.$$

Eliminating dt, we get

$$\frac{db}{dk} = \left(\frac{avm - 1}{\theta}\right) - \left(\frac{a}{\theta}\right)\frac{k}{b}. \tag{6}$$

This gives us the slope in the bk plane of the required curve for any pair of values of b and k. Hence, starting from the "floor," we can proceed by small steps, in the direction calculated from (6), to the "ceiling," and conversely.

3

Mr. Harrod's Dynamic Theory*[1]

By J. R. HICKS†

MR. HARROD's book may be regarded as falling into two parts. One of them (Chapters 1, 3 and 4) outlines a new "dynamic" theory of economic progress and of the trade cycle; the other (Chapters 2 and 5) is specially concerned with interest. There is, of course, some overlapping; but the two parts are fairly well separated. One could, I think, say a good deal about the part on interest without much reference to the other part; and one can certainly say a good deal about the dynamic theory without any reference to the part on interest. Personally, I find the dynamic theory a good deal more interesting. I can find quite enough to say about it to fill the space which could conveniently be allotted to me on this occasion; I propose, therefore, to take the drastic step of leaving the part on interest altogether on one side.

Dynamics, according to Mr. Harrod, is a study of "an economy in which rates of output are changing." This definition is contrasted with that given in my own *Value and Capital*—"that part of economic theory in which all quantities must be dated"—and also with that used by the econometricians, such as Frisch and Kalecki, which Mr. Harrod takes to be particularly concerned with the effects of lags. Certainly there is no need to fight over definitions; I have myself no desire to defend the *Value and Capital* definition for purposes outside its immediate context. It had convenience as a means of organising a particular discussion; I would claim no more for it. But I think that both the econometricians and myself have the right to enquire whether Mr. Harrod has paid sufficient regard to the aspects of a dynamic process to which we have drawn attention. In fact, he seems to be open to some criticism on both grounds. It is very awkward to analyse a dynamic process (in his sense) without paying more regard than he does to the question of dating; and once one begins to date, it is hardly possible to slide over the question of lags. But instead of arguing this matter in general terms, let us look at it in terms of the details of Mr. Harrod's theory.

---

* *Economica*, n.s. XVI (May 1949). Reprinted by courtesy of *Economica* and the author.
† All Souls College, Oxford University.
[1] R. F. Harrod, *Towards a Dynamic Economics* (London: Macmillan & Co., Ltd., 1948).

The central feature of that theory is a certain equation[2] which (modifying Mr. Harrod's notation a little[3]) I will write in the form $gc = s$. s is saving, expressed as a proportion of income (or output); g is the rate of growth of output (increment of output expressed as a proportion of output); c is the ratio of investment to the increment of output. Those whose minds (like my own) find it difficult to think in terms of these ratios will prefer to multiply up by income or output (Υ). $g\Upsilon$ is then identifiable as the increment of output during the period, which could be written $d\Upsilon/dt$. The equation thus becomes $c\dfrac{d\Upsilon}{dt} = s\Upsilon$. This is recognisable as our old friend, the equation of Saving and Investment. (Υ, it should be understood, is measured in terms of goods, not in terms of money or of "wage-units.")

The reason why Mr. Harrod prefers to write a familiar equation in this unfamiliar form is that he is anxious to stress the dependence of investment on the rate of change of output—the "Relation" which other economists have called the "acceleration principle." In given conditions of technique, and with a given rate of interest, the ratio (c) between *ex-ante* investment and the change in income may perhaps be properly regarded as more or less constant. If this is so, and if the saving ratio s may also be regarded as constant, then the fundamental equation $c\dfrac{d\Upsilon}{dt} = s\Upsilon$ can be treated as a differential equation, and solved as such. The solution is $\Upsilon = \Upsilon_0\, e^{gt}$, where Υ_0 is the level of income at time zero, which must be supposed to be given, and g is now *defined* as s/c, where both s and c are now to be taken as given constants. The economic meaning of this solution is, of course, that the economy expands at a constant rate g.

The solution is got by assuming that the economy is all the time in a state of Keynesian equilibrium, with *ex-ante* investment equal to *ex-ante* saving. The path defined by the solution is therefore not the path which will actually be followed; it is the path which would be followed if the system remained continually in this sort of equilibrium. (Mr. Harrod calls it the "warranted" rate of growth.) And that means, as we shall see, very little more than that it is *a possible* path of development.

The use of the concept of equilibrium in such matters as this is very tricky. In the Keynesian system, we were first told that the savings-investment equation determined the level of output; then it became clear that it only determined the equilibrium level of output; the actual level, at any particular time, might depart from the equilibrium level. This was an important qualification, with many consequences not yet all of them fully appreciated;

---

[2] This equation first appeared in his "Essay in Dynamic Theory" (*Economic Journal*, 1939).

[3] Mr. Harrod writes the equation $GC = s$. I have replaced his big letters by small ones because I prefer to keep big letters for the main economic quantities, such as Υ, using small letters for their ratios.

but it did not in itself seriously affect the usefulness of the Keynesian construction, because the Keynesian equilibrium is *stable*. If *ex-ante* saving exceeds *ex-ante* investment (under Keynesian or near-Keynesian assumptions) output will tend to fall, thus tending to restore equilibrium. And *vice versa*. Because there are these stabilising forces tending to hold the system to an equilibrium position (or, as we might say, more dynamically, to hold it on an equilibrium path), it is probable that divergences from a Keynesian equilibrium would be limited. Great divergences must be short lived. Thus, in so far as the Keynesian system is valid, it does not only explain "tendencies"; it does, at least in a rough sort of way, explain the facts. If it is valid, then it is a first approximation to what does actually happen. It has this property in virtue of its mathematical *stability*. The ordinary supply and demand theory for a single commodity has the same property for the same reason.

Mr. Harrod's equilibrium path—his "warranted rate of growth"—does not have this property. His system is mathematically unstable. A rise in the rate of saving (s) raises the warranted rate of growth (g), thus causing the equilibrium path to slope more steeply upwards. There is sense in this. With the demand for the use of savings coming from the increase in output, an increased supply of savings can only be absorbed if output increases more rapidly than before. But an increase in s will not cause the economy to move on to this new path. Just as in the Keynesian case a rise in s causes *ex-ante* saving to exceed *ex-ante* investment, and therefore tends to diminish output. But this means (under Mr. Harrod's assumptions) that the system tends at once to move away from its equilibrium rate of advance. Instead of expanding as it "ought" to do, it starts to contract.

Mr. Harrod is, of course, well aware of this instability; he draws a number of interesting conclusions from it, some of them, I think, very important conclusions. In a sense he welcomes the instability of his system, because he believes it to be an explanation of the tendency to fluctuation which exists in the real world. I think, as I shall proceed to show, that something of this sort may well have much to do with the tendency to fluctuation. But mathematical instability does not in itself elucidate fluctuation. A mathematically unstable system does not fluctuate; it just breaks down. The unstable position is one in which it will *not* tend to remain. That is all that the condition of mathematical instability tells us. But, on being barred from that position, what will it do? What path will it follow? Mere knowledge of the unstable position does not tell us.

Perhaps I may put my difficulty graphically. In Fig. 1 time is measured on the horizontal axis, and output on the vertical (the latter, as seems appropriate for these "growth" problems, being reckoned on a logarithmic scale). We begin with output OA at time zero. s and c being given, AA' is an equilibrium path. Suppose that this path is followed from A to B, but that at B the rate of saving (s) rises. The new equilibrium path will be such as BB'. But the rise in the rate of saving does not cause the economy to move along BB', or along anything like it. It has the opposite effect, causing a divergence to the other side of BA′. But about the course of that divergence and about its direction we learn practically nothing. In practice, with these strong centrifugal forces at work, we must suppose that we shall almost always be dealing

FIG. 1

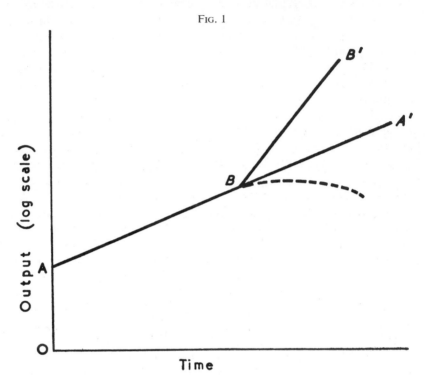

with an economy which is somewhere or other on some such divergent path. So long as the actual course of events on such a path is left undetermined, little use can be made of the theory. It is extraordinarily hard to use it either for the explanation of events, or for the prediction of what is likely to result from changes introduced by policy.

II

Faced with this difficulty, I have been tempted to go beyond the ordinary functions of a reviewer, and to enquire whether it is not possible, by some modification of Mr. Harrod's assumptions, to overcome the deficiency. The prize is a great one, for no one can study Mr. Harrod's work at all deeply without feeling that results of really great significance are just round the corner. What we have to do is to introduce just sufficient frictions to give the model mathematical stability, while not sacrificing the economic instability on which the substance of the argument depends. Can this be done?

It can be done as soon as we are allowed to make some use of lags. It is not generally realised (Mr. Harrod has certainly failed to realise it) that the great function of lags in this sort of dynamic theory is to impart just that measure of stability in the small—day-to-day stability we might call it—as is required in order to make the movement of the system economically determinate. The lags are needed to hold the system to a given path. Mr. Harrod's theory, in the form he has given it, may be regarded as an indirect proof of this; because he will have no lags, his system explodes out of the time dimension. A dynamic system which is economically unstable, having a high propensity to fluctuate, cannot be efficiently studied unless some of the variables are lagged.

The easiest way to introduce lags is to work in terms of period analysis. Instead of treating time as continuous, we break it up into successive periods. The increment of output, which formerly appeared as $d\Upsilon/dt$, will now appear as $\Upsilon_n - \Upsilon_{n-1}$. If there are no lags, the basic equation will then have to be written

$$c(\Upsilon_n - \Upsilon_{n-1}) = s\Upsilon_n \qquad (1)$$

the properties of which are substantially the same as those of Mr. Harrod's equation.[4]

But as soon as the equation is written in this form, it does at once look decidedly queer. It is not really reasonable to assume that current investment should depend upon the increment of output *in the same period* (especially if periods are fairly short), and still less is it reasonable to assume that saving depends wholly upon the income of the same period. If we make the simplest possible lagging assumptions, we shall make investment depend upon the increment of income in the preceding period, and *consumption* upon the income of the preceding period. Current saving would then equal $\Upsilon_n - (1 - s)\Upsilon_{n-1}$, so that the basic difference equation becomes

$$c(\Upsilon_{n-1} - \Upsilon_{n-2}) = \Upsilon_n - (1 - s)\Upsilon_{n-1}$$

or

$$\Upsilon_n = (1 - s + c)\Upsilon_{n-1} - c\Upsilon_{n-2} \qquad (2)$$

An equation of this kind is completely stable in the short run, for an increase in s reduces Υ_n as it should. It can therefore be used to trace out a path which is such that an economy might possibly follow it.

The properties of such paths have been widely studied by mathematical economists.[5] Without going into detail, the following general conclusions

---

[4] For its solution gives g (the proportional increment of output) equal to $s/(c - s)$. When s is small relatively to c, this is approximately the same as s/c.

[5] The best general description of this work, in non-mathematical language, is that by Hansen and Samuelson, in *Fiscal Policy and Business Cycles*, ch. 12. The best account in terms of fairly elementary mathematics is in A. Smithies, "Equilibrium Analysis and Process Analysis," *Econometrica*, 1942.

may be mentioned. s and c being given, the path is completely determined when *two* initial positions (say Y_0 and Y_1) are given. Associated with any particular difference equation, there will be a "full equilibrium" position, which is such that it can be maintained indefinitely if it is once fully established. For very low values of c, the system approximates to the Keynesian type, and therefore moves steadily towards its full equilibrium. For very large values of c, the system tends away from full equilibrium. For intermediate values, it oscillates about the equilibrium position, the oscillations having a diminishing amplitude if c is less than 1, and an increasing amplitude if c is greater than 1. These are the results for the "second-order" equation, in which Y_n depends upon its *two* previous values. Similar, but mathematically much more complex, results appear to hold for difference equations of higher orders.

These results have attracted much attention because they seem to show that on quite simple assumptions a system may be constructed which has an automatic tendency to develop fluctuations. But the more one works with this structure, interesting as it is, the more one feels that its fluctuations are really too simple. They do not take account of some of the most elementary features of the real problem, which must surely find a place, and a central place, in a realistic theory. The mathematical economists do seem to have got hold of a part of the mechanism, but there are other things which they have left out which need to be brought in.

Now Mr. Harrod has got some of these other things. Although his system will not do in the small, it is better than theirs in the large. Is it impossible to build up a construction which will combine the merits of each?

III

The reader may have noticed that the lagged Harrod equation (2) would, in itself, be unsatisfactory for the purposes of the mathematical theory which we have just described. For if we seek to determine its full equilibrium level of output (which can always be determined from a difference equation by putting its various Ys equal to one another) the answer must clearly come out as $Y = 0$. This would not perhaps worry Mr. Harrod very much, because he is seeking to analyse a dynamic process, not an equilibrium situation. He does not want his system to settle down to "equilibrium."

But this means that the only solution of the difference equation in which he will be interested is that which occurs when c is relatively large, so that the system becomes "explosive." He is quite ready for his system to explode, provided that it does not explode too fast!

Nevertheless, since the system is to fluctuate, having down-tracks as well as up-tracks, it is important that the down-tracks should be checked somewhere. After all, slumps do have bottoms; something has to be introduced to stop the slump tending to an "equilibrium" with no output at all.

The only provision which Mr. Harrod makes to meet this need is the suggestion that some part of the investment of a period may be "long-range" —so that its "worthwhileness is not deemed to have any relation to current requirements." I believe that this is the solution; but by treating this long-range investment as a fraction (presumably in principle a constant fraction) of current income, Mr. Harrod makes it impossible for it to give him any really substantial help. For whether the long-range investment depends upon Υ_n, Υ_{n-1} or Υ_{n-2}, its introduction in this guise only affects the coefficients in the difference equation; and no juggling with the coefficients will prevent an equation of the form

$$\alpha \Upsilon_n + \beta \Upsilon_{n-1} + \gamma \Upsilon_{n-2} = 0$$

from having its equilibrium solution at zero output.

I believe that the readiest way out is to make the long-range investment depend, not upon current output, but upon the trend value of output. Evidently we must not treat long-range investment as a constant; for if we did so, though we should get a bottom to our slumps, we should lose the possibility of the upward trend, on the introduction of which into the model Mr. Harrod sets so much store. If, however, we make the assumption that the long-range investment depends, other things being equal, upon the natural growth of the economy (in productivity and perhaps population), we can get a bottom to our slumps and still retain the general progressive movement.

I would therefore suggest that we introduce a term $H(1 + g)^n$ for the long-range investment, where H is a constant, and g (also a constant) is now Mr. Harrod's *natural* rate of growth. The introduction of this term certainly seems to be worth trying, and it proves to have the most interesting effects.

IV

On introducing this term, the difference equation (2) is transformed into

$$H(1 + g)^n + c(\Upsilon_{n-1} - \Upsilon_{n-2}) = \Upsilon_n - (1 - s)\Upsilon_{n-1} \qquad (3)$$

This equation is just a shade harder to handle than (2), but in fact by a simple device we can reduce it to an equivalent form.

The nearest thing to an equilibrium solution which is possible for this new equation is that which gives a steady advance at the *natural* rate. At such a steady advance, we should have $\Upsilon_n = E(1 + g)^n$, where E is a constant. Substituting this trial solution in (3), we find

$$H(1 + g)^n = E(1 + g)^n - (1 - s + c)E(1 + g)^{n-1} + cE(1 + g)^{n-2}$$

whence

$$E = \frac{H(1 + g)^2}{(1 + g)(s + g) - cg} \qquad (4)$$

If, as we may properly assume, there is enough saving to look after the investment engendered in the steady advance, E will be positive.

Now write $\Upsilon_n = E(1 + g)^n(1 + y_n)$, so that y_n is the proportion by which actual income in the nth period exceeds (or, if y_n is negative, falls short of) its *moving* equilibrium value. Substituting this value in (3) and using (4), we get

$$y_n - \frac{1 - s + c}{1 + g} y_{n-1} + \frac{c}{(1 + g)^2} y_{n-2} = 0 \tag{5}$$

which is a simple difference equation of exactly the same type as (2). Its full equilibrium solution is at $y_n = 0$; but this no longer corresponds to zero output, but to the output which gives a steady advance.

What we have now found is that in our revised model, the proportional divergences from the moving equilibrium output will obey the same laws as were obeyed by the level of output itself in the simple model (2). Thus if $c/(1 + g)^2$ is small, any displacement from the moving equilibrium will be followed by a steady movement back to the equilibrium. The moving equilibrium can then be regarded as stable. For larger values of c, we should get fluctuations about the moving equilibrium, which (as c increased) would first be damped, and would then become "explosive." Finally, for very large values of c, we should get a steady divergence from equilibrium as the result of any chance displacement.

Now it is, I think, these latter possibilities (relatively neglected by the econometrists) to which Mr. Harrod seeks to draw our attention. In order to study them conveniently, we may perhaps fix our attention upon one particular value of c, which makes the difference equation more than usually easy to handle. This is the minimum value which gives a steady divergence from equilibrium, without there being any fluctuations induced by the difference equation itself. It can be calculated to be $c = (1 + \sqrt{s})^2$. Substituting this value of c in (5), we get

$$y_n - 2\lambda y_{n-1} + \lambda^2 y_{n-2} = 0 \tag{6}$$

where $\lambda = (1 + \sqrt{s})/(1 + g)$. It is obviously safe to assume that $\lambda > 1$.

The solution of equation (6) is $(nA + B)\lambda^n$, where A and B are constants, depending on the initial positions. Thus if we start from a position which is such that A is positive, y will steadily increase (at least after a limited number of initial periods), and if we start from a position in which A is negative, y will steadily diminish (subject to the same proviso). We have therefore verified that we are dealing with an "explosive" equation; and we may be sure that for higher values of c we should get cases which would be still more explosive.

If we start from an equilibrium position, with $y_0 = 0$, we are bound to have $B = 0$, since by putting $n = 0$, we see that $y_0 = B$. A is determined by the value of y in period 1, being equal to y_1/λ when $B = 0$. Applying the general formula, we see that $y_n = n\lambda^{n-1}y_1$. Thus if we began with an upward displacement, so that y_1 was positive, y_n would increase from period to period in a ratio which at first exceeded λ, but gradually approached the limiting value λ as n became large.

V

Thus the difference equation tells us that if there chances to be an upward displacement from the equilibrium level, y will expand indefinitely. But y cannot expand indefinitely! For y, it will be remembered, is not the equilibrium level of output, which *can* expand indefinitely, given sufficient time; it is the proportion in which actual output exceeds the moving equilibrium output, and in that moving equilibrium the natural growth of the system has already been allowed for. It is therefore reasonable to assume that there is some maximum level which y cannot exceed—something which we may call the Full Employment level. Until that limit is reached, output can expand, both by natural growth and by a reduction in the percentage of unemployed resources. Once, however, the limit is reached, only natural growth is possible. And that means that y has reached its maximum value.

Let us write the full employment limit of y as f. Then if we have started, as before, from the moving equilibrium, and have encountered the full employment ceiling in the nth period after the initial divergence, we have the following situation. $y_{n-2} = (n-2)\lambda^{n-3}y_1$; $y_{n-1} = (n-1)\lambda^{n-2}y_1$; but y_n does not equal $n\lambda^{n-1}y_1$, but is kept down to the lower value f. What then happens to y_{n+1}? In order to discover this, we have to go back to the difference equation (6), for there is no reason why it should not continue to hold.

$$y_{n+1} = 2\lambda f - \lambda^2 y_{n-1}$$

This may be greater or less than f, but if it is greater than f, it will have to be replaced by f, since f is its greatest possible value. We pass on to y_{n+2}. Applying the difference equation to this, we see that its maximum possible value is $2\lambda f - \lambda^2 f = f[1 - (\lambda - 1)^2]$. This is definitely less than f; so that, *having reached its full employment limit, the system must begin to turn round again and output to go down, at least relatively to the trend.*

This conclusion is quite generally true. If we go back to the more general equation (5), we see that two successive ys which are equal and positive must be followed by a third which is lower than they are. This follows from the same inequality as gave us our fundamental condition that the (moving) equilibrium level of output should be positive.

What happens next? Effectively we are now starting from two successive ys which are both equal to the same positive magnitude f. We have to use the difference equation to work out the ensuing path. It is not difficult to show that successive ys will continue to fall, and that a point must be reached at which output does not merely fall relatively to its moving equilibrium, but falls absolutely.

When this happens, I think that we must reconsider our difference equation. If the system continued on the path determined by the same difference equation, output would ultimately fall to zero; our model, having agreed with experience quite well up to this point, would therefore at this point begin to diverge sharply. Can we see why? The induced investment, on which so much has depended, is investment induced by an *expansion* in output; if we maintained the same difference equation on the downswing as on the upswing, we should be letting it go into reverse and becoming negative when output began to fall. This does not look right. It is true that there are some sorts of investment (investment in working capital) for which a construction of this sort might be plausible. Increases in output induce investment in working capital, of the sort which we have so far taken into account; and it is reasonable to suppose that reductions in output will cause entrepreneurs to find their working capital excessive, so that they will take steps to reduce their excessive stocks. So far as fixed capital is concerned, however, this is not possible. There does therefore seem to be a changed situation in the downswing from what there was in the upswing, and it is reasonable to allow for this change by changing the form of the difference equation. Let us say, as a first approximation, that when output turns absolutely downwards, the induced investment term $c(\Upsilon_{n-1} - \Upsilon_{n-2})$ simply drops out. It becomes zero, but does not become negative. Suppose this occurs, what happens?

The difference equation now takes the form

$$H(1 + g)^n = \Upsilon_n - (1 - s)\Upsilon_{n-1} \tag{7}$$

instead of the form expressed in equation (3). This is a much easier equation to handle than equation (3), but it will be convenient to set out its solution in similar form. It will have a similar moving equilibrium, which we may write $L(1 + g)^n$, and the value of the constant L can be determined by a similar substitution. We get

$$H(1 + g)^n = L(1 + g)^n - (1 - s)L(1 + g)^{n-1}$$

or

$$L = \frac{1 + g}{s + g} H \tag{8}$$

Comparing this with the expression previously got for E [(4) above], we see that L will always be less than E, so that the new moving equilibrium will always be lower than the old.

Now write $\Upsilon_n = L(1 + g)^n(1 + z_n)$, so that z_n is the proportion in which actual income exceeds the new (lower) moving equilibrium level. Substituting this in (7) and using (8) we get

$$z_n = \frac{1 - s}{1 + g} z_{n-1}$$

The coefficient $(1 - s)/(1 + g)$ is necessarily positive and less than unity. Starting, therefore, from a given value of z_0, the successive zs get smaller and smaller, in geometrical progression. By what is essentially the Kahn convergent series, the system tends towards its lower moving equilibrium $L(1 + g)^n$.

But it will not get there. For once z has fallen so far as to become less than a certain ratio (which, as can readily be verified, is the not particularly small ratio g/s), the fall in the proportion z by which actual output exceeds the lower moving equilibrium output becomes less than the rate at which that moving equilibrium is itself rising; and once this happens, actual output will begin to rise. The original difference equation should then come back into operation, and that will start a new expansion *relatively to the natural growth*.

The simplest way of proving that this must be so is the following. Suppose, for a moment, that there is no induced investment until the lower equilibrium has actually been reached. Then the system will start taking up successive positions which are actually on the lower equilibrium line. In these positions the ys (measured, as before, from the upper equilibrium) are negative and equal. Now if y_0 and y_1 are both equal to $-a$, we shall have [by (6)] $y_2 = -2\lambda a + \lambda^2 a$, so that $y_2 - y_1 = (\lambda - 1)^2 a$, which is certainly positive. It can further be shown, by the usual methods, that $y_n - y_{n-1} = (n - 1)\lambda^{n-2} \times (\lambda - 1)^2$, which will always be positive. The same result can be shown to hold for the more general case, in which we assume a larger value for c.

Thus, if the system actually hits its lower equilibrium, it will then be bound to start an upward expansion. If induced investment appears before it has hit the lower equilibrium, that is simply a further expansionary influence. The output so generated will then be greater, for each period, than that which we have just calculated. The expansion is therefore demonstrated *a fortiori*.

VI

Our model is now complete; and by our algebraic method, we have shown its internal consistency. For further discussion, it will be convenient to have a graphical representation.

Fig. 2 represents the same variables as Fig. 1: time on the horizontal axis, and on the vertical the logarithm of output (or investment). Steady progress is therefore represented by a straight line which slopes upwards, and steady progress at the "natural rate of growth" by a straight line of given slope. There are four such lines which play a part in our model. First, there is the Full Employment line F. Secondly, there is the "upper equilibrium" line E; and thirdly there is the "lower equilibrium" line L. Finally, there is the "long-range investment" line H, the upward slope of which is responsible for the upward slopes of E and L. It should again be emphasized that output is being measured in real terms, so that F may slope upwards, on account of an upward trend in productivity, even if population is constant. H slopes upwards at the natural rate of growth, because, by assumption, it is geared to the trend. E and L slope upward because they depend on H.

FIG. 2

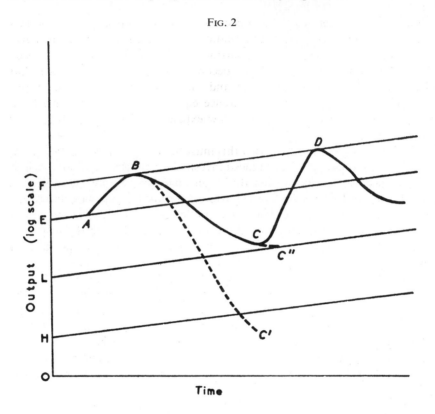

We know that L must lie above H, because of the Keynesian multiplier argument. We know that E must lie above L, because E includes the multiplier effect of induced investment (at the natural rate of growth of output) as well as the multiplier effect of the long-range investment. We shall assume for the present that E lies below F, though it should be noticed that we have not proved that it must do so.

The E line is such that the economy could possibly advance along it in a smooth manner without fluctuation. But it will do so only if it is held to it in some manner, for any chance divergence in either direction will set up a movement away from the equilibrium E. Suppose that there is a chance divergence in an upward direction. Output then begins to grow at more than its natural rate of growth, and though there may be some tendency for the actual rate of growth to slow up after some time has elapsed, the actual rate will always exceed the natural rate (at least according to the value which we have given to c). And that means that the actual path AB must hit the ceiling F sooner or later. But when it hits the ceiling, the rate of increase in output is slowed up, and therefore (in the next period) induced investment is cut down. But the induced investment, which corresponds to an increase in output at the natural rate (which is all that is allowed by the ceiling F) is only sufficient to engender a level of output which approximates to the E line, not one which goes along the F line. Output therefore tends to move back, on the course BC′, towards the E line. But as output moves back, the rate of increase in output falls below the natural rate, and in consequence actual output tends to fall below the E line. The track which would be generated, on this principle, after the "upper turning-point" B had been passed, would plunge downwards indefinitely, tending towards an output of zero. I show it on the diagram by the dotted line BC′.

It was, however, at this point that we felt it necessary to introduce our second complication. A downward movement in actual output, when it becomes an absolute fall, not merely a fall relatively to the natural rate of growth, should not be thought of as causing induced investment to become negative (or at least as only doing so to a minor extent). The path BC′ is therefore too pessimistic. If zero is the lowest point to which induced investment can fall, then on the down-track we have a situation in which the only investment occurring is that which is represented by H. And L is the equilibrium to which the system will tend when the only investment is that represented by H. The system will therefore move along a path BC″, which is determined by the familiar multiplier theory of Keynes (or Kahn). This path will merge into the L line at a point C″.

But since the L line is upward sloping, the path BC″ will have begun to turn upwards at a point C, which precedes C″. At this point the "accelerator" comes back into gear. It must then bring about a positive induced investment, which will cause the actual path to diverge from CC″ in an upward direction. The rate of growth will then soon be in excess of the natural rate, and the path CD must therefore intersect the E line sooner or later. When it does so, it will still have a rate of growth in excess of the natural rate, and will therefore keep on rising. Finally, it must hit the F line, and when it does so, it is bound to turn down as before, for exactly the same reason as before.

There has thus been engendered a complete cycle, and a cycle which is completely self-perpetuating. It must turn down when it gets to the top, and when it approaches the bottom it must turn up. So long as the fundamental data remain unchanged, actual output must fluctuate between the limits L and F, and will do so indefinitely.

VII

Further, what has been accomplished is something more than the making of a special model, which happens to show a fluctuation, something like the observed sort, for certain values of its parameters. We have used special values for purposes of illustration, but the cycle which has been engendered does not depend on the special values chosen. All that is necessary is (1) that the relations between income and consumption, on the one hand, and between investment and changes in income, on the other, should be such as to impart a rather strong tendency to instability in the level of output; (2) that the system should have an upward trend, and that some investment should be geared to that upward trend; (3) that the supply of resources, at any given time, should not be inexhaustible; (4) that falls in output should not induce disinvestment, in the way that rises in output induce investment, except (possibly) to a minor extent. These conditions are certainly not at all restrictive; all of them (except possibly the first) are things which we should naturally expect to be true. And the first condition, though its validity is certainly far from self-evident, is not intrinsically unplausible. We do therefore seem to have shown that a cycle, which is strongly reminiscent of that which we experience, can be explained on the basis of a minimum number of hypotheses, each of which is very reasonable in itself. It is hardly possible for a *theory* of the Cycle to do more than that.

Besides, from this point we can again go forward. The next thing to do should be to reconsider the very simple difference equation on which our formal analysis (though not the real essence of our argument) has been based. It is, as a matter of fact, most unlikely that the two relations (between income and consumption, and between investment and change in income) are as simple in form as we have assumed them to be. We have taken a simple form, in order to keep our main difference equation down to the second order; but there can be little doubt that the equation we thereby got is over-simplified, though it should be noticed that the mathematical difficulties accumulate very rapidly when we introduce additional complications in this direction. There is, however, one generalisation which can be made without incurring these mathematical difficulties. We can allow for the probability that a part of consumption will depend upon current income as well as a part on previous income; an amendment in this direction makes the system *more* liable to fluctuate.[6] This has a bearing on the weakest of the four assumptions listed in the previous paragraph. It will probably have been noticed that in order to get our model to work, we did apparently need a rather large value for the capital coefficient c; it looked as if it had to be distinctly larger than unity.[7] So large a value for c is not altogether unplausible (Mr. Harrod is evidently prepared to accept a value of this order of magnitude); nevertheless when we

---

[6] We can also allow for the possibility that a part of consumption may be geared to the trend of income without introducing additional difficulties. The effect of this amendment would be to diminish the amplitude of fluctuations, but not to diminish the probability of their occurrence.

[7] When $c = 1$, it means that an increase in real output by £100 millions (at given prices) causes an increase in investment by £100 millions (at prices which correspond).

remember that "long-range" investment is being otherwise allowed for, a doubt must remain whether so large a value of c is realistic. It is therefore useful to notice that if only a part of consumption is lagged, we can manage to work our model with much smaller values of c. The value of c can be appreciably less than unity, and we can still get the required instability in the level of output.

Such things evidently need much further enquiry; but the way to that enquiry is now open. It will then be of great importance to study the changes in the model which may occur through changes in the sizes of some of the parameters, and to enquire whether they have any correspondence with observed changes in the behaviour of the actual economy through various cycles. If it could be shown that there is such correspondence, the theory would receive striking confirmation. I am in fact inclined to think that some of this confirmation can be sighted without looking very far. One thing which clearly could happen would be that the value of c was not large enough for the upward swing (AB or CD in Fig. 2) to hit the Full Employment ceiling. If this were to happen, the boom would turn down before it hit the ceiling; but the rest of the cycle could apparently go on as before. Does not this look very like the case of the boom which "peters out"? Mr. Harrod has done some useful work on the factors determining the size of c; by using his researches on this point, and concentrating on the effects of changes in his factors in this direction, it does look as if the theory we have been advancing should be capable of some indirect verification.

Again, it is clearly not realistic to assume that the "height" of the H line (the long-range investment) will, as we have drawn it, be constant in all circumstances. Such things as wars and their aftermaths (and maybe other disturbances too) must be thought of as causing "autonomous" fluctuations in long-range investment. The effects of such fluctuations could be analysed. A considerable upward hump in the H line could, for instance, push the corresponding E *above* the Full Employment line. If this happened, there would be no tendency for output to turn down when it reached the Full Employment level. Let us consider the matter, for instance, in terms of equation (6). We saw that in a system which was "driven" by that equation, two successive ys which were both equal to f would be succeeded by a third which was equal to $f - (\lambda - 1)^2 f$; if f is positive, this must be smaller than f. But if f is negative, as in the case we are considering, the third y will be *larger* than f; being above the Full Employment level, it will then have to be replaced by f. Thus the system can remain in Full Employment as long as the hump in the H-curve lasts.

This is itself a highly suggestive result; one further modification, which can be introduced into our structure, not only without damage but with benefit, makes it more suggestive still. It is not quite right to treat "Full Employment," as we have done hitherto, as a rigid barrier; it is better to regard it as a zone which, if penetrated, calls forth rapidly increasing resistances to the expansion of output, but in which some increase of output can, up to a point, still be attained. This modification makes no real difference to the structure of our theory; the slowing-up of expansion, due to the resistances, will still cause output to turn downwards once the zone is fairly penetrated, so long as the equilibrium level E is lower than the level at which the resistances begin. But if we allow that the resistances begin (as I think they do) at a level of output which is short of that where there is a tendency to definite inflation, we get another important result. We can see why it is that the ordinary commercial boom, carried by induced investment, is most unlikely to penetrate through the resisting medium so far as to cause any serious inflation; the resistances will cause it to turn downwards before it gets to that point. It is only when there is a big hump in the H-curve, pushing the equilibrium level well into the Full Employment zone, that the system can have enough "steam" in it to carry it to the inflationary point. The ordinary commercial boom is unlikely to do that. Our theory therefore affords a ready explanation of another well-established practical generalisation, which was previously rather out of touch with theory; it shows why it is that inflation is so liable to occur in conditions of war and post-war reconstruction, but rarely (if ever) results from a purely commercial boom.

I should, however, not like it to be inferred from these arguments that a continued boosting of the H-curve, so as to keep E above F, is a desirable solution of the cycle problem. For what is bound to happen, in this "over-employment" situation, is that induced investment is kept steadily below its normal relation to current output. And since, on the whole, the induced investment is *needed* in order to enable output to be produced efficiently, its repression (certainly its continued repression) is bound to have adverse effects on the efficiency of production. Thus even if the danger of open inflation can be somehow averted, this "solution" can cure the cycle only at the price of a severe loss in efficiency. The true object of policy should be to keep the equilibrium line as near as possible to the Full Employment mark, but not to push beyond it. If this is done, it will also be necessary to have measures at hand to correct the downward divergences from equilibrium, which are then liable to occur. This policy is much harder than its alternative; but if it can be achieved, its results will be infinitely preferable.

4

Economic Fluctuations and Growth*

By ARTHUR SMITHIES†

The central purpose of this article is to produce a model that will explain both fluctuations and growth through the operation of endogenous forces. It thus attempts a synthesis of business cycle theories of the Tinbergen type and growth theories of the Harrod type. The model stresses those factors that, in the opinion of the author, explain the great depression of the 1930's and the continued growth (subject to minor fluctuations) of the economy since the war. It does not seek to explain the minor fluctuations that have occurred in the last decade. This article has been arranged, at the cost of some repetition, to meet the requirements of nonmathematical and mathematical readers.

I. INTRODUCTION

THE LAST twenty-five years have seen a wealth of "business cycle theories" which attempt to explain fluctuations about a growth trend but leave the trend itself largely unexplained. Many of the dynamic theories of the postwar period have been preoccupied with the conditions for steady growth and have neglected what happens when the economy leaves its narrow exponential path. Bridges between these two types of theory are infrequent and by no means satisfactory. This article attempts a synthesis and seeks to show how fluctuations can be generated by the process of growth; how growth can occur without fluctuations; and how fluctuations can occur independently of growth.[1]

The model is empirical in the sense that I do not believe that any of the possibilities it suggests can be excluded by the available evidence. But it is not numerical. In fact, I doubt whether satisfactory numerical models can be constructed so long as we have to rely heavily on the evidence of time series—and I do not see how we can escape that. For anything like statistical reliability

* *Econometrica*, Vol. XXV (January, 1957). Reprinted by the courtesy of the Econometric Society and the author. [At the request of the editors the author has condensed sections of the original article.]

† Harvard University.

[1] This article was written during a sabbatical year at Oxford. I am most grateful to the Oxford economists for listening to it at various stages during its fluctuating growth, and I wish particularly to thank D. G. Champernowne, G. D. A. MacDougall, L. R. Klein, and G. D. N. Worswick.

to be attained, the economist must commit himself to a single model for a twenty- or thirty-year period. But if the model is simple enough to be manageable, its structure is likely to change within such a period. For instance, a model with unchanging structure is unlikely to fit the 1920's, the 1930's, and the postwar period.

Consequently, numerical models that are adequate from the theoretical point of view are unlikely to be useful instruments of prediction. Prediction, in my view, must depend on cruder statistical methods, supplemented by judgment. But judgment can be sharpened and improved by knowledge of what can happen under specified conditions. And this is where a model that exhibits a variety of possibilities becomes useful, even though it does not furnish numerical estimates.

The present model is constructed with the United States economy mainly in mind and therefore focusses on the factors that are critical to the behaviour of that economy. I believe the most critical of those factors is the rate at which the capacity to produce behaves in relation to total demand; and that the most serious difficulties arise when capacity increases faster than demand in prosperity periods. I say virtually nothing about foreign trade and the balance-of-payments which are so critical for other economies. Nor do I stress labor or capacity bottlenecks which have played a prominent part in several recent business cycle theories. Also a model in terms of constant prices may be more valid for the United States than for other economies.

The model is constructed of familiar materials. Its claims to novelty rest on the synthesis it achieves of ideas put forward by others. The main authors to whom I feel particularly indebted include Tinbergen, Klein, Kalecki, Harrod, Domar, Hicks, Goodwin, Schumpeter, Modigliani, Duesenberry, the Brookings Institution, Frisch, and, of course, Keynes.

More generally I am greatly indebted to the work of Fellner, Kaldor, Samuelson, and especially Joan Robinson. I am not aware, however, that adoption or rejection of their ideas has been responsible for specific elements in my own model.

That concludes my list of major acknowledgments on the theoretical side. But no list could be complete without referring to the monumental work of data collection undertaken by Kuznets, Goldsmith, and the National Income Division of the U.S. Department of Commerce.

II. CONCEPTS AND DEFINITIONS

Full-Capacity Output

A central feature of the model is the concept full-capacity output and the difference positive or negative between full-capacity and actual output. By full-capacity output I mean the output that the existing stock of equipment is intended to produce under normal working conditions with respect to hours of work, number of shifts, and so forth. It corresponds to the notion of full capacity used in the steel and other industries. And, in *America's Capacity to Produce* [Edwin G. Nourse], an estimate was made for the whole American economy. I see no reason why such estimates should not be made regularly on a sample basis and a great deal of reason why the attempt should be made —since the measurement of capital involves even greater difficulties.

The problem of the relation of capital to output, however, cannot be avoided at the margin. We do need to know how full-capacity output responds to investment, and this involves the use of marginal capital-output ratios. A given amount of (gross) investment will itself increase capacity output, but to estimate the increase in capacity in a given year account must also be taken of the capacity output that is lost through physical depreciation and obsolescence. These in turn must be values in terms of the investment that is needed to make up for the loss. Net investment will then mean gross investment minus depreciation and obsolescence, calculated in this way.

Actual output can exceed or fall short of full-capacity output. An excess of actual output may be achieved by the use of reserve capacity or by more intensive use of capacity through additional shifts or overtime. And it may create conditions of excessive demand in particular areas. A deficiency of actual output, on the other hand, produces a condition of excess capacity which will only be removed when output increases or existing capacity is extinguished.

Full-capacity output can also differ from full-employment output. An excess of the latter means that actual output must exceed full-capacity output in order to achieve full employment. In extreme situations, such as prevailed in the bomb-damaged areas of Europe after the war, shortage of capacity may simply prevent the attainment of full employment. An excess of capacity output over full-employment output means that full utilization of capacity requires abnormal overtime or additions to the labor force; and labor shortages may be sufficiently acute to prevent full use of capacity.

Along with changes in capacity output go changes in the general complexion of the economy, the emergence of new products, the revolutions in the techniques of production, the growth of cities and the decline of agriculture. These changes in turn affect economic behaviour with respect to consumption, investment, and government activity. In what follows I shall use the difference between this year's and last year's full-capacity output as a general indicator of economic change.

Ratchet Effects

The operation of the model will depend critically on ratchet effects, introduced into the modern theory of consumer behaviour by Modigliani and Duesenberry. The ratchet effect means that the highest level of income or product attained so far prevents the economy falling back to previous low levels in the event of a depression. This effect permits growth and fluctuations to occur at the same time, without the assistance of outside trends. I maintain that ratchet effects are not simply related to the behaviour of consumers but represent a pervasive economic phenomenon.

The idea of the ratchet is not really a modern discovery. It is inherent in Schumpeter's notion of the role of equilibrium in economic development, first published in 1912. Equilibrium in his system not only constitutes fetters through which the entrepreneur must break. But the subsequent process of expansion and adaptation (recession) establishes equilibrium at a new and higher level. Thus in his system the tendency towards equilibrium represents both a ratchet and a brake.

A satisfactory model would take into account possible brake effects as well as ratchet effects. Moreover, it would allow for the ratchet to exert a diminishing force as time went on. But for the sake of simplicity of exposition, I resist the inclination to include such refinements.

In the model, I shall make the following simplifying assumptions:

1. Prices remain stable and no significant changes occur in relative prices.
2. The ratio of compensation of employees to GNP remains constant. This in conjunction with (1) implies that money wages rise proportionately to the average productivity of labor.
3. The supply of credit to finance investment is elastic in the sense that the banking system will provide any amount of loans supported by given collateral on constant terms and conditions.
4. The economy is closed in the sense that exports and imports are always equal.
5. Government budgetary policies are neutral in their effects. This requires not only that the government's budget is always balanced but that the impacts of taxation and expenditures are "diffused" so as not to alter the distribution of income between wages and profits or among individuals.

The operation of the model is governed by four basic relations:

1. A consumption function which determines consumers' expenditures in relation to income and trend variables.
2. An investment function which does the same thing for gross investment expenditures.
3. A short-run equilibrating relation which states that consumption and investment so determined add up to the GNP in every year without excessive demand or supply—or that gross saving is equal to gross investment.
4. Relations that determine the increase in full-capacity output in response to gross investment, and the losses of capacity resulting from depreciation and obsolescence.

Relations (1), (2), and (3) then determine change in the actual level of aggregate demand and output, while (4) determines changes in its full-capacity level. There is no reason why actual and full-capacity output should increase at the same rate. In fact it seems to be of the essence of economic change that they should change at different rates, leading to "persistent exhilaration," equilibrium growth, or repeated fluctuations. But before going further we must examine the constituent relations of the model.

The Investment Function

In the formulation of the investment function, I shall follow Tinbergen, Kalecki, Klein, and Meyer and Kuh[2] and maintain that the endogenous variable of the system that has the dominant influence on the rate of gross investment decisions is the level of present or past gross profits. The influence of profits is twofold. They provide a basis for expectations concerning the returns to be obtained from investment and they influence the terms and conditions on which firms can finance their investment.

Investment is clearly affected by factors other than profits, such as the rate of growth achieved in the past, the rate and character of technical change, and the structure of final demand. The justification for using profits as a central variable is that changes in those factors favorable to investment are also likely to result in an increase in the level of profits.

From the point of view of finance, businesses have a decided preference for investing their own funds, rather than raising new money in the market. Moreover the terms on which they can borrow money in the market depend on the amounts they can provide themselves. Thus an increase in the level of profits reduces the cost of financing a given amount of investment.

It is reasonable to suppose, however, that entrepreneurs are not guided merely by their current level of profits. In a recession, the high levels of profits previously attained are likely to influence expectations of the future. Thus the ratchet level of profits should be included as a factor affecting investment decisions.

Even in a simple aggregative model, however, the state of excess or deficient capacity should be recognized as an influence on investment. But the current state of excess capacity does not seem to be the correct indicator, since investment does take place in the midst of excess capacity. The critical question, rather, is whether capacity appears to be excessive from the point of view of a normal level of operations. This suggests that, in terms of the concepts of the model, the rate of investment should depend on the difference between current capacity and its ratchet level.

In addition to endogenous factors, however, exogenous trends must be recognized as an important influence on investment. The rate of population growth, which I shall not undertake to explain by economic factors, is the most obvious example. Regardless of the immediate or past level of profits, changes in the rate of population growth can influence profit expectations and hence the rate of investment. And although no new geographical frontiers remain to be crossed in the United States, the development or the restoration of regions in the South and West can have effects similar to new frontiers on the rate of investment.

---

[2] J. R. Meyer and E. Kuh, *The Investment Decision* (Cambridge: Harvard University Press, 1957).

Since we are assuming that gross profits are proportional to GNP, the latter can be used as a variable of the investment function instead of profits. Let I = gross investment, Y = GNP, $\overline{Y}$ = highest level of GNP so far, and Y_F = full-capacity GNP. All the variables are expressed in real terms. Then assuming investment is linearly related to the variables, the investment function is

$$I = \beta_1 Y_{-1} + \beta_2 \overline{Y} - \beta_3 (Y_{F-1} - \overline{Y}) + k\,!$$

Current investment depends on lagged rather than current values of the output variables Y and Y_F in recognition of the fact that investment plans precede actual investment. Since I am not concerned with numerical estimation, I shall assume that this lag is one year.

The first term denotes dependence on profits from both the inducement and the supply-of-funds points of view; the second, on the ratchet level of profits; the third, on the existence of excess or deficient capacity. The final term indicates the independent influence of trends, such as population growth, on investment.

The Consumption Function

The relation of consumers' expenditures must be considered in two parts: first, the relation of disposable consumers' income to GNP and, second, the relation of consumers' expenditures to disposable income.

In our simplified economy, wages and salary payments and gross profits are each a constant proportion of GNP. In a steadily growing economy, it can also be assumed that distributions out of gross profits to stockholders and bondholders will be a constant proportion of gross profits. This proportion will result from the competing desires of the stockholders for dividends and the desires of management to provide for investment by internal financing. In a fluctuating economy, however, distributions are subject to ratchet effects. The most striking example is the maintenance of dividend payments for several years after the 1929 downturn even though net profits had virtually disappeared. Putting these factors together, we can say as a rough approximation that current disposable income depends on the current level of GNP and its ratchet level.

With respect to the relation of consumer expenditures to disposable income, I accept as a rough approximation, the Duesenberry-Modigliani hypothesis that consumption tends to be a constant ratio of a steadily growing income, but is subject to ratchet effects. However, I am more interested in asserting that there is no demonstrable tendency in the long-run ratio to decline than to maintain its constancy. There is no need to stress the fact that in the short run consumer expenditures are affected by capital gains, as in 1929; by liquid asset accumulations, as in the postwar period; and by fluctuations in the demand for durables.

Since disposable income depends on GNP and its ratchet value, consumption depends on disposable income and its ratchet value; and since ratchet disposable income depends on ratchet GNP, we can conclude that consumption depends on GNP and on ratchet GNP. If the relations are linear, the consumption function is

$$C = (1 - \alpha_1)Y + \alpha_2 \overline{Y}$$

where C denotes real consumption expenditures. The long-run marginal (or average) propensity to consume, where $Y = \overline{Y}$, is $1 - \alpha_1 + \alpha_2$ and the short-run marginal propensity is $1 - \alpha_1$. The corresponding propensities to save are α_1 and $\alpha_1 - \alpha_2$.

I shall not formally include trend influences on consumption in the model. But they can exist and can be taken into account in the same manner as trend influences on investment.

Short-Run Equilibrium

I shall assume that investment and consumers' expenditures determined by their respective functions together determine the level of GNP at any particular time; and, in that sense, the system is in short-run equilibrium. This means that the multiplier process is assumed to work itself out in a period that is short relative to the investment planning period and that there are no impediments to rapid upward or downward changes in production. While output can exceed full-capacity output, I assume that output is not limited by shortages of equipment or labor—except where this possibility is explicitly recognized.

These simplifications rule out some minor sources both of disturbance and stability, but I cannot see that they affect the course of the economy to any major extent.

With these assumptions we have

$$Y = C + I$$

or

$$Y - C = I = S$$

where S denotes gross savings.

Changes in Full-Capacity Output and the Productivity of Labor

To complete the model, we need to examine the effect of investment on full-capacity output.

The possibility of discrepancies between changes in actual output and changes in full-capacity output is the critical feature of the model. In line with Harrod and Domar, the increase in actual output depends on the increase in effective demand which in turn depends on the increase in gross investment plus the multiplier effects on consumption. That is determined by the relations already set out. The increase in full-capacity output depends on the technical consequences of net investment, which is the matter now under examination.

Before coming to this question directly, it is necessary to observe that by no means all increases in capacity output require gross investment, and by no means all gross investment, as it is usually classified, results in increased output.

Capacity output can increase because of increased skill and improved training of the labor force and increased willingness to work, both more intensively and a greater number of shifts. It can increase because of the increased skill of management in organizing business and in achieving good labor relations. In fact, most of the possibilities of Marshallian increasing returns, which explicitly exclude technological change, may be realized with little or no investment needed to put them into effect. Because of the need to impose limits on this discussion, I deal with these matters as trend influences.

Investment, as a statistical category, is necessarily somewhat arbitrary and does not correspond exactly with the economists' notion of productive capital. Much of it is more closely akin to consumers' durables. Consider, for instance, housing construction. New housing that removes impediments to needed relocation of the labor force or reduces absenteeism through improving public health clearly counts as productive investment. But housing that does none of these things but merely increases standards of comfort, however desirable on social grounds, has little to do with increasing capacity output.[3] Similar questions can be raised with respect to commercial building—shops and hotels. The upshot is that a qualitative analysis of a country's investment is needed to determine how much of the total is relevant from the point of view of increasing output capacity.

Subject to these qualifications, every act of gross investment in itself increases full-capacity output, whether or not the investment is undertaken in response to technological change. In a hypothetical economy not subject to technological change the ratio of capacity output increase to investment will remain constant or decrease. It will remain constant if capital is simply widened with a flexible and increasing supply of labor. In an economy that is subject to technological change the ratio may increase or decrease from time to time depending on the character of the innovations that technology makes feasible. In this way production can become more or less capital-intensive without further specification. But technological change affects not only the increase in capacity output per unit of investment, but also its increase in relation to the employment of additional labor. The output-investment

---

[3] Of course, it can be argued that the improved services rendered by the improved housing themselves constitute increases in output. But this argument is almost, if not wholly, tautological and practically confusing.

ratio may increase by more or less than the output-labor ratio. The change in capacity output, however, depends on net investment—that is, on gross investment *minus* depreciation and obsolescence, as defined in the last section. We must now specify the relations of these items to the variables of the model.

If it could be assumed that equipment retains its usefulness to the end of its useful life, that the life of all kinds of equipment was the same *n* years, and that none of it died prematurely on account of obsolescence, then physical depreciation today would be equal to the replacement cost of the equipment constructed *n* years ago. If the economy had been growing at a steady rate during the intervening period, this figure could be taken as proportional to full-capacity output. Actually depreciation depends in a complicated way on the history of investment over the lifetime of existing equipment. The interruptions of wars or extreme depressions may have affected the age distribution of equipment, so that current depreciation is subject to "echo effects" from the past and varying rates of obsolescence have a bearing on the amount of equipment that is allowed to reach the end of its useful physical life.

In view of these complexities, I have the choice of making the artificial assumption that depreciation is proportional to full-capacity output or regarding it as a changing datum of the problem. From this point of view changes in depreciation fall in the category of shocks that can only be anticipated by a continuing qualitative examination of the existing stock of equipment. For the practical economists' purposes, the latter approach is essential. For present pedagogic purposes I shall resort to the artificial assumption that a fixed proportion of full-capacity output is lost each year. To be more specific, I shall assume that on account of depreciation, full-capacity output this year is reduced by a fixed proportion of last year's full-capacity output.

By obsolescence, I mean the abandonment of equipment before the end of its useful physical life. Obsolescence can be directly related to gross investment in the sense that a decision to construct new equipment may involve a decision by the same firm to abandon existing equipment prematurely. And even if the economy is growing steadily without interruption, successful innovation will force competitors to abandon equipment prematurely. I suggest therefore that there is a category of obsolescence that can be described as "normal" and which is proportional to the rate of gross investment.

There is, however, a second category: "extraordinary obsolescence." If demand is low relative to capacity output, abnormal abandonment can be expected. If demand is relatively high, equipment that would normally be abandoned may be retained in operation, and extraordinary obsolescence is negative. Thus high rates of gross investment can be followed by high or low rates of obsolescence, and the expectations of those who undertake investment can be satisfied even though others are profoundly dissatisfied with the situation. As will be seen later, obsolescence in this way exercises an automatic stabilizing influence on the economy. With relatively low demand abandonment will be accelerated.

As a simple hypothesis I shall assume that this second type of obsolescence, positive or negative, is proportional to the difference between full-capacity and actual output. Thus, with respect to obsolescence as a whole, I shall assume that full-capacity output this year depends on the rate of gross investment last year and on the difference between full-capacity and actual output last year.

The argument of this section can now be summarized symbolically. The rate of increase in full-capacity output depends on the rate of gross investment and on the losses of capacity output through depreciation and obsolescence. If D_1 and D_2 denote physical depreciation and extraordinary obsolescence, respectively, we have

$$Y_F - Y_{F-1} = \sigma I_{-1} - D_1 - D_2 + I'$$

and

$$D_1 = \delta_1 (Y_F)_{-1} \, ,$$
$$D_2 = \delta_2 [(Y_F)_{-1} - Y_{-1}]^4.$$

The coefficient σ (Domar's symbol) takes into account the direct effects of gross investment on capacity minus the losses of capacity due to normal obsolescence. It depends on the rate and character of technological change. While it may be assumed constant for moderate periods, it clearly changes over longer periods. Moreover, even in short periods changes in σ may occur if the economy encounters factor shortages that induce a greater relative intensiveness of capital. The trends factor I' has been introduced to take into account changes in capacity output that may occur independently of the rate of investment.

III. THE OPERATION OF THE MODEL—VERBAL ANALYSIS

I shall now give a *verbal* description of how the model works. This will be followed by a more precise mathematical analysis, which is necessary to prove many of the propositions that can only be dealt with on an intuitive basis in the present discussion.

The model can be divided into two interrelated parts. The first determines the behaviour of aggregate demand (with the model continually in short-run equilibrium). The second relates to the change in full-capacity output.

---

[4] I have arbitrarily assumed that the lag periods in these relations is the same as that in the investment function. In a model that arrived at numerical results, the two lag periods would each have to be estimated. The assumption of a single lag period, however, does not affect the validity of the model as a basis for quantitative discussion. It should be emphasized that D_1 and D_2 denote losses of capacity output, and not losses of equipment. If losses of equipment are valued at the replacement cost of equivalent capacity, depreciation and obsolescence will be D_1/σ and D_2/σ respectively.

Aggregate demand changes as a result of the inducement to invest and the multiplier. In addition to trend influences, investment depends first on (lagged) profits, which in turn depend on (lagged) GNP, Y. The second influence on investment is the (lagged) difference $\overline{Y} - Y_F$. A relative shortage of capacity is a stimulus to investment and relative excess capacity a deterrent. Thus investment can turn down while Y is increasing provided $\overline{Y} - Y_F$ is decreasing sufficiently. While Y increases in response to aggregate demand, Y_F depends on the influences tending to increase or decrease capacity—the second part of the model.

The rate of change in Y_F depends on the rate of gross investment which increases Y_F according to the investment-output ratio. But it also depends on depreciation and obsolescence which tend to decrease it. While the rate of depreciation, in fact, depends on the life history of past investment, I am assuming that it depends simply on the existing level of Y_F. Its obsolescence on the other hand depends on the degree to which capacity is being used, i.e., on $Y - Y_F$. Excess capacity accelerates obsolescence while abnormal use of capacity tends to retard it.

A second basic distinction to be made is between those situations where the ratchet effects are felt and those where the economy has no need of ratchet support. If Y (and Y_F) increase continually without fluctuation, the present level of output is equal to the "highest level so far," i.e., Y is identical with $\overline{Y}$. On the other hand, where fluctuations occur $\overline{Y}$ exceeds Y after a downturn in Y and the ratchets act as sustaining influences until Y returns to its previous peak level. We thus have, in effect, two models for different states of the economy. State 1 will denote conditions under which $\overline{Y} \equiv Y$ and State 2 those where $Y < \overline{Y}$.

Reasonable values of the coefficients of the model are consistent with continued economic growth or with fluctuations. Neither possibility can be excluded without specific knowledge of the economy under consideration. Moreover, I maintain that conditions in one economy can change from time to time, so that in one decade, for instance, a continued growth model may be appropriate while in another a fluctuating model is needed, depending on conditions outside the present frame of reference. I shall therefore consider first the possibilities of continued growth (or continued decline) revealed by the model and then the possibilities of fluctuations. In both cases it is instructive to examine first how the economy behaves endogenously—without the aid or obstacle of trends; and then to consider how that behaviour is modified by trend influences.

Continued Growth

(a) *Equilibrium Growth.* A useful path of reference for the study of continued growth is the Harrod "warranted rate." In the present context, this is a state where the economy grows continually with Y always equal to Y_F:

the disturbing difference $Y - Y_F$ is ruled out of account; and, of course, ratchet influences are absent. This kind of growth seems entitled to the name "equilibrium growth," since it represents an orderly and simple state of the economy and is a useful path of reference for considering other situations.

If equilibrium growth is assumed to occur, the model reduces to very simple terms. On the "aggregate demand side," gross investment is a fixed proportion of lagged GNP, gross saving is a fixed proportion of current GNP, and savings and investment are equal. On the supply side the increase in GNP depends on gross investment, physical depreciation, and normal obsolescence.

In symbols,

$$I = \beta Y_{-1}, \tag{1}$$

$$S = \alpha Y, \tag{2}$$

$$I = S, \tag{3}$$

$$Y - Y_{-1} = \sigma I_{-1} - \delta_1 Y_{-1}. \tag{4}$$

Equations (1), (2), and (3) determine the rate of increase of aggregate demand, and equation (4) determines the increase of output on the supply side. For steady growth to continue, the rate of increase in output derived from (1), (2), and (3) must equal its rate of increase derived from (4).

From (1), (2), and (3) we have

$$\alpha Y = \beta Y_{-1}, \quad \text{or} \tag{5}$$

$$Y = \frac{\beta}{\alpha} Y_{-1}.$$

This relation states that output at any time is equal to the current rate of investment (βY_{-1}) multiplied by the multiplier $(1/\alpha)$. Under these conditions output will increase from year to year at a constant proportionate rate. For

$$\frac{Y - Y_{-1}}{Y_{-1}} = \frac{\beta}{\alpha} - 1. \tag{6}$$

For instance, suppose $\alpha = 20\%$ and $\beta = 21\%$; then the percentage rate of growth will be 5%.

Another formula for the proportionate rate of growth can be derived from (4). Since $I = S$, we can write αY_{-1} for I_{-1}. and (4) consequently becomes

$$Y - Y_{-1} = (\sigma\alpha - \delta_1)Y_{-1},$$

and the proportionate rate of growth is

$$\frac{Y - Y_{-1}}{Y_{-1}} = \sigma\alpha - \delta_1. \tag{7}$$

This expression states that the rate of growth of full-capacity output depends on the proportion (α) of its current output the economy is prepared to devote to increasing output; on the technical effectiveness of investment in increasing output (σ), and on the rate at which existing capacity output is being reduced through depreciation (δ_1). It is in fact the Harrod-Domar warranted rate of growth. Their analysis runs in terms of net output and net investment, so that their rate of growth is simply the $\sigma\alpha$ appropriate to the net concepts.

To illustrate (7) numerically, suppose $\sigma = 0.60$, implying a marginal investment output ratio of 1.7, $\alpha = 0.20$, and $\delta_1 = 0.07$. Then the proportionate rate of growth of full-capacity output will also be 5%.[5]

For steady growth to occur, the rates of growth in (5) and (6) must be equal. If (5) is greater than (6), there will be a persistent tendency for aggregate demand and current output to exceed capacity output and if less there are likely to be recurrent tendencies for the economy to generate excess capacity.

Harrod argues, in effect, that if steady growth is once attained, entrepreneurs will in general be satisfied with the results and will tend to maintain it. In the present terminology, if they have hit on the required value of β, will they be satisfied? If they are, it will be in a very limited sense. β is the resultant of many investment decisions. Some investors are satisfied and others disappointed. Those who gain in the competitive struggle during one period may be the losers in others. Those who are successful in any period may try to increase their gains, and the losers may increase their investment in order to recover their losses or may contract it in order to protect their financial positions. "A tolerable state of unrest" would be a better descriptive term than "a general state of satisfaction."

That being so, there can hardly be any tendency for β to attain the correct level. Conceivably an all-wise planning authority could calculate $\alpha\sigma$ and the other factors and consequently achieve the right value of β. But even planning authorities make mistakes. In a private economy each entrepreneur would have to forecast his competitors' behaviour with respect to β and the behaviour of the whole economy with respect to α and σ. And even if he could do that, there is no reason to believe that the general action of all entrepreneurs would tend to produce steady growth.

The point of view of this paper is that steady growth is unlikely. However, the economy is not disorderly. In the absence of external disturbances, such as wars or the special circumstances that prevailed in 1929, the economy follows a reasonably steady course. It is therefore worth inquiring whether β, α, and σ are related to each other in ways that will tend to preserve stability. Suppose the economy is already in a state of steady growth and one of these

---

[5] These numerical illustrations show, incidentally, the danger of using aggregative models as methods of estimating rates of growth. Suppose in the last example $\sigma = 0.70$, $\alpha = 0.22$, and $\delta_1 = 0.05$, then the rate of growth will be 10% instead of 5%. Widely differing results thus follow from values of the determining factors that are close together from the point of view of statistical reliability. The usefulness of such models lies in their validity as a device for thinking about the questions they pose.

factors changes, can changes in the others be expected that will tend to keep the economy on a steady growth path?

Changes in β can occur, e.g., through changes in credit policy, that do not directly affect α or σ. But for steady growth to be maintained an increase in β must induce either an increase in σ or an increase in α or both. First with respect to σ, an increase in β will tend to raise interest rates and reduce the availability of finance. If the change is expected to last for some time, it may induce a shift towards less capital-intensive methods of production and hence reduce σ; and a decrease in β may have the opposite effect. With respect to α, business savings are directly related to investment plans, so that an increase in β can have an influence on α. Further, if an increase in β has inflationary consequences and thus induces a shift to profits, it may again tend to increase α. Changes in σ can result from changes in the nature of technological change. An increase in σ, meaning less capital intensity, may increase β and steady growth will continue at an accelerated rate, although the eventual outcome is grim to contemplate. It seems more likely, however, that a continued tendency for σ to increase will reduce β, and for steady growth to be maintained α must also be reduced. But this is a possibility. In constructing the model I have assumed that profits are a fixed proportion of GNP. But an increase in σ may also reduce the gross profits margin: the forces of competition would be increased by the ability to achieve a given increase in output with smaller investment. A reduction of the profit margin would reduce α and β. But the reduction in β might well be the smaller. Although the reduction of profits would in itself reduce the incentive to invest, the new technical possibilities inherent in the increase in σ might provide an offsetting tendency, so that β/α could increase as σ increases.

There is, however, another possibility. If the increase in σ produces a tendency toward excess capacity, producers may intensify their efforts to sell their products and hence utilize their capacity. These efforts, if successful, will mean a reduction of α. This is not merely a short-run phenomenon, but may alter the long-run complexion of the economy. I believe the American economy does have a greater tendency to generate excess capacity than other economies; and this may help to account for the fact that salesmanship is more pronounced in the United States than elsewhere.

Increases in α can come about through changes in the age distribution of the population, changes in depreciation accounting methods, or changes in depreciation allowances resulting from changing rates of accumulation in the past. An increase in α unrelated to β or σ will have a deflationary effect on the economy, and the monetary consequence will be a tendency for interest rates to fall. This in turn may induce increases in σ and β which will tend to offset the effects of the increase in α on the course of steady growth.

Thus there are stabilizing tendencies in a steadily growing economy. In fact if β is a decreasing function of the rate of interest and σ is an increasing function, and if the rate of interest itself depends on β, α, and the money supply, a self-adjusting model of steady growth could easily be constructed, provided awkward ceilings or floors were not encountered. But the self-adjustment depends on refined static substitution effects. The behaviour of σ, for instance, is likely to depend much more on technological factors than on closely-calculated changes in capital intensity resulting from changes in interest rates.

While there are thus reasons to believe that there will not be chaotic departures from the equilibrium growth conditions, this does not mean that there is much likelihood that equilibrium growth will in fact be achieved. This may be due not only to failure of the conditions already specified to be realized, but also to "initial conditions" which keep the economy off its steady path.

So far we have ignored the influence of the trends in the rate of investment and the rate of growth of full-capacity output. These must now be taken into account.

An upward trend in investment will affect the rate of growth of income and output; it will have multiplier effects on consumption and will also affect the rate of endogenous investment. Through its influence on current income it will affect the level of profits and through its effect on the rate of growth of the economy, it may affect the value of β itself since β depends on the rate of growth generated endogenously or exogenously. The greater the proportional trend rate of growth the greater will be the value of β. In short the trend is likely to affect the structure of the endogenous model.

The rate of growth of full-capacity output, however, will be $\sigma\alpha - \delta_1$ whether or not there is an upward trend in investment. This rate of growth depends on the proportion of its current output, α, the economy is prepared to devote to investment and does not depend on how investment demand arises (this, of course, assumes that σ is independent of the origins of investment demand and that α is independent of the level of income).

Consequently, for actual output and full-capacity output to increase by the same proportions year after year, actual output must again increase at the constant percentage rate $\sigma\alpha - \delta_1$. This can only occur if the trend in investment grows at the same rate as the endogenous rate of increase of output. If, for instance, the trend is represented by a geometrical series k^t, the proportional increase in trend investment from one year to the next will be $k - 1$. Equilibrium growth will be possible only if

$$k - 1 = \frac{\beta_1}{\alpha} - 1 = \sigma\alpha - \delta_1.\,^{6}$$

---

[6] This argument is only approximately correct. For $Y \equiv Y_F$, the proportional rate of growth will initially be greater than the endogenous equilibrium rate, but will approach the latter rate with t sufficiently large. An accurate statement is given in the following mathematical section. But I find it impossible to translate the mathematical argument into intelligible literary terms.

If the trend influence is greater than this critical value, it will change a state of endogenous equilibrium growth into one of exhilaration. If that influence is smaller (including a downward trend with $k < 1$), the economy will tend to produce excess capacity. The trend will slow down the rate of growth of demand by more than it will slow down the growth of capacity.

An independent upward trend in Y_F is inconsistent with equilibrium growth. The point is that while the trend adds to capacity, it does not add to effective demand. If the conditions for endogenous expansion are fulfilled, the addition of such a trend will create excess capacity and hence depress the rate of investment below the equilibrium rate so that the economic process as a whole will generate excess capacity. On the other hand a downward trend in Y_F will have the opposite effect. It will raise the rate of expansion above the endogenous equilibrium rate. The moral of this is not that an upward trend in Y_F is a disadvantage (it is after all the "cheapest" way to increased productivity) but that it needs to be offset by endogenous conditions that tend to make Y increase faster than Y_F.

(b) *Persistent Exhilaration.* The next possibility to consider is that Y may be persistently greater than Y_F for a considerable period of time. This may be termed "persistent exhilaration." To analyze this situation, we must have recourse to the complete model for State 1, and in particular recognize the influence of the factor $Y - Y_F$ as a stimulus to investment and as a delayer of obsolescence.

Even though the foregoing equilibrium condition is fulfilled, initial shortage of capacity such as that which has occurred after wars, will increase investment both through its direct influence and indirectly through raising income and profits. Thus there will be an additional factor increasing the rate of increase of Y. But this added investment will also make Y_F increase more rapidly. As time goes on the difference between Y and Y_F may widen or narrow. In the former case the state of exhilaration will persist until the economy is again affected by some autonomous change. In the latter, it will return towards the equilibrium path.

Such initial conditions may supervene not on an economy that would otherwise be in equilibrium but on one that otherwise generates capacity faster than demand. In such circumstances, the exhilaration is indeed a fool's paradise. Exhilaration can also occur even though Y and Y_F are initially equal. If $(\beta/\alpha) - 1 > \sigma\alpha - \delta_1$, Y will exceed Y_F and the influence of $Y - Y_F$ on investment will come into play. This will merely accentuate the tendency for Y to exceed Y_F. Aggregate demand will be persistently greater than full-capacity output; and so far as the model is concerned the economy can go on indefinitely on that basis. Shortages of capacity need not grow cumulatively but a fixed proportion between actual and full-capacity output may be maintained.

The state of exhilaration can be reinforced or offset by trends in investment or full-capacity output. In line with what is said above, a trend in investment that is rising more rapidly than $\sigma\alpha - \delta_1$ will accentuate endogenous exhilaration or even produce it, and one that is rising less rapidly or falling will act as an offset. Also a trend in full-capacity output will tend to offset or produce exhilaration according to whether it is rising at any rate or falling.

Under conditions of exhilaration, with or without trends, the economy can continue to grow just as steadily as if the full Harrod conditions are fulfilled. In fact the growth may be more steady since downward disturbances of investment may not reduce the rate of growth below the warranted rate and hence produce excess capacity. And upward disturbances will not necessarily be more disturbing than if they impinge on an equilibrium situation.

There is, however, the possibility that a persistent state of exhilaration may alter the structure of the model so as to reinforce itself. If the great majority of investors find their expectations more than realized, their willingness to invest in response to given levels of profits, etc. may increase. Such tendencies may eventually lead to bottleneck situations with respect to labor and equipment and hence have inflationary consequences. But the monetary and fiscal authorities can keep the degree of exhilaration within due bounds. I see no reason why a moderate degree of exhilaration should not be an enduring state or a feasible objective of policy.

(c) *Persistent Excess Capacity.*   Conditions opposite to those specified for exhilaration can yield expansion under conditions of chronic excess capacity.

Even though the equilibrium condition is satisfied, initial excess capacity with $Y_F > Y$ can result in continued excess capacity even though the economy grows. Depending on the magnitude of the influence of $Y_F - Y$ on investment, the system may eventually return to the equilibrium path or it may remain persistently away from it. Suitable adaptations of this idea may be needed to explain the duration of the depression of the 1930's.

If Y and Y_F are initially equal, the economy will tend to generate excess capacity persistently if $(\beta/\alpha) - 1 < \sigma\alpha - \delta_1$, but the model may nevertheless result in continual expansion of Y and Y_F. Again it is possible that Y and Y_F may both decline steadily, usually with Y_F greater than Y, but possibly with Y greater than Y_F. However, if this is the outcome of State 1, the economy will enter State 2, and may experience damped fluctuations in that state. Conceivably, even State 2 may involve continual decline.

These latter cases, however, can hardly be regarded as practical possibilities. They may represent the operation of the endogenous forces of the economy, which, in fact, are offset by the influence of rising trends, say of investment. If such offsetting influences are not present, a persistent tendency to grow and to generate excess capacity would be likely to indicate an unstable state of the economy or an unsatisfactory state of the model. The influence of excess capacity on investment would be likely to increase, and this would tend to produce fluctuations rather than continued growth.

Fluctuations of Output and Capacity Output

Before the complexities of transitions from State 1 to State 2 are introduced, it is instructive to consider the fluctuating solution of State 1 alone. If we assume that the economy never enters State 2, despite fluctuations, we have a model of the conventional Tinbergen-Kalecki type where the cyclical process does not engender growth, and growth depends entirely on trends.

The model for State 1 can have a cyclical solution if $(\beta/\alpha) - 1 < \sigma\alpha - \delta_1$. Cycles then arise from the influence of $Y - Y_F$ on investment. If this influence is great enough (but not too great) in the model it will produce fluctuations rather than continued growth or decline. The precise conditions are given in the following mathematical section.

To illustrate the cyclical process, suppose the economy is initially in a state where actual and full-capacity output are equal. In that event, gross investment may expand, owing to the influence of profits, and output can increase. The expansion of output means greater profits and further increases of gross investment. But full-capacity output will increase faster than actual output and from the outset will exceed it. This excess capacity will tend to deter investment. It will result in a decreasing rate of increase and eventually a downturn of gross investment, and consequently of output.

Despite the downturn in gross investment, full-capacity output will continue to increase so long as net investment remains positive. But eventually the forces of depreciation and obsolescence will bring about a decline in full-capacity output. Loss of equipment will be going on continually because of physical mortality, and in addition the decline in total demand will hasten obsolescence. The depression will then continue until full-capacity output has fallen in relation to actual output and a relative shortage of capacity brings about a revival of investment. The subsequent prosperity will then be stimulated both by increasing profits and the shortage of equipment. But the shortage of equipment will decline and will eventually disappear and excess capacity will emerge and, in due course, a new depression will commence.

During the course of the depression, gross investment may fall to zero or well below zero while inventories are being decumulated. As the model is constructed, zero gross investment means zero consumption. But there must be a cut-off point where consumption ceases to be a fixed proportion of GNP and declines no further. Zero gross investment and minimum consumption provide floors to the model. These floors also limit the height of the subsequent boom. The model does not represent a continuous cyclical process, but it starts off afresh after lying on the floor for an appropriate time. If the consumption floor remains constant in terms of real output and the gross investment floor is zero, the model will generate successive fluctuations of equal amplitude, with relatively long depressions and relatively short prosperity periods.

This state of the model is clearly unsatisfactory. Depressions are not normally long in relation to booms. (The depression of the 1930's is an exception when aggravating factors not taken into account in the present model were at work.) Furthermore, when the model becomes cyclical in its effects, it ceases to explain the growth of the economy. For this reason, outside trends are frequently introduced, as in the Hicks model, to account for economic growth. For instance, an upward trend in investment or in consumption standards will raise the floor of the model, and, consequently, the peaks, from cycle to cycle. While the importance of trends cannot be denied, the possibilities of endogenous growth should be explored before they are relied on. This brings us to the question of ratchet effects.

The ratchets on consumption and investment take hold when the model has passed its peak and continue to influence its course throughout the following depression and also during the following recovery until the previous peak level of output has been passed. Beyond that point the ratchet comes off and may, as suggested above, be replaced by a brake effect. The ratchet effect on consumption reflects the fact that property owners, particularly bond and stockholders, have acquired a vested interest in their prosperity levels of income; and that consumers have acquired new consumption standards which they try to maintain despite a subsequent fall in their incomes. The ratchet effect on investment is twofold. First, the profits expectation of investors can reasonably be supposed to be influenced not only by their depression level of profits, but also by previous prosperity levels. Second, their estimates of whether capacity is excessive or deficient should be related to the output they regard as normal rather than to its depression level.

The ratchet metaphor is not entirely satisfactory. A mechanical ratchet holds the mechanism, such as a jack or a cogwheel, in a fixed position when the ratchet takes hold—unless the ratchet actually breaks. The economic ratchet effect rather suspends the economy from a peg by an elastic cord. The effect on the economy depends on the height of the peg and the elasticity of the cord.

With the ratchet effects, the cyclical process described by the model becomes more realistic and reasonable. There are forces that prevent the economy from descending to the depths, once a depression starts. Nor is such a descent necessary to generate the forces of recovery. Recovery will begin when full-capacity output has been reduced in relation to its normal rather than to its depression level. The ratchet effect can be strong enough to ensure that each depression is reached at a higher level than the preceding one. But more than this is required. The influences that mitigate depressions also diminish the strength of subsequent booms by denying the economy the momentum for cyclical expansion it would otherwise require. The ratchet effects must not be so strong as to prevent the economy, while still in State 2, from exceeding its previous peak. In other words State 2 must be "explosive." Provided State 1 is explosive, the ratchet effects can be such as to meet the required conditions; and a process of endogenous fluctuating growth is possible.

If the ratchet effects are not strong enough to ensure that each depression is less severe than the previous one, the economy will fluctuate around some floor or trend level, as in the case where State 1 prevailed throughout. The intervention of State 2 will reduce the severity of both booms and depressions, but will not affect the general character of fluctuations.

A further endogenous possibility is that State 2 may involve damped fluctuations. This may be due to the fact that the ratchet effects are too strong, or to the fact that State 1 itself is too weak (State 2 is always more damped or less explosive than State 1). In that event once the economy gets into State 2, it remains there forever so far as endogenous forces are concerned. It may be

Fig. 1

$Y =$ —— $Y_F =$ – – –

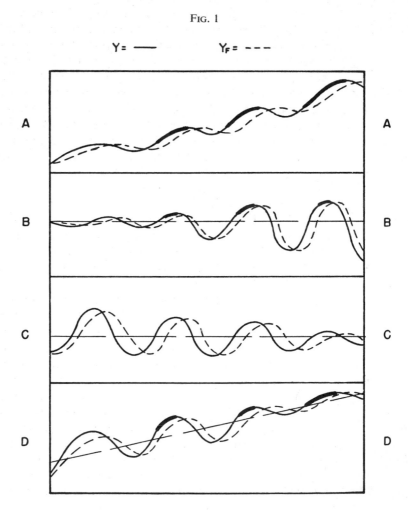

expected, however, that as time goes on the influence of the ratchets diminishes and State 2 comes to approximate State 1.

We can now turn, finally, to the influence of trends. As is well known, in the Tinbergen type of model, changes in trends do not affect the existence of fluctuations, but can affect their amplitude and phase.

In the present model, trends have more significant consequences. The intervention of a downward trend in investment, for instance, could offset endogenous expansion and keep the economy indefinitely in State 2. Similarly an upward trend investment may be strong enough to lift the economy out of State 2, even though its solution is damped, and thus the forces of endogenous expansion would be added to those of the trend.

When changes in trends are considered, however, the possible effects of those changes on the structure of the model itself must not be ignored. The values of coefficients of this or any other model depend on expectations. Insofar as trend changes affect expectations of output, profits, etc., they are likely to affect the investment equation. The occurrence of a sharp upward trend in investment may change the endogenous model from one of fluctuation to one of continued expansion.

Various possibilities of fluctuation are illustrated in Figure 1.

These charts indicate the behaviour of Y and Y_F. The solid lines denote Y and the dotted lines Y_F. The Y lines are heavy during the periods when the model is in State 1. For the remainder of the time—most of it in fact—the model is in State 2. Chart A indicates fluctuating endogenous growth with each peak and each depression occurring at a higher level of Y than the preceding one. Chart B represents the case where the ratchet effect is not strong enough to ensure growth, as defined, and the model produces explosive fluctuations about some zero level of Y. In C, the endogenous forces for expansion are so weak that fluctuations are so weak that the economy remains perpetually in State 2. In D, trend influences are superimposed on C, and are strong enough to bring the model into State 1 during prosperity periods.

IV. THE OPERATION OF THE MODEL—MATHEMATICAL ANALYSIS

With this introduction, the operation of the model can now be examined explicitly in terms of the equations. The model results in two sets of equations: those that hold when the ratchets are operating and those that are in effect when the economy expands beyond the ratchet level of output. In either case it is instructive, from the economic point of view, to consider the model as consisting of two simultaneous difference equations, one with actual output and the other with full-capacity output as the dependent variable.

To recapitulate, the model consists of the following equations:

$$I = \beta_1 Y_{-1} + \beta_2 \overline{Y} - \beta_3 (Y_{F-1} - \overline{Y}) + k^t, \tag{1}$$

$$C = (1 - \alpha_1)Y + \alpha_2\overline{Y}; \quad \text{or} \quad S = \alpha_1 Y - \alpha_2\overline{Y}, \tag{2}$$

$$Y = C + I \quad \text{or} \quad I = S, \tag{3}$$

$$Y_F - Y_{F-1} = \sigma I_{-1} - D_1 - D_2 + l^t, \tag{4}$$

$$D_1 = \delta_1 Y_{F-1}, \tag{5}$$

$$D_2 = \delta_2(Y_{F-1} - Y_{-1}). \tag{6}$$

Where the ratchet is not operating, $\overline{Y} = Y_{-1}$ in (1) and $\overline{Y} = Y$ in (2). The "aggregate demand" side of the system is obtained by solving (1), (2), and (3). The equation for full-capacity output is obtained from (4), (5), and (6), and by substituting $(\alpha_1 - \alpha_2)Y_{-1}$ for I_{-1}. Consequently we have the two basic difference equations.

$$Y = aY_{-1} + bY_{F-1} + gk^t; \tag{7}$$

$$Y_F = cY_{-1} + dY_{F-1} + l^t \tag{8}$$

where

$$a = \frac{\beta_1 + \beta_2 + \beta_3}{\alpha_1 - \alpha_2},$$

$$b = \frac{-\beta_3}{\alpha_1 - \alpha_2},$$

$$c = \sigma(\alpha_1 - \alpha_2) + \delta_2,$$

$$d = 1 - \delta_1 - \delta_2,$$

$$g = \frac{1}{\alpha_1 - \alpha_2}.$$

This system will be referred to throughout as State 1 of the economy. Where the ratchet effect is operative, the system is

$$Y = a'Y_{-1} + b'Y_{F-1} + r\overline{Y} + g'k^t \tag{9}$$

and

$$Y_F = c'Y_{-1} + d'Y_{F-1} + s\overline{Y} + l^t \tag{10}$$

where

$$a' = \frac{\beta_1}{\alpha_1},$$

$$b' = \frac{\beta_3}{\alpha_1},$$

$$c' = \sigma\alpha_1 + \delta_2,$$

$$d' = 1 - \delta_1 - \delta_2,$$

$$g' = \frac{1}{\alpha_1},$$

$$r = \frac{\alpha_2 + \beta_2 + \beta_3}{\alpha_1},$$

$$s = -\sigma\alpha_2.$$

This system will be referred to as State 2.

If State 1 is a process of noncyclical expansion with Y continually increasing, State 2 never becomes relevant. On the other hand, if Y fluctuates it sometimes falls below $\bar{Y}$, and the economy then comes into State 2 until Y again exceeds $\bar{Y}$. (There is also the possibility that the economy may enter State 2 and lack the power ever to return to State 1—which did not seem an absurd idea in the 1930's.) Consequently I shall first examine the solution of State 1 and the possibilities of continued expansion, and then the possibilities of fluctuations, which will involve both State 1 and State 2.

Solution of State 1

Equations (7) and (8) can be solved in terms either of Y or Y_F. But from the economic point of view, the behaviour of Y and Y_F in relation to each other is of great interest and importance. Hence I shall examine both solutions. To simplify the exposition, I shall assume that only one of the trend terms k^t or l^t is operative at any given time.

The solutions for Y and Y_F (ignoring the trend term l^t) are

$$Y = m_1 y'_1 + m_2 y'_2 + \lambda k^t, \tag{11}$$

$$Y_F = n_1 y'_1 + n_2 y'_2 + \mu k^t \tag{12}$$

where y_1 and y_2 are solutions of the homogeneous part of the system; and (assuming we are concerned only with integral values of t) m_1, m_2, n_1, n_2, λ and μ are constants that satisfy the requirement that the equations hold simultaneously, and satisfy the system when Y and Y_F take on arbitrary initial values, Y_0 and $(Y_F)_0$, at $t = 0$.

y_1 and y_2 are the solutions of the characteristic equation of the matrix

$$\begin{pmatrix} a & b \\ c & d \end{pmatrix}.$$

Thus,

$$y = \frac{a + d \pm \sqrt{(a - d)^2 + 4bc}}{2}. \tag{13}$$

As will be shown later, there are no general empirical grounds for excluding the possibilities that y_1 and y_2 are real and positive or complex, or greater or less than unity in absolute value. However, I shall assume that negative roots can be excluded as economically unrealistic.

The requirement that equations (11) and (12) hold simultaneously imposes the following conditions on the coefficients:

$$m_1 = n_1 \frac{b}{y_1 - a} = n_1 \frac{y_1 - d}{c},$$

$$m_2 = n_2 \frac{b}{y_2 - a} = n_2 \frac{y_2 - d}{c}, \qquad (14)$$

$$\lambda = \frac{k - d}{c} \mu.$$

If the trend l^t is considered in place of k^t and λ' and μ' are the corresponding coefficients, the relation between them is

$$\lambda' = \frac{b}{k - a} \mu'.$$

This result is obtained by substituting the solutions for Y and Y_F given by (11) and (12) in (7) and (8). In this way a pair of homogeneous equations in y_1^t, y_2^t, and k^t is obtained. For these to hold simultaneously, the coefficients of each of the variables must be identically zero. This requirement leads to the stated conditions.

Under these conditions, we can find the solution. The procedure is to find a particular solution of the system that will give λ and μ and then find m_1 and m_2 so that the initial conditions are satisfied. We find

$$m_1 = \frac{Y_0(a - y_2) + bY_{F0} - \lambda(k - y_2) + k}{y_1 - y_2},$$

$$m_2 = \frac{Y_0(a - y_1) + bY_{F0} - \lambda(k - y_1) + k}{y_2 - y_1},$$

$$\lambda = \frac{gk(k - d)}{(k - y_1)(k - y_2)}.$$

When the l^t replaces k^t, we have

$$\lambda' = \frac{bl}{(l - y_1)(l - y_2)}.$$

For purposes of economic interpretation (and also for mathematical purposes), it is convenient to separate the terms that are influenced by the trend term k from those that are not.

Let

$$M_1 = \frac{Y_0(a - y_2) + bY_{F0}}{y_1 - y_2}$$

and

$$M_2 = \frac{Y_0(a - y_1) + bY_{F0}}{y_2 - y_1},$$

and let N_1 and N_2 have corresponding values, given by (14).
The solution for Y and Y_F in State 1 then are

$$Y = M_1 y_1' + M_2 y_2' + \lambda \left(-\frac{k - y_2}{y_1 - y_2} y_1' - \frac{k - y_1}{y_2 - y_1} y_2' + k^t \right), \qquad (15)$$

$$Y_F = N_1 y_1' + N_2 y_2' + \mu \left(-\frac{k - y_2}{y_1 - y_2} y_1' - \frac{k - y_1}{y_2 - y_1} y_2' + k^t \right).^7 \qquad (16)$$

The trend influence when l^t replaces k^t is obtained by substituting λ', μ', and l for λ, μ, and k in (15) and (16).

The Possibilities of Continued Growth

If y_1, y_2, k, or l are all real, the economy represented by (15) and (16) will grow or decline without fluctuation. (However, in the complete model State 2 must be considered in the event of decline.) To discuss the noncyclical solutions in a general way is a complicated matter. The best course seems to be to discuss the conditions under which $Y \equiv Y_F$ for all t. This is Harrod's "warranted rate of growth," and can reasonably be described as "equilibrium growth." Although the required conditions are unlikely to be completely fulfilled in practice, "equilibrium growth" serves as a useful path of reference, and its solution is simple and comprehensible. The other noncyclical case that is economically interesting is the one where Y increases over time and is or tends to be greater than Y_F. This can be termed "persistent exhilaration." I shall argue that other noncyclical solutions which may be called persistent excess capacity, such as Y_F persistently greater than Y or continual decline in both, reveal unstable states of the model rather than significant economic possibilities.

(a) *Equilibrium growth.* In approaching the question of equilibrium, it is convenient first to consider the possibility of endogenous growth—omitting the trend terms—and then to consider the influence of trend. Under these

---

[7] From the mathematical point of view this method of stating the solution makes clear what happens when $k \to y_1$ or y_2. Although under those circumstances, λ and $\mu \to \infty$, the total trend influences can readily be seen to approach finite limits.

conditions, for $Y \equiv Y_F$, it is necessary and sufficient that only one of the solutions y_1 and y_2 remain in the complete solution, and that its coefficients in (15) and (16) be equal.

Suppose therefore $M_1 = N_1$; then from (14)

$$M_1 = M_1 \frac{c}{y_1 - d}.$$

Thus,

$$y_1 = c + d = a + b;\tag{17}$$

and under these conditions,

$$y_2 = a - c = d - b.\tag{18}$$

In terms of the economic coefficients these conditions mean

$$y_1 = \frac{\beta_1 + \beta_2}{\alpha_1 - \alpha_2} = \sigma(\alpha_1 - \alpha_2) + 1 - \delta_1,\tag{17a}$$

and

$$y_2 = \frac{\beta_1 + \beta_2}{\alpha_1 - \alpha_2} - \sigma(\alpha_1 - \alpha_2) - \delta_2 = 1 - \delta_1 - \delta_2 + \frac{\beta_3}{\alpha_1 - \alpha_2}.\tag{18a}$$

Substituting these values of y_1 and y_2 in the formulas for M_1 and M_2, the complete solution of the endogenous model is

$$Y = \frac{cY_0 + bY_{F0}}{c + b} y_1^t + \frac{b(Y_0 - Y_{F0})}{c + b} y_2^t,\tag{19}$$

$$Y_F = \frac{cY_0 + bY_{F0}}{c + b} y_1^t - \frac{c(Y_0 - Y_{F0})}{c + b} y_2^t.\tag{20}$$

Interpretation of these results is facilitated if they are rearranged

$$Y = Y_0 y_1^t - \frac{b(Y_0 - Y_{F0})(y_1^t - y_2^t)}{b + c},\tag{19a}$$

$$Y_F = Y_{F0} y_1^t + \frac{c(Y - Y_{F0})(y_1^t - y_2^t)}{b + c}.\tag{20a}$$

y_1, on economic grounds, can be assumed to be greater than unity. $y_1 < 1$ implies $\sigma(\alpha_1 - \alpha_2) < \delta_1$—which means that the economy is not even maintaining its productive capacity. Even if there is an upward trend in Y_F, it seems hardly likely that $c + d < 1$. Hence if the equilibrium conditions are fulfilled, they can be taken to result in growth. y_2, however, can be greater or less than unity, as $\beta_3/(\alpha_1 - \alpha_2) \gtrless \delta_1 + \delta_2$, according to (18a). There is no necessary economic reason for regarding either possibility as the more likely.

If initially $Y_0 = Y_{F0}$, the solution reduces to

$$Y = Y_{F0} = Y_0 y_1^t,\tag{21}$$

and equilibrium growth is achieved, with a proportionate rate of growth of $y_1 - 1$.

If however $Y_0 \neq Y_{F0}$, the second term of (19a) and (20a) becomes operative. It should first be observed that the influence of this term is positive or negative according to whether $Y_0 \gtrless Y_{F0}$—for $y_1 \gtrless y_2$ implies $b + c \gtrless 0$.

Subtracting (20) from (19), we obtain

$$Y - Y_F = (Y_0 - Y_{F0})y_2^t. \tag{22}$$

Hence if $y_2 < 1$, equilibrium can still be achieved eventually, despite $Y_0 \neq Y_{F0}$. In that event the equilibrium path will be given by the first terms of (19) and (20). The proportionate rate of growth will be the same as before, $(y_1 - 1)$, but the absolute value of Y will be affected by the initial conditions. If $Y_0 - Y_{F0}$ is sufficiently great, the absolute rate of growth may be too great to be sustainable on account of factors not taken into account in the model—such as labor bottlenecks. On the other hand if $Y_{F0} - Y_0$ is sufficiently great, the equilibrium path may approach zero or may even mean a progressive decrease in output. Thus even though the structure of the economy is "fundamentally sound," unfavorable initial conditions may prevent its soundness from being realized. This kind of phenomenon may have been witnessed during the prolonged depression of the thirties.

Thus if $y_2 < 1$, equilibrium is in a sense stable. Despite disturbances, the economy will return to the same proportionate rate of change. But the level of output and the direction of change may be affected.

If $y_2 > 1$, equilibrium is unstable. If $Y_0 > Y_{F0}$, it is clear from (22) that the absolute size of the discrepancy between Y and Y_F will increase progressively. Whether the state of exhilaration is sustainable will depend on the magnitude of y_2 and the speculative and other consequences the state of exhilaration may induce. If $Y_{F0} > Y_0$, then Y_F will persistently exceed Y even though the economy is expanding. Such a situation clearly cannot go on indefinitely. If initial conditions produce this result, they are likely to alter the structure of the model so that the solution becomes cyclical.

The discussion so far is an analysis of the Harrod-Domar problem of warranted growth. The equilibrium rate of growth $\sigma(\alpha_1 - \alpha_2) - \delta_1$ is the Harrod warranted rate, expressed in terms of gross rather than net product. This exercise in reformulation seems to me to be worthwhile both because it distinguishes sharply between the demand for investment and the effects of investment on increasing capacity (which are not the same thing) and because it permits an examination of the stability or instability of the equilibrium path.

It remains now to consider the influence of the trend terms on equilibrium growth. I shall consider first the influence of k^t and shall ignore l^t.

For equilibrium growth to continue in the presence of an upward trend, it is evident from the foregoing argument that $Y \equiv Y_F$ is only possible in the special case where $k = y_1 = a + b$ or $c + d$. Under these conditions the total trend influences in (15) and (16) are necessarily equal by virtue of (14) and can be shown to approach a limit as $k \to y_1$, which is

$$gc\left[\frac{ty_1'}{y_1 - y_2} + \frac{y_1 y_2'}{(y_1 - y_2)^2}\right].$$

This whole trend influence is positive. This is obviously the case where $y_1 > y_2$. Where $y_1 < y_2$, the expression is clearly positive for values of t sufficiently large. It can also be seen to be positive for small values of t. I induce that it is positive for all values of t.

For the economy to attain a path of equilibrium growth, it is now necessary and sufficient that $y_2 < 1$, so that the second term in this expression will approach zero. If this is so, and in addition $Y = Y_{F0}$, the equilibrium path of growth is obtained by adding this trend term to (21), and we have

$$Y = Y_{F0} = \left[Y_0 + \frac{mct}{y_1 - y_2}\right]y_1'. \tag{23}$$

Whereas in the endogenous case the proportional rate of growth will be $y_1 - 1$, in this case it will initially exceed this rate but will approach it with t sufficiently large. Only in this exceptional case is a geometric trend consistent with equilibrium growth. In general an upward trend in investment will produce disequilibrium if endogenous equilibrium growth is possible. From (17) we have

$$\lambda = \frac{c}{k - d}\mu. \tag{24}$$

Thus if $k > c + d$, the trend influence will tend to produce persistent exhilaration with $Y > Y_F$; and $k < c + d$ will produce a persistent tendency for $Y_F > Y$. Since $k > 1$ and $d < 1$, there is no possibility that λ and μ should be of opposite sign.

When we ignore k^t and consider an upward trend in Y_F represented by l^t, equilibrium growth again requires $l = a + b = c + d$, but the trend influence in this case is

$$b\left[\frac{ty_1'}{y_1 - y_2} + \frac{y_1 y_2'}{(y_1 - y_2)^2}\right]$$

and again $y_2 < 0$ is required for equilibrium growth. But since $b < 0$, the total trend influence is negative. If the endogenous rate of equilibrium expansion were maintained, the economy would generate excess capacity through the addition of the trend influence. The equilibrium path analogous to (23) is then

$$Y = Y_{F0} = \left[Y_0 + \frac{bt}{y_1 - y_2}\right]y_1'. \tag{25}$$

Here the proportional rate of growth will initially be less than $y - 1$. It will decrease as t increases and with t sufficiently large Y will decline at the rate $y_1 - 1$. In short, equilibrium *growth* is impossible under these circumstances.

From the economic point of view, this conclusion does not, of course, mean that an upward trend in Y_F is bad for the economy—merely that its effect should be offset by endogenous exhilaration to yield satisfactory results.

In this discussion of equilibrium growth, with or without trends, I have so far adhered strictly to the logic of the argument and have set out the conditions under which $Y \equiv Y_F$ in the strict sense. Even though these conditions are not fulfilled, it is quite possible that the combined influences of initial conditions, trend influences, and the internal structure of the economy may produce offsetting tendencies that will result in approximate equality of Y and Y_F for substantial periods of time. Such combinations of circumstances, however, may lead to persistent tendencies for Y to diverge from Y_F—which will now be considered.

(b) *Persistent Exhilaration.* Using the equilibrium growth as a path of reference, there are various possibilities for Y to exceed Y_F.

(1) Even though equilibrium is achieved in other respects, initial conditions may produce such a tendency. From (22), if $Y_0 > Y_{F0}$ and $y_2 > 1$, $Y > Y_F$. The difference $Y - Y_F$ will grow at a proportionate rate of $y_2 - 1$. However, whether this difference is an increasing or decreasing proportion of Y will depend on whether $y_2 \gtrless y_1$ as can be seen from (19) and (20).

Forces in the aggregate may produce an approximation to equilibrium, as suggested above, or a tolerable or an intolerable disequilibrium situation. For instance, the endogenous forces may produce persistent excess capacity, but the trend influence on investment may be strong enough to raise Y and Y_F. And an endogenous tendency toward exhilaration can be offset by a trend in Y_F.

Suppose the model yields a state of persistent exhilaration. Then can such a state in fact persist? Clearly it can unless the state is affected by factors not taken into account in the model or unless such a state induces changes in the structure of the model itself. With respect to the first possibility it should be noted that $Y > Y_F$ does not necessarily imply labor bottlenecks, monetary stringency, or inflation. Furthermore, Y can exceed Y_F significantly without causing capacity bottlenecks. However, $Y > Y_F$ does mean that in general the degree of capacity use exceeds expectations. Conceivably the *persistence* of such a state may increase the investment function so that $(a + b)$ increases in relation to $(c + d)$: the exhilaration may cumulate and lead to bottlenecks and inflation. But such tendencies if they occur can be counteracted by monetary and fiscal measures. In short, I can see no reason why a "moderate" excess of Y over Y_F should not be considered a permanent and satisfactory state of the economy and, indeed, a suitable objective of policy.

(2) If the equilibrium conditions fail because $a + b > c + d$, it follows that $y_1 > c + d$, and $y_1 > y_2$. Consequently from (14) $M_1 > N_1$. Therefore Y will exceed Y_F, even though an initial excess of Y_F over Y may temporarily depress Y below Y_F.

(3) An upward trend in investment k^t, with $k > y_1$, will produce in a situation that is otherwise in equilibrium a persistent tendency for Y to exceed Y_F. A similar tendency will be produced with a downward trend l^t, with $l < 1$, in Y_F.

(c) *Persistent Excess Capacity.* Noncyclical solutions can occur with both Y and Y_F increasing, but with $Y_F > Y$.

If in the endogenous case $(a + b) < (c + d)$, y_1 and y_2 can nevertheless be real and greater than unity. But in this case $y_1 < c + d$ and $y_1 > y_2$. Consequently from (14) $N_1 > M_1$ and $N_2 > M_2$. This ensures that whatever the effect of initial conditions, the economy will eventually achieve growth with $Y_F > Y$. Trend influences, however, may offset or reinforce this tendency.

(It is possible, however, that y_1 and y_2 are real and less than unity. The solution of State 1 would then be continual decline with $Y_F > Y$. But in this event, the economy would pass into State 2 and remain there. The most likely outcome would then be damped fluctuations in State 2—although conceivably the solution for State 2 would also be continual decline.)

I shall not pursue the question of persistent excess capacity further since I believe that unless offset by trend influences, a persistent tendency for $Y_F > Y$ (whether the economy is growing or declining) reveals an unstable state of the model, and is likely to result in changes in its structure, so that the solutions for y_1 and y_2 become complex. The discriminant of (13) in terms of the economic parameters is

$$\left[\frac{\beta_1 + \beta_2 + \beta_3}{\alpha_1 - \alpha_2} - (1 - \delta_1 - \delta_2) \right]^2 - \frac{4\beta_3(\sigma(\alpha_1 - \alpha_2) + \delta_2)}{\alpha_1 - \alpha_2}, \tag{26}$$

which must be positive for real solutions. This implies that the investment coefficients β_1 and β_2 retain their values despite the persistent generation of redundant capacity. Under these conditions the most likely (but not the only) possibility seems to be that $\beta_1 + \beta_2$ will decline relatively to α_1 and α_2 and render y_1 and y_2 complex.

The Possibilities of Fluctuations

If the solutions of (13) are complex, and the solution of State 1 consequently cyclical, we have to consider the system in its successive movements through State 1 and State 2. Or it may remain in State 2 permanently. The model then offers the following possibilities:

1. In all cases the critical factor is the difference $Y \quad Y_F$ or $\bar{Y} - Y_F$ as the case may be. A boom ends and a depression begins when Y_F has increased relative to Y to such an extent that total investment is reduced—and this in turn reduces consumption. The depression continues until depreciation and obsolescence reduce Y_F in relation to Y sufficiently to produce a revival of investment and, consequently, consumption. During the prosperity Y_F increases faster than Y

and hence the stage is set for another depression. If State 1 were the only state of the economy, such cycles would represent deviations—explosive or damped—from a growth trend. The existence of State 2, however, opens up other possibilities.

2. The economy may alternate between States 1 and 2 in a process of fluctuating endogenous growth without the aid of trends. This is the most interesting possibility suggested by the model. By fluctuating growth I mean that each depression and each boom respectively occurs at a higher level of output than the preceding one.

3. These alterations may occur with depressions increasing in severity, but not so severe as if State 1 prevails throughout. So long as State 1 is modified by State 2 to any extent, depressions will have a smaller amplitude but a longer duration than booms.

4. The forces of endogenous expansion may not be strong enough to drive the economy out of State 2 once it gets into that state. The result will then be a series of damped fluctuations determined exclusively by the State 2 model. But in this case allowance should be made for the possibility that the memory of the past will grow dimmer and the ratchet influences in State 2 may diminish so that a State 1-type model becomes reestablished.

5. Trend influences can modify the foregoing situations materially: (a) An upward trend in $Y(k > 1)$ or a downward trend in $Y_F(l < 1)$ can reinforce situation (1) or convert situations (2) and (3) into (1). (b) Trends in the opposite direction will tend to modify situation (1) in the direction of (2), and (1) and (2) in the direction of (3).

Leaving out trends for the time being the general solution for Y of State 1 will be as before.

$$Y = M_1 y_1^t + M_2 y_2^t, \tag{27}$$

$$Y_F = N_1 y_1^t + N_2 y_2^t. \tag{28}$$

That of State (2) will be

$$Y = M_1' y_1''^t + M_2' y_2''^t + R\bar{Y}, \tag{29}$$

$$Y_F = N_1' y_1''^t + N_2' y_2''^t + S\bar{Y}, \tag{30}$$

where y_1' and y_2' are the roots for State 2 and $R\bar{Y}$ and $S\bar{Y}$ are the constant "solutions" of (9) and (10)—omitting the trend terms, and

$$R = \frac{r(1 - d') + b's}{1 - (a' + d') + a'd' - b'c'}$$

and

$$S = \frac{rc' + s(1 - a')}{1 - (a' + d') + a'd' - b'c'}.$$

R and S measure the sustaining effect of the ratchet influences; and, as can be seen intuitively as well as analytically, their values depend directly on β_2, β_3, and α_2.

We can now examine these possibilities in terms of the mathematical analysis.

(1) *The Cyclical Mechanism.* To demonstrate how fluctuations are generated we can examine the cyclical solutions of State 1 and State 2. This discussion should furnish a sufficient indication of what occurs when those states occur in sequence.

First of all the solutions for State 1 *can* be complex. Considering the discriminant of (13) as set out in (26), there is no necessary economic obstacle to a complex solution.

Next if y is complex, y' must necessarily also be complex. The discriminant for the equation for y' is obtained by omitting the terms β_2 and α_2 from (26). These omissions necessarily decrease its value.

The absolute value of y is given by

$$|y|^2 = ad - bc = \frac{\beta_1 + \beta_2 + \beta_3}{\alpha_1 - \alpha_2}(1 - \delta_1 - \delta_2) + \beta_3\sigma + \frac{\beta_3\delta_2}{\alpha_1 - \alpha_2}. \qquad (29)$$

$|y'|$ is obtained by omitting β_2 and α_2 from this expression entirely and β_3 from the first term. Consequently $|y'| < |y|$. Thus if the solution of State 1 is explosive, that of State 2 may be explosive or damped. If State 1 is damped, State 2 is also damped.

The period of the cycles of State 1 will be $2\pi/\theta$, where

$$\cos\theta = \frac{a+d}{\sqrt{ad-bc}}.$$

By inspection it can be seen that $\cos\theta' > \cos\theta$ where θ' relates to State 2. Hence $\theta' < \theta$, and $2\pi/\theta' > 2\pi/\theta$.

We can now examine the relations of Y and Y_F in States 1 and 2. From (14)

$$M_1 = N_1 \frac{y_1 - d}{c},$$

and similarly for State 2

$$M_1' = N_1' \frac{y_1' - d}{c}.$$

Moreover,

$$\frac{y_1 - d}{c} = \frac{a - d + \sqrt{[-4bc - (a-d)^2]}i}{2c}.$$

If $a - d > 0$, the angle of $(y_1 - d)/c$ will be >0 and $<\pi/2$. If $a - d < 0$, the angle will be $<\pi$ and $>\pi/2$; and consequently Y will always lead Y_F. $a - d$ can usually be assumed to be positive. d is necessarily less than unity. But

$$a = \frac{\beta_1 + \beta_2 + \beta_3}{\alpha_1 - \alpha_2}.$$

For anything but severely damped cycles $a > 1$. Certainly $a > 1$ for all explosive situations. For $|y| = \sqrt{ad - bc}$; and since $d < 1$ and $c < 1$, and $a > -b$, $|y| > 1$ requires $a > 1$. Similar reasoning can be applied to State 2.

Next we can examine the behaviour of $Y - Y_F$ in relation to Y. Subtracting (28) from (27),

$$Y - Y_F = (M_1 - N_1)y_1^t + (M_2 - N_2)y_2^t,$$

and applying (14),

$$Y - Y_F = M_1\left(1 - \frac{y_1 - a}{b}\right)y_1^t + M_2\left(1 - \frac{y_2 - a}{b}\right)y_2^t.$$

We can determine the time relation of $Y - Y_F$ to Y by examining the properties of $1 - (y_1 - a)/b$:

$$1 - \frac{y_1 - a}{b} = \frac{a - d + 2b}{2b} - \frac{\sqrt{-4bc - (a-d)^2}}{2b}i.$$

Since i has a positive coefficient, the angle of this expression is between 0 and π; and, consequently $Y - Y_F$ will lead Y. This means that $Y - Y_F$ will increase during the earlier, and decline during the later stages of prosperity. It will decline still further during the initial stages of depression but will increase during the latter stages.

(2) *Fluctuating Endogenous Growth.* With these preliminaries, we can now examine the question of fluctuating endogenous growth and determine sufficient—and, approximately, necessary—conditions for its occurrence.

For each peak to be higher than the preceding one, it is both necessary and sufficient that State 2 carry the economy higher than the preceding peak. Otherwise State 1 will never be reached. For this to occur it is clearly sufficient that the solution of State 2 be explosive, i.e., $|y'| > 1$.

This condition may not be necessary. It is mathematically possible that even a slightly damped solution of State 2 can produce this result. However, to formulate the necessary condition precisely seems to be a refinement that is not worth undertaking.

If each peak is higher than the preceding one, each depression will occur at a higher level of output than the preceding one, if and only if the depression level of Y exceeds some positive fraction of the previous peak level, $\bar{Y}$.

Expressed in terms of real variables the general solution will be given by

$$Y = 2(M')|y|^t \cos(\theta't + \varepsilon) + R\bar{Y}.$$

Letting $t = 0$ when $Y = \bar{Y}$, we have

$$\bar{Y} = 2|M'| \cos \varepsilon + R\bar{Y}.$$

Consequently,

$$2|M'| = \frac{\bar{Y}(1 - R)}{\cos \varepsilon}.$$

Hence the general solution of State 2 is

$$Y = \left[\frac{1 - R}{\cos \varepsilon} |y'|^t \cos(\theta' t + \varepsilon) + R \right] \overline{Y}. \tag{31}$$

The depression level of Y will occur approximately where $t = \pi/\theta'$. Hence an approximation for the depression level will be

$$Y_D = [-(1 - R)|y|^{\pi/\theta'} + R] \overline{Y}. \tag{32}$$

But the required condition is that $Y_D > \gamma \overline{Y}$, where γ is a positive fraction. This means that

$$\frac{R - v}{1 - R} > y^{\pi/\theta'}.$$

But Y_D will increase over time even though $\gamma \to 0$. Hence the required condition is, approximately

$$\frac{R}{1 - R} > |y'|^{\pi/\theta'}. \tag{33}$$

Since $|y'| > 1$ to satisfy the peak condition, it follows that $R/(1 - R) > 1$ or $R > 1/2$. Hence $R > \frac{1}{2}$ and $|y'| > 1$ are *sufficient* conditions for endogenous fluctuating growth.

R measures the strength of the combined ratchet effects. It is plausible to assume that an increase in the ratchet influence is associated with a decrease in the influence of current income. For instance, in the consumption relation $C = (1 - \alpha_1)Y + \alpha_2 \overline{Y}_1$ it seems reasonable to suppose that the existence of ratchet influences in fluctuating situations will not affect consumption under conditions of continued growth. If this is the case, $(1 - \alpha_1 + \alpha_2)$ is unaffected by size of the ratchet effect. Consequently an increase in α_2 is associated with a decrease of $(1 - \alpha_1)$. Thus an increase in R will be associated with a decrease in $|y'|$.

It is evident from (31), and from common sense, that an increase in R increases Y_D and thus diminishes the severity of depressions. It seems intuitively evident that this same influence diminishes the strength of the subsequent booms. Consider the position where Y subsequently attains the value $\overline{Y}$, and the model returns to State 1. It is clear from the structure of the model that $Y - Y_F$ will be smaller than if the economy had remained in State 1 throughout. Hence the conditions for continued expansion are less favourable than they would have been had there been no ratchet effects. To put the point in more concrete economic terms: the maintenance of income that occurs during the depression diminishes the obsolescence that occurs during that period, and, consequently, the decks are not cleared as thoroughly as they would be under the rigors of severe depression.

(3) *Explosive Fluctuations.* If the foregoing conditions are not fulfilled, fluctuations will assume a different character. If condition (33) fails but y' is

greater than unity, the economy will fluctuate explosively about a zero (or constant or trend) level of Y; and as $R \to 0$, State 1 will tend to prevail throughout. In this event boundary conditions that restrain the explosiveness will inevitably become operative.

(4) *Damped Fluctuations.* If $|y'| < 1$ fluctuations will be damped and so far as the mathematics is concerned the economy will converge to a constant output of $R\overline{Y}$. However, the influence of $\overline{Y}$ is unlikely to persist indefinitely. The situation is likely to be transformed into one of damped or explosive fluctuations under State 1.

(5) *The Influence of Trends.* We turn finally to the influence of trends on fluctuations. The trend influence on State 1 is given by (15) and (16), and that on State 2 by corresponding formulas.

The existence of trends will not affect the existence of fluctuations. But it will affect their character. The trend does more than add its direct effect to the endogenous cycle, as is frequently assumed. Inspection of (11) and (12) shows that the trend affects the amplitude and phase of a cycle through its influence on m_1 and m_2. But I have been unable to formulate any reasonably simple rules concerning these effects.

More important for the present model is the fact that any upward trend in investment, with $k > 1$, hastens the advent of State 1 and exposes the economy longer to its expansionary influence—which serves to lengthen booms and shorten depressions. And even though $|y'| < 1$, the trend influence can bring the economy into State 1, and if $|y| > 1$, fluctuations can continue so long as the trend persists. A downward trend, with $k < 1$, will have opposite effects and may keep the economy in State 2 for an extended period even though $|y'| > 1$.

A trend in Y_F with $l \gtrless 1$ will have effects opposite to those produced by $k \gtrless 1$.

V. QUALIFICATIONS

The various and drastic simplifying assumptions that surround the model have been stated in the course of the argument. I shall not attempt to remove those assumptions here, but shall merely remind the reader of some of the main ones and suggest how their relaxation would affect the argument.

(1) *The Employment of Labor.* Very little has been said about the level of employment. I have assumed implicitly that the level of employment is determined by the level of output, the level of capacity output, and the techniques prevailing at the particular time. With reference to a given labor force, the model may yield unemployment or more than full employment. In a complete analysis the matter should not be allowed to rest there. First, the

labor force is not independent of the demand for labor. Excess demand brings new recruits and deficient demand promotes retirements. Second, employment and unemployment depend on relative prices and wages in ways that the model does not reveal. A reduction of wages and prices in a particular industry under the pressure of unemployment does not necessarily leave total employment unchanged—for both monetary and nonmonetary reasons.

The most important question from our present point of view is how full employment affects the operation of the model. If we adhere rigidly to the theory of the model, full employment, if interpreted as an inflexible upper limit, will prevent Y from increasing, but investment will continue to increase Y_F; and the consequent excess capacity will reduce investment and hence Y. This is essentially the answer given by Harrod and Hicks. But there are other possibilities. The full-employment situation may render profitable investment in labor-saving methods. These would permit Y to increase and would limit the increase in Y_F. Or the outcome may be Keynesian inflation, with investment and consumption industries competing for resources. To analyze the possibilities would carry us far afield; and the excursion would hardly be worthwhile for the U.S. economy where labor bottlenecks do not appear to be of critical importance.

(2) *Capacity Bottlenecks.* Some authors, for example Joan Robinson, rely on bottlenecks in segments of the investment-goods industries as the cause of cyclical downturns. The argument seems to be that bottlenecks in particular segments, such as steel, may call a halt to the increase in investment or even produce a decline. This, through the multiplier, prevents aggregate demand from increasing and results in under-use of the new capacity that is becoming available as the result of prior investment. But the shortage of steel may give rise to increased investment in steel. In terms of the model the result would be not that investment is slowed down, but that the rate of increase of Y_F is reduced. In this event the shortage of steel capacity would tend to prolong the boom rather than cut it off. Or again these bottlenecks would result in competition between investment and consumers' goods industries for the products of the bottleneck industry; and the situation would have to be analyzed in terms of its inflationary consequences. Again, I doubt the importance of such bottlenecks in explaining fluctuation in the United States; and their possible effects seem to be too complex to be incorporated in a simple general model.

(3) *Depreciation: Echo Effects.* As I have pointed out, the assumption that physical depreciation is proportional to current capacity output is unjustified. Depreciation is likely to show echo effects depending on past fluctuations of investment. But in an economy subject to rapid technological change and obsolescence, the prediction of the extent and timing of these effects is extremely difficult. They are best regarded as disturbances giving rise to changes in Y_F and consequently in $Y - Y_F$.

(4) *Inventory Fluctuations.* The assumption that investment and saving are determined by the equations of the model rules out involuntary, miscalculated, or speculative accumulation or decumulation of inventories. Inventory recessions and booms are of obvious importance—as witness the behaviour of the U.S. economy in 1949 and 1953. But they seem to me to defy incorporation in a general model; for practical purposes they should be considered as disturbances. The model is useful, however, in appraising the possible consequences of inventory fluctuations. An inventory recession is less likely to bring on a general recession when the forces of expansion included in the model are operating strongly than when there is a precarious balance between expansion and contraction.

(5) *The Distribution of Income.* One of the assumptions of the model most in need of reexamination is that gross profits are a fixed proportion of GNP. From both the short- and the long-run points of view this assumption covers up a major and complex subject for investigation. The national income statistics of the United States provide a strong *prima facie* case for long-run stability as far as private GNP is concerned. If prosperity years alone are considered, the ratio of gross profits to private GNP shows remarkable stability over the period 1929 to date.

Whether this stability indicates the operation of some identifiable economic law, as Douglas contends, or whether it is the net result of a combination of circumstances is open to question. With our present state of knowledge on the subject, I suggest that economists should not commit themselves to the view that the ratio will be constant for the long-run future.[8] In the short run, the gross profit ratio does appear to increase during periods of prosperity. From the point of view of the model, this shift to profits tends to increase both saving and investment—with no clear-cut effect on the character of the cycle.

(6) *The General Price Level.* The model rests on the implied assumption that changes in the general price level do not affect its operation. This ignores the well-known speculative phenomena associated with cyclical price movements; but I cannot see how the direction of change indicated by the model can be affected thereby.

From the long-run point of view the direction of price changes is relevant to the effect of the burden of debt on the operation of the economy. An upward price trend that results in steady liquidation of indebtedness must be more favorable to investment than a downward trend, which has the opposite effect. And provided the long-run trend is accompanied by uncertainty concerning short-run price behaviour, there is no reason why a long-run upward trend should become cumulative.

---

[8] These remarks are in part prompted by opinions of the Department of Commerce which lean in the direction of constancy. See *Survey of Current Business*, January, 1956.

Price trends also have a bearing on depreciation allowances. If depreciation allowances are based, as they are to a large extent, on original money cost, and prices remain stable, the allowances currently made in a growing economy will necessarily exceed current replacement requirements—in the same way as life insurance premiums exceed disbursements on policies with a growing population. This will be true even if techniques of production remain unchanged. It will be even more true as increasing productivity in the capital goods industries reduces net replacement costs. Consequently a rising price trend may be required to keep the real value of depreciation allowances in line with replacement requirements.

(7) *Foreign Trade and the Balance of Payments.* For the United States, the assumption that exports and imports balance may well provide a sufficient first approximation when the general course of the economy is being considered, because foreign trade is small in relation to domestic trade and because the United States need not adjust its domestic economy to the requirements of balance in its international payments. But for any other Western country foreign trade can exert an important, and in some cases a decisive, influence on the domestic economy; and the model must be amended accordingly.*

(8) *Money, Credit, and Interest.* From the formal point of view, money and interest can easily be introduced into the model. The rate of interest can be included explicitly in the investment and consumption equations; and a new Keynesian liquidity preference equation can be added to the system. This would relate the rate of interest to the GNP and the quantity of money. But to give anything like an adequate portrayal of the monetary system would be far more complicated.

My opinion is that "finance" is still the province of literary economics rather than econometrics, even in the broad sense in which I use the latter term. I infer that, particularly in this area, the practical economist should attempt to devise satisfactory trial and error methods and readily reversible measures.

(9) *Government Expenditures and Taxation.* In order to isolate the operation of the private economy, I have assumed that both expenditures and taxes are always equal and that both expenditures and taxation are "diffused" throughout the economy so that relative disposable income shares are unaffected by changes in the size of the budget.

Whether these assumptions are enough to render the budget neutral in its effects raises interesting questions. If the government spends a constant

---

* This paragraph is reprinted as it was written as a warning to economists who attempt to forecast. By the time the present volume appears the paragraph may have regained some validity.

amount, in real or money terms, all groups have an incentive to increase their incomes in order to diminish the severity of taxation.

The incidence of expenditures does not lend itself to theorizing but must depend on (extremely difficult) empirical investigation of particular cases. The incidence of taxation has lent itself to abundant theorizing, but the theories are highly inconclusive from the empirical point of view. The diffusion assumption may be as valid as the opposite extreme: that the tax system leaves the distribution of income before taxes unaffected. From the point of view of the model the important distinction to be made is between taxes whose main initial effect is to deter investment and those whose initial impact is on consumption. While it may be reasonable to assume, say, that reduction of deductable depreciation allowances initially affects investment and increases of the first bracket of the income tax primarily affect consumption, the effects of other taxes are far more open to doubt. It is interesting to note that national income statisticians are forced to assume that all indirect taxes are diffused.

The balanced-budget assumption is almost certain to be invalid during the course of fluctuations. In the United States there is considerable "built-in flexibility" in the federal budget. Expenditures on many programs rise and fall automatically as production and employment move in the opposite directions; and changes in the yield of the progressive tax system are even more pronounced if output changes are accompanied by corresponding price changes, since decisions concerning taxation and also expenditures, to a large extent, are made in money rather than real terms. These automatic tendencies are likely to be stronger than any deliberate attempts that may be made to keep the budget in balance during the course of fluctuations.

In the long run there may be a tendency toward a budget surplus. As the economy grows the yield of a progressive tax system will increase progressively. Expenditures can also be expected to increase (leaving out fluctuations in defense needs), but not necessarily progressively. However, if a surplus rather than a reduction of a deficit is actually achieved under these circumstances, political pressure for tax reduction may well extinguish it.

VI. THE USEFULNESS OF THE MODEL

Despite those qualifications, I consider the model to have some practical usefulness both in explaining the past and in serving as a guide to the policymaker.

With respect to the past in the United States, I have been greatly influenced by the conclusion of the Brookings Institution that the 1929 collapse can be ascribed to the tendency of the American economy to generate capacity faster than demand. The speculative optimism of the late 1920's, however, prolonged the boom, and its collapse deepened the depression. Had the model alone been at work, the depression would have occurred earlier and been milder.

As it was, the economy entered the depression with excess capacity estimated by Brookings at 17 percent; and capacity became even more excessive as the depression deepened. The depression continued until excess capacity was reduced by depreciation and obsolescence sufficiently for revival to occur. And as it continued, the ratchet effects may have exerted a diminished influence on both investment and consumption.

The first decade of the postwar period can plausibly be described as one of persistent exhilaration, induced by initial shortages of capacity in the area of consumers' durables as well as houses, plant, and equipment, and by fiscal policies that contributed to that state. The "real" forces were reinforced by the high liquidity of the economy at the end of the war. At the present time (June, 1956) the main danger seems to be that the economy is reverting to a fluctuating state of the model.

From the standpoint of 1963, it appears that the monetary and fiscal policies employed, largely for balance-of-payments reasons, have produced a persistent tendency to generate excess capacity.

With respect to policy, stabilization measures can be corrective or anticipatory. The corrective approach is to deal with fluctuations after they have begun. They can be allowed to run their course if minor. Otherwise fiscal and monetary stimulants are applied to restore high levels of demand. The main danger of this approach is political. There will be strong pressure to apply the stimulants in those areas where supply already tends to be excessive. If there is unemployment in the automobile or housing industries, measures to stimulate production in areas of relatively short supply rather than to encourage further production of automobiles and houses should be undertaken. The latter course, however, is the one most likely to be adopted and may store up trouble for the future.

An anticipatory policy on the other hand would prevent the occurrence of serious depressions. Our discussion has shown that fluctuations are not inherent in the process of growth. Fiscal and monetary policies that will achieve continued growth, interrupted only by partial maladjustments, should be possible. They could have equilibrium growth as their objective. But, to be on the safe side, they might well aim at a mild degree of exhilaration.

5

A Linear Model of Cyclical Growth*

By HYMAN P. MINSKY[†]

PROFESSOR SAMUELSON's path-breaking article on the "Interaction Between the Multiplier Analysis and the Principle of Acceleration" appeared in this *Review* almost twenty years ago. A large literature has developed in which the basic ideas of that article have been applied to both business cycle and economic growth problems. In a considerable portion of that literature, Samuelson's warning that "the representation is strictly a *marginal* analysis to be applied to the study of small oscillations" has been overlooked.[1]

Samuelson's warning can be interpreted as meaning that the time series generated by any particular solution of the model will determine actual income for only a short time. Given the mathematical model, the relevant particular solution can change due either to (1) the accelerator or the multiplier coefficients changing (as Samuelson suggests), or (2) the imposition of new initial conditions. Goodwin[2] has examined various models in which the accelerator coefficient is a variable. These nonlinear models are mathematically complex, and the specific limit cycles that Goodwin derives obviously are due to the special assumptions he makes about how the path of income affects the accelerator coefficient. Hicks[3] has investigated how an otherwise explosive accelerator model will be affected by floors and ceilings. In this paper such floors and ceilings will be interpreted as imposing new initial conditions, and therefore this paper can be considered a reinterpretation of Hicks's setup.[4]

---

* *The Review of Economics and Statistics*, Vol. XLI (May, 1959). Reprinted by courtesy of *The Review of Economics and Statistics* and the author.

† University of California, Berkeley. The major portion of this article was completed while the author was a Visiting Associate Professor at the University of California, Berkeley, and he wishes to thank those graduate students who patiently sat through the presentation of this material, as well as Professors Irma Adelman and Roger Miller.

[1] P. A. Samuelson, "Interactions Between the Multiplier Analysis and the Principle of Acceleration," this REVIEW, Vol. XXI (May, 1939), p. 78. Reprinted in *Readings in Business Cycles* (Philadelphia, 1944), p. 269.

[2] R. M. Goodwin, "The Non-Linear Accelerator and the Persistence of Business Cycles," *Econometrica*, Vol. XIX (January, 1951), pp. 1–17.

[3] J. R. Hicks, *A Contribution to the Theory of the Trade Cycle* (Oxford, 1949).

[4] References to the influence of initial conditions upon the time series generated by an

We will work with a slightly modified version of Samuelson's model, and assume that

$$C_t = \alpha_0 + \alpha_1 Y_{t-1} \tag{1}$$

$$I_t = \beta(Y_{t-1} - Y_{t-2}) \tag{2}$$

so that

$$Y_t = (\alpha_1 + \beta)Y_{t-1} - \beta Y_{t-2} + \alpha_0 \tag{3}$$

where C_t, I_t, and T_t are the tth day's consumption, investment, and income; α_0 is the "zero income" consumption; α_1 is the marginal propensity to consume; and β is the accelerator coefficient.[5] The solution to equation (3) is

$$Y_t = A_1 \mu_1^t + A_2 \mu_2^t + k_0 \tag{4}$$

where the roots μ_1 and μ_2 depend upon α_1 and β, the coefficients A_1 and A_2 are determined by the initial conditions, and k_0 [$= \alpha_0/(1 - \alpha_1)$] is determined by the "zero income" consumption. In the solution equation (4), k_0 has a natural intepretation as the income at which consumption equals income.[6]

The α_1 and β coefficients will be assumed to be constants with values such that an explosive time series will be generated, i.e., in equation (4) $\mu_1 > \mu_2 > 1$.[7] As α_1 and β are constants, so are μ_1 and μ_2. Rather than assume

---

accelerator process are scarce. One such is "But he [Hicks] (correctly) argues that disinvestment is limited to the size of the depreciation allowances. This implies that after a downswing we do not follow the course of the cycle which produced the previous upswing. Instead we start a new cycle on the basis of new initial conditions." J. S. Duesenberry, "Hicks on the Trade Cycle," *Quarterly Journal of Economics*, Vol. LXIV (February, 1950), p. 465.

[5] Samuelson's equation (1) is $C_t = \alpha_1 Y_{t-1}$ and his equation (2) is $I_t = \beta(C_t - C_{t-1})$. The modification of equation (2) does not change the essential character of the results and it is mathematically convenient. The modification of equation (1) will enable us to introduce the effects of changes in k_0 (either through a Duesenberry ratchet effect or a Tobin-Pigou asset effect) into our analysis. For the mathematical details of the derivation of equation (4) see either W. J. Baumol, *Economic Dynamics* (New York, 1951) or R. G. D. Allen, *Mathematical Economics* (London and New York, 1956).

[6] In equation (3), if $Y_t = Y_{t-1} = Y_{t-2}$, then $Y_t = k_0$.

[7] The μ_1 and μ_2 in the solution equation $Y_t = A_1 \mu_1^t + A_2 \mu_2^t + k_0$ are the roots of the characteristic equation $f(x) = x^2 - (\alpha_1 + \beta)x + \beta$ to the second-order difference equation $y_t = (\alpha_1 + \beta)y_{t-1} - \beta y_{t-2}$. The roots are determined by setting $f(x) = 0$. The following is known about $f(x)$: (1) $f(0) = \beta$, (2) $f(1) = 1 - \alpha_1 > 0$, (3) $f(\alpha_1 + \beta) = \beta$, (4) the minimum value of $f(x)$ is $f\left(\dfrac{\alpha_1 + \beta}{2}\right)$, (5) for $0 < x < \dfrac{\alpha_1 + \beta}{2}$, $f(x)$ is decreasing, (6) for $0 < \dfrac{\alpha_1 + \beta}{2} < x < \beta, f(x)$ is increasing. For two distinct real roots to exist it is necessary that $f\left(\dfrac{\alpha_1 + \beta}{2}\right) < 0$. (Two identical roots exist if $f\left(\dfrac{\alpha_1 + \beta}{2}\right) = 0$.) With $0 < \alpha_1 < 1, f(1) = (1 - \alpha_1) > 0$ will be on either the negatively or the positively sloped arm of $f(x)$. If it is on the negatively sloped arm, then $\dfrac{\alpha_1 + \beta}{2} > 1$ and both $\mu_1 > 1$ and $\mu_2 > 1$. If it is on the positively sloped arm, then $\dfrac{\alpha_1 + \beta}{2} < 1$ and both $0 < \mu_1 < 1$ and $0 < \mu_2 < 1$. It is *impossible* to have $\mu_1 > 1$ and $\mu_2 < 1$; $(\alpha_1 + \beta)^2 - 4\beta > 0$ and $\beta > 1$ are the conditions for $\mu_1 > \mu_2 > 1$.

that the accelerator and multiplier coefficients change, the marginal nature of the formulation will be taken into account by intermittently imposing new initial conditions. The initial conditions will be interpreted as reflecting effective supply constraints.

The particular formulation to be used has the aggregate supply of income increase at an exogenously given rate and the floor to income depend upon the capital consumption rate. The nature of the time path of income generated by the model depends upon whether the rate of growth of ceiling income is greater than, equal to, or less than the minor (smaller) root of the solution equation. By also taking into account a "ratchet" in the consumption function, the apparatus to be developed can generate either (a) steady growth, (b) cycles, (c) booms, or (d) long depressions.

Formally, it will be shown that the simple linear accelerator-multiplier model can be used as a flexible framework for the analysis of both economic growth and business cycles and that there is no analytical need to separate the two problems: that is, the model generates both the trend and the cycle.[8]

ECONOMIC ASSUMPTIONS

In order to use a linear accelerator-multiplier model as a flexible framework for the analysis of growth and cycles, the flexibility must be built into the economic assumptions. Of course the fundamental assumption is that the accelerator-multiplier apparatus can be used to represent the intertemporal generation of aggregate demand. The validity of this assumption depends upon whether this apparatus yields satisfactory interpretations or predictions of events. No further argument for the validity of the accelerator hypothesis is offered in this paper.

The other economic assumptions made are:

1. The consumption function can be represented by a straight line, $C_t = \alpha_0 + \alpha_1 Y_{t-1}$. The value of α_1 is constant and the value of α_0 depends upon factors which, in turn, can be represented as depending upon past income. By assuming that α_0 changes intermittently and increases more readily than it decreases, a ratchet is built into the consumption function.
2. At each date there exists an exogenously determined ceiling to income which depends upon population growth and technological change, and which does not depend upon the existing capital stock.
3. During each time period, there exists a maximum possible amount of net disinvestment, which depends upon the capital stock and a technologically determined depreciation rate. The consumption function is a determinant of

---

[8] A. Smithies, "Economic Fluctuations and Growth," *Econometrica*, Vol. XXV (January, 1957), pp. 1–52 [reprinted in this volume], has a similar perspective and uses many of the same ingredients.

S. S. Alexander, "The Accelerator as a Generator of Steady Growth," *Quarterly Journal of Economics*, Vol. LXIII (May, 1949), p. 174, demonstrated that such an accelerator apparatus could not be used to generate both steady growth and the business cycle without additional stabilizing factors. This paper negates Alexander's results.

aggregate demand, whereas the ceiling and floor to income are determinants of aggregate supply.

The assumption that α_0, the zero income consumption level, depends upon past incomes is based upon two, not necessarily mutually exclusive, hypotheses. One is the Duesenberry changing preference system hypothesis,[9] which in our interpretation has α_0 depend upon previous peak income. The other is the Tobin-Pigou type of asset (wealth) consumption relation,[10] which in our interpretation has α_0 depend upon the real value of assets. As far as the mechanics are concerned either interpretation would suffice. However, the Duesenberry ratchet is insensitive to changes in the relative prices of assets and income, whereas a Tobin-Pigou ratchet reacts to such changes. Thus, a Tobin-Pigou ratchet can transmit financial market developments to the real sector. As both preference systems and asset holdings do change over time, an eclectic interpretation of the ratchet in the consumption function is both useful and defensible.

As the accelerator-multiplier apparatus is here interpreted, it is simpler to consider changes in the relative prices of income and wealth as exogenous factors which influence the generation of aggregate demand by affecting α_0. Therefore, in the formal model, α_0 will be assumed to depend upon the previous peak income. In interpreting events, any development which raises (lowers) the ratio of consuming units' wealth to income will tend to increase (decrease) α_0. In more concrete terms, a large increase in the ratio of monetary assets to income (such as took place during World War II) will tend to raise α_0, whereas a large fall in the market price of assets relative to income (such as took place in the fall of 1929) will tend to lower α_0. It will be shown that by feeding financial and money market developments into the formal model through the ratchet in the consumption function, booms and depressions of varying amplitude and length can be generated.

The form adopted for the consumption function implies that there is a positive equilibrium level of income at which consumption equals income. If there is a trend in peak income and if α_0 is a linear function of peak income, the equilibrium income will exhibit the same trend. By appropriate assumptions with regard to depreciation, the same trend can be introduced into the floor to income. With these trend assumptions a model is constructed which generates a constant relative amplitude cycle. It will be shown that if these trends are not postulated, the model generates cycles with increasing relative amplitude.

At each date, the ceiling real income is the income which that date's

---

[9] J. S. Duesenberry, *Income, Saving and the Theory of Consumer Behavior* (Cambridge, 1949).

[10] J. Tobin, "Relative Income, Absolute Income and Saving," in *Money, Trade and Economic Growth* (New York, 1951), pp. 135–56; A. C. Pigou, *Employment and Equilibrium*, 2nd ed. (London, 1949), pp. 131–34.

labor force could produce, given the date's technology, if the optimum capital stock existed. As the actual capital stock is less than or equal to the optimum capital stock, the ceiling income is not necessarily the existing capacity income. Ceiling income will change due to changes in the labor force and technology. It is assumed that a technologically progressive society is being considered and that the labor force is growing. As a result, the ceiling real income, $Y_t^{(c)}$, is always growing independently of what the actual income and capital stock may be. That is, $Y_t^{(c)} = \tau Y_{t-1}^{(c)}$, where $\tau > 1$ and is also greater than the rate at which the labor force is growing. In the formal analysis, the assumption will be made that τ is a constant.[11]

The validity of the assumption about the behavior of the income ceiling is questionable. This paper, at a formal level, can be interpreted as an examination of the joint implications of the accelerator-multiplier and the ceiling hypotheses. However, as will be shown, the rate of growth of ceiling income can vary within considerable limits without affecting the qualitative characteristics of the model. Therefore, if desired, this rigid assumption can be relaxed.

The maximum possible disinvestment during any period is determined by the technical fact that at least a portion of the capital stock, fixed capital, is long lived. Hence, during any period only a small part of such capital can be consumed. We will assume that the ratio of capital consumption to peak income capital stock is a constant. Thus, given the capital stock being consumed, the maximum disinvestment which can take place per period is determined. To determine the floor to income, this maximum possible disinvestment has to be joined to behavior assumptions which determine the behavior of equilibrium income, k_0, when income is falling. This maximum possible disinvestment is a supply condition, since it determines the greatest possible excess of consumption over income.

The disinvestment assumption is quite heroic. The ratio of possible disinvestment per period to the capital stock certainly depends upon the composition of the capital stock. As an example, the higher the ratio of working to fixed capital, the higher can be the ratio of a period's disinvestment to the capital stock. It can be expected that the ratio of working capital to fixed capital will be higher at the beginning than during the later part of a downturn. Thus, there is some expectation that the maximum possible disinvestment per period decreases as a depression wears on.

---

[11] R. F. Harrod, *Towards a Dynamic Economics* (London, 1948), defines a natural rate of growth which is the rate of growth of the labor force. Our rate of growth of ceiling income can be interpreted as a "converted" natural rate, to allow for technological change. However, Harrod's result, that there is a knife-edge equilibrium rate of growth, when the "natural" rate is equal to the "warranted" (full-employment savings equal investment) rate of growth, is not borne out by our analysis.

R. M. Solow, "A Contribution to the Theory of Economic Growth," *Quarterly Journal of Economics*, Vol. LXX (February 1956), pp. 65–94, also negates the Harrod conclusion of a knife-edge equilibrium rate of growth of income.

In addition, the size of the capital stock being consumed during any period is open to debate. Is the maximum possible capital consumption during a period based upon the the largest amount of capital which existed during any previous period, or is it based upon the capital stock in existence at the beginning of the period? If the first assumption is made, the maximum possible disinvestment will not decrease when net disinvestment is taking place, whereas the second assumption implies that net disinvestment per period will decrease as a depression continues. Once again, since the mechanics of the model is independent of which assumption is made, we will assume that the disinvestment ceiling is determined by the maximum prior existent capital stock. The qualitative impact of variation in the amount of maximum disinvestment will be considered in the verbal discusssion.

GENERAL CHARACTERISTICS OF THE MODEL

In the models to be considered, the accelerator-multiplier process in conjunction with the initial conditions determines aggregate demand. Actual, or realized, income is determined by the interaction of aggregate demand and supply. We will assume that aggregate supply is a limitational factor determined either by the autonomously growing ceiling or the floor to income. Aggregate demand determines actual income unless the income so determined is inconsistent with the aggregate supply conditions. Whenever this occurs actual income is determined by aggregate supply, and simultaneously a new relation will be determined which generates subsequent aggregate demand.

Given that the accelerator and the consumption coefficients are constants, the two roots, μ_1 and μ_2, of the solution equation are also constants; and we assume that μ_1 and μ_2 are real and greater than one. With k_0 (the consumption-equals-income income) known, two observed incomes are needed as initial conditions to determine A_1 and A_2 in the solution equation. A solution equation with A_1 and A_2 determined by specific initial conditions will be called a particular solution equation. As long as aggregate demand generated by a particular solution equation falls in the range determined by the ceiling and floor to income, actual income will be generated by this particular solution equation. However, it is assumed that μ_1, the dominant root of the solution equation, is very large compared with possible rates of growth of ceiling (decline of floor) income. Hence, income as generated by a particular solution equation will, in time, exceed (fall below) the ceiling (floor) income; whenever this happens, supply conditions will determine actual income. Such actual incomes determined by supply conditions will be the initial conditions in determining new values of A_1 and A_2 and this new particular solution will generate successive aggregate demands.

It will be shown that the qualitative behavior of the model depends upon the relative values of the minor (smaller) root of the solution equation and the rate of growth of ceiling (decline of floor) income. If the rate of growth of ceiling (decline of floor) income is equal to or greater than the minor root of the solution equation, then aggregate demand as determined by the particular solution equations will continuously press against the ceiling (floor) so that steady growth (decline) of actual income will take place. If the rate of growth of ceiling (decline of floor) income is smaller than the minor root, then actual income will bounce off the ceiling (floor), that is, a turning point will be generated. A succession of such bounces between the ceiling and the floor generates a cycle in actual income.

When the ceiling becomes the effective determinant of income, a portion of real aggregate demand is not realized. This cutback can be effected by (1) investment falling proportionately more than consumption, (2) consumption falling proportionately more than investment, or (3) investment and consumption falling to the same extent. If investment is cut back proportionately more than consumption, a capital goods deficiency tends to be created. This could increase β. If consumption is cut back proportionately more than investment, a deficiency in final demand occurs, which could decrease β. Such endogenously determined changes in β make the model nonlinear, of the type which Goodwin has studied. We will not examine the case of changing β in detail. However, it can be shown that $d\mu_1/d\beta > 0$ and $d\mu_2/d\beta < 0$, so that if hitting the ceiling increases β, the minor root of the solution equation decreases; this makes the conditions for steady growth easier. On the other hand, if β decreases, the condition for steady growth becomes more difficult to satisfy.[12]

In the third case, where investment and consumption fall to the same extent, the reasons given above for β changing do not apply. However, the manner in which the adjustment between the demand and ceiling incomes is effected can be assumed to depend upon financial arrangements. If all investment and consumption demand is financed, money income will equal demand income even though real income is equal to the ceiling income. We can assume that consumption and investment are reduced proportionately. The difference between demand income and ceiling income will be adjusted by

---

[12] We have that $\mu_1 = \dfrac{\alpha_1 + \beta + \sqrt{(\alpha_1 + \beta)^2 - 4\beta}}{2}$

and $\mu_2 = \dfrac{\alpha_1 + \beta - \sqrt{(\alpha_1 + \beta)^2 - 4\beta}}{2}$

so that $\dfrac{d\mu_1}{d\beta} = \tfrac{1}{2} + \tfrac{1}{2}\dfrac{(\alpha_1 + \beta - 2)}{\sqrt{(\alpha_1 + \beta)^2 - 4\beta}}$ and $\dfrac{d\mu_2}{d\beta} = \tfrac{1}{2} - \tfrac{1}{2}\dfrac{(\alpha_1 + \beta - 2)}{\sqrt{(\alpha_1 + \beta)^2 - 4\beta}}$

As $\mu_1 > \mu_2 > 1$, $\dfrac{\alpha_1 + \beta}{2} > 1$ and as $\sqrt{(\alpha_1 + \beta)^2 - 4\beta} > 0$, $\dfrac{d\mu_1}{d\beta} > 0$. Also

$\mu_2 = \dfrac{\alpha_1 + \beta - \sqrt{(\alpha_1 + \beta)^2 - 4\beta}}{2} > 1$, $(\alpha_1 + \beta - 2) > \sqrt{(\alpha_1 + \beta)^2 - 4\beta}$ so that

$\dfrac{\alpha_1 + \beta - 2}{\sqrt{(\alpha_1 + \beta)^2 - 4\beta}} > 1$. Therefore, $\dfrac{d\mu_2}{d\beta} < 0$.

a price rise. By assuming that the succeeding period's real demand for consumption and investment depends upon the change in real income, such price
level changes can be ignored in our analysis.[13]

Throughout the body of this paper it is assumed that the roots of the characteristic equation are real and greater than one. If the roots are conjugate
complex numbers with a modulus greater than one, the solution path is
inherently oscillatory; and if the modulus is greater than the rate of growth
of ceiling income, in time the ceiling will become the effective determinant
of income. In the Appendix it is shown that in this case income will always
bounce off the ceiling, so that the qualitative characteristics of the time series
are not affected by the existence of the ceiling. The rich results we obtain by
assuming the roots to be real and greater than one are not available in the
explosive oscillatory case.

The income floor is determined by the consumption-equals-income income
and the maximum possible capital consumption per period. The maximum
capital consumption per period is determined by the capital necessary to
produce the previous peak income. With an invariant consumption-equals-
income income, the relative amplitude of the cycle generated by income
bouncing between the ceiling and the floor will increase: the cycle is really
explosive. However, by adopting the Duesenberry hypothesis that the consumption-equals-income income shifts upward whenever income turns down
from a peak, the income floor is raised and a constant relative amplitude
cycle results.

The accelerator-multiplier process generates income as a deviation from
the consumption-equals-income income, and the rate of growth of income
as generated by any solution equation refers to income so measured. The
natural interpretation of the rate of growth of ceiling income refers to income
measured from its natural origin, i.e., from zero. It will be shown that a
given rate of growth of ceiling income must be multiplied by the ratio of income measured from the natural origin to income measured as a deviation
from equilibrium income before being compared with the smaller root of
the solution equation to determine whether income will continuously press
against or bounce off the ceiling. If the rate of growth of ceiling income so
multiplied is equal to or greater than the smaller root of the solution equation,
steady growth of income measured from the natural origin will result. If the
constant term in the consumption function only increases intermittently, as
the Duesenberry hypothesis suggests, then the ratio of income measured
from the natural origin to income measured as a deviation from the consumption-equals-income income decreases during a period of steady growth.
At some date, given that the rate of growth of ceiling income is smaller than
the smaller root of the solution equation, the state of steady growth will

---

[13] For an examination of monetary factors and such accelerator models see Hyman
P. Minsky, "Monetary Systems and Accelerator Models," *American Economic Review*,
Vol. XLVII (December, 1957), pp. 859–83.

come to an end and income will turn down. Hence, it is possible for actual income to press against the ceiling for a number of periods and then turn down. This generates a cycle with a long boom; and the greater the ratio of income measured from natural origin to income measured as a deviation from the consumption-equals-income income at the date the ceiling to income becomes the effective determinant of actual income, the longer will the economy be in such a state of steady growth.

The above result follows from the introduction of the Duesenberry ratchet in the consumption function. If the Tobin-Pigou effect is interpreted as affecting the ratio of the consumption-equals-income income to ceiling income, then financial market developments will result in the generation of cycles with booms of varying length. If the Tobin-Pigou effect is continuously operative and the ratio of consumption-equals-income income to ceiling income remains constant, steady growth can result.

A symmetric argument applies to the behavior of the system with respect to the income floor, although the postulate that the income floor is steadily falling is not economically natural. If the income floor is a constant during a depression, the only possible result of the process being analyzed is that income bounces off the floor. Note that the prosperity phase generated by this model can be longer than the depression phase.

Since the ratio of the consumption-equals-income income to ceiling income can be considered a variable, the model can generate cycles of varying amplitudes and periods. Also, by utilizing the Tobin-Pigou effect this apparatus makes it possible to integrate real and monetary aspects of cycles and growth.

THE FORMAL MODEL

Obviously the results stated in the previous section must be derived. It may surprise some that new results can be achieved by looking once again at a formulation that has been as well explored as the accelerator-multiplier model. However, the typical formulations ignored the constant term in the linear consumption function and used the initial conditions only once, to start the solution equation off from the equilibrium position. The possibility of booms of different lengths and amplitudes depends upon the interpretation of the constant term in the consumption function. The possibility that either steady growth or a turning point will result when the ceiling (floor) income constrains an otherwise explosive accelerator process follows from imposing initial conditions at the ceiling (floor) income rather than at the consumption-equals-income income.

We must distinguish between actual, aggregate demand (as generated by a particular solution equation), ceiling, and floor incomes. These different incomes will be identified by superscripts, thus:

$Y_t^{(a)}$ is the tth date's actual income,

$Y_t^{(d)}$ is the tth date's aggregate demand income,

$Y_t^{(c)}$ is the tth date's ceiling income,

$Y_t^{(f)}$ is the tth date's floor income.

We also take account of the intermittently imposed initial conditions in our notation by writing the date of the initial conditions in parenthesis after $Y_t^{(d)}$, A_1, and A_2 and subtracting the date of the first initial condition from t in the solution equation, e.g.,

$$Y_t^{(d)}(n, n + 1) = A_1(n, n + 1)\mu_1^{t-n} + A_2(n, n + 1)\mu_2^{t-n} + k_0(n + 1). \quad (5)$$

Equation 5 states that the particular solution was derived by using the nth and $(n + 1)$st dates' actual incomes as the initial conditions. By writing μ_1^{t-n} and μ_2^{t-n} the initial conditions dates are the zero and first powers of the roots. The writing of the equilibrium income as $k_0(n + 1)$ denotes that the $(n + 1)$st date's income was the peak income which determined a Duesenberry ratchet in the consumption function.

In the next three sections, where the values of the A_1 and A_2 coefficients and the effects of the income floor and ceiling are derived, the consumption-equals-income income will be constant. In these sections, it will be mathematically convenient to measure income as a deviation from the consumption-equals-income income. A lower-case y will be used when income is so measured.

Determination of A_1 and A_2

To determine A_1 and A_2 it is necessary to know the actual incomes of two dates, $Y_0^{(a)}$ and $Y_1^{(a)}$. We have

$$y_0^{(a)} = Y_0^{(a)} - k_0 = A_1(0, 1) + A_2(0, 1)$$

$$y_1^{(a)} = Y_1^{(a)} - k_0 = A_1(0, 1)\mu_1 + A_2(0, 1)\mu_2.$$

Assuming k_0 is known and that $y_1^{(a)} = \bar{\mu}y_0^{(a)}$ we have

$$A_1(0, 1) = \left[\frac{\bar{\mu} - \mu_2}{\mu_1 - \mu_2}\right] y_0^{(a)} \quad (6)$$

$$A_2(0, 1) = \left[\frac{\mu_1 - \bar{\mu}}{\mu_1 - \mu_2}\right] y_0^{(a)}. \quad (7)$$

Assuming $y_0^{(a)} > 0$ since $\mu_1 > \mu_2$, if $\mu_1 > \mu_2 > \bar{\mu}$ then $A_1(0, 1) < 0$, $A_2(0, 1) > 0$ whereas if $\mu_1 > \bar{\mu} > \mu_2$ then $A_1(0, 1) > 0$, $A_2(0, 1) > 0$.[14]

---

[14] Note that in equations (6) and (7) only the numerators differ. If $|\bar{\mu} - \mu_2| < |\mu_1 - \bar{\mu}|$ then $|A_1(0, 1)| < |A_2(0, 1)|$. It is also obvious that if $\mu_2 = \bar{\mu}$, then $A_1(0, 1) = 0$ and if $\mu_1 = \bar{\mu}$, $A_2(0, 1) = 0$. Also if $\bar{\mu} > \mu_1 > \mu_2$, then $A_1(0, 1) > 0$, $A_2(0, 1) < 0$ with

In any particular solution equation, $y_t^{(d)} = A_1(0, 1)\mu_1^t + A_2(0, 1)\mu_2^t$, the income of any period is an average of μ_1 and μ_2 with weights $A_1(0, 1)\mu_1^{t-1}$ and $A_2(0, 1)\mu_2^{t-2}$. As t increases, $A_1(0, 1)\mu_1^{t-1}/A_2(0, 1)\mu_2^{t-1}$ increases so that the weight of μ_1 in determining aggregate demand increases. In time, μ_1 dominates the behavior of the time series. Nevertheless, if $|A_2(0, 1)|$ is very much greater than $|A_1(0, 1)|$ for small t the behavior of the series will be dominated by $A_2(0, 1)\mu_2^t$ so that, even with $A_1(0, 1) < 0, y_t > y_{t-1}$ is possible.

Assume $y_1 > y_0 > 0$ and $\mu_1 > \bar{\mu} > \mu_2$. Then $A_1(0, 1)$ and $A_2(0, 1)$ are both positive, and all incomes generated by this particular solution equation will be positive and the rate of growth of income will increase, approaching μ_1 as a limit. On the other hand, if $\mu_2 > \bar{\mu}$ then $A_1(0, 1)$ is negative. For small t income will be positive and can even be increasing, though at a diminishing rate. However, as t increases, $A_1(0, 1)\mu_1^t$ takes over, so that income will fall and in time becomes negative $[Y_t^{(d)}(0, 1) < k_0]$. Unless constrained, the rate of increase of negative income will increase, approaching μ_1 as a limit.

Therefore, if $y_1 > y_0 > 0$ but $y_1 < \mu_2 y_0$, $A_1(0, 1)$, the coefficient of the dominant root, will be negative. This particular solution equation, with roots (μ_1 and μ_2) large enough to generate an explosive time series, will in fact have one upper turning point. As a result of the initial displacement not being large enough, the explosion will take place in the opposite direction from its "start."

Symmetrically, the above holds for $y_n < y_{n-1} < 0$, i.e., if $y_n > \mu_2 y_{n-1}$, ($\mu_2 > \bar{\mu}$) then $A_1(n - 1, n)$ will be positive and $A_2(n - 1, n)$ will be negative, so that one lower turning point will be generated.

The Ceiling to Income

The task of this section is to examine the relation between particular solution equations that yield a monotonically increasing income and the income ceiling. The larger root of the solution equation is assumed to be greater than the rate of growth of ceiling income, so that in time the ceiling becomes effective. The problem is whether, once the ceiling becomes effective, income will bounce off the ceiling, yielding an upper turning point, or will continue to press against the ceiling resulting in a state of steady growth. Two cases must be examined: (1) when the smaller root of the solution equation is greater than the rate of growth of ceiling income, and (2) when the smaller root of the solution equation is equal to or smaller than the rate of growth of ceiling income. It will be shown that the first case results in

---

$|A_1(0, 1)| > |A_2(0, 1)|$. This leads to the uninteresting case of growth at essentially μ_1.

If $y_0 = 0$ and $y_1 = \delta > 0$, then $A_1(0, 1) = \dfrac{\delta}{\mu_1 - \mu_2} > 0$ and $A_2(0, 1) = \dfrac{\delta}{\mu_2 - \mu_1} < 0$.

This special case is the one considered by all those who, once and for all, impose initial conditions as a deviation from equilibrium.

income bouncing off the ceiling and the second case results in income continuing to press against the ceiling.

1. *Smaller Root Greater than Ceiling Rate of Growth.* To make the exposition simpler, we assume that λ is a constant rate of growth of the ceiling income measured as a deviation from k_0, i.e., $y_{t+n}^{(c)} = \lambda^n y_t^{(c)}$. We also have that $y_0^{(d)} = A_1 \mu_1^t + A_2 \mu_2^t$; and we first assume that $\mu_1 > \mu_2 > \lambda > 1$.

Since it does not matter where we break into the time series, we begin with two positive, arbitrarily dated incomes, $y_0^{(a)}$ and $y_1^{(a)}$. Both incomes are less than the ceiling of their respective dates and also $\mu_1 > y_1^{(a)}/y_0^{(a)} > \mu_2$. These initial conditions determine positive $A_1(0, 1)$ and $A_2(0, 1)$. The particular solution equation thus started will generate a monotonically increasing series with an increasing (approaching μ_1) rate of increase of income. In time, say at the nth date, the income generated by this particular solution equation will become greater than the ceiling income, i.e., $y_n^d = A_1(0, 1)\mu_1^n + A_2(0, 1)\mu_2^n > \lambda^n y_0^{(c)}$.

As long as the particular solution equation yields an income less than the ceiling income (or greater than the floor income), the income so determined will be the actual income. Whenever a particular solution equation tends to generate an income inconsistent with the constraint, actual income is equal to the constraint (ceiling or floor) income. And whenever actual income is determined by a constraint, it will be interpreted as imposing new initial conditions. Inasmuch as two initial incomes are needed to determine A_1 and A_2 such an actual-equals-constraint income and one other income is needed. This other income will be either the income just prior to or the income immediately following the first income at which the constraint becomes effective.

Hence, if $y_n^{(d)} > \lambda^n y_0^{(c)}$ then the actual income will be $y_n^{(a)} = \lambda^n y_0^{(c)}$. If $y_n^{(a)}/y_{n-1}^{(a)} = \bar{\mu}(n, n-1) > \mu_2 > \lambda$ then the particular solution equation using $y_n^{(a)}$ and $y_{n-1}^{(a)}$ as the initial conditions will generate an income $y_{n+1}^{(d)}$ greater than the $(n+1)$st date's ceiling income.[15] Therefore, the actual income of $(n+1)$ will be determined by the ceiling income, and new initial conditions

---

[15] The ratio of the two initial periods income $\bar{\mu}$

$$= \frac{A_1(n-1, n)}{A_1(n-1, n) + A_2(n-1, n)}\mu_1 + \frac{A_2(n-1, n)}{A_1(n-1, n) + A_2(n-1, n)}\mu_2$$

is a weighted average of μ_1 and μ_2 and the ratio of the weights of μ_1 and μ_2 is $\frac{A_1(n-1, n)}{A_2(n-1, n)}$. From the solution equation $y_{n+1}^{(d)} = A_1(n-1, n)\mu_1^2 + A_2(n-1, n)\mu_2^2$ and

$$y_{n+1}^{(d)}/y_n^{(d)} = \frac{A_1(n-1, n)\mu_1}{A_1(n-1, n)\mu_1 + A_2(n-1, n)\mu_2}\mu_1 + \frac{A_2(n-1, n)\mu_2}{A_1(n-1, n)\mu_1 + A_2(n-1, n)\mu_2}\mu_2 \text{ so}$$

that the ratio of the weights of μ_1 and μ_2 is $\frac{A_1(n-1, n)\mu_1}{A_2(n-1, n)\mu_2}$. As $\mu_1 > \mu_2$ the weight of μ_1 in determining the ratio $y_{n+1}^{(d)}/y_n^{(d)}$ is greater than its weight in determining the ratio $y_n^{(d)}/y_{n-1}^{(d)}$. Hence, $y_{n+1}^{(d)} > \bar{\mu}y_n^{(d)}$. As $y_n^{(d)}$ is a ceiling income, then $y_{n+1}^{(d)} > \lambda y_n^{(d)}$ so that $y_{n+1}^{(a)} = y_{n+1}^{(c)} = \lambda y_n^{(d)}$.

are imposed. As $y_n^{(a)}$ and $y_{n+1}^{(a)}$ are both ceiling incomes $y_{n+1}^{(a)}/y_n^{(a)} = \lambda$, so that a negative $A_1(n, n+1)$ coefficient will be determined. This new particular solution equation, $y_t^{(d)}(n, n+1) = A_1(n, n+1)\mu_1^{t-n} + A_2(n, n+1)\mu_2^{t-n}$, will generate future incomes smaller than the ceiling incomes of the respective dates. Therefore, the ceiling will no longer be an effective constraint and, until such time as the floor becomes effective, actual incomes will be generated by this solution equation.

If $\mu_2 > y_n^{(a)}/y_{n-1}^{(a)} > \lambda$, then the solution equation using $y_{n-1}^{(a)}$ and $y_n^{(a)}$ as initial conditions will determine $A_1(n-1, n) < 0$. If the absolute value of $A_1(n-1, n)$ is very small, the positive component, $A_2(n-1, n)$ can dominate, so that $y_2^{(d)}(n-1, n) > \lambda^{n+1}y_0^{(c)}$. If this is true, then once again $y_n^{(a)}$ and $y_{n+1}^{(a)}$ will be used to determine $A_1(n, n+1)$ and $A_2(n, n+1)$ and this case becomes the same as the one above. On the other hand, if $|A_1(n-1, n)|$ is not so small, then $y_{n+1}^{(d)}(n-1, n) \le \lambda^{n+1}y_0^{(c)}$, the ceiling is not effective and this solution equation will determine the actual incomes of succeeding periods.

Regardless of whether the ceiling income is an effective constraint for one or two periods, as long as $\mu_2 > \lambda > 1$, the "initial conditions" will determine a negative coefficient for the dominant root. Income will bounce off the ceiling and, unless constrained by a floor, the solution equation will in time generate an income that approaches $-\infty$, at a rate determined by μ_1.

2. *Smaller Root Equal to or Smaller than Ceiling Rate of Growth.* Assume that $\mu_1 > \lambda > \mu_2 > 1$ and that the actual incomes of the nth and $(n+1)$st dates are ceiling incomes. A particular solution equation determined by using these dates' incomes as initial conditions will have positive A_1 and A_2. This particular solution equation will yield only positive and increasing incomes and $y_{n+2}^{(d)}$ generated by this equation will be greater than $y_{n+2}^{(c)}$.

As a result of $y_{n+2}^{(a)}$ being determined by the ceiling constraint rather than by the solution equation, new initial conditions are effective. The new coefficients are $A_1(n+1, n+2) = \left[\dfrac{\lambda - \mu_2}{\mu_1 - \mu_2}\right]\lambda y_n = \lambda A_1(n, n+1)$ and $A_2(n+1,$

$n+2) = \left[\dfrac{\mu_1 - \lambda}{\mu_1 - \mu_2}\right]\lambda y_n = \lambda A_2(n, n+1)$. Therefore, the new solution equation is $y_t^{(d)}(n+1, n+2) = \lambda[A_1(n, n+1)\mu_1^{t-(n+1)} + A_2(n, n+1)\mu_2^{t-(n+1)}]$. This will be repeated as long as the ceiling income is the effective determinant of the actual income, so that $y_t^{(d)}(n+h, n+h+1) = \lambda^h[A_1(n, n+1)\mu_1^{t-h} + A_2(n, n+1)\mu_2^{t-h}]$ where t is either h or $h+1$.

By continuously imposing new initial conditions which are determined by a sufficiently large constant rate of growth of ceiling income, steady growth is generated. Note that this growth state is not a "knife edge," for the rate of growth of ceiling income can vary between μ_1 and μ_2 without causing either "runaway" expansion or a downturn.

The Floor to Income

As was argued earlier, a simple disinvestment assumption is that the maximum disinvestment per period is some constant percentage, ρ, of the capital stock required to produce the previous peak income. It has been shown that a peak income is in the neighborhood of a ceiling income so that the capital stock to be depreciated is $\beta[k_0 + \lambda^n y_0^{(c)}]$ and the maximum possible capital consumption per period is $\rho\beta[k_0 + \lambda^n y_0^{(c)}]$. The floor income following a particular peak income is given by

$$Y_{n+h}^{(f)}(n) = k_0(n) - \frac{\rho\beta(k_0(n) + \lambda^n y_0^{(c)})}{1 - \alpha_1}$$

or

$$y_{n+h}^{(f)}(n) = -\frac{\rho\beta(k_0(n) + \lambda^n y_0^{(c)})}{1 - \alpha_1}.$$

Assume that the income determined by the ruling particular solution equation for the $(n + h)$th date is lower than the floor income, so that actual income equals the floor income. A new particular solution equation with $y_{n+h}^{(f)}$ as one of the initial conditions is determined. The arguments in the previous section examining the ratio between $y_{n+h-1}^{(a)}$ and $y_{n+h}^{(a)}$ could be repeated; however, it is sufficient to argue from the assumption that both $y_{n+h}^{(a)}$ and $y_{n+h+1}^{(a)}$ are equal to the floor income.

These two floor incomes determine a new particular solution equation with

$$A_1(n + h, n + h + 1) = \left[\frac{1 - \mu_2}{\mu_1 - \mu_2}\right]\left[\frac{-\rho\beta(k_0 + \lambda^n y_0^{(c)})}{1 - \alpha_1}\right] > 0$$

and

$$A_2(n + h, n + h + 1) = \left[\frac{1 - \mu_2}{\mu_2 - \mu_1}\right]\left[\frac{-\rho\beta(k_0 + \lambda^n y_0^{(c)})}{1 - \alpha_1}\right] < 0.$$

As the coefficient of the dominant root is positive, y_{n+h+2} will be greater than the floor income, and a monotonic expansion will be set off.

With a constant floor to income, it is impossible for income to glide along the floor. For income to glide along the floor it is necessary that the rate of decrease of the negative floor income be greater than or equal to μ_2. This would require either an increase in ρ, the percentage of capital that can be consumed per period, or a decline in k_0, the equilibrium income. To the extent that one wishes to interpret business cycle events using this framework, a deep depression—or a stagnation—could only be the result of ρ or k_0 changing. These assumptions would result in establishing formal symmetry between the floor and the ceiling.

Generation of an Explosive Cycle

In this section it will be shown that in the case where income bounces between the ceiling and the floor the assumption that the consumption-equals-income income does not change implies that in time the absolute amplitude of the cycle will be greater than income. It follows that the assumption of an unchanging equilibrium income has to be abandoned, and in the next section the implications of various assumptions as to the behavior of equilibrium income will be derived.

The amplitude of a cycle is defined as the difference between a peak income and the succeeding trough income and is approximately equal to the difference between a ceiling and a floor income. The floor income of a cycle which begins by either bouncing off or falling away from a ceiling income $Y_n^{(c)}$ is $k_0 - \dfrac{\rho\beta Y_n^{(c)}}{1 - \alpha_1}$ and the amplitude of the cycle is $Y_n^{(c)} - \left(k_0 - \dfrac{\rho\beta Y_n^{(c)}}{1 - \alpha_1}\right)$

$= \left(1 + \dfrac{\rho\beta}{1 - \alpha_1}\right) Y_n^{(c)} - k_0$. If m periods elapse before the next peak income, the amplitude of the succeeding cycle will be $\left(1 + \dfrac{\rho\beta}{1 - \alpha_1}\right) \tau^m Y_n^{(c)} - k_0$ where τ is the constant rate of growth of ceiling income measured from its natural origin. In time $\rho\beta\tau^m Y_n^{(c)}/1 - \alpha_1$ will be greater than k_0, so that eventually the amplitude of the cycle will be greater than peak income.

The relative amplitude of the cycle, defined as the ratio of the amplitude to the beginning peak income, is $\left(1 + \dfrac{\rho\beta}{1 - \alpha_1}\right) - \dfrac{k_0}{\tau^m Y_n^{(c)}}$. In addition to implying negative income at the trough of the cycle, the assumption that k_0 is a constant implies that the amplitude of the cycle will be an increasing percentage of an exponentially growing ceiling income; the cycle generated will be truly explosive.

The Ratchet in the Consumption Function

The assumption that k_0, the consumption-equals-income income, does not change leads to an economically unacceptable result. Hence, it is necessary to abandon that assumption, and in this section we shall derive the implications of the assumption that a ratchet in the consumption function exists. It will be shown that, depending upon the assumptions made as to its determinants, a ratchet in the consumption function leads to a number of interesting results, namely cycles with (1) constant relative amplitude, (2) varying relative amplitude, and (3) booms (or depressions) of differing length. The first two results follow almost immediately from the differing specification of how k_0 changes, the third result requires an investigation of the relation between the rate of growth of income measured from zero and the rate of growth of income measured as a deviation from the consumption-equals-income income.

The specification of the Duesenberry ratchet in the consumption function to be used is that

$$\alpha_0(n) = \gamma Y_n^{(c)} \text{ where } Y_n^{(a)} = Y_n^{(c)}, \ Y_{n+1}^{(a)} < Y_{n+1}^{(c)}$$

$$\text{and } Y_{n+h}^{(a)} \le Y_{n+h}^{(c)}, \ h > 1,$$

i.e., that whenever a downturn (or a "falling off" from the ceiling) occurs, α_0 increases. From this specification it follows that α_0 is a constant within a cycle, including any periods in which income glides along the ceiling, but it increases whenever income bounces off or falls away from the ceiling.

As a result, k_0 also changes intermittently, in fact $k_0(n) = \dfrac{\alpha_0(n)}{1 - \alpha_1} = \dfrac{\gamma}{1 - \alpha_1} Y_n^{(c)}$. It follows that the amplitude of each cycle is $\left(1 + \dfrac{\rho\beta}{1 - \alpha_1}\right) Y_n^{(c)} - \dfrac{\gamma}{1 - \alpha_1} Y_n^{(c)}$, and the relative amplitude is $1 + \dfrac{\rho\beta}{1 - \alpha_1} - \dfrac{\gamma}{1 - \alpha_1}$ which is a constant. The Duesenberry ratchet in the consumption function liquidates the embarrassing explosiveness of the cycle generated by bouncing between the income ceiling and floor.

If it is desired to consider α_0 (or γ) as depending upon financial or monetary phenomena in addition to previous peak income, the relative amplitude of the cycle can be a variable. If a downturn in income occurs when assets are a large percentage of income, k_0 will be high and the relative amplitude of the cycle that follows will be small. On the other hand, if a downturn in income is associated with a financial crisis, so that the ratio of the value of assets to income falls, then k_0 will also fall, leading to a cycle with a high relative amplitude. By allowing financial developments to affect the consumption function, the basic accelerator-multiplier process can generate cycles of varying amplitude.

Note that if ρ, the depreciation ratio, is interpreted as a behavior rather than a technical coefficient, it too would be affected by the same monetary and financial factors. That is, if a downturn in income is associated with financial ease, the carrying costs of excess capacity and the need by firms for additional liquidity are both low, and ρ would tend to be small. On the other hand, if a financial crisis occurs, the carrying costs of excess capacity are high and firms would need additional liquidity, and ρ would tend to be high. Hence, financial ease would be associated with low amplitude fluctuations and financial stringency with large amplitude fluctuations. This effect of financial developments on the depreciation ratio would tend to reinforce the effect of financial developments on the consumption function.

In addition to differing in amplitude, cycles differ in duration. The ratchet in the consumption function and the Tobin-Pigou asset effects can also affect the duration of the boom and the depression.

In order to examine the determinants of the duration of a cycle, it is necessary to note that the solution equation always determines the rate of growth of income as a deviation from the equilibrium income, k_0. The natural interpretation of the rate of growth of ceiling income is as the rate of growth of income measured from its natural origin. In previous sections we assumed that there was a constant rate of growth of income measured as a deviation from the equilibrium income. We will now investigate the relation between τ, the constant rate of growth of income measured from the natural origin, and λ, the variable rate of growth of income measured as a deviation from k_0.

The numerical growth of ceiling income between any two dates is the same measured from either origin, i.e.,

$$y_{t+1}^{(c)} - y_t^{(c)} = Y_{t+1}^{(c)} - Y_t^{(c)}.$$

Therefore,

$$\lambda - 1 = \frac{y_{t+1}^{(c)} - y_t^{(c)}}{y_t^{(c)}}$$

and as

$$Y_{t+1}^{(c)} - Y_t^{(c)} = (\tau - 1)Y_t^{(c)}$$

we have

$$\lambda = 1 + \frac{Y_t^{(c)}}{y_t^{(c)}} (\tau - 1).^{16}$$

If k_0 does not change, λ is a variable, greater than τ. As the limit of $Y_t^{(c)}/y_t^{(c)}$ is 1, the lower limit of λ is τ.

On the other hand, if k_0 increases at the same rate as $Y_t^{(c)}$, which could be the result of interpreting the Tobin-Pigou effect as reflecting the increase in the net worth of households that accompanies investment activity, then $\tau = \lambda$ for $y_{t+1}^{(c)} - y_t^{(c)} = Y_{t+1}^{(c)} - Y_t^{(c)} - k_0(t+1) + k_0(t)$ so that $(\lambda - 1)y_t^{(c)} = (\tau - 1)[Y_t^{(c)} - k_0(t)] = (\tau - 1)y_t^{(c)}.^{17}$

In determining whether income will bounce off or press against the ceiling once it becomes the effective determinant of income, it is λ, rather than τ, that is relevant. Once the income ceiling becomes effective the necessary

---

[16] If income grows at three percent per period ($\tau = 1.03$) and if the equilibrium income is $\frac{2}{3}$ actual income, so that $Y_t^{(c)}/y_t^{(c)} = 3$, then $\lambda = 1.09$. That is, a three percent rate of growth of income in natural units is equivalent to a nine percent rate of growth of income measured as a deviation from equilibrium income.

[17] Note that $k_0 = \alpha_0/(1 - \alpha_1)$, so that if k_0 grows at the same rate as ceiling income so does α_0. Since $C_t^{(c)} = \alpha_0(t-1) + \alpha_1 Y_{t-1}^{(c)}$ at a date when actual income equals ceiling income then

$$C_t^{(c)}/Y_{t-1}^{(c)} = \frac{\alpha_0(t-1) + \alpha_1 Y_{t-1}^{(c)}}{Y_{t-1}^{(c)}} = \frac{[\alpha_0(0) + \alpha_1 Y_0^{(c)}]\tau^{t-1}}{\tau^{t-1}Y_0^{(c)}} = \frac{\alpha_0(0) + \alpha_1 Y_0^{(c)}}{Y_0^{(c)}}$$

which is a constant. Those authors who write $C_t = \alpha_0 Y_{t-1}$ rather than $C_t = \alpha_0 + \alpha_1 Y_{t-1}$ can be interpreted as assuming that the equilibrium income increases at the same rate as the ceiling income, which can be identified as following from the specification that equilibrium income is affected by the result of investment activity in increasing the net worth of households.

and sufficient condition for $A_1 \geq 0$ is for $\lambda(n, n+1) \geq \mu_2$. Hence, if the income ceiling is the effective determinant of actual income beginning at the nth date, steady growth will continue as long as

$$\lambda(n+h-1, n+h) = 1 + (\tau - 1)\left[\frac{Y_{n+h-1}^{(c)}}{y_{n+h-1}^{(c)}}\right]$$

$$= 1 + (\tau - 1)\left[\frac{Y_n^{(c)} + \xi}{y_n^{(c)} + \xi}\right] \geq \mu_2.$$

The border between a positive and a negative A_1 is

$$\xi = \left(\frac{\tau - 1}{\mu_2 - \tau}\right)Y_n^{(c)} - \left(\frac{\mu_2 - 1}{\mu_2 - \tau}\right)y_n^{(c)}.$$

Since $\xi = (\tau^{h-1} - 1)Y_n^{(c)}$ we have

$$\tau^{h-1} = 1 + \left(\frac{\tau - 1}{\mu_2 - \tau}\right) - \left(\frac{\mu_2 - 1}{\mu_2 - \tau}\right)\frac{y_n^{(c)}}{Y_n^{(c)}}$$

$$h - 1 = \log\left(1 - \frac{y_n^{(c)}}{Y_n^{(c)}}\right)\left(\frac{\mu_2 - 1}{\mu_2 - \tau}\right) \div \log \tau$$

$$h = 1 + \log\frac{k_0(n)}{Y_n^{(c)}}\left[\frac{\mu_2 - 1}{\mu_2 - \tau}\right] \div \log \tau$$

where h is the number of periods after the ceiling first becomes effective that income will press against rather than fall away from (or bounce off) the ceiling. Obviously, with a fixed rate of growth of ceiling income the higher the ratio of the equilibrium to the actual income at the date the ceiling first becomes effective, the longer the boom; and the smaller the minor root of the solution equation, the longer the boom.[18]

As the length of the period of sustained growth depends upon the ratio of the equilibrium to actual income at the date the ceiling first becomes

---

[18] The following table gives the proximate value of h, the number of periods for which the model will exhibit steady growth after reaching the ceiling income, for various values of $k_0(n)/Y_n^{(c)}$, the ratio of equilibrium income to actual income at the date the ceiling first becomes the effective determinant of income, and μ_2, the smaller root of the solution equation, assuming that τ is 1.03.

$k_0(n)/Y_n^{(c)}$	μ_2	h
1.0	1.05	33
0.8	1.05	24
0.6	1.05	15
1.0	1.07	20
0.8	1.07	12
0.6	1.07	3
1.0	1.10	13
0.8	1.10	6
0.6	1.10	1

effective, any phenomenon which tends to increase this ratio will tend to stretch out this period. The interpretation of the Tobin-Pigou effect adopted in this paper would result in financial market and monetary developments affecting the equilibrium income. In particular, a period following a rise in the ratio of the money value of households' assets to income would be characterized by long intervals of sustained growth during which income glides along (or presses against) the ceiling, whereas a period following a fall in this ratio would be characterized by cycles in which income bounces off the ceiling.

The monetary and financial developments which tend to stretch out the boom also tend to decrease the amplitude of the fluctuations, and the developments which tend to shorten booms are associated with deep depressions. A deep depression after a long boom can result if the falling away from the ceiling income were associated with a financial crisis.

The floor to income becomes effective wherever income generated by a solution equation tends to be lower than the floor. Measuring from the natural origin the floor to income is $Y^{(f)}_{n+h}(n) = k_0(n) - \dfrac{\rho \beta Y^{(c)}_n}{1 - \alpha_1}$, but the particular solution equation generates income as a deviation from the equilibrium income at the date it became effective. If at the date the floor becomes effective, the rate of decline of the floor to income is greater than the smaller root of the solution equation, the new particular solution equation would have negative A_1 and A_2 coefficients. This lowering of the floor would have to be the result of changes in $k_0(n)$ or in ρ; and this, of course, could be the results of a continuing financial crisis. Hence, long and deepening depressions in this model result from a stretched-out period of financial stringency.

This model is incapable of generating stagnation, that is, a relatively long period of stable, low income.

CONCLUSION

It has been shown that a model which combines the explosive accelerator-multiplier hypothesis and an exogenously determined rate of growth of ceiling income is capable of generating a wide variety of alternative types of time series. In particular, it was shown that one process is capable of simultaneously generating the trend and the cycle of observable series. The variability among the types of time series generated can be imputed to the effects of presumable observable events. As a result the model does provide a useful framework for economic analysis.

In particular, the model seems capable of serving as an explanatory device for the great postwar boom. Wartime shortages of capital equipment resulted in the ceiling income being much greater than actual income, and the great expansion of the net worth position of households due to the high wartime savings resulted in a relatively high consumption-equals-income income.

In addition, the exploitation of various wartime technological changes for civilian use made the rate of growth of ceiling income high. The combination of these factors enabled income to press against the ceiling for considerable periods of time. Whenever income fell away from the ceiling—as in 1948 and 1954 in the United States—the financial ease, carried over from the war, resulted in a relatively high and nonfalling floor in income, so that recovery was quick.

In order for more serious depressions to occur it is necessary for the ratio of equilibrium income to ceiling income to decrease or for depreciation ratios to increase. Within the framework adopted in this paper, this could occur if the downturn were accompanied by a financial crisis or if the preceding boom had been associated with a relatively small increase or even a decrease in the liquid asset position of households and firms.

APPENDIX

In the text the case where $\mu_1 > \mu_2 > 1$ is examined. In this appendix the cyclically explosive case, where the roots of the solution equation are conjugate complex numbers with a modulus greater than 1, is examined.

The solution equation to $y_t = (\alpha_1 + \beta)y_{t-1} - \beta y_{t-2}$ can be written as $y_t = M^t(A_1 \cos t\theta + A_2 \sin t\theta)$ in the cyclical case, where M, the modulus, is equal to $\beta^{\frac{1}{2}}$ and θ is defined by the conditions $\cos \theta = \dfrac{\alpha_1 + \beta}{2\beta^{\frac{1}{2}}}$ and $\sin \theta = \dfrac{\sqrt{4\beta - (\alpha_1 + \beta)^2}}{2\beta^{\frac{1}{2}}}$.

For the cyclically explosive case the modulus must be greater than 1, so that $\beta^{\frac{1}{2}} > 1$. Once again A_1 and A_2 are determined by the initial conditions.

If $\beta^{\frac{1}{2}} \leq \lambda$ the ceiling to income does not affect the time series generated; the interesting case occurs when $\beta^{\frac{1}{2}} > \lambda$. To examine this case we will assume that $y_0^{(a)}$ and $y_1^{(a)}$ are both ceiling incomes. The problem is whether $y_2^{(d)} > y_2^{(c)}$ so that $y_2^{(a)} = y_2^{(c)}$ and a new particular solution equation based upon $y_1^{(a)}$ and $y_2^{(a)}$ as initial conditions is established. It will be shown that with a cyclically explosive solution $y_2^{(d)} < y_2^{(c)}$, so that income always bounces off the ceiling.

Using the initial conditions we have that $y_0^{(c)} = \beta^{0/2}(A_1 \cos 0^\circ + A_2 \sin 0^\circ)$ so that $A_1 = y_0^{(c)}$. Also, $y_1^{(c)} = \lambda y_0^{(c)} = \beta^{\frac{1}{2}}(A_1 \cos \theta + A_2 \sin \theta)$ so that

$$A_2 = \frac{2\lambda - (\alpha_1 + \beta)}{\sqrt{4\beta - (\alpha_1 + \beta)^2}} y_0^{(c)}.$$

Therefore, the particular solution equation is

$$y_t^{(d)} = \beta^{t/2}(\cos t\theta + \frac{2\lambda - (\alpha_1 + \beta)}{\sqrt{4\beta - (\alpha_1 + \beta)^2}} \sin t\theta)y_0^{(c)}.$$

The problem is to determine the relation between $y_2^{(d)}$ and $y_2^{(c)}$.

$$y_2^{(d)} = \beta(\cos 2\theta + \frac{2\lambda - (\alpha_1 + \beta)}{\sqrt{4\beta - (\alpha_1 + \beta)^2}} \sin 2\theta)y_0^{(c)}.$$

We know that if $\cos \theta = \dfrac{\alpha_1 + \beta}{2\sqrt{\beta}}$ and $\sin \theta = \dfrac{\sqrt{4\beta - (\alpha_1 + \beta)^2}}{2\sqrt{\beta}}$

then $\cos 2\theta = \dfrac{(\alpha_1 + \beta)^2}{2\beta} - 1$ and $\sin 2\theta = \dfrac{(\alpha_1 + \beta) \sqrt{4\beta - (\alpha_1 + \beta)^2}}{2\beta}$.

Therefore, $y_2^{(d)} = [\lambda(\alpha_1 + \beta) - \beta]y_0^{(c)}$. If the ceiling is to be effective, it is necessary that $y_2^{(d)} > \lambda y_1^{(c)} = \lambda^2 y_0^{(c)}$. Therefore, $y_2^{(d)} = [\lambda(\alpha_1 + \beta) - \beta]y_0^{(c)} > \lambda^2 y_0^{(c)}$ is a necessary condition for the ceiling to be effective. This yields $\lambda^2 - (\alpha_1 + \beta)\lambda + \beta \leq 0$ or $\lambda^2 - (\alpha_1 + \beta)\lambda + (\beta + k) = 0$ $(k > 0)$ and

$$\lambda = \frac{\alpha_1 + \beta \pm \sqrt{(\alpha_1 + \beta)^2 - 4(\beta + k)}}{2}.$$

However, λ is real, and since $\dfrac{\alpha_1 + \beta \pm \sqrt{(\alpha_1 + \beta)^2 - 4\beta}}{2}$ is assumed complex, $(\alpha_1 + \beta)^2 - 4(\beta + k) < 0$, so that $\lambda(\alpha_1 + \beta) - \beta > \lambda^2$ contradicts our assumption. Therefore, $[\lambda(\alpha_1 + \beta) - \beta]y_0^{(c)} < \lambda^2 y_0^{(c)}$ and $y_2^{(d)} < y_2^{(c)}$.

140425

6

The Nature and Stability of
Inventory Cycles*

By LLOYD A. METZLER†

BUSINESS CYCLE explanations may conveniently be classified, for the purpose of comparison, according to their implicit stability assumptions. On this basis there are two principal groups, one in which the economy is assumed to be in unstable equilibrium and one in which market relations are assumed to be stable. Proponents of the first group envisage cyclical movements as the consequence of (1) an initial disturbance that sets in motion a cumulative process, and (2) certain limiting stabilizers which reverse the direction of the cumulative movement but which are not operative except in extreme positions, such as full employment, etc. Wicksell's analysis of prices and interest rates provides a good example of this type of theory. In the second group, on the other hand, movements of output and employment represent a process of adaptation to cyclical changes in the parameters of a system that would otherwise be stable. The idea of a determinate relation between changes in the level of noninduced investment and changes in total income, for example, belongs to this group.

Corresponding to either type of cycle theory are two sets of relations, a series of sequences defining time-paths for the variables of the system, and a set of simultaneous equations expressing equilibrium or stationary values of the variables.[1] From this point of view, the distinction between the unstable- and the stable-economy theories is largely one of emphasis. No tendency exists, according to the former, for the economy to approach an equilibrium; consequently, the dynamic system receives most attention. And since an unstable economy obviously does not move steadily upward or downward, the analysis of "turning points" is highly important.[2] The stable-economy

---

* *The Review of Economic Statistics*, Vol. XXIII (August, 1941). Reprinted by courtesy of *The Review of Economics and Statistics* and the author.

† University of Chicago.

[1] Cf. P. A. Samuelson, "The Stability of Equilibrium: Comparative Statics and Dynamics," *Econometrica*, Vol. IX (1941), pp. 97–120.

[2] See Gottfried Haberler, *Prosperity and Depression* (Geneva, 1940), *passim*, but especially Chapter 11.

theories, on the other hand, emphasize the character of the static system; for this system is regarded as a norm toward which the economy is moving, and which would ultimately be attained except for disturbances in the parameters of the system. Dynamic sequences are relevant for this type of theory only in so far as they indicate the manner in which the economy moves from one equilibrium to another. Indeed, if the period of adjustment is relatively short, the dynamic system may be neglected entirely and time-movements attributed simply to changes in the parameters of the static system.

I

These relations of comparative statics to economic dynamics are presented in an interesting and important form in recent discussions of the determinants of total output. Use of the Multiplier in analyzing income and investment, as noted above, obviously constitutes static analysis of a system that is assumed to be *stable* in equilibrium. That is, an equilibrium level of income is assumed to correspond to any given level of noninduced investment, and the system is assumed to move toward this equilibrium. And yet the implications of such a stability assumption have never been fully explored. From early formulations of the investment-income relation it is not apparent exactly *how* the system moves from one equilibrium to another and *why* it tends to approach equilibrium at all.[3] In the *General Theory* of Mr. Keynes, for example, one searches in vain for a description of the time sequence of events by which an increase of net investment produces a rise of income. Thus, although static relations are worked out in some detail, the dynamic equivalent of the income equation is not fully specified.

Needless to say, an infinite number of dynamic sequences having the Keynes income-investment equation as an equilibrium limit could be formulated. In the group of possible models, however, two types of time relation seem most important. The first of these is the lag in the expenditure of income behind its receipt. This receipts-expenditure period, associated as it is with the income velocity of circulation of money, has much to do with the rate at which a system moves from one equilibrium of income to another.[4] The second important lag is the period required for a change in revenue from sales to produce a change in total output. This period determines the time

---

[3] See R. F. Kahn, "The Relation of Home Investment to Unemployment," *Economic Journal*, Vol. XLI (1931), pp. 173–98; Colin Clark, *National Income and Outlay* (London, 1936), Chapter 12; J. M. Keynes, *The General Theory of Employment, Interest, and Money* (New York, 1936), *passim*. The geometric series which Kahn uses in developing his employment multiplier suggests a dynamic sequence, but the exact character of the lag is never fully explained.
[4] I do not wish to imply that the lag of expenditure behind receipt of income is identical with the inverse of income velocity, but only that, *ceteris paribus*, a reduction of the receipt-expenditure lag increases income velocity. See A. H. Hansen, *Fiscal Policy and Business Cycles* (New York, 1941), pp. 268–70.

rate at which an alteration in money demand is converted into a change in income paid out.

Shortly after publication of the *General Theory*, both types of lag were utilized in the formulation of dynamic systems of which the Keynes scheme was a static limit. Mr. D. H. Robertson developed a sequence in which the first type was utilized,[5] while Mr. Erik Lundberg examined the consequences of a system containing the second.[6] Briefly, the Robertson sequence was built upon the following assumptions:[7] (1) The expenditure of income was assumed to occur one period after its receipt. (2) Businessmen were assumed to respond to an increase in money demand with an immediate increase of output, so that income produced in a particular period could be measured by the sum of consumption plus net investment. Mr. Robertson assumed, in other words, a length of unity for the receipts-expenditure period and a zero lag in the response of output to a change in consumer demand.

Mr. Lundberg, on the other hand, built his models upon the following assumptions: (1) Consumers' demand was assumed to respond immediately to a change of income (i.e. the receipts-expenditure period was assumed to be zero). (2) A lag of one period was assumed in the output of consumers' goods behind a change in revenue from sales. In other words, businessmen were assumed to base their production in period t upon sales in period $t - 1$. Thus a discrepancy between *total output* and *total sales* might arise. This discrepancy was assumed to be balanced by a change of inventories.

The foregoing summaries of the Roberston and Lundberg dynamic sequences should indicate clearly that the latter is in most respects the converse of the former. The Robertson model assumes a period of unity for the first type of lag (expenditure behind receipt of income) and a period of zero for the second (output behind revenue from sales), while Mr. Lundberg assumes a zero period for the first and a unit period for the second. For relatively simple sequences, both systems lead to substantially the same results, i.e., a given increase of investment causes total income to approach steadily a new level determined by the Multiplier and the amount of added investment. Both systems, in this case, are stable when the marginal propensity to consume is less than unity, and otherwise unstable. But when more complex sequences are considered, and particularly when allowance is made for the possibility of induced investment, the behavior of the two systems may differ even with the same values of the marginal propensity to consume and the accelerator. Hence it is important to know (*a*) which

---

[5] D. H. Robertson, "Some Notes on Mr. Keynes' General Theory of Employment," *Quarterly Journal of Economics*, Vol. LI (1936), pp. 168–91.

[6] Erik Lundberg, *Studies in the Theory of Economic Expansion* (London, 1937), Chapter 9.

[7] In addition to the enumerated assumptions, both the Robertson and Lundberg sequences, as well as those developed in this paper, assume the existence of unemployed resources, so that output may be expanded without a rise of prices.

scheme more accurately describes the existing state of affairs, and (*b*) in what respects the two lead to different results.

No doubt some lag exists, in the real world, both in expenditure of income behind its receipt and in the output decisions of businessmen behind changes of monetary demand. Indeed, the mere fact of inventory fluctuations is adequate demonstration of the latter lag, while the periodic character of income payments lends support to the argument for the former. Logically, of course, there is no reason why a system including both types could not be devised. But as a practical matter, the solutions of such hybrid systems are quite complex, and useful results from them are difficult to derive. Moreover, if the length of one of the lag periods is quite short compared with the other, either the Robertson or the Lundberg sequence will give a close approximation to the true situation, the selection depending upon which lag is the shorter. If, for example, businessmen make production plans on a yearly basis, while the average interval between receipt and expenditure of income is only one-half month, the assumptions of a zero length for the receipts-expenditure lag and a unit period for the sales-output lag will not be seriously unreal. Error will arise only on account of the half-month period at the end of the production year. In other words, except for this half-month interval, the assumption that income paid out within a given production period is spent (or saved) in the same production period is correct. In this case the Lundberg sequence is appropriate. Conversely, if businessmen revise their plans from day to day, so that the sales-output lag is short compared with the receipts-expenditure period, the Robertson sequence best fits the facts.

Which of the two lags is likely, in fact, to be the shorter? If we measure the receipts-expenditure period by one-half the average interval between income payments, this period is quite short. For wages are paid on a weekly or bi-weekly basis, while salaries are paid monthly, and dividends and interest, which are paid out over longer intervals, represent a smaller proportion of the national income. From this point of view, the Lundberg sequence would seem more realistic. It must be remembered, however, that the length of the receipts-expenditure period is conditioned not only by the average interval between income payments, but also by the nature of consumer habits. In most cases, a rise of income will not lead to an immediate increase of consumption even with a very short payment interval, for some time is essential to adapt oneself to a higher standard of living. Likewise, a fall of income will usually take time to bring about a reduction of consumer demand.[8] Such consumer inertia makes an appraisal of the average lag between income receipt and expenditure extremely difficult. And even if this average could be determined empirically, the length of the second lag (sales-output) would still remain to be determined.

---

[8] Mr. Colin Clark finds a lag of about two years for changes in consumption of the British well-to-do behind changes in their incomes (*op. cit.*, p. 254).

Because of uncertainty regarding the comparative lengths of the two periods, a contrast of the behavior of an economy subject to the Robertson lag with that of an economy where the Lundberg lag is assumed to be most important seems desirable. Since the Robertson model has been elaborated by Professors Hansen[9] and Samuelson,[10] through the introduction of induced investment, I shall confine myself to variants of the Lundberg sequence.*

II

Consider, first, a dynamic model based upon the following assumptions:

1. Entrepreneurs have adequate inventories so that any discrepancy between output and consumer demand may be met by inventory fluctuations rather than price changes.
2. Output in a given period is based upon sales of the preceding period.
3. Consumers' goods are produced entirely in anticipation of sales with no attempt to replenish inventory losses or to get rid of accumulated stocks.
4. Income is equal to the production of consumers' goods plus net investment.
5. Consumption within the sales-output period depends upon income of the same period.
6. All income produced is paid out, i.e., there are no business savings.

These assumptions will be recognized as those of the Lundberg first sequence, except that I have excluded business savings. I make this change because it simplifies the numerical examples while retaining all of the essential features of the Lundberg models. In any case, if business savings represent permanent additions to (private) capital which never enter into the stream of income paid out, they may be considered in our models simply by changing the marginal propensity to consume. This amounts to assuming that corporations pay out income to themselves and that the community marginal propensity is computed by including such corporations as "persons" whose marginal propensity to consume is zero. For example, a community in which 75 percent of all income produced is paid out, and in which consumers spend all of the income they receive, will have a marginal propensity to consume of 75 percent, related to income produced. Likewise, a community whose corporations pay out 80 percent of income produced, and whose citizens spend 90 percent of income received, will have a marginal propensity to consume of $(0.90)(0.80) = 0.72$, again related to income produced. Thus, so long as business savings are *permanent* their effect may be summarized in

---

[9] *Op. cit.*, Chapter 12.

[10] P. A. Samuelson, "Interactions Between the Multiplier Analysis and the Principle of Acceleration," this *Review*, Vol. XXI (1939), pp. 75–78.

* [Added note: When I wrote this paper, there was little evidence upon which to decide whether the Robertson sequence or that of Lundberg was more realistic. Subsequently, however, I have made a study which confirms the Lundberg sequence. See L. A. Metzler, "Three Lags in the Circular Flow of Income," *Income, Employment and Public Policy: Essays in Honor of Alvin H. Hansen* (New York: W. W. Norton and Co., 1948).]

the marginal propensity to consume, and explicit recognition of them in our model sequence is unnecessary.[11]

If v_o represents the amount of noninduced net investment, while $y(t)$ and $u(t)$ represent total income produced and consumers' goods produced, respectively (in period t), we know that[12]

$$y(t) = u(t) + v_o .$$

This relationship simply expresses the fact that income produced is equal to the output of consumers' goods plus net investment. But output of consumers' goods in a given period, t, is equal to sales of the preceding period, by assumption (2). Hence if β is the marginal propensity to consume, related to income produced, $u(t) = \beta y(t - 1)$ and

$$y(t) = \beta y(t - 1) + v_o . \tag{1}$$

Equation (1) shows how income of a given period is related to income of the preceding period and to the amount of net investment. It depicts a sequence identical with the Robertson model. Thus for simple dynamic systems, the behavior of a model is not changed by substituting a sales-output lag for a receipts-expenditure lag.

A numerical example of the way the system approaches equilibrium is given in Table 1. I assume there that the marginal propensity to consume is 0.6, that net investment (v_o) is 400, and that the economy is initially in equilibrium with a total income of 1000, 600 of which represent consumers' goods. I assume, also, that inventories of consumers' goods amount to 500. Equilibrium is disturbed, in the second period, by an increase of net investment to 500. Production of consumers' goods being 600, total income in period 2 is 1100. Hence consumption is 660, of which 600 represent current production and 60 a reduction of inventories. In the third period, entrepreneurs produce 660 units (last period's sales), and, assuming investment to be maintained at 500 per period, income of this period is 1160, so that sales amount to 696. Again, sales represent partly current production (660) and partly a reduction of inventories (36).

The sequence continues in this manner, with the increase of output and income of each period being smaller than that of the preceding period. Ultimately a new equilibrium of 1250 units of income is approached, and, as long as net investment remains at 500, this level of income will be maintained.

---

[11] If undistributed profits are not permanently invested, but simply retained for a period longer than our "unit period," the dynamic sequence becomes quite complex. In this case, simply to change the marginal propensity to consume does not suffice, since business savings of a given period are likely to be balanced by subsequent disbursements in excess of earnings.

[12] To compare net investment with consumption, we must specify a unit of measurement common to both. We may assume either that all magnitudes are in wage units, or, alternatively, that they are in currency units which, because of unemployed resources and constant costs, do not change in value.

Changes of income and inventories are depicted in Chart 1. For the moment, we need only note that (1) income approaches its new equilibrium steadily; (2) inventories decline by the exact amount of the increase in sales per period; and (3) the income equilibrium is not affected by the inventory reduction, since this represents only a temporary source of disinvestment.

TABLE 1

BEHAVIOR OF A SYSTEM WITH PASSIVE INVENTORY ADJUSTMENTS

$(\beta = 0.6)$

(1) Production of Consumers' Goods for Sale	(2) Net Noninduced Investment	(3) Income Produced (1) + (2)	(4) Sales	(5) Inventories at Close of Period
600	400	1000	600	500
600	500	1100	660	440
660	500	1160	696	404
696	500	1196	718	382
718	500	1218	731	369
731	500	1231	739	361
739	500	1239	743	357
743	500	1243	746	354
746	500	1246	748	352
748	500	1248	749	351
..	..	..	..	..
..	..	..	..	..
..	..	..	..	..
750	500	1250	750	350

None of the conclusions based upon Table 1 is novel. All of them may be found in Mr. Lundberg's first sequence, and part of them in the Robertson analysis. I have, nevertheless, included the table and figure in order to facilitate comparison with more complex sequences to follow.

The passive nature of inventory changes in Table 1 makes the sequence rather unrealistic. Businessmen will ordinarily attempt to replenish inventories depleted by an unforeseen rise in demand, or to reduce inventory accumulations resulting from unpredicted depressions. We ought, therefore, to consider a dynamic model in which allowance is made for such adjustments. We may retain all of the assumptions of the first sequence except No. 3. Rather than assuming inventories to be completely passive (No. 3 of the first sequence), we shall now assume that an attempt is made to maintain them at a constant, "normal" level, s_o. Otherwise, we shall assume as before that production for sale in a given period (as distinguished from production for stocks) is based upon sales of the preceding period. Thus we have the following value for income produced in period t:

$$y(t) = u(t) + s(t) + v_o$$

where $u(t)$ represents production for sale, $s(t)$ production for inventory purposes, and v_o net noninduced investment.

We wish to know how production for sale, $u(t)$, and production for inventories, $s(t)$, are related to income and sales of preceding periods. As before, production for sale is assumed equal to sales of the preceding period so that $u(t) = \beta y(t - 1)$.

CHART 1

BEHAVIOR OF A SYSTEM WITH PASSIVE INVENTORY ADJUSTMENTS:
THE BASIC LUNDBERG SEQUENCE

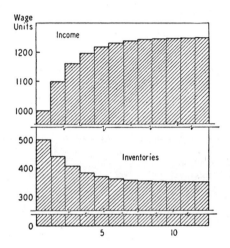

The second item, $s(t)$, may be either positive or negative. If stocks exceed the normal level, s_o, which business wishes to maintain, businessmen will produce fewer consumers' goods than they expect to sell in the hope that by so doing they can reduce inventories. In this case $s(t)$ is negative. On the other hand, if stocks are lower than the normal level, s_o, an attempt will be made to replenish inventories so that $s(t)$ will be positive. Whether positive or negative, however, production for inventories in period t will equal the difference between the normal level, s_o, and the actual level of stocks at the *close* of period $t - 1$. But in period $t - 1$, entrepreneurs *intended* to produce enough so that stocks at the close of that period would equal the normal level, s_o; i.e., they produced an amount sufficient to cover expected sales plus whatever was needed (positive or negative) to make stocks equal s_o. If actual sales exceeded those anticipated, entrepreneurs were forced to sell goods they had intended for inventories. Conversely, if actual sales fell short of expected sales, entrepreneurs were forced to hold goods they had intended for sale. In either case, the difference between the normal level, s_o, and the actual level at the close of period $t - 1$ is simply the difference between actual and anticipated sales of that period.

It follows immediately that production for inventories in period t is equal to the difference between actual and anticipated sales of period $t-1$. In common-sense terms, we say that production for stocks in a given period is equal to the unintended inventory loss of the preceding period. But anticipated sales of $t-1$ were $\beta y(t-2)$, while actual sales were $\beta y(t-1)$. Hence

$$s(t) = \beta y(t-1) - \beta y(t-2).$$

Combining the expressions for $u(t)$, $s(t)$, and v_o, income in period t may be described as follows:

$$y(t) = 2\beta y(t-1) - \beta y(t-2) + v_0. \tag{2}$$

The behavior of this system may be illustrated by another numerical example. In Table 2, I assume, as before, that the marginal propensity to

TABLE 2

RESULT OF ATTEMPTING TO MAINTAIN INVENTORIES: THE PURE INVENTORY CYCLE

$(\beta = 0.6)$

(1) Production of Consumers' Goods for Sale	(2) Production of Consumers' Goods for Stocks	(3) Net Noninduced Investment	(4) Income Produced (1) + (2) + (3)	(5) Sales	(6) Inventories at Close of Period
600	0	400	1000	600	500
600	0	500	1100	660	440
660	60	500	1220	732	428
732	72	500	1304	782	450
782	50	500	1332	799	483
799	17	500	1316	790	509
790	-9	500	1281	769	521
769	-21	500	1248	749	520
749	-20	500	1229	737	512
737	-12	500	1225	735	502
735	-2	500	1233	740	495
740	5	500	1245	747	493
747	7	500	1254	752	495
752	5	500	1257	754	498
754	2	500	1256	754	500
754	0	500	1254	752	502
752	-2	500	1250	750	502

consume is 0.6, and that we start from a position of equilibrium in which net noninduced investment is equal to 400, income is 1000, total sales 600, production for sale 600, and production for inventories zero. These figures are in the first line of the table. In the second period, I assume that equilibrium is disturbed by an increase of noninduced investment to 500, an increase which is subsequently maintained. Total income thus rises to 1100, and sales to 660, causing an inventory reduction of 60, since anticipated sales (and hence output) in period 2 were only 600. Suppose, now, that entrepreneurs attempt to maintain their inventories at a level of 500. Then in period 3 they will produce 660 units for sale plus 60 units for inventory. Adding to this the 500 units of noninduced investment, we get a total income produced in period 3 of 1220, with sales of 732. Thus actual sales have once again exceeded anticipated sales, so that inventories remain below the normal level of 500.

This is characteristic of the early prosperity phase of a pure inventory cycle. For a time, added income generated by production for inventories plus the secondary effects of increased investment will cause sales to exceed those anticipated by more than production for inventory purposes. Hence inventories actually decline despite. attempts to increase them. Sales, however, cannot continue to rise as rapidly as income because of the dampening influence of savings. As a result, the excess of actual sales over anticipated sales declines, and inventories begin slowly to accumulate. But this causes income to rise at a still slower rate, since less is produced each period for inventory purposes. In turn, the decline of the *rate of growth* of income and sales accelerates the increase of stocks. Ultimately (period 6 of the table) actual sales fall short of those expected, and inventories rise above the normal level. Thereafter, attempts of entrepreneurs to reduce stocks lead to a cumulative decline of income because (1) less is produced than is expected to be sold, and (2) the initial decline reduces expectations and hence production for sale in subsequent periods. Moreover, once income begins to decline actual sales fall short of those anticipated so that attempts to reduce stocks are abortive.

Once again, however, the stabilizing influence of savings prevents a continuous movement in one direction. With a marginal propensity to consume less than unity, the decline of sales is less than the decline of total income, which means that the depression cannot continue to "feed upon itself." In other words, actual sales cannot continue to fall short of expected sales by as much as the inventory surplus. Eventually, therefore, attempts at inventory reduction will succeed, so that inventories are brought down slowly to the normal level. At this point income begins to rise by reason of the fact that entrepreneurs are no longer attempting to produce less than they sell. Thus the cycle repeats itself, but each time with smaller amplitude.

This is the simplest form of inventory cycle. I have discussed it in some detail because it contains many features common to more complex sequences. The nature of the cycle is more clearly seen in Chart 2. The following points may be noted:

1. The cycles are damped, so that income eventually approaches a new equilibrium of 1250, determined by the Multiplier and the increase of noninduced investment.
2. Induced investment for purposes of inventory accumulation does not affect the income equilibrium.

3. Inventories lag behind the movement of income. So long as inventories remain below the normal level, income rises; whenever they are above normal, income falls. Income reaches a maximum at the point where inventories have finally accumulated to the normal level, and a minimum at the point where they have *fallen* to this norm.

The cycle pictured in Chart 2 is a pure inventory cycle in the sense that it is produced entirely by investment (or disinvestment) for inventory purposes.

CHART 2

THE PURE INVENTORY CYCLE

(Income and Inventory Figures from Table 2)

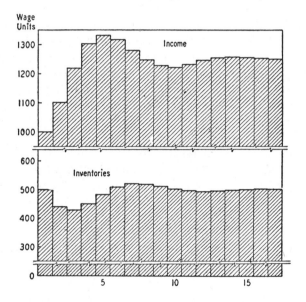

It may be shown that *any disturbance in a dynamic system such as (2) will produce cyclical oscillations about a new level of income provided the marginal propensity to consume is less than unity.* Thus the results of Table 2 do not depend upon any special values of our coefficients. If the marginal propensity to consume were greater than unity, the system would not oscillate when disturbed by an increase of noninduced investment, but would diverge steadily.

III

The dynamic models of Tables 1 and 2 introduce a somewhat artificial assumption about business expectations. In both cases entrepreneurs are assumed to base their expectations of sales in a given period upon sales of the preceding period. It is natural to object that expectations of future sales may depend not only upon the past *level* of sales, but also upon the *direction of change* of such sales. Thus a level of sales of 500 in period $t - 1$ which was reached from a level of 400 in $t - 2$ might give rise to expectations in period t entirely different from what they would have been had the sales of 500 been approached from a level of 600 in $t - 2$. In the former case, sales would normally be expected to exceed 500 in period t, whereas in the latter they would probably be expected to fall short of 500.

To discuss the role of expectations, I shall make use of a coefficient of expectation (η) defined as the ratio between the expected change of sales between periods t and $t - 1$ and the observed change of sales between periods $t - 1$ and $t - 2$. To see what this means, let us consider some examples. Suppose observed sales in periods $t - 1$ and $t - 2$ were 500 and 400 respectively. Then the expected change of sales between $t - 1$ and t would be the product of the coefficient of expectation by the observed change of sales between $t - 2$ and $t - 1$ (100 units). If the coefficient were one half, e.g., sales would be expected to increase by 50 between $t - 1$ and t; in other words, expected sales would be 550. Likewise, if the coefficient were zero, no change at all would be expected, so that anticipated sales in t would equal actual sales in $t - 1$. Other results for this same example may be tabulated as follows:

Coefficient of Expectation	Anticipated Sales
-1	400
-0.5	450
0	500
0.5	550
1	600

Remembering that actual sales in $t - 1$ and $t - 2$ were 500 and 400 respectively, we may make the following observations:

1. If the coefficient of expectation is unity, a given rate of change is expected to continue undiminished.
2. If the coefficient of expectation is zero, a given level of sales is expected to continue.
3. If the coefficient is -1, any change between $t - 2$ and $t - 1$ is expected to be only temporary, so that sales in period t are expected to return to the level of period $t - 2$.

In the sequences to follow, the coefficient of expectation will be assumed to lie between the limits $-1 \leq \eta \leq 1$. Although the argument might easily be extended to other values, I believe that this range is sufficiently wide to include most actual cases.[13]

---

[13] It is useful to compare this coefficient with Hicks' "elasticity of expectation" (J. R. Hicks, *Value and Capital*, London, 1939, p. 205). In my terminology, the Hicks elasticity concept is defined as the ratio of the expected relative change between $t - 2$ and t to the *actual* relative change between $t - 2$ and $t - 1$. If a parameter has the values π_2 and π_1 in periods $t - 2$ and $t - 1$, and if these values lead to an expectation of π_0 in period t, the

Again we may suppose, as in the first two sequences, that income is spent (or saved) in the period in which it is received. But rather than assuming production for sale to be determined by sales of the past period, we shall now suppose it is related to sales of the *two* preceding periods by the coefficient of expectation, in the following manner:

$$u(t) = \beta y(t-1) + \eta[\beta y(t-1) - \beta y(t-2)]$$

or

$$u(t) = (1+\eta)\beta y(t-1) - \eta\beta y(t-2).$$

If no attempt is made to adjust inventories, total income produced is equal to the output of consumers' goods for sale plus net noninduced investment. Hence

$$y(t) = (1+\eta)\beta y(t-1) - \eta\beta y(t-2) + v_o. \tag{3}$$

Equation (3) is simply an extension of the Lundberg first sequence obtained by introducing a coefficient of expectation. In fact, the Lundberg sequence is the special case of (3) in which $\eta = 0$. It is therefore important to know how the behavior of this basic sequence changes with an alteration of the coefficient of expectation.

Numerical examples of sequence (3) are presented in Table 3. In each example the marginal propensity to consume is 0.6. Hence any differences between the three cases presented may be attributed to the coefficient of expectation. The initial disturbance, as before, is a rise of 100 in the level of noninduced net investment.

An explanation of Table 3, Part A will suffice, since all three parts of the table are constructed according to the same principles. We begin from a position of equilibrium, with sales per period of 600, noninduced investment of 400, and total income of 1000, and we suppose this equilibrium disturbed by an increase in net noninduced investment per period to 500. Income rises in the first period of added investment to 1100, and sales to 660, so that inventories decline to 440. Thus far the results are the same as in Table 1. The coefficient of expectation being positive, however, the rise of sales creates an expectation of a further rise. The coefficient assumed in Table 3A is 0.2. Thus expected sales in period 3 (and hence production of consumers' goods) are $660 + 0.2(660 - 600) = 672$. With production of consumers' goods of 672 and net noninduced investment of 500, total income produced in the third period is 1172, and sales are 703. These sales in turn create an expectation

---

elasticity of expectation is $\dfrac{\pi_0 - \pi_2}{\pi_2} \div \dfrac{\pi_1 - \pi_2}{\pi_2}$, whereas my coefficient of expectation is $\dfrac{\pi_0 - \pi_1}{\pi_1 - \pi_2}$. If e represents the elasticity of expectation while η, as above, represents the *coefficient* of expectation, it is easily shown that $\eta = e - 1$. Thus a range of variation for e between zero and unity (the range which Hicks considers) corresponds to a range for η between -1 and zero.

that revenue in the next period will be $703 + 0.2(703 - 660) = 712$, and so on. The following features of the table may be noted:

1. Income approaches steadily a new equilibrium determined by the Multiplier and the amount of net noninduced investment.
2. For the values of the coefficient of expectation and the marginal propensity to consume of Table 3A, dependence of output upon the rate of change of sales does not change the mode of approaching a new equilibrium, but merely accelerates the speed with which the new level is approached. Thus with a positive coefficient of expectation, income moves more rapidly from the old equilibrium to the new than with a zero coefficient.
3. While sales advance by 150 per period in the new equilibrium, inventories decline only by 120 even though no attempt is made to maintain them.

TABLE 3

EFFECT OF EXPECTATIONS UPON THE BASIC LUNDBERG SEQUENCE

Part A: $\beta = 0.6$; $\eta = 0.2$

(1) Production of Consumers' Goods for Sale	(2) Net Noninduced Investment	(3) Income Produced (1) + (2)	(4) Sales	(5) Inventories at Close of Period
600	400	1000	600	500
600	500	1100	660	440
672	500	1172	703	409
712	500	1212	727	394
732	500	1232	739	387
741	500	1241	745	383
746	500	1246	748	381
747	500	1247	748	380
748	500	1248	749	379
749	500	1249	749	379
..	..	..	..	..
..	..	..	..	..
..	..	..	..	..
750	500	1250	750	380

Part B: $\beta = 0.6$; $\eta = 0.5$

600	400	1000	600	500
600	500	1100	660	440
690	500	1190	714	416
741	500	1241	745	412
760	500	1260	756	416
762	500	1262	757	421
757	500	1257	754	424
752	500	1252	751	425
749	500	1249	749	425
748	500	1248	749	424
..	..	..	..	..
..	..	..	..	..
..	..	..	..	..
750	500	1250	750	425

TABLE 3 (*cont.*)

Part C: $\beta = 0.6$; $\eta = 1$

(1) Production of Consumers' Goods for Sale	(2) Net Noninduced Investment	(3) Income Produced (1) + (2)	(4) Sales	(5) Inventories at Close of Period
600	400	1000	600	500
600	500	1100	660	440
720	500	1220	732	428
804	500	1304	782	450
832	500	1332	799	483
816	500	1316	790	509
781	500	1281	769	521
748	500	1248	749	520
729	500	1229	737	512
725	500	1225	735	502
733	500	1233	740	495
745	500	1245	747	493
754	500	1254	752	495
757	500	1257	754	498
756	500	1256	754	500
754	500	1254	752	502
750	500	1250	750	502
..	..	..	..	..
..	..	..	..	..
..	..	..	..	..
750	500	1250	750	500

The second and third parts of Table 3 differ from Table 3A only in the value of the coefficient of expectation. In 3B, η has a value of 0.5, while in 3C, the coefficient is unity. Comparison of 3B and 3C with 3A suggests the following points:

1. All three sequences are stable, for income approaches a new equilibrium in each case.
2. The income equilibrium is independent of the coefficient of expectation; it depends only upon the propensity to consume and the amount of noninduced investment.
3. For large values of the coefficient of expectation, income does not approach its new equilibrium steadily, but tends to oscillate about this new level in a series of damped cycles.

Explanation of these cycles may be found in the relation of η to the marginal propensity to consume. The initial rise of income leads to expectations of a further rise. And the combined influence of high expectations with the secondary effects of higher noninduced investment may create a level of income above the level justified by the amount of noninduced investment. When this happens, income must necessarily decline. For, with a marginal propensity to consume less than unity, an expansion of production in antici-pation of a rise in sales cannot *by itself* create an increase of sales as great as the increase in consumers' goods output. Hence expectations are disappointed, which leads to lower expectations in subsequent periods, with a slowing down in the rate of growth of incomes and further unrealized expectations. The process continues until income actually begins to decline.

Once the decline is started, a further decline is inevitable since businessmen restrict output in expectation of fewer sales. Again, however, savings act as a stabilizer and reverse the direction of change. With a marginal propensity to consume less than unity, the mere expectation of a decline cannot in itself lead to a reduction of sales as great as the reduction of output. Eventually, therefore, expectations become less pessimistic, owing to the fact that they have not been fully realized in the past. When this occurs, output, although still lower than sales of the previous period, may exceed output of the previous period so that income again begins to rise. And thus the cycle repeats itself, each time with a smaller amplitude, as indicated in Parts B and C of Table 3.

We have seen that a positive coefficient of expectation may lead to (1) a steady approach to equilibrium of the same type as in the Lundberg first sequence, only more rapid, or (2) cyclical oscillations about the new equilibrium. Whether the system behaves in the first manner or the second depends upon the relation of the marginal propensity to consume to the coefficient of expectation. The nature of this relation is indicated in Chart 3. A sequence of the type (3) will approach equilibrium steadily for any values of β and η in the region S, while it will oscillate about the new equilibrium if its β and η lie in the region S_o.[14] Thus a positive coefficient of expectation is more likely to lead to cyclical movements the smaller is the marginal propensity to consume. In other words, a smaller coefficient of expectation is required to "overstep the mark" if the system is damped by large savings than if most income is consumed.

With a negative coefficient of expectation, behavior of the system is quite different. The cycle is replaced by a cobweb movement. To show how this cobweb arises, suppose that an economy has a marginal propensity to consume of unity and a coefficient of expectation of -1. And suppose that, because of a change in noninduced investment, income and sales rise from 1000 to 1100 units. Since $\eta = -1$, we know that any change of sales is expected to be temporary, so that entrepreneurs anticipate sales of 1000 in the next period after the change. Consequently, they produce only 1000 units, and if the burst of noninduced investment is not maintained, actual income and sales are 1000. The drop in sales from 1100 to 1000, in turn, leads to sales expectations of 1100 for the next succeeding period; as a result, actual production and sales are 1100. In this manner an initial burst of investment produces an undamped cobweb with income and sales alternating

---

[14] The region S_o is separated from S by the line $\beta(1 + \eta)^2 = 4\eta$. The inequality $\beta(1 + \eta)^2 < 4\eta$ is simply the condition that the roots of the "characteristic equation" $\rho^2 - (1 + \eta)\beta\rho + \eta\beta = 0$ shall be imaginary.

between 1000 and 1100. The system is in *neutral* equilibrium. Had the marginal propensity to consume been less than unity, however, the cobwebs would have been damped, and equilibrium stable. More generally, any model whose β and η lie within the region S_c of Chart 3 represents a stable system

CHART 3

INFLUENCE OF EXPECTATIONS UPON A SYSTEM WITH PASSIVE INVENTORY ADJUSTMENTS

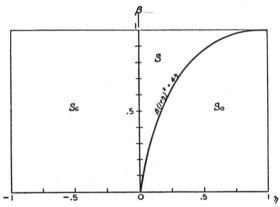

which approaches equilibrium through a combination of (1) a damped cobweb and (2) a steady change at an exponential rate.

Although expectations may temporarily be negative, the kind of alternate periods of optimism and pessimism depicted in a literal interpretation of a negative coefficient of expectation is probably seldom found in the actual world. Analysis of the case is included, nevertheless, to show that negative expectations do not change the condition of stability (i.e., $\beta < 1$).

An interesting parallel is found between our third sequence and the Hansen-Samuelson extension of Robertson's dynamic model. Without attempting a detailed discussion of the Hansen-Samuelson case, its essential features may be enumerated as follows:

1. A lag of one period is assumed in the expenditure of income behind its receipt.
2. Entrepreneurs are assumed to produce, in a given period, whatever amounts of consumers' goods are demanded in that period (the sales-output lag is zero).
3. Aside from noninduced investment, a part of the production of capital goods in a particular period is assumed to be a linear function of the rate of change of sales in the same period (the acceleration principle).

With these assumptions, a dynamic model is constructed which is found to (1) converge steadily, (2) converge cyclically, (3) diverge cyclically, or (4) diverge steadily according to the values of the marginal propensity to consume and the accelerator.

Comparison of equation (3) with the Samuelson equation reveals that the two are identical except that the coefficient of expectation (η) has replaced the accelerator (α in Samuelson's notation). Thus the coefficient of expectation apparently bears the same relation to the basic Lundberg sequence that the acceleration principle bears to the Robertson sequence. Indeed, the right half of my Chart 3 is the same as Samuelson's figure (with η substituted for α) except that I have excluded values of η greater than unity.

So long as inventories are merely a passive factor of adjustment, our discussion of sequence (3) demonstrates that a nonzero coefficient of expectation between -1 and $+1$, while changing the method of approach toward equilibrium, cannot alter either the level of equilibrium or stability of the system. The situation is otherwise if entrepreneurs attempt to maintain their stocks of goods at a constant level. In this case, a positive coefficient places important restrictions upon the conditions of stability. The character of these restrictions may be determined by developing another model.

We may assume, as in the third sequence, that sales anticipations are related to sales of the two preceding periods through the coefficient of expectation, η. Rather than supposing inventories to be entirely passive, however, we now assume that an attempt is made to maintain them at a constant level, s_o. Otherwise, all assumptions of the basic Lundberg sequence are maintained.

We have seen above that income produced in the consumers' goods industries may be divided into two parts: (1) an amount $u(t)$ produced in anticipation of sales; and (2) an amount $s(t)$ produced for stocks. The first item, production for sale, is related to past sales through the coefficient of expectation, exactly as in our third sequence, so that

$$u(t) = (1 + \eta)\beta y(t - 1) - \eta\beta y(t - 1).$$

To complete the sequence, production for stocks, $s(t)$, must be related to income (or sales) of preceding periods. In developing our second sequence, we found that attempting to maintain inventories is equivalent to producing for stocks in each period an amount equal to unintended inventory reductions of the preceding period, and that unintended inventory reductions of a given period are simply the difference between actual and anticipated sales of that period. In other words, production for stocks in period t was found equal to the difference between actual and anticipated sales of period $t - 1$. So it is here. Only, now, anticipated sales of period $t - 1$ are no longer equal to sales of $t - 2$, but are related to sales of the *two* preceding periods through the coefficient of expectation, as follows: expected sales in period $t - 1 = (1 + \eta)\beta y(t - 2) - \eta\beta y(t - 3)$. Hence $s(t)$, the difference between actual and anticipated sales of period $t - 1$, is

$$s(t) = \beta y(t - 1) - (1 + \eta)\beta y(t - 2) + \eta\beta y(t - 3).$$

Remembering that income produced in period t is equal to total production of consumers' goods for all purposes plus net noninduced investment,

TABLE 4

<small>Effect of Expectations when Entrepreneurs Attempt to Maintain Inventories</small>
Part A: Unstable Case; $\beta = 0.6$; $\eta = 1$

(1) Production of Consumers' Goods for Sale	(2) Production of Consumers' Goods for Stocks	(3) Net Noninduced Investment	(4) Income Produced (1) + (2) + (3)	(5) Sales	(6) Inventories at Close of Period
600	0	400	1000	600	500
600	0	500	1100	660	440
720	60	500	1280	768	452
876	48	500	1424	854	522
940	−22	500	1418	851	589
848	−89	500	1259	755	593
659	−93	500	1066	640	519
525	−19	500	1006	604	421
568	79	500	1147	688	380
772	120	500	1392	835	437
982	63	500	1545	927	555
1019	−55	500	1464	878	641
829	−141	500	1188	713	616
548	−116	500	932	559	489
405	11	500	916	550	355
541	145	500	1186	712	329
874	171	500	1545	927	447

Part B: Stable Case; $\beta = 0.6$; $\eta = 0.5$

600	0	400	1000	600	500
600	0	500	1100	660	440
690	60	500	1250	750	440
795	60	500	1355	813	482
845	18	500	1363	818	527
820	−27	500	1293	776	544
755	−44	500	1211	727	528
702	−28	500	1174	704	498
693	2	500	1195	717	476
724	24	500	1248	749	475
765	25	500	1290	774	491
786	9	500	1295	777	509
779	−9	500	1270	762	517
754	−17	500	1237	742	512
732	−12	500	1220	732	500
727	0	500	1227	736	491
738	9	500	1247	748	490

we have

$$y(t) = (2 + \eta)\beta y(t - 1) - (1 + 2\eta)\beta y(t - 2) + \eta\beta y(t - 3) + v_0. \qquad (4)$$

In Table 4 behavior of sequence (4) is illustrated by two numerical examples. The two examples differ only in the value of the coefficient of expectation;

in Part A, η has a value of unity, while in Part B it is one half. The marginal propensity to consume is 0.6 in both cases. Let us consider Part A of Table 4. We begin, as always, from a position of equilibrium, with noninduced investment of 400, income of 1000, sales of 600, production for sale of 600, and production for inventory of zero. Equilibrium is disturbed in the second period by a rise of noninduced investment to 500. This increases sales to 660 and reduces inventories to 440. In the third period, production for sale is related to sales of the two preceding periods, just as in Table 3, by the coefficient of expectation. Since this coefficient is unity in Table 4A, sales of 600 and 660 in the first two periods create an expectation that sales of the third period will be 720. In addition to this amount produced for sale, 60 units are produced to make good the unintended inventory reduction of the previous period. Adding to these items the 500 units of noninduced investment, we obtain a total income produced of 1280 units for the third period. In this manner the entire sequence may be built up. Table 4B is constructed in exactly the same manner except that a coefficient of expectation of one half is used in computing the column, "production of consumers' goods for sale."

CHART 4

<small>INCOME AND INVENTORY MOVEMENTS AS DESCRIBED BY DATA IN TABLE 4, PART A</small>

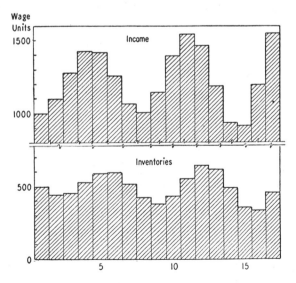

Income and inventory figures from the two parts of the table are plotted in Charts 4 and 5. Both charts exhibit the characteristic inventory cycle, with changes in the level of stocks lagging one-fourth cycle behind changes of income. The two charts differ, however, in an important respect. In Chart 4, the amplitude of the cycles grows larger as the sequence develops, whereas in Chart 5 the fluctuations are damped. In other words, the sequence in Table 4B represents a stable system while 4A is essentially unstable. The de-stabilizer in 4A is obviously the coefficient of expectation, for the two parts of the table differ from each other only in the value of this coefficient. Thus, apparently, whenever entrepreneurs attempt to maintain inventories at a constant level, a high coefficient of expectation may create an unstable situation even with a marginal propensity to consume less than unity.

CHART 5

INCOME AND INVENTORY MOVEMENTS AS DESCRIBED BY DATA IN TABLE 4, PART B

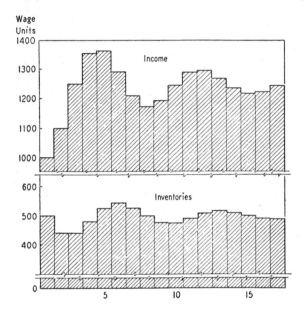

Exactly how large η must be to produce instability is indicated in Chart 6. A system of the type (4) is stable for any values of η and β contained in region S_o; disturbances of equilibrium in such cases produce damped inventory cycles.[15] A system with values of η and β in region U_o, on the other hand, is unstable; disturbances of equilibrium here produce explosive cycles such as those of Chart 4. Examination of our stability chart suggests the following points:

1. For values of the coefficient of expectation less than one half, conditions of stability are no more restrictive than in our previous sequences; such models are stable for any marginal propensity to consume less than unity.

---

[15] The lines dividing the stable from the unstable regions are determined from the conditions that the roots of the characteristic equation, $\rho^3 - (2 + \eta)\beta\rho^2 + (1 + 2\eta)\beta\rho - \eta\beta = 0$, shall lie within the unit circle of the complex plane.

2. Severity of stability conditions increases very rapidly with an increase in the coefficient beyond one half. In general, β, the marginal propensity to consume must be less than $\frac{1}{2\eta}$. How severe this condition really is may be shown by a few numerical examples. If η is unity (i.e., a given rate of change of sales is expected to continue), the system will not be stable unless the marginal propensity to consume is less than one half. Likewise, with $\eta = \frac{3}{4}$, stability requires that β be less than two thirds.

For negative expectations between 0 and -1, the system is stable, in our sequence, for any marginal propensity to consume less than unity. This is the region, $S_{c,o}$, of Chart 6. Movement toward equilibrium in such cases

CHART 6

STABILITY DIAGRAM FOR SEQUENCE (4)

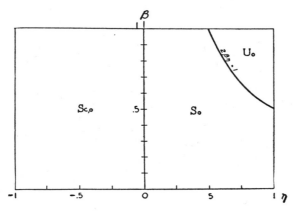

is a combination of a damped cobweb and a cyclical movement, the former attributable to the negative coefficient of expectation and the latter representing a simple inventory cycle.

IV

The inventory cycles analyzed in the preceding section were a direct result of attempts by entrepreneurs to maintain stocks at a constant level, which in many cases probably represents a reasonable approximation to the actual situation, particularly if one considers only short-run adjustments. In other cases, however, the assumption that the desirable level of stocks is somehow related to the expected level of sales may be more accurate. In general, the amount of inventories which entrepreneurs regard as "normal" will vary directly with the expected volume of business. Thus, the economy may be subject to the influence of an accelerator as well as a coefficient of expectation, for inventory production will then be related to the rate of change of sales. A complete examination of dynamic systems having a sales-output lag therefore requires analysis of the relations between the inventory accelerator and our coefficient of expectation.

We may begin with the inventory accelerator alone. Suppose that entrepreneurs attempt to maintain inventories at a constant proportion, α, of expected sales. Suppose, further, that sales in a given period (say t) are expected to equal sales of the preceding period (i.e., $\eta = 0$). Income produced, as before, is equal to production for sale, $u(t)$, plus production for stocks, $s(t)$, plus noninduced investment. Anticipated sales being equal to sales of the preceding period, we know that

$$u(t) = \beta y(t - 1).$$

Production for inventory purposes, on the other hand, is equal to the difference between the desired level of inventories, $\alpha\beta y(t - 1)$, and actual stocks on hand at the close of the previous period, $k(t - 1)$; i.e.,

$$s(t) = \alpha\beta y(t - 1) - k(t - 1).$$

But $k(t - 1)$ would have been equal to $\alpha\beta y(t - 2)$ except for unintended reductions or increases in stocks during the period $t - 1$. And, just as in the previous section, these unintended changes of inventories are the difference between actual sales, $\beta y(t - 1)$, and expected sales, $\beta y(t - 2)$. Hence $k(t - 1) = \alpha\beta y(t - 2) - \beta y(t - 1) + \beta y(t - 2)$ so that

$$s(t) = (1 + \alpha)\beta y(t - 1) - (1 + \alpha)\beta y(t - 2).$$

Adding the amounts of production for sale, $u(t)$, and production for inventory, $s(t)$, to noninduced investment, v_o, we obtain the following expression for income of the period t:

$$y(t) = (2 + \alpha)\beta y(t - 1) - (1 + \alpha)\beta y(t - 2) + v_o. \tag{5}$$

This equation, except for minor changes, is Mr. Lundberg's second sequence.

Two numerical examples of the model are given in Table 5. In Part A the assumption is made that $\beta = 0.5$ and $\alpha = 0.5$, while Part B is constructed upon the assumptions that $\beta = 0.6$ and $\alpha = 1$. The only feature of the tables requiring explanation is the second column, "production of consumers' goods for stocks." Amounts in this column are those needed to bring stocks up to the given proportion, α, of expected sales. In the third line of Part A, for example, expected sales are 550 and inventories of the previous period only 200. Since $\alpha = 0.5$, sales expectations of 550 should be accompanied by total inventories of 275. Consequently, production for stocks in the third period is 75.

Both parts of Table 5 reveal the usual inventory cycles. In Part A, however, the cycles are damped, while in Part B they are explosive. The inventory accelerator thus appears to act as a de-stabilizer in much the same manner as a positive coefficient of expectation. Stability of the economy cannot be discussed without knowing what combinations of α and β will produce

TABLE 5

THE INVENTORY ACCELERATOR

Part A: Stable Case; $\alpha = 0.5$; $\beta = 0.5$

(1) Production of Consumers' Goods for Sale	(2) Production of Consumers' Goods for Stocks	(3) Net Noninduced Investment	(4) Income Produced (1) + (2) + (3)	(5) Sales	(6) Inventories at Close of Period
500	0	500	1000	500	250
500	0	600	1100	550	200
550	75	600	1225	612	213
612	93	600	1305	652	266
652	60	600	1312	656	322
656	6	600	1262	631	353
631	−38	600	1193	596	350
596	−52	600	1144	572	322
572	−36	600	1136	568	290
568	−6	600	1162	581	271
581	19	600	1200	600	271
600	29	600	1229	614	286
614	21	600	1235	617	304
617	4	600	1221	610	315
610	−10	600	1200	600	315
600	−15	600	1185	592	308
592	−12	600	1180	590	298

Part B: Unstable Case; $\alpha = 1$; $\beta = 0.6$

600	0	400	1000	600	600
600	0	500	1100	660	540
660	120	500	1280	768	552
768	216	500	1484	890	646
890	244	500	1634	980	800
980	180	500	1660	996	964
996	32	500	1528	917	1075
917	−158	500	1259	755	1079
755	−324	500	931	559	951
559	−392	500	667	400	718
400	−318	500	582	349	451
349	−102	500	747	448	250
448	198	500	1146	688	208
688	480	500	1668	1001	375
1001	626	500	2127	1276	726
1276	550	500	2326	1396	1156
1396	240	500	2136	1282	1510

damped cycles, as in Part A, and what combinations will lead to explosive cycles, as in Part B. Solution of this problem is depicted in Chart 7. Any economy whose marginal propensity to consume and inventory accelerator lie in the region S_o is a stable economy that approaches equilibrium through a series of damped cycles. Both U_o and U, on the other hand, are regions of instability. No economy whose α and β lie in these regions has any tendency at all to approach equilibrium. Systems with α and β in U_o oscillate in explosive cycles when disturbed, as in Part B, while those with α and β in U diverge steadily.[16]

CHART 7

STABILITY DIAGRAM FOR SEQUENCE (5)

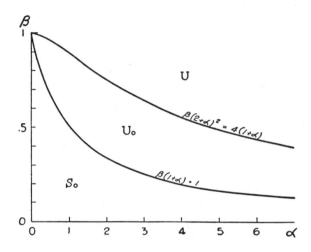

Introduction of the accelerator imposes severe limitations upon stability of the system, particularly if entrepreneurs attempt to maintain inventories at a large multiple of sales. If, for example, α is unity (i.e., entrepreneurs attempt to maintain stocks equal to sales), the economy will not be stable unless the marginal propensity to consume is less than one half. Likewise, if α is 2, stability requires a marginal propensity to consume less than one third.[17]

---

[16] Separation of the stable region from the unstable regions is determined from the conditions that the roots of $\rho^2 - (2 + \alpha)\beta\rho + (1 + \alpha)\beta = 0$ shall lie within the unit circle of the complex plane. Separation of U_o from U, on the other hand, is determined from the conditions that the roots of the above equation shall be real.

[17] Mr. Lundberg's failure to solve his difference equations has led him to draw an incorrect conclusion from one of his models. In his second sequence, which is the same as sequence (5) above, he assumes that 80 percent of all income produced is paid out, and that 90 percent of all income paid out is consumed. This amounts to assuming that our β, the marginal propensity to consume related to income produced, is $(0.8)(0.9) = 0.72$. He also assumes that entrepreneurs attempt to maintain stocks at 50 percent of sales (i.e., $\alpha = 0.5$). From Chart 7 it is evident that the point $\beta = 0.72$, $\alpha = 0.5$ lies in the region U_o. In other words, for these values of the marginal propensity to consume and the inventory accelerator, the economy is unstable; any disturbance produces a series of explosive cycles. And yet Mr. Lundberg concludes from his numerical example that the system approaches *asymptotically* a new equilibrium determined by the Multiplier and the amount of noninduced investment. As a matter of fact, a sequence such as this one never behaves in this manner,

In Chart 8, stability conditions for our fifth sequence are compared with those of its analogue, the Hansen-Samuelson model. The region S represents values of α and β which yield stable results for either model. Similarly, values of α and β in the region U produce instability in both sequences.

CHART 8

Stability of the Hansen-Samuelson Model Compared with That of Sequence (5)

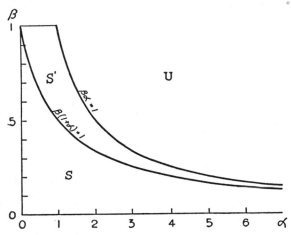

Any pairs of the two parameters found in S', however, will yield stable results if applied to the Hansen-Samuelson model, but will represent an unstable system in the present case. If α is equal to unity, for example, the Hansen-Samuelson model will be stable for any β less than unity, whereas stability of sequence (5), as noted above, requires a β less than one half. Thus an inventory accelerator places much more severe restrictions upon stability conditions of the basic Lundberg sequence than does the ordinary accelerator upon the Robertson sequence.

The explanation of this difference is simple. The acceleration principle is usually developed from the assumption that either technological or economic factors require a constant ratio between output of consumers' goods and certain types of capital goods. And then it is shown that, *ignoring changes in replacement demand*, the demand for capital goods is a linear function of the rate of change in demand for consumers' goods. This is the α of the Hansen-Samuelson model. If the capital goods in question are extremely durable, ignoring changes of replacement demand will not vitiate the results of a short-run analysis. In the present case, however, the capital goods

---

although it may approach a new equilibrium through a series of damped inventory cycles.

The Lundberg error provides a good illustration of the treacherous nature of numerical examples. It is unsafe to draw general conclusions from them, for one never knows to what extent the conclusions depend upon special characteristics of the examples chosen.

subject to the acceleration principle are inventories, perhaps the least durable of all. Hence replacement demand should not be neglected.

The manner of considering replacement is clearly seen in equation (5). In formulating this equation, production in period t of goods for stock was put equal to $(1 + \alpha)\beta y(t - 1) - (1 + \alpha)\beta y(t - 2)$. Now this expression may be divided into two parts. The first, $\alpha[\beta y(t - 1) - \beta y(t - 2)]$, is the simplified accelerator, which ignores replacement demand. The second, $\beta y(t - 1) - \beta y(t - 2)$, is the amount produced to replace unintended inventory reductions of the preceding period. Such unintended changes of stock occur, of course, because actual sales differ from those expected. Without this second item (production for replacement) the Lundberg second sequence would require exactly the same conditions for stability as the Hansen-Samuelson model. When unintended inventory changes are adjusted, however, the inventory accelerator becomes a de-stabilizer with the same force that is possessed by an ordinary accelerator, one unit larger. An inventory accelerator of unity, for example, imparts as much instability to a system as an ordinary accelerator of two.

The sequence summarized in equation (5) was developed from the assumption of a positive inventory accelerator and a zero coefficient of expectation. Development of sequence (4), on the other hand, required a positive coefficient of expectation and a zero inventory accelerator. A dynamic system more general than either (4) or (5) may be obtained by assuming both the coefficient of expectation and the inventory accelerator to be positive.

Let η and α, as above, represent these two parameters. Production of consumers' goods in a given period may now be divided into three parts: (1) production for anticipated sales; (2) production to replace unintended inventory losses; and (3) production to bring output up to the given proportion, α, of expected sales. Call these three items $u(t)$, $s_r(t)$, and $s_a(t)$, respectively. We have seen above that $u(t)$, production for sale, is related to sales of the two preceding periods in the following manner:

$$u(t) = (1 + \eta)\beta y(t - 1) - \eta\beta y(t - 2).$$

Likewise, unintended inventory reductions (or accumulations) in period $t - 1$ are equal to the difference between actual and anticipated sales in that period, so that

$$s_r(t) = \beta y(t - 1) - (1 + \eta)\beta y(t - 2) + \eta\beta y(t - 3).$$

Finally, $s_a(t)$, production on account of the "pure accelerator," is equal to the difference between anticipated sales in period t and in period $t - 1$ multiplied by the accelerator; i.e.,

$$s_a(t) = \alpha[(1 + \eta)\beta y(t - 1) - (1 + 2\eta)\beta y(t - 2) + \eta\beta y(t - 3)].$$

Since total income produced equals production of consumers' goods for all purposes plus noninduced net investment, we have, upon adding the expressions for $u(t)$, $s_r(t)$, and $s_a(t)$,

$$y(t) = [(1 + \eta)(1 + \alpha) + 1]\beta y(t - 1)$$
$$- (1 + 2\eta)(1 + \alpha)\beta y(t - 2)$$
$$+ (1 + \alpha)\eta\beta y(t - 3) + v_o . \tag{6}$$

The difference equation (6) is the most general dynamic system to be considered. Many of our other sequences are simply special cases of this model. Thus by putting $\eta = 0$ we obtain equation (5), while equation (4) is the special case in which $\alpha = 0$. Likewise, equation (3) may be obtained by setting both η and α equal to zero in (6).

Behavior of an economy subject to both an inventory accelerator and a coefficient of expectation might be illustrated, as in previous cases, by numerical examples. Both the method of constructing such examples and the character of inventory movements, however, should by now be thoroughly familiar. And inventory cycles corresponding to this more general model are not different, in principle, from those of the special cases. Consequently, I leave it to the reader to construct any examples which seem appropriate to verify the conclusions set out below.

Although income and inventory movements are much the same for the general case (6) as for (4) and (5), the range of values of the parameters α, β, and η within which an economy is stable requires further consideration. For stability of this general system, the marginal propensity to consume, the inventory accelerator, and the coefficient of expectation must satisfy the following inequalities:[18]

$$\left.\begin{array}{r}(1 + \alpha)(2 + \alpha)\eta\beta^2 - (1 + \alpha)(1 + 2\eta)\beta + 1 > 0 \\ 3 - \beta(2\alpha + 3) \qquad\quad > 0\end{array}\right\} \tag{7}$$

In order clearly to grasp just what this means, we may consider some special cases. Let us suppose, as before, that η may have any values between zero and unity; and let us consider only these limiting values. If $\eta = 0$, the system will be stable, as in (5), provided only that $\beta < \dfrac{1}{1 + \alpha}$. If $\eta = 1$, on the other hand, stability requires that $(1 + \alpha)(2 + \alpha)\beta^2 - 3(1 + \alpha)\beta + 1 > 0$ where, because of the second of the inequalities (7), the relevant root of the quadratic in β is the lowest positive root.

The nature of these restrictions is best understood by referring to Chart 9. All values of the marginal propensity to consume and the inventory accelerator below the line marked "$\eta = 0$" yield stable results when the coefficient of expectation is zero. This is simply case (5). If the coefficient of expectation

---

[18] Again, stability of the system is determined from the condition that the roots of $(\rho) = 0$ shall lie within the unit circle, where $f(\rho) = 0$ is the characteristic equation of (6).

is unity, however, the economy will not be stable unless β and α lie below the line "$\eta = 1$." The chart shows clearly that the coefficient of expectation places very severe restrictions upon our stability conditions—so severe, indeed, that an economy with a unitary coefficient must almost certainly be unstable.

CHART 9

<small>INFLUENCE OF EXPECTATIONS UPON THE STABILITY OF A SYSTEM CONTAINING AN INVENTORY ACCELERATOR [SEQUENCE (6)]</small>

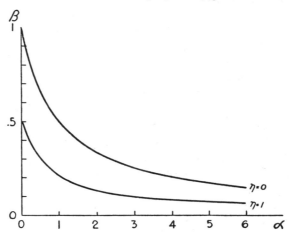

Suppose, for example, that businessmen attempt to keep inventories equal to one half of sales (i.e., $\alpha = 0.5$). If $\eta = 1$, Chart 9 shows that the economy will not be stable unless the marginal propensity to consume is less than (approximately) three tenths. Even with $\alpha = 0$ (no inventory accelerator), stability of a system with a unitary coefficient of expectation requires a marginal propensity to consume less than one half. It is doubtful whether propensities as low as these could be found, even in the most wealthy countries. We may conclude either (a) that the coefficient of expectation cannot conceivably be as large as unity, or (b) that the economy is essentially unstable except for the operation of certain limiting stabilizers.

If we accept conclusion (a), we place ourselves with the group who envisage cyclical fluctuations as a result of variations in the parameters of an otherwise stable economy. In this case, discussions of an income equilibrium corresponding to a given level of noninduced investment are relevant. The Multiplier, in other words, becomes an important if not a dominant factor in the determination of income. Acceptance of conclusion (b), on the other hand, makes necessary an explanation of why the economy exhibits any stability at all. The level of income and employment must be explained, not by the Multiplier and the amount of noninduced net investment, but by the operation of limiting stabilizers. A comprehensive discussion of such stabilizers is beyond the scope of this paper. An enumeration of them, however, would certainly include flexible interest rates, full employment, credit restrictions (other than interest rate changes), and cyclical changes in the coefficient of expectation, to mention only a few. How important these stabilizers are, and at what points they begin to operate, are questions for empirical investigation. Probably no very useful generalizations may be made about them.

V

The dynamic sequences (1) through (6) were intended to show what types of behavior are possible for a system containing a sales-output lag. The following conclusions seem to be the most important:

1. An economy in which businessmen attempt to recoup inventory losses will always undergo cyclical fluctuations when equilibrium is disturbed, provided the economy is stable. This is the pure inventory cycle.
2. The assumption of stability imposes severe limitations upon the possible size of the marginal propensity to consume, particularly if the coefficient of expectation is positive.
3. The inventory accelerator is a more powerful de-stabilizer than the ordinary acceleration principle. The difference in stability conditions is due to the fact that the former allows for replacement demand whereas the usual analytical formulation of the latter does not. Thus, for inventories, replacement demand acts as a de-stabilizer. Whether it does so for all types of capital goods is a moot question, but I believe cases may occur in which it does not.
4. Investment for inventory purposes cannot alter the equilibrium of income, which depends only upon the propensity to consume and the amount of noninduced investment.
5. The apparent instability of a system containing both an accelerator and a coefficient of expectation makes further investigation of possible stabilizers highly desirable.

7

Monetary and Real Factors Affecting Economic Stability: A Critique of Certain Tendencies in Modern Economic Theory*

By GOTTFRIED HABERLER†

I. INTRODUCTION

IT IS THE conclusion of the present paper that a large part of contemporary economic theory has laid undue stress on "real" factors and that "monetary" factors and the closely related phenomena of institutional price and wage rigidities have been neglected or their importance grossly underestimated. Instability in general economic activity as well as in the external balances of payments are explained in terms of physical rigidities, fixed coefficients of production, stubborn inelasticities of demand and supply instead of being attributed to faulty monetary arrangements and policies, to price and wage rigidities and similar factors.

II. THE MEANING OF INSTABILITY

Let me explain first what I mean by instability. I define it as fluctuations in aggregate output and employment. However, even with stable aggregate output and employment, price instability is possible in the sense of changes in relative prices as well as of the price level (in any one of the possible meanings of this ambiguous term). Price instability introduces instability in the income distribution which may well present very serious social and economic problems. Sharp changes in the terms of foreign trade, which are an especially serious matter for highly specialized primary producing countries, are an example on the international level. But there can be no doubt that in most

---

* *Banca Nazionale del Lavoro Quarterly Review*, Vol. IX (September, 1956). Reprinted by courtesy of the Banca Nazionale del Lavoro and the author. The present article is an abridged and slightly altered version of a paper read at the *First Congress of the International Economic Association* held in Rome, 6–11 Sept. 1956.

† Harvard University.

cases violent changes in the terms of trade between large segments of the economy on the national or international level are the consequences or concomitants of fluctuations in aggregate output and employment in the industrial countries.

For this reason I shall concentrate in this paper on the short-run fluctuations—the business cycle in the industrially developed countries.

In the "underdeveloped" countries economic instability is to a very large extent either the reflection of the business cycle in the industrial world or the consequence of autonomous inflationary policies. Much has been made of changes in demand, technology, and import policies of the industrial countries which may destabilize the external balances of highly specialized primary producing countries. Without wishing entirely to discount the importance of these factors, I venture to say, however, that from a global standpoint such sources of instability are of minor importance compared with the business cycle and inflation.

Inflation, to which I shall return briefly later in my paper, is by no means an unimportant matter. On the contrary, I am convinced that long-run (continuous or intermittent) inflation not only introduces price instability but is also a factor seriously retarding economic growth. But intellectually the problem of rapid secular inflation[1] is much less challenging than the problem of the business cycle to which I turn my attention now.

Business cycles I take in the sense in which the term is used by the National Bureau of Economic Research—that is, ups and downs in aggregate activity, more precisely in aggregate output and employment, changes in output due to changes in employment.[2] (Output can, of course, change without changes in employment—harvest changes being the most important example. But the short-run changes in aggregate output that constitute the business cycle are clearly not of that nature—which does not, however, exclude that crop changes as well as other exogenous disturbances may have great causal significance for the cycle.)

I follow Mitchell and Burns in defining the cycle as the shortest observable fluctuations in activity. In their words, "business cycles vary from more than one year to ten or twelve years and are not divisible into shorter cycles of similar character with amplitudes approximating their own."[3] Furthermore, I make no attempt at finding a regular sequence or pattern of "minor" and "major" cycles (as Hansen thinks there exists). Cycles do, of course, differ

---

[1] The slow, "creeping" kind of inflation which is now going on in many developed countries is again a more insidious process, much harder to diagnose and to evaluate than the rapid, open inflation from which many underdeveloped countries suffer.

[2] In identifying fluctuations in activity with fluctuations in aggregate output and employment, I deviate somewhat from the great masters of the National Bureau. The deviation is, however, slight because their cyclical chronology for "activity" is almost perfectly matched by the cyclical chronology in aggregate output and employment series.

[3] See Burns and Mitchell, *Measuring Business Cycles*, p. 3. Seasonal fluctuations are not of "similar character."

greatly in duration and enormously in amplitude; some depressions are mild, others severe; some upswings strong, others weak and abortive.[4] But the most careful investigations in *Measuring Business Cycles* have convinced me that no regular and persistent pattern exists or at any rate has yet been discovered; that it is not possible to interpret the succession of cycles of different length and amplitude as resulting from the superimposition of independent or interdependent cycles of different length (Schumpeter's three-cycle schema); that it is even less defensible to assign different quasi-independent cyclical mechanisms to the different superimposed cycles. Each cycle or depression is, in a sense, an historically unique case; that is to say it is the joint product of endogenous and exogenous forces. The result of interaction between the cyclical mechanism and the historical environment and external disturbances is a complicated chemical compound and not a mechanical mixture whose constituent parts are separable by more or less mechanical statistical devices. The statistical decomposition of time series in cycles and trend is an insoluble problem.[5] But this does by no means exclude that it is often possible to explain particular cycles or phases (depressions or expansions) in terms of exogenous forces or endogenous processes or to point to strongly intensifying or mitigating factors which explain the mildness or severity of a particular depression, or weakness or strength of a particular upswing. Let me mention only one or two examples—more will follow later. The intensification of the boom following the outbreak of the war in Korea does not require any further explanation than reference to the wave of governmental and private spending engendered by the war.[6] The great depression of the 1930's in the United States, whatever its deeper causes, was undoubtedly tremendously intensified by the collapse of the banking system.

[4] This makes me doubt the usefulness of the averaging procedure adopted by N.B.E.R. even with all the caution and reservations expressed by the illustrious authors of *Measuring Business Cycles*.

[5] It is perhaps more correct to say that the problem is meaningless, at least in the sense in which it is—or rather *was*, for it is no longer a very live issue—usually formulated. The question is usually framed as a causal one: How to separate the effects of the causes responsible for the cycle from the effects of the causes responsible for the trend. The further assumption is made that the two sets of effects are additive. This assumption is surely unwarranted. The causes making for cyclical fluctuations, when impinging on a growing system, will produce very different results than they would produce in a stationary system. And similarly the growth factors would produce different results in an economic system that, unlike the one we live in, is not subject to cyclical fluctuations. As a consequence, if we could make the experiment of abstracting from the actual system which is subject to the joint operation of both sets of causes, first those that make for cycles, and second those that make for trend, the sum of the two effects would not be equal to, but would probably greatly exceed the total observed change.

[6] It should be observed, however, that in the United States the lower turning point following the mild recession of 1948-49 had occurred already in the middle of 1949. The war in Korea was therefore not necessary to pull the American economy out of a depression, but was superimposed on an upswing that had started independently.

It is disturbing that economists do not see eye to eye on all these matters. But we can take consolation in the fact that despite great divergences in the interpretation and explanation, different writers agree about the dates of cyclical turning points and about certain basic characteristics of the short cycle. For example, cyclical chronologies established independently by the most careful investigations of the N.B.E.R., by Edwin Frickey's painstaking researches,[7] and by Schumpeter's more impressionistic methods agree almost entirely. (Divergences in the dates for turning points of a few months are hardly surprising and serious in view of the complexity of the underlying data.)

While the contours of the short-run business cycle are, thus, fairly clear and generally accepted—further characteristics which throw light on the role of money in its causation will be discussed presently—the long "waves" which go under the name of Kondratief cycles, secondary or trend cycles, are a much more hazy thing. They find their expression mainly in wholesale prices and interest rates. But the chronology varies considerably from writer to writer and from country to country; and it is not quite clear whether the ups and downs in prices are always associated—as they invariably are in the short cycle—with ups and downs in output and employment.

It is better not to identify the problem of long run stability with a hypothetical long cycle—a phrase which suggests an endogenous mechanism and a degree of regularity that simply do not exist. We should rather think of the occurrence or recurrence at irregular intervals of rising or falling price trends stretching over several short cycles which may or may not be associated with similar trends in real output.

III. A STRIKING CHARACTERISTIC OF THE SHORT CYCLE

One of the most striking and revealing characteristics of the short cycle is that the ups and downs in output and employment are closely correlated with ups and downs in price levels. *A fortiori* fluctuations in *real* magnitudes (output, employment, real income) are paralleled by fluctuations in *money* flows (money income, money value of output). It should be noted that this does not follow from our definition of the cycle which runs in *real* terms. Conceivably, prices as well as money values could be uncorrelated or negatively correlated with fluctuations in real output.

It seems to me that this actual, almost[8] perfect parallelism cannot be a

---

[7] Edwin Frickey, *Economic Fluctuations in the United States* (Cambridge, Mass., 1942).

[8] I say "*almost* perfect" because there are sometimes shortlived deviations at the turning points between the movement of prices on the one hand and that of real activity on the other. But note that even if the timing between prices and real volume is not perfect, it is still possible (and probably the case) that money flows (price times quantities) are perfectly correlated with volumes.

For the hypothetical long cycle the parallelism is certainly much less close. This surely is a reflection of the fact that in the long run price and wage flexiblility is much greater than in the short run.

chance phenomenon. In fact, an increasing number of business cycle analysts explicitly or implicitly agree that the *proximate* cause of fluctuations in output and employment is fluctuations in aggregate expenditure or effective demand. To be sure there is plenty of disagreement on the deeper forces and processes that are responsible for the cyclical fluctuations in aggregate expenditure. It is nevertheless highly significant that very diverse theories agree on the role of expenditure fluctuations. To this group belong not only the various types of monetary theories of the cycle, but also all the modern "capital stock adjustment theories" which rely on some sort of interaction of multiplier and acceleration principle to construct an endogenous oscillating mechanism and even Schumpeter's theory, whose logical structure is entirely different, belongs to this group. All these theories explain in different ways why expenditures fluctuate in cycles; it is then easy to see how this produces cycles in output and employment—so easy indeed that the necessary assumption of some sort of price and wage rigidity is rarely made clear. Let me add that a very large part of currently employed methods of forecasting the future course of business consists of attempts to form a judgment on the probable course of various segments of the expenditure stream—business spending on investment (plant and equipment, inventories), consumer spending, government spending, foreign demand, etc.

The proposition that fluctuations in aggregate effective demand or expenditure are the proximate cause of the business cycle does by no means imply that is it always monetary factors in the sense of active measures of monetary policy on the part of the monetary authorities or of the banks that bring about the fluctuations in expenditures. The line of causation does not necessarily always run from the monetary to the real factors, although it can hardly be doubted, in my opinion, that monetary factors do often greatly contribute to cyclical instability and that, on the other hand, skilful monetary policy can help to counteract instability caused by "real" factors.[9] Suppose our economic system were not subject to cyclical fluctuations; it would then be an easy task to produce by monetary measures a business cycle with all the familiar features of alternating periods of expansion and contraction in output and employment associated with ups and downs in prices and aggregate demand. All that is required to bring about such a result would be to expand and contract credit or to produce sufficiently large surpluses and deficits in the government budget.

---

[9] Hardly anybody doubts this anymore. In that respect the situation is different from what is was at the time of the outbreak of the Great Depression. But let me add that this remark does not imply the endorsement of a naive version of "functional finance." However the criticism of the latter (see especially the forceful and convincing strictures by Milton Friedman) is based on the realization of the difficulties in diagnosis and timing of policies owing to lags and uncertainties and not on a denial of the basic proposition that correctly timed and properly dosed injections of money can counteract (although not always completely compensate) fluctuations in aggregate real activity.

IV. REAL AND MONETARY FACTORS BEHIND THE
FLUCTUATIONS IN AGGREGATE EXPENDITURE

In order to gain perspective let me briefly enumerate and survey various possibilities of explaining cyclical fluctuations in aggregate spending by "monetary" and "real" factors and their interaction—starting from cases of "purely monetary" causation and proceeding to cases of increasing preponderance of "real" factors.

At the one extreme we have the purely monetary explanations of the cycle which assume that the real economic system is inherently stable and that instability is introduced by misbehavior or mismanagement of money. (It should be remembered that what may be purely monetary is the causal mechanism; the thing to be explained, the cycle, we have defined in real terms.)

Of modern writers who have proposed purely monetary explanations, Irving Fisher and R. G. Hawtrey come at once to mind. Fisher flatly denied that there was such a thing as a cycle except to the extent that quasicyclical instability was introduced by monetary instability which he conceived in terms of changes in the purchasing power of money. Professor Hawtrey's endogenous theory, consisting of a dynamic mechanism of lagged interactions of monetary circulation, cash drains, and credit policy of the banks, changes in short-term interest rates inducing changes in inventory investment, is well known.[10]

Another school that explains the cycle by monetary factors starts from Wicksell's distinction between the market or money rate of interest, on the one hand, and the natural or equilibrium rate on the other. Wicksell himself did not hold a purely monetary theory of the cycle, but Mises and Hayek, to mention only two, did. They believe that the initiating cause of the cycle can always be found on the monetary side, on the supply side of money. Excessive supply of credit (that is to say, credit creation in excess of "voluntary savings"—the precise criterion of excessiveness not being always the same) depresses the market or money rate of interest below its equilibrium level; this starts a Wicksellian cumulative process which necessarily ends in crisis and depression.

In these monetary theories, which stress changes in the supply side of money, it is assumed explicitly or tacitly that the demand for money and credit, or to put it differently, the natural or equilibrium rate of interest is determined by the (physical) marginal productivity of capital which is fairly stable over time, although perhaps subject to a gradual downward shift as the capital stock increases.

Nonmonetary factors make their appearance as soon as it is realized that

---

[10] It seems safe to say that his theory would have made a greater impression if it had been worked out in mathematical form.

the demand for money and credit (or the equilibrium rate of interest) is neither stable nor determined solely by the physical productivity of capital.

The main factors making for instability of investment demand, or in the terminology of the Wicksellian School, for changes in the equilibrium rate of interest (if we still permit ourselves under these circumstances to think of an equilibrium rate existing at any given moment) are as follows, arranged in the approximate order of increasing "physicalness": "psychology," i.e. waves of optimism and pessimism; investment changes induced by changes in income or consumption as postulated in the different variants of the acceleration principle (including that of Kaldor); inventions and innovations and the forces giving rise to the "bunching" of innovational investment as described by Schumpeter; "lumpiness" of investment due to the durability and indivisibility of capital instruments together with the asymmetry in the operation of the accelerator, the replacement waves and "echo effects" which follow from the fact that capital goods are durable; speaking of bunching and lumpiness of capital investment we cannot forget in the world in which we live the most powerful external factor causing intense concentration (and hence instability) of investment, namely, wars and preparation for wars.

All these factors have been used, singly or in combination, to explain the business cycle. But in all these theories, although they are no longer purely monetary, monetary factors enter more or less importantly—and not only in the trivial sense that everything that happens in a money economy (as distinguished from barter) wears a monetary garb.

The theories which use the various "building blocks" just mentioned vary greatly not only in content but also as to the degree of formal refinement.

Let me·first say a word on the latter aspect. The earlier theories have relied on verbal analysis and rough estimates of magnitudes. Since the pioneering article of Frisch, "Propagation Problems and Impulse Problems in Dynamic Economics"[11] Lundberg's celebrated *Studies in the Theory of Economic Expansion*, and especially since the formal marriage of multiplier and acceleration principle (who earlier lived together under different names in ill-defined relationship), a great change has come over business cycle theorizing. The theory has been formalized in complete endogenous sequence models using difference and differential equations. The earlier models were linear but soon nonlinear models with "floors," "ceilings," "asymmetries," "stochastic variables," and "exogenous shocks" were added. Not only mathematical blueprints but full-blown econometric models relating to individual countries or even to the whole world with constants and parameters statistically evaluated are pouring from single scholars' studies and statistical laboratories like automobiles from the assembly line.

This surely is a very interesting development and this type of approach

---

[11] *Economic Essays in Honour of Gustav Cassel*, London, 1933. [Reprinted in this volume.]

is undoubtedly worth trying and perfecting. But there can be hardly a doubt any more that so far the results have been most disappointing. The multiplicity of more or less inconsistent models, many of them based on broadly plausible assumptions and, if of the econometric type, fitting the data from which they are derived fairly well, but none of them standing up to the test of extrapolation beyond the period from which the data were taken—this is a spectacle that is not calculated to inspire confidence.

But let me return to the substantive question concerning the role of monetary forces in the cycle. It would seem to be a valid generalization that purely monetary explanations have become increasingly unpopular, and although most current theories are mixed in the sense that monetary and real factors interact, the monetary factor has been more and more deemphasized and relegated to a merely passive or permissive role.

Let me consider, as an example, Hicks' classic *Contribution to the Theory of the Trade Cycle*—the most elegant and most carefully elaborated specimen of a great variety of similar systems.

His principal model runs almost entirely in "real" terms: Consumption expenditure is a function of real income; investment a function of the rate of change in *real* income; there is a physical ceiling which may or may not be hit and, owing to the *physical* impossibility of using up durable capital faster than it wears out, the accelerator is weaker on the downgrade than on the upgrade. Wages are supposed to be perfectly rigid and so are prices (with minor qualifications).

In the basic model money plays a purely passive role; monetary circulation automatically expands during the upswing and automatically contracts during the downswing of the cycle.[12] Money is a mere veil or rather a tricot (as Mises used to put it[13]) which faithfully reflects without distortion the contours of the economic body and all its changes.

Although Hicks regards the "real" model as the heart of this theory and the latter as an adequate picture of reality, he is too much of a realist to rely entirely on the "real" part of his theory for the explanation of actual cyclical experience. In the last two chapters of his book he introduces the "monetary factors" as a very active element and thus modifies his theory more drastically than appears on the surface or than he himself seems to admit. But let me spend a few more minutes on the "real" models.

---

[12] Monetary complications are, however, invoked to explain one feature of actual cyclical experience which in Hicks' opinion cannot be accounted for by his "real" model. He thinks that after the downturn the contraction of output usually proceeds faster than the multiplier-acceleration mechanism would lead one to expect. So he introduces as an intensifier what Pigou many years ago (in his *Industrial Fluctuations*, 1926, which to this day has kept remarkably fresh) called the detonation of bankruptcies and business failures into which the upswing explodes. For this concession to realism Hicks was promptly rebuked by Kaldor, who believes that also this particular feature of the cycle can be explained by the "real" mechanism.

[13] Needless to say Mises did not accept the view that money was a mere tricot.

Although in these models money plays no active role in the sense that no deliberate inflationary measures, or rising prices, falling interest rates or lowered credit standards are required to explain a cyclical upswing—nor the opposite of all this to account for the depression phase—money is nevertheless essential because the upswing could not proceed unless the supply of money were elastic in the sense that either M or V increased without sharp rises in the interest rates.[14] If there is not sufficient scope for V to expand the monetary authorities must permit the necessary expansion in M; if V can expand it is sufficient that they refrain from counteracting the increase in V by contracting M.

The downturn is brought about entirely by the "real" mechanism and during the downswing the role of money is even less important than in the upswing; for while the monetary authorities can always stop or slow down an expansion they can do nothing or very little to soften a contraction (although they could presumably intensify it). When the "real" forces "decree a contraction," MV shrinks inexorably and if monetary policy prevents M from shrinking (or expands it) the result is simply an offsetting drop in V.

There can be hardly a doubt that this account greatly underestimates the importance of monetary factors in producing the major cyclical swings of actual experience. What is open to question is the degree of distortion of the true picture. While I realize that many of those who have put forward real models of the cycle would be ready to admit that their picture of the cycle is liable to be changed somewhat by the operation of monetary factors, I still believe that modern theory has tended grossly to underestimate the importance of the monetary factors. Not only in the field of business cycles, but in other areas as well alleged stubborn "structural" and "real" instabilities and impediments to necessary adjustment have been overemphasized and overestimated at the expense of monetary factors and the closely related element of price and wage rigidity. This is a matter of great importance which has far-reaching policy implications.[15]

V. MONETARY FACTORS IN DEPRESSIONS

The operation of monetary forces is especially conspicuous in depressions. But the seeds of depression are sown during the boom and they are not entirely of "real" origin.

Let me enumerate a few instances in which monetary factors have notoriously greatly intensified depressions although perhaps not brought them about.

---

[14] It is true there has been a strong tendency to discount the importance of the interest rate but it has hardly gone so far as to deny that sharply rising interest rates would act as a brake on the expansion.

[15] Thus it was necessary to "rediscover monetary policy." See Prof. Ellis' celebrated article "The Rediscovery of Money." The same felicitous phrase was used independently by Prof. M. A. Heilperin.

The Great Depression of the 1930's in the United States was made much more severe than it would otherwise have been by the wholesale destruction, through bankruptcies, of banks and bank money. It is surely not an essential feature of the real cycle that the banking system should collapse during the depression. The same thing happened in several other countries and the breakdown of the gold standard, the liquidation of the gold exchange standard, and the international scramble for liquidity is essentially the same monetary process on the international level.

It is gratifying to see a prominent champion of the "real" cycle theory like Professor Hicks himself emphatically stressing the basically monetary nature of the Great Depression thereby flatly rejecting "real" explanations of the events of the 1930's, his multiplier-acceleration theory, as well as the "secular stagnation" thesis.

Let me quote the relevant passage hidden away in a footnote:

I do not see that there is any adequate reason to suppose that the real boom of 1927–9 was at all an exceptional boom; if the accelerator mechanism, and nothing else, had been at work, it should not have been followed by an exceptional slump. But the slump impinged upon a monetary situation which was quite exceptionally unstable. The main cause of this instability was not the purely superficial speculative over-expansion which had occurred in New York in 1928–9; its roots went much further back. The monetary system of the world had never adjusted itself at all fully to the change in the level of money incomes which took place during and after the war of 1914–18; it was trying to manage with a gold supply, which was in terms of wage-units extremely inadequate. Difficulties in the postwar adjustment of exchange rates (combined with the vast changes which the war had produced in the creditor-debtor position of important countries) had caused the consequential weakness to be particularly concentrated in certain places; particular central banks, as for instance the Bank of England and the Reichsbank, were therefore particularly incapable of performing their usual function as "lenders of last resort."[16]

This explanation of the Great Slump has long been propounded by continental European economists, notably by the late Charles Rist, but has not found many supporters among Anglo-American economists.

Two general observations are called for. First, it should be stressed that price rigidity, which is in practice primarily wage rigidity, is an essential prerequisite of any monetary explanation. This remark must, however, not be interpreted to mean that everything would be put right and cyclical instability could be banished by introducing wage flexibility. The problem is much more complicated, because of the existence of fixed contracts and possible adverse dynamic and expectational repercussions of a perfectly flexible wage and price system.

---

[16] *Loc. cit.*, p. 163. This explanation does not quite fit the American case. It cannot well be said that the monetary (gold) base of the U.S. economy was too narrow even though the dollar was later devalued in terms of gold. The speculative orgies of the late 1920's were not as superficial as Hicks thinks; they surely contributed much to the collapse of the banking system.

Second, it is well known that throughout the 19th century the British monetary system operated on a very narrow gold reserve. This narrowness of the monetary base made for a jerky credit policy, because it forced the Bank of England to react sharply to slight cash drains. Thus it contributed to monetary instability throughout the 19th century.[17] The growing wage rigidity in the 20th century made that system unworkable.

It is well known, although often forgotten, that monetary mismanagement, namely, the revaluation of sterling after the first world war, without the necessary wage adjustments, was responsible for the semistagnation of the British economy during the 1920's.[18]

The Great Depression of the 1870's offers many parallels with that of the 1930's. It too was greatly intensified by monetary factors, both in the United States and in Europe. In the United States large budget surpluses followed the deficits during the Civil War and the premium on gold was gradually reduced from 57 percent in 1865 to zero in 1879,[19] the terminal year of the depression—a situation which in many respects resembles the British position in the 1920's. True, the general economic background—19th century United States vs. 20th century Britain—is entirely different, but the difference in the surrounding conditions makes the similarity of the outcome all the more remarkable and serves to support the hypothesis that the monetary factors were in both cases of decisive importance.

These are conspicuous and notorious cases in which depressions have been intensified by monetary factors. Similar though less conspicuous and serious monetary disturbances entailing credit contraction, pessimistic expectations and inducement to increase liquidity (reduction in V) can be found in practically every but the mildest depression.

VI. MONETARY FACTORS DURING BUSINESS CYCLE UPSWINGS

While it is, thus, easy to point to instances in which depressions have been greatly intensified by monetary factors and policies during the depression and while, following Pigou and Hicks, we may venture the generalization

---

[17] On all this and for references to the contemporary literature see especially Viner, *Studies in the Theory of International Trade*, chapter V.

[18] This outcome was correctly foretold by Keynes in his pamphlet *The Economic Consequences of Mr. Churchill*, 1925.

As Prof. Hayek has pointed out (*Monetary Nationalism and International Stability*, London, 1937, p. 44) Keynes' warning was based on orthodox teaching. A hundred years ago (1821) Ricardo in a letter to Wheatley said, "I never should advise a government to restore a currency, which was depreciated 30%, to par; I should recommend... that the currency should be fixed at the depreciated value." (Ricardo, Sraffa edition, Vol. IX, p. 73.) Under 20th century conditions of wage rigidity, most economists would say that a 10% overvaluation is too much to be dealt with by deflation rather than by devaluation of the currency.

[19] See R. Fels, "American Business Cycles 1865–79," in *American Economic Review*, June, 1951, pp. 325–49.

that in many less conspicuous cases than those mentioned the severity of depressions has been enhanced by monetary repercussions of financial crises, the role of monetary factors in the upswing and boom phase of the cycle is much more controversial and difficult to assess.

I take it that hardly anyone would defend nowadays the proposition, and I certainly would not do so myself, that the tapering-off of the upswing and the subsequent depression could be avoided either by keeping M, or MV (in some sense) or some general price level constant. Hence the failure of money or monetary policy to conform to any simple rule cannot be held responsible for the fact that booms do not last forever and are always followed by depressions. But from the fact that it is difficult or impossible to discover a monetary rule which, if observed during the upswing, would guarantee perpetual prosperity, it does not follow that the behavior of money or monetary policy during the upswing cannot greatly contribute to the severity of the following contraction.

The length and severity of depressions depend partly on the magnitude of the "real" maladjustment which developed during the preceding boom and partly on the aggravating monetary and credit factors already mentioned —the scramble for liquidity by financial institutions as well as by others, destruction of bank money by bank failures, and similar events on the international level.

While monetary arrangements and policies during the upswing probably cannot entirely prevent the emergence of real maladjustments—except perhaps by preventing the upswing itself—imprudent monetary policies surely can aggravate them; moreover, the financial crises which frequently mark the downturn of the cycle and the monetary and financial complications during the depression are partly the consequence of monetary forces and policies operating during the preceding expansion.

The term "real maladjustment" must not be interpreted in a narrow, exclusive sense.[20] There are alternative types of such maladjustments and I do not wish to suggest that there is a presumption that every boom breeds the same kind of trouble. Let me mention only two or three types.

The Harrod-Hicks theory (envisaged also by other writers) that when an expansion runs head on into a full employment ceiling (which need not be a rigid barrier but may be a flexible bottleneck zone) induced investments will collapse,[21] describes one kind of real maladjustment.

---

[20] In the economic literature it is closely associated with F. A. Hayek's theory of the cycle. However, the "real maladjustment" which Hayek describes, "over extension of the period of production" (the concept is not easy to define in operational term) is only one kind of maladjustment out of a multitude of possibilities, and not the most likely or most easily ascertainable one.

[21] In other words, "capital widening" comes to an end and since "capital deepening" cannot quickly take up the slack, aggregate investment is bound to fall and a depression ensues.

Another type of maladjustment is the one described by Schumpeter. It can be characterized as a temporary exhaustion of investment opportunities in the particular area in which the boom was concentrated. The chances that there should be a *general* and *chronic* dearth of investment outlets for current savings (as distinguished from a temporary one in a particular area) are so remote and *sub specie historiae* so farfetched that we can ignore them.[22]

While these real maladjustments are closely tied up with growth and expansion itself and are most difficult to diagnose and to avoid (except by preventing the expansion itself) most upswings are characterized in varying degrees by excesses which at least *postfestum* appear unnecessary, undesirable and avoidable, even though the line which separates them from the maladjustments mentioned earlier cannot always be drawn neatly at the time when things are going well.

What I mean are speculative excesses in the real as well as in the financial sphere: overoptimistic overproduction in particular lines of industry and overbuilding, speculative land booms and speculative overinvestment in inventories,[23] and in the financial sphere, excessive speculation on the stock exchanges.

It is mainly in this area that money and monetary policy become important during the upswing. These "unhealthy" developments are not possible, or at least not possible on the large and disturbing scale on which they actually occur, without excessive credit expansion. It is, of course, often difficult to diagnose such developments when they occur and a most difficult task of monetary policy to prevent inflationary excesses without endangering expansion itself; no easy rule such as stabilizing some general price level will be sufficient. It is nevertheless a fact, I believe, that these things do happen in every major upswing and that they breed financial upheavals and revulsions which then greatly contribute to the severity of the succeeding deflation and depression.

---

[22] This does not, however, alter the fact that in every severe depression we experience a revival in lay and expert circles alike of the theory that most if not all depressions are the consequence of a chronic lack of investment opportunities—only to be given up during the following upswing and replaced in the minds of many by the opposite point of view to the effect that we have at last conquered the business cycle and entered the "new" era of perpetual prosperity. This illustrates the "Konjunkturgebundenheit" of economic thinking and can be claimed as supporting evidence by those economists who stress the importance of the "psychological" factor in the generation of the business cycle. In recent years Prof. W. A. Jöhr has dwelt upon the "psychological factor" in his monumental volume on business cycles.

[23] I suspect that the "nonspeculative" inventory cycle based on a multiplier-acceleration mechanism (analyzed in masterly fashion in Metzler's celebrated articles) is only a small part of the real story and that inventory cycles without price speculation and monetary stimuli (elements which play no part in Metzler's theory) would be mild and uninteresting affairs.

VII. THE COMPARATIVE IMPORTANCE OF MONETARY AND REAL FACTORS IN THE CYCLE

My general conclusion is that monetary factors and policies play an important role in generating economic instability. A large part of modern cycle theory has unduly neglected monetary factors and overplayed the "real" factors, although most proponents of "real" theories of the cycle find it necessary to bring in monetary factors as modifying elements at some stage before applying their theories to the cycle of the real world.

Let me now raise the quantitative question: Suppose the various de-stabilizing monetary complications which I have enumerated could be avoided by institutional reforms and skilful monetary policy; would that damp down the cycle drastically or would it not make much difference? In other words, is the "real" cycle without the so-called "complications" really a very serious problem?

This is, of course, an extremely complicated question. I cannot hope in the course of one lecture to formulate it with all the care and precision which it requires, let alone to give a well-documented answer.

But let me make bold and suggest tentative answers to some subdivisions of the main query.

If the wholesale destruction of bank money during depressions through bank failures, runs on banks, lack of confidence in the financial institutions as well as analogous phenomena in the international sphere could be avoided —a modest minimum program of monetary reform—catastrophic slumps as in the 1930's would be eliminated. Avoidance of mistakes such as in the re-valuation of the pound after the first world war and a modest policy of monetary expansion (I am speaking now of monetary policy, not of fiscal policy, i.e. the creation of counter cyclical budget deficit in a depression) would make prolonged periods of semistagnation like that of the British economy in the 1920's extremely unlikely.

If, in addition to this, inflationary and speculative excesses during cyclical expansions were prevented and a mild counter cyclical budget policy adopted, cyclical instability would be damped down to moderate proportions. In other words, the "real" cycle without the monetary "complications" (comprehensively defined) is, in my judgment, a rather mild affair.

What are the chances that the "monetary complications" will in fact be avoided henceforth? I think that a majority of economists would agree that the chances are good as far as antidepression policy is concerned. Runaway deflation, like in the 1930's, is, I believe, out of the question everywhere, even in the most capitalistic countries. More than that, as far as antidepression policy is concerned, there is certainly more danger in most countries of too soon and too much rather than of too late and too little. Does that mean that we have reached the millenium of economic stability? Now, as far as employment is concerned, there is probably little chance anywhere of prolonged mass unemployment due to a deficiency of effective demand. True, this does not exclude unemployment due to a lack of cooperating factors. But dislocations where that happens on a large scale are exceedingly rare.[24]

VIII. SECULAR INFLATION

But for other dimensions of economic stability than employment, for example, for price stability, the outlook is definitely not so good. The low tolerance for unemployment, the strong inclination to suspect an incipient major depression in every slight actual or imagined dip in economic activity, the high propensity to apply antidepression measures—all that coupled with the powerful urge to invest and develop, the constant pressure of organized labor for higher wages and, in some countries, of organized agriculture for higher prices, makes for secular, intermittent or continuous, creeping or galloping inflation.

Continuous galloping inflation is found in some underdeveloped countries —Chile is perhaps the most extreme recent example. There can be no doubt that it retards growth (through lowering the allocative efficiency of the economy and discouraging saving) even if acute depressive reactions can be avoided.

In the advanced industrial countries secular inflation threatens in the form of a creeping and intermittent rise in prices. That is to say, prices rise over the long pull at an *average* rate of a few percent per annum, not steadily but in waves, periods of rapidly rising prices being interrupted by shorter periods of stable or even slightly falling prices. This is an insidious process which is not easy to diagnose and on the consequences of which there is little agreement between economists, at least so long as the average price rise is not more than, say, 2–3% a year.

---

[24] Such conditions existed after the war in war-ravaged countries due to a lack of raw materials, machinery, and transportation. The spectre of that kind of unemployment arose in some countries such as in Britain during severe balance of payments crises; but it never came to pass. Some theorists have played with the idea that this kind of unemployment exists *chronically* (!) in disguised form in underdeveloped countries. It is based on the assumption of constant coefficients of production, that is to say that capital and labor can be combined only in one or two fixed proportions (rectangular or at least angular production functions). Capital is scarce, hence much labor must remain unemployed. The assumption that such conditions should exist in the long run not for particular narrowly defined industrial processes but for industry as a whole or broad subdivisions, seems to me unrealistic to the point of being preposterous. It must be pointed out, however, that this same phantastic assumption underlines the famous Harrod-Domar model of long-run economic growth.

These theories constitute other extreme examples of the modern propensity to overemphasize real factors and to look for real, in this case literally physical rigidities, instead of for monetary factors, price and wage rigidities and the like. (For an able criticism of the Harrod-Domar model see L. B. Yeager, "Some Questions about Growth Economics," in *American Economic Review*, March, 1954.)

I am not going to speculate about the average annual speed and time shape at which secular inflation will begin to have serious consequences. I shall instead discuss one aspect of the causal mechanism which brings about this condition and one of its consequences on the international level.

As Bronfenbrenner[25] points out, there are two different explanations of the tendency in the industrial countries of the West towards secular creeping inflation. The one school blames the pressure groups of organized labor and organized agriculture; the other blames monetary policy which has become lax under the influence of the Keynesian thinking of our time. According to the first, the price level is gradually pushed up by rising wages; according to the other view, it is pulled up by monetary policy.

Money plays, of course, its role in both schemes. Labor unions could not push the price level up unless monetary policy gave way. It should also be observed that it is not necessary that labor be organized in one huge bloc (as it actually is in some countries) and force up the whole wage level in one big push. For the inflationary mechanism to work, it is a sufficient condition that big chunks of wages be forced up here and there by some of the large unions. The forces of competition and actions of other unions can then be relied upon rapidly to generalize these increases. Pull and push always interact once the upward movement has started. Thus the difference between the two schools seems to degenerate into one of the hen and egg variety.

But there remains an important operational difference. Although both schools agree that despite union pressure on wages the price level could be held, if monetary policy stood firm (as it had to under the gold standard), the pressure group school asserts (or implies) that if monetary policy does stand firm, wages (or some wages) will be pushed up anyway. As a consequence unemployment will appear and monetary authorities are then confronted with the dilemma either to "create" a certain amount of unemployment or to tolerate at least from time to time a rise in the price level.

The other school takes a more optimistic position. According to them there is no such dilemma. If the monetary authorities stand firm wages will not rise or will rise only a little. A small amount of unemployment or the mere threat of unemployment will sufficiently persuade the unions to desist from wage demands in excess of the gradual increase in overall labor productivity.

Given the fact that the tolerance for unemployment in our time is low, the difference of opinion between the two schools thus reduces to one's estimate of the power and policy of labor unions and employer reactions. Obviously much depends also on public opinion and government policy.

I am inclined to side on this issue with the pessimists.[26] But this is certainly a question on which it would be unwise to take a dogmatic position.

---

[25] "Some Neglected Implications of Secular Inflation," in *Post-Keynesian Economics* (1954).

[26] Bronfenbrenner too (*op. cit.*) is on the pessimistic side and so is the dean of American "labor economists," S. H. Slichter. The optimistic view is represented by members of the

The power and policies of labor unions as well as the behavior of employers, reactions of public opinion and government policy differ from country to country and although the trend has been everywhere in the free world in the direction of increased union power towards a "laboristic society" (Slichter), this trend obviously depends on political and social forces whose future course cannot be foreseen. The economist has certainly no special expert qualifications for making such prophecies.

IX. INSTABILITY OF THE INTERNATIONAL BALANCE OF PAYMENTS

I now come to my last topic which dramatically illustrates the modern tendency to look for deepseated structural defects and to see stubborn real stumbling blocks to the maintenance of stable equilibrium where in reality faulty monetary policies and the rigidity of certain key prices provide a perfectly satisfactory explanation for the existing disequilibrium or instability.

While in a closed economy with a unified monetary and banking system, free mobility of funds and a fair degree of mobility of labor, a secular inflation of 2–3 % per year may not have deleterious effects for quite some time, at least not clearly visible ones, in the actual world, consisting as it does of different countries with different monetary systems and policies, little or no mobility of capital funds and labor between them, even a small deviation in the rate of inflation between different countries must almost immediately lead to balance of payments disequilibria.

What holds of differences in the degree of secular inflation is, of course, also true of deviations in timing and magnitude of cyclical and other short-run expansions and contractions. Analytically it is, moreover, only the other side of exactly the same problem, if the disequilibrium in the balance of payments has been caused initially by a shift in international demand (however brought about). In that case the persistence of the disequilibrium can be said to be due to the failure of the monetary mechanism to bring about an *equilibrating* divergency between the rate of expansion in the surplus country and that in the deficit country,[27] while in the cases mentioned before the disequilibrium in the balance of payments was caused by the appearance of a *disequilibrating* divergence of the same sort.

"Chicago School." See e.g. Milton Friedman, "Some Comments on the Significance of Labor Unions for Economic Policy" in *The Impact of the Union*, New York, 1951, and W. K. Morton, "Trade Unionism, Full Employment, and Inflation," *American Economic Review*, March, 1950.

[27] The equilibrating mechanism can be of the gold standard type (stable exchanges, expansion in the surplus countries and contraction in the deficit countries) or it can use the technique of flexible exchanges under which no expansion and contraction in the local currency circulation is necessary. Complications caused by price and wage rigidities and consequential changes in employment or by speculative movements of capital cannot be discussed here.

But let me concentrate on the chronic case, because it illustrates most clearly the point I wish to make, namely, the contemporary propensity to overemphasize "real" factors and to neglect monetary factors and institutional rigidities.

There is today much more agreement than there was a few years ago on the proposition that the basic reason for the chronic (continuous or intermittent) balance of payments deficit, *alias* "dollar shortage," from which many countries are suffering is to be found in the fact that the deficit countries have, for a variety of reasons, a higher "propensity to inflate" than the surplus countries. (It should be stressed, however, that it is grossly misleading to speak of a shortage of the U.S. dollar only. The same shortage applies just as much to the Canadian dollar, Mexican peso, Venezuelan bolivar, Swiss franc, more recently also to the German mark, Dutch guilder and other currencies which are more or less freely convertible into U.S. dollars.)

The reasons for a high propensity to inflate are, of course, many. Some are of an "ideological," "political," and "social" nature, others are deeply rooted in the recent or more distant historical development of a country; still others are very "real." It is, for example, easy to understand why for some time after the war it was almost impossible for war-torn and ravaged countries to restrain inflation (of the "open" or "repressed" variety); moreover, it stands to reason that countries with a low tolerance for unemployment, an elaborate social welfare establishment, exhorbitant rates of direct taxation, aggressive trade unions, will constantly strain against the leash; similarly, it is not surprising at all that poor and backward countries when they wake up and set their minds to develop in a hurry and to catch up with the more developed countries, are continuously tempted to overspend their meagre resources and to live beyond their means.

With such a wealth of explanatory material available which offers unlimited opportunities for bringing into play "propensities," "asymmetries,"[28] "demonstration effects" and many other gadgets dear to the heart of the economic theorist, it is difficult to understand why anyone should find it necessary to fall back on such implausible and farfetched hypotheses as the sudden appearance in the fourth decade of the 20th century of stubborn real inelasticities of international demand (of whole continents and a great variety of countries) or on the equally bizarre theory that, again beginning with the third or fourth decade of our century, balances of payments (and terms of trade) must turn inexorably in favor of the most rapidly progressing countries.

---

[28] See e.g. C. Kindleberger, *"L'asymétrie de la balance des paiements," Revue Economique,* 1954, pp. 166–89.

X. SUMMARY AND CONCLUDING REMARKS

My main conclusion is: Monetary factors comprehensively defined bear a heavy share of responsibility for short-run economic instability—for the ordinary business cycle (again comprehensively defined) as well as for the instability and chronic disequilibria in the balances of payments.

By "monetary factors" I do not merely mean active policies of inflation or deflation—the latter having become almost inconceivable since the Great Depression and the rise of Keynesian thinking—but also monetary repercussions of financial crises which frequently mark the upper turning point of the cycle or occur during the downswing—irrespective of whether the downturn itself can or cannot be attributed to monetary factors. For example, the collapse of the American banking system in the 1930's, the downfall of the gold standard, the ensuing sudden liquidation of the gold exchange standard, withdrawal of international credits, hot money flows and the general scramble for liquidity—all these and similar events on the national and international level are monetary factors. If these things could be avoided, catastrophes like the Great Depression would be impossible and other cycles would be mitigated.

If we define the concept "monetary factor" somewhat more comprehensively so as to include as its effects that part of existing instability which would disappear in the event that monetary policy succeeded (in addition to preventing the monetary disturbances mentioned above) in imparting a mildly anticyclical pattern to the supply of money and credit—monetary factors would be responsible for a still larger share in economic instability. In other words, the amplitude of the cycle would be sharply reduced if monetary factors in that comprehensive sense became inoperative (which would require, of course, acts of commission as well as of omission on the part of the monetary authorities).

This does, however, by no means imply that nonmonetary factors are of no importance.

First of all, the monetary factors operate in an environment or impinge on a system which possesses certain nonmonetary features that make the system respond to the monetary forces as it does. One could easily imagine an economic system in which the monetary factors would not produce large swings in output and employment but only fluctuations in prices, which would be a much less serious matter. If, for example, deflation did not breed pessimism and inflation did not produce exaggerated optimism,[29] if in addition wages and prices were flexible and there were no large fixed monetary contracts, the effects of monetary instability on aggregate output and employment would be much smaller than they are in the real world.

The "monetary" factor, the "psychological" factor and the "rigidity" factor are complementary in the strict sense of the word and reinforce each

---

[29] Prolonged and too rapid inflation may, of course, produce pessimistic reactions.

other. The resulting instability is their joint product and it is therefore quite legitimate to attribute to each of these factors a substantial share of the existing economic instability in such a way that the sum of their (alternative) shares greatly exceeds the total.[30]

Second, I do not wish to discount completely—for short-run purposes—fixity of capital coefficient as postulated by the acceleration principle—although even in the short run the capital-output ratio (and labor-output ratio) is not as rigid as many modern business cycle models assume.[31] Nor would I ignore the multiplier. But the acceleration principle plus multiplier, unless combined with and reinforced by monetary factors, psychology and rigidities would hardly produce more than mild and inconsequential fluctuations. All these factors together bring it about that our economic system is subject to cumulative, self-reinforcing processes of expansion and contraction.

Third, there are autonomous changes in aggregate expenditure, especially the concentrations followed later by slumps of investment demand (including demand for consumer durables) caused by technological innovations and above all by wars and preparations for war. These "real factors" obviously do contribute their share to economic instability. But in my judgment it is mainly in their role as starters, intensifiers and interrupters of cumulative processes that they do their destabilizing work. That is to say, the "propagation problem" is more important than the "impulse problem." And in the propagation mechanism, the way in which the economy responds to outside impulses, the monetary factor plays a decisive role.

One important reason for this hypothetical evaluation is the historical experience that modern economies frequently take terrific impulses and shocks in their stride while on other occasions they seem to react strongly to modest shocks. Recent history offers numerous examples. Let me mention the transition from peace to war and the transition from war to peace, the latter entailing a tremendous sudden drop in government expenditures; another example is the reconstruction of war-torn countries—such as Italy, Germany, Austria—and the subsequent levelling out of these economies into a more normal course of development. These shocks, which were absorbed with surprising ease, were certainly incomparably more severe than those that are supposed to have started the Great Depression.

I conclude that the response mechanism is more important than the severity of the external shocks and in the response mechanism monetary factors play a most important role.

---

[30] This has been pointed out many years ago by A. C. Pigou in his *Industrial Fluctuations*, 2nd ed., London, 1929.

In Part I, Chapter 22, he says: "It is possible that more than one factor may be a dominant cause of fluctuations in the sense that, if it were removed, the amplitude of these fluctuations would be reduced to insignificant proportions." (See *op. cit.*, Table of Contents, p. xiiii.)

[31] To assume that it is rigid in the long run or subject only to autonomous changes (due to technological innovations) and not to equilibrating adjustments seems to me hopelessly unrealistic.

II. METHODOLOGY

8

Introduction

As NOTED in the Preface, mathematical formulation of theory and an econometric approach to empirical work are probably the two outstanding (and interrelated) developments in the recent business cycle literature. Frisch's paper, with which this section opens, charted as early as 1933 the course that was to be followed by future builders of aggregative dynamic models. It combines an internal mechanism which may be cyclical by itself with external shocks which may be either random or autonomous. (The Adelmans' paper, reprinted in Part III, demonstrates the importance of random disturbances in generating cycles, and the rapid growth of the public sector points up the need for study of the effects of autonomous impulses.) Frisch's theoretical paper, together with the pioneering econometric work of Tinbergen, set the stage for much of the recent empirical work in the field of business cycles.

At the same time that model-building and econometric research (which starts with the formulation of hypotheses in mathematical terms) have been becoming increasingly popular, detailed empirical investigations of a non-econometric sort continue to be carried on. The outstanding practitioner of such detailed empirical work is the National Bureau of Economic Research.[1] The publication in 1946 of the long-awaited *Measuring Business Cycles*, by Arthur F. Burns and Wesley Mitchell, led to the critical review article by Tjalling Koopmans which is reprinted here. There followed a spirited debate between Koopmans and Rutledge Vining, also reprinted here, which bears rereading. The former's "Additional Comment," published ten years after the original debate, reflects a more sympathetic attitude toward the "simple methods of statistical inference" used by the National Bureau than was suggested by the original "Measurement without Theory."

Another interesting methodological debate, at about the same time as Vining's first reply to Koopmans, involved not only the National Bureau's and the econometric but also the "quantitative-historical" approach to business cycle research.[2] Further material bearing on these debates as to

---

[1] The *Annual Reports* of the National Bureau provide a convenient source of information on its research in progress.

[2] See the papers by R. A. Gordon and T. C. Koopmans, with discussion by J. W. Angell, Arthur F. Burns, and Gottfried Haberler, in *American Economic Review : Papers and Proceedings*, Vol. XXXIX (May, 1949), pp. 47–88.

method may be found in other sections of the present volume. In Parts III and IV, for example, the reader will find examples of recent econometric work as well as the informative review by Geoffrey Moore of the recent and current work of the National Bureau. Mention should also be made of the approach underlying what has come to be known as the Munich Business Test, which is described in the section on forecasting.

9

Propagation Problems and Impulse Problems in Dynamic Economics*[1]

By RAGNAR FRISCH†

I. INTRODUCTION

THE MAJORITY of the economic oscillations which we encounter seem to be explained most plausibly as free oscillations. In many cases they seem to be produced by the fact that certain exterior impulses hit the economic mechanism and thereby initiate more or less regular oscillations.

The most important feature of the free oscillations is that the length of the cycles and the tendency towards dampening are determined by the intrinsic structure of the swinging system, while the intensity (the amplitude) of the fluctuations is determined primarily by the exterior impulse. An important consequence of this is that a more or less regular fluctuation may be produced by a cause which operates irregularly. There need not be any synchronism between the initiating force or forces and the movement of the swinging system. This fact has frequently been overlooked in economic cycle analysis.

If a cyclical variation is analysed from the point of view of a free oscillation, we have to distinguish between two fundamental problems: first, the *propagation* problem; second, the *impulse* problem. The propagation problem is the problem of explaining by the structural properties of the swinging system what the character of the swings would be in case the system was started in some initial situation. This must be done by an essentially dynamic theory, that is to say, by a theory that explains how one situation grows out of the foregoing. In this type of analysis we consider not only a set of magnitudes in a given point of time and study the interrelations between them, but

* From *Economic Essays in Honor of Gustav Cassel* (London: George Allen and Unwin, Ltd., 1933). Reprinted by courtesy of the author.

† University of Oslo.

[1] The numerical results incorporated in the present study have been worked out under my direction by assistants in the University Institute of Economics, Oslo, established through generous grants from the Rockefeller Foundation, New York, and A/S Norsk Varekrig, Oslo. As directors of the Institute, Professor Wedervang and I take this opportunity of expressing our sincere thanks for the support received from these institutions.

we consider the magnitudes of certain variables in different points of time, and we introduce certain equations which embrace at the same time several of these magnitudes belonging to different instants. This is the essential characteristic of a dynamic theory. Only by a theory of this type can we explain how one situation grows out of the foregoing. This type of analysis is basically different from the kind of analysis that is represented by a system of Walrasian equations; indeed in such a system all the variables belong to the same point of time.

In one respect, however, must the dynamic system be similar to the Walrasian: it must be determinate. That is to say, the theory must contain just as many equations as there are unknowns. Only by elaborating a theory that is determinate in this sense can we explain how one situation grows out of the foregoing. This, too, is a fact that has frequently been overlooked in business cycle analysis. Often the business cycle theorists have tried to do something which is equivalent to determining the evolution of a certain number of variables from a number of conditions that is smaller than the number of these variables. It would not be difficult to indicate examples of this from the literature of business cycles.

When we approach the study of business cycles with the intention of carrying through an analysis that is truly dynamic and determinate in the above sense, we are naturally led to distinguish between two types of analyses: the micro-dynamic and the macro-dynamic types. The micro-dynamic analysis is an analysis by which we try to explain in some detail the behaviour of a certain section of the huge economic mechanism, taking for granted that certain general parameters are given. Obviously it may well be that we obtain more or less cyclical fluctuations in such sub-systems, even though the general parameters are given. The essence of this type of analysis is to show the details of the evolution of a given specific market, the behaviour of a given type of consumers, and so on.

The macro-dynamic analysis, on the other hand, tries to give an account of the fluctuations of the whole economic system taken in its entirety. Obviously in this case it is impossible to carry through the analysis in great detail. Of course, it is always possible to give even a macro-dynamic analysis in detail if we confine ourselves to a purely *formal* theory. Indeed, it is always possible by a suitable system of subscripts and superscripts, etc., to introduce practically all factors which we may imagine: all individual commodities, all individual entrepreneurs, all individual consumers, etc., and to write out various kinds of relationships between these magnitudes, taking care that the number of equations is equal to the number of variables. Such a theory, however, would only have a rather limited interest. In such a theory it would hardly be possible to study such fundamental problems as the *exact time shape* of the solutions, the question of whether one group of phenomena is lagging behind or leading before another group, the question of whether one part of the system will oscillate with higher amplitudes than another part, and so on. But these latter problems are just the essential problems in business cycle analysis. In order to attack these problems on a macro-dynamic basis so as to explain the movement of the system taken in its entirety, we must deliberately disregard a considerable amount of the details of the picture. We may perhaps start by throwing all kinds of production into one variable, all consumption into another, and so on, imagining that the notions "production," "consumption," and so on, can be measured by some sort of total indices.

At present certain examples of micro-dynamic analyses have been worked out, but as far as I know no determinate macro-dynamic analysis is yet to be found in the literature. In particular no attempt seems to have been made to show in an exact way what the relations between the propagation analysis and the impulse analysis are in this field.

In the present paper I propose to offer some remarks on these problems.

II. LE TABLEAU ÉCONOMIQUE

In order to indicate the most important variables entering into the macro-dynamic system we may use a graphical illustration as the one exhibited in Fig. 1.

FIG. 1

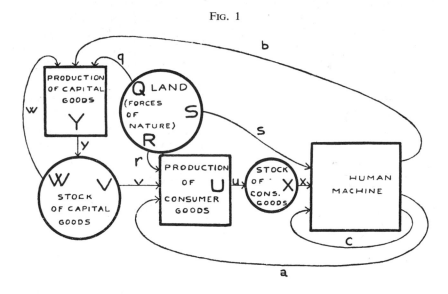

The system expressed in Fig. 1 is a completely closed system. All economic activity is here represented as a circulation in and out of certain sections of the system. Some of these sections may best be visualized as receptacles (those are the ones indicated in the figure by circles), others may be visualized as machines that receive inputs and deliver outputs (those are the ones indicated in the figure by squares). There are three receptacles, namely, the forces of nature, the stock of capital goods, and the stock of consumer goods. And there are three machines: the human machine, the machine producing capital goods, and the machine producing consumer goods.

The notation is chosen such that capital letters indicate stocks and small letters flows. For instance, R means that part of land (or other forces of nature) which is engaged in the production of consumer goods, r is the services rendered by R per unit time. Similarly V is the stock of capital goods engaged in the production of consumer goods and v the services rendered by this stock per unit time. Further, a is labour (manual or mental) entering into the production of consumer goods, so that the total input in the production of consumer goods is $r + v + a$.

The complete macro-dynamic problem, as I conceive of it, consists in describing as realistically as possible the kind of relations that exist between the various magnitudes in the Tableau Économique exhibited in Fig. 1, and from the nature of these relations to explain the movements, cyclical or otherwise, of the system. This analysis, in order to be complete, must show exactly what sort of fluctuations are to be expected, how the length of the cycles will be determined from the nature of the dynamic connection between the variables in the Tableau Économique, how the damping exponents, if any, may be derived, etc. In the present paper I shall not make any attempt to solve this problem completely. I shall confine myself to systems that are still more simplified than the one exhibited in Fig. 1. I shall commence by a system that represents, so to speak, the extreme limit of simplification, but which is, however, completely *determináte* in the sense that it contains the same number of variables as conditions. I shall then introduce little by little more complications into the picture, remembering, however, all the time to keep the system determinate. This procedure has one interesting feature: it enables us to draw some conclusion about those properties of the system that may account for the cyclical character of the variations. Indeed, the most simplified cases are characterized by monotonic evolution without oscillations, and it is only by adding certain complications to the picture that we get systems where the theoretical movement will contain oscillations. It is interesting to note at what stage in this hierarchic order of theoretical set-ups the oscillatory movements come in.

III. SIMPLIFIED SYSTEMS WITHOUT OSCILLATIONS

We shall first consider the following case. Let us assume that the yearly consumption is equal to the yearly production of consumers' goods, so that there is no stock of consumers' goods. But let us take account of the stock of fixed capital goods as an essential element of the analysis. The depreciation on this capital stock will be made up by two terms: a term expressing the depreciation caused by the use of capital goods in the production of consumers' goods, and a term caused by the use of capital goods in the production of other capital goods. For simplicity we shall assume that in both these two fields the depreciation on the fixed capital goods employed is proportional to the intensity with which they are used, this intensity being measured by the volume of the output in the two fields. If h and k are the depreciation coefficients in the capital producing industry and in the consumer goods industry respectively, the total yearly depreciation on the nation's capital stock will be $hx + ky$, where x is the yearly production of consumers' goods and y the yearly production of capital goods. Our assumption amounts to saying that h and k are technically given constants.

What will be the forces determining the annual production of capital goods y? There are two factors exerting an influence on y. First, the need to keep up the existing capital stock, replacing the part of it that is worn out. Second, the need for an increase in total capital stock that may be caused by the fact that the annual consumption is increasing. This latter factor is essentially a progression (or degression) factor, and does not exist when consumption is stationary. I shall consider these two factors in turn.

First let us assume that the annual consumption is kept constant at a given level x. How much annual capital production y will this necessitate? This may be expressed in terms of the depreciation coefficients in the following way. Let total capital stock be denoted Z. The rate of increase of this stock will obviously be

$$\dot{Z} = y - (hx + ky) \tag{1}$$

Since the stationary case is characterized by $\dot{Z} = 0$, the stationary levels of x and y must obviously be connected by the relation $y = hx + ky$, i.e.

$$y = mx \tag{2}$$

where

$$m = \frac{h}{1 - k}$$

The constant m represents the *total* depreciation on the capital stock associated with the production of a unit of consumers' goods, when we take account not only of the *direct* depreciation due to the fact that fixed capital is used in the production of consumer goods, but also take account of the fact that fixed capital has to be used in the production of those capital goods that must be produced for replacement purposes. This follows from the way in which (2) was deduced, and it may also be verified by following the depreciation process for an infinite number of steps backwards. Indeed, the production of x causes a direct depreciation of hx. In order to replace these hx units of capital, a further depreciation of khx is caused, and this amount has to be added to the annual capital replacement production. But adding the amount khx to the annual capital production means that the annual depreciation is increased by $k . (khx) = k^2hx$, which also has to be added to the annual capital production, and so on. Continuing in this way, we find that the total annual capital production needed to maintain the constant consumption x (with no change in the total capital stock) is equal to

$$hx + khx + k^2hx + \ldots = \frac{h}{1-k} x = mx$$

which is formula (2). For this reason m may be called the *total*, h and k the *partial* depreciation coefficients.

Now let us consider the other factor that affects the annual capital production, namely, the *change* $\dot{x}$ in the annual production of consumption goods.

Let us take a simple example. Suppose that a capital stock of 1,000 units is needed in order to produce a yearly national income (i.e. a yearly national consumption) equal to 100 units, then if the production of consumer goods rests stationary at a level of 100 units per year, it is only necessary to produce each year enough capital goods to replace the capital worn out, namely, $m . 100$, m being the constant in (2).

But if there is in a given year an *increase*, say, of 5 units, in the production of consumer goods, then it is necessary during that year to increase the stock of capital goods. Indeed, in order to maintain a yearly production of consumer goods equal to 105, there is needed a capital stock equal to 1,050. During the year in question it is therefore necessary to produce an additional 50 units of capital goods. We are thus led to assume that the yearly production of capital goods can be expressed in a form where there occurs not only the term (2) but also a term that is proportional to $\dot{x}$, i.e. y will be of the form

$$y = mx + \mu\dot{x} \qquad (3)$$

where m and μ are constants. The constant m expresses the wear and tear on capital goods caused directly and indirectly by the production of one unit of consumption, and μ expresses the size of capital stock that is needed directly and indirectly in order to produce one unit of consumption per year. In other words, μ is the total "production coefficient," in the Walrasian sense, for the factor capital.

The two influences expressed by the two terms in (3) have been the object of a certain discussion in the literature which ought to be mentioned here. Professor Wesley C. Mitchell, in one of his studies, observed that the maximum in the production of capital goods preceded the maximum in the production of consumer goods (or, which amounts to the same, the sales of consumer goods if stock variations of consumer goods are disregarded). From this he drew the conclusion that it is rather in production than in consumption we ought to look for the factors that can explain the turning point of the cycle. Professor J. M. Clark objected to this conclusion. He said that the *rate of increase* of consumption exerts a considerable influence on the production of capital goods, and that the movement of this rate of increase precedes the movement of the absolute value of the consumption. Indeed, during a cyclical movement the rate of increase will be the highest, about one-quarter period before the maximum point is reached in the quantity itself.

The effect which Clark had in mind is obviously the effect which we have expressed by the second term in (3). If we think only of this term, disregarding the first term, we will have the situation where y is simply proportional to the rate of increase of x. If the movement is cyclical, we would consequently have a situation as the one exhibited in Fig. 2.

Fig. 2

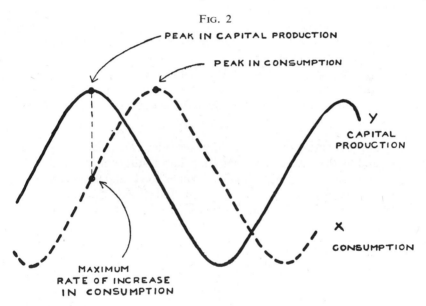

In Fig. 2 we notice that the peak in consumption comes after the peak in capital production, but if we compare production with the *rate of increase* of consumption, we find that there is synchronism: the maximum rate of increase in consumption occurs at the same moment as the peak in the actual size of capital production. The fact observed by Mitchell can, therefore, just as well be explained—as Clark did—by saying that it is consumption which exerts an influence on production. This is an interesting observation, and it is correct if taken only as an expression for *one* of the factors influencing production.[2]

---

[2] Clark, in his discussion of this question, went further than this. He tried to prove that the fact here considered could by itself explain the turning point of the business cycle, but this is not correct. Indeed, equation (3) is only one equation between two variables. Consequently many types of evolutions are possible. See the discussion between Professor Clark and the present author in the *Journal of Political Economy*, 1931–32.

In order to have a complete and correct picture we must, however, take account of both terms in (3), and we must also look for some other relation between our variables. So far the problem is not yet determinate.

In order to make the problem determinate we need to introduce an equation expressing the behaviour of the consumers. We shall do this by introducing the Walrasian idea of an *encaisse désirée*. This notion will be introduced here only as a parameter by means of which we express a certain feature of the behaviour of the consumers. The parameter is going to be introduced in the equations and then eliminated. Its introduction, therefore, does not mean that we are actually elaborating a monetary theory of business cycle. It is only an intermediary parameter introduced in order to enable the formulation of a certain simple hypothesis.

The *encaisse désirée*, the need for cash on hand, is made up of two parts: cash needed for the transaction of consumer goods and producer goods respectively. The first of these parts may of course always be written as a certain factor r times the sale of consumer goods, and the second part as a certain factor s times the production of capital goods, provided the factors r and s are properly defined. In other words, the *encaisse désirée* ω may be written

$$\omega = rx + sy \tag{4}$$

As a first approximation one may perhaps consider r and s as constants given by habits and by the nature of existing monetary institutions.

When the economic activity both in consumer goods and in producer goods production increase, as they do during a period of expansion, the *encaisse désirée* will increase, but the total stock of money, or money substitutes, cannot be expanded *ad infinitum* under the present economic system. There are several reasons for this: limitations of gold supply, the artificial rigidity of the monetary systems, psychological factors, and so on. We do not need to discuss in detail the nature of these limiting factors. We simply assume that, as the activity and consequently the need for cash increases, there is created a *tension* which counteracts a further expansion. This tension is measured by the expression (4). It seems plausible that one effect of the tightening of the cash situation, and perhaps the most important one, will be a restriction in consumption. In the boom period when consumption has reached a high level (in many cases it has extended to pure luxuries), consumption is one of the elastic factors in the situation. It is likely that this factor is one that will yield first to the cash pressure. To begin with this will only be expressed by the fact that the rate of increase of consumption is slackened. Later, consumption may perhaps actually decline. Whatever this final development it seems plausible to assume that the *encaisse désirée* ω will enter into the picture as an important factor which, when increasing, will, after a certain point, tend *to diminish the rate of increase* of consumption. Assuming as a first approximation the relationship to be linear, we have

$$\dot{x} = c - \lambda\omega \tag{5}$$

where c and λ are positive constants. The constant c expresses a tendency to maintain and perhaps expand consumption, while λ expresses the reining-in effect of the *encaisse désirée*.

Introducing into (5) the expression for the *encaisse désirée* taken from (4), we get

$$\dot{x} = c - \lambda(rx + sy) \tag{6}$$

This equation we shall call the consumption equation.

The two equations (3) and (6) form a determinate system in the two variables x and y. If the parameters μ, m, λ, etc., are constants, the system may easily be solved in explicit form. By doing so we see that the system is too simple to give oscillations. Indeed, by eliminating $\dot{x}$ between (3) and (6) we get a linear relation between x and y. Expressing one of the variables in terms of the others by means of this relation and inserting in one of the two equations (3) or (6) we get a linear differential equation in a single variable. The characteristic equation is consequently of degree one, and has therefore only one single real root. This means that the variables will develop monotonically as exponential functions. In other words, we shall have a secular trend but no oscillations.[3]

The system considered above is thus too simple to be able to explain developments which we know from observation of the economic world. There are several directions in which one could try to generalize the set-up so as to introduce a possibility of producing oscillations. One idea would be to distinguish between saving and investment. The fact that, in an actual situation, there is a difference between these two factors will tend to produce a depression or an expansion. This is Keynes' point of view. It would be exceedingly interesting to see what sort of evolution would follow if such a set of hypotheses were subject to a truly dynamic and determinate analysis.

Another way of generalizing the set-up would be to introduce the fact that the existence of debts exerts a profound influence on the behaviour of both consumers and producers. This is the leading idea of Irving Fisher's approach to the business cycle problem.

A third direction would be to introduce the Marxian idea of a bias in the distribution of purchasing power. This idea may—with a slight change of emphasis—be expressed by saying that under private capitalism production will not take place unless there is a prospect of profit, and the existence of profits tends to create a situation where those who have the consumption power do not have the purchasing power, and *vice versa*. Thus, under private capitalism, production must more or less periodically kill itself.

A fourth direction would be the introduction of Aftalion's point of view with regard to production. The essence of this consists in making a distinction between the quantity of capital goods whose production is *started*

---

[3] Incidentally this shows that the fact pointed out by Clark does not necessarily lead to a development giving a turning point.

and the activity needed in order to *carry to completion* the production of those capital goods whose production was started at an earlier moment. The essential characteristics of the situation that thus arises are that the activity at a given moment does not depend on the decisions taken at that moment, but on decisions taken at earlier moments. By this we introduce a new element of discrepancy in the economic life that may provoke cyclical oscillations. I do not think that Aftalion's analysis as originally presented by himself can be characterized as a determinate analysis. By putting his argument into equations one will find that he does not have as many equations as unknowns. But his idea with regard to production is very interesting, and, if properly combined with other ideas, will lead to a determinate system. Not only that, but it may lead to a system giving rise to oscillations. I now proceed to the discussion of such a system.

IV. A MACRO-DYNAMIC SYSTEM GIVING RISE TO OSCILLATIONS

Let y_t be the quantity of capital goods whose production is *started* at the point of time t. We shall call y_t the "capital starting" or the "production starting," and we shall assume that this magnitude is determined by an equation of the form (3.3). A capital object whose production is started at a certain moment will necessitate a certain production activity during the following time in order to complete the object. The productive activity needed in the period following the starting of the object will, as a rule, vary in a certain fashion which we may, as a first approximation, consider as given by the technical conditions of the production. Let D_τ be the amount of production activity needed at the point of time $t + \tau$ in order to carry on the production of a unit of capital goods started at the point of time t. The function D_τ we shall call the "advancement function."

This being so, the amount of production work that will be going on at the moment t will be

$$z_t = \int_{\tau=0}^{\infty} D_\tau y_{t-\tau} \, d\tau \tag{1}$$

The magnitude z_t we shall call "the carry-on-activity" at the point of time t.

In the formula of the *encaisse désirée* it is now z that will occur instead of y, so that the consumption equation will be

$$\dot{x} = c - \lambda(rx + sz) \tag{2}$$

where c, λ, r and s are constants.

The three equations (3.3), (1) and (2) form now a determinate system in the three variables x, y and z.

If the carry-on function D_τ is given, the above system may be solved. If D_τ is given only in numerical form, the system has to be solved numerically, taking for granted a certain set of initial conditions. If D_τ is given as a simple mathematical expression, the system may under certain conditions be solved in explicit form. As an example we shall assume

$$D_\tau = \begin{cases} 1/\varepsilon & 0 < \tau < \varepsilon \\ 0 & \tau \gtreqless \varepsilon \end{cases} \tag{3}$$

where ε is a technically given constant. This simply means that a given element of capital starting will cause a certain constant amount of carry-on-activity per unit time over the ε units of time following the starting, and that in this point the object is finished, so that no further carry-on-activity is needed. This is obviously a simplified assumption, but may perhaps be taken as a first approximation.

In this case we get from (1) by differentiating with respect to time

$$\varepsilon \dot{z}_t = y_t - y_{t-\varepsilon} \tag{4}$$

For certain purposes it will be convenient to differentiate also the equation (2) in order to get rid of the constant term, which gives

$$\ddot{x} = -\lambda(r\dot{x} + s\dot{z}) \tag{5}$$

The three equations to be considered now are (2), (3.3) and (4) (or possibly (5) may replace (2)). This is a mixed system of differential and difference equations. It is therefore to be expected that the solution will depend, not only on the initial conditions of the system in a given *point* of time; as initial conditions we shall have to consider the shape of the curve over a whole interval of length ε.

We shall in particular investigate whether the system is satisfied if each of the variables is assumed to be made up of a number of *components*, each component being either an exponential or a damped oscillation, i.e. a damped sine curve. It is easier to handle the formulae if each such term is written in the complex exponential form, that is to say in the form

$$a_1 e^{(-\beta + i\alpha)t} + a_2 e^{(-\beta - i\alpha)t} \qquad i = \sqrt{-1} \tag{6}$$

where a_1 and a_2 are constants. For brevity we may write (6)

$$a_1 e^{\rho_1 t} + a_2 e^{\rho_2 t} \tag{7}$$

where ρ_1 and ρ_2 are complex numbers.

This applies to a single component. Considering now several components in each variable, we may express the above assumption by saying that the variables x, y and z considered as time series are of the form

$$\begin{cases} x = a_* + \Sigma_k a_k e^{\rho_k t} \\ y = b_* + \Sigma_k b_k e^{\rho_k t} \\ z = c_* + \Sigma_k c_k e^{\rho_k t} \end{cases} \tag{8}$$

where ρ_k are complex or real constants, and where a, b and c are also constants. By convention we let the numbering in (8) run $k = 0, 1, 2 \ldots$. Does there exist a set of functions of the form (8) which satisfy the system consisting of the equations (3.3), (2) and (4)? Such functions do exist. The exponential characteristics ρ_k of these functions are determined by the structural constants ε, λsm, $\lambda s\mu$, λr that enter into the system considered. On the contrary, the coefficients, a, b and c in (8) will depend on the initial conditions.

It is easy to verify this and to determine how the exponential characteristics ρ_k depend on the structural constants. This is done by differentiating the various expressions in (8) and inserting the results obtained into the equations of the system. If this is done, one will find that the coefficients a, b and c must satisfy the relations

$$
\begin{cases}
\dfrac{c_k}{a_k} = -\dfrac{\lambda r + \rho_k}{\lambda s} \\[2ex]
\dfrac{b_k}{a_k} = m + \mu\rho_k \\[2ex]
\dfrac{c_k}{b_k} = \dfrac{1 - e^{-\varepsilon\rho_k}}{\varepsilon\rho_k} \\[2ex]
(k = 0, 1, 2 \ldots)
\end{cases}
\tag{9}
$$

This condition entails that all the ρ_k must be roots of the following characteristic equation:

$$
\frac{\varepsilon\rho}{1 - e^{-\varepsilon\rho}} = -\lambda s \frac{m + \mu\rho}{r\lambda + \rho}
\tag{10}
$$

This equation may have complex or real roots. For the numerical computation it is therefore convenient to insert into (10)

$$
\rho = -\beta + i\alpha \qquad i = \sqrt{-1}
\tag{11}
$$

and to separate the real and imaginary parts of the equation after having cleared the equation of fractions. Doing this, we get the following two equations to determine α and β (assuming ε and $\lambda s\mu = 0$).

$$
1 + \lambda s\mu e^{\varepsilon\beta}\frac{\sin \varepsilon\alpha}{\varepsilon\alpha} = \frac{m\dfrac{\varepsilon^2}{\mu^2}(m - \lambda r\mu)}{\left(\varepsilon\beta - m\dfrac{\varepsilon}{\mu}\right)^2 + (\varepsilon\alpha)^2}
\tag{12}
$$

$$
-\frac{\varepsilon\beta - \lambda r\varepsilon + m\dfrac{\varepsilon}{\mu}}{\varepsilon\beta - m\dfrac{\varepsilon}{\mu}} + \lambda s\mu\frac{1 - e^{\varepsilon\beta}\cos\varepsilon\alpha}{\varepsilon\beta - m\dfrac{\varepsilon}{\mu}} = \frac{m\dfrac{\varepsilon^2}{\mu^2}(m - \lambda r\mu)}{\left(\varepsilon\beta - m\dfrac{\varepsilon}{\mu}\right)^2 + (\varepsilon\alpha)^2}
\tag{13}
$$

The terms of these equations have been ordered in the particular form indicated in order to facilitate the numerical solution.

The roots (β, α) of these two equations will determine the shape of the time curves x, y and z. It is obvious from (12) and (13) that if (β, α) is a root, then $(\beta, -\alpha)$ will also be a root. In other words, if complex roots occur they will be conjugate, which means that the corresponding component of x, y and z will actually be a damped sine curve. If there exists a magnitude β such that $(\beta, 0)$ is a root, then the corresponding component will be a secular trend in the form of an exponential.

In order to study the nature of the solutions, I shall now insert for the structural coefficients ε, μ, m, etc., numerical values that may in a rough way express the magnitudes which we would expect to find in actual economic life. At present I am only guessing very roughly at these parameters, but I believe that it will be possible by appropriate statistical methods to obtain more exact information about them. I think, indeed, that the statistical determination of such structural parameters will be one of the main objectives of the economic cycle analysis of the future. If we ask for a real *explanation* of the movements, this type of work seems to be the indispensable complement needed in order to co-ordinate and give a significant interpretation to the huge mass of empirical descriptive facts that have been accumulated in cycle analysis for the past ten or twenty years.

Let us first consider the constant ε. It expresses the total length of time needed for the completion of big units of fixed capital: big industrial plants, water-power plants, railways, big steamers, etc. This span of time includes not only the actual time needed for the technical construction (the erection of the buildings, etc.) but also time needed for the planning and organization of the work. Indeed, the variable τ in (1) is measured from the moment when the initiative was taken. In many cases the items planning and organization take more time than the actual technical construction.

It seems that we would strike a fair average if we say that the actual production activity needed in order to complete a typical plant of the above-mentioned kind will be distributed over time in such a way that in general it takes place around three years after the planning began. Some work will of course frequently be done before and some after this time, but three years can, I believe, tentatively be taken as an average. In making this guess I have taken account of an important factor that tends to pull the average up, namely, the fact that in a given individual case the activity will as a rule not be distributed evenly over the period (as assumed in the simplified theoretical set-up) but the peak activity will be concentrated near the *end* of the period. If three years is taken as the *average* lag of the various elements of production activity after the beginning of the planning, we shall have to put $\varepsilon = 6$ in (3), and consequently in (4); indeed in the case of equal distribution, as assumed in (3), the *average* lag will be half the *maximum* lag.

Furthermore, let us put $\mu = 10$, which means that the total capital stock is

TABLE 1

Characteristic Coefficients of the Components Obtained

		Trend ($j=0$)	Primary Cycle ($j=1$)	Secondary Cycle ($j=2$)	Tertiary Cycle ($j=3$)
Frequency	α	$\rho_0 = -0.08045$	0.73355	1.79775	2.8533
Period	$p = \dfrac{2\pi}{\alpha}$		8.5654	3.4950	2.2021
Damping exponent	β		0.371335	0.5157	0.59105
Damping factor per period	$e^{-2\pi\beta/\alpha}$		0.0416	0.1649	0.2721
Consumption x { Amplitude	A	-0.32	0.6816	0.27813	0.17524
Consumption x { Phase	ϕ		0	0	0
Production starting y { Amplitude	B	0.09744	5.4585	5.1648	5.0893
Production starting y { Phase	ψ		1.9837	1.8243	1.7582
Carry-on-activity z { Amplitude	C	0.12512	-10.662	-10.264	-10.147
Carry-on-activity z { Phase	θ		1.9251	1.7980	1.7412

ten times as large as the annual production. Further, let us put $m = 0.5$, which means that the direct and indirect yearly depreciation on the capital stock caused by its use in the production of the national income is one half of that income, i.e. 20% of the capital stock. Finally, let us put $\lambda = 0.05$, $r = 2$, and $s = 1$. These latter constants, which represent the effect of the *encaisse désirée* on the acceleration of consumption, are of course inserted here by a still rougher estimate than the first constants. There is, however, reason to believe that these latter constants will not affect very strongly the length of the cycles obtained (see the computations below).

Inserting these values in the two characteristic equations (12) and (13) we get a numerical determination of the roots. In the actual computation it was found practical to introduce $\varepsilon\alpha$ and $\varepsilon\beta$ as the unknowns looked for. By so doing, and utilizing an appropriate system of graphical and numerical approximation procedures, the roots may be determined without too much trouble. A good guidance in the search for roots is the fact that the solutions in α are approximately the minimum points of the function

$$\frac{\sin \varepsilon\alpha}{\varepsilon\alpha} \tag{14}$$

that is to say, a first approximation to the frequencies α will be every other of the roots of the equation

$$tg\varepsilon\alpha = \varepsilon\alpha \tag{15}$$

The roots of this equation are well known and tabulated.[4] The results of the computations are given in the first columns of Table 1.

The first component ($j = 0$) is a trend, which in all the three variables x, y and z is composed of an additive constant and a damped exponential term. We may write these trends in the form

$$\begin{cases} x_0(t) = a_* + a_0 e^{\rho_0 t} \\ y_0(t) = b_* + b_0 e^{\rho_0 t} \\ z_0(t) = c_* + c_0 e^{\rho_0 t} \end{cases} \tag{16}$$

---

[4] The above characteristic equation was worked out and the roots numerically determined by Mr. Harald Holme and Mr. Chr. Thorbjörnsen, assistants at the University Institute of Economics. In brief the following procedure was used: The right member of equations (12) and (13) was put equal to a parameter q, and (12) solved with respect to $\varepsilon\beta$, and (13) with respect to $\cos \varepsilon\alpha$. From (15) a first approximation to α was determined and the corresponding β taken as the value determined by putting $q = 0$ in (12). This value of β was as a rule immediately corrected by using (12) with the value of q that followed from the above preliminary determination of α and β. This gave a new value of q that was inserted in (13), thus determining a new value of α. Starting from this new value of α the whole process was iterated. This method gave good results except for very small values of λ, in which case it was found better to start by guessing at the value of β.

These expressions are nothing but the first terms in the composite expressions (8). The damping exponent ρ_0 is the first root of the characteristic equation, it is real and negative; $\rho_0 = -0.08045$ (see Table 1). The additive constants a_*, b_* and c_* are also determined by the structural coefficients ε, λsm, etc. Indeed, if $t \to \infty$ the functions (16) will approach the stationary levels a_*, b_* and c_*. Since the derivatives will vanish in this stationary situation, we get from (3.3), (1) and (2)

$$b_* = ma_* \qquad\qquad c_* = b_* \qquad\qquad \lambda ra_* + \lambda sc_* = c \qquad\qquad (17)$$

putting as an example $c = 0.165$ this determines uniquely the three constants $a_* = 1.32$, $b_* = 0.66$, and $c_* = 0.66$.

The coefficients a_0, b_0 and c_0 are not determined uniquely by the structural coefficients, but one initial condition may be imposed on them—for instance, a condition that determines a_0. When a_0 is determined, b_0 and c_0 follow from (9). If, as a numerical example, we impose the condition that x_0 shall be unity at origin, we get the functions x_0, y_0, z_0 in (23a).

Besides the secular trend, there will be a primary cycle with a period of 8.57 years, a secondary cycle with a period of 3.50 years, and a tertiary cycle with a period of 2.20 years (see Table 1). These cycles are determined by the first, second and third set of conjugate complex roots of (10). These sets are denoted $j = 1, 2, 3$ in Table 2. There will also be shorter cycles corresponding to further roots of (10), but I shall not discuss them here.

TABLE 2

Step-by-Step Computation of the Primary Cycle

t	x	y	z	$\dot{x}$	$\dot{z}$	y_{t-6}
0	0	5.0000	−10.000	0.5000	6.4264	−33.5581
0.16667	0.08333	4.4229	− 8.929	0.4381	6.6811	−35.6634
0.33333	0.15635	3.8297	− 7.8155	0.3752	6.7865	−36.8894
0.50000	0.21887	3.2329	− 6.6844	0.3124	6.7592	−37.3221
0.66667	0.27093	2.6435	− 5.5579	0.2508	6.6153	−37.0480

The presence of these cycles in the solution of our theoretical system is of considerable interest. *The primary cycle of 8.57 years corresponds nearly exactly to the well-known long business cycle.* This cycle is seen most distinctly in statistical data from the nineteenth century, but it is present also in certain data from the present century; in the most recent data it actually seems to come back with greater strength.

Furthermore, the secondary cycle obtained is 3.50 years, which corresponds nearly exactly to the short business cycle. This cycle is seen most distinctly in statistical data from this century, but it is present also in older series. As better monthly data become available back into the nineteenth century the short cycle will become quite evident also here I believe.

The lengths of the cycles here considered depend, of course, on all the structural coefficients; but it is only ε that is of great importance. The other coefficients only exert a very small influence on the length of the cycles. Choosing, for instance, $\lambda = 0.1$, $s = 1$, $r = 2$, $\mu = 5$, and different values for m, we find

m	Period p	Damping Factor $e^{-2\pi\beta/\alpha}$
0.7	8.53	0.042
0.5	8.43	0.043
0.0	8.20	0.048

In other words, even an extreme variation in the total depreciation factor m leaves both the period and the damping factor nearly unchanged.

A change in the constant λ that expresses the "reining-in" effect of the *encaisse désirée* exerts a considerable influence on the damping factor, but a relatively small influence on the length of the period. For $\lambda = 0.001$, $s = 1$, $r = 2$, $\mu = 5$ and $m = 0.5$, we find, for instance, $p = 10.6$ years, $e^{-2\pi\beta/\alpha} = 0.000002$. In other words, the period is still of the same order of magnitude, but the damping is now enormous, the amplitude being brought down to two millionths in the course of one period. This means that the cycle in question is virtually non-existing.

It is interesting to interpret the last result in the light of the limiting case where $\lambda = 0$, i.e. where the need for cash as a brake on the development of production is eliminated. In this case it follows immediately from (2) that x will evolve as a straight line with *positive* inclination (c being assumed positive). Hence by (3.3) y must also be a straight line, and by (4) $\dot{z}$ must be a constant, hence z linear. The movement of the system will consequently be a steady evolution towards higher levels of consumption and production without the setbacks caused by depressions.

Of course, the results here obtained with regard to the length of the periods and the intensity of the damping must not be interpreted as giving a final explanation of business cycles; in particular it must be investigated if the same types of cycles can be explained also by other sets of assumptions, for instance, by assumptions about the saving-investment discrepancy, or by the indebtedness effect, etc. Anyhow, I believe that the results here obtained, in particular those regarding the length of the primary cycle of $8\frac{1}{2}$ years and the secondary cycle of $3\frac{1}{2}$ years, are not entirely due to coincidence but have a real significance.

I want to go one step further: I want to formulate the hypothesis that if the various statistical production or monetary series that are now usually studied in connection with business cycles are scrutinized more thoroughly, using a more powerful technique of time series analysis, *then we shall probably discover evidence also of the tertiary cycle, i.e. a cycle of a little more than two years.*

Now let us consider the other features of the cycles: phase, etc. We write the various cyclical components

$$\begin{cases} x_j(t) = A_j e^{-\beta_j t} \sin(\phi_j + \alpha_j t) \\ y_j(t) = B_j e^{-\beta_j t} \sin(\psi_j + \alpha_j t) \\ z_j(t) = C_j e^{-\beta_j t} \sin(\theta_j + \alpha_j t) \\ (j = 1, 2 \dots) \end{cases} \tag{18}$$

$j = 1$ means the primary cycle, $j = 2$ the secondary cycle, etc. The frequencies α and the damping coefficients β are uniquely determined by the characteristic equation, but the phases ϕ, ψ, θ and the amplitudes A, B, C are influenced by the initial conditions. For the primary cycle ($j = 1$) two such conditions may be imposed. We may, for instance, require that $x_1(0) = 0$ and $\dot{x}_1(0) = \frac{1}{2}$. This leads to $\phi_1 = 0$, $A_1 = \dfrac{1}{2\alpha_1}$. And when the phase and amplitude for the primary cycle in x is thus determined, the phases and amplitudes of the primary cycles in y and z follow by virtue of (9). Similarly, if ϕ_2 and A_2 are determined by two initial conditions imposed on the secondary cycle in x, for instance, by the conditions $x_2(0) = 0$ and $\dot{x}_2(0) = \frac{1}{2}$, the phases and amplitudes of the secondary cycles in y and z are also determined by (9).

When the conditions (9) are formulated in terms of phases and amplitudes, we get

$$\begin{cases} B \sin(\psi - \phi) = A\mu\alpha \\ B \cos(\psi - \phi) = A(m - \mu\beta) \end{cases} \tag{19}$$

$$\begin{cases} C \sin(\theta - \phi) = -\dfrac{A\alpha}{\lambda s} \\ C \cos(\theta - \phi) = \dfrac{A(\beta - \lambda r)}{\lambda s} \end{cases} \tag{20}$$

These equations hold good for all the cycles, that is, for $j = 1, 2, 3 \dots$. They show that the lag between x, y and z are independent of the initial conditions and depend only on the structural coefficients of the system. From (18) and (19) we get indeed

$$\begin{cases} tg(\psi - \phi) = \dfrac{\mu\alpha}{m - \mu\beta} \\ tg(\theta - \phi) = -\dfrac{\alpha}{\beta - \lambda r} \end{cases} \tag{21}$$

Similarly the relations between the amplitudes may be reduced to

$$\begin{cases} |B| = \sqrt{(\mu\alpha)^2 + (m - \mu\beta)^2} \cdot |A| \\ |C| = \dfrac{\sqrt{\alpha^2 + (\beta - \lambda r)^2}}{\lambda s} \cdot |A| \end{cases} \tag{22}$$

where the square roots are taken positive. If the amplitudes are taken positive, $\sin(\psi - \phi)$ has the same sign as $\mu\alpha$ and $\sin(\theta - \phi)$ the same sign as $-\alpha/\lambda s$.

A given set (18) (for a given j) does not—taken by itself—satisfy the dynamic system consisting of (3.3), (2) and (4). It will do so only if the structural constant $c = 0$. If $c \neq 0$ the constant terms a_*, b_* and c_* must be added to (18) in order to get a correct solution. If these constant terms are added, we get functions that satisfy the dynamic system, and that have the property that any linear combination of them (with constant coefficients) satisfy the dynamic system provided only that the sum of the coefficients by which they are linearly combined is equal to unity. This proviso is necessary because any sets of functions that shall satisfy the dynamic system must have the uniquely determined constants a_*, b_* and c_*.

The sets (18), with no constants a_*, b_* and c_* added, are solutions of the system obtained by leaving out c in (2). Or, again, (18) may be looked upon as solutions of the system obtained by letting (5) replace (2).

If we impose on the trends the initial condition that x_0 shall be unity at origin, and on each cycle in x the condition that it shall be zero at origin and with velocity $=\frac{1}{2}$, we get the functions in (23a, b, c, d). The corresponding cycles are represented in Figs. 3–5.

$$\begin{cases} x_0 = 1.32 - 0.32e^{-0.08045t} \\ y_0 = 0.66 + 0.09744e^{-0.08045t} \\ z_0 = 0.66 + 0.12512e^{-0.08045t} \end{cases} \tag{23a}$$

$$\begin{cases} x_1 = 0.6816e^{-\beta_1 t} \sin \alpha_1 t \\ y_1 = 5.4585e^{-\beta_1 t} \sin(1.9837 + \alpha_1 t) \\ z_1 = -10.662e^{-\beta_1 t} \sin(1.9251 + \alpha_1 t) \end{cases} \tag{23b}$$

$$\begin{cases} x_2 = 0.27813e^{-\beta_2 t} \sin \alpha_2 t \\ y_2 = 5.1648e^{-\beta_2 t} \sin(1.8243 + \alpha_2 t) \\ z_2 = -10.264e^{-\beta_2 t} \sin(1.7980 + \alpha_2 t) \end{cases} \tag{23c}$$

$$\begin{cases} x_3 = 0.17524e^{-\beta_3 t} \sin \alpha_3 t \\ y_3 = 5.0893e^{-\beta_3 t} \sin(1.7582 + \alpha_3 t) \\ z_3 = -10.147e^{-\beta_3 t} \sin(1.7412 + \alpha_3 t) \end{cases} \tag{23d}$$

(The α and β are given in Table 1.)

From the constants given in Table 1, and from the shape of the curves in
Figs. 3–5, we see that the shorter cycles are not so heavily damped as the long
cycle. Furthermore, we see that the lead or lag between the variables x, y and
z is, roughly speaking, the same in the primary, secondary and tertiary cycles.
To study the lag it is therefore sufficient to consider only one of these types
—for instance, the tertiary cycle (Fig. 5).

FIG. 3

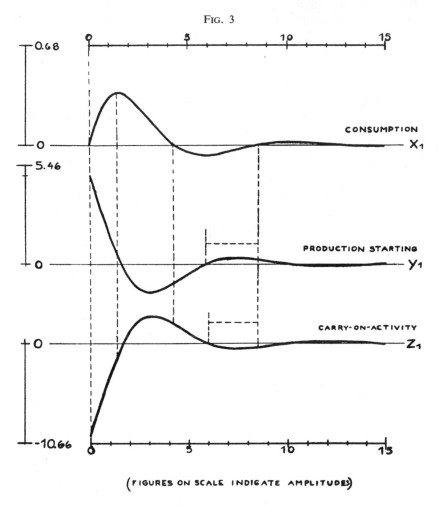

(FIGURES ON SCALE INDICATE AMPLITUDES)

Let us first compare consumption with production starting. Apart from
the fact that the cycles in Fig. 5 are damped, the relation between x and y is
very much the same as in Fig. 2, i.e. production has its peak nearly at the
same time as the *rate of change* of consumption is at its highest. The reason
for this is that the constant μ in our example is chosen rather large in comparison to m. This means that our example refers to a highly capitalistic

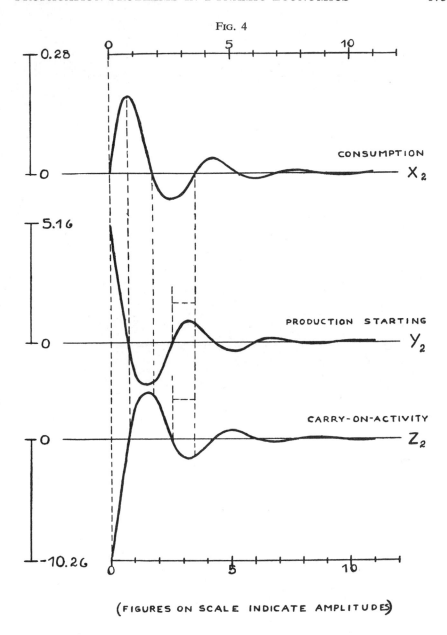

Fig. 4

(FIGURES ON SCALE INDICATE AMPLITUDES)

society where the annual depreciation is relatively small. By reducing the size of the capital stock in relation to the output (i.e. reducing μ) and increasing the annual depreciation (i.e. m) the peak in production starting will advance so as to arrive nearer the peak in consumption.

Next, comparing consumption with the carry-on-activity, we see that the

Fig. 5

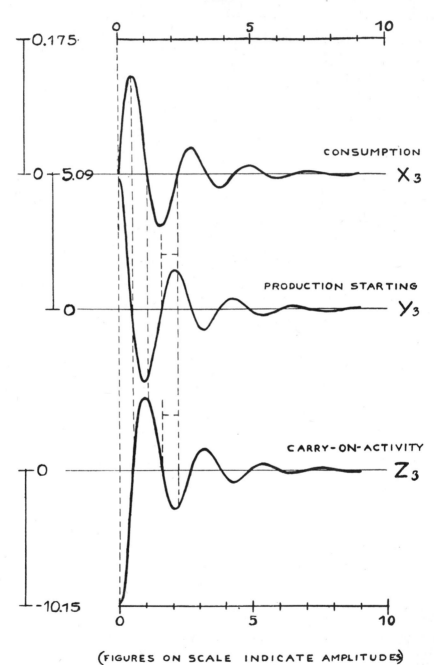

(FIGURES ON SCALE INDICATE AMPLITUDES)

former is leading by a considerable span of time, i.e. in the depression the carry-on-activity starts to increase only when the upswing in consumption is well under way, and the carry-on-activity continues to increase even after consumption has started to decline.

The way in which the structural relations determine the time shape of the solutions may perhaps be rendered more intuitively by a method of successive numerical approximation.

In order to show this, we take for granted that the time shape of one of the curves—for instance, y_1—is known in the interval $-6 < t < 0$. That is to say, in this interval we simply consider the values of y_1 as given by the expression (23b). Then we want by the dynamic equations to determine the solutions numerically from the point $t = 0$ and onwards.

With the numerical constants ε, μ, m, etc., inserted, the dynamic system (where c in (2) is left out) will now be

$$\left\{ \begin{array}{l} y = 0.5x + 10\dot{x} \\ \dot{x} = -0.1x - 0.05z \\ -6\dot{z}_t = y_{t-6} + 0.5(x_t + z_t) \end{array} \right. \tag{24}$$

We shall use (24) for a step-by-step computation. Since $x = 0$ and $\dot{x} = 0.5$ are given at the origin, $z = -10$ may be determined from the second equation in (24). Furthermore, since y_{t-6} is given, we may compute $\dot{z}$ in origin by means of the third equation in (24), and finally y may be computed by the first equation in (24). Thus we have all the items in the first line of Table 2. Since we know x and $\dot{x}$ in origin, we may by a straight linear extrapolation determine x and z in the next point of time, that is to say, in the second line of Table 2. And knowing x and z in this point, we may from the second equation of (24) compute $\dot{x}$. Further, taking the value of y_{t-6} as given also in the next line we can compute $\dot{z}$, etc. In this way we may continue from line to line and determine the development of all the three variables x, y and z. A comparison

TABLE 3

PRIMARY CYCLE COMPUTED DIRECTLY BY FORMULA (23b)

t	x	y	z
0	0	5.0000	—10.0000
0.16667	0.07814	4.4138	— 8.9058
0.33333	0.14581	3.8179	— 7.7817

between the values in Table 2 for x, y and z with the values in Table 3 (determined by the explicit formulae (23b) and represented in Fig. 3) will give an idea of the closeness of the approximation obtained by the numerical step-by-step solution.

V. ERRATIC SHOCKS AS A SOURCE OF ENERGY IN MAINTAINING OSCILLATIONS

The examples we have discussed in the preceding sections, and many other examples of a similar sort that may be constructed, show that when an economic system gives rise to oscillations, these will most frequently be damped. But in reality the cycles we have occasion to observe are generally not damped. How can the maintenance of the swings be explained? Have these dynamic laws deduced from theory and showing damped oscillations no value in explaining the real phenomena, or in what respect do the dynamic laws need to be completed in order to explain the real happenings? I believe that the theoretical dynamic laws do have a meaning—much of the reasoning on which they are based are on *a priori* grounds so plausible that it is too improbable that they will have no significance. But they must not be taken as an immediate explanation of the oscillating phenomena we observe. They only form *one* element of the explanation: they solve the propagation problem. But the impulse problem remains.

There are several alternative ways in which one may approach the impulse problem and try to reconcile the results of the determinate dynamic analysis with the facts. One way which I believe is particularly fruitful and promising is to study what would become of the solution of a determinate dynamic system if it were exposed to a stream of erratic shocks that constantly upsets the continuous evolution, and by so doing introduces into the system the energy necessary to maintain the swings. If fully worked out, I believe that this idea will give an interesting synthesis between the stochastical point of view and the point of view of rigidly determined dynamical laws. In the present section I shall discuss this type of impulse phenomena. In the next I shall consider another type which exhibits another—and perhaps equally important—aspect of the swings we observe in reality.

Knut Wicksell seems to be the first who has been definitely aware of the two types of problems in economic cycle analysis—the propagation problem and the impulse problem—and also the first who has formulated explicitly the theory that the source of energy which maintains the economic cycles are erratic shocks.[5] He conceived more or less definitely of the economic system as being pushed along irregularly, jerkingly. New innovations and exploitations do not come regularly he says. But, on the other hand, these irregular jerks may cause more or less regular cyclical movements. He illustrates it by one of those perfectly simple and yet profound illustrations: "If you hit a wooden rocking-horse with a club, the movement of the horse will be very different to that of the club."

---

[5] See, for instance, his address, "Krisernas gåta," delivered to the Norwegian Economic Society, 1907, *Statsøkonomisk Tidsskrift*, Oslo, 1907, pp. 255–86.

Wicksell's idea on this matter was later taken up by Johan Åkerman, who in his doctorial dissertation[6] discussed the fact that small fluctuations may be able to generate larger ones. He used, among others, the analogy of a stream of water flowing in an uneven river bed. The irregularities of the river bed will cause waves on the surface. The irregularities of the river bed illustrate in Åkerman's theory the seasonal fluctuations; these seasonals, he maintains, create the longer cycles. Unfortunately Åkerman combined these ideas with the idea of a *synchronism* between the shorter fluctuations and the longer ones. He tried, for instance—in my opinion in vain—to prove that there always goes an exact number of seasonal fluctuations to each minor business cycle. This latter idea is, to my mind, very misleading. It is also, as one will readily recognize, in direct opposition to Wicksell's profound remark about the rocking-horse.

Neither Wicksell nor Åkerman had taken up to a closer mathematical study the *mechanism* by which such irregular fluctuations may be transformed into cycles. This problem was attacked independently of each other by Eugen Slutsky[7] and G. Udny Yule.[8] In this connection may also be mentioned a paper by Harold Hotelling.[9]

Slutsky studied experimentally the series obtained by performing iterated differences and summations on random drawings (lottery drawings, etc.). Yule only used second order differences, but tried to interpret the random impulses concretely as shocks hitting an oscillating pendulum. By the experimental numerical work done by these authors, particularly by Slutsky, it was definitely established that some sort of swings will be produced by the accumulation of erratic influences, but the exact and general law telling us what *sort* of cycles that a given kind of accumulation will create was not discovered.

Later certain mathematical results which are of interest in connection with this problem were given by Norbert Wiener.[10]

But still the main problem remained, both with regard to the mechanism by which the *time shapes* of the resulting curves are determined and with regard to the concrete economic interpretation. In the present section I shall offer some remarks on these questions. For a more detailed mathematical analysis the reader is referred to a paper to appear in one of the early numbers of *Econometrica*.

Consider for simplicity an oscillating pendulum whose movement is hampered by friction. If y denotes the deviation of the pendulum from its vertical

---

[6] *Det ekonomiska livets rytmik*, submitted 1925, published Lund, 1928.

[7] *The Summation of Random Causes as the Source of Cyclic Processes*, Vol. III, No. 1, Conjuncture Institute of Moscow, 1927. (Russian with English summary.)

[8] "On a Method of Investigating Periodicity in Disturbed Series," *Trans. Royal Society*, London, A, Vol. 226, 1927.

[9] "Differential Equations Subject to Error," *Journal of the American Statistical Association*, 1927, pp. 283–314.

[10] "Generalized Harmonic Analysis," *Acta Mathematica*, 1930.

position, the equation governing the movement of the pendulum will be

$$\ddot{y} + 2\beta\dot{y} + (\alpha^2 + \beta^2)y = 0 \tag{1}$$

where $\dot{y}$ and $\ddot{y}$ are the first and second derivatives of y with respect to time, and β and α are positive constants, β expressing the strength of the friction. The equation expresses the fact that the net force acting on the pendulum (and being expressed by the acceleration $\ddot{y}$) is made up of two factors. First a factor which tends to make the force proportional to the deviation y (and of opposite sign). This gives the gross force expressed by the last term of the equation. From this gross force must be subtracted the effect of the friction, and this effect is proportional to the *velocity* $\dot{y}$ and is expressed by the second term of the equation.

It is easily verified that the solution of (1) is a function of the form

$$He^{-\beta t} \sin(\phi + \alpha t)$$

where α and β are the constants occurring in (1).

The amplitude H and the phase ϕ are determined by the initial conditions. For our present purpose it is convenient to write the solution in such a way that we can see immediately how the initial conditions determine the curve. If y_0 and $\dot{y}_0$ are the values of y and $\dot{y}$ respectively at the point of time $t = t_0$ the solution may be written in the form

$$y(t) = P(t - t_0) \cdot y_0 + Q(t - t_0) \cdot \dot{y}_0 \tag{2}$$

where $P(\tau)$ and $Q(\tau)$ are two functions independent of the initial conditions and defined by

$$P(\tau) = \frac{\sqrt{\alpha^2 + \beta^2}}{\alpha} e^{-\beta\tau} \sin(v + \alpha\tau) \tag{3}$$

$$Q(\tau) = \frac{1}{\alpha} e^{-\beta\tau} \sin \alpha\tau \tag{4}$$

where

$$\sin v = \frac{\alpha}{\sqrt{\alpha^2 + \beta^2}} \qquad \cos v = \frac{\beta}{\sqrt{\alpha^2 + \beta^2}} \tag{5}$$

By convention the square root in (3) and (5) may be chosen positive. By insertion into the equation (1) it is easily verified that (2) is a function that satisfies the equation and the specified initial condition. $P(\tau)$ may be looked upon as the solution of (1), which is equal to unity and whose derivative is equal to zero at the origin $\tau = 0$, and $Q(\tau)$ may be looked upon as the solution which is equal to zero and whose derivative is equal to unity at the origin. These functions satisfy indeed the equation, and we have

$$\begin{cases} P(0) = 1 & \qquad Q(0) = 0 \\ \dot{P}(0) = 0 & \qquad \dot{Q}(0) = 1 \end{cases} \tag{6}$$

Suppose that the pendulum starts with the specified initial conditions at the point of time t_0 and that it is hit at the points of time t_1, $t_2 \cdots t_n$ by shocks which may be directed either in the positive or in the negative sense and that may have arbitrary strengths. Let y_k and $\dot{y}_k$ be the ordinate and the velocity of the pendulum immediately before it is hit by the shock number k. The ordinate y_k is not changed by the shock, but the velocity is suddenly changed from $\dot{y}_k$ to $\dot{y}_k + e_k$, where e_k is the strength of the shock; mechanically expressed it is the quantity of motion divided by the mass of the pendulum. The concrete interpretation of the shock e_k does not interest us for the moment. The essential thing to notice is that at the point of time t_k the only thing that happens is that the velocity is increased by a constant e_k. Let us consider separately the effects produced by the two terms $\dot{y}_k$ and e_k. From (2) we see that the initial conditions enter linearly. Consequently we can consider $\dot{y}_k$ and e_k as two independent contributions to the later ordinates of the variable. In other words, the fact of the shock may simply be represented by letting the original pendulum move on undisturbed but letting a *new* pendulum start at the point of time t_k with an ordinate equal to zero and a velocity equal to e_k. This argument may be applied to all the points of time. We simply have to start in each of the points of time t_1, $t_2 \cdots t_n$ a new pendulum with an ordinate equal to zero and a velocity equal to the strength of the shock occurring at that moment, and then let all these pendulums continue their undisturbed motion into the future. The sum of the ordinates of all these pendulums at any given point of time t will then be the same as the ordinate $y(t)$ of a single pendulum which has been subject to all the shocks. In other words, the ordinate $y(t)$ will simply be

$$y(t) = P(t - t_0) \cdot y_0 + Q(t - t_0)\dot{y}_0 + \sum_{k=1}^{n} Q(t - t_k)e_k \qquad (7)$$

If the point t is very far from the initial point t_0, and if β is positive so that there is actually a dampening, then the influence of the initial situation y_0 and $\dot{y}_0$ on the ordinate $y(t)$ will be negligible, that is, the ordinate will be

$$y(t) = \sum_{k=1}^{n} Q(t - t_k) \cdot e_k \qquad (8)$$

This means that the ordinate $y(t)$ of the pendulum at a given moment will simply be the *cumulation* of the effects of the shocks, the cumulation being made according to a system of weights. And these weights are simply the shape of the function $Q(\tau)$. That is to say, $y(t)$ is the result of applying a linear operator to the shocks, and *the system of weights in the operator will simply be given by the shape of the time curve that would have been the solution of the determinate dynamic system in case the movement had been allowed to go on undisturbed.*

The fundamental question which arises is, therefore: If we perform a cumulation where the weights have the form $Q(\tau)$, what sort of time shape will

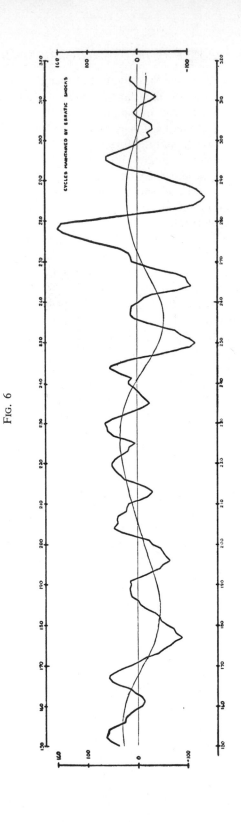

FIG. 6

the function $y(t)$ get? The answer to this question is given by studying the effects of linear operators on erratic shocks. The result of this analysis is that the time shape of the curve will be a *changing harmonic* with the same frequency α as the one occurring in $Q(\tau)$. By a changing harmonic I understand a curve that is moving more or less regularly in cycles, the length of the period and also the amplitude being to some extent variable, these variations taking place, however, within such limits that it is reasonable to speak of an *average* period and an *average* amplitude. In other words, there is created just the kind of curves which we know from actual statistical observation. I shall not attempt to give any formal proof of these facts here. A detailed proof, together with extensive numerical computations, will be given in the above-mentioned paper to appear in *Econometrica*. Here I shall confine myself to reproducing the graph (see Fig. 6) of a changing harmonic produced experimentally as the cumulation of erratic impulses, the weight function being of the form (4).

Thus, by connecting the two ideas: (1) the continuous solution of a determinate dynamic system and (2) the discontinuous shocks intervening and supplying the energy that may maintain the swings—we get a theoretical set-up which seems to furnish a rational interpretation of those movements which we have been accustomed to see in our statistical time data. The solution of the determinate dynamic system only furnishes a part of the explanation: it determines the *weight system* to be used in the cumulation of the erratic shocks. The other and equally important part of the explanation lies in the elucidation of the general laws governing the effect produced by linear operations performed on erratic shocks.

VI. THE INNOVATIONS AS A FACTOR IN MAINTAINING OSCILLATIONS

The idea of erratic shocks represents one very essential aspect of the impulse problem in economic cycle analysis, but probably it does not contain the whole explanation. There is also present another source of energy operating in a more continuous fashion and being more intimately connected with the permanent evolution in human societies. The nature of this influence may perhaps be best exhibited by interpreting it in the light of Schumpeter's theory of the innovations and their role in the cyclical movement of economic life. Schumpeter has emphasized the influence of new ideas, new initiatives, the discovery of new technical procedures, new financial organizations, etc., on the course of the cycle. He insists in particular on the fact that these new ideas accumulate in a more or less continuous fashion, but are put into practical application on a larger scale only during certain phases of the cycle. It is like a force that is released during these phases, and this force is the source of energy that maintains the oscillations. This idea is also very similar to an idea developed by the Norwegian economist, Einar Einarsen.[11] In mathematical language one could perhaps say that one introduces here the idea of an auto-maintained oscillation.

Schumpeter's idea may perhaps be best explained by a mechanical analogy. Personally, I have found this illustration very useful. Indeed it is only after I had constructed this analogy that I really succeeded in understanding Schumpeter's idea. After long conversations and correspondence with Professor Schumpeter I believe the analogy may be taken as a fair representation of his point of view.

Suppose that we have a pendulum freely suspended to a pivot. Above the pendulum is fixed a receptacle where there is water. A small pipe descends all along the pendulum, and at the lower end of the pendulum the pipe opens with a valve which has a peculiar way of functioning. The opening of the valve points towards the left and is larger when the pendulum moves towards the right than when it moves towards the left. Concretely one may, for example, assume that the valve is influenced by the air resistance or by some other factor that determines the opening of the valve as a function of the velocity of the pendulum. Finally we assume that the water in the receptacle is fed from a constantly running stream which is given as a function of time. The stream may, for instance, be a constant.

Now, if the instrument is let loose it is easy to see what will happen. The water will descend through the pipe, and the force of reaction at the lower end of the pendulum created by the fact that the water is emptying through the valve will push the pendulum towards the right, and this movement will continue until the force of gravitation has become large enough to pull the pendulum back again towards its equilibrium point. During the return the opening of the valve and consequently the force that tends to push the pendulum towards the right will diminish, and thus the movement back towards the central position will be accelerated. The pendulum which is now returning with considerable speed will work up an amount of inertia that will push it behind its equilibrium point away over to a position at the left, here again the gravitation will start to pull it back towards the centre, and now the valve will widen, and by doing so will increase the force which accelerates the movement towards the right. In this way the movement will continue, and it will continue even although friction is present. One could even imagine that the movement would be more than maintained, i.e. that the oscillations would become wilder and wilder until the instrument breaks down. In order to avoid such a catastrophe one may of course, if necessary, add a dampening mechanism which would tend to stabilize the movement so that the amplitude did not go beyond a certain limit.

The meaning of the various features of this instrument as an illustration of economic life is obvious. The water accumulating in the receptacle above the

---

[11] *Gode og daarlige tider*, Oslo, 1904.

pendulum are the Schumpeterian innovations. To begin with they are kept a certain time without being utilized. Some of them will perhaps never be utilized, which is illustrated by the fact that some of the atoms in the receptacle will rest there indefinitely. But some others will descend down the pipe, which illustrates that these new ideas are utilized in economic life. This utilization constitutes the new energy which maintains the oscillations.

The instrument as thus conceived will give a picture of the *oscillations* but not of the secular or perhaps supersecular tendency of evolutions. This tendency seems to us to be irreversible because we have not yet lived long enough to see the decline. It is not difficult to complete the instrument in such a way that it will express also this secular or supersecular movement. We may, for instance, imagine that the pivot to which the pendulum is suspended is not fixed but slides in a crack in the wall, the crack ascending towards the right. This being so, the whole instrument will move by jumps, and each jump will carry it to a higher position than before. We only have to feed the instrument by a constantly running stream of water. The impulsion which the water creates as it leaves the valve will maintain the oscillations, and these oscillations will constitute the jumps which carry the instrument steadily to higher levels. Thus there will be an intimate connection between the oscillations and the irreversible evolution.

It would be possible to put the functioning of this whole instrument into equations under more or less simplified assumptions about the construction and functioning of the valve, etc. I even think this will be a useful task for a further analysis of economic oscillations, but I do not intend to take up this mathematical formulation here.

10

Measurement without Theory*[1]

By *TJALLING C. KOOPMANS*†

THE EMPIRICAL APPROACH

WHEN TYCHO BRAHÉ and Johannes Kepler engaged in the systematic labor of measuring the positions of the planets, and charting their orbits, they started with conceptions and models of the planetary system which later proved incorrect in some aspects, irrelevant in others. Tycho always, and Kepler initially, believed in uniform circular motion as the natural basic principle underlying the course of celestial bodies. Tycho's main contribution was a systematic accumulation of careful measurements. Kepler's outstanding success was due to a willingness to strike out for new models and hypotheses if such were needed to account for the observations obtained. He was able to find simple empirical "laws" which were in accord with past observations and permitted the prediction of future observations. This achievement was a triumph for the approach in which large scale gathering, sifting, and scrutinizing of facts precedes, or proceeds independently of, the formulation of theories and their testing by further facts.

The book by Burns and Mitchell,[2] discussed here, approaches the problems of cyclical fluctuations in economic variables in the same empirical spirit. The book has two main purposes: first, a detailed exposition, with experimental applications, of the methods of measuring cyclical behavior, developed by the National Bureau of Economic Research; secondly, a search, with the help of these methods, for possible changes in cyclical behavior of economic variables over time, whether gradual, abrupt, in longer cycles, or otherwise.

---

* *The Review of Economic Statistics*, Vol. XXIX (August, 1947). Reprinted by courtesy of *The Review of Economics and Statistics* and the author.

† Yale University.

[1] This article was reprinted as part of Cowles Commission Papers, New Series, No. 25. I am indebted to several friends, including Dr. A. F. Burns, for comments on an earlier draft. These comments have helped me to bring out more clearly the issues raised in this review, for which, of course, I remain exclusively responsible. T.C.K.

[2] Arthur F. Burns and Wesley C. Mitchell, *Measuring Business Cycles* (National Bureau of Economic Research, Studies in Business Cycles, No. 2) (New York, 1946).

The approach of the authors is here described as empirical in the following sense: The various choices as to what to "look for," what economic phenomena to observe, and what measures to define and compute, are made with a minimum of assistance from theoretical conceptions or hypotheses regarding the nature of the economic processes by which the variables studied are generated.

In fact, Burns and Mitchell are more consistently empiricist than Kepler was. The latter made no secret of his predilection for the principle of circular motion until observations spoke decisively for the elliptical orbit. He held other speculative views as to the role of the five regular solids and of musical intervals in the proportions of the planetary system, which now appear as irrelevant. Burns and Mitchell do not reveal at all in this book what explanations of cyclical fluctuations, if any, they believe to constitute plausible models or hypotheses.

The undertaking commands respect, and the precedent holds great promise: For, in due course, the theorist Newton was inspired to formulate the fundamental laws of attraction of matter, which contain the empirical regularities of planetary motion discovered by Kepler as direct and natural consequences. The terms "empirical regularities" and "fundamental laws" are used suggestively to describe the "Kepler stage" and the "Newton stage" of the development of celestial mechanics. It is not easy to specify precisely what is the difference between the two stages. Newton's law of gravitation can also be looked upon as describing an empirical regularity in the behavior of matter. The conviction that this "law" is in some sense more fundamental, and thus constitutes progress over the Kepler stage, is due, I believe, to its being at once more elementary and more general. It is more elementary in that a simple property of mere matter is postulated. As a result, it is more general in that it applies to all matter, whether assembled in planets, comets, sun or stars, or in terrestrial objects—thus explaining a much wider range of phenomena.

It appears to be the intention of Burns and Mitchell—in any case it is the opinion of the present reviewer—that their book represent an important contribution to the "Kepler stage" of inquiry in the field of economics. It is concerned exclusively with cyclical fluctuations. Its hypotheses are concerned with the character of such fluctuations, rather than with the underlying economic behavior of man.

The auspicious precedent in the history of celestial mechanics suggests that this is a promising procedure, which may expect to be rewarded in due course by further development of theory. Nevertheless, this reviewer believes that in research in economic dynamics the Kepler stage and the Newton stage of inquiry need to be more intimately combined and to be pursued simultaneously. Fuller utilization of the concepts and hypotheses of economic theory (in a sense described below) *as a part of the processes of observation and measurement* promises to be a shorter road, perhaps even the only possible road, to the understanding of cyclical fluctuations. Such a course, in addition, promises as by-products greater insight into noncyclical and even nondynamic problems of economics.

While a systematic argument in support of this position would surpass the bounds of a review, I shall attempt to adduce some of the arguments in the course of this discussion of the book. It is then my duty to point out in what respects, in my opinion, the present state of business cycle analysis differs from the situation in which Tycho and Kepler approached the phenomenon of planetary motion. I hasten to add that the parallel with the classical problems of celestial mechanics is not mentioned by, and may not have been in the minds of, the authors. It is merely the best example, known to the reviewer, of a case where the empirical approach paved the way for the discovery of fundamental laws.

The example has been selected because it is favorable to the empiricist position. Needless to say, the history of science knows of many cases in which "fundamental" hypotheses, more or less integrated into a theory of the phenomena studied, have played a much larger role. However, the spectacular success, achieved in the case here chosen as an example, has set a pattern which has ever since, consciously or unconsciously, been in the minds of scientific workers in widely diverse fields.

MEASURES OF CYCLICAL "BEHAVIOR"

The authors formulate their objective in the following terms:

> Whatever their working concepts, . . . , all investigators cherish the same ultimate aim—namely, to attain better understanding of the recurrent fluctuations in economic fortune that modern nations experience. This aim may be pursued in many ways. The way we have chosen is to observe the business cycles of history as closely and systematically as we can before making a fresh attempt to explain them (p. 4).

The point of departure is a definition of business cycles, derived from experience, and to be tested in the light of further experience:

> Business cycles are a type of fluctuation found in the aggregate economic activity of nations that organize their work mainly in business enterprises: a cycle consists of expansions occurring at about the same time in many economic activities, followed by similarly general recessions, contractions, and revivals which merge into the expansion phase of the next cycle; this sequence of changes is recurrent but not periodic; in duration business cycles vary from more than one year to ten or twelve years; they are not divisible into shorter cycles of similar character with amplitudes approximating their own (p. 3).

As is often the case in statistical work, a vast amount of data—represented here by (mostly monthly) observations of many economic variables over long periods—is to be reduced and summarized by computing a smaller number of "derived" measures, incorporating what is relevant and informative, omitting what is accidental or devoid of interest. The first eight chapters essentially consist in making reasoned choices as to what measures are relevant and informative. In that undertaking, the definition just quoted—itself the result of an earlier volume by Mitchell in the same series—is the main guide.

The *first* group of measures selected concerns location in time and duration. For each variable, lower and upper turning points are determined, as well as time intervals between them (expansion, contraction, trough-to-trough duration of *specific* cycles). In addition, turning points and durations are determined for *reference* cycles, i.e., points around which the corresponding specific cycle turning points of a great many variables are concentrated. Leads and lags are found as differences between corresponding specific cycle and reference cycle turning points. All turning points are determined after elimination of seasonal variation but without prior trend elimination, using as much as possible monthly or otherwise quarterly data.

The *second* group of measures relates to movements of one variable within one cycle, which may be either a cycle specific to that variable, or a reference cycle. For the computation of these measures, each variable is expressed in percent of its mean over the cycle concerned—a procedure which eliminates intercycle trend but preserves intracycle trend. For each cycle, a pattern of nine successive "standings" is then computed, i.e., a sequence of nine averages, indicated by Roman numerals, of which I, V, and IX are generally three-month averages centered at successive trough, peak, and trough months, respectively, and those numbered II, III, IV, and VI, VII, VIII are averages arising from subdivision, into three approximately equal parts, of the intermediate periods of expansion and contraction, respectively. The result is a specific cycle pattern, or a reference cycle pattern, of the variable concerned, depending on what kind of turning points were employed. These patterns are plotted on a time scale reflecting whatever inequality there is in duration between expansion and contraction. For specific cycles the following measures of amplitude are considered: "rise" $(V - I)$, "fall" $(V - IX)$, and "rise and fall" $(2V - I - IX)$, both in absolute terms, and on a per month basis to indicate steepness of rise and fall. Reference cycle amplitudes are computed in a similar manner, but the three stages involved are not necessarily the reference stages I, V, IX, but rather such reference cycle stages (with constant Roman numeral) as are most frequently or closely coincident in timing with specific cycle stages I, V, IX.

The foregoing measures have been described for a single cycle. Averages of these measures for a sequence of cycles are likewise computed, and are qualified by presenting the average deviation as a measure of variation between cycles.

The *third* group of measures expresses conformity of specific cycles of a variable to business cycles. These comprise ratios of average reference cycle amplitudes to average specific cycle amplitudes of the same variable, for expansions and contractions combined. They further comprise indexes of conformity expressing the proportion of all reference cycles covered in which the signs of (V − I), of (V − IX), and of (V − I)-per-month plus (V − IX)-per-month, respectively, are positive. In order to do justice to cases where specific cycles show regular lags or leads in relation to reference cycles, these measures are supplemented by similar conformity measures in which the reference cycle standings I, V, and IX are replaced by the three reference cycle standings described above, selected to reflect the average lag or lead shown by each type of specific turning point.

This somewhat lengthy, though still incomplete, enumeration of the various measures employed may serve to show the main preoccupation of the authors: faithful observation and summarizing of the cyclical characteristics of a large number of economic series. The tool kit of the theoretical economist is deliberately spurned. Not a single demand or supply schedule or other equation expressing the behavior of men or the technical laws of production is employed explicitly in the book, and the cases of implicit use are few and far between.

THE DIFFICULTIES OF INQUIRY WITHOUT PRECONCEPTIONS

As indicated above, I am here concerned mainly with evaluating this empiricist position taken by the authors, and with showing its implications and limitations. My *first argument*, then, is that even for the purpose of systematic and large scale observation of such a many-sided phenomenon, theoretical preconceptions about its nature cannot be dispensed with, and the authors do so only to the detriment of the analysis. It has already been mentioned that the latter and more interesting part of the book (Chapters 9–12) is devoted to a search for possible changes in cyclical "behavior" over time, with a view to qualifying the meaning of average measures of cyclical "behavior" computed from a sequence of cycles. This analysis employs the following seven series, arranged here as classified on page 372:

Relating to	Series
Durable goods market	1. Pig iron production
	2. Railroad freight car orders
Money market	3. Yields of high-grade railroad bonds[3]
	4. Call money rates[3]
Stock market	5. Railroad stock prices[3]
	6. Number of shares traded[3]
Volume of payments	7. Deflated bank clearings

There is no systematic discussion of the reasons for selecting these particular variables as most worthy of study. As a justification for this choice the following few lines are given on page 384:

These series cover processes that rank high among the activities stressed in theoretical studies of business cycles. Partly for this reason, partly because of the comparatively long stretch of time covered by these records, we regard our small sample as fairly satisfactory for the present purpose.

---

[3] Quoted on New York Stock Exchange.

The choices made may have been the best possible ones. But "good" choices means relevant choices. What is relevant can only be determined with the help of some notions as to the generation of economic fluctuations, and as to their impact on society. In the light of such notions, wide fluctuations in call money rates may be unimportant if total employment is relatively stable. Fluctuations in the production of durable producers' goods would be less serious if they were approximately offset by opposite fluctuations in the production of consumers' goods. The choices as to what variables to study cannot be settled by a brief reference to "theoretical studies of business cycles." These issues call for a systematic argument to show that the best use has been made of available data in relation to the most important aspects of the phenomena studied.

Earlier in the book (pp. 71–76), some discussion is indeed devoted to the "meaning" of individual variables, in particular with a view to determining whether a single variable or aggregate might be used to locate turning points of reference cycles. The shortness of the periods for which broad aggregates— like national income, an index of total production, or employment—are available rules out such series for all purposes requiring a long period of observation. But the use of a small number of aggregates is also warned against as being insufficient in principle. This question, it seems to me, admits of different answers in different cases, depending on the scope, the objective, and the underlying assumptions of each particular piece of analysis.

The lack of guidance from theoretical considerations is perceivable also in the choice of the measures computed from the variables selected. These are intended to be measures of cyclical "behavior." The use of the term "behavior" does not mean, however, that the authors intend to study the behavior of groups of economic agents (consumers, workers, entrepreneurs, dealers, etc.) whose modes of action and response, in the social organization and technological environment of the society studied, are the ultimate determinants of the levels of economic variables as well as their fluctuations. Instead, they study the "behavior" (in a more mechanical sense) of certain measurable joint effects of several of those actions and responses. This shift of attention from underlying human responses to their combined effects is a decisive step. It eliminates all benefits, described more fully below, that might be received from economic theory—by which I mean in this context the theoretical analysis of the aggregate effects of assumed patterns of economic behavior of groups of individuals. It also divorces the study of fluctuations from the explanation of the levels or trends around which the variables fluctuate, since such theoretical analysis is needed to bring out the common features in both groups of problems.

The rejection of the help that economic theorizing might give leaves a void. For now there is a need for some organizing principle to determine on what aspects of the observed variables attention should be concentrated. Here the definition of business cycles quoted above comes into operation. But it does not quite fill the gap. It does not become altogether clear why the cyclical forms of movement should receive such exclusive attention. With the great variety in types of movement in the real world, it is not even always clear what a cycle is. The gap left by the barring of explicit formal theory is thus filled with methodological quasi-theory concerned with delineating the object of study. There are lengthy discussions of questions like these: What is a turning point? When is a certain movement of a variable to be recognized as a specific cycle? (pp. 61–62). When are certain concurrent movements of a number of variables to be recognized as a business cycle? (pp. 87–94). In first instance the criteria employed are mechanical applications of clauses in the definition of business cycles quoted above, like limitations on the length of time between two successive turning points, or the rule that no "cycle" be divisible into shorter cycles with amplitudes approximating its own (even if those shorter cycles would escape recognition because of their shortness). Difficulties then arise in periods of war or important changes in economic policies. Reference is made to judgment and indeed to explanatory factors where those are clearly visible (tie-ups through weather or strike, economic effects of war, changing policies in the early "new deal" period). Arbitrary formal criteria are here combined with good though incidental pieces of causal analysis to answer what are, in frequent borderline cases, essentially irrelevant questions. The authors' insistence on seeing, counting, and measuring cycles before anything else reminds one of Kepler's preference for circular motion.

A similar group of questions, sometimes permitting only arbitrary answers, arises in deciding how to match the cycles specific to one variable with recognized business cycles, for certain comparisons. One of these questions is whether the variable concerned is to be treated on a positive (i.e., trough-to-trough cycle) or on an inverted (peak-to-peak) plan. We learn on page 115 the highly interesting fact that raw material stocks held by manufacturers tend to be positively related to business cycles, whereas stocks of finished products tend to be related invertedly. The authors do not at this stage ask for the motives or determining factors of this behavior of dealers or manufacturers. Instead they discuss formal rules to establish positive or inverted "behavior" of a variable on the basis of frequencies of concurrent or opposite directions of movement.

On the whole, the same measures are computed for all variables studied, irrespective of their economic nature. The importance of the economic phenomenon expressed by any particular variable is duly stressed (pp. 140–41) with reference to the interpretation to be placed on the measures computed, but is in general not permitted to influence the choice of measures used. An exception is found in the discussion of criteria for positive or inverted treatment, which contains hints of postulated behavior relationships (p. 117). This analysis would need to be made more explicit to remove the impression that somewhat scholastic distinctions are used in the discussion of how to relate specific and reference cycles (p. 118).

The notion of a reference cycle itself implies the assumption of an essentially one-dimensional basic pattern of cyclical fluctuation, a background pattern around which the movements of individual variables are arranged in a manner dependent on their specific nature as well as on accidental circumstances. (There is a similarity here with Spearman's psychological hypothesis of a single mental factor common to all abilities.) This "one-dimensional" hypothesis may be a good first approximation, in the same sense in which the assumption of circular motion provides a good first approximation to the orbits of the planets. It must be regarded, however, as an assumption of the "Kepler stage," based on observation of many series without reference to the underlying economic behavior of individuals. It is in this sense, I believe, that the authors refer (p. 3) to their definition of business cycles as "a tool of research, similar to many definitions used by observational sciences, and like its analogues subject to revision or abandonment if not borne out by observation." I believe that the authors would not object to the addition: "or by the logical implications of observations of a wider range of phenomena."

SCANT GUIDANCE FOR MAKERS OF POLICIES

The examples given illustrate the authors' scientific strategy, in which measurement and observation precede, and are largely independent of, any attempts toward the explanation of economic fluctuations. The plan of inquiry envisaged by the National Bureau is therefore to follow up the present methodological work by a series of monographs in which the techniques of measurement developed are applied comparatively to various industries, countries, or broad markets. Ultimately, it is intended to "weave the results established by the monographs together with existing knowledge into a theoretical account of how business cycles run their course."[4]

The wording of this statement of intentions still admits of the interpretation that even the ultimate objective of the authors is only a generalizing description of the typical course of a business cycle. However, I believe, and will assume for the purpose of this discussion, that more is meant, namely, a genuine explanation of economic fluctuations, i.e., an explanation in which only extra-economic phenomena are accepted as "data" without further inquiry, all relevant economic phenomena being subject to explanation in terms of assumed behavior patterns of men in a given institutional and technological environment. I am not sure whether a still further objective is included, which extrapolates the idea of explanation: the prediction, within the narrowest attainable limits of error, of the effects of stated hypothetical measures of economic policy on the level and movements of economic variables. However, I feel that such prediction is actually the most important

---

[4] P. 22. A less ambitious "preview" of this final volume is promised shortly under the title *What Happens During Business Cycles: A Progress Report*, by Wesley C. Mitchell.

objective of the analysis of economic fluctuations. The criterion of social usefulness of scientific analysis gives us the right to discuss the merits of any particular approach to the problem of economic fluctuation on the basis of the guidance it gives to economic policy, even if such guidance were not claimed by the authors.

Let us, then, now consider the question whether the development that led from the empirical regularities observed by Kepler to the general theory of gravity discovered by Newton might find a counterpart in similar discovery of the laws of economic motion on the basis of carefully described regularities. I shall mention and discuss a few important differences between the two scientific situations.

Newton's achievement was based, not only on the regularities observed by Kepler, but also on the experiments conducted on the surface of the earth by Galileo. Economists are not in a position to perform experiments with an economic system as a whole for the sole purpose of establishing scientific truth (although deliberate changes in parts of the system have been under-taken at various occasions for other than scientific purposes, and have in-cidentally added to our information). It is therefore not possible in many economic problems to separate "causes" and "effects" by varying causes one at a time, studying the separate effect of each cause—a method so fruitful in the natural sciences.

On the other hand, economists do possess more elaborate and better established theories of economic behavior than the theories of motion of material bodies known to Kepler. These economic theories are based on evidence of a different kind than the observations embodied in time series: knowledge of the motives and habits of consumers and of the profit-making objectives of business enterprise, based partly on introspection, partly on interview or on inferences from observed actions of individuals—briefly, a more or less systematized knowledge of man's behavior and its motives. While much in these theories is incomplete and in need of reformulation and elabora-tion (particularly in regard to behavior over time under conditions of un-certainty), such theory as we have is an indispensable element in understanding in a quantitative way the formation of economic variables. For according to that theory the relevant economic variables are determined by the simul-taneous validity of an equal number of "structural" equations (of behavior, of law or rule, of technology). The very fact that so many relations are simul-taneously valid makes the observation of any one of them difficult, and sometimes even impossible. For any observed regularity between simultaneous and/or successive values of certain variables may have to be ascribed to the validity of several structural equations rather than any one of them. The mere observation of regularities in the interrelations of variables then does not permit us to recognize or to identify behavior equations among such regular-ities. In the absence of experimentation, such identification is possible, if at all, only if the form of each structural equation is specified, i.e., in particular, if we can indicate the set of variables involved in each equation, and perhaps also the manner in which they are to be combined. In each case, a preliminary study of the system of structural equations held applicable is required to decide whether the specifications regarding any particular equation are sufficiently detailed to permit its identification. Without such identification, measurement of the structural equation involved is not possible, and should therefore not be attempted.

One might object: why should measurement of the behavior equations of consumers, workers, entrepreneurs be necessary? If observed regularities are due to the simultaneous validity of several behavior equations, these regularities will persist as long as each of the underlying (unknown) behavior patterns persists. However, there are important arguments to counter this objection. Sheer scientific curiosity still urges us on to penetrate to the underlying structural equations. This curiosity is reinforced and justified (if you wish) by the awareness that knowledge of the behavior patterns will help in understanding or analyzing different situations, for instance, problems of secular trend, or cyclical problems in other countries or periods—in the same way (although one would not expect with the same exactness) in which the law of gravitation explains celestial and terrestrial phenomena alike. This point has particular relevance with regard to the different situations expected to arise in an impending future period of the same country that has been studied. Behavior patterns are subject to change: gradually through changing habits and tastes, urbanization and industrialization; gradually or unevenly through technological change; abruptly through economic policies or the economic effects of political events. While one particular behavior pattern may be deemed fairly stable over a certain period, a much greater risk is involved in assuming that a whole system of structural equations is stable over time. An observed regularity not traced to underlying behavior patterns, institutional rules, and laws of production is therefore an instrument of unknown reliability. The predictions it yields cannot be qualified with the help even of known trends in behavior or technology. It is of no help whatever in assessing the probable effects of stated economic policies or institutional changes.

There is no sign in the book of an awareness of the problems of determining the identifiability of, and measuring, structural equations as a prerequisite to the practically important types of prediction. Measurable effects of economic actions are scrutinized, to all appearance, in almost complete detachment from any knowledge we may have of the motives of such actions. The movements of economic variables are studied as if they were the eruptions of a mysterious volcano whose boiling caldron can never be penetrated. There is no explicit discussion at all of the problem of prediction, its possibilities and limitations, with or without structural change, although surely the history of the volcano is important primarily as a key to its future activities. There is no discussion whatever as to what bearing the methods used, and the provisional results reached, may have on questions of economic policy.

This, then, is my *second argument* against the empiricist position: Without resort to theory, in the sense indicated, conclusions relevant to the guidance of economic policies cannot be drawn.

CHANGES IN CYCLICAL "BEHAVIOR" OVER TIME

There is a highly interesting analysis in the last four chapters, already referred to, in which the following question is treated (phrasing by the reviewer): Is there evidence that such structural changes as have taken place during the period studied have led to changes in cyclical "behavior" of the variables studied? A search is made (Chapter 10) for secular changes, in duration, amplitude (absolute and per month) and timing of the specific cycles, and in the pattern of reference cycles, of the seven American variables selected for intensive study. A hypothesis by Mills linking durations of business cycles in various countries to stages of industrialization, and the hypothesis of a break in average duration and amplitude of specific cycles of the seven American series due to the first world war are tested. A search is also made (Chapter 11) for long cycles in cyclical characteristics. Possible statistical connections with the long wave in building activity, and various long cycle hypotheses formulated by Wardwell, Kondratieff, Schumpeter, and Kitchin, respectively, are tested.

There appears to be a tendency in this chapter to select a hypothesis for testing because it has been stated in a scientific publication rather than on the basis of possible arguments in favor of it. Nevertheless, the hypotheses (granted that they concern the "behavior" of variables rather than of men) cover a wide range of possibilities. In particular the hypotheses of secular trend in cyclical characteristics, that of a break in structure due to war, and that of an influence of the long cycle in construction are of great theoretical and practical interest.

The most remarkable outcome of this whole group of tests is the extent to which mild traces of systematic change, of one type or another, in cyclical "behavior" are almost drowned by wide and apparently random variability between cycles. It is true that interesting particular changes are found. Money markets are found more susceptible to secular changes in cyclical behavior than industrial or security markets. The lead in the cyclical revival of pig iron production and freight car orders in early cycles is found to have disappeared in later cycles. The latter effect may be wholly or partly an automatical result of a diminishing rate of growth, given the fact that turning points are defined without prior elimination of secular trend.[5] It would indeed be interesting to determine whether the gradual decrease in cyclical lead would remain if turning points were determined after trend elimination.

---

[5] See the discussion in Chapter 7, Section III.

If so, there is a parallel phenomenon in the gradual decrease in the responsiveness of demand for railway rolling stock to changes in traffic and profitability, in the United Kingdom during a period preceding the first world war, apparently from one of Tinbergen's investigations.[6]

One of the results interpreted as a possible sign of longer cycles in cyclical behavior might be merely the effect of considerable random variation between cycles, combined with correlation between the various characteristics of a cycle. I am referring to the differences found between average characteristics of the first and last cycles of groups of successive cycles separated by severe depressions. For such averages are obtained by a process of selection of cycles that start and end, respectively, in especially deep depressions. The authors stress this selection effect when they deal with Schumpeter's hypothesis that each Juglar cycle contains three Kitchin cycles, but do not seem to give it sufficient emphasis in relation to their own grouping of cycles just described.[7]

However this may be, any systematic effects present are found to be greatly obscured and dominated by random variation of the characteristics of individual cycles. The authors themselves express surprise (p. 413) at the slight manifestations of structural change (other than mere growth, largely eliminated by the use of relatives to cycle means) in data covering a period known to have witnessed thoroughgoing changes in economic organization. They state their intention to press the search for secular changes in cyclical behavior in subsequent studies concerned with particular industries or markets.

ISOLATING THE SOURCES OF RANDOM VARIATION

The presence of random variability in economic data gives rise to methodological requirements which do not arise in the study of planetary motion. In the latter case, the phenomenon studied can for all practical purposes be treated as a deterministic process, with some randomness entering into the data only through errors of measurement. In dynamic economics, the phenomenon itself is either essentially a stochastic process or needs to be treated as such because of the great number of factors at work.[8] Hence the analysis and interpretation of economic data call for the application of the methods of statistical inference.

---

[6] J. Tinbergen, *Statistical Testing of Business Cycle Theories: I. A Method and Its Application to Investment Activity*, Graph V.2 on page 120.

[7] I do not understand the reasoning at the top of page 460, where evidence independent of selection is claimed.

[8] It has been stated by H. Hotelling ("Differential Equations Subject to Error and Population Estimates," *Journal of the American Statistical Association*, Vol. 22, 1927, pp. 283–314, quotation on p. 287), that celestial mechanics would for the same reason have developed as a statistical science, had the "solar" system to which the earth belongs contained several bodies of mass comparable to that of the sun. The full quotation is given and commented on by H. T. Davis, *The Analysis of Economic Time Series* (Bloomington, Indiana, 1941), see pp. 2–4.

The main problem of inference is the choice of "statistics," i.e., those functions of the observations—fewer in number than the observations themselves—which are to be used for estimation of parameters or for the testing of hypotheses. The question should therefore now be raised whether the authors' finding of strong domination of random variation over possible traces of systematic change in cyclical "behavior" is not at least partly due to the choice of the particular "statistics" studied. At the risk of becoming monotonous, I wish to state that explicit dynamic theory of the formation of economic variables is needed to throw light on this question. Most theories of this kind recently constructed have in common the attempt to describe the fluctuating economy by a complete system of structural equations which, as to their form, are stochastic difference equations. They are difference equations (embodying dynamic theory), in that they describe responses subject to time lags: past values of economic variables affect current actions of individuals. They are stochastic equations in that the behavior of any group of individuals, and the outcome of any production process, is determined in part by many minor factors, further scrutiny of which is either impossible or unrewarding. Such further scrutiny is not necessary provided that the analysis of each structural equation be pushed to the point where the joint effect of unanalyzed factors can indeed be regarded as random (if not necessarily independent) drawings from a reasonably stable probability distribution. To attain this end, it is often necessary to introduce explicitly so-called "exogenous variables," representing the effects of wars, political events, population growth, economic policies, or technological developments which are not routine responses to economic conditions, etc.

Systems of this kind may possess a tendency for the variables to evolve in cyclical movements. Even if the random disturbances (or shocks) in individual equations possess a fairly stable distribution, however, there is no need for the ensuing cycles to be very regular or similar in duration or amplitude. Current values of economic variables are the cumulative effect both of a sequence of random shocks over the recent past, and of the impulses exerted by exogenous variables in the recent past.[9] Because of this tendency to cumulation of effects, relatively small shocks may have considerable effects over time on such "cyclical characteristics" as duration and amplitudes of cycles. Also, different impulses exerted successively by the same exogenous variables may produce different cycles of quite diverse appearance.

Now any rigorous testing of hypotheses according to modern methods of statistical inference requires a specification of the form of the joint probability distribution of the variables. In principle, such specification does not need to take on a "parametric" form, as when linear, parabolic or exponential

---

[9] How long this "recent past" is to be taken depends on the degree of damping of the system, which in turn depends on the parameters or curves representing the several structural equations.

functions, or normal distributions, are specified—although parametric assumptions usually admit more accurate estimation or more powerful tests whenever they are justified. In any case, however, it is necessary to hypothesize in what manner randomness enters into the formation of economic variables. It is for this reason that the form of each structural equation should be specified and/or determined to the point where at least a conceptual isolation of the random influences at work is attained.

The authors do not discuss randomness in terms of a definite distributional hypothesis, although the idea of random factors as one of the determinants of economic variables is clearly in their minds.[10] They accordingly recognize (p. 392) that the analysis of variance tests applied by them to durations, amplitudes, time lags, are not rigorous, since such measures need not be independent in successive cycles. More important yet is the fact that those tests are not particularly powerful in discerning structural change under the welter of random variation. For on the one hand, these tests fail to take into account the influence of measurable exogenous variables, and to take advantage of the known time series of such variables—a possible advantage particularly important in periods of war or of new departures in economic policy. On the other hand, the basic cyclical measures they analyze are cumulative effects of random shocks, of which observations are limited to the number of cycles covered by the study. The additional information about the individual structural equations and the disturbances therein, contained in the more numerous original data, is thus lost.

In their defense of the application of analysis of variance, the authors mention that the original items of economic time series are even less independent serially than cycle durations or amplitudes. Probably they do not mean to imply a statement (which has often been fallaciously advanced) that the high serial correlation of economic time series precludes the use of such data (as distinct from "cyclical" measures derived therefrom) in any statistical tests or estimation procedures. Statistical theory is sufficiently flexible to face such situations. In the first place, it may be found that serial correlation in economic variables measured annually, say, is due only to their being determined by difference equations, with no serial correlation present in the disturbances (shocks) operating in individual equations—a situation which may be confirmed by tests based on the "residuals" obtained from fitting such equations. But even a situation of serially correlated disturbances—which is likely to prevail in any case in quarterly or monthly figures—is in principle amenable to statistical treatment. The mathematical and computational difficulties inherent in such a situation pose technical problems which need to be overcome, to enable us to extract all information about the structure of our economy from statistical records.

---

[10] This can be seen from the discussion of the causal interpretation of averages, particularly on page 506, where there is a groping for distinctions which only mathematical formulation can clarify.

The amplitudes, durations, and measures of conformity used by Burns and Mitchell are poor measures from this point of view. They waste an unknown but probably considerable amount of information contained in the original data. Their averages are unstable[11] because of the occurrence of borderline cases under the rules for recognizing cycles, because turning points are located without allowance for secular trend, and because of great variability between cycles.[12]

However, the extraction of more information from the data requires that, in addition to the hypotheses subject to test, certain basic economic hypotheses are formulated as distributional assumptions, which often are not themselves subject to statistical testing from the same data. Of course, the validity of information so obtained is logically conditional upon the validity of the statistically unverifiable aspects of these basic hypotheses. The greater wealth, definiteness, rigor, and relevance to specific questions of such conditional information, as compared with any information extractable without hypotheses of the kind indicated, provides the *third argument* against the purely empirical approach.

Let me wind up the argument with a statement combining exhortation and prophecy. In the monographs dealing with specific markets, in preparation or planned by the National Bureau of Economic Research, situations will frequently be encountered where the applicability of the behavior schedules of economic theory is more directly obvious, less beset with doubts on the score of unhomogeneity of commodities or individuals, and the connected difficulties of aggregation. Also, certain relationships between aggregates seem more strongly established *a priori* than others. The aggregate consumption function, a subject which the National Bureau is now investigating, so far stands on firmer ground than the investment schedule: consumption decisions are more of one kind than investment decisions. Among the latter decisions, inventory policies seem to be subject to a smaller number of considerations, more readily rationalized, than investment in productive equipment. Thus, the use of behavior schedules will inevitably force itself on the mind of an investigator dealing with some of the more specific partial subjects of dynamic economics. Such a development is both predictable and highly desirable. The combination of theoretical and statistical analysis into an explanation of cyclical fluctuations and an exploration of the means to influence them must necessarily proceed from detailed studies of individual relationships. Conversely, the statistical methods used in those detailed studies should recognize and take into account the fact that the specific relationship studied is part of a complete network of interrelations connecting the variables involved in many ways.

---

[11] See the discussion of conformity indexes on pages 184–85.

[12] In two cases, on page 425 and page 433, the exclusion of the "exceptional" reference cycle 1927–33 from an average makes a sufficient difference to the test comparison being made to be mentioned (recommended?) in the text. Addition to the averages of the 1933–38 cycle (which is not included in the tests discussed above) might well have a similarly large effect.

This already lengthy review could well end here. However, I cannot forego the opportunity to append a few brief comments on various specific points of method raised in the volume.

INDEX NUMBERS, TIME UNITS, SMOOTHING, SINE CURVES VERSUS TRIANGULAR PATTERNS

The authors' preference for the study of many individual series rather than index numbers doubtless derives from their basic decision to place the large-scale study of facts before theoretical concepts and hypotheses regarding the formation of economic variables. But their arguments provide a challenge to those who believe that the most relevant phenomena of economic fluctuation can fruitfully, or even better, be analyzed through aggregates or index numbers. To withstand critical examination, this belief needs to be argued more cogently than is usually done. It will be necessary to specify the purposes index numbers are required to serve, and to show theoretically and statistically to what extent these purposes are actually served efficiently and without undue loss of relevant information.

The authors' views that quarterly or monthly data contain much information which is lost by reduction to annual averages deserves strong sympathy. It is true that several of the particular measures on which the National Bureau concentrates are especially vulnerable to such reduction, as the authors amply demonstrate. But also if the purpose is one of estimating the parameters of structural equations, the presence and dynamic importance of relatively small time lags in many equations, as well as the shortness of available time series, makes the use of at least quarterly figures an important objective of the analysis of economic fluctuations.

The authors' rejection of the use of smoothing formulae is similarly appropriate. One could add to their arguments that, if explicit mathematical formulation of the distribution of the observations is introduced to guide the choice of estimation or test procedures, smoothing is found both to be wasteful of information and to complicate mathematical treatment, because it mixes up the effects of successive disturbances as well as blurs the time-shape of exogenous variables. In fact, one of the reasons why business cycle analysis is a difficult undertaking is that the economic system itself is such an effective smoothing agent of the random shocks to which it is exposed. The analytical problem is one of de-smoothing rather than smoothing.

Exception must be taken to a statement appearing on page 369:

When averages are struck for all cycles covered by a series, the erratic factors in the measures for single cycles have an additional opportunity to cancel out.

This is true generally, but is not applicable to the average standings at troughs (I, IX) and peaks (V). A selection effect is operative through the location of troughs and peaks at local minima and maxima of the curve, giving downward and upward biases to average trough and peak standings respectively, which will be especially pronounced if erratic disturbances persist for at least three months. This point is important because of the authors' statement (p. 157) that a "triangular" cyclical pattern often gives a better approximation to reality than the sine-curve pattern (whose dominance in the literature the authors attribute particularly to the prevalent habit of smoothing time series before analysis (p. 343). An important theoretical question is involved: the rounded curve seems connected with the idea of a natural equilibrium level or trend line around which fluctuations take place; in particular, pure sine curves suggest linearity of the equations describing the economy, whereas less symmetric but still rounded curves are compatible with nonlinear systems where no effective limits are placed on the range of the variables involved. However, the broken straight line pattern suggests one-sided movement as the natural condition of the economic system, reversed by capacity limits or other physical or incidental factors. Now the trough and peak standings are the crucial observations in making a choice between these two hypotheses. The selection effect mentioned produces a bias toward the triangular hypothesis, disqualifying average cyclical patterns as a means of testing the issue mentioned.

The authors are aware of the possibility of such bias,[13] but seem to feel that it will be unimportant except in series with pronounced erratic movements.[14] However, their graphs suggest a widespread occurrence of this bias. While all of the ten specific-cycle patterns in Chart 16 on page 56 show sharply defined kinks at the turning points, definite cusps are developed most clearly in the series most subject to erratic fluctuations (shares traded, total exports, sugar meltings). This does not mean that the issue between rounded curves and triangular patterns is to be decided in favor of the former. Other evidence, less marred by methodological doubts, is adduced to show that at least a substantial proportion of cycles have kinked peaks and troughs: slightly over two thirds of the turning points in five American series are not shifted in time if determined after trend elimination instead of before (p. 277).

CONCLUSION

To sum up: the book is unbendingly empiricist in outlook. Granted this basic attitude, it shows great perseverance and circumspection on the part of the authors in handling a vast amount of statistical data. In the latter part of the book, hypotheses of theoretical and practical relevance, referring to the characteristics of cyclical movements of the economy as a whole, are tested.

---

[13] See page 334, footnote 30; page 346; and the third graph in the first column of Chart 47 on page 345.

[14] The authors refer on page 347 to an opposite bias due to the mild smoothing involved in the use of three-month averages for trough and peak standings. However, this bias is likely to be smaller than the bias due to selection, owing to the smallness of the three-month period compared with the average duration of cycles.

But the decision not to use theories of man's economic behavior, even hypothetically, limits the value to economic science and to the maker of policies, of the results obtained or obtainable by the methods developed. This decision greatly restricts the benefit that might be secured from the use of modern methods of statistical inference. The pedestrian character of the statistical devices employed is directly traceable to the authors' reluctance to formulate explicit assumptions, however general, concerning the probability distribution of the variables, i.e., assumptions expressing and specifying how random disturbances operate on the economy through the economic relationships between the variables.

11

Koopmans on the Choice of Variables to Be Studied and of Methods of Measurement*

By RUTLEDGE VINING†

THE CRITICAL review by T. C. Koopmans of the recent study by Burns and Mitchell[1] would apparently cast doubt on the efficiency of almost any method of analysis that is not essentially identical with the methods adopted and developed by Koopmans and his associates. While these methods are intriguing and the results of their application will be awaited with keen interest, they are as yet untested. Acceptance of them as the only, or the best, method must hinge on results, not on any advance statement, no matter how persuasive, of their potential merits. Until such evidence is available, they must be considered an exceedingly narrow class of methods, and an insistent appeal to use them, and them alone, as an invitation to put a strait jacket on economic research. I would therefore like to discuss some of the questions raised by Koopmans. Sometimes, it seems, a paper such as this one of Koopmans may be more referred to than read. It should be recorded somewhere that some of the points emphasized by Koopmans are more controversial than they appear as stated. I hope it will be clear from what follows that I am not attempting in this paper a critique of the particular methods adopted by Koopmans. It would be presumptuous of me to undertake such a task. Moreover, it follows from my general position that the only satisfactory test of the usefulness of these methods is their fruits, and these have not yet been attained, or if attained, have not yet been made generally available.

1. Koopmans classifies the stages of development of a theory into the "Kepler stage" and the "Newton stage"—the analogy being the development

---

* *The Review of Economics and Statistics*, Vol. XXXI (May, 1949). Reprinted by courtesy of *The Review of Economics and Statistics* and the author.

† University of Virginia.

[1] T. C. Koopmans, "Measurement Without Theory," this REVIEW, Vol. XXIX (1947), pp. 161–72. This is a review article of the book by A. F. Burns and W. C. Mitchell, *Measuring Business Cycles* (National Bureau of Economic Research) (New York, 1946). [Reprinted in this volume.]

of celestial mechanics from the systematic accumulation of measurements through the discovery of simple empirical laws to the formulation of Newton's law of gravitation. The book by Burns and Mitchell is regarded as a contribution to the Kepler stage. "Nevertheless," says Koopmans,

> this reviewer believes that in research in economic dynamics the Kepler stage and Newton stage of inquiry need to be more intimately combined and to be pursued simultaneously. Fuller utilization of the concepts and hypotheses of economic theory *as a part of the process of observation and measurement* promises to be a shorter road, perhaps even the only possible road, to the understanding of cyclical fluctuations. . . .
>
> My *first argument*, then, is that even for the purpose of systematic and large scale observation of such a many-sided phenomenon, theoretical preconceptions about its nature cannot be dispensed with, and the authors do so only to the detriment of the analysis. . . .
>
> There is no systematic discussion [for example] of the reasons for selecting these particular variables as most worthy of study [in the search for possible changes in cyclical behavior over time]. . . . The choices made may have been the best possible ones. But "good" choices means relevant choices. What is relevant can only be determined with the help of some notions as to the generation of economic fluctuations, and as to their impact on society. . . . The choices as to what variables to study cannot be settled by a brief reference to "theoretical studies of business cycles." These issues call for a systematic argument to show that the best use has been made of available data in relation to the most important aspects of the phenomena studied.

His second argument is that,

> The prediction, within the narrowest attainable limits of error, of the effects of stated hypothetical measures of economic policy . . . is actually the most important objective of the analysis of economic fluctuations . . . [and] without resort to theory, in the sense indicated, conclusions relevant to the guidance of economic policies cannot be drawn.

The third argument is explicitly a matter of statistical estimation.

> Now any rigorous testing of hypotheses according to modern methods of statistical inference requires a specification of the form of the joint probability distribution of the variables. . . . [The measures used by Burns and Mitchell are poor measures in that] they waste an unknown but probably considerable amount of information contained in the original data. . . . The extraction of more information from the data requires that, in addition to the hypotheses subject to test, certain basic economic hypotheses are formulated as distributional assumptions, which often are not themselves subject to statistical testing from the same data. . . . The greater wealth, definiteness, rigor, and relevance to specific questions of such conditional information, as compared with any information extractable without hypotheses of the kind indicated, provides the *third argument* against the purely empirical approach.

The elaboration of these arguments introduces a somewhat new element into the discussion of the old controversy regarding the relation between theory and quantitative research. Briefly, Koopmans argues that without a theoretical framework having the *form* that he specifies, statistical data cannot be used efficiently—this term being used in the sense given it by modern theoretical statistics. The discussion seems somewhat strained to me, and without defending the particular methodological procedures of the National Bureau or attacking the procedures of the Cowles Commission, I believe that one might raise the possibility that Koopmans' argument contains a misleading emphasis if not an error.

One need not doubt the importance of the statistical research going forward at the Cowles Commission in order to hold that a work that does not make use of the methods being developed there is not by that condition alone subject to criticism. It isn't that the work of the National Bureau on trade fluctuations is barren of results that are capable of development, for Koopmans refers to certain phenomena that these less elegant methods turned up as materials for further hypotheses. And Koopmans lays no claim that by his methods he has already reached these same results more "efficiently." Instead, he gives a preview of the potentialities of his new methods and proceeds to argue that the results that may be expected of his methods will be *better* results. But, surely, in arguing so, Koopmans has left the realm in which modern theories of tests of hypotheses provide criteria that are unambiguously applicable. The work of Burns and Mitchell that is being criticized purports to be a work of discovery and hypothesis-seeking, and it is not clear at all what meaning should be given to "efficiency" in this context. Statistical efficiency is an attribute of an estimation and testing procedure rather than of a procedure of "search," and problems of statistical efficiency may be trivial, or almost so, in the prospecting and probing phase of the development of the understanding of a phenomenon. Discovery has never been a field of activity in which elegance of conception and equipment is of prime consideration; and foreign to the nature of exploration is the confinement involved in the requirements that the procedure followed shall be characterized by theoretical preconceptions having certain prescribed forms and shall yield findings that are directly subject to the rather restricted tests provided by the ideas included in the Neyman-Pearson theory of estimation.

Koopmans, in arguing that the results yielded by the methods of the National Bureau are inferior to those that we may expect from his methods, takes a definite stand on the issue of the nature of the variation to be accounted for in the study of trade fluctuations. This step, I think, has always been the core of the controversy over what is generally referred to as the problem of the role of theory in quantitative research. It would seem that we need not bother over whether or not a really discerning observer of phenomena approaches his materials with a theoretical or hypothetical framework in mind. We may take for granted that he does. The controversy might turn not so much upon assertions of the existence or absence of a hypothetical framework as upon the nature of the entity the behavior of which is to be accounted for. Koopmans presumably does not like the unit of analysis used in the Burns and Mitchell study—the "business cycle" of a given category of economic activity. I too feel that this unit of analysis is limited and, at least, should be regarded as strictly tentative—as it undoubtedly is regarded by these users; but I think that Koopmans' alternative unit—the individual economizing agent—is possibly even more fundamentally limited in the study of many aspects of aggregate trade fluctuations. But what we think will not settle these issues. We must try things to see.

A developing understanding of the population phenomenon of trade variation in its many aspects will of course draw upon many types of study. It seems unnecessary for us to accept the not infrequent assumption that a theoretical system based upon individual motivation and developed primarily for the discussion of welfare problems must also be *the* theoretical system to which we must turn in accounting for systems of variation representing the behavior of population phenomena. I believe that in our discussions of trade fluctuations, national and international, we deal with the behavior of an entity that is not a simple aggregate of the economizing units of traditional theoretical economics. I think that we need not take for granted that the behavior and functioning of this entity can be exhaustively explained in terms of the motivated behavior of individuals who are particles within the whole. It is conceivable—and it would hardly be doubted in other fields of study—that the aggregate has an existence apart from its constituent particles and behavior characteristics of its own not deducible from the behavior characteristics of the particles. We should work toward an explicit delineation of the entity itself—its structure and functioning—and the role that hypothesis and formal theory play in the earlier stages of this growth of understanding is subtle and irregular.

I, therefore—primarily in defense of empiricism as a fundamental part of scientific procedure—shall offer three points counter to these arguments of Koopmans: First, his conception of the character or extent of the variation to be accounted for appears to be unduly narrow, and a broadening of this conception raises the question often posed as to whether economics, as a science of variation rather than as an argument in political philosophy, has approached any nearer than has biology to a state where a comprehensive mathematizing of knowledge of variation is feasible. This point does not question the crucial importance of mathematics in the investigation of special or subsidiary hypotheses. But a prime source of these ideas to be analyzed in the abstract is the explorative work such as this of Burns and Mitchell, who obviously do not proceed without the guidance of tentative hypotheses. Second, the position taken that present research is to be evaluated from the point of view of social action is entirely questionable. And, third, modern theories of statistical estimation and of tests of hypotheses with their emphasis upon distributional hypotheses, upon the extraction of maximum information, upon the power of a test, and the like, are almost beside the point in attempts to derive hypotheses, the exploratory stage that characterizes a great part of the work in all developing fields of knowledge.

2. With respect to the first point, Koopmans seems convinced that without Kepler we have witnessed the emergence of what will pass as a first approximation to or a supporting framework for a Newtonian phenomenon. Some of his discussion suggests that we have already at hand a theoretical model that is a sort of social counterpart of Newtonian mechanics. But this is not asserted; rather, he argues that a way must be found (or has been found) to perform the Keplerian and Newtonian tasks together. Koopmans doesn't give his hypotheses specific economic content. He discusses the mathematical form that the model should (or must) take; and suggests the kind of content it should have in very general terms, such as "the behavior of groups of economic agents," "underlying human responses," "knowledge of man's behavior and its motives." But apparently all he has to insist upon at present is the mathematical form, and from his discussion it appears not unfair to regard the formal economic theory underlying his approach as being in the main available from works not later than those of Walras. Once workers began to apply correlation methods to economic quantities and to rationalize or "identify" the resulting regression equations as demand or supply schedules, it was almost inevitable that before long someone would be computing as many such equations as the number of variables designated to be "explained." This of course was the general line followed in the work of Tinbergen published by the League of Nations some nine years ago. In connection with a particular detail, Koopmans remarks that:

The mathematical and computational difficulties inherent in such a situation pose technical problems which need to be overcome to enable us to extract all information about the structure of our economy from statistical records.

In a sense, these are the only problems that have been attacked by this entire line of development—the problem of statistical estimation that would be presented by the empirical counterpart of the Walrasian conception. Add to Walras the simple notion of lagged effects (if it is not already there) and certain devices of the nature of the difference equation, and the problem is wholly statistical as contrasted with economic.

Now a formal theoretical model based upon postulated and fixed individual motives and transformation functions might be just the conception that we need for accounting for and analyzing the uniformities discoverable among human individual and population phenomena. But such has not been demonstrated and until evidence of the adequacy of this model is made available, it is an unnecessary restriction upon economic research to insist that the method used shall be essentially that adopted and developed by Koopmans and his associates. As indicated above, some of us may feel that the unit of analysis and the entity the behavior of which it is of interest to study is not the individual economizer in his conscious, problem-solving state of mind.[2] I believe that much of the statistical regularities that are to be

_____

[2] With reference to this inclination on the part of some to regard a quantitative work

that is not built upon the neo-classical theoretical model as being essentially without a theoretical foundation at all, there is a point of moderate interest to the modern history of economic doctrines. Not all of the neo-classical writers look upon this model as a particularly useful framework for quantitative studies. While there is all manner of subclassifications that could be contrived, the writings of F. H. Knight would be classed in general among those of the deductive schools of economics: the Marshallians, the Walrasians, the Austrians and Wicksellians. A school of statistical economics has sprung from this tradition, and "econometricians" have for some time been engaged in the statistical estimation of systems of demand, supply, and other relations formulated in Marshallian and Walrasian economics. This work is conceived of as being of the nature of a refinement, extension and quantitative expression of neo-classical economics, and it is in good color within the tradition; for it appears to have been the rule rather than the exception for economists of the classical school to look upon the ability quantitatively to predict responses of given economic variables resulting from known changes in other given factors as the utltimate objective of the development of their science. Rough and ready (and more or less casual) calculations demonstrating an alleged predictive value of certain theoretical formulations are found in almost all treatises on economic theory; and econometricians who profess an adherence to the classical tradition have made a point of giving references to passages in the works of the older writers such as Marshall, Pareto, Jevons, and the like in which this goal is expressed explicitly.

Knight, however, stands out against this conception of the role and prospective development of traditional theoretical economics. This latter is not even the beginning of the development of a social analogue for Newtonian mechanics, the knowledge represented being fundamentally different from the knowledge of relations between inert entities. The characteristically social and human problems are problems of freely establishing bases of agreement on the conditions of social organization, and the use of economic theory is instrumental in the discussion of the conditions under which an economic problem is to be solved. It purports to describe the results of economistic behavior under conditions that are fixed by postulate. As a basis for the discovery of predictive laws, as Newtonian mechanics, for example, is a basis for the derivation of differential equations describing the expected behavior of certain physical phenomena, it is fundamentally limited in that economistic behavior is "active" and developmental, in a sense that he discusses in detail, and not of the nature of phenomena that are subject to cause-and-effect explanation. The component of behavior that is positive is not motivated, and a model based upon conscious motivation would not be expected to be particularly relevant in the scientific search for "explanations" of uniformities and statistical regularities. The social analogue for Newtonian mechanics has yet to be developed, and perhaps it is biology that has the more cogent analogues anyway.

Institutionalism, following from or through the writings of Veblen, emphasizes this component of behavior that is positive and based upon non-deliberative, habitual behavior forms. Knight, I think, is critical of institutionalism, as a school of thought and as a social science to take the place of traditional economics, primarily because of the extremity of its positivism. Institutionalism does not touch upon what Knight regards as the distinctively "social" problems raised in the "active" seeking on the part of individuals for grounds of agreement and consensus. It has had a bias toward the development of instrumental knowledge for control purposes, the objectives being more or less taken for granted. Agreement on objectives, however, presents the real social problems for Knight, and traditional economics has developed to facilitate and improve the quality of social discussion. Knight, a traditional and deductive economist, is critical of institutionalism for its incomplete conception of the nature of a "social" problem, but at the same time he is as critical as the institutionalists are of the "scientism" and methods of the econometricians who base their work on the traditional economistic model. It would be of some interest to outline the basis for Knight's point of view and to note where Veblen's criticism of traditional economic theory as a framework of reference for the development of a positive social science has a good bit in common with this position. Both men classify human behavior and social phenomena into "active," deliberative, problem-solving *procedure* on the cne hand and objective, passive, non-deliberative *process* on the other. Knight's emphasis is upon the philosophical or ethical problems involved in the first component in its impact upon matters of social

observed in population phenomena and that are relevant for the discussion of economic problems involves the behavior of social organisms that are distinctly more than simple algebraic aggregates of consciously economizing individuals. I think that in a positive sense the aggregate has an existence over and above the existence of Koopmans' individual units and behavior characteristics that may not be deducible from the behavior of these component parts. This notion is of the nature of a postulate or hypothesis to be investigated, and I have suggested at another place[3] a fuller picture of a conception that I propose to investigate. I seek to view a great nation such as ours as an interlacing of definite population structures. An interspersing of population "clusters" exists with lines of union connecting these clusters. Along these lines flows of commerce may be observed in their concrete forms. Measures of the magnitudes and rates of change of these flows between and within these "clusters" suggest random and unruly variation. But patterns of behavior are suggested when these measures are observed as statistical distributions. This conception has reference to a population system, but the behavior described may nevertheless be regarded as "economic" if by that term we class together phenomena relevant in the discussion of socio-economic problems. The national series which we study in our business cycle inquiries may plausibly be interpreted as averages of measurements of such "organic" flows having a spatial dimension; and from this point of view the studies of Burns and Mitchell represent an accumulation of knowledge that may later play a part in a more complete account of a vast and immensely complex system of variation. An assertion that the development of Koopmans' methods is the best and simplest means by which we may account for the events *in space and time* that take place within the spatial boundary of such a system of population structures—and this is what an "understanding of cyclical fluctuations" might be broadened out to mean—seems to me a quite extraordinary statement in the present state of our knowledge. But if Koopmans should give a demonstration

---

organization that are subject to conscious deliberation. Veblen's emphasis is upon the instrumental knowledge of non-deliberative, unconscious process. To the extent that my reading and understanding has progressed, Veblen seems to me not strong on positive and constructive points of methodology in the study of this material, and Knight regards the study of this phenomena as outside his field of interest. But the writings of each would appear to imply that the search, in so far as it purports to be scientific, should be for rules of order and uniformities in space and time that are either absolutely invariant with respect to individual thought processes or that are subject to deliberate policy change if discovered and made known to society as a group. For Veblen's argument see, for example, *The Place of Science in Modern Civilization and Other Essays*, "Economics and Evolution," pp. 73 ff., and, "The Limitations of Marginal Utility," pp. 234 ff. (New York, 1919). For Knight's position see in particular, "Science, Philosophy, and Social Procedure," *Ethics*, Vol. 52 (1942), pp. 253–74; and "Fact and Value in Social Science," *Science and Man* (edited by Ruth Anshen, New York, 1942). Both essays are reprinted in *Freedom and Reform* (New York), 1947.

[3] "Measuring State and Regional Business Cycles," *Journal of Political Economy*, August, 1947, p. 350, and, "The Region as a Concept in Business Cycle Analysis," *Econometrica*, July, 1946, pp. 201–218.

of the generality of his methods, then we would move awed and gladly on—or at least we *should* move gladly[4]—to unexplained fields of problems.

A more complete account of the philosophy or theory of the method of Koopmans' group is to be found in Trygve Haavelmo's *The Probability Approach in Econometrics.*[5] This book appears to be an important piece of work that should somehow be presented in a form that would have more currency among economists than it now has. Haavelmo gives a rough fourfold classification of the main problems encountered in quantitative research: first, the construction of tentative theoretical models; second, the testing of theories; third, the problem of estimation; and fourth, the problem of prediction. It may be noticed that the first problem (possibly the second, depending upon one's interpretation) is the only one of the four that is not a problem of strictly modern statistical theory. He goes on to say that the "explanation" of phenomena "consists of digging down to more fundamental relations than those that appear before us when we 'stand and look.' " The more fundamental relations are those that have a great degree of invariance or autonomy with respect to the ordinary or reasonably expected changes in economic structure, and a theory is a construction of a system of autonomous relations. He illustrates the notion of an autonomous relation by considering the possibility of establishing a functional relationship between the distance of the accelerator from the floor of the automobile and the corresponding maximum speed of the car on a dry, flat road. Such a study might provide information sufficient to operate the car at a prescribed speed, but it would not tell us anything at all about the inner mechanism of an automobile. The relation depends on many other relations, some of which are transitory.

On the other hand, the general laws of thermodynamics, the dynamics of friction, etc., etc., are highly autonomous relations with respect to the automobile mechanism, because these relations describe the functioning of some parts of the mechanism irrespective of what happens in some other parts.

Let us turn from this analogy to the mechanism of economic life. Economic theory builds on the assumption that individuals' decisions to produce and to consume can be described by certain fundamental behavioristic relations, and that, besides, there are certain technical and institutional restrictions upon the freedom of choice (such as technical production functions, legal restrictions, etc.).[6]

In statements of this sort there is no doubt but that these men are considering the vast and rich field of economic variation, where systematic

---

[4] I recall a very telling passage in J. S. Mill's *Autobiography* giving an account of his introspection into how gladly he would have moved on if all the critical problems in which he had involved himself were suddenly solved. An acute depression of guilt, we are told, resulted from this introspective inquiry.

[5] *Econometrica*, Vol. 12, Supplement, July, 1944. In connection with this matter of probability and phenomena of economic variation, this book seems to highlight a point of interest. Classical theoretical economics has drawn heavily for concepts upon classical mechanics, but the word "statistical" in *statistical economics* carries an entirely different connotation from the same word in *statistical mechanics*.

[6] *Ibid.*, p. 28.

classification and description have hardly begun, but where flows and movements of things may be observed—flows of objects within and between economic or social organisms. The functioning of the great supraorganisms which we see as population agglomerations, their growth and decline, their interdependencies, give rise to quantities having both a spatial and a temporal dimension. Are we ready to accept the particular list of economic relations given in the above quotation as *the* fundamental autonomous relations, sufficient for our purposes and not dependent on other relations transitory in character? Haavelmo mentions our faith in the existence of certain elements of invariance in relations between real phenomena, which are discoverable provided that we hit upon the right arrangement of our materials and ideas. But are we certain that those relations represent the right arrangement of ideas, and who has inquired into the degree of invariance exhibited by these relations?[7] Is it not something of a mighty jump to imply that the postulated preference function of an individual is in some sense analogous to the general laws of thermodynamics, the dynamics of friction, etc., etc.? Is the Walrasian conception not in fact a pretty skinny fellow of untested capacity upon which to load the burden of a general theory accounting for the events in space and time which take place within the spatial boundary of an economic system? When we think of the enormous body of factual knowledge digested and systematized in the other fields of variation and the meagerness of our own results from efforts to systematize, are we quite ready to leave Haavelmo's first problem and launch into the last three problems in estimation theory? When generations later and after vastly more systematic observation and taxonomic work has been done, is it a foregone conclusion that the hypotheses of Koopmans will be regarded as overwhelmingly more comprehensive in what they will be able to explain than those that must inhabit the minds of such workers as Burns and Mitchell as they choose their quantities and arrange their materials? Burns and Mitchell presumably are still on Problem 1. Koopmans has vaulted over, some would say hastily if the research is in the field of economics, to Problems 3 and 4. This is not to deny the very great interest that economic research has in the results of Koopmans' group on Problems 3 and 4. But it is to express the belief that, so long as a field of knowledge continues to develop, workers will be puttering around, and not in vain, within the unexplored expanses of Problem 1—the searching for regularities and interrelations of regularities and the feeling around for interesting theoretical models. Not all of this work will find formal mathematics of immediate use, and much of it will be of such an explorative

---

[7] Where Haavelmo speaks of the invariance or autonomy of these behavioristic relations and technological restrictions, Veblen ends up a long discussion of these same relations with, "The wants and desires, the end and aim, the ways and means, the amplitude and drift of the individual's conduct are functions of an institutional variable that is of a highly complex and wholly unstable character." *Op. cit.*, pp. 242–43.

character as to render almost meaningless the notion of a planned maximization of information from given data.

3. I shall not argue the second point. The work of the National Bureau will bear comparison with the work of other research agencies from the point of view of social usefulness. But aside from this, easy illustrations may be cited of the unpredictability of the use of any given piece of knowledge, and it would appear unnecessary for us to put much stock in Koopmans' criterion of social usefulness in judging economic research. This insistence that research be pointed up to some topical problem of policy is put somewhat more baldly in the field of economics than seems to be the case with other fields of knowledge. J. B. S. Haldane makes certain comments regarding the conservatism with which scientific investigators should approach problems of public policy. Genetics has developed into a beautiful science, but this leading contributor to the development states: "I hold that a premature application of our rather scanty knowledge will yield little result, and will merely serve to discredit the branch of science in which I am working."[8] If knowledge in this field is scant, we have next to no knowledge at all in the field of economic variation. But we do not lack exponents of the application of knowledge in economics. Haldane, in denying that genetics as a science has been advanced far enough to provide knowledge upon which social policy might be based, offered the suggestion that while the relation between eugenics and genetics could only unfairly be regarded as similar to the relation between astrology and astronomy, the analogy provided in the history of the latter is not without point. Now, it would be clearly unjust and inappropriate to speak of the relation between economics as currently used in discussions of positive policy and economics as a study of a field of variation as being similar to the relation between astrology and astronomy. But fortune telling provided the principal support of many of the prominent early astronomers, and is fortune telling too hard an expression for much of what we do?

4. Regarding the third point, we may note that in those fields of investigation where modern statistics has found its greatest development there is much fundamental work done without assistance from theories of estimation and of tests of hypotheses of the Neyman-Pearson type. There are important schools of biology where statistics is not taught, and there are significant contributors to biological knowledge who make scarcely any use at all of modern theoretical statistics. To biology, microscopy is important no less than statistics. One of the more distinguished members of the University of Virginia faculty has spent the greater part of a fruitful scientific career studying the transparent tail of a tadpole—a ridiculous occupation to the lofty workers in our own field who occupy themselves with nothing less than the pathology of civilizations. But

---

[8] *Heredity and Politics* (London), 1938, pp. 8 and 175.

this person has succeeded in developing microscopic and photographic techniques by which the growth and functioning of living cells and organisms may be watched.[9] As I look at the motion pictures that he has succeeded in recording, the flows of identifiable objects, the motion of cells in action and cells in growth, the random, palpitating variation that somehow assumes form in the aggregate—all of this rich array of motion reminds me of what I think I can see reflected in the motion of economic quantities. Professor Speidel's contributions have been in the uncovering of knowledge not discernible by the unaided eye; that is, he has been engaged in Haavelmo's digging down process, finding more fundamental relations that those that appear when we merely "stand and look." But his tools include neither the Neyman-Pearson theory of estimation nor any mathematical formulation; and while modern principles of experimental design could perhaps be brought to bear in this work, such has not been done in its present stage. Mr. Speidel is not just a photographer. He is a highly regarded biologist, and as he arranges his materials for experiment and observation he obviously has in mind hypotheses or theories that are to be inquired into. No less do such workers as Burns and Mitchell have hypotheses in mind, and workers in neither field at this classificatory and descriptive level need be burdened down with the emphasis on an advanced and fascinating theory of estimation. There are numerous problems where modern statistics comes into full use—where quantities have been defined, where units of study or "organisms" have been tentatively delineated and their functioning described, where hypotheses regarding numerical aspects of relations have been formulated.[10] Koopmans presumably regards his work as in this stage. But it is not the stage of all economic research.

The excessive emphasis of modern statistics upon certain types of problems was stressed in a part of the discussion of a paper read by M. G. Kendall a few years back.[11] Kendall had remarked that "the estimation of properties of a population from a sample is the most important practical problem in statistics and is long likely to continue so." Mr. Yule denied this proposition:

It never was, in my opinion, the most important practical problem in statistics, and so cannot continue to be that which it never was. The initial problem of the statistician is simply the description of the data presented; to tell us what the data themselves show. To this initial problem the function of sampling theory is in general entirely secondary or ancillary; to inform the investigator as to the limits within which his descriptive measures can be trusted, so far as fluctuations of simple sampling alone are concerned. The development of theory during my own lifetime

---

[9] For a description of this work see Carl C. Speidel, "Living Cells in Action," *American Scientist*, April, 1948, pp. 237–57.

[10] For example, Frank L. Kidner's problem in his *California Business Cycles* is to some considerable extent a problem of estimation. See, e.g., a review article on this book, "Measuring State and Regional Business Cycles," *Journal of Political Economy*, August, 1947.

[11] M. G. Kendall, "The Future of Statistics," *Journal of the Royal Statistical Society*, New Series, Vol. CV, Part II, pp. 69–72.

followed at first the natural course suggested by this fact. Primarily it was new methods that were developed, and investigations of the "probable errors" involved only followed in their train. More recently methods, with few exceptions (time-series in economics, factor-methods in psychology), have been almost neglected, while there has been a completely lopsided development—almost a malignant growth—of sampling theory. I hope there may be a swing back towards the study of method proper, and as methods only develop in connection with practical problems, that means a swing back to more practical work and less pure theory. . . .

There are quite large fields of statistics into the discussion of which sampling theory hardly enters at all. . . . Even in the field of experimental work, if the investigator possesses caution, common sense and patience, those qualities are quite likely to keep him more free from error in his conclusions than the man of little caution and common sense who guides himself by a mechanical application of sampling rules. He will be more likely to remember that there are sources of error more important than fluctuations of sampling. . . . No: I cannot assign the place of highest importance to sampling theory—a high place perhaps, but not the highest.[12]

Mr. E. S. Pearson, whose name adorns one of the more important pieces of modern statistical apparatus, suggested that the following questions be put to mathematical statisticians:

How far do we practice what we preach in journal contributions, classroom or meeting-hall? Exactly how important a part do numerical probability measures play in the practical decisions following from our analysis of statistical data? Is our confidence in probability theory related to the simplicity of the technique used? How often are we completely satisfied that the assumptions of randomness and so on have been met? Frankly, for my part I do not know the answers, and I see no way of obtaining them except by attempting to keep a brief case-history of every problem with which I am concerned in which a numerical probability measure is calculated to guide a practical decision.[13]

Kendall then went on to say that there was less difference between Mr. Yule and himself than might appear.

I would agree with Mr. Yule that, for practical purposes, a great deal of the modern developments of the theory of sampling has taken place at the expense of other and more important practical work. Perhaps we have let mathematics run away with us a little. It is interesting to see from Professor Pearson's remarks that he may feel something of the same kind when he suggests that we should keep running records of the cases in which we make inferences from data and note how often we really rely solely upon the theory of probability and not intuitive judgments.[13]

Thus, I am not alone in feeling that an excessive emphasis is placed by modern statistics upon the sampling problem. To be sure, Koopmans is an important contributor to new statistical method in the sense used by Yule— the method of measuring simultaneous relations. Yet, it appears to me that he emphasizes somewhat heavily the estimation aspects of his problem. For example, his insistence upon a "distributional hypothesis" is based upon

---

12 *Ibid.*, pp. 83, *et seq.*
13 *Ibid.*, pp. 87, 90.

estimation considerations rather than upon a primary interest in the distribution itself. Sampling and estimation theory is important to a student of economic variation, but in a sense it is secondary. A worker in this explorative field might work in close contact with the statistical specialist in seeking a solution of his sampling and estimation problems. But for the basic work with his materials statistical theory in its broader meaning is fundamental. At the observational level it plays a role in economic research similar to that played by microscopy in biology. It must aid us in seeing our materials, and methods of arranging our data must be discovered by which there will be revealed any orderliness that exists in the welter of motion and confusion shown by the disorderly units of the study. This latter point may be extended beyond the meaning of mere method of observation. The statistical point of view is a conception of nature no less useful in the study of economic variation than in the study of physical phenomena. Much orderliness and regularity apparently only becomes evident when large aggregates are observed, and theoretical treatment involves a probability interpretation. Distributions of economic variates in as large groups as can be obtained should be studied and analyzed, and the older theories of the generation of frequency distributions should be brushed off, put to work, and further developed. That is to say, statistical economics is too narrow in scope if it includes just the estimation of postulated relations. Probability theory is fundamental as a guide to an understanding of the nature of the phenomena to be studied and not merely as a basis for a theory of the sampling behavior of estimates of population parameters the characteristics of which have been postulated. In seeking for interesting hypotheses for our quantitative studies we might want to wander beyond the classic Walrasian fields and to poke around the equally classic fields once cultivated by such men as Lexis, Bortkiewicz, Markov, and Kapteyn.

These are the roles that I should like statistics to play, and it seems to me that this is in fair conformance with the views of Burns and Mitchell. In any event, I should feel much safer in bringing my little work before the Commissar of Research if that chair were occupied by Burns or Mitchell than if Koopmans were the occupant. I would feel that the first question put by Commissar Koopmans would be, "Where are your difference equations?", and I would have to answer that I did not have any to speak of. When the next question was put, "Where is your argument showing that the best use has been made of available data in relation to the most important aspects of the phenomena studied?", I would have to admit that I was still in a state of puzzlement regarding the most important aspect of the phenomena that I study. My liquidation as an inquirer would be just preceded by the obvious reframing of the above question, "Where is your assurance that in what you have done you have wasted no information?", for I would have to answer that I was fairly confident that I had in fact wasted worlds of it. There would clearly be no point in the Commissar going into the power of my tests. But such grounds for the liquidation of methods of research would, I think, be gravely unfortunate. Most of us feel that we have got beyond a state of dilettantism, but, even so, dilettantes have played a quite remarkable role in the history of science and of ideas in general—and a reading of Koopmans' review may throw a little light upon why this might have been the case.

12

A Reply*

By TJALLING C. KOOPMANS[1]

QUESTIONS OF methodology are among the most difficult to reach agreement on or even to find a basis of discussion for. Undeniably, intuitive elements enter into our choice of scientific methods, and states of expectation or confidence affect our attitudes toward specific principles of scientific procedure. Equally obvious is the desirability to formulate explicitly and scrutinize rationally the assumptions and anticipations underlying these choices and attitudes. I fully agree with Vining that the only conclusive test of methods is results ultimately attained (postponing for further discussion under (c) below what is to be the meaning of the term "results"). In view of the insufficiency and inconclusiveness of "results" reached so far in quantitative economics, the only remaining criteria of choice are partly formal (logical clarity and consistency), partly empirical (analogies from other and older sciences that have attained more satisfactory results), and partly, indeed, intuitive.

It is unfortunate that some of the expressions employed by Vining might lead one to think that the issue before us is a dispute between two particular research institutions over their pet methods and procedures. The "econometric approach" to economic dynamics has been initiated and developed in many places by men like Fisher, Frisch, Tinbergen, Marschak, Kalecki, Ezekiel, Haavelmo, Tintner, Stone, Hurwicz, Klein, and others.[2] Similarly, the "empiricist" position has been embraced by many a scholar outside the National Bureau of Economic Research.

The substance of Vining's criticism can perhaps be summarized in the following four sentences:

a To seek a basis for economic dynamics in the analysis of the economizing behavior of the individual agent may not be necessary or even particularly desirable.

b A narrow mathematical form has been imposed on a theoretical model for the study of economic dynamics.

---

* *The Review of Economics and Statistics*, Vol. XXXI (May, 1949).

[1] I am indebted to my colleagues in the Cowles Commission for Research in Economics for valuable comments and criticism of an earlier draft of this reply.

[2] It is, therefore, embarrassing to me to see the methodological approach that resulted from the cumulative effort of these men referred to as "Koopmans' methods" or the "methods of Koopmans' group."

c Social usefulness is hardly a relevant criterion in the evaluation of economic research.
d The present theories of statistical inference are of little help in a process of exploration and hypothesis seeking.

I shall attempt to explain why I remain in fundamental disagreement on the first point (*a*); that I believe (*b*) can be met by further clarification of my position; that I do not think we are far apart on (*c*); and that (*d*) points to important gaps and unsolved problems in the theory of statistical inference.

(*a*) With respect to the first statement, I cannot understand the meaning of the phrase that "the aggregate has an existence apart from its constituent particles and behavior characteristics of its own not deducible from the behavior characteristics of the particles." If a theory formulates precisely (although possibly in probability terms) the determination of the choices and actions of each individual in a group or population, in response to the choices and actions of other individuals or the consequences thereof (such as prices, quantities, states of expectation), then the set of these individual behavior characteristics is *logically* equivalent to the behavior characteristics of the group. Such a theory does not have an opening wedge for essentially new group characteristics. Any *deus ex machina* who should wish to influence the outcome can only do so by affecting the behavior of individuals. This does not deny the existence of essentially social phenomena, based on imitation, such as fads and fashions, waves of optimism and pessimism, panics and runs; or based on power struggles, such as price wars, trust formation, lobbying; or based on a social code or sense of responsibility, such as the acceptance of personal sacrifice for a common objective. It is maintained only that such social phenomena are necessarily acted out by individuals[3] as members of a group.

The logical equivalence of group behavior to the set of individual behavior characteristics does not imply that the mathematical definition and derivation of aggregate behavior equations from individual behavior equations is a simple problem, or even a problem soluble with present mathematical tools. Neither should we exclude the possibility that group behavior will "look" surprisingly different from the individual behavior from which it is derived. On page 171 of my review[4] I have expressed some uneasiness at the lack of concern, in many econometric studies, with an explicit justification of aggregate behavior equations. The position has been taken by Arrow[5] that

---

[3] It is true that the choices of individuals are restrained by a framework of institutional rules enforced or adhered to by the government, the banking system and other institutions. These rules (tax schedules, reserve requirements, etc.) can to some extent be taken as given for the analysis of economic fluctuations. In a deeper analysis, these rules and the changes in them would need to be explained further from choices by individuals interacting, in various degrees of association with each other, through political processes.

[4] "Measurement Without Theory," this REVIEW, Vol. XXIX (1947), pp. 161–72. [Pp. 186–203 of the present volume.]

[5] In a paper "Summarizing a Population of Behavior Patterns" presented at the Chicago meeting of the Econometric Society, December, 1947. An abstract of this paper appeared in *Econometrica*, Vol. 16, No. 2, April, 1948.

such aggregate equations are not even necessary for macro-analysis: the relevant information can be conveyed by frequency distributions of individual behavior parameters in the group considered.

Neither does what I have said so far imply that for the analysis of group behavior it is necessary or even worthwhile to build on the foundation of individual analysis. Boyle established the (aggregate) gas laws by experiments before anyone worried about their derivation from hypothetical properties of molecules. However, on pages 166–67 of my review I have adduced what I believe to be strong arguments (not commented on by Vining) for the necessity of seeking a basis in theories of individual decisions. The first of these is the inavailability of experimentation to determine separately the relevant aggregate behavior equations (if I may continue in that terminology in spite of the doubts just expressed). The third (to interchange the order) is the necessity for identification[6] of separate aggregate behavior equations if the effect of policies is to be predicted—to that argument I shall return when discussing Vining's point (*c*). The second argument is the availability of direct knowledge about individual behavior. While it was long possible and sometimes tempting for physicists to deny the usefulness of the molecular hypothesis, we economists have the good luck of being some of the "molecules" of economic life ourselves, and of having the possibility through human contacts to study the behavior of other "molecules." Besides introspection, the interview or questionnaire, and even small scale experiments, are available as means of acquiring or extending knowledge about individual behavior. Thus we, indeed, have direct access to information already recognized as essential.

(*b*) The discussion now flows over into Vining's next point: that I am attempting to impose on the study of business fluctuations the strait-jacket of a narrow mathematical form. Vining correctly notes that I do not in the present context propose a definite content for the theory of individual behavior. The truth is that I am at this stage not even concerned with any very specific *mathematical* form of this theory. I am, for instance, quite unhappy about difference equations. They are clumsy instruments that treat time as if it comes in indivisible pieces of one year or one quarter each. The only excuses for their use are simplicity in exposition and the fact that statistical theory concerning the estimation of their parameters is further advanced than that for alternative, more realistic forms. I am hoping, however, that statisticians will soon teach us how to treat equation systems in which behavior responses are allowed to be subject to continuously distributed lags and in which probability enters through "disturbances" that are stochastic processes of a continuous time variable. Similarly, I should be happy to follow Arrow's suggestion to scrap the notion of aggregate behavior equations, should he demonstrate that the notion of a frequency distribution of individual

---

[6] In another paper ("Identification Problems in Economic Model Construction," published in *Econometrica*, April, 1949) I have given an exposition of this group of problems.

behavior parameters suffices for the objectives discussed under (*c*) below, and should we be able to collect the data relevant to the measurement of these concepts.

I do emphasize what might be called the *logical* form of a science of economic dynamics, or, if you like, its mathematical form in a very broad and general sense. At the basis: hypotheses regarding the behavior of individual consumers, laborers, entrepreneurs, investors, etc., in the markets indicated by these terms. In so far as we assume rational behavior, these hypotheses may be of the utility-maximizing or profit-maximizing type or, in situations involving strategy, of the type studied by Morgenstern and von Neumann.[7] Even then, time lags arise from the process of transmission of information and of decision taking. But we need not and should not confine ourselves to assuming rational behavior. What we need to measure is actual behavior, as shaped by habit, culture, ideals, imitation, advertising, prejudice and misinformation as well as by the narrower economic motives usually referred to as rational. Therefore, besides using deductions from the economic motive, we need to formalize and strengthen our knowledge of other motives of modern economic man, through observation, interview, and sampling study, drawing on whatever results other social sciences have to offer.

The basic assumption is that the numerically measurable effects of the implementation of individual decisions have a relatively persistent relationship to the principal numerically measurable aspects of the information that has gone into the making of these decisions—persistent, if not for a given individual, then in some average or aggregate sense for a group of individuals. Since the relationship is between numerical entities, it is necessarily mathematical; since not all pieces of information relevant to the decision can be statistically traced and perhaps also because of basic erratic elements in all human behavior, the relationship has the form of a probability distribution of decision effects which depends on the decision data (some of which are exogenous, i.e., non-economic).

Not all economic variables are determined directly through individual decisions. Some are set by government or bank officials acting under law or conventional rule (as pointed out in footnote 3). Some are the outcome of productive processes, described by transformation functions possibly involving further time lags, new random elements and additional exogenous variables.

Whether or not the relationships of behavior, rule, and technology are sufficiently persistent to merit study, it must, I believe, be granted that they are a logically complete set of elements (building blocks) for explaining the formation of economic variables. If these relationships are valid, any other interesting relationships between the same variables or aggregates thereof must be dependent on (deducible from) these. So must, for instance, relationships between regional aggregates. Such aggregates are determined through

---

[7] *Theory of Games and Economic Behavior* (Princeton, 1944).

behavior, rule, and technology in Virginia, Illinois, and other states, in interaction. That is, regional analysis does not enter as a new and independent principle of research. It directs interest to one particular (geographical) mode of aggregation.

(*c*) I have always felt that social usefulness as an objective should and does receive greater emphasis in economics than, for instance, in the natural sciences (other than technology). But even physicists have become alarmed and worried at the thought that the social usefulness of their latest discoveries may well be negative. Political economy has traditionally sought justification for its speculations in the search of a scientific basis for public policy in economic matters.

However, this is clearly a matter of personal choice and emphasis. And even if the criterion of usefulness is adopted as the ultimate guide, this does not exclude in any way that a piece of knowledge obtained for knowledge's sake may some day turn out to have greater social usefulness than knowledge sought with a particular policy problem in mind. Indeed, the case for measurement of identifiable relationships expressing average economic behavior of individuals does not rest on the acceptance of a research criterion of social usefulness. It rests rather on the criterion that relevant knowledge should enable us to predict outcomes in not yet observed (future or past) situations. There has been a good deal of experience (Harvard barometer, etc.) to show that relationships between economic variables observed over a period of time but not traced to underlying behavior equations are unreliable as instruments for prediction. The reason, so excellently explained by Haavelmo in the study quoted by Vining, is that such apparent relationships may well depend for their validity on several behavior equations, and will fail even if only one of the latter fails, either because of a change in the response pattern itself or because some policy or exogenous variable affects the response. Changes in policies and in external conditions occur continually, and methods of prediction that fail whenever some such change occurs somewhere are of very limited use.[8]

Vining counters with the question whether even the most autonomous behavior equations can themselves be expected to have much persistence through time. Calling now on the criterion of social usefulness to reinforce an argument independent of it, I submit that this is an empirical question of great social importance. Suppose these behavior relationships are so fickle and transitory as to escape measurement. Then the best we can expect from past observation is the type of information collected by Burns and Mitchell: statistical averages and frequency distributions of cyclical characteristics like the depth of depressions, the steepness of upswing or decline, etc. That is,

---

[8] See also J. Marschak, "Economic Structure, Path, Policy, and Prediction," *American Economic Review*, May, 1947, pp. 81–84; especially Section III.

assuming that for some unknown reason at least these averages and distributions possess stability over time, we can then form expectations as to what, on the average, the future has in store for us. But if some of this expected variety of events turns out to be detrimental to welfare, we shall then have no knowledge as to how to prevent or reduce the damage. Now, if we do not learn how to introduce greater stability in the economy by the indirect inducements of money supply, tax schedules, and other general incentives or deterrents to individual action—either because such knowledge is impossible or because we do not seek it—political processes and social necessities will make us move more to the method of direct administrative prescription of individual behavior. Thus, a question of social method and organization in which many noneconomic issues and problems are involved may be decided in a particular way because lack of the quantitative knowledge of economic behavior required for one possible solution prevents an informed comparison of the alternatives before us.

(*d*) I am in agreement with much that is said by Vining under the last heading. Probability, randomness, variability, enter not only into estimation and hypothesis testing concerning economic behavior parameters. These concepts are an essential element in dynamic economic theory, in the model we form of the conditioning (rather than determination) of future economic quantities by past economic developments. I submit that the concept of an aggregate behavior equation, or of a frequency distribution of individual behavior parameters, is an excellent example of the "orderliness and regularity" which "only becomes evident when large aggregates are observed," referred to by Vining. I believe that his term "statistical theory in its broader meaning" is used in the same sense in which the econometricians speak of "model construction." It is the model itself, as a more or less suitable approximation to reality, which is of primary interest. The problems of estimation of its parameters or testing of its features have a derived interest only. But this derived interest is strong: it has long been emphasized by Tinbergen and others, and recently again by Friedman,[9] that quantitative conclusions regarding cyclical movements and the influence of policies thereon depend critically on the numerical values of time lags and other response parameters.

I come now to the distinction between problems of "hypothesis-seeking" and problems discussed in the theory of estimation or in the Neyman-Pearson theory of "hypothesis-testing." This touches on unsolved problems at the very foundations of statistical theory, and I must confess that I do not see clearly through the issues involved. It is possible to take a formal view and argue that hypothesis-seeking and hypothesis-testing differ only in how wide a set of alternatives is taken into consideration. In the Neyman-Pearson theory a

---

[9] Milton Friedman, "A Monetary and Fiscal Framework for Economic Stability," *American Economic Review*, June, 1948, pp. 245–64; see especially Section IIIB.

choice between only two alternatives (single or composite) is made. In estimation, a choice is made from an infinite number of alternatives which are neatly arranged in a continuous finite-dimensional space. Obviously these are only two special cases of a much broader problem. Statisticians are often compelled to use solutions to these special problems in situations requiring a broader approach (which has not yet been developed). For instance, we constantly take hints from the data regarding the choice of hypotheses to be tested from the same data—although we know that the degree of confidence to be placed in the test is affected by that practice. These and similar[10] difficulties can only be resolved by a theory or theories permitting choice of hypotheses from a wider range of alternatives than hitherto considered.

To the extent that hypothesis-seeking is an activity that can be formalized by such a theory, there is little doubt that the concept of statistical efficiency will remain relevant. It will also remain true, I believe, that choices between alternative hypotheses can be made with greater power of discrimination on the basis of explicit mathematical formulation of these alternatives, in the form of probability models describing the generation of the observations. However, there remains scope for doubt whether all hypothesis-seeking activity can be described and formalized as a choice from a preassigned range of alternatives. If not, there is further doubt whether the concept of statistical efficiency or discriminatory power of a method of selecting hypotheses can be given a definite meaning.

Having thus granted the principle of Vining's remark, I hasten to add that my criticism of the statistical measures used by Burns and Mitchell is not, I believe, affected thereby. On page 170[11] of my review I indicated that these measures are found to be inefficient tools if the range of alternative hypotheses is restricted by the use of economic theory concerning the behavior patterns underlying the formations of economic variables. I adduced the availability of more efficient tools, and, indeed, of the yardstick of efficiency, as a strong reason for accepting such a restriction of alternatives, in order to attain greater sharpness of conclusion, at the price of attaining only a conclusion conditional on basic hypotheses not tested from the same data.

Arrow has pointed out to me in conversation that scientific progress has often been made in the past by narrowing down the range of alternatives in such a manner that a crucial experiment or test can be devised. He mentions as a striking example the historical dispute between corpuscular and wave theories of light. Progress was made just because this issue was believed settled in favor of the wave theory by experiments devised for the purpose, at a time when the synthesis of wave and corpuscular theory envisaged by modern quantum theory was not regarded as an available alternative. These and similar

---

[10] I discuss further limitations of present statistical theory in Section 6 of the article cited in footnote 6.

[11] In the middle of the second column. [Page 200 of the present volume.]

examples suggest a scientific strategy of not discarding basic theoretical notions and assumptions before they "cause trouble," that is, before observations are made which come in conflict with these basic notions and assumptions.

It may be added that it becomes extremely difficult, if not impossible, to assess the appropriateness of any statistical technique if resort is not taken to some narrowing down of alternatives. If "hypothesis-seeking" means just looking for hypotheses which find some support in the data (without specifying what alternative hypotheses find less support) it will be hard to prove that tools as formal and elaborate as those employed by Burns and Mitchell are better than, as good as, or not greatly inferior to other possible measures or test criteria.

Vining's jocular remarks about a commissariat of research should, I am sure, have made me throw up my hands in horrified protest at the mere idea of such an anomalous office. Instead (I confess) they set me daydreaming as to what questions I really would ask if for one day I were to be so installed (much like a schoolboy who is allowed to act as the mayor of the town for one whole day). I felt that my first official action would be to make available ample resources for the exploration of the basic principles of statistical inference. Then I would ask economists to overhaul their theories of individual behavior, modified in the light of sociology and social psychology, and express these theories in mathematical form. I would ask government economists for an enumeration and description of the possible instruments of policy, and welfare economists for a statement of (complementary or alternative) objectives of policy. Next I would ask mathematicians to perform such aggregations of individual behavior equations as would bring out the most important (aggregate) behavior parameters, knowledge of which would guide policy toward any of the relevant objectives. I would then ask statisticians to get ready for the collection of the necessary data (if not already available) and to devise methods to estimate these parameters. . . .

At this point disturbing thoughts occurred to me. What if I had forgotten some important link in the chain? What if each of these groups conceived of their tasks in such a way that their respective results could not be fitted together? These thoughts rather spoiled the daydream, and I abandoned it before it could turn into a nightmare ending in my liquidation for inefficiency.

13

A Rejoinder*

By RUTLEDGE VINING

PROFESSOR KOOPMANS has replied with patience and restraint, and one who has questioned his position cannot but appreciate his attitude. But his reply seems not to be a satisfactory resolution of our differences. Point (*a*) appears to me to be left somewhat in the air. Moreover, in the discussion of the other three points there are conveyed what I believe to be misconceptions. In my opinion, the attainments of the recent work in econometrics are primarily in the extension of the theory of regression, and on the basis of what has been published it seems misleading to imply that in this extension new truth has been discovered in the field of economic relations. Finally, I read from the reply what must surely be a misconception with regard to the type of empiricism represented by the work of Burns and Mitchell. I shall comment upon point (*a*) and upon the nature of the presumed misconceptions.

In his discussion of the appropriate unit of analysis, Koopmans is of course not maintaining that the effect of two or more "causes" acting together is necessarily equivalent to the sum of the individual "causes" acting independently. This kind of linearity, we are told by physicists, characterizes classical mechanics but not the phenomena stressed in modern physics. In this latter field the equation system is nonlinear, and the effect of two or more causes acting jointly is not the sum of the individual effects. Neither is Koopmans intimating that anything at all can be inferred as *necessary* about the real world from first principles. The development of science has been a series of surprises. Mathematical systems and systems of logic contain no necessary truth about empirical phenomena. They are axiomatized systems of relations invented to deal with reality as found, and there is not just one algebra or one geometry.

Neither does he deny the *possibility* that an important component of motivated and problem-solving individual behavior is indeterminate and fundamentally unpredictable—in the sense that he would perhaps admit as unpredictable the outcome of his own problem-solving behavior. But he presumably does assert that a knowledge of all there is to know about individual behavior together with a mathematics with which the individual behavior

* *The Review of Economics and Statistics*, Vol. XXXI (May, 1949).

equations may be combined would yield all of the parameters of group behavior relations, these latter in turn containing the properties of the structure of an economic system. He makes no claim that his present knowledge of the "individual behavior equations" is much more than trivial, and he states that the mathematics has perhaps not yet been invented.

One could quibble here. If individual behavior should have only a statistical stability and predictability, is the error term that is attached to the individual equations or the "expected value" of individual effects an attribute of a population or of the constituent individual? And is it the individual that Koopmans regards as the unit anyway? Perhaps his unit is the family or the firm, in some instances a grouping of families and in many instances a grouping of firms.

But the point at issue is more clear-cut than this. I maintain that it is gratuitous for anyone to specify any particular entity as necessarily the ultimate unit for the whole range of inquiry within some general and essentially unexplored field of study. Scientific procedure has involved working from observed regularities in space and time to logical inferences of other space-time relations. Theories, subject to test by observation, are developed in this process, the simplest theory accounting for observed phenomena being that which uses the least number of postulated and "unexplained" relations. What this implies with respect to the unit of analysis is an empirical matter. Koopmans in demonstrating the efficiency of his choice among possible units must establish the relative simplicity of his empirically tested theory.

Koopmans presents his position in the form of a syllogism that is clearly faulty in its formulation. What he implies in his premise goes beyond what must necessarily be granted. There is implied that all actions and configurations associated with human beings are subject ultimately to individual determination. No room is left for the possibility of structural features and dynamic behavior characteristics that are invariant with respect to human decisions. His conclusion includes a term, "behavior characteristics of the group," which is not defined and which appears to be used in such a way that the statement is reduced to a tautology. No issue would be involved over the triviality that in moving a house one must move the constituent bricks; but no one would contend that from the properties of individual bricks one could infer all the properties of the house being constructed. There is more to the developing house than can be learned from the bricks. Whether or not this is the case with regard to human beings and the structural and functional characteristics of evolving societal forms is not a matter of logic, but rather a matter of fact.

These considerations seem so obvious that I am inclined to think that our differences are largely verbal. Koopmans' analogies are drawn primarily from physics, and he is thinking perhaps of "aggregate" in terms, say, of the total or joint effect of the bombardment of a screen by many atomic particles. I used the word "aggregate" or "population," following analogies drawn from biology, in the sense in which certain populations are regarded as fundamental

biological entities. Certain aspects of a termite colony are studied by considering the entire organization as an integrated organism, just as the eye or the
heart or the nervous system may be looked upon as a "population" of cells.
These entities have structural and functional properties that are studied by
observing the organism as a unit. Similarly, we may learn of structural and
functional characteristics of human social forms by studying a social structure
as a unit. From this point of view, Koopmans' conception of "structure"—as
suggested by his use of "structural equations" and "structural coefficients"
and by his reference to Arrow's comments—strikes me as being excessively
formal; and his notion of the "aggregation problem" seems to me to be confined to the formal realm of arithmetic. A look at the older sciences, as
Koopmans recommends, shows morphologists or their counterparts engaged
in the study of the more concrete and "pictorial" aspects of structure and
function in all the empirical sciences. To assume that *all* structural properties
of an economic system may be expressed and most effectively studied as
different modes of adding or combining "structural equations" appears to me
not only to beg baffling questions but also to aspire to more generality than
has been achieved in the "older sciences."

The point of the discussion, of course, has to do with where Koopmans
thinks we should look for "autonomous behavior relations." He appeals to
experience but in a somewhat oblique manner. He refers to the Harvard
barometer "to show that relationships between economic variables . . . not
traced to underlying behavior equations are unreliable as instruments for
prediction." He might have gone back to a period prior to the Harvard
barometer and been reminded of the research preceding the Federal Reserve
Act which led to the reliably "planned" alternation of what was regarded as a
socially undesirable extreme seasonality in the money markets. His argument
would have been more effectively put had he been able to give instances of
relationships that *have been* "traced to underlying behavior equations" *and*
that have been reliable instruments for prediction. He did not do this, and
I know of no conclusive case that he could draw upon. There are of course
cases of economic models that he could have mentioned as having been
unreliable predictors. But these latter instances demonstrate no more than the
failure of the Harvard barometer: all were presumably built upon relations
that were more or less unstable in time. The meaning conveyed, we may
suppose, by the term "fundamental autonomous relation" is a relation stable
in time and not drawn as an inference from combinations of other relations.
The discovery of such relations suitable for the prediction procedure that
Koopmans has in mind has yet to be publicly presented, and the phrase
"underlying behavior equation" is left utterly devoid of content.

In the lively exchange between Keynes and Tinbergen in 1939,[1] Keynes
remarked that Tinbergen was anxious not to claim too much. "If only he is

---

[1] *Economic Journal*, Volume 49 and Volume 50.

allowed to carry on, he is quite ready and happy at the end of it to go a long way towards admitting, with an engaging modesty, that the results probably have no value." But econometrics has faced up to its responsibilities since those faraway days, and Koopmans now confronts us with the awful portent of authoritarianism as the alternative to success in his venture. Keynes was heavily critical of the procedures used by Tinbergen. Econometricians have in general held that the criticisms were the conclusions of a sadly misinformed and misguided man. But I judge that with the arguments simply put, many economists today would agree with most of what Keynes had to say; and those points upon which he was misinformed they would regard as among the less important. Moreover, in my judgment, many economists, given a full account in simple terms of the theoretical and technical developments since Tinbergen's models of 1939, would find the present models as intellectually unsatisfying as the models of Tinbergen, and for the same basic cosmological reason. Many would simply remain unconvinced that the real thing is put together in any such fashion as is implied. They could be readily convinced of the validity of these procedures through empirical demonstrations. But many economists remain unimpressed by what has been made available.

Tinbergen's procedure amounted to a glorified multiple correlation project. He arranged to have a complete system of equations, "complete" being used primarily in an algebraic sense. His methods of estimating the parameters of these equations are now regarded as capable only of yielding biased estimates, the term "bias" being used in a sense defined in theoretical statistics. Statisticians have understandably found stimulation and interest in the hunt for unbiased methods of estimating the parameters of a system of equations. But my judgment is that many economists, while commending the reduction in bias of estimation, would be more impressed with the possibilities of biases introduced by the philosophical postulates of the "economic analysis." Tinbergen computed standard errors, but as then computed they are not regarded as valid measures of reliability. Confidence intervals, it is contended, may now be computed appropriate for the model adopted. But the meaning of "confidence" must be construed with care. It is not a confidence in the model for purposes of predicting the future. Nor is it a confidence in the model for purposes of predicting the effects of policy decisions. When Koopmans speaks of introducing "greater stability in the economy by indirect inducements" he has reference to a planned alteration of some of his estimated coefficients or to the "suppression of a structural equation." So far as I know, Koopmans has no practicable basis for feeling any confidence one way or another regarding such a refurbishing of his estimated equation system.

It is along these lines, I think, that the general economist can be misled by the econometricians' characterization of their own attainments. Econometricians, on the other hand, may apparently mislead themselves when they attempt to characterize the research efforts of economists. Consider, for example, Koopmans' characterization of the work of Burns and Mitchell. As the last resort for economists frustrated by failures in other efforts and as something, alas, inadequate for our stand against direct administrative prescription of individual behavior, he describes "the type of information collected by Burns and Mitchell: statistical averages and frequency distributions of cyclical characteristics." But this is a misconception. The book under review is not a terminal book and was explicitly designed to outline in detail certain methods of measurement that have been adopted in an explorative study of economic variation. However uninspiring these particular procedures may seem to us, we have grounds for confidence in the investigators responsible for them. I would want the reader to refer back to Burns' *Production Trends in the United States since 1870*, and to pass judgment upon the nature of the knowledge provided in that book. To me, the book holds a magnificent portrayal of the dynamic growth of industrial America, implying an intricate theoretical structure. Perhaps this theoretical structure may be systematized in terms of simpler elements than those used, and maybe some later scholar will see in these evolutions of growth a generalizing principle. But having done our best towards systematizing, let a comparison be made between that which may be read from this book and the economic theory underlying one of Koopmans' models. This work should suggest expectations from the work on business cycles, even if a knowledge of Mitchell's work through the years had not already induced a confidence that an understanding of real processes would be furthered. Koopmans uses somewhat loosely the term "empiricist position" and associates it with the National Bureau. But, again, let the reader study the work of Friedman and Kuznets, *Income from Independent Professional Practice*, and answer whether or not economic and statistical theory are brought to bear and furthered. Or let him study the forthcoming volume on inventories by Abramovitz and answer whether or not the theory of the role of inventory investment in business fluctuations is furthered.

These are works that come to mind and of course others could be added. To some they evidence a growing understanding of the structure of an economic system, of how the variety of industrial behaviors are interwoven, and of the stresses and strains of a great economy in motion. In Koopmans' remarks there is no indication of a realization of this.

Additional Comment*

By TJALLING C. KOOPMANS

. . . THE PROCESSING of a larger number of observations places a premium on simple methods of statistical inference, possibly at some sacrifice in information extracted. Suggestions in that direction are contained in the work of the National Bureau of Economic Research, which has studied various order statistics such as leads and lags in turning points, and amplitudes and periods of fluctuation, for a large number of available time series. Used originally mainly as a means of measuring past cyclical experience, similar techniques have been studied by Moore as a possible means of prognosis of his work on diffusion indices. The selection of the particular order statistics used has been made largely on intuitive grounds. At first sight, the selection of just a few items out of a time series, or the utilization of directions of change rather than magnitudes of change may appear as a somewhat wasteful use of information. However, in regard to nonlinear models that recognize ceilings and floors to the movements of some variables, the theory of statistical inference might show such measures to be reasonably efficient summaries of a large part of the relevant information contained in the series. If this were to be the case, the intuitions that led to the adoption of such measures would be vindicated. . . .

* Quotation from Tjalling C. Koopmans, "The Interaction of Tools and Problems in Economics," the third of *Three Essays on the State of Economic Science* (New York: McGraw-Hill Book Co., Inc., 1957), pp. 215–16. [This has been added here at the suggestion of the author and with permission of the publisher.]

III. ECONOMETRIC MODELS

14

Introduction

THE FIRST attempts to construct economy-wide econometric models were chiefly concerned with testing business cycle theories and establishing such cyclical properties as periodicity, phase timing, and amplitudes. There was some concern with stabilization policies, but the Keynesian revolution shifted the emphasis heavily in this latter direction. The need for accurate forecasting techniques in order to implement government policies directed econometricians toward building models that would explain the levels of employment and activity at any given time and project them into the near-term future. Their research expanded with the mathematical elaboration of the Keynesian system, the gathering of reasonably reliable social accounting information, and the development of methods of statistical inference from nonexperimental data.

This Keynesian outgrowth is perhaps best illustrated in Daniel Suits' paper in the section on forecasting, where he takes up the accuracy of econometric prediction, policy applications of models, and evaluation of realistic multipliers. The econometric models in the present section, however, emphasize more recent applications to the original objectives of pure cycle problems that motivated Tinbergen in his celebrated League of Nations Study.

The papers by Duesenberry, Eckstein, and Fromm and by the Adelmans use the technique of simulation, whereby a model is put through its cyclical paces under hypothetical conditions. The Duesenberry–Eckstein–Fromm account studies the U.S. economy, through the eyes of a model, in recession phases of the business cycle. In this connection, it is important that they are able to use quarterly data. The Adelman paper uses the modern electronic computer to simulate a fairly large-scale model of the American economy over a future time span under assumed exogenous conditions. They find that the pure propagation mechanism, in the language of Frisch, produces only a severely damped cycle that does not resemble realistic business fluctuations. They do find, however, that the model under repeated random impulses, again in the sense of Frisch, propagates cycles that have average characteristics very much like those recorded by the National Bureau of Economic Research over the past 100 years.

The Adelman paper raises basic questions as to the endogenous or exogenous character of business cycles, and their research is carried further in another study published by Mrs. Adelman in 1962.[1] The theory of nonlinear cycle models is based on the assumption that cycles are endogenous. This is especially true of the contributions of Goodwin and Hicks in Part I. The stochastic shock theory of cycles emanates from a fundamental paper by E. Slutsky, which we decided not to reprint because of its highly mathematical nature.[2]

The model serving as a basis for the simulation studies of the Adelmans, known as the Klein-Goldberger model, is separately published in a book, and Carl Christ's review article conveniently summarizes the system of equations and appraises it in the context of the whole development of macroeconometric models. Since we could not reprint two review articles on the same book, the reader may be referred to Karl Fox's review, which gives an independent appraisal.[3]

The number of econometric models that have been constructed for various countries continues to grow rapidly. Two recent trends have been toward use of quarterly data and toward greater disaggregation. Some further comments on the use of econometric models in forecasting will be found in our introduction to Part VII.

---

[1] I. Adelman, "Business Cycles—Endogenous or Stochastic?" *Economic Journal*, Vol. LXX (December, 1960), pp. 783–96.

[2] E. Slutsky, "The Summation of Random Causes as the Source of Cyclic Processes," *Econometrica*, Vol. V (April, 1937), pp. 105–46.

[3] K. Fox, "Econometric Models of the United States," *Journal of Political Economy*, Vol. LXIV (April, 1956), pp. 128–42.

15

A Simulation of the United States Economy in Recession*

By *JAMES S. DUESENBERRY*,† *OTTO ECKSTEIN*,†
and *GARY FROMM*‡

PART I

A. INTRODUCTION

FOR SOME years economists have been saying that the American economy is
now much more stable than it was before World War II. It has been argued
that, for various reasons, business investment is now far more stable than was
formerly the case. Moreover, it has been held that the "automatic stabilizers"
—i.e., high marginal tax rates, and transfer payments responsive to income—
reduce the impact of any change in business investment or government
expenditure. Finally some attention has been given to the effect of rapid
population growth on the stability of demand for consumer goods and for
housing. The logic behind these arguments has been reinforced by the success
with which we have weathered the three postwar recessions.

Pronouncements to the effect that the business cycle is over have not,
however, been unanimously accepted. Many writers have been doubtful about
the new stability of business investment. And while everyone agrees that the
postwar levels of tax and transfer payments help to stabilize the economy,
in 1949 and 1954 they were reinforced by fortuitous changes in tax rates.
In addition, the strength of durable goods consumption in 1954 was probably
due more to luck than to built-in stability. Moreover, the economy performed

* *Econometrica*, Vol. XXVIII (October, 1960). Reprinted by the courtesy of the Econometric Society and the authors. This paper (condensed for this reprinting) was presented at
the Chicago Meetings of the Econometric Society, December 28, 1958. We thank the Harvard Economic Research Project which provided us with research aid and made available
the time of one of the authors. We also thank the Social Science Research Council for
financial assistance to defray the cost of computations and other research expenses.
The paper was prepared for a conference on economic stability organized by the Council.
  † Harvard University.
  ‡ The Brookings Institution, Washington, D.C.

very nicely in minor depressions in the twenties although we know now that it was in fact very unstable.

It seems desirable therefore to examine the stability of the system in a systematic way. In this paper we have attempted to gauge the response of the economy to various hypothetical shocks by constructing an econometric model and then calculating the time sequence generated by the model and predetermined sequences for certain autonomous variables.

The logic of the theory of income determination suggests that the stability of the economy is determined by three sets of factors—(1) the stability of the sum of business investment, residential construction, and government purchases of goods and services, (2) the systematic response of consumer expenditures and inventory in GNP, and (3) the residual variance in consumer expenditure and inventory change.

In this paper we have concentrated on the last two problems. We have constructed an econometric model of quarterly movements of the GNP. In this model government purchases of goods and services, gross private domestic fixed capital investment and foreign investment, are taken to be autonomous. The equations of the model explain the movements of consumption and inventory investment.

The model was constructed by starting with the relation that disposable income equals GNP less taxes, transfers, and gross retained corporate earnings (and some minor items). We then constructed equations to explain each of the components of the difference between GNP and disposable income. The variables in those equations were current values of GNP, its components, or autonomous variables such as population. We next constructed a consumption function in which real consumption per capita is a function of lagged real income per capita and lagged real consumption per capita. Finally, we constructed an inventory investment equation in which real inventory investment is a function of current and past GNP components, lagged inventory stock, and changes in unfilled orders for durable goods.

Given the values for the autonomous variables for a particular period t, and values of GNP and its components for the previous period, it is possible to estimate consumption and inventory investment for period t and therefore to compute GNP for period t. It is also possible to compute disposable income in period t. The results of that computation plus a new set of values for the autonomous variables for $t+1$ can be used to compute GNP and its components for period $t+1$ and so on.

Using this procedure it is possible to estimate how the GNP will move during a period of several quarters in response to any set of initial conditions and any set of movements of the autonomous variables. It also is possible to judge the effectiveness of the so-called automatic stabilizers. Finally it is possible to judge the probable effect of changes in the tax system or unemployment compensation system on the stability of our economy.

We have computed a number of different sequences of values of GNP over a period of seven quarters. In doing so we have used four different sequences of movements of the autonomous variables. With each of those four autonomous sequences we have computed three sequences of GNP values, one based on the original parameter estimates for our model, one based on the same parameters except for an increase in unemployment compensation benefits, and one based on the original parameters except for a change in the personal income tax function. In the last case personal income tax rates are made to vary automatically with the decline in GNP. The results of the twelve sequences are discussed in detail in Sections D and E.

In the computations just mentioned we assumed that each of our behavior equations held exactly. We know, of course, that that is not so. We therefore wished to investigate the variations in movements of GNP which could result from superimposing random variations in the behavior equations on the movements of the autonomous variables. To do that we determined the standard error of estimate from each of our equations. We then computed new GNP sequences in the following way: (1) a sequence of values for the autonomous variables was used as before, (2) in computing the value of any variable for any quarter we first computed the value of the variable from the appropriate equation as before, (3) we then added a number drawn at random from a normal distribution with a mean of zero and a standard deviation equal to the standard error of estimate for the equation in question.

We used two of the sequences of autonomous variables previously used and made 50 sets of random drawings with each of them. The results of those calculations are discussed in Section I.

B. SOME GENERAL CHARACTERISTICS AND THE DATA FOR THE MODEL

The level of aggregation of the model follows the national income accounts of the Department of Commerce. In the case of some transfers and taxes there is some further disaggregation, but the relationships that are established are designed to correspond to the national income account figure.

The fundamental time period of the model is one quarter of a year. Thus we seek to estimate the quarterly movements of the national income accounts. In some instances, an even shorter period would have been desirable because some dynamic interactions, particularly in inventories and consumption, move so quickly. But since the national income accounts are published on a quarterly basis, that particular interval was chosen. Annual data are inadequate for studies of the economy in recession because the postwar declines have been of such short duration and have not coincided with calendar years. A quarterly model does appear to be able to reflect much of the dynamics of recession.[1]

---

[1] The Department of Commerce has recently published a revised set of national income figures. Our analysis was completed before the new figures appeared. The parameters of the model thus apply to the unrevised figures.

The variables are expressed in real rather than monetary terms.[2] Generally, relationships which abstract from price changes tend to be more stable, and within recessions, price movements have been small in the postwar years. In the case of the tax and transfer functions, particularly the personal income tax, it is the monetary relationship which is stable, however; the increase in revenue is the same whether a rise in personal income is due to inflation or to an increase of real income. In such instances, the relationship was established in current dollars.

Seasonally adjusted variables were used, thus divorcing our model from the calendar. In the "real world," seasonal fluctuations can reinforce business cycle movements, and there is some evidence that this did occur in the postwar recessions. But the magnitude of seasonal fluctuations prevents the identification of the cyclic properties of the system in data which contain the seasonal variation.

All relationships, except for some structural tax coefficients, are established from time series data. In the case of the consumption function, quarterly time series covering both the prewar and postwar periods were used. In the rest of the model only postwar data were employed; the tax and transfer system has been drastically altered since the prewar period. For several of the equations dealing with taxes and transfers, as well as for our profit equation, the system is assumed to behave differently in recession than at other times. Data drawn only from recession periods were used to estimate these functions.

As a consequence, the model is appropriate only for recession.[3] It is not designed to explain the upper turning point in the business cycle, nor is it appropriate for periods of general prosperity. Some of the equations, including the important consumption, inventory, and personal income tax equations, are fitted for all normal peacetime conditions, and the rest of the system could be estimated for other economic circumstances; but the present study confines itself to the case of recession. A model fitted to a wider range of business cycle conditions might not have been able to reflect the stability properties of the system.

C. THE NATURE OF THE MODEL

The model divides itself into two parts; first, the total gross national product is built up; second, the disposable income which would be generated is computed. Given the disposable income, consumption is estimated; also,

---

[2] Because the Department of Commerce does not yet publish quarterly deflated data, it was necessary to deflate the various series. Deflators were constructed, using the annual implicit deflators for GNP components as benchmarks.

[3] In this respect we differ from the Klein-Goldberger model. L. R. Klein and A. S. Goldberger, *An Econometric Model of the United States, 1929–1952* (Amsterdam: North-Holland Publishing Co., 1955), esp. pp. 142–154. Work is currently in progress, however, to extend the quarterly analysis to the complete cycle.

given sales, unfilled orders and inventories, a value for inventory investment is derived. The rest of the demand for GNP is determined autonomously. Government expenditures for goods and services are either estimated from budget projections, or in some experiments, by arbitrary assumption. Similarly, fixed investment[4] and foreign investment are determined from outside the system, though the assumptions used in our experimental iterations are designed to reflect specific recession conditions, and thus implicitly contain some allowance for induced effects.[5]

Given a level of GNP, we estimate the impact of the various automatic stabilizers, including tax declines, increases in several categories of transfer payments, as well as changes in business saving. We allow for some of the trends in the system which would continue in recession, stabilizing trends such as increased retirements and diminished tax collections due to population growth, and destabilizing trends such as increased property tax collections and growing capital consumption allowances. With disposable income known, consumption is estimated for the succeeding quarter, the next period's inventory investment is determined, and given the assumptions for the autonomous components, GNP is computed.

There are several lags in the system. Consumption depends on preceding disposable income; inventory investment depends on several variables at an earlier date; dividends depend on their level in the preceding quarter, and there are several trends. Thus the system is a dynamic model rather than an equilibrium one.

The model is completely recursive, rather than interdependent, however.[6] Once the initial conditions and the assumptions about the autonomous demands are specified, it is possible to compute the path of the system step-by-step, without treating any of the equations as simultaneous. While this consideration played little role in our choice of the model, its recursive nature permits the use of simple least squares methods without introducing the bias that would be caused by simultaneous equations.

D. SIMULATION OF MACROECONOMIC BEHAVIOR

1. *Experiment I: A Medium Recession, Active Government*

In our first experiment we have tried to show the effects of the various stabilizing and destabilizing influences in our economy in a realistic context.

---

[4] We also treat investment in farm inventories as autonomous.

[5] Our model may be contrasted to the notable model prepared by Lusher and others within the federal government. See David W. Lusher, "The Stabilizing Effectiveness of Budget Flexibility," and Comment by Samuel M. Cohn, in National Bureau of Economic Research, *Policies to Combat Depression* (Princeton, New Jersey: Princeton University Press, 1956), pp. 77–100.

[6] For the technical definitions of these terms, see R. Bentzel and B. Hansen, "On Recursiveness and Interdependence in Economic Models," *Review of Economic Studies*, Vol. XXII (3) (June, 1955), p. 153.

A set of hypothetical values for GNP and its components, quarterly from the 4th quarter of 1957 through the 2nd quarter of 1959, were computed. To do that we constructed series for Gross Private Domestic Investment, Government Purchases of Goods and Services, and Net Foreign Investment for the seven quarters. For the 4th quarter of 1957 to the 3rd quarter of 1958 we used approximately the actual values. For the remaining quarters we estimated government purchases from various newspaper forecasts; net foreign investment was set arbitrarily at 1 billion dollars for the period; business plant and equipment expenditures were estimated from the reports of the SEC-OBE anticipation survey through the end of 1958. For subsequent quarters the consensus of "outlook" experts was applied.[7]

TABLE I

EXPERIMENT I: THE PSEUDO-REALISTIC SITUATION

	Quarter							
	1957:3 1	1957:4 2	1958:1 3	1958:2 4	1958:3 5	1958:4 6	1959:1 7	1959:2 8
1. GNP	440.0	431.6	425.8	419.7	420.8	428.0	439.8	453.1
minus								
2. Depreciation	37.4	37.9	38.6	39.3	39.9	40.6	41.2	41.9
3. Indirect business taxes	37.1	37.0	37.1	37.1	37.3	37.6	38.0	38.5
4. Subsidies + statistical discrep.	1.7	0.5	0.5	0.5	0.5	0.5	0.5	0.5
5. Corp. income taxes	20.9	18.7	17.1	16.4	16.3	17.4	19.2	21.3
6. Retained corp. earnings	7.4	5.6	4.4	4.1	4.3	5.6	7.4	9.4
7. Contributions to social ins.	14.6	14.2	14.0	13.8	13.9	14.1	14.5	15.0
plus								
8. Transfers	26.0	27.8	28.7	29.7	29.8	29.2	28.1	26.8
equals								
9. Personal income	346.9	345.3	342.8	338.2	338.4	341.5	347.0	353.4
minus								
10. Personal taxes	43.6	43.2	42.8	42.0	42.1	42.7	43.9	45.2
equals								
11. Disposable income	303.3	302.1	300.0	296.2	296.4	298.8	303.1	308.2
12. Consumption	283.6	280.2	280.3	279.6	277.6	278.7	281.3	285.2
13. Inventory change	+2.3	−2.0	−6.6	−5.3	−5.5	−2.8	+1.1	+5.6
14. Autonomous demand	154.1	153.4	152.0	145.4	148.7	152.2	157.4	162.3

---

[7] Contrasting the movement in GNP in experiment I with the actual historical movements, the magnitude of the decline was approximated closely, 20.3 billion in the model versus 22.6 billion actual. The time pattern of decline and recovery corresponds to the actual movements, including a flat trough of two quarters followed by vigorous recovery. However, a delay in peak inventory decumulation by a quarter, plus error terms in other equations, makes the simulation fall behind actual developments by a quarter. Also, the assumed recovery in autonomous elements is somewhat smaller than actual events.

We wish to emphasize that these figures did not in any sense represent a forecast. They were used only to provide an illustration for data whose absolute and relative magnitudes are familiar. Such a choice seemed desirable in order to make it easy for the reader to see the implications of the model. But we did not make any serious forecast of either government expenditures or private investment. We are here only concerned with illustrating the implications of a predetermined set of movements for those variables.

We also had to construct a series for unfilled orders for durable goods. That series was constructed in such a way as to provide a rough consistency between the order series and the assumed path of government purchases and private investment. We used actual values through the third quarter of 1958 and then used the slope of a regression of changes in unfilled orders in quarter t on sales in $t + 1$. The relation between orders and sales is not a precise one so that we only needed to establish rough consistency between the two. Part of the movement of orders is autonomous.

Finally, a number of our equations involve lags. For the initial lagged values we used the actual data for the 2nd and 3rd quarters of 1957, adjusting for price changes to the 3rd quarter of 1957. The results are therefore in constant, 3rd quarter 1957 prices. The assumed data for government purchases and private investment were not price corrected, however, since prices for sales to these sectors did not rise on the average.

Our procedure was as follows:

1. Using lagged values, we computed consumption for the 4th quarter, 1957.
2. The consumption figure plus the autonomous elements gave us final product sales for the 4th quarter. That figure with the lagged data for sales and inventory change and inventories and autonomous unfilled order data gave inventory investment.[8]
3. Previous inventory stock plus inventory investment gave inventories at the end of the 4th quarter.
4. Consumption plus government purchases, foreign investment, private fixed investment and inventory change gave 4th quarter GNP.
5. The GNP figure was then used to compute disposable income for the 4th quarter.

In our model the sum of the autonomous elements, private fixed investment, government purchases, and net foreign investment, falls from 154.1 billion in the 3rd quarter of 1957 to a low of 145.4 in the second quarter of 1958. It rises by 3.3 billion in the 3rd quarter and then rises quite rapidly to 162.3 by the 2nd quarter of 1959. In the upswing that movement represents a combination of low and steady private investment and strongly rising government expenditure.

The result is a rapid decline in GNP from a high of 440 billion in the 3rd quarter of 1957 to a low of 419.7 billion in the 2nd quarter of 1958, another quarter near the bottom followed by a vigorous and accelerating recovery

---

[8] Inventory investment was first computed in 1947 prices and then inflated to 1957 prices using a price index of 140, which was based on a rough computation of the relative importance of changes in durable and non-durable inventories.

to 453.1 billion in the second quarter of 1959. The 20.3 billion dollar reduction in GNP from peak to trough consists of a decline of 7.6 billion in inventory investment, an 8.7 billion dollar decline in private investment and government expenditures, and a decline in consumption of 4.0 billion. Inventory investment hit its trough a quarter earlier, with a net decline in its rate of 8.9 billion. Consumption hit its bottom a quarter after the GNP trough, a further decline of 2 billion. The small decline in consumption is due in part to the effect of the automatic stabilizers and in part to the impact of a steady increase in population.

The effect of the various stabilizers can be shown by an analysis of changes in components of personal income and personal disposable income from peak to trough. Of the 20.3 billion decline in GNP, only 8.7 billion was reflected in personal income. The difference was due to a decline of 4.5 billion in corporate taxes, of 3.3 billion in retained earnings, a rise of 3.7 billion in transfer payments, and a fall of 0.8 billion in contributions for social insurance. Those stabilizers were offset by a rise of 0.7 billion in non-corporate depreciation. Of the decline of 8.7 billion in personal income, 1.7 billion was absorbed by reduction in the yield of personal taxes. Finally, the increase in population raised consumption (over what it would have been with constant population and the same aggregate income) by 1.6 billion between the peak and trough. Population growth has a continual impact on consumption during the recovery period. Continual population growth thus operates as a stabilizer of considerable importance.

The upshot is that the automatic stabilizers operate so effectively that in a recession of the scale envisaged here, the reduction in GNP produced only a modest reduction in consumption, less than a third of the decline in GNP. On the other hand, income was greatly reduced by inventory changes. In the model sequence, changes in inventory investment account for (in quarter 3) 62 percent of the change in GNP, and for 37 percent at the trough. Fortunately the rate of decline in inventories is reduced very shortly after government expenditure and private fixed investment begin to rise. That is so primarily because of the impact of changes in unfilled orders on inventory investment. In that connection it is important to note that the placement of government orders has an influence on inventory investment before government expenditures are actually made.

It should also be noted that an inventory cycle is possible even without any feedback from inventory investment to consumption. That is due to (1) the feedback of inventory decumulation by one producer on sales of another and (2) the effect of order changes and order backlogs on inventory investment.

2. *Experiment II*: *A More Severe Recession—The Disaster Model*

Our second model was constructed in the same general way as the first, including the same pattern of decline of autonomous demands. But whereas the second quarter of 1958 sees a reversal of this decline in autonomous demands in Experiment I, these demands continue to fall here by 2.6 and 2.3 billion and thereafter by 1 billion a quarter.

In this experiment GNP falls continuously from 440 billion in the 3rd quarter of 1957 to 406 billion in the 1st quarter of 1959. It then begins to recover very slightly in the 2nd quarter. Of the decline from peak to trough, 14.9 billion was due to a change in autonomous expenditures, 9.0 billion to a decline in consumption, and 10.1 to a reduction in inventory investment.

The major difference between the two cases is not in the magnitude of the secondary effects of the change in autonomous expenditures but in their time path. In our second model GNP fell farther than in the first because there was a much greater decline in autonomous expenditure. The maximum rate of inventory disinvestment was only 1.7 billion higher than in the first case. The maximum decline in consumption was 3.4 billion more than in the first case.

In our first model, however, the rate of disinvestment in inventories reached its maximum in the second quarter of 1958 and then became smaller, turning to positive accumulation by the second quarter of 1959. In the second case, inventory disinvestment was still 5.7 billion per year in the first quarter of 1959. Thus, the increase in government expenditure in the first case, which is the rising component of autonomous demand, had not only a direct effect on income but also an indirect influence through inventories. It is to be noted that the stimulus of government action worked through orders as much as through actual expenditures. The effect of government expenditures on inventories was more important than its effect on consumption. That is at least partly due to the fact that the automatic stabilizers work both ways, absorbing much of the impact of declining GNP on consumption, but also absorbing much of the increase.

3. *Experiment III: An Analogue to the Simple Multiplier*

Our third experiment sought to parallel the conventional multiplier analysis. A once-and-for-all change in the level of autonomous expenditure of 13.1 billion dollars was postulated, and the subsequent path of the system toward a new equilibrium was iterated. Our inventory function was not used; only the effect on disposable income and the subsequent consumption reaction were traced.[9] It was found that the induced effects were extremely small. After the initial drop caused by the autonomous change, GNP falls only

---

[9] Since a term for inventory change enters our profit equation, it was necessary to postulate the amount of inventory decumulation that would occur. We assume that inventory accumulation, which was at a rate of 3.0 billion during the period of initial condition, falls to zero and remains at the level thereafter. This drop is part of the decline of the autonomous components, i.e., government outlays and fixed investment are assumed to fall by 10.1 billion.

another 1.8 billion, and thereafter begins to rise very slowly. Thus there is a tremendous amount of damping in the multiplier reaction. The various stabilizers, including business savings, constitute such a large leakage that the effect on consumption is only 40 percent of the autonomous change. To draw the analogy to the conventional multiplier, our experiment suggests a value of 1.34, defining the multiplier as the ratio of change in GNP, peak to trough, to change in autonomous expenditure.

TABLE II

PERCENT OF AUTONOMOUS DECLINE OFFSET BY VARIOUS STABILIZERS[1]

	Experiment III (Quarters)		Experiment IV (Quarters)	
	1 to 3	1 to 8	1 to 4	1 to 8
Depreciation	− 6.8	−26.8	− 6.9	−50.0
Indirect business taxes	− 0.6	− 4.2	− 0.7	− 3.9
Corporation income taxes	23.9	24.4	19.3	38.9
Retained corporate earnings	18.2	13.1	14.5	8.9
Transfers	17.6	25.6	16.4	44.4
Contributions to social insurance	4.1	3.6	3.6	3.9
Personal taxes	6.8	9.5	9.1	10.6
Total offsets	64.4	45.2	55.3	52.8

[1] The percentages represent the ratio of the absolute decline or increase in the item to the decline in GNP.

Table II shows the relative significance of the various stabilizers (including depreciation which is a destabilizer), measured from peak to trough and from the beginning to the end of the period. It will be seen that the destabilizing effect of depreciation rises with time, that the effect of declines in retained earnings diminishes, but that personal income taxes gradually become a stronger stabilizer. Sixty-four percent of the decline in GNP is offset, with corporation income taxes and retained earnings accounting for 42 percent.

4. *Experiment IV: Analogue to the Multiplier with Inventory Reaction*

The fourth model follows the preceding one, except that inventory investment is allowed to adjust in accordance with our inventory equation. Departing from the same initial conditions, autonomous demand for GNP is assumed to fall by 10.1 billion. We assume a large fraction of the decline to be concentrated in government demand for hardware items and in the demand for producers' durables; this is reflected in our assumptions by a large decline of unfilled orders in the preceding quarter. The resultant path of the system produces its lowest value of GNP, 412.5, in the third quarter of the decline, a drop of 27.5 billion. Thus, the autonomous decline is amplified by 172.3%, or there is a "super multiplier" (including inventory reaction) of 2.72.

Subsequent to the quick decline, GNP rises by two to three billion a quarter. The rapid decline is due to the sharp plunge of inventories as orders and sales drop, and to the initial round of repercussions in consumption. This fall is reversed as orders fall no further and inventories shrink with sales leveling off. The subequent slow rise is caused by a continuing improvement in inventory investment, plus the rising consumption caused by population and the rise in disposable income. The percentage breakdown of the stabilizers for this experiment is also given in Table II.

E. USE OF THE MODEL TO TEST POLICIES

To illustrate the potential use of the model to test various fiscal policy measures, some of the equations for taxes and transfers have been changed to correspond to potential policy changes. Repeating some of the simulations of the earlier experiments, the net effect of the policy changes can be seen and the resultant behavior of the economy indicated. Thus, policies can be given a trial run in the laboratory, so to speak. In this work we follow the pioneering efforts of Frisch and Tinbergen.[10]

A trial run of this sort does not constitute a full test of potential policies, of course. There may be severe practical and political difficulties. Even strictly within the realm of economics, there may be allocative distortions or other peculiar microeconomic side effects, or perhaps long-run growth or distributive effects, which may make a policy less (or more) attractive than the short-run macroeconomic simulation test suggests. And the model itself, besides being inevitably imperfect when applied to future data, is stochastic and hence produces a range of outcomes for any policy.

Nevertheless, as we hope to demonstrate with the following three experiments, the macroeconomic implications of new policies revealed by the model are neither obvious nor uninteresting. At the least, the over-all magnitudes of the impacts are indicated and can be seen in relation to the movements of the system as a whole. In the stochastic experiments reported below, two further pieces of information are produced: first, an estimate of the probability distributions of possible outcomes is given, making clear the uncertainty of any statements about policy effects; second, by comparing the probability distributions of outcomes under new policies with the distributions under present policies, the impact of the policy change on the stochastic properties of the system is shown. For example, a highly effective and quick-acting stabilizing policy may reduce the variance of outcomes by neutralizing

---

[10] See R. Frisch, "A Memorandum on Price-, Wage-, Tax-, Subsidy-, Policies in Maintaining Optimum Employment," U.N. Document, partly republished in *Metroeconomica*, Vol. VII (1955), p. 111, and J. Tinbergen, *Economic Policy: Principles and Design* (Amsterdam: North-Holland Publishing Co., 1956).

any errors in consumption, inventory investment, or in other functions of the model.

The particular policies that were tested are relatively simple, and are not meant to be applied in the precise form here given. For a full-scale test, a statutory change has to be specified and its implications on the equations of the system worked out. In particular, realistic estimates of the time lags must be made and the possibilities of error through residual discretionary elements explored. Thus the policies tested below are somewhat utopian.

1. *Experiment V: Improved Unemployment Insurance Benefits*

Experiment V shows the effect of strengthening the unemployment insurance system. Total benefit payments are assumed to be increased by 50 percent, a reform which is well within the range of feasibility. Contributions by employers are assumed unchanged. With present benefits no more than a third of average weekly wages, a 50 percent increase would still leave the benefits below one half of wages; part of the increase could also be effected by extending coverage to more people. The assumptions about autonomous demands in this experiment are the same as in Experiment 2.

A comparison of the results of these experiments reveals the net effect of this policy change in a disaster situation. As a consequence of increasing transfer payments by 2.4 billion, the decline in GNP, peak to trough, is reduced from 34 billion to 32 billion; the decline in consumption from 9 billion to 6.6 billion. These results show that this policy change has a fairly modest effect. While unemployment insurance is a perfect stabilizer insofar as it turns itself on and off with very little time lag and increases with the amount of decline that the economy has experienced, the total payments involved are simply too small, even after the policy change. Also, the inventory movements which constitute a large part of the changes in GNP are affected only by 0.4 billion by this policy. The experiments suggest, in summary, that the stability of the economy is somewhat improved by higher unemployment benefits but that this measure alone will leave the system quite unstable.

2. *Experiment VI: Automatic Rate Changes in the Federal Personal Income Tax*

The second policy experiment involves more drastic changes, a proposal which has been advocated for a number of years, but would admittedly run into considerable political difficulty. The policy would reduce the amount of income tax collected by a percentage which depends on the decline in GNP from its peak value. Tax collections would stop completely when GNP falls by one-sixth, which would correspond to unemployment somewhat greater than 10 million persons. For smaller declines the reduction in tax collections would be proportionately smaller: for example, a decline in GNP of one-twelfth would cut the tax by 50 percent. Thus federal personal tax collections are

$$T'_{pf} = \alpha T_{pf},$$

where T_{pf} is the tax collected under the regular rate structure and

$$\alpha = 1 - 6\left(\frac{\text{GNP}_o - \text{GNP}_t}{\text{GNP}_o}\right).$$

This form of automatic variation in tax collections is a very strong policy measure. By tying the rate cuts to declines in GNP rather than to unemployment it moves more quickly, since unemployment often does not develop until after a recession is well started. A more rapid compilation of GNP figures would be necessary, however. There would also be some administrative difficulties in cutting the tax so quickly, but since a large part of revenues is produced by withholding, much of the effect could be felt almost without lag,[11] and would initially be concentrated among wage and salary recipients.

The power of this stabilizer can be seen by contrasting the movement of GNP in Experiments II and VI; the decline in GNP falls from 34 billion to 20.2 billion, with consumption rising slightly through the recession. Before the end of the period, the favorable trends in population plus the upturn in the inventory reaction are sufficient to reverse the movement in GNP. Recovery would still be very slow as long as autonomous demands keep on declining by the assumed billion a year, but the depth of the depression would have been cut greatly.

The total cost to governments would not be very great, because the collections of other taxes and lower unemployment insurance costs would offset part of the loss of income tax revenue. The actual loss is an average of 4.2 billion per year, with an average income tax loss of 8 billion offset by 3.8 billion of other revenues and transfer reductions. Even at the bottom of this drastic recession, over 70% of the full-rate income tax revenues would be collected.

3. *Experiment VII–VIII: Combination of the Two Policies*

When the two policies are applied simultaneously, the stability of the system is further enhanced, though the effects of the two policies are approximately additive. The decline in GNP in the disaster situation is cut from 34 billion to 19.7 billion; consumption rises somewhat more, and the lower turning point becomes a little more decisive.

---

[11] End-of-year tax liabilities could be computed on the usual basis, with a reduction in liability allowed which is equal to the tax saving of the affected weeks. Some provision would have to be made to prevent abuse, such as bunching of large incomes in the recession weeks, but the cure to that problem is surely not beyond the ingenuity of tax lawyers.

TABLE III

EXPERIMENT VIII:

POLICY MODEL IV—BOTH POLICIES APPLIED TO PSEUDO-REALISTIC SITUATION

	Quarter							
	1957:3 1	1957:4 2	1958:1 3	1958:2 4	1958:3 5	1958:4 6	1959:1 7	1959:2 8
1. GNP	440.0	431.6	429.9	427.3	431.0	437.5	445.2	454.2
minus								
2. Depreciation	37.4	37.9	38.6	39.3	39.9	40.6	41.2	41.9
3. Indirect business taxes	37.1	37.0	37.2	37.3	37.5	37.8	38.2	38.5
4. Subsidies + statistical discrep.	1.7	0.5	0.5	0.5	0.5	0.5	0.5	0.5
5. Corp. income taxes	20.9	18.7	17.5	17.5	17.8	18.9	20.2	21.4
6. Retained corp. earnings	7.4	5.6	4.8	5.0	5.6	6.8	8.0	9.2
7. Contributions to social ins.	14.6	14.2	14.2	14.1	14.2	14.4	14.7	15.0
plus								
8. Transfers	26.0	29.4	29.9	30.6	30.2	29.4	28.3	27.1
equals								
9. Personal income	346.9	346.9	347.0	344.3	345.7	347.9	350.8	354.8
minus								
10. Personal taxes	43.6	39.4	38.6	36.9	39.0	42.7	44.6	45.5
equals								
11. Disposable income	303.3	307.5	308.4	307.4	306.6	305.1	306.2	309.3
12. Consumption	283.6	280.2	284.7	285.9	285.6	285.5	284.8	286.3
13. Inventory change	+2.3	−2.0	−6.8	−4.0	−3.4	−0.2	+3.0	+5.6
14. Autonomous demand	154.1	153.4	152.0	145.4	148.7	152.2	157.4	162.3
15. Tax adjustment factor	1.00	0.89	0.86	0.83	0.88	0.97	1.00	1.00

The combination of policies has also been applied to the pseudo-realistic assumptions used in Experiment I (Table III). Here the decline in GNP has been cut from 20.3 billion to 12.7 billion, with consumption rising by 2 billion. The initial inventory reaction is still about as strong as without the policies; it is hard to envisage any fiscal stabilization scheme that would ameliorate it. But the reaction is briefer and the economy turns up after just one quarter at the bottom. Incidentally, the total cost to governments of the two policies in this experiment is only 1.8 billion, a very small price for cutting the recession in half.

4. *Concluding Comments on Policy Experiments*

The preceding policy experiments show that it is possible to reduce the instability of the system considerably, and at relatively little financial cost to governments. But none of the actual automatic stabilizers nor the two policies tested have the capability to lift the economy back to full employment. Only if the private part of the system has the inherent tendency to reverse itself will the economy as a whole work itself completely out of a recession. The trend terms in transfers, consumption, taxes, and depreciation have a net positive effect, gradually raising the system, but it is much too small an effect, and in terms of employment, would certainly do no more than absorb the normal increase in the labor force. For the private economy to have the requisite capability to provide the stimulus for full recovery, the decline in autonomous investment must be of such form that the inventory decumulation reverses itself with sufficient vigor.

The reason for the inadequacy of the stabilizing mechanism, actual and proposed, is that it is composed almost exclusively of proportional corrections, as defined by Phillips.[12] These raise demand by some fraction of the decline from full employment levels, and hence depend on the persistence of the deviation. As full employment is approached, they become weaker. Phillips suggests that integral corrections, that is policies which depend on the cumulated past deviations, are needed to make the system reverse itself fully, but that these so increase the instability of the system that derivative corrections (which move according to the rate of change of GNP) must also be added to prevent oscillations. Clearly, to make the system completely stable automatic stabilizers with properties stronger than proportional corrections are needed. But then complete stabilization may be an undesirable objective!

F. POPULATION AS A STABILIZER

The role of population changes in our model is worthy of some comment. The regular growth of population serves as an automatic stabilizer in two ways: first, it reduces the yield of the personal income tax to the extent of $125 per baby; second, it reduces per capita disposable income in the consumption function, which raises the consumption-income ratio, and thereby the total amount of consumption. Table IV illustrates these effects for a hypothetical case. Personal income is assumed constant over 5 quarters, using 1957:3 values of the unrevised Department of Commerce series as initial conditions. The resultant movements of disposable income and of consumption are traced. It can be seen that with constant personal income, disposable income rises by 100 million dollars a quarter, while consumption rises by 600 million. Over the whole year, the level of consumption rises by 2.7 billion dollars, a significant amount by any standard.

This analysis does not exhaust the stabilizing potential of population

---

[12] A. W. Phillips, "Stabilization Policy in a Closed Economy," *Economic Journal*, June, 1954, pp. 290–323, and "Stabilisation Policy and the Time Form of Lagged Responses," *ibid.*, June, 1957, pp. 265–77. [The latter is reprinted in this volume.]

TABLE IV

EFFECT OF POPULATION GROWTH ON DISPOSABLE INCOME AND CONSUMPTION[1]
(Billions of Dollars)

	Quarter				
	1	2	3	4	5
Personal income	346.9	346.9	346.9	346.9	346.9
Disposable income	303.3	303.4	303.5	303.6	303.7
Consumption	281.0	281.6	282.5	283.1	283.7

[1] The computation assumes the actual population growth from 1957:3 to 1958:2, and a rate of 750,000 a quarter thereafter.

growth. There is also some effect on investment in residential construction, and perhaps on other items. On the other hand, the decline in economic activity will lower the birth rate, reducing the effect of this stabilizer (though with a lag, of course).

G. PRICE LEVEL CHANGES AND STABILITY

All of the calculations in our model have been based on the assumption of constant prices. If we had put prices explicitly into the model it would have been necessary to introduce a theory of price change in the system or to treat price changes as autonomous and predict them. We have not developed a theory of the price level at this point. On the other hand, the introduction of arbitrary movements in prices would have obscured the effects of the other autonomous variables. Prices have therefore been left out of our calculations but it seems desirable to make a few comments on their effects on the stability of real income.

Let us first consider the effects of uniform changes in prices and wages. Such changes affect the stability of real income because certain types of income and expenditure are fixed in money terms. Let us start with a given GNP in real terms and consider the effect on personal income of a 1% rise in the general level of prices and wages. The rise in prices increases the money value of GNP by 1%. Excise tax revenue will rise by 1%, but property taxes will not rise so that Indirect Business Taxes will rise by less than 1%. Depreciation will not rise. Corporate profits will therefore increase but most of the increase will go to corporate income taxes and retained earnings. There will be a slight increase in dividends. Transfer payments will remain fixed. Contributions for social insurance will rise by slightly less than 1%.

The net result is a very small change in the real value of personal income. For example, in the 4th quarter of 1957, GNP was 437 billion dollars. Personal income was 352 billion. A 1% rise in the price level would increase real personal income if the resultant increase in the sum of the items making up the difference between GNP and personal income were less than 0.85 billions; the latter figure is 1% of 437–352 billion dollars. Excise and sales taxes would increase by 0.18 billions, gross corporate profits by 0.56 billions, and contributions for social insurance by 0.14 billions. The total of 0.88 billion dollars would be offset by a very small change in dividends. The result therefore would be an increase in personal income of just a shade over 1%, almost exactly matching the price level rise. On this account then, general price level changes may be regarded as effectively neutral with regard to personal income.

Disposable income, however, would increase by less than the change in prices; given the elasticity of income tax collections, disposable income would rise by approximately 0.93%. For a 10% rise in prices, real disposable income would shrink by 0.7%.

Other types of price level change may have different effects. An increase in wage rates without an increase in prices will, of course, result in a reduction in gross corporate profits and a corresponding increase in personal income. Such a change will therefore lead to an increase in real disposable income and consumption.

A rise in the prices of agricultural commodities has a more complex effect. Because the demand for agricultural products is inelastic, consumption of those goods will not decline much in response to the price increase. Incomes of farmers will increase as a result and expenditure on non-farm commodities will fall. A high proportion of the decline in expenditure will be borne by gross corporate profits. As a result, personal income of farmers will rise almost in proportion to the price increase while non-farm personal incomes will fall by a small amount. The effects of increases in charges for professional services, in rents charged by noncorporate landlords, and in prices for services produced by unincorporated businesses are similar.

General price level changes have relatively little effect on the relation between personal income and GNP, but relative price changes of the type described above have effects of some magnitude.

H. STOCHASTIC PROPERTIES OF THE SYSTEM: RANDOM ERROR EXPERIMENTS

In the experiments just described we are concerned with what might be called the central tendency of the response of income to various sequences of values of the autonomous variables. We know, however, that the demand for GNP is influenced by a large number of variables which have not been taken into account whose net effect seems to be random. It is of some importance to know how far GNP can drift away from its expected value (for a given sequence of values of the autonomous variables) under the influence of random factors.

To estimate the magnitude of that drift, 50 experimental calculations were made for the autonomous sequences used in experiments I and II and for the autonomous sequence used in experiment I but with the variable tax rate function built in. To perform those experiments we calculated the standard error of estimate of each of our equations. We then calculated the sequence of values of income associated with a sequence of values of the autonomous variables in the same way as before except that the value of each variable in each quarter was set equal to its expected value, plus a random term. The random term was drawn from a universe having a mean of zero and a standard deviation equal to the standard error of estimate for the equation in question.

This procedure was justified by investigation of the properties of the distributions of the error terms of the equations. First, it was found that the errors in different equations were not correlated with each other over time. Second, according to the Durbin-Watson ratio test, the errors in none of the major equations were significantly autocorrelated. Third, the errors are normally distributed, though for some of the equations there are too few observations for a conclusive test.

For each of the three sequences of values of the autonomous variables we obtained 50 sequences of values of GNP and of all the other variables. The results in terms of the GNP sequences can be described as follows:

(1) The mean of the 50 values of GNP for each quarter in each of the three sequences was quite close to the corresponding value of the GNP obtained by running the same sequence without any random terms. That result was to be expected in view of the fact that the model's behavior is approximated by a linear system within recessions. The distributions are symmetrical and roughly normal.

(2) The variance of the distribution of the 50 values of GNP in each of the three models increased from quarter to quarter in an irregular way. A gradual increase in variance is to be expected because the linearity of the system makes the deviations from expected values linear combinations of the random terms. The absolute variance of such linear combinations expands as the number of drawings increases.

(3) We calculated correlation matrices showing the correlations of the values of the GNP in one quarter with the values of GNP from the same sequence in all other quarters. These correlations measure the relation between deviations in different quarters. Thus high correlations would show that a deviation from the mean path is likely to persist.

In a system with no feedbacks other than those of the multiplier sequence type, one would expect fairly high correlations between GNP values for successive quarters. The existence of processes of the lagged multiplier type implies that GNP is proportional to a moving average of exogenous inputs and therefore implies a correlation between the GNP values for successive quarters. The correlation will weaken with the passage of time and the speed of decline in correlation will be higher the more rapid the convergence of the multiplier process.

We found that the correlations were quite high for GNP values in adjacent quarters but declined rapidly. Thus in Model I the correlation between GNP in quarter 1 and GNP in quarter 2 was 0.74 but the correlations between GNP in quarter 1 and GNP in quarter 3 was only 0.57. Between GNP in quarter 1 and GNP in quarters 4, 5, 6 and 7 the correlation was negligible.

It should be noted that the inventory equation tends to produce negative correlations between quarters. If there is extra high inventory accumulation in one quarter, there is a tendency for decumulation in later quarters. That effect as well as the low value of the multiplier may help to explain the rapid decline in the correlations between GNP values in different quarters.

(4) The deviations of GNP from the expected value were almost identical in Models I and II. This seems to show that the effects of the autonomous variables and the random terms are essentially independent.

(5) In the sequences using the flexible tax rate scheme the variance of the values of GNP was somewhat smaller than in the other cases, and the correlations among quarters were smaller as well. The adjustment of taxes

TABLE V

RESULTS OF RANDOM SEQUENCES[1]

Qtr.	Model I			Model II			Flexible Tax Model		
	Mean	Expected Value	Variance	Mean	Expected Value	Variance	Mean	Variance	Expected Value
(1) 57:4	431.9	431.6	5.5	431.9	431.6	5.5	431.9	5.5	431.6
(2) 58:1	426.9	425.8	8.6	425.9	425.8	8.6	430.0	7.3	428.9
(3) 58:2	421.8	419.7	9.9	419.8	417.8	9.9	427.6	7.5	426.0
(4) 58:3	423.1	420.8	9.2	415.9	413.6	9.2	431.0	6.7	429.6
(5) 58:4	430.5	428.0	9.6	410.3	407.9	9.6	437.9	7.3	436.4
(6) 59:1	441.8	439.8	10.6	408.0	406.0	10.6	446.1	8.7	444.5
(7) 59:2	454.7	453.1	11.5	408.2	406.7	11.5	455.7	10.1	453.6

[1] GNP in billions of 1957:3 dollars.

CORRELATIONS

GNP in Quarter 1 Against GNP in Indicated Quarter

Qtr.	Model I	Model II	Tax Model
2	0.74	0.74	0.61
3	0.57	0.57	0.38
4	0.33	0.33	0.09
5	0.12	0.12	−0.0008
6	−0.14	−0.14	−0.17
7	−0.16	−0.15	−0.10

to income changes works to offset part of the effect of the random terms as well as much of the effect of variation in the autonomous variables.

1. *Significance of Random Variation*

The absolute size of the variance in GNP resulting from the random runs deserves some comment. The results of the random sequences can be looked at as indicating what kind of batting average a forecaster operating under very favorable conditions can expect. The forecaster is assumed to know the correct values of the parameters of the system and he knows the correct values of the autonomous variables. If he makes predictions based on the equations his errors for prediction of next quarter's income will have a variance of over 5 billion dollars. (Actually because of the high correlation between the deviations in successive quarters he would reduce the error substantially if he used the changes in the variables rather than absolute magnitudes.)

Most of the time the knowledgeable forecaster would not do much better than a naive forecaster assuming no change or projecting a simple trend. He would, however, have a much better batting average on recessions like that of 1958 when the change in GNP from the 4th quarter of 1957 to the 1st quarter of 1958 was 13 billion dollars. For forecasts 7 quarters ahead he would do much better than a naive forecaster. In Model II, for example, he would forecast a decline of GNP of 30 billion with a standard error of about 10 billion. His score in such situations would be much better than that of an unsophisticated predicter.

PART II: THE SHORT-RUN MODEL IN DETAIL

A. THE CYCLIC RESPONSE OF DISPOSABLE INCOME

1. *Outline of the Section*

This section presents a detailed analysis of the response of Disposable Income to changes in Gross National Product. This response is of critical importance to the stability of the system because of the influence of disposable income on consumption. The analysis closely adheres to the concepts of the National Income accounts. Following the Commerce Department definitions, we let

Disposable Income = Gross National Product − Capital Consumption Allowances − Indirect Business Taxes + Net Subsidy to Government Enterprises − Statistical Discrepancy − Corporation Income Taxes − Retained Corporate Earnings + Transfers − Contributions to Social Insurance − Personal Income Taxes.   (1.1)

Our task is to estimate the cyclical sensitivity of each of these components and then to derive the over-all sensitivity of disposable income. We shall proceed through each of the components in turn.

2. Depreciation

The total amount of depreciation has been on a steady upward trend in the last ten years. Even in recession depreciation has continued to increase at a slightly diminished rate. Most of the depreciation allowance is related to the existing stock of old capital; although the additions to capital slow down and the accounting depreciation of some old plant and equipment is completed, the resultant deviation from the upward trend is small. There are three reasons. First, new capital in a period is only a small fraction of the capital stock; this is particularly true when the period of analysis is a quarter of a year. Second, because of the long-run inflation, the money value of the plant and equipment being written off the books is much smaller than current investment levels. Third, the tax provisions for depreciation have been gradually liberalized, first through the rapid amortization certificates, and since 1954, through the new depreciation methods. Since 1955, an increasing fraction of new capital is being written off under the new methods, reinforcing the upward trend.

Fitting the trend to the quarterly total capital consumption allowances,[13] we get[14]

$$Ca = 30.7160 + 0.6571(t - 1955 : 1), \qquad r = 0.9996 . \qquad (2.1)$$
$$(0.0123)$$

In the event of prolonged depression, with capital accumulation seriously curtailed, formula (2.1) will, after some period, overstate depreciation. A more sophisticated estimate, more closely tied to actual movements in investment, can be derived by a method recently outlined by Schiff.[15] Applying this approximation to aggregate data, we derive an estimate of depreciation; we get

$$\text{Dept.} = -0.64 + \underset{(0.0209)}{0.9989} \left[\sum_{t=-29}^{t=0} \frac{I_{pt}}{30} + \sum_{t=-9}^{t=0} \frac{I_{et}}{10} \right] , \qquad r = 0.9987. \qquad (2.2)$$

Where Dept. is total depreciation, I_{pt} is private construction in year t, and I_{et} is gross investment in producers' durables in year t.[16] Autonomous

---

[13] This includes depreciation, accidental damage to fixed capital, and capital outlays charged to current expense.

[14] The trend term rises by the quantity one each quarter, with the base quarter defined equal to zero.

[15] Eric Schiff, "Gross Stocks Estimated from Past Installations," *Review of Economics and Statistics*, May, 1958, pp. 174–77.

[16] The stock series were constructed by using Goldsmith's data in original costs for 1945 as a bench mark (using his lower estimate for residential construction) (R. W. Goldsmith, *Saving in the United States*, Vol. III, pp. 26–29), adding cumulated national income

estimates of the other components of total capital consumption allowances need to be added. In recent years these have been equal to from 3.5 to 3.8 billion; they can be expected to fall somewhat in depression.[17]

3. Indirect Business Taxes

Indirect business taxes have remained a remarkably constant fraction of GNP since 1947. The decrease in some federal excise tax rates in 1954 and the erosion of specific taxes by inflation have been offset by gradual increases in state and local tax rates. Equation (3.1) shows the regression between quarterly indirect businesss taxes and GNP, 1947–1957.

$$T_b = -1.9955 + 0.0886\text{GNP}, \qquad r = 0.9925. \qquad (3.1)$$
$$(0.0016)$$

The elasticity implicit for these taxes with respect to changes in GNP, for 1957 figures, is 1.07.

This figure is relatively high in view of the usually assumed regressivity of these taxes. It can be explained in terms of the upward trend in the tax structure[18] and particularly by the adoption of general sales taxes by 9 states and the increase in rates in 10 others. Gasoline, cigarette and liquor taxes have also been instituted in several states or have been increased. For purposes of this study, however, the long-run elasticity of the tax is not the relevant magnitude, since it overstates the reaction of the tax when GNP falls. Several of the most important taxes have yields which tend to be irreversible. The consumption of gasoline, liquor, and tobacco is little curtailed in recession, nor do property taxes or motor vehicle licenses decline. In major depression, even these items are affected, of course.

Because of the changes in tax structure that have taken place in recent years, it is not possible to derive the recession elasticity of this group of taxes from aggregate time series data on revenue. We constructed a synthetic estimate from the elasticities of the individual taxes and of the taxed commodities.

---

account figures for total private construction and producers' durables, minus estimates of the capital whose assumed economic life has expired. Thus the stock figures are estimates of the cumulated investment of the preceding 30 and 10 years respectively. For equipment, gross capital formation 10 years earlier was derived from national income figures; for construction 30 years earlier, Goldsmith's change in total private structures was used.

[17] The behavior of depreciation in depression can be seen from the following example: Assume that plant and equipment expenditures each fall to 20 billion dollars in the first year and then fall to 10 billion in the next two years. Assuming 1957 as the point of departure, depreciation would rise by 1.4 billion the first year, stay constant the next year, and then fall by 1.1 billion. If gross capital formation halted completely, depreciation would fall by 2.5 billion.

[18] For a historical survey of recent state tax activity, see Tax Foundation, Inc., *The Financial Challenge to the States*, New York, 1957, pp. 17–19. Postwar tax revision has come in three waves, in 1947, 1951, and 1955—in each case after excessively pessimistic revenue forecasts.

TABLE VI

ESTIMATES OF INCOME ELASTICITIES OF INDIRECT TAX SOURCES

Tax	Amount (in Millions of Dollars)	Long-run Elasticity		Recession Elasticity	Depression Elasticity
Property	10,928	$0.55^{(3)}$	$0.22^{(8)}$	$0^{(5,9)}$	$0.53^{(4)}$
Liquor	3,622	$0.10^{(1)}$	$0.33^{(8)}$	$0^{(5)}$	
Tobacco	2,173	$0.42^{(1)}$	$0.63^{(8)}$	$0^{(5)}$	$0.37^{(4)}$
Gasoline	4,416	$0.42^{(1)}$	$0.36^{(8)}$	0	$0.24^{(4)}$
Other excises (federal)	4,088	$1.0^{(2)}$		$1.0^{(2)}$	$1.0^{(2)}$
General sales (state)	3,144	$1.0^{(8)}$	$1.0^{(8)}$	$1.0^{(8)}$	$1.0^{(8)}$
Customs duties	743	1.0		1.0	
Other taxes and local sales taxes	3,551	$0.5^{(6)}$		$0.5^{(6)}$	$0.5^{(6)}$
Non Taxes	1,663	$0^{(7)}$		$0^{(7)}$	
Motor vehicle licenses	797	0		$0^{(5)}$	$0.37^{(4)}$
—Federal Refunds	—125				
Total	35,000	0.54		0.28	

[1] Cross-section data, *LIFE Study of Consumer Expenditures*, Vol. I, 1957.

[2] Otto Eckstein and John V. Krutilla, "Social Cost of Capital, Hells Canyon, and Economic Efficiency," *National Tax Journal*, March, 1958, p. 11.

[3] Walter A. Morton, *Housing Taxation* (Madison, Wisconsin: University of Wisconsin Press, 1955), p. 49, based on cross-section data.

[4] Based on peak to trough changes, 1929–33.

[5] Based on recession of 1937, 1949, 1954. These zero elasticities may represent a combination of positive elasticities plus a time trend. The data do not permit us to distinguish between these two hypotheses. Their quantitative implications in future recessions are very similar, however.

[6] This includes local sales and gross receipts taxes (30% of total) and miscellaneous other taxes.

[7] Includes water and utility charges, liquor store revenues, and licenses. There is probably some slight elasticity in this item.

[8] Estimates of H. M. Groves and C. H. Kahn, "The Stability of State and Local Tax Yields," *American Economic Review*, March, 1952, p. 90.

Table VI lists estimates of these income (or rather GNP) elasticities. We give three sets of elasticities: (1) long-run elasticities based on cross-section demand data and on time series spanning at least one business cycle; (2) recession elasticities based on behavior in recent recessions, and (3) depression elasticities based on 1929–1933. It will be seen that the long-run elasticities are largest, the recession elasticities are very low, and the depression elasticities tend to be closer to long-run values.

For this study the recession elasticities are most pertinent. Our estimate of the average elasticity of indirect business taxes is 0.28. For 1957 values, this corresponds to the equation[19]

$$T_b = 26.573 + 0.0238\text{GNP} + 0.160(t - 1957:3) . \qquad (3.2)$$

---

[19] Property taxes have been rising at an annual rate of 630 million dollars a year over the last ten years, including recession years. We assume the trend to continue and introduce the last term in (3.2) for this purpose.

4. Net Subsidies to Government Enterprises

This item is treated as if it were a negative excise tax. It consists of the losses of the Post Office, of public power agencies, and other miscellaneous business-type public enterprises. The figure has risen very sharply since 1955, reaching 1.7 billion in 1957. We shall treat it as a constant in the absence of a change in government policy.

5. Statistical Discrepancy

This component of GNP is certainly the most difficult to explain. If it were a truly random error, with mean value of zero, we could ignore it, at least in single-valued estimates of our model. But Gartaganis and Goldberger have found that the statistical discrepancy is not a random error term. For seasonally adjusted quarterly data, 1939–1953, they find that the series is autocorrelated, with a mean of 0.7 billion. For recent years, 1952–1957, the mean has been 2.1 billion. We shall assume that this value will persist.[20]

6. Corporate Profits

To estimate corporation income taxes and retained earnings, two leakages between GNP and disposable income, we first estimate corporate profits, compute the tax, and then apply a dividend function; this leaves retained earnings as the residual. Since the federal corporation income tax (as well as most such state taxes) is almost a flat rate tax, this leakage can be estimated with precision. Similarly, dividend disbursement can be estimated from well-established functions. The behavior of corporate profits in recession involves much greater uncertainty.

There are at least two competing theories of corporate profits in recession, that of Modigliani,[21] and Lintner.[22] While both have influenced the concepts underlying our equation, the function derived for the model departs from their formulations.[23]

Rising prices generate inventory profits; it is reassuring that the aggregate Department of Commerce figures which are computed by a rather complicated procedure on an industry-by-industry basis correlate well with changes in

---

[20] A. J. Gartaganis and A. S. Goldberger, "A Note on the Statistical Discrepancy in the National Accounts," *Econometrica*, April, 1955, p. 172.

[21] Franco Modigliani, "Fluctuations in the Saving-Income Ratio: A Problem in Economic Forecasting," *Studies in Income and Wealth*, Vol. 11, (New York: National Bureau of Economic Research, 1949), pp. 371–441.

[22] John Lintner, "The Determinants of Corporate Savings," in Walter W. Heller *et al.* (eds.), *Savings in the Modern Economy* (Minneapolis: University of Minnesota Press, 1953), pp. 230–55.

[23] Both Modigliani and Lintner employ a form of ratchet effect, as we do below.

wholesale prices.[24] The equation is

$$\text{I.V.A.} = -0.2971 - 0.8193 \underset{(0.0027)}{} \frac{\Delta p_w}{p_w}, \qquad r = 0.9597. \qquad (6.1)$$

Our model treats prices as constant in recession, insofar as this is a reasonable assumption. We therefore assume the inventory valuation adjustment to be zero. This corresponds closely to the average value for the recession of 1954. In 1949 the adjustment reached a value of 1.9 billion; but the relative constancy of wholesale prices in the 1958 recession suggests that the I.V.A. will again be small. To make the I.V.A. an endogenous variable, a complete price theory would need to be incorporated. Where estimates of wholesale prices are available, equation (6.1) can be used to estimate the adjustment.

Neither a pure ratchet theory nor a theory which assumes a flatter slope to the profit-income relation in recovery than in decline appears to explain the profit data. A regression fitted to the pooled statistics for the 1949 and 1954 recessions (1948:4–1950:2 and 1953:3–1955:1) is as follows:

$$P_{a_0} - P_{a_t} = -1.426 + 0.362 \, (Y_{n_0} - Y_{n_t}), \qquad r = 0.773 \qquad (6.2)$$
$$(0.082)$$

where P_a is corporate profit after the inventory valuation adjustment.

This regression corresponds to the purely symmetric ratchet and is not very satisfactory.[25] It is clear that profits react strongly to declines in national income; but the simple relationship is inadequate for explaining the timing of the decline in profits within the cycle. This is not surprising; the decline in profits depends on the industrial composition of the decline, the decline in sales as opposed to the decline in production, the movements of wage-price relationships in oligopolistic industries, the degree of utilization of the capital stock at the peak in various industries, the degree of flexibility of existing technology under changes in output, and other factors.

A relationship which accounts for a good deal of the timing of the profit decline within recession is the following, which has also been fitted to pooled data of the recessions of 1949 and 1954 (48:4 to 50:2 and 53:3 to 55:1):

$$\Delta \pi_{g_0} \equiv P_{a g_0} - P_{a g_t} = -0.253 + 0.230[S_{f_0} - S_{f_t}] \qquad (6.3)$$
$$(0.098)$$

$$+ 0.558[\Delta \text{Inv}_0 - \Delta \text{Inv}_t], \qquad R = 0.902.$$
$$(0.118)$$

---

[24] The Department of Commerce seeks to eliminate capital gains on inventories from national income through the I.V.A. It seeks to put all sales on a LIFO basis. As industry adopts LIFO more widely, the I.V.A. should shrink in relation to price changes; but so far the evidence seems to be the reverse. (We owe these comments to E. F. Denison.)

[25] Using GNP instead of National Income produces very similar results. The equation is

$$P_{a_0} - P_{a_t} = -2.53 + 0.325 \, (\text{GNP}_0 - \text{GNP}_t), \qquad r = 0.778. \qquad (6.2a)$$
$$(0.073)$$

P_{ag} is gross corporate profit before depreciation but after the inventory valuation adjustment; S_f is final sales, equal to GNP minus inventory investment; ΔInv is inventory investment. The equation states that the decline in profits from its peak value depends on the decline in final sales and the decline in inventory investment.

Gross corporate profits before depreciation are used because they are the total return on fixed assets; depreciation, after all, is no more than an accounting convention, which continues to rise in recession and puts a downward trend into the figures for profits after depreciation. Final sales rather than GNP are used as the measure of economic activity because profits are earned on sales, not on production.

Inventory decumulation affects profits at least via two routes. First, when much of final sales is out of inventory, sales in intermediate stages of production fall. The amplified decline in the sales figures for the manufacturing and wholesale sectors in recession bears evidence on this phenomenon. But corporate profits, to a large extent, are earned in these earlier stages of production. Therefore they fall when inventory decumulation supplies an extraordinary share of the goods for final sale.

Railroad profits are particularly important from this point of view. Freight car loadings fall far more than final sales, partly because railroads are more important in the shipment of materials and intermediate goods than in finished products. Given their large fixed overhead, profits fall sharply with inventory decumulation. Other important industries, such as steel, power, and automobile manufacturing, are in an analogous position.

The other influence of inventory change on profits is more indirect. Inventory change is an indicator of the state of the market. It is when decumulation is large that business conditions are at their worst. Expectations are poor, and companies strike the worst bargains to get rid of inventory. Thus, profit margins shrink, accentuating the decline in total profits.

We use equation (6.3) in our model. To derive profits after depreciation, we employ equation (6.4) which reflects the upward trend of corporate depreciation:

$$\text{Depc}_t = \text{Depc}_{t-1} + 0.4 . \tag{6.4}$$

7. Corporation Income Taxes

Changes in the ratio of corporate tax liability to corporate profits have largely been due to changes in the tax structure; for example, the drop in 1954 was due to repeal of the excess profits tax. The recent level of the ratio corresponds closely to the rate of the federal tax. This is due to two offsetting factors, the favorable tax treatment accorded a few industries, such as petroleum and insurance, compensated by the revenue from state corporation income taxes. We shall assume the recent ratio to persist until there is some change in the tax structure. Thus

$$T_c = 0.51 P_a \tag{7.1}$$

where T_c is the corporate income tax liability, and P_a is corporate profit after inventory valuation adjustment.

8. *Dividends and Retained Earnings*

We estimate retained earnings (R.E.) by subtracting dividends (Dv) from total profit after taxes (P_{l_t}). Lintner's formula[26] for dividends has been applied to quarterly data, 1947–57. Where Lintner, using annual data for 1918–41 found the relation

$$\text{Dv}_t = 0.352 + 0.150 P_{l_t} + 0.700 \text{Dv}_{t-1}, \qquad R = 0.967, \tag{8.1}$$

quarterly data yield

$$\text{Dv}_t = -0.53 + 0.079 P_{l_t} + 0.91 \text{Dv}_{t-1}, \qquad R = 0.962. \quad \delta^2/s^2 = 2.23 \tag{8.2}$$
$$\qquad\quad (0.028) \qquad (0.04)$$

Lintner's formula is based on the theory that dividend decisions are couched in terms of net change from the preceding dividend and that management moves toward a preconceived dividend-payout ratio, closing a constant fraction of the gap between actual dividends and the level suggested by the desired ratio. In moving from annual to quarterly dividends, one would expect the influence of preceding dividends to become stronger and of present profits to become weaker. Annual dividends can be viewed as a cumulation of decisions about net changes—hence reflecting a larger influence of earnings. Thus the change in the coefficients in the dividend function is what would be expected under the Lintner theory. In terms of retained earnings, (8.2) becomes

$$\text{R.E.}_t = +0.53 + 0.921 P_{l_t} - 0.91 \text{Dv}_{t-1} \tag{8.3}$$

9. *Transfer Payments*

The major categories of transfer payments are old age and survivor benefits and direct relief, unemployment insurance, net interest paid by government, and other government transfers and insurance payments. We shall treat these categories separately.

a. Old Age and Survivor Benefits and Direct Relief. Old age and survivor benefits have been rising steadily in the last ten years. The number of older people has been growing, the percentage eligible for pensions has risen due to the lengthening history of the system and the statutory broadening of coverage,

---

[26] John Lintner, "Distribution of Incomes of Corporations Among Dividends, Retained Earnings, and Taxes," *American Economic Review*, May, 1956, pp. 97–113.

and benefit minima and maxima have been raised. Thus the fundamental movement in this series has been an upward trend. While there appears to be a small cyclic factor in retirements, this is not statistically significant and is swamped by movements caused by statutory changes.

Coverage of pensions has now been extended to almost everyone except physicians. Therefore, the rate of increase in beneficiaries will slow down, once the present backlog of new candidates has been depleted. According to the official projections of the OASDI System,[27] benefits of that system rise by 1 to 1-1/2 billion a year in the period 1956–59, but rise by only 500 to 600 million a year thereafter. For the period for which our model applies, a trend of 425 million a quarter is assumed, which makes allowance for trends in the other pension systems, including civil service, veterans, and railroad retirement.

Direct relief payments are also on a steady upward trend, but are significantly affected by cyclic factors. A multiple regression on total unemployment and trend yields

$$\text{Re} = 1.369 + 0.000108 U_T + 0.0335(t - 1946\!:\!4), \qquad R = 0.97 . \qquad (9.1)$$
$$\quad\;\;(0.000029) \quad\;\; (0.0014)$$

The relation between total unemployment (in thousands) and the decline of GNP from its peak is

$$U_{T_t} = 3093 + 85.96\,(\text{GNP}_o - \text{GNP}_t), \qquad r = 0.84 . \qquad (9.2)$$
$$\quad\;(13.74)$$

Substituting (9.2) in (9.1) we get

$$\text{Re} = 1.703 + 0.0093(\text{GNP}_o - \text{GNP}_t) + 0.0335(t - 1946\!:\!3) \qquad (9.3)$$

b. *Unemployment Insurance.* The relation of unemployment insurance payments to declines in GNP depends on four factors: (1) the amount of unemployment generated by the recession, (2) the fraction of the unemployed insured in the system, (3) the percent of wages which average benefits represent, and (4) the percent who have exhausted their benefits.

The amount of unemployment for a given decline of GNP depends, to some extent, on the degree to which the work-week is shortened, the industrial composition of the decline, additions to the labor force, and a host of minor factors. The fraction of the unemployed who are insured also depends on the industry mix of the decline, the geographic and industrial coincidence of recent labor force accretion with the unemployment, and so on. Because insured unemployment is less dependent on changes in the labor force, its relation to GNP is more stable.

---

[27] *Actuarial Cost Estimates and Summary of Provisions of the Old-Age, Survivors, and Disability Insurance System as Modified by the Social Security Amendments of 1958*, prepared for the use of the Committee on Ways and Means by Robert J. Myers, Actuary of the Committee, Sept. 2, 1958, p. 10.

Not all of the insured unemployed collect benefits, however. In the past two recessions between 77% and 91% collected checks. There are at least three causes of ineligibility: first, most states require at least a week of unemployment to elapse; second, people who leave their jobs voluntarily are ineligible; and third, some fraction exhaust their benefits. One would expect a time lag between changes in GNP and benefit exhaustions since the average period of eligibility is 22 weeks; but the actual lag is very small or non-existent. The reason appears to be the following: there is always a stock of candidates for eligibility exhaustion. When employment conditions worsen, many more of this group fail to find jobs, and so exhaustions rise quickly.[28] The temporary extension of the benefit period by 50% in many of the big industrial states in 1958–59 greatly reduced the importance of exhaustions.

In the absence of significant time lags, a concurrent relation between the number collecting unemployment insurance and the decline in GNP can be established:

$$U_b = 1423.46 + 66.90 \, (\text{GNP}_o - \text{GNP}_t), \qquad r = 0.917, \qquad (9.4)$$
$$(7.30)$$

where U_b is the number of people collecting, in thousands.

The ratio of weekly average benefits to average wages has fluctuated from 32 to 40 percent, depending on the generosity of state laws and their time lag behind changes in the price level. In early 1958 the ratio was 34 percent, which yielded a weekly benefit check of $30.90. Putting this figure, at an annual rate, into (9.4) yields

$$U = 2.287 + 0.1075(\text{GNP}_o - \text{GNP}_t) \qquad (9.5)$$

where U is total unemployment benefits in billions.

c. Net Interest Paid by Government. This item primarily depends on the average interest rate on the federal debt, and hence can be expected to fall in recession. The decline will be fairly small and irregular, depending on the amount of refinancing required in the period and the specifics of debt management and monetary policy. We shall assume interest as a fixed item, treating changes as part of autonomous policy. The 1957 value is 6.0 billion dollars.

d. Other Transfer Payments. The remaining 2,252 million dollars of transfers for 1956 consist of government life insurance benefits, cash sickness compensation, and some veterans benefits. We assume this item is constant during recession.

---

[28] For a more elaborate analysis of exhaustion, including a probabilistic model that could conceivably be applied to national aggregates, see W. S. Woytinsky, *Principles of Cost Estimates in Unemployment Insurance*, Federal Security Agency, Social Security Administration, Bureau of Employment Security, 1948.

10. *Contributions to Social Insurance*

This quantity, which includes employer, employee, and self-employed contributions to the various federal and state systems, moves almost proportionately, in the short run, with wages and salaries.

The ratio of contributions to wages and salaries has been rising steadily, climbing from 3.9 percent in 1948 to 6.0 percent in 1957. This is largely caused by upward revisions of the rates of OASI. Broader coverage, the institution of the self-employment tax, and changes in some of the other pension systems have also served to raise the percentage. Unemployment tax rates have moved rather irregularly, but have, for the post-war period as a whole, been falling. The ratio of wages and salaries to GNP has been little affected by recessions. The level has risen from 0.52 to 0.54–0.55 from the late 1940's to 1952–57, but a cyclic pattern is not discernible. Nor does there appear to be a lead or lag.[29]

Applying the ratio of 0.55 of recent years, we derive the relation between contributions to Social Insurance, H_t, and GNP,

$$H_t = 0.0330 \text{GNP}^t . \tag{10.1}$$

11. *Personal Tax and Non-tax Payments*

All government personal tax and non-tax payments have comprised approximately 12% of national income in recent years. The federal income tax, however, constitutes much the largest part of the total (about 90%), though the other items are not negligible by any means.

a. The Federal Income Tax.   There have been several recent studies of the cyclic properties of the Federal income tax. The most detailed study is by Pechman.[30] For the period 1948–53, he found that the tax base, i.e., taxable income, increased by 65% of the increase in adjusted gross income; he also found that both the average and the marginal effective tax rate applied to that tax base, assuming 1953 tax laws, would have remained constant at 27%, i.e., a rate of 17–18% on adjusted gross income. After the 10% rate reduction of 1954, he estimated that the marginal tax rate would be 15% to 16% of adjusted gross income, which would correspond to 14% to 15% of personal income.

Brown and Kruizenga[31] have recently found formulas for estimating

---

[29] D. Creamer, *Personal Income During Business Cycles*, National Bureau of Economic Research (Princeton: Princeton University Press, 1956), p. xiii.

[30] Joseph A. Pechman, "Yield of the Individual Income Tax During a Recession" in *Policies to Combat Depression*, National Bureau of Economic Research (Princeton: Princeton University Press, 1956), pp. 123–44. See the paper by Brown and Kruizenga discussed below for a survey of the literature.

[31] E. C. Brown and R. J. Kruizenga, "Income Sensitivity of a Simple Personal Income Tax," *Review of Economics and Statistics*, August, 1959, pp. 260–69.

taxable income which are extremely precise for the period 1929 to 1953. One formula is the following:[32]

$$\frac{Y_T}{Y_p} = 0.1669 + 0.200 \frac{Y_p}{\text{pop.} \times 10^{-3}} - 0.158 \frac{E}{\text{pop.} \times 10^{-3}}, \quad R = 0.986 \quad (11.1)$$

where Y_T is taxable income, Y_p is personal income, pop. is population, and E is the total value of exemptions. This formula makes the fraction of personal income which is taxable depend on per capita personal income and the exemption level.

Since the exemption level has been constant at $600 since 1948, equation (11.1) has been refitted for the years 1948 to 1955, omitting that variable. The result is

$$\frac{Y_T}{Y_p} = 0.1499 + \underset{(0.0049)}{0.1435} \frac{Y_p}{\text{pop.} \times 10^{-3}}, \quad r = 0.9933 . \quad (11.2)$$

This equation yields the same constant term as (11.1), making allowance for elimination of the exemption variable, but has a lower regression coefficient. This suggests that the rate of increase of the ratio of taxable to personal income declines over large changes in the level of per capita personal income,[33] but over the small range of short run changes with which we are concerned in this study. (11.2) is an extraordinarily good approximation. Tax payments were predicted by means of (11.2) for 1956 and 1957, yielding estimates which were in error by less than 300 million dollars, or about 0.7%.[34]

(11.2) can be rewritten

$$Y_T = 0.1499 Y_p + \frac{0.1435 Y_p^2}{\text{pop.} \times 10^{-3}} . \quad (11.3)$$

From this form it can be seen that

$$\frac{dY_T}{dY_p} = 0.1499 + 0.2870 \frac{Y_p}{\text{pop.} \times 10^{-3}} \quad (11.4)$$

---

[32] Brown and Kruizenga recommend a logarithmic version of this equation of the form,

$$\log\left(1 - \frac{Y_T}{Y_p}\right) = 0.0219071 - \underset{(0.00014)}{0.00257} \log \frac{Y_p}{\text{pop.} \times 10^{-3}}$$

$$+ \underset{(0.000255)}{0.0014598} \log \frac{E}{\text{pop. } 1000}, \quad R^2 = 0.9907 .$$

They prefer this form because it has the property that Y_T/Y_p will only approach 1.0 asymptotically, whereas the linear form can exceed 1.0 at a sufficiently high level of per capita income ($5,900 in formula (11.2) as compared with a 1957 level of $2,000). We use the linear form for simplicity, since it is a very close approximation over the range in question.

[33] This lends support to the logarithmic form of the equation.

[34] Because figures for taxable income for these years were not available as yet, average effective tax rates were estimated and applied to the projected tax base. Thus the resultant revenue estimates were derived from a combination of two projections—the tax base and the tax rate. Assuming the relative distribution of income to remain constant, the average effective tax rate was calculated to rise by 0.002 in 1956 and in 1957, bringing it to 0.2425.

which equals 0.72 for 1957 values. This is a somewhat higher figure than Pechman's estimate of base flexibility; but for the period studied by Pechman, say, 1950, (11.2) yields a flexibility of 0.58 with personal income, which is the same as his estimate.

Also

$$\frac{dY_T}{d(\text{pop.} \times 10^{-3})} = -\frac{1435 Y_p^2}{(\text{pop.} \times 10^{-3})^2}.$$ (11.5)

Thus, for 1957 values, an increase of population by one million persons with constant personal income will reduce the tax base by 0.574 billion dollars.

The average effective tax rate to be applied to this base was found to be relatively constant by Pechman from 1948 to 1953 despite the rise in income. This is attributable to the entry of people into the lowest taxable bracket who previously earned no taxable income and to the gradual erosion of the law; these were sufficient to offset the rise of other taxpayers into higher brackets. Also, because of the $4,000 breadth of brackets and the exemptions and deductions, the effective tax rate is almost constant up to an adjusted gross income of $15,000, the income level below which 70% of the tax was collected in 1955. However, the fraction of income remaining below the taxable level has been falling, and the fraction of income over $15,000 has been rising, so that the average effective tax rate must now be assumed to have some slight elasticity. Our computations suggest an elasticity of the average effective tax rate of about 0.10. At 1957 values, this corresponds to the equation

$$T_{pf} = -3.710 + 0.2667 Y_T.$$ (11.6)

Combining (11.3) and (11.6), we get an equation for federal income tax payments:

$$T_{pf} = 0.03998\ Y_p + 0.03828\ \frac{Y_p^2}{\text{pop.} \times 10^{-3}} - 3.710.$$ (11.7)

At 1957 values, this corresponds to a marginal tax rate[35] on personal income of 19%, or to an elasticity of 1.8.

b. *Other Personal Tax and Non-tax Payments.* These payments fall into three groups: federal estate and gift taxes, state and local income taxes, and miscellaneous state and local revenues, including special local property assessments and some charges for government services. For the state and local income taxes we assume an income elasticity of 1.5, following Groves and Kahn,[36]; actual revenues have risen much more, but this is due to structural changes. The yield of federal estate and gift taxes has recovered since the

---

[35] This assumes constant population. The increase in population would reduce the marginal rate. An increase of personal income of 10 billion dollars in a year, combined with normal population growth would yield a marginal rate of 15%.

[36] Groves and Kahn, *op. cit.*, p. 90.

decline caused by the drastic statutory liberalization of 1948. The yield is difficult to forecast because it depends on the small number of very wealthy people who may die in a year, as well as on such variables as security prices. The average annual increase, 1950 to 1956, was 90 million dollars a year, a trend we assume will persist.

The other revenues, including non-tax sources, are little related to cyclic factors; they have been rising at a rate of 300 million dollars a year for the last four years. There is reason to believe that this rate of growth will continue, if not accelerate.

Expressing these assumptions as an equation under 1957 conditions, we obtain the following equation for other personal tax and non-tax payments.

$$T_{ps_t} = (0.0075 Y_{p_t} - 0.750) + (T_{e_{t-1}} + 0.165) \tag{11.8}$$

where T_{ps_t} is all personal tax and non-tax payments other than federal income tax, in quarter t. The terms in the first brackets yield our estimate for state and local income taxes. The terms in the second brackets estimate the other items in this category, $T_{e_{t-1}}$ being the value of these items in the preceding quarter.

B. INVENTORY INVESTMENT

In attempting to develop an inventory investment equation we recognized at the outset that it would be desirable to use separate explanations for inventories of retailers, wholesalers, manufacturers and others, to separate durable goods from non-durables, and to treat work in process, raw material and finished product inventories separately. That would have involved a large system of equations including not only the explanation of each sector's behavior but additional equations to explain the relations among the sectors. With the time and resources at our disposal, it was impossible to attempt so ambitious a project. We decided that it was necessary to do as well as possible with a single equation relating total inventories to Gross National Product or some other variable at that level of aggregation. We obtained a series for total inventories in 1947 prices which was developed from the Department of Commerce data for changes in inventories.

We began with the hypothesis that inventory investment can be explained in terms of a stock adjustment process. Assume (1) that the desired level of inventories is proportional to Final Product Sales (GNP less consumer and government services, less inventory change), (2) that planned inventory investment (positive or negative) takes place when actual inventories deviate from desired inventories, (3) that expected sales in one quarter equal actual sales in the preceding quarter. Then $\Delta I_{p_t} = 4 \cdot F(a S_{t-1} - I_{t-1})$ where ΔI_{p_t} is planned inventory investment, S_{t-1} is deseasonalized sales in the previous quarter, I_{t-1} is inventory at the end of the last quarter, a is the desired ratio of inventories to sales, and F is the fraction of the discrepancy to be removed in one quarter (the 4 is needed if we measure flows at annual rates to make the adjustment between annual rates and absolute quarterly changes in stocks).

Actual inventory investment will differ from planned investment by an amount related to the change in sales from one quarter to the next. The equation for inventory investment then becomes:

$$\Delta I_t = 4F(aS_{t-1} - I_{t-1}) + b\Delta S_t.$$

We fitted that equation using quarterly data for 1948–57, deseasonalized and deflated, for inventories, final product sales and changes in sales. We did not have data for durable and non-durable goods inventories separately. However, we did have separate sales data for durables and non-durables. We therefore tried fitting an equation in which a single inventory was related to the two types of sales. That approach had to be abandoned, however, because durable and non-durable final product sales are linearly (though not proportionally) related to one another in the postwar period with a very high correlation. The results of the calculation were disappointing. The multiple correlation obtained from the equation described above was only 0.3.

We tried leaving out the data for the Korean War period but the results were not better. We then had to consider whether the basic hypotheses was wrong, whether the basic idea was right but was expressed in too crude a form in our equation, or whether some important additional variable was needed. We noted that, although inventory change is not well explained by the assumption that firms are trying to keep inventories proportionate to final product sales, inventories themselves are linearly related to final product sales. Moreover, Ruth Mack's studies seem to lead up to an equation of the same general type.[37] Her work, of course, suggests that no adjustment of inventories takes place when the ratio of inventories to sales lies within a certain range. An equation corresponding exactly to her description of inventory behavior would be a good deal more complicated than ours.

Those considerations suggested that the low correlation obtained might be due to the fact that sales and inventories in the postwar period move with a strong trend but with relatively little variance about the trend. If the basic hypothesis were correct, we might still get a poor explanation of quarterly inventory investment because of (1) the crudeness of our model, (2) errors in the data, (3) our failure to take account of the indifference range postulated by Ruth Mack.

We therefore tried to find some data which would show wider discrepancies between desired and actual inventories and therefore give the stock adjustment process more chance to work. For that purpose we used the National Industrial Conference Board data for inventories and shipments of a sample of manufacturing firms from 1929 through 1940.[38] We fitted the stock adjustment equation described above to those data. The multiple correlation was

---

[37] R. P. Mack and Victor Zarnowitz, "Changes in Retailers Buying," *American Economic Review*, March, 1958.

[38] National Industrial Conference Board, *Economic Record*, December 26, 1940. Inventories, Shipment Orders 1929–40.

0.68 which is not so bad for quarterly data involving changes in a stock. However, only one of the three coefficients (the one for sales) was significant. That result was not terribly impressive but it did suggest that the original hypothesis was not completely off the track.

We then gave some further thought to the crudely aggregate nature of our model. We noted that manufacturers' sales vary much more than in proportion to sales of final product. We constructed some simple multi-sector models and concluded that the explanation of that fact is that inventory accumulation or decumulation for one firm produces changes in sales of others which are not reflected in final product sales. Those models also suggested that inventory change would be better explained by adding the previous period's rate of change of inventories to the explanatory variables.

We tried that with spectacular results. The lagged inventory change raised the correlation to 0.8. However, the results did not seem satisfactory in other respects. When the predicted change in inventories was plotted against the actual change, we found that the prediction equation was always one quarter too late at the turns. Moreover, the regression coefficient for current inventory change on lagged inventory change was much too large. We concluded that lagged inventory change though possibly relevant in itself was also a proxy for some other variable.

We therefore looked for another variable having a fairly strong serial correlation. At that point, Mr. Michael Lovell showed us the results of some computations directed toward the explanation of raw material and work-in-process inventories for manufacturing. Those computations indicated that a good explanation could be obtained by using a stock adjustment equation plus change in unfilled orders for durables lagged a quarter. We fitted the equation

$$\Delta I_t = 4F(aS_t - I_{t-1}) + b\Delta S_t + c\Delta O_{t-1} + dO_{t-1} + e$$

where O_t is unfilled orders for durables at the end of period t. The resulting multiple correlation was 0.86, which seems very satisfactory for quarterly data.

We had reasoned, however, that lagged inventory change should be relevant, so we put it back into the equation. It had a significant regression coefficient of much smaller size than the one obtained before using the orders variable. We concluded that it would be desirable to make use of the lagged inventory variable as part of the explanation of inventories.

Our final equation (fitted for 1948:4–1957:4) was

$$\Delta I_t = 0.295\,S_t - 0.947\,I_{t-1} - 0.333\,\Delta S_t + 0.771\,\Delta O_{t-1} + 0.115\,O_{t-1}$$
$$\quad(0.078)\quad\;(0.267)\qquad\;\;(0.107)\qquad\;(0.139)\qquad\qquad(0.054)$$

$$+\,0.341\,\Delta I_{t-1} + 8.508, \qquad R = 0.90,\; S_e = 1.74 \qquad \delta^2/S^2 = 2.27$$
$$\;\;(0.115)$$

A number of observations on the equation and its significance are, in order:

(1) The constant term arises, in part at least, from the fact that there is a difference between the inventory ratios for durable and non-durable goods and a linear relation (with a constant term) between them. The constant term may, of course, also reflect nonlinearity or average deviations from the regression not equal to zero.

(2) All the coefficients are highly significant with the possible exception of the lagged value for unfilled orders. The standard error of estimate of the equation, however, is rather high. Even if the world actually conformed to the statistical model underlying our regression procedure, we could not claim a very high degree of predictive accuracy.

(3) The coefficients on the first two terms can be written in the form $4 \times 0.237(0.31S_t - I_{t-1})$ which suggests (a) an inventory final product sales ratio at 0.31 and (b) that about one-fourth (0.237) of the deviation of actual from desired inventories will be removed each quarter if there is no further change in sales.

(4) The correlation of inventories with sales is 0.94 and the regression coefficient of inventories on sales is 0.35, which is consistent with the estimate obtained above. The 0.31 figure is a little lower than the actual average ratio because durable and non-durable inventories are weighted by the marginal ratios in the regressions.

(5) In view of those correlations, it seems likely that the variances of the sales and inventory coefficients in the equation are not independent. Both reflect the variance of F, the coefficient of speed of adjustment of actual inventories to desired inventories. We should expect F to be more variable than the desired ratio itself.

(6) The fact that the stock adjustment part of the equation explains so little of the variance of inventory investment, although the coefficients seem perfectly sensible, requires explanation. One possible interpretation is to say that in the period in question there was a strong trend in sales. The stock adjustment process produced a strong trend in inventories while the other variables explained variations around the trend. The stock adjustment equation then can be regarded as explaining why the average value of inventory change was positive while the other variables explain deviations about that average.

(7) Finally, we must ask why changes in unfilled orders play so important a role. It was noted above that changes in unfilled orders are related to raw material and work-in-process inventories with a lag. That suggests that when orders rise above sales and therefore increase the order backlog, production is increased, causing an increase in raw material and work-in-process inventories in the following quarter with the change in sales coming still later.

On the whole, we feel that the equation given above has coefficients which make sense in terms of signs and orders of magnitude. The combination of a stock adjustment process with a reaction to changes in order backlogs has a good rationale. In addition, it is consistent with data for manufacturing alone. Obviously, a great deal more work needs to be done before we have a really satisfactory explanation of inventories.

One final point must be noted. The coefficients in these equations reflect the actual relation between durable and non-durable purchases in a postwar world. That relation would not hold up in a deep depression. Except to the extent that the unfilled orders variable provides a corrective, our equation may understate changes in inventories in deep depressions.

C. THE CONSUMPTION FUNCTION

In the twenty years since Keynes introduced the concept of the consumption function, we have made a good deal of progress in our understanding of consumer behavior. To some extent that progress has consisted of finding out how little we know and how much remains to be found out.

In the *General Theory*, Keynes, though emphasizing the importance of the income variable as a determinant of consumption and saving, gave at least a sketchy account of the influence of other factors. But in the early empirical work and the early theoretical applications of the consumption function notion the income variable received almost exclusive attention. That was appropriate enough since income is certainly the most important determinant of consumer expenditure and saving. But we have progressed beyond that stage. We cannot here review the enormous mass of literature on consumption which has appeared in the last twenty years. A list of the more important conclusions on which most economists will probably agree will suffice.

(1) There is a fairly strong association between changes in disposable income and changes in consumer expenditures. (2) There is a considerable unexplained variance in quarter-to-quarter changes in consumption. That remains true even when we use a complicated consumption function and include the non-income variables which seem most relevant. (3) There is little reason to believe that the proportion of income saved tends to rise merely because of the secular increase in per capita real income. It will be noted that this is a negative statement. It does not assert that the savings ratio is a constant but only that the ratio is *not* a function of the absolute level of income. (4) Consumer expenditures are influenced not only by current income, but also by some type of average of past incomes and by expected future levels of income. (5) The rate of consumer expenditures is influenced by several aspects of the asset and debt position of households. (6) The rate of consumer expenditures is influenced by demographic factors, e.g., age distribution, distribution of families by years of marriage, etc. It is also influenced by the distribution of income jointly with the demographic variables and by its distribution among farmers, entrepreneurs, and others. (7) The savings ratio is probably influenced by a complex of institutional arrangements such as pension plans, mortgage amortization arrangements and availability of credit.

We wished to develop a consumption function which could be used in a quarterly model. We concluded at once that we could not deal with distributional variables or with institutional change. We did, however, attempt to take account of the influence of liquid assets, consumer debt (other than mortgages), and the number of recent marriages. Data for those variables are available; two of them, liquid assets and consumer debt, have received a good deal of attention in the literature.

Because of the argument given by Enthoven[39] we had some doubt whether consumer debt would in fact be an important factor in the explanation of consumption. We also had some doubt about the importance of liquid assets in the aggregate because the ownership of liquid assets is so concentrated. We began from the point of view that in addition to assets, debt, and recent marriages, we should include some variable which would represent the influence of past income or past consumption. Such a variable would take account of the effects of both "permanent income" considerations and habit persistence. Three ways of introducing these considerations suggested themselves: (1) to make the ratio of consumption to income depend on the ratio of current or recent past income to previous peak income; (2) to make current consumption depend on current income and consumption in the previous quarter—thus making consumption depend on a moving average of income; (3) to make current consumption depend on a moving sum of past consumption—this would have the same effect as (2) but would reduce the effect of random variations in consumption in one quarter on consumption in the succeeding one.

The equations involving the previous peak income were fitted in ratio form. The equations in the absolute form suffered from collinearity. In the first difference form there was some indication of interactions of the type described by Haavelmo. The ratio forms seemed to be fairly free of both problems. Dividing all the variables except the recent marriage one by an income variable seemed to eliminate the effects of trends and seemed to eliminate the cause and effect problem which appeared in the first difference form. We therefore concentrated our attention on the equations in ratio form.

We found that the marriage variable was correlated with the other variables in such a way that whenever it was used, all the coefficients became very unstable. The marriage variable never had a statistically significant coefficient, but, because of the intercorrelations, that does not indicate that marriages do not have an influence on consumption. We had no choice but to drop out the marriage variable and concentrate our attention on the other variables.

We concluded that while assets and debt probably have some influence on consumption, it cannot be very powerful and must be measured with finer instruments than time series regression. Data for the joint distribution of

---

[39] Alain C. Enthoven, "Installment Credit and Prosperity," *American Economic Review*, December, 1957.

liquid assets and debt with demographic variables might give more satisfactory results. In that connection the work now being done by Professor
Orcutt is very promising.[40] Meanwhile we must do the best we can. After
some experimentation with lags we finally concluded that the best equation
has the form[41]

$$\frac{c_t}{y_{t-1}} = \alpha + \beta \frac{y_{t-1}}{y_{o_{t-1}}} + \gamma \frac{c_{t-1}}{y_{t-2}}$$

when c_t is deflated consumption per capita, y_t is deflated disposable income
per capita, y_o is the highest value of deflated disposable income prior to
period t. We fitted this equation for the periods 1929–38, 1948–57, and the
two periods together. We also fitted the same form of the equation with the
variables, per capita debt over disposable income, and per capita liquid assets
over disposable income, added. The six equations which resulted are given
in Table VII.

After some study of the correlation matrices we concluded that the intercorrelations of assets, debt, and income in the prewar period had distorted
the coefficients in equation 4. In the postwar period income has never
declined much so we judged that postwar data alone would not give any
significant information on the relative importance of previous peak income
and previous consumption. We concluded therefore, that the most reliable

---

[40] Guy H. Orcutt, "Decision Models and Simulation of the United States Economy,"
unpublished paper (mimeographed), Harvard University, December, 1957.

[41] It is interesting to note that this equation may also be expressed in the form of a
Friedman (*The Theory of the Consumption Function*) permanent income type consumption
function. Robert Dorfman made this observation and was kind enough to bring it to the
authors' attention.

Let: $\qquad\qquad\qquad\qquad\qquad x_t = c_t/y_{t-1}$

Assume (a Koyck transformation):

$$x_t = \alpha + \beta \frac{y_{t-1}}{y_{o_{t-1}}} + \beta\gamma \frac{y_{t-2}}{y_{o_{t-2}}} + \beta\gamma^2 \frac{y_{t-3}}{y_{o_{t-3}}} + \ldots$$

Then:

$$\gamma x_{t-1} = \alpha\gamma + \beta\gamma \frac{y_{t-2}}{y_{o_{t-2}}} + \beta\gamma^2 \frac{y_{t-3}}{y_{o_{t-3}}} + \ldots$$

and:

$$x_t - \gamma x_{t-1} = \alpha(1 - \gamma) + \beta \frac{y_{t-1}}{_o y_{t-1}} .$$

Therefore, since $x_t = c_t/y_{t-1}$

$$\frac{c_t}{y_{t-1}} = \alpha(1 - \gamma) + \beta \frac{y_{t-1}}{y_{o_{t-1}}} + \gamma \frac{c_{t-1}}{y_{t-2}} .$$

The empirical results in no way prove or disprove any particular theoretical interpretation of the statistically derived equation. Several hypotheses, including Friedman's, are
consistent with the given function which, seemingly, fairly accurately describes aggregate
consumer behavior.

TABLE VII

Consumption Functions
(Deseasonalized, 1947–49 Dollars, Per Capita)

1930—1938   1948—1957

1. $\dfrac{c_1}{y_{t-1}} = 0.5353 - \underset{(0.0217)}{0.1366} \dfrac{y_{t-1}}{y_{0t-1}} + \underset{(0.0457)}{0.5704} \dfrac{c_{t-1}}{y_{t-2}}$

   $R = 0.9106$
   $S_e = 0.0168$
   $\delta^2/S^2 = 2.18$

2. $\dfrac{c_t}{y_{t-1}} = 0.4914 - \underset{(0.0251)}{0.1361} \dfrac{y_{t-1}}{y_{0t-1}} + \underset{(0.0450)}{0.5577} \dfrac{c_{t-1}}{y_{t-2}} + \underset{(0.0284)}{0.0262} \dfrac{D_t}{y_{t-1}} + \underset{(0.0056)}{0.0130} \dfrac{A_t}{y_{t-1}}$

   $R = 0.9183$
   $S_e = 0.0161$

1930—1938

3. $\dfrac{c_t}{y_{t-1}} = 0.5826 - \underset{(0.0472)}{0.1685} \dfrac{y_{t-1}}{y_{0t-1}} + \underset{(0.0669)}{0.5472} \dfrac{c_{t-1}}{y_{t-2}}$

   $R = 0.8959$
   $S_e = 0.0217$

4. $\dfrac{c_t}{y_{t-1}} = 0.8703 - \underset{(0.2059)}{0.6490} \dfrac{y_{t-1}}{y_{0t-1}} + \underset{(0.0565)}{0.5474} \dfrac{c_{t-1}}{y_{t-2}} + \underset{(0.2187)}{0.8895} \dfrac{D_t}{y_{t-1}} - \underset{(0.0324)}{0.0561} \dfrac{A_t}{y_{t-1}}$

   $R = 0.9376$
   $S_e = 0.0170$

1948—1957

5. $\dfrac{c_t}{y_{t-1}} = 0.8218 - \underset{(0.0819)}{0.6250} \dfrac{y_{t-1}}{y_{0t-1}} + \underset{(0.0526)}{0.7843} \dfrac{c_{t-1}}{y_{t-2}}$

   $R = 0.9306$
   $S_e = 0.0069$
   $\delta^2/S^2 = 1.84$

6. $\dfrac{c_t}{y_{t-1}} = 0.7771 - \underset{(0.0981)}{0.5951} \dfrac{y_{t-1}}{y_{0t-1}} + \underset{(0.0710)}{0.7417} \dfrac{c_{t-1}}{y_{t-2}} + \underset{(0.0167)}{0.0317} \dfrac{D_t}{y_{t-1}} + \underset{(0.0085)}{0.0116} \dfrac{A_t}{y_{t-1}}$

   $R = 0.9376$
   $S_e = 0.0065$

estimates would be obtained from using data for the whole period, i.e., either equation 1 or 2. The coefficients on assets and debt in equation 2 were both small relative to their standard errors and the sign for debt was incorrect. We therefore decided to drop them and use equation 1.

PART III: CONCLUDING COMMENTS

Without repeating the conclusions that our various experiments suggest, some concluding comments are in order.

1. We believe that there will continue to be variations in autonomous GNP demands.

2. Given a shock of this nature, it takes very little to generate an inventory reaction, which will lower production considerably, but this will reverse itself fairly quickly if autonomous demands do not continue to deteriorate.

3. The reaction on consumption is likely to be small, however, because of the automatic stabilizers. Of these, much the most important is the modern corporation, the profits of which suffer a large share of the decline in incomes, but which almost maintains its dividends.

4. Present stabilizers do not have the power to return the system to full employment.

5. Better stabilizers are possible, including some which would have the capability to restore the system to full activity. Such stabilizers would substantially reduce the violence of recessions below the levels that occur now; but damping of the inventory reaction is extremely difficult, if not impossible.

6. The stability properties of the system change with time, as tax rates are changed and as population and the social insurance systems impose different trends. Thus models such as this one must be revised periodically.

7. The deviations introduced by random error terms into our simultations cumulate only to a very moderate extent, far from becoming explosive.

8. The variance of these deviations is independent of the size of the decline of the autonomous demands.

9. Self-correcting stabilization policies, such as variable tax rates, decrease the variance of deviations caused by random errors and reduce the serial correlation of the deviations.

10. The model simulated the 1958 recession closely, using only data from earlier periods, suggesting that it has some predictive value. Obviously, better models, using a lower degree of aggregation, can, and should, be built. The present relatively crude model can, however, provide useful estimates of the macroeconomic results of present and potential policies.

16

The Dynamic Properties of the Klein-Goldberger Model*

By IRMA ADELMAN and FRANK L. ADELMAN†

1. INTRODUCTION

ONE OF THE MOST vexing of the unsolved problems of dynamic economic analysis is that of constructing a model which will reproduce adequately the cyclical behavior of a modern industrial community. None of the schemes so far advanced have (yet) offered a satisfactory endogenous explanation of the persistent business fluctuations so characteristic of Western capitalism. It is true that there exist theories which lead to oscillatory movements, but, except under very special assumptions, these swings either die down, or else they are explosive in nature.[1] In the latter case, appeal is usually made to externally imposed constraints in order to limit the fluctuations of the system,[2] while, in the former case, exogenous shocks must be introduced from time to time to rejuvenate the cyclical movement.[3] Since recourse to either of these devices is rather artificial, it is of interest to seek a more satisfactory mechanism for the internal generation of a persistent cyclical process.

While it is desirable for an economic model (or any other model, for that matter) to be as simple as possible, it is almost certain that an adequate explanation of the business cycle cannot be found through approaches as idealized as those usually suggested. It may be of interest, therefore, to

---

* *Econometrica*, Vol. XXVII (October, 1959). Reprinted by courtesy of The Econometric Society and the authors.

† The Johns Hopkins University and Institute for Defense Analysis, Washington, D.C. Formerly at Stanford University and at the Livermore branch of the University of California Lawrence Radiation Laboratory. We are grateful to the Computation Division of the Radiation Laboratory for the use of their facilities. Also, we wish to express our appreciation to Arthur Goldberger for his helpful discussion of this paper.

[1] P. A. Samuelson, "The Interaction of the Accelerator and the Multiplier," *Review of Economic Statistics*, Vol. XXI (1939), pp. 75–78.

[2] J. R. Hicks, *A Contribution to the Theory of the Trade Cycle* (Oxford, 1939).

[3] R. Frisch, "Propagation Problems and Impulse Problems in Dynamic Economics," *Economic Essays in Honor of Gustav Cassel* (London, 1933), pp. 171–205. [Reprinted in the present volume.]

278

examine, from this point of view, the most complicated econometric description of the United States published in recent years—the 1955 forecasting scheme of Klein and Goldberger.[4] This structure, which consists of 25 difference equations[5] in a corresponding number of endogenous variables, is nonlinear in character, and includes lags up to the fifth order. By its very nature it constitutes a description of a dynamic world, rather than a portrayal of comparative statics. Not only are the endogenous variables in each period functions of exogenous inputs, but also of lagged endogenous quantities and of stock variables. Thus, even if all the exogenous magnitudes were held constant, the economy represented by these equations would still vary with time.

But, while this model has been applied to yearly projections of economic activity in this country with some success, its dynamic properties have been analyzed only under highly simplifying assumptions. In particular, it would be interesting to find out whether this construct really offers an endogenous explanation of a persistent cyclical process. We should like to learn whether the system is stable when subjected to single exogenous shocks, what oscillations (if any) accompany the return to the equilibrium path, and what is the response of the model to repeated external and internal shocks.

The purpose of this paper, then, is to investigate these issues in some detail. There are perhaps two major reasons which indicate why this work has not previously been done. First of all, the fact that Klein and Goldberger used observed quantities as inputs for their annual forecasts, rather than values generated by the model from earlier data, prevented them from studying, at the same time, the type of dynamic paths which would be traversed by the system in the absence of external interference. Secondly, the complexity of the model requires the use of modern high-speed computers for the long-run solution of the system in a reasonable length of time. Since the problem is about the right size for the IBM 650 calculator, and since the appropriate computing facilities exist at the University of California Radiation Laboratory, we programmed the equations for that machine.

2. THE MODEL

The Klein-Goldberger econometric model of the United States[6] is a system of 25 difference equations in as many endogenous variables. Some of the equations are accounting identities, while others, behavioral in nature, were derived from statistical fits to empirical data. Generally speaking, each

---

[4] L. R. Klein and A. S. Goldberger, *An Econometric Model of the United States*, 1929–52 (Amsterdam, 1955).

[5] Including 5 tax equations.

[6] For an excellent, more detailed description of this model, see C. F. Christ, "Aggregate Economic Models," *American Economic Review*, Vol. XLVI (1956), pp. 385–408. [Reprinted in the present volume.]

equation describes some significant feature of the economy. The real sector of the model includes, in addition to the usual consumption and investment relationships, a production function, a corporate profits equation, and a corporate savings function. Also taken into account are private employee compensation, farm income, imports, and depreciation. The monetary sector consists of two liquid asset functions, two interest rate equations, a wage adjustment relationship, and an agricultural price equation. There are also five tax equations, which represent the impact of government tax policies upon the economy, and five accounting identities. Of the exogenous variables, the most important (aside from time) are government expenditures, population size, and the distribution of the labor force among the several sectors of the economy. All these equations are given in Appendix A, together with the definitions of the symbols used.

For this study of the Klein-Goldberger system several changes were introduced into the most recent Klein-Goldberger model, some for convenience and some for consistency or logic. First, whenever the standard error of estimate of a regression coefficient was more than twice as large as the coefficient itself, we dropped the corresponding term from the equations. The justification for so high a level of significance is that, for our purposes, we felt it less serious an error to ascribe to a zero coefficient a nonzero value than to ignore a regression coefficient which has an economic existence. The alterations made in accordance with this criterion are indicated in Appendix B, Section 1. In principle, of course, one should correct the equations for these omissions. However, since we were not interested in accurate prediction, but, rather, in the dynamic performance of the model, we felt that the required modifications were small[7] and would not add to the value of the study.

A second departure from the original system was to delete the import equation. This was done because, during the sample period, the calculated quantities of imports constituted a poor approximation to the values observed.[8] After imports had been dropped from the list of endogenous variables, it seemed reasonable also to omit both imports and exports from the model. For, since both would now be exogenous, and since their difference contributes only a small amount to GNP, it is difficult to see how their exclusion could alter the dynamic character of the system.

A modification of quite another sort was made in the form of the tax equations. Since those given by Klein and Goldberger were not intended to be applicable for more than a few years,[9] we had to re-estimate all the tax relationships. Therefore, at the suggestion of A. Goldberger,[10] we adopted

---

[7] Indeed, in all cases, the quantitative changes which would have been required lay within the standard errors of the constants to be altered.
[8] Cf. Klein-Goldberger, *op. cit.*, p. 95 and Figure 29, p. 102.
[9] Klein-Goldberger, *op. cit.*, pp. 96–102.
[10] Private communication.

a new set of tax functions, which assumed that the tax policies of 1952, interpreted as relationships between real variables, would continue indefinitely into the future. These are incorporated into the tax equations which appear in Appendix B.1.

We were also forced to alter the interest rate equations. Since the excess bank reserves, R_t, are taken as exogenous, the short term interest rate $(i_S)_t$ and the long term rate $(i_L)_t$ can both be computed without reference to the rest of the system. With the small values of R_t typical of the postwar period, it is evident from the short-term interest rate equation [Eq. (15)] that $(i_S)_t$ will double (roughly) every decade. And yet there is no restoring force within the system to keep this quantity at a reasonable value! Similarly, $(i_L)_t$ will, ultimately, become equal to about $0.7(i_S)_t$. In view of the fact that such a projection would eventually result in economic nonsense, we decided to suppress the interest rate equations and to fix (arbitrarily) the short term rate at 2.5% and the long term rate at 3.5%.

Lastly, the agricultural price equation was re-evaluated, using only the postwar data. The reason for this alteration was the admittedly unsatisfactory behavior of the form used by Klein and Goldberger.[11]

We were still not in a position to follow the long-term development of this system, however, as it was necessary to extrapolate the exogenous variables far into the future. This was done, in some instances, by fitting a least-squares straight line to the postwar data. But, in the case of governmental expenditures, the discontinuity because of the Korean War and the subsequent intensification of military preparedness, imparted a trend to the postwar data much steeper than could reasonably be expected to continue. Therefore, we estimated the rate of increase of government expenditures by fitting a straight line to both the prewar and the postwar points, omitting only those of 1951 and 1952. The level was chosen to coincide, more or less, with that of those latter two years. With this procedure we found that our extrapolation leads to numbers which appear to be consistent with current experience.

On the other hand, agricultural subsidy income and the number of farm operators have a declining trend. For these quantities it seemed more appropriate to use a fit of the form

$$X = a + \frac{b}{t - \alpha},$$

in order that they never become negative. Finally, since there was no obvious trend, during the postwar period, for the index of hours worked and the index of farm exports, both were taken as constant. The extrapolations of all the exogenous quantities appear in Appendix B.2. The initial values of the lagged variables are listed in Appendix B.3.

---

[11] Klein-Goldberger, *op. cit.*, p. IX and Fig. 31, p. 105.

3. CALCULATIONAL PROCEDURE

The modified Klein-Goldberger model to be investigated thus consists of a set of 22 simultaneous equations in a corresponding number of endogenous variables. What we must do in order to evaluate the magnitudes of the endogenous variables for the year t is to insert into these equations the values for the $(t-1)$st and preceding years, as required, along with appropriate exogenous numbers, and solve the equations simultaneously. Using the newly found endogenous quantities for the tth year plus the required exogenous magnitudes, we can then solve the system for the endogenous variables of the $(t+1)$st period. This process is continued until we have traveled sufficiently far into the future to satisfy our curiosity.

At first glance the system we wish to analyze would appear to be highly nonlinear. The substitution of $q = 1/p$ as a variable, however, instead of the price level p itself, leaves us with only a single nonlinear equation (18), the wage and salary identity. Of course, it is much easier to solve a set of simultaneous *linear* equations than it is to evaluate a nonlinear system. For this reason it was decided to "linearize"[12] (18), and then to utilize a successive approximation procedure to find the solution of the nonlinear set to the desired degree of accuracy. Our criteria for an acceptable solution were that the value of each variable appearing in the nonlinear equation must differ from its previous approximation by less than $\frac{1}{2}\%$ and that the original form of that equation also be satisfied to that accuracy. Since convergence was quite rapid, even when the initial guess was poor, our criteria appear to be sufficiently stringent to assure convergence to the economically relevant solution of the system (in case there is more than one solution).

Before actually programming the equations for the IBM 650, however, it was possible, by appropriate algebraic substitutions, to reduce the 22 equations down to a set of four simultaneous equations in four unknowns. The investment relation (2) could be evaluated from exogenous and lagged data, while the equations remaining after the completion of the algebra could be solved *seriatim* as soon as the answers to the first five were available. This procedure was advantageous, if not actually necessary, because the computation time required for the solution of a simultaneous linear system by matrix inversion is proportional to the cube of the rank of the matrix.

. After all the preceding considerations were taken into account, it turned out that neither memory space nor running time was a serious limitation on the use of the IBM 650. Therefore, the problem was coded for the machine in a straightforward manner. As a matter of interest, the computations for one year could be made during an operating time of about one minute.[13]

---

[12] To do this, we wrote the equation in terms of differences from initial (extrapolated) guesses, which must be consistent with the integral form of the equation.

[13] The actual time depends on the number of iterations required for convergence; in the linear part of the time path, the first guess is adequate.

4. THE DYNAMIC NATURE OF THE MODEL

Now, we are finally in a position to study some of the problems raised in the Introduction. First of all, what is the dynamic nature of the Klein-Goldberger model? That is, what sort of time path will these equations generate in the absence of additional external constraints or shocks? *A priori*, it is conceivable that the long-run extrapolation of this short-run predictive system will indicate that the economy so described is subject to a business cycle more or less analogous to that observed in modern industrialized societies. On the other hand, it is also possible that this model cannot offer even a qualitative picture of the economic growth process in the real world.

Fig. 1

KLEIN-GOLDBERGER TIME PATHS

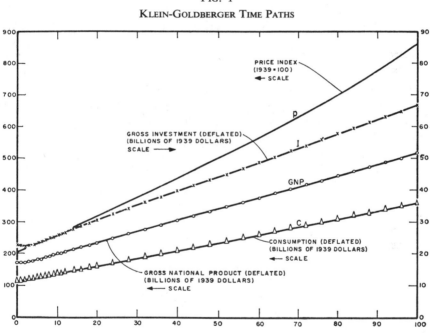

Our first machine data decided the issue unequivocally. After a brief "settling-down" period, the system is quite monotonic and essentially linear. There is no hint whatever of any internally generated business cycle, and, indeed, even in the first few years, the shock of start-up is not sufficient to induce more than a single turning point in any variable. Of course, since most of the exogenous trends are fitted by straight lines, it is not surprising that the overall character of the solution is linear, rather than, say, quadratic, but the absence of oscillations is less obvious (*a priori*) and more significant.

The time paths of several of the more important quantities are depicted in Figure 1. The several curves in Figure 1 represent the projections of the price index and of the real values of GNP, consumer expenditures, and gross private investment, respectively. The approximate behavior of the rest of the variables may be inferred from the information in Table 1.[14]

In an attempt to see whether the qualitative properties of the solution are at all sensitive to the starting conditions, we reduced the magnitudes of all but seven[15] of the initial values of the real quantities by 10 percent. The results of this calculation possessed the same general character as had been observed previously. As might have been anticipated, the new ordinates were invariably lower, and, except for corporate savings, the slopes of the curves tended to be the same or smaller. The linearity was even more marked with the reduced inputs; indeed, only two variables showed any turning points at all. These were corporate savings and corporate surplus, both of which were actually negative for several periods. Since, in view of these results, it was felt that small variations in our input would not lead to significant differences in the *nature* of our solution, a more detailed investigation of the influence of initial values upon the operation of the model was postponed to a future date.

The implications of these results are quite clear. Since the economic variables in the Klein-Goldberger model grow almost linearly with time, it is apparent that this scheme does not contain an intrinsic explanation of a persistent oscillatory process. That is, the complete lack of even a broad hint of cyclical behavior in the absence of shocks precludes the application of the Klein-Goldberger analysis to economies in which oscillations are presumed to develop spontaneously. The conclusions one may draw from this observation lie anywhere between the two extreme positions which follow. On the one hand, if one wishes to retain the hypothesis that periodic cumulative movements are self-generated in the course of the growth process in a realistic economy, one may contend that the Klein-Goldberger model is fundamentally inadequate, and hence that it is inapplicable to further business cycle theory. On the other hand, one may hold that, to the extent that the behavior of this system constitutes a valid qualitative approximation to that of a modern capitalist society, the observed solution of the Klein-Goldberger equations implies that one must look elsewhere for the origin of business fluctuations. Under the latter assumptions, cyclical analysis would be limited to an investigation of the reaction of the economic system to various perturbations. And, since the Klein-Goldberger model does present a more or less detailed description of the interactions among the various sectors of the economy, it could itself be utilized in the examination of the mechanism of response to shocks. Actually, as we shall see, exploitation of the latter alternative can prove extremely profitable.

---

[14] The authors will be happy to furnish, upon request, the detailed results of their computations.

[15] The ones excluded were N_W, h, N_E, N_F, N_G, N, N_P (for explanation of symbols, see Appendix A).

TABLE 1

BEHAVIOR OF KLEIN-GOLDBERGER MODEL THROUGH TIME

Variable* (years)	24 (first year)	30	60	90	120
$Y + T + D$	171.5	186.0	291.1	396.3	501.5
$\Delta(Y+T+D)$	.294	3.42	3.51	3.51	3.51
C	115.1	125.1	199.3	273.9	348.7
ΔC	.015	2.42	2.48	2.49	2.49
W_1	80.6	86.7	137.5	188.4	239.3
ΔW_1	—.046	1.64	1.70	1.70	1.70
A_1	9.0	9.5	12.6	15.9	19.2
ΔA_1	.008	.100	.108	.109	.110
I	22.9	24.0	37.9	51.5	64.9
ΔI	—.289	.434	.455	.450	.448
K	45.9	65.3	163.0	260.8	357.1
ΔK	3.75	3.05	3.24	3.23	3.20
D	18.5	21.0	34.6	48.2	62.2
ΔD	.396	.429	.458	.452	.448
P_C	14.9	15.4	22.5	29.6	36.8
ΔP_C	—.454	.245	.233	.237	.240
P	33.1	33.8	44.3	54.7	65.3
ΔP	—.667	.361	.343	.349	.353
S_P	.44	.57	2.17	2.85	3.16
ΔS_P	—.192	.082	.032	.015	.007
B	.63	2.96	48.80	125.71	216.51
ΔB	.250	.65	2.20	2.86	3.16
N_W	54.2	53.6	64.7	75.7	86.9
ΔN_W	—1.06	.352	.365	.370	.373
L_1	70.5	71.7	80.6	89.6	98.7
ΔL_1	.037	.288	.299	.301	.301
L_2	40.8	45.9	79.4	112.7	146.0
ΔL_2	1.40	1.00	1.12	1.11	1.11
w	344	443	1043	1817	2776
Δw	15.9	17.3	22.9	29.0	35.2
p	206	238	412	604	825
Δp	4.1	5.8	6.0	6.9	7.9
p_A	318	363	604	871	1179
Δp_A	5.7	8.1	8.3	9.6	11.0
T	14.5	15.8	25.5	35.3	45.0
ΔT	.028	.315	.324	.324	.324
T_W	7.6	9.0	19.2	29.3	39.5
ΔT_W	.069	.329	.338	.339	.339
T_A	.47	.49	.65	.82	.99
ΔT_A	.0003	.0050	.0055	.0056	.0056
T_C	9.4	9.6	12.9	16.0	19.3
ΔT_C	—.204	.110	.105	.108	.108
T_P	12.9	13.2	19.4	26.0	32.8
ΔT_P	—.268	.198	.212	.225	.231

For any quantity Q, $\Delta Q = Q_{t+1} - Q_t$.

5. STABILITY OF THE SYSTEM

It is apparent from the preceding discussion that, under ordinary conditions, the Klein-Goldberger model is non-oscillatory in nature. It remains to be seen whether the economy described by this system is stable under large exogenous displacements.

In order to study this point, we solved the equations as in the preceding section, until the system was essentially on its long-run equilibrium path (about 8 years). Then, in the ninth period, we suddenly reduced the real magnitude of federal outlays from its extrapolated level of 37.5 to the much lower figure of 10; in the succeeding years government expenditures were returned to the values they would have had in the absence of external interference.

While it is obvious that such a discontinuity in an exogenous variable is basically equivalent to a change in initial conditions, it is equally obvious that the response of a dynamic system to large displacements may be quite different from its behavior under small perturbations.[16]

Figure 2 presents some of the calculated results of this extremely severe shock to the economy.[17] As is evident from these curves, the community was immediately thrown into a very deep depression by the sudden drop in federal outlays. The restoration of a normal governmental budget during the following year alleviated the situation only slightly, but, by the second year after the dip, the business world had more than recovered. The next period saw the return of national income, farm receipts, and total employment to their pre-shock trends. However, it was not until the fourth year after the disturbance that real private employee compensation achieved its unperturbed level, as the price index rose more rapidly than the wage rate. Meanwhile, possibly as a result of the fact that consumer expenditures lagged yet another period, there was a mild business recession in the fourth year, the effects of which were felt throughout the rest of the economy for the next two periods. The subsequent boom reached its peak (with respect to its unperturbed trend) about eight years later, and then tapered off extremely slowly over an additional 22 years or so. While calculations were not continued beyond this point, it appears that, after this 34-year cycle, the economy has essentially returned to its basic equilibrium path, except for the price and wage indices[18] and for the cumulative corporate surplus (all of which remained lower).

While the details of the response of a Klein-Goldberger economy to a

---

[16] E.g., consider a marble trapped in a horizontal saucer. If the disturbance is not large enough to cause the marble to cross the saucer rim, the system is stable. However, once the marble crosses the rim, it will not return to the saucer without the application of external forces. See also, P. A. Samuelson, *Foundations of Economic Analysis* (Harvard, 1953), pp. 200–62.

[17] More data are, of course, available for this case, and will be provided upon request.

[18] The real wage rate, however, does return to its equilibrium trend by the end of the cycle.

strong shock will depend on the nature of the perturbation, it would appear likely from this calculation that even a very strong shock will not permanently distort the long-run path of the economy. In other words, the Klein-Goldberger system is stable. Nevertheless, a sharp disturbance does suffice to

FIG. 2

SHOCKED TIME PATHS

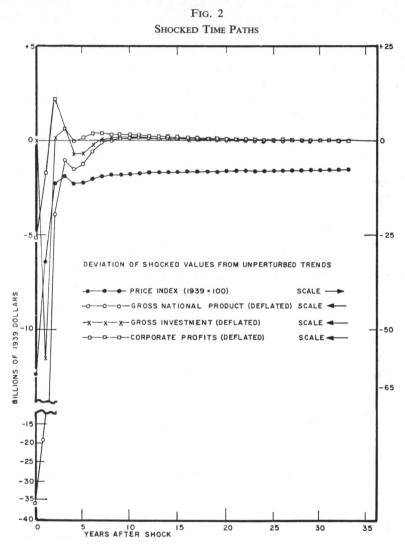

create a business cycle of depth comparable to that which one would expect in an actual economy under a corresponding impulse. And, while the duration of the cyclical movement is much longer than that normally observed in practice, it is probable that the later stages of such a cycle, if it really existed, would be obscured by the intervention of new exogenous shocks.

6. INTRODUCTION OF RANDOM SHOCKS

So far, we have studied the dynamic properties of the Klein-Goldberger system by treating it as if it were composed of a set of exact functional relationships. That is to say, we have abstracted from the random elements which are inherent in the statistical specification of the equations. Furthermore, we have used smooth extrapolation procedures for predicting the magnitudes of the exogenous variables. We saw that under those assumptions the Klein-Goldberger equations are inadequate as an explanation of the cyclical behavior of our economy.

We cannot yet assess the validity of the Klein-Goldberger equations, however, as a representation of the United States economy over a long period of time because we must still analyze the time path of their system under the impact of random shocks.[19] After all, as was pointed out by Haavelmo,[20] a model which differs from empirical fact by comparatively small and nonsystematic external factors may still be useful. It is therefore of great interest to see whether or not the introduction of relatively minor uncorrelated perturbations into the Klein-Goldberger structure will generate cyclical fluctuations analogous to those observed in practice.

With these considerations in mind, we exposed the Klein-Goldberger system to two distinct varieties of random impulses. First of all, random shocks were superimposed upon the extrapolated values of the exogenous quantities (shocks of type I). Secondly, random perturbations were introduced instead into each of the empirically fitted Klein-Goldberger equations (shocks of type II). In addition we made a set of calculations in which both kinds of disturbances were present.

7. SHOCKS OF TYPE I

Shocks of type I arise logically whenever exogenous quantities are projected in a smooth manner over long periods of time, for, while it is convenient to extrapolate these variables in a continuous fashion, even a cursory glance at the data over a period of a few years shows that these magnitudes tend to jump more or less erratically with respect to any smooth curve one might draw. It is, of course, obvious that a system that incorporates such statistical fluctuations may not be completely satisfactory for quantitative purposes. On the other hand, it may still prove fruitful to compare with economic experience the frequency of occurrence and the amplitudes of whatever cycles may arise.

---

[19] The idea that economic fluctuations may be due to random shocks was first suggested in 1927 by E. Slutzky, "The Summation of Random Causes as the Source of Cyclical Processes," translated into English in *Econometrica*, Vol. 5 (1937), pp. 105 ff. It was also suggested independently by R. Frisch, *op. cit.*

[20] T. Haavelmo, "The Inadequacy of Testing Dynamic Theory by Comparing Theoretical Solutions and Observed Cycles," *Econometrica*, Vol. 8 (1940), p. 312.

We shall therefore modify our method of extrapolation of the exogenous variables in order to see what effects these random perturbations may have. For this purpose we define the value of an exogenous variable y_t at time t as its trend value $\bar{\bar{y}}_t$ plus the shock term δy_t and assume that δy_t has a Gaussian distribution[21] with a mean of zero. In order that the shocks inflicted upon the system be of a more or less realistic magnitude at all, times, we evaluate the standard deviation of δy_t over that portion of the data for which our least squares fit was made,[22] and, for our subsequent calculations, we maintain the ratio of the standard deviation of δy_t to y_{t-1} at a value independent of time. It is interesting to note that these standard deviations (see Appendix B.4) are, in general, quite small; in fact, only three of them exceed 10 percent of the trend value of the corresponding variable.

In examining the behavior of the twelve exogenous variables[23] over the sample period, it becomes evident that there exists a high degree of correlation between the long- and the short-term interest rates, and between the size of government payrolls and the number of government employees.[24] It is therefore appropriate to assume that these pairs of variables move together and that the determination of a shock on one variable of each pair automatically sets the size of the corresponding shock on the other. Hence we are left with a set of ten random exogenous shocks, whose magnitudes and signs are to be established.

The technique employed for this purpose was to divide the normal curve of error into 100 regions of equal area. To each region we assigned both the normal deviate associated with the midpoint of its interval and a previously unassigned integer between 00 and 99, inclusive. Then selecting a two-digit random number, we effectively chose at random a specific region of the Gaussian distribution and the corresponding normal deviate. Multiplying this deviate by the standard deviation of δy_t, we found the magnitude and direction of a shock on the variable y at time t. Since the selection of an interval in this manner was thus purely random, and since all intervals defined the same area under the curve, this method produced a normally distributed[25] *random* shock upon the variable in question. By repeating this procedure for each of the exogenous variables and adding the calculated shocks to the appropriate trend values, we arrived at a set of shocked exogenous quantities

---

[21] This assumption also underlies the principle of least squares fits.

[22] It will be recalled that we used data from 1946–52 for our least squares extrapolations of all exogenous variables except government expenditures, G; for G, data for 1929–40 and 1946–50 were used.

[23] These variables, it will be recalled, are the short-term i_S and long term interest rates i_L, the index of hours worked h, government employee compensation W_2, government expenditures G, the index of agricultural exports F_A, agricultural subsidies A_2 and five population and labor force variables (N_P, N, N_E, N_F, and N_G).

[24] The correlation coefficient between government payrolls W_2 and government expenditures G for the sample years 1946–52 is 0.97 and that between the interest rates is 0.89.

[25] Since we have divided the normal curve into discrete intervals, we actually have only a (good) approximation to a normal distribution.

to use as inputs for the tth period. The values of the endogenous variables for this period were then found, of course, as before.

Some of the results obtained with shocks of type I are summarized in Figure 3. The solid lines in this graph portray the computed time paths

Fig. 3

SELECTED TIME PATHS UNDER TYPE I IMPULSES

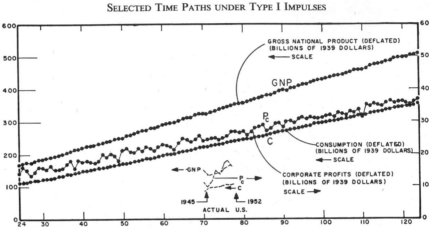

of GNP, consumption, and corporate profits, while the dotted lines represent actual time paths of these variables for the postwar portion of the sample period.[26] From this figure, it would seem that the introduction of forces of type I into the model generates 3 to 4 year swings in the variables of the system. However, the same graph also reveals that the average amplitude of the "cycles" induced by random shock on exogenous quantities is unrealistically small. It would appear, then, that type I perturbations of reasonable magnitude superimposed upon the Klein-Goldberger model will not produce the sort of cyclical behavior observed in the actual economy. We shall therefore proceed to see whether shocks of type II will prove more promising.

8. SHOCKS OF TYPE II

To understand the origin of shocks of type II, one should recall that, in the process of fitting their empirical data, Klein and Goldberger endowed each of their behavioral equations with a random error term.[27] At least three sources of irregularity could produce this term. In the first place, simplifying assumptions are inevitable whenever one wishes to construct a concrete

---

[26] The data for the actual time paths are taken from Klein-Goldberger, *op. cit.*, pp. 131–33.

[27] This is standard econometric procedure; cf. Klein-Goldberger, *op. cit.*, pp. 42–46.

model of a realistic economy. Some of these abstractions are made for convenience, others because the precise equations of motion of an economic system are not yet known. Variables which in practice exert a direct influence upon the solution may be suppressed from several of the equations, made exogenous, or omitted entirely; similarly, relationships which are an integral part of the description may be lost in the process of approximation. Moreover, in predictive models, inherently nonlinear relationships are often treated in a linear approximation for the sake of expediency. In view of these considerations, it is reasonable to expect that the inexactness of the functional form of the Klein-Goldberger equations as a representation of the economic behavior of our society contributes to the size of the random error term.

Secondly, even if the Klein-Goldberger relationships did have a functional form derived from indisputable theory, the fact that the coefficients are based upon empirical data would imply a random error term, as a result of the usual sampling fluctuations. These include, for example, the uncertainty of the degree to which the sample is representative of the universe, as well as the changes in accounting practices, coverage, and reporting techniques which generally occur in the collection of data over a long period of time.

A third potential contributor to the size of shocks of type II is of quite a different character. It arises from the possibility that some of the economic relationships which compose the Klein-Goldberger system may *never* be valid as exact equations. This situation will result if the aggregation of microeconomic quantities into macroeconomic variables is not a legitimate procedure. For example, if the value of total consumption depends upon the distribution of income as well as on its magnitude, a precise macroeconomic relationship between overall consumption and aggregate income will not exist. A similar effect, which will also be reflected in the size of the random error term, would occur if decision functions are probabilistic rather than single-valued.

It is therefore evident from the above discussion that the residuals of the several empirically fitted equations included in the Klein-Goldberger model can be attributed to a number of different types of irregularity. Since there would appear to be no *a priori* correlation among the many individual sources of fluctuation, the random error terms can be assumed for all practical purposes to be distributed in a Gaussian manner. We therefore postulate that each error term is distributed normally about a mean of zero, and we evaluate its standard deviation, just as in the case of shocks of type I, from the standard errors observed for the sample period (see Appendix B.5).

In order to introduce perturbations of type II into the Klein-Goldberger model, we added a random error term to the right-hand side of each of the original non-definitional relationships.[28] Then the same process of algebraic

---

[28] The equations involved are (1)–(8) and (10)–(13) of Appendix A.

substitution which was used in the simplification of the unshocked system was applied to this new group of equations. These operations left us with a set of equations in which the several error terms appear as parameters, analogous to the exogenous and the lagged variables. Once the sizes and directions of these endogenous shocks are determined (by the selection of two-digit random numbers, as in the case of type I impulses), the system is solved as before. A similar procedure can be used to investigate the behavior of the Klein-Goldberger equations when both shocks of type I and shocks of type II are present simultaneously.

FIG. 4

SELECTED TIME PATHS UNDER TYPE II IMPULSES

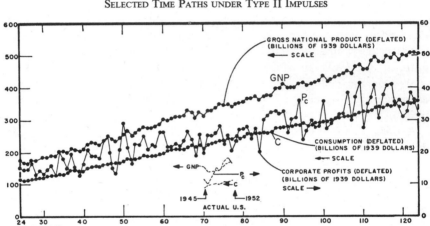

Some of the results of the computation with shocks of type II are plotted in Figure 4. As in Figure 3, the solid lines represent the calculated behavior of GNP, consumption, and corporate profits, respectively, while the dotted lines depict the time paths traversed by the same quantities during the postwar period in the United States.[26] As before, we see that the shocked Klein-Goldberger system produces oscillatory movements with periods of 3 to 4 years. But, unlike the behavior of the model under the action of forces of type I, the swings generated here compare favorably in magnitude with those experienced by the United States economy after World War II. Thus, the superposition of impulses of type II upon the Klein-Goldberger equations leads to cycles whose gross properties are reasonably realistic.

Since the effects of shocks of type II are much larger than those of type I disturbances, the same statement can be made for a system in which both kinds of perturbations are present. And, in view of the fact that, on *a priori* grounds, either type of shock may be present in an actual economy, it would seem appropriate to carry out our more detailed analysis for the case in which both forces are present.

9. ANALYSIS OF COMPUTED CYCLES

It is encouraging, of course, to find that the amplitudes and the periods of the oscillations observed in this model are roughly the same as those which are found in practice. But, this much agreement is merely a necessary condition for an adequate simulation of the cyclical fluctuations of a real industrial economy. We must investigate further to find out whether or not a shocked version of the Klein-Goldberger system really produces business cycles in the technical sense.[29] Specifically, how nearly all-pervasive are the cumulative movements which arise? How are the various oscillations correlated? Is there any consistent phase relationship among the several economic series? Do the time paths of the individual variables of the model correspond to those observed in the United States economy? In other words, if a business cycle analyst were asked whether or not the results of a shocked Klein-Goldberger computation could reasonably represent a United States-type economy, how would he respond?

To answer these questions we shall apply to the data techniques developed by the National Bureau of Economic Research (NBER)[30] for the analysis of business cycles.

One property of cyclical fluctuations in an industrial economy is a marked tendency for a clustering of peaks and troughs of individual economic time series about particular reference dates. It is, in fact, precisely this characteristic of business cycles that Burns and Mitchell use as their criterion for the dating of turning points in the United States economy.[31] And, inasmuch as the oscillations in the Klein-Goldberger model occur in response to random (i.e., noncorrelated) perturbations, a study of the simultaneity of occurrence of peaks (and troughs) will provide us with quite a stringent test of the validity of the model.

As in the normal NBER procedure,[32] we first date the specific cycles;[33] i.e., we determine all the turning points of each of the several time series.

---

[29] R. A. Gordon, for example, defines business cycles in the following manner: "Business cycles consist of recurring alternations of expansion and contraction in aggregate economic activity, the alternating movements in each direction being self-reinforcing and pervading virtually all parts of the economy." *Business Fluctuations* (Harpers, 1952), p. 214.

[30] The methods and results of the NBER work are summarized in A. F. Burns and W. C. Mitchell, *Measuring Business Cycles* (National Bureau, 1946) and in W. C. Mitchell, *What Happens During Business Cycles* (National Bureau, 1951).

[31] Mitchell, *op. cit.*, pp. 10–11.

[32] See Burns and Mitchell, *op. cit.*, Ch. 2.

[33] In the rest of this paper we will need the definitions of several quantities prevalent in the literature of business cycles. See, for example, Mitchell, *op. cit.*, pp. 9–11, or Gordon, *op. cit.*, p. 232.

(1) Reference dates are those dates which mark the turning points of overall business activity in the economy.

(2) A reference cycle of an economic variable V represents the behavior of V between the reference dates marking two consecutive minima of overall business activity.

(3) A specific cycle of V represents the behavior of V between the dates marking two consecutive minima of V itself.

Then, to establish the reference dates[33] for the turning points of the *overall* business cycle, we examine the data for bunching (in time) of specific cycle peaks and troughs.[34]

Table 2 is a summary of some of the relevant characteristics of the business cycles observed in our shocked Klein-Goldberger economy. In examining this table, one should recall that intervals and dates can have significance only to the nearest year, inasmuch as the Klein-Goldberger computation was made on a year-to-year basis. The first two columns give the reference dates for the peaks and troughs, respectively. Since one can identify 23 complete business cycles (measured either from trough to trough or from peak to peak) occurring in the 93 years included in our calculation, the average length of a cycle is 4.0 years. This result is in startling agreement with the 4 year post-World War II cycles in the United States economy, as well as with the mean length of American peacetime business cycles since 1854.[35]

The Klein-Goldberger cycles are broken down, in columns 3 and 4, to indicate the duration of the expansion and contraction phases of each cycle. The average expansion covered 2.6 years, while the normal contraction occupied only 1.5. The agreement with the observed figures for the United States (2.1 and 1.8, respectively)[36] is surprisingly good when one considers the fact that the length of a single business cycle stage in our Klein-Goldberger computation can be estimated only to an integral number of years.

The validity of this comparison of United States and Klein-Goldberger business cycles is dependent, of course, upon the degree of reliability with which the reference dates have been determined. One criterion which can be used is the extent to which specific cycle peaks (troughs) tend to cluster at times coincident with the maxima (minima) of the overall business cycles. In our Klein-Goldberger data, 51 percent of the individual series, on the average, have maxima coincident with an upper turning point of general business activity, and 52 percent have minima which coincide with a reference trough. The corresponding figures for the United States economy are 58 per cent and 52 percent respectively.[36] In addition, the proportions of specific cycles which lead or lag the business cycle in our computed data is quite similar to the

[34] Our procedure corresponds to that of the NBER (cf. Mitchell, *op. cit.*, pp. 10–12). As a basis for establishing the reference dates we used all the Klein-Goldberger endogenous quantities except the 5 tax variables. A reference peak (trough) was said to occur (in our data) during any year in which the modal number of specific cycle peaks occurs, provided that at least 10 peaks (troughs) are found in a two-year period which includes the modal year.

[35] Computed from the NBER dating for the period 1854–1949, reproduced in Gordon, *op. cit.*, p. 216. We omitted from our averages the Civil War cycle and those corresponding to the two World Wars.

[36] These percentages were estimated from Chart 3 (pp. 16–17) of G. H. Moore, *Statistical Indicators of Cyclical Revivals and Recessions* (National Bureau Occasional Paper 31, 1950). Moore's graph was presented on a monthly basis and included the years 1885–1940.

TABLE 2

REFERENCE DATING FOR SHOCKED KLEIN-GOLDBERGER MODEL

Reference Dates		Elapsed Time (Years)		Number of Series at Peaks Which:			Number of Series at Troughs Which:		
Trough (T)	Peak(P)	T→P	P→T	Lag One Year	Coin-cide	Lead One Year	Lag One Year	Coin-cide	Lead One Year
–	27	–	2	–	–	–	–	–	–
29	31	2	1	2	8	6	1	6	4
32	37	5	1	1	8	5	4	7	4
38	42	4	1	1	10	0	1	13	1
43	45	2	1	2	7	4	0	10	0
46	51	5	2	2	11	1	3	8	3
53	54	1	2	4	12	1	2	10	4
56	59	3	1	1	10	1	1	11	4
60	63	3	1	2	7	6	4	6	2
64	68	4	2	6	6	3	5	7	1
70	72	2	1	2	7	3	1	13	1
73	74	1	1	2	9	1	2	8	2
75	77	2	1	2	8	4	0	10	2
78	79	1	1	2	8	2	3	9	3
80	83	3	2	2	12	1	1	7	3
85	86	1	2	4	12	2	2	11	2
88	90	2	1	2	12	2	1	11	4
91	94	3	2	3	10	1	3	11	3
96	98	2	4	5	8	3	1	9	3
102	106	4	1	3	12	2	3	10	2
107	109	2	1	4	9	1	5	11	2
110	113	3	1	2	11	4	5	7	1
114	116	2	1	5	7	4	3	13	0
117	119	2	1	1	8	8	4	9	3
120	–	–	–	–	–	–	–	–	–
Totals		59	34	60	212	65	55	217	54
Average per cycle		2.56	1.48	2.61	9.22	2.82	2.39	9.43	2.34
Percent of Specific Cycles Represented		–	–	14.5	51.2	15.7	13.3	52.4	13.0

analogous figure[37] for the United States economy. Our numbers are given in the last line of Table 2.

All in all, it would appear that there is a remarkable correspondence between the characteristics of fluctuations generated by the superposition of random shocks upon the Klein-Goldberger system and those of the business cycles which actually occur in the United States economy. The resemblance is not restricted to qualitative parallelism, but is, indeed, ·quantitative, in the sense that the duration of the cycle, the relative length of the expansion and contraction phases, and the degree of clustering of peaks and troughs are all in numerical agreement (within the accuracy of measurement) with empirical evidence. Therefore, we shall study the Klein-Goldberger cycles in more detail.

Table 3 summarizes, for the shocked Klein-Goldberger model, some of the significant features of the specific cycle patterns observed in the endogenous variables. As can be seen from columns 6, 7, 14, and 15, the segregation of the Klein-Goldberger economic variables into leading, coincident, and lagging series is quite similar to the division of the analogous quantities in the United States economy by the NBER. (Columns 2–5 and 10–13 give the data which lead to our grouping; the NBER separation into categories is taken from Mitchell.)[37] Of the 20 series listed, 12 are classified as coincident series at both peaks and troughs. These are gross national product ($Y + T + D$), national income Y, gross investment I, private employee compensation W_1, non-wage non-farm income P, employment N_W, corporate profits P_C, corporate savings S_P, corporate surplus B, capital stock K, the general price index p, and the index of agricultural prices p_A. In addition, consumption C coincides at peaks, but has a tendency to lead at troughs. All of these results are in accord with NBER experience (when available), except that the United States specific cycles for consumption coincide, rather than lead at the troughs.

Three additional variables (corporate liquid assets L_2, real wages w/p, and the capital-output ratio K/Y) are in inverse coincidence with the business cycle, in the sense that their troughs tend to occur at reference peaks and vice versa. Unfortunately, we were unable to find the identical items among the NBER data; however, on both theoretical and empirical grounds, these inverse relationships are eminently reasonable. As far as L_2 is concerned, for example, both transactions demand and investment opportunities are reduced as business activity falls and therefore liquid surpluses should begin to accumulate.[38] Indeed, the NBER has some experimental data to support the proposition that the cash component of L_2, at least, tends to rise as the downturn develops (and vice versa).[39]

---

[37] Mitchell, *op. cit.*, Table 15, pp. 154–55, Table 16, pp. 159–67, and Table 42, pp. 312–25.

[38] An excellent description of this process can be found in Gordon, *op. cit.*, pp. 270–71.

[39] Mitchell, *op. cit.*, p. 148.

TABLE 3

COMPARISON OF KLEIN-GOLDBERGER AND NBER SPECIFIC CYCLES

Variable	Frequencies and Other Properties at Peaks								Frequencies and Other Properties at Troughs								Remarks
	One Year Lead	Coincide	One Year Lag	Other	K-G Classification	NBER Classification	K-G Index of Conformity (%)	NBER Index of Conformity (%)	One Year Lead	Coincide	One Year Lag	Other	K-G Classification	NBER Classification	K-G Index of Conformity (%)	NBER Index of Conformity (%)	
$Y+T+D$	1	21	1	1	Coincident	Coincident	+100	*+100	2	21	0	1	Coincident	Coincident	+92	*+50	
Y	1	21	1	1	Coincident	Coincident	+100	*+100	1	22	0	1	Coincident	Coincident	+100	*+50	
C	1	8	3	0	Coincident	Coincident	+100	*+100	5	5	1	1	Leading-Coincident	Coincident	−17	*+50	
I	4	20	0	3	Coincident	Coincident	+100	*+100	0	23	1	3	Coincident	Coincident	+100	*+100	
W_1	2	10	3	2	Coincident	Coincident	+83	*+100	1	10	3	3	Coincident	Coincident	+8	*+50	
A_1	6	8	7	7	Irregular	Coincident	−4	+60	8	5	5	10	Irregular	Coincident	−33	+12	
P	4	19	0	4	Coincident	Coincident	+91	—	0	22	1	4	Coincident	Coincident	+100	—	
N_w	4	18	2	2	Coincident	Coincident	+91	+100	3	19	2	2	Coincident	Coincident	+100	+100	
P_c	4	20	0	4	Coincident	Coincident	+100	*+100	3	20	1	4	Coincident	Coincident	+92	*+100	
S_P	4	16	0	4	Coincident	Coincident	+83	+100	1	17	4	3	Coincident	Coincident	+100	+50	
B	0	5	1	1	Coincident	—	+100	—	1	5	3	0	Coincident	—	−42	—	
K	1	9	6	0	Coincident	—	+87	—	0	11	3	1	Coincident	—	+33	—	
D	10	6	3	6	Leading	—	+22	—	10	7	4	5	Leading	—	−25	—	
L_1	14	4	5	3	Leading	—	+13	—	5	6	9	5	Lagging-Irregular	—	+8	—	
L_2	4	15	0	4	Coincident	—	−65	—	2	17	3	1	Coincident	—	−83	—	Inverse
p	3	17	2	0	Coincident	Coincident	+100	+64	0	20	2	0	Coincident	Coincident	+83	+82	
p_A	4	17	2	5	Coincident	Coincident	+100	+50	6	14	4	4	Coincident	Coincident	+42	+60	
w	0	1	9	1	Lagging	Lagging	+83	+100	0	4	7	0	Lagging	Coincident	−67	−50	
w/p	2	17	1	5	Coincident	—	−74	—	0	21	0	4	Coincident	—	−100	—	Inverse
K/Y	4	19	1	4	Coincident	—	−100	—	5	19	1	3	Coincident	—	−100	—	Inverse

With respect to the capital-output ratio, it too should fall in times of expansion and climb during a contraction. From a theoretical point of view, as shown by Duesenberry,[40] a non-decreasing capital-output ratio during a business expansion would imply a rising marginal efficiency of investment. But the marginal efficiency of investment cannot increase unless the capital-output ratio drops. Therefore, the capital-output ratio must fall during the boom phase. Furthermore, the time required for the formation and depletion of the capital stock exceeds the time lag inherent in the production of consumer goods; this too implies that the capital-output ratio will move in a direction opposite to that of the general level of economic activity.

With regard to w/p, both Marshall[41] and Keynes[42] suggested that real wages tend to vary inversely with the level of output and employment. This theorem, which has been thoroughly discussed in the literature,[43] is consistent with our observations. In addition, experimental data concerning the movement of real wages in industrial economies,[44] while somewhat inconclusive, tend to confirm the calculated inverse behavior of this variable.

Of the remaining four quantities, the NBER considers farm income A_1 to concur with the general business cycle and money wage rates w to coincide at troughs and to lag at peaks. We, on the other hand, find the former series to be irregular and the latter to lag everywhere. But, as is evident from Table 3, the NBER data for agricultural incomes do not show a very high degree of conformity to the overall business cycle (especially at the troughs), and farm output itself (in real terms) tends to have a higher correlation with meteorological cycles than with business cycles.[45] For wages, the disagreement between the behavior of the shocked Klein-Goldberger model at the troughs and the NBER analysis may simply be a reflection of the fact that the Klein-Goldberger equations do not appear to allow enough interaction between unemployment and wage rates.[46]

---

[40] J. S. Duesenberry, *Business Cycles and Economic Growth* (McGraw-Hill, 1958), p. 112.

[41] A. Marshall, *Principles of Economics*, 8th ed. (Macmillan, 1947), p. 620.

[42] J. M. Keynes, *The General Theory of Employment, Interest and Money* (Harcourt Brace, 1935), p. 10.

[43] See, e.g., J. T. Dunlop, "The Movement of Real and Money Wage Rates," *Economic Journal*, Vol. 48 (1938), pp. 413–34; L. Tarshis, "Changes in Real and Money Wages," *Economic Journal*, Vol. 49 (1939), pp. 150–54; R. Ruggles, "The Relative Movements of Real and Money Wage Rates," *Quarterly Journal of Economics*, Vol. 55 (1940), pp. 130–49; S. C. Tsiang, *The Variations of Real Wages and Profit Margins in Relation to the Trade Cycle* (London, 1947), pp. 10–12; and K. W. Rothschild, *The Theory of Wages* (New York, 1956), pp. 128–31.

[44] Roughly speaking, statistical evidence seems to support the proposition if we take account of *product wages* (i.e., money wages deflated by an index of wholesale prices) (see Tsiang, *op. cit.*, Ch. III) and to undermine it if we consider money wages deflated by a cost of living index (see Dunlop, *op. cit.*, and Tarshis, *op. cit.*). It should be noted that the deflator used for real wages in our computations is the implicit deflator for GNP, and therefore that our (w/p) is closer to the product wage rate than to the measure of real wages analyzed by Dunlop and Tarshis.

[45] Mitchell, *op. cit.*, p. 56, and Gordon, *op. cit.*, pp. 347–50.

[46] D. Creamer and M. Bernstein, *Behavior of Wage Rates During Business Cycles*

In our study personal liquid assets L_1 tend to lead at peaks and to lag somewhat irregularly at troughs. We have not encountered comparable NBER series. However, one might attribute a lead in personal liquidity at a peak to the de facto financing of the last stages of the boom by dishoarding on the part of overoptimistic consumers, and the lag at a trough to the satisfaction of pent-up demand in the light of renewed income prospects.

Finally, depreciation D leads, in our calculations, at both troughs and peaks. While Fabricant[47] has found that depreciation charges tend to show much less cyclical fluctuation than corporate gross income or physical output, our computations do not exhibit this behavior. But, it should be noted that, first of all, the Klein-Goldberger depreciation is deflated and more complicated than that of Fabricant, and, secondly, that Fabricant's data cover only the first fourteen years immediately following World War I. We feel, therefore, that existing empirical work is inconclusive on this point, especially in view of the complex nature of any realistic measure of depreciation.

Columns 8–9 and 16–17 of Table 3 present the indices of conformity[48] of the specific cycles to the expansions and contractions of the business cycles of both the Klein-Goldberger data and the NBER statistics.[49] These indices measure the correlation between the direction of movements in the individual series which comprise the business cycle and that of the overall economic fluctuations which result. In evaluating the data, one should note that those NBER indices which are preceded by an asterisk in the table are based upon only four complete cycles and therefore that they can assume no numerical values other than 0, ± 50, and ± 100. While, by definition, an index of $+100$ denotes perfect concurrence in direction of specific cycles with the general business cycle for all four cycles, an index of $+50$ for these data states merely that, in exactly three out of the four cases examined, the series expanded during the reference expansion (or contracted during the reference contraction).

As can be seen from this table, there is reasonably good agreement between the Klein-Goldberger indices of conformity and those of the NBER,

---

(National Bureau Occasional Paper 34) applied the NBER method to British and American statistics and found an average lag of wages behind general business activity of about 7 months at the major turning points, and longer for the minor ones.

[47] S. Fabricant, *Capital Consumption and Adjustment* (NBER, 1938), p. 197.

[48] The index of conformity of a set of specific cycles to the expansion of the overall business cycle is the percentage of conforming movements minus the percentage of non-conforming movements. A conforming movement occurs when the value of the variable at a reference peak is higher than its value at the preceding trough. If the two values are equal, the movement does not contribute to the index (although it is counted as an event in computing the percentages). A non-conforming movement is a movement opposite in direction to a conforming movement. The index of conformity to reference contractions is defined in an analogous manner.

[49] The NBER data are taken from Mitchell, *op. cit.*, Table 15, pp. 154–55, Table 16, pp. 159–67, and Table 42, pp. 312–25.

especially during expansions.[50] A major discrepancy appears, however, in agricultural incomes A_1, where the tendency for irregular behavior of the Klein-Goldberger series observed in the classification process is confirmed by the low values of the conformity indices; the NBER conformity is somewhat higher. We also find that the Klein-Goldberger total payrolls W_1 do not conform as well to business contractions as the NBER data would suggest they should. This is probably due primarily to the failure of money wages w to contract sufficiently in the model. This tendency for rigidity in money wages during contractions, however, is confirmed in the NBER data. Finally, Klein-Goldberger consumption C appears to have little or no tendency to fall during business contractions. This behavior, which agrees with post-World War II United States experience, may be due to the fact that a strong upward trend in consumption expenditures (and in the economic variables in general) has been built into our extrapolation of the Klein-Goldberger model. It is, however, conceivable that there exists a real difference in consumption patterns since World War II, as compared with the prewar era (from which the NBER data were taken). Such a shift would be reflected, at least partially, in the Klein-Goldberger statistical fits.

Generally speaking, then, the specific cycles generated in the Klein-Goldberger model by random shocks thus bear an obvious resemblance to those of cycles found in the United States economy. The division of the Klein-Goldberger data into leading, lagging, and coincident series is almost identical to that of the NBER (when available), and is in accord with theoretical expectations. Similarly, the indices of conformity to the business cycle are reasonably consistent with those given by Mitchell[51] for the United States economy.

10. CONCLUSIONS

Our investigation into the dynamic nature of the econometric model of Klein and Goldberger suggests that their equations do not offer an immediate explanation of an internally generated cyclical process. For, in the absence of perturbations, the time paths of the economic variables are monotonic and essentially linear in character. Furthermore, the behavior of the model is remarkably stable, as evidenced by the fact that the solution resumes its unperturbed equilibrium growth trend even after a strong exogenous disturbance.

On the other hand, when random shocks of a realistic order of magnitude

---

[50] In an economy with a prevalent upward trend, conformity to expansions is more regular than conformity to contractions. Therefore, for the Klein-Goldberger data, a conformity index of $+60$ to expansions is fairly low. However, since the rising trend also tends to weaken the conformity to expansion of series with inverted timing, a conformity -60 to expansions is high.

[51] Mitchell, *op. cit.*, pp. 154–55, 159–67, and 312–25.

are superimposed upon the original form of the Klein-Goldberger equations, the cyclical fluctuations which result are remarkably similar to those described by the NBER as characterizing the United States economy. The average duration of a cycle, the mean length of the expansion and contraction phases, and the degree of clustering of individual peaks and troughs around reference dates all agree with the corresponding data for the United States economy. Furthermore, the lead-lag relationships of the endogenous variables included in the model and the indices of conformity of the specific series to the overall business cycle also resemble closely the analogous features of our society. All in all, it would appear that the shocked Klein-Goldberger model approximates the behavior of the United States economy rather well.

In view of these results, it is not unreasonable to suggest that the gross characteristics of the interactions among the real variables described in the Klein-Goldberger equations may represent good approximations to the behavioral relationships in a practical economy. There are, of course, a number of significant defects in the detailed workings of the Klein-Goldberger system. For example, the treatment of the monetary quantities and the interconnections between them and the real sector both need improvement. Nevertheless, the representation would seem to offer a good working basis for the investigation of cyclical fluctuations, especially if the deficiencies mentioned above are corrected.

But, the behavior of the Klein-Goldberger system under random perturbations is also suggestive from another point of view. Ever since the path-breaking article of Frisch on the propagation of business cycles, the possibility that the cyclical movements observed in a capitalistic society are actually due to random shocks has been seriously considered by business cycle theorists. The results we have found in this study tend to support this possibility. For, the agreement between the data obtained by imposing uncorrelated perturbations upon a model which is otherwise non-oscillatory in character is certainly consistent with the hypothesis that the economic fluctuations experienced in modern, highly developed societies are indeed due to random impulses.

Of course, these random impulses are not necessarily synonymous with an exogenous theory of the business cycle. For, as we saw in Section 8 above, it was primarily shocks of type II which led to agreement between the cyclical behavior of the model and that of the United States economy. And, the reader will recall, these shocks may reflect inexactness in the model, statistical inaccuracies in the fits, or inherent randomness in the decision functions of the economic units themselves. While none of these factors is, strictly speaking, endogenous to the particular Klein-Goldberger system investigated, this does not imply that the type of perturbations actually responsible for the observed cyclical behavior are exogenous to economic theory in general.

In conclusion, we should like to emphasize that, while we have shown that the shocked Klein-Goldberger model offers excellent agreement with economic fact, we have not proved either that the Klein-Goldberger model itself is a good representation of the basic interactions among the several sectors of our economy or that random shocks are the prime cause of business cycles. In view of the remarkable quantitative correspondence with reality, however, we are very tempted to suggest that the second of these hypotheses is true and that, in addition, the Klein-Goldberger system is, except for the deficiencies discussed, not very far wrong.

APPENDIX A

1. *Explanation of Symbols*

$Y + T + D$	Gross national product, 1939 dollars
C	Consumer expenditures, 1939 dollars
I	Gross private domestic capital formation, 1939 dollars
G	Government expenditures for goods and services, 1939 dollars
p	Price index of gross national product, 1939: 100
F_E	Exports of goods and services, 1939 dollars
F_I	Imports of goods and services, 1939 dollars
W_1	Private employee compensation, deflated
W_2	Government employee compensation, deflated
D	Capital consumption charges, 1939 dollars
P_C	Corporate profits, deflated
S_P	Corporate savings, deflated
T	Indirect taxes less subsidies, deflated
T_W	Personal and payroll taxes less transfers associated with wage and salary income, deflated
T_P	Personal and corporate taxes less transfers associated with nonwage nonfarm income, deflated
T_C	Corporate income taxes, deflated
T_A	Taxes less transfers associated with farm income, deflated
K	End-of-year stock of private capital, 1939 dollars from arbitrary origin
F_A	Index of agricultural exports, 1939: 100
p_A	Index of agricultural prices, 1939: 100
p_I	Index of prices of imports, 1939: 100
N_P	Number of persons in the United States
N	Number of persons in the labor force
N_W	Number of wage-and-salary-earners
N_G	Number of government employees
N_F	Number of farm operators
N_E	Number of nonfarm entrepreneurs
h	Index of hours worked per year, 1939: 100
w	Index of hourly wages, 1939: 122.1
P	Nonwage nonfarm income, deflated
A_1	Farm income, deflated
A_2	Government payments to farmers, deflated
i_L	Average yield on corporate bonds, percent
i_S	Average yield on short term commercial paper, percent
R	Excess reserves of banks as a percentage of total reserves

L_1	End-of-year liquid assets held by persons, deflated
L_2	End-of-year liquid assets held by businesses, deflated
t	Time trend, years, $t = 1$ is 1929
B	End-of-year corporate surplus, deflated, from arbitrary origin

2. Klein and Goldberger's Equations

(1)* $\quad C_t = -22.26 + 0.55\,(W_1 + W_2 - T_W)_t + 0.41\,(P - T_P - S_P)_t$
$\qquad\qquad + 0.34(A_1 + A_2 - T_A)_t + 0.26C_{t-1} + 0.072(L_1)_{t-1} + 0.26(N_P)_t$

(2)* $\quad I_t = -16.71 + 0.78(P - T_P + A_1 + A_2 - T_A + D)_{t-1} - 0.073K_{t-1}$
$\qquad\qquad + 0.14(L_2)_{t-1}$

(3)* $\quad (S_P)_t = -3.53 + 0.72(P_C - T_C)_t + 0.076(P_C - T_C - S_P)_{t-1} - 0.028B_{t-1}$

(4)* $\qquad\qquad\qquad (P_C)_t = -7.60 + 0.68P_t$

(5)* $\qquad\qquad D_t = 7.25 + 0.10\,\dfrac{K_t + K_{t-1}}{2} + 0.044(Y + T + D - W_2)_t$

(6)* $\quad (W_1)_t = -1.40 + 0.24(Y + T + D - W_2)_t + 0.24(Y + T + D - W_2)_{t-1}$
$\qquad\qquad + 0.29t$

(7)* $\quad (Y + T + D - W_2)_t = -26.08 + 2.17[h(N_W - N_G) + N_E + N_F]_t$
$\qquad\qquad + 0.16\,\dfrac{K_t + K_{t-1}}{2} + 2.05t$

(8)* $\quad w_t - w_{t-1} = 4.11 - 0.74(N - N_W - N_E - N_F)_t + 0.52(p_{t-1} - p_{t-2}) + 0.54t$

(9)* $\quad (F_I)_t = 0.32 + 0.0060(W_1 + W_2 - T_W + P - T_P + A_1 + A_2 - T_A)_t$
$\qquad\qquad + 0.81(F_I)_{t-1}$

(10)* $\quad (A_1)_t\,\dfrac{p_t}{(p_A)_t} = -0.36 + 0.054(W_1 + W_2 - T_W + P - T_P - S_P)_t\,\dfrac{p_t}{(p_A)_t}$
$\qquad\qquad - 0.007(W_1 + W_2 - T_W + P - T_P - S_P)_{t-1}\,\dfrac{p_{t-1}}{(p_A)_{t-1}} + 0.012(F_A)_t$

(11)* $\qquad\qquad\qquad (p_A)_t = -131.17 + 2.32p_t$

(12)* $\quad (L_1)_t = 0.14(W_1 + W_2 - T_W + P - T_P - S_P + A_1 + A_2 - T_A)_t$
$\qquad\qquad + 76.03(i_L - 2.0)_t^{-0.84}$

(13)* $\quad (L_2)_t = -0.34 + 0.26(W_1)_t - 1.02(i_S)_t - 0.26(p_t - p_{t-1}) + 0.61(L_2)_{t-1}$

(14)* $\qquad\qquad (i_L)_t = 2.58 + 0.44(i_S)_{t-3} + 0.26(i_S)_{t-5}$

(15)* $\qquad\qquad 100\,\dfrac{(i_S)_t - (i_S)_{t-1}}{(i_S)_{t-1}} = 11.17 - 0.67R_t$

(16) $\qquad\qquad C_t + I_t + G_t + (F_E)_t - (F_I)_t = Y_t + T_t + D_t$

(17) $\qquad\qquad (W_1)_t + (W_2)_t + P_t + (A_1)_t + (A_2)_t = Y_t$

(18) $\qquad\qquad h_t\,\dfrac{w_t}{p_t}\,(N_W)_t = (W_1)_t + (W_2)_t$

(19) $$K_t - K_{t-1} = I_t - D_t$$

(20) $$B_t - B_{t-1} = (S_P)_t$$

(21) $$T_t = 0.0924(Y + T + D)_t - \frac{275.4}{p_t}$$

(22) $$(T_W)_t = 0.1549(W_1)_t + 0.1310(W_2)_t - \frac{1398.1}{p_t}$$

(23) $$(T_C)_t = 0.4497(P_C)_t + \frac{548.2}{p_t}$$

(24) $$(T_P)_t = 0.248(P - T_C - S_P)_t + 0.2695\frac{p_{t-1}}{p_t}(P - T_C - S_P)_{t-1}$$
$$+ 0.4497(P_C)_t - \frac{1162.1}{p_t}$$

(25) $$(T_A)_t = \frac{50.0}{p_t}$$

APPENDIX B

1. *The equations that, for the actual calculations, replaced their counterparts of Appendix A*

(3) $$(S_P)_t = -3.53 + 0.72(P_C - T_C)_t - 0.028B_{t-1}$$

(9) $$(F_I)_t = (F_E)_t$$

(10) $$(A_1)_t \frac{p_t}{(p_A)_t} = 0.054(W_1 + W_2 - T_W + P - T_P - S_P)_t \frac{p_t}{(p_A)_t} + 0.012(F_A)_t$$

(11) $$(p_A)_t = 1.39p_t + 32.0$$

(13) $$(L_2)_t = 0.26(W_1)_t - 1.02(i_S)_t - 0.26(p_t - p_{t-1}) + 0.61(L_2)_{t-1}$$

(14) $$(i_L)_t = 3.5$$

(15) $$(i_S)_t = 2.5$$

(16) $$C_t + I_t + G_t = Y_t + T_t + D_t$$

(21) $$T_t = 0.0924(Y + T + D)_t - 1.3607$$

(22) $$(T_W)_t = 0.1549(W_1)_t + 0.131(W_2)_t - 6.9076$$

(23) $$(T_C)_t = 0.4497(P_C)_t + 2.7085$$

(24) $$(T_P)_t = 0.248(P - T_C - S_P)_t + 0.2695\frac{p_{t-1}}{p_t}(P - T_C - S_P)_{t-1}$$
$$+ 0.4497(P_C)_t - 5.7416$$

(25) $$(T_A)_t = 0.0512(A_1 + A_2)_t$$

2. Extrapolations

$$(W_2)_t = 1.82 + .578t$$

$$(N_E)_t = 3.70 + .118t$$

$$(N_F)_t = 4.01 + \frac{2.12}{t-15}$$

$$(N_G)_t = 2.01 + .321t$$

$$(N_P)_t = 97.39 + 2.589t$$

$$N_t = 44.53 + .964t$$

$$h_t = 1.062$$

$$G_t = 19.892 + .567t$$

$$(A_2)_t = .108 + \frac{.0746}{t-16}$$

$$(F_A)_t = 171.86$$

3. Initial values used in calculations

Endogenous Variables	1951 $(t-2)$	1952 $(t-1)$	Exogenous Variables	1952 $(t-1)$	1953 (t)
$Y + T + D$	—	172.0	h	—	1.062
C	—	111.4	W_2	15.12	15.70
W_1	—	78.65	G	—	33.5
A_1	—	7.3	A_2	0.1187	0.1173
I	—	24.3	F_A	—	171.86
K	—	41.5	N_P	—	159.6
D	—	19.35	N	—	67.63
P_C	—	16.51	N_E	—	6.53
P	—	35.17	N_F	—	4.25
S_P	—	1.9	N_G	—	9.71
B	—	0.19	i_S	2.5	2.5
N_W	—	56.0	i_L	3.5	3.5
L_1	—	95.2			
L_2	—	38.1			
w	—	326.2			
p	197.5	202.4			
p_A	—	303.0			
T	—	14.51			
T_W	—	8.63			
T_A	—	0.38			
T_C	—	10.14			
T_P	—	13.72			

4. *Standard deviations used for Type I shocks* (*upon exogenous variables*)

Variable	$\sigma_{\delta y_t}$	$\dfrac{\sigma_{\delta y_t}}{y_{t-1}}$
i_S	0.512	0.20
i_L	0.146	0.0423
h	0.0185	0.018
W_2	1.77	0.123
G	0.88	0.026
A_2	0.0192	0.16
F_A	12.2	0.071
N_P	0.086	0.00054
N	0.125	0.0018
N_E	0.114	0.017
N_F	0.234	0.055
N_G	0.975	0.10

5. *Standard deviations used for Type II shocks* (*upon equations*)

Variable	Equation	$\sigma_{\delta y_t}$	$\dfrac{\sigma_{\delta y_t}}{y_{t-1}}$
C	(1)*	0.958	0.0086
I	(2)*	2.946	0.12
S_P	(3)	5.428	0.29
P_C	(4)*	0.700	0.044
D	(5)*	0.699	0.036
W_1	(6)*	1.0325	0.013
$Y + T + D$	(7)*	2.319	0.013
w	(8)*	4.861	0.015
A_1	(10)	0.955	0.13
L_1	(12)*	0.017575	0.00059
L_2	(13)	1.2911	0.034
p_A†	(11)	15.716	0.052

† Based on residuals from our re-estimated equation for p_A for the years 1946-52.

17

Aggregate Econometric Models*

By CARL F. CHRIST†

THIS ARTICLE is a review of Klein and Goldberger's recent contribution[1] to the series of aggregate econometric models of the U.S. economy that have followed in the footsteps of Tinbergen.[2] Section I describes the general nature of such models. Section II briefly compares five of them with respect to the kinds of equations they use. Section III examines the main equations of the two Klein-Goldberger models in some detail. Section IV discusses the relative merits of the least-squares and limited-information methods of estimating economic parameters, and discusses the merits and consequences of experimenting with estimates of different forms of each equation before choosing among them. Section V discusses the predicting ability of the Klein-Goldberger models. Section VI is a brief conclusion.

I. NATURE OF AGGREGATE ECONOMETRIC MODELS

The aggregate econometric model grew out of a blend of several different streams of work. One of these is the mathematical economics stream springing from Walras, according to which the economy can be represented by a system of simultaneous equations. Another, or perhaps part of the first, is the work of Frisch and others in the theory of economic dynamics. Others are: The stream of work in statistical inference associated with Pearson and his successors, from which we learn how to estimate the values of unknown parameters with the aid of *a priori* assumptions and observed data; the development by King, Kuznets and others of numerical estimates of national income and expenditure and their components, in real as well as money terms; and the formulation of economic theories that deal in aggregates such as income,

---

* *American Economic Review*, Vol. XLVI (June, 1956). Reprinted by courtesy of the American Economic Association and the author.

† The Johns Hopkins University.

[1] Lawrence R. Klein and Arthur S. Goldberger, *An Econometric Model of the United States 1929–1952*. (Amsterdam: North-Holland Pub. Co. 1955. Pp. xv, 165. $4.50.) All subsequent page references not otherwise identified are to this volume.

[2] *Statistical Testing of Business Cycle Theories*, II. *Business Cycles in the United States of America 1919–1932* (Geneva, 1939).

consumption, and investment, along the lines pursued by Kahn and Keynes in the 'thirties. All of these streams are evident in Tinbergen's pioneering work, and in later models as well.

The general character of these models may be briefly described thus: There is a system of N equations, each equation representing some important sector or feature of the economy. Some of the equations are definitions (sometimes called identities) of the type found in national accounting. These are supposed to hold exactly in every time-period, and they contain no unknown magnitudes. Examples are "consumption plus investment plus government expenditure plus net exports equals national expenditure," and "average money wage rate times quantity of labor input equals total money wage bill."

The remaining equations, *i.e.*, those other than the definitions, are supposed to hold only approximately, and their errors are assumed to be small and randomly determined. An example is "consumption equals a constant proportion of disposable income, plus another constant, plus a random disturbance." The supposition that the disturbances are random rather than systematic is highly convenient for the purpose of estimating the values of the constants statistically. It is sometimes justifiable even if the disturbances contain systematic parts, for if those parts are numerous and small and independent of each other, then their sum behaves approximately *as if* it were random. Thus in formulating a model of this type, one hopes to include in each equation explicitly all the important systematic influences that bear upon it, so that the only systematic components contained in the disturbance will be small ones.

Equations containing random disturbances are called stochastic equations, since in statistics "stochastic" means randomly determined. Some of the stochastic equations refer to the *behavior* of an important group in the economy, such as consumers, investors, holders of money, etc. Some refer to technological or institutional *restraints* such as production functions, tax laws, etc. And some refer to the *adjustment* process that occurs when there is a disequilibrium in a particular market, such as for labor, money to hold, goods, etc. These four types of equations (definitional, behavior, restraint, and adjustment) are called structural equations, for each is supposed to describe some more or less well-defined part of the structure of the economy.

The equations contain variables and parameters; the latter are supposed to be constant in value. Since there are more variables than equations, the system cannot determine the values of all the variables. Some of the variables are supposed to be determined by forces completely outside the system, and their values given. These called exogenous variables. Examples are weather (which is hardly ever used in a model), government policy variables, foreign demands, etc. The other variables, whose values are determined by the system when the values of the parameters and exogenous variables and disturbances are given, are called endogenous. There must be N of them, *i.e.*, the same number as the number of equations in the typical case, if the system is to be complete. The system may specify that the endogenous variables of the current period are affected not only by exogenous variables, but also by lagged endogenous variables, *i.e.*, values of the endogenous variables determined by the operation of the system in previous periods. It is often useful to distinguish the current endogenous variables from the group of exogenous and lagged endogenous variables. Accordingly the former group is known as predetermined variables. (Note that it is unnecessary to distinguish current and lagged exogenous variables, for both are determined outside the system.)

Any system containing lagged endogenous variables has a dynamic character, for the current endogenous variables then depend not only on the parameters, exogenous variables, and disturbances, but also on the past history of the system. Simple systems containing lags can generate cycles and/or long-term growth or decline, even with no changes in the parameters or exogenous variables or disturbances. Another device for making a system dynamic is to use cumulated variables, such as capital stock as the sum of net investments in the past, etc.[3]

Suppose that now we solve the system for the N current endogenous variables, expressing each in terms of the parameters, predetermined variables, and disturbances.[4] The result is called the reduced form of the system. Its parameters depend on the parameters of the original system of structural equations. It can be used to make forecasts of future values of the current endogenous variables if the values of its parameters and the predetermined variables are known or estimated in advance.

There has been much interest in the dynamic properties of such models: under what circumstances does one find cycles, growth, etc.? To examine these dynamic properties it is useful to eliminate algebraically from each reduced-form equation the lagged values of all endogenous variables other than the one

---

[3] Another way to dynamize a system is to introduce year-to-year changes in its variables, instead of lags. This is formally equivalent to using lags, as we can quickly see. Let the symbol x_t stand for the value of x in period t, and x_{t-1}, x_{t-2}, etc., for values of x lagged one period, two periods, etc., and Δx_t for the change of x between periods $t-1$ and t. Then by definition

$$\Delta x_t = x_t - x_{t-1}$$

This is called the first difference of x_t. The second-order difference is the first difference of first differences,

$$\Delta^2 x_t = \Delta x_t - \Delta x_{t-1} = x_t - 2x_{t-1} + x_{t-2}$$

By these and similar equations, a difference of any order can be expressed in terms of x and lags up to that same order. Similarly, a lag of any order can be expressed in terms of x and differences up to that same order. One may use derivatives with respect to time instead of differences, *i.e.*, dx/dt, d^2x/dt^2, etc. Both differences and derivatives express rates of change over time, the former as averages during whole periods, and the latter instantaneously. Fluctuations and growth can be generated by either, the former yielding small jumps once per period, and the latter yielding continuous change. Econometric models so far have generally used differences instead of derivatives. Cumulating is the reverse of taking differences, just as integration is the reverse of taking derivatives, for if Δx is the first difference of x, then x is the cumulation of Δx.

[4] If the system has a determinate solution, this can always be done in principle, though it becomes unwieldy if the system is large and nonlinear.

explained by that equation. The results so obtained have been called final equations by Tinbergen.[5] Each final equation is essentially a difference equation in one endogenous variable, expressing the current value of that variable as a function of a number of its lagged values, and of parameters and exogenous variables and disturbances. If the latter three are held constant and if the required number of consecutive values of an endogenous variable are given, say x_1, x_2, x_3 in the case of a final equation with three lags, then from these the final equation determines the next value, x_4; and on the basis of x_2, x_3, x_4 it determines x_5; and so on indefinitely. The time-path of x_t generated in this way is called the solution of the final equation, and it can be examined to see under what conditions it contains cycles, growth, decline, etc.

Much of the literature on the mathematical theory of economic dynamics is devoted to this kind of inquiry, and in particular to the question of what the system's time-path is like in its later stages, after the short-lived effects of the initial situation have died away. It should be remembered, however, that in reality the exogenous variables do not stay constant. Hence a system never reaches the later stages of a time-path because exogenous changes set it off on a new time-path from a new initial situation almost every year. Hence it is at least as important to study the first two or three years of a time-path as to study its later stages. Klein and Goldberger recognize this when they estimate a one-year and a two-year multiplier for their models (pp. 85, 111–14).

So far nothing has been said about how one attaches numerical values to the unknown and supposedly constant parameters of the structural equations. They are estimated by fitting the equations to data giving the values of the current endogenous and predetermined variables in several time periods. If the equations were perfectly correct and the data contained no errors of measurement, of course the fit would be perfect and one could find the values of the parameters exactly.[6] In reality, the equations are approximately correct at best, and the data do contain errors, so that one never finds an exact fit.

II. A COMPARISON OF FIVE MODELS

Let us now compare several large econometric models of the U.S. economy. By "large" I mean "having a relatively large number of equations," say a dozen or more. I have chosen the following five, all based on annual data beginning some time between the first and second world wars: Tinbergen's

---

[5] *Op. cit.*, p. 130. In principle, if the system is determinate, the final equations can always be obtained algebraically from the reduced form, but it is cumbersome if the reduced form is nonlinear.

[6] Except for any parameters that are not identified. For a good introductory exposition of this problem see T. C. Koopmans, "Identification Problems in Economic Model Construction," *Econometrica*, Vol. XVII (April, 1949), pp. 125–44. Reprinted in William C. Hood and T. C. Koopmans (eds.), *Studies in Econometric Method*, Cowles Commission Monograph 14 (New York: Wiley, 1953).

original model,[7] Klein's model III,[8] my model,[9] and Klein and Goldberger's models 1 and 2.[10] All of these models are nonlinear in variables. Tinbergen's model is linear except for the use of certain "threshold" variables, *i.e.*, variables assumed to have no effect at all unless they exceed a certain minimum level.[11] Even equations of the form "price times quantity equals value" are linearized.[12] The other four models are linear except for the use of certain compound variables involving the use of products and/or quotients of other variables in the system, such as price ratios and deflated variables. All the models are dynamic, using lagged variables and cumulated variables. The first two models cover the interwar period only, and the latter three extend as well into the period following the second world war. The number of years covered varies from 14 to 22. The number of equations varies from 14 to 20, except that Tinbergen used 48 equations. Some of the important individual characteristics of the five models are described in Table 1.

Tinbergen's model is distinguished by its large number of equations and endogenous variables. Most of the differences in size between Tinbergen's and the others is due to two things. First, he has a fairly detailed financial sector (note, however, that taxes and government expenditures do not appear except through their effect on the financial variables). Second, he treats the major expenditure items in both current dollars and deflated terms, introducing a price-level variable for each and an identity of the form "price times quantity equals value."[13]

Klein's model III sets the pattern for the other models discussed here. It deals mainly with deflated variables, though the general price level enters (so does the rent index, but this and the equations and other variables belonging to the housing market are dropped from some later models). It has consumption and investment equations on the final demand side, with government expenditure exogenous. Tax receipts are also exogenous. It has a demand-for-labor equation on the factor-demand side. It has adjustment equations for the interest rate, the rent index, and total output. The output-adjustment equation says that changes in output occur in response to unintended inventory changes, as measured by the error made by the inventory-demand equation. The

---

[7] *Op. cit.*, esp. pp. 196–97.

[8] L. R. Klein, *Economic Fluctuations in the United States 1921–1941* (New York, 1950), esp. pp. 108–13.

[9] C. F. Christ, "A Test of an Econometric Model for the United States 1921–1947," in Universities-National Bureau Committee, *Conference on Business Cycles* (New York, 1951), esp. pp. 72–77.

[10] Esp. pp. 51–53, 90–92.

[11] *Op. cit.*, pp. 97–98, 108.

[12] This is done by expressing each variable, say p, as the sum of its average value $\bar{p}$ over the period in question plus its deviation Δp from average, $p = \bar{p} + \Delta p$. Then $pq = v$ becomes $(\bar{p} + \Delta p)(\bar{q} + \Delta q) = \bar{v} + \Delta v$, or $\bar{p}\Delta q + \bar{q}\Delta p = \Delta v + \bar{v} - \overline{pq}$, neglecting the small term $\Delta p \Delta q$. Here Δp, Δq, and Δv are the variables, and $\bar{p}$, $\bar{q}$, and $\bar{v} - \overline{pq}$ are the parameters.

[13] See the preceding note. I shall argue below at the end of Section III that this is the only conceptually correct approach.

TABLE 1
A Comparison of Five Aggregate Models

	Years	Est. Meth.[a]	Stochastic Equations Definitions Total Equations	Endogenous Variables	Main Exogenous Variables	Dynamic Features
Tinbergen	1919–32	LS	42 6 — 48	4 consumption variables (2 farm, 2 nonfarm) 4 investment components 5 output variables 11 income components 11 price variables 13 stocks (2 real, 11 financial)	exports and imports building costs required reserves 5 financial stocks 3 financial flows agricultural supply	lags up to 4 years cumulated profits cumulated investment
Klein III	1922–41	LS and LI	12 3 — 15	consumption 4 net investment components private output disposable income wage income price level interest rate rent level capital stock 2 money stock components % vacant housing	government expenditure taxes plus corp. saving excise taxes capital goods prices excess reserves	lags of 1 and 2 years cumulated investment

			No.	Endogenous variables	Exogenous variables	Lagged variables
Christ	1922–47 (not incl. 1942–45)	LS and LI	10 4 — 14	consumption 4 net investment components private output private employment disposable income wage income price level wage rate interest rate rent level capital stock	government expenditure taxes plus corp. saving excise taxes capital goods prices money stock	lags of 1 and 2 years cumulated investment
Klein-Goldberger 1	1929–50 (not incl. 1942–45)	LI	14 5 — 19	consumption gross investment depreciation imports corporate saving private employees national income and 4 components price level wage level 2 interest rates capital stock 2 liquid assets components corporate surplus	government expenditure 4 components of direct taxes indirect taxes import prices excess reserves 5 population and labor force variables weekly hours	lags of 1, 2, 3, and 5 years cumulated investment cumulated corp. savings
Klein-Goldberger 2	1929–52 (not incl. 1942–45)	LI	15 5 — 20	farm price level other variables same as model 1	same as model 1	same as model 1

[a] Estimation methods: LS, least-squares; LI, limited-information.

output-adjustment equation proved unworkable and was dropped from later models.

My model was obtained by testing Klein's model III against data of two postwar years, retaining equations that described those data satisfactorily, and revising or replacing the ones that did not. It contains essentially the same kinds of equations as Klein's model III, except that it has a production-function instead of an output-adjustment equation, and it contains a wage-adjustment equation and employment and the money wage rate.[14]

The Klein and Goldberger models 1 and 2 can be discussed together, for they are essentially alike.[15] On the demand side there are equations for consumption, gross investment, and imports. There are a production-function, a demand-for-labor equation, a wage-rate-adjustment equation, a corporate-saving equation, and an equation describing the relation of corporate profits to property income. There is a depreciation equation, for which Klein and Goldberger have constructed estimates of depreciation at replacement cost in deflated terms. There is a pair of equations for long and short-term interest rates, another pair for liquid asset holdings of households and firms, a farm income equation, and (in model 2 only) a farm-price equation. There are five definitions, giving capital stock as cumulated net investment; corporate surplus as cumulated undistributed profits; gross national product as the sum of final expenditures; national income as the sum of incomes of farmers, non-farm wage and salary earners, and all others; and wage and salary income as the hourly wage rate times employment in man-hours.

III. THE KLEIN-GOLDBERGER MODELS

Let us now examine more closely some of the equations in the Klein-Goldberger models. Unless otherwise stated, the same equation was fitted to both 1929–50 and 1929–52 (omitting the war years 1942–45 in each case). The numbering of equations below does not correspond to that in the book.

(1) The consumption function contains three disposable income variables, which I shall call farm, labor, and property incomes.[16] It also contains lagged

---

[14] Klein's model III contains two equations describing the demand for active and idle cash balances. I dropped these two equations and the two cash-balances variables, because the variables appear nowhere else in Klein's model.

[15] Model 2, in addition to being fitted to a slightly longer series of data, has an additional equation to explain an additional variable, the farm price level. There are other small changes; see pp. 89–90.

[16] Farm income includes essentially the income of corporate and unincorporated farm enterprise. Labor income includes essentially wages and salaries and supplements. Property income is the remaining part of national income. The disposable income components were obtained from Commerce Department national income figures by allocating taxes and transfers among the three groups; see L. Frane and L. R. Klein, "The Estimation of Disposable Income by Distributive Shares," *Rev. Econ. and Stat.*, Vol. XXXV (November, 1953), pp. 333–37. It would have been preferable to impute wages to individual proprietors, and thus allocate part of unincorporated enterprise income to labor and only the residual to property.

consumption, household liquid asset holdings at the start of the year, and population. All coefficients are statistically significantly different from zero by the usual *t*-test at the $2\frac{1}{2}$ percent level of significance,[17] except the liquid assets coefficient for 1929–50. No slope coefficient changes much when the years 1951–52 are added to the sample in fitting model 2, except that the liquid assets coefficient increases and the coefficient of the population variable declines. The fits to the data are very good, no residual in either sample period being as great as 2 billion 1939 dollars and most being less than \$1 billion. The percentage errors are all less than 2 percent.

The three income variables are quite highly correlated with each other, and hence it would be impossible to discover accurately the separate effect of each on total consumption if one used only time-series estimation methods. The authors avoid this difficulty by the ingenious device of obtaining from multivariate cross-section analyses the ratios among the three marginal propensities to consume, then obtaining the value of one propensity as a sort of numeraire from the time-series data, and then obtaining the values of the other two propensities from the ratios. The cross-section studies used were based on the postwar Surveys of Consumer Finances.[18] The short-run and long-run marginal propensities to consume they obtain for 1929–52 are:[19] farm income, 0.34 and 0.46; property income, 0.41 and 0.55; labor income, 0.55 and 0.74.

I believe that these estimates overstate the difference between labor income receivers and the other two groups, on the following grounds: Labor incomes are less variable than others. Hence among the highest labor incomes in a given year there will be a smaller proportion of incomes that are unusually high than in the cases of farm and property incomes. And similarly, among the lowest labor incomes in a given year there will be a smaller proportion of unusually low incomes than in the cases of farm and property incomes. Hence the consumption of the best-paid laborers in a given year will give a relatively good picture of the consumption of laborers who are accustomed to that income-bracket, while the consumption of the best-remunerated farmers and property-income receivers will give a relatively poor picture (too low) of the consumption of such people who are accustomed to that income bracket. A symmetrical result holds for the low-income people in each of the three groups. Therefore the cross-section estimate of the marginal propensity to consume is a more serious underestimate for farmers and property-income receivers than for wage and salary earners. Hence Klein and Goldberger's

---

[17] Here and in further references to the *t*-test of significance of coefficients, I use a one-tail test because the algebraic sign of the coefficient is presumed to be known if it is not zero. For a criticism, see Section IV.

[18] See L. R. Klein "Statistical Estimation of Economic Relations from Survey Data," in L. R. Klein (ed.), *Contributions of Survey Methods to Economics* (New York, 1954).

[19] See p. 90 for the short-run propensities. The long-run propensities are obtained by setting lagged consumption equal to current consumption and solving for the latter, as explained on pp. 62–64.

ratios show too great a difference between labor income and other income.

(2) The gross private domestic investment equation relies mainly on a "profit" variable, lagged disposable property income (gross of depreciation allowances). It also contains capital stock and business liquid assets at the start of the year. The authors say that they tried fitting equations including the interest rate as a variable, but that they finally omitted it because in all their attempts its coefficient turned out to be not significantly different from zero, and positive—suggesting that high interest rates stimulate investment (pp. 67–68). The profit variable's coefficient is statistically significantly different from zero for both 1929–50 and 1929–52 at the 1 percent level and beyond, but the other variables' coefficients are not at the 5 percent level, though they have the expected algebraic signs. Only the capital coefficient is much affected by adding 1951–52 to the sample; it becomes less important.

Like the other investment equations known to me, this one makes large errors in 1938 and 1949, when it overestimates investment by 4.9 and 5.6 billion 1939 dollars respectively.[20] It also makes a substantial overestimate in 1932 ($4.5 billion) and substantial underestimates in 1929, 1950, and 1951 ($4.1, $3.5, and $3.6 billion respectively).[21] These errors can be put in perspective by noting that they amount to between 13 and 80 percent of actual gross investment in the respective years. An examination of the authors' graphs of their data[22] strongly suggests that the current rather than the lagged value of their profit variable (disposable property income gross of depreciation) would serve much better in explaining investment, for the current value of the profit variable coincides with investment in peaks and troughs quite well in 1929, 1932–33, 1937, and 1938, and fairly well after the war, while the lagged value misses the major turning points by a year. The authors state (p. 67) that they used the lagged value because they did not find reasonable estimates of equations containing both current and lagged earnings. One wonders whether they tried the current value alone.

Total investment includes housing construction, which one would expect to respond to labor income as well as or instead of property income, and to household liquid assets as well as or instead of business liquid assets. The authors recognize this in their discussion, and also the possibility of attempting to treat inventory investment separately as Klein's model III did (pp. 11, 68).

(3) The production function expresses real gross business product as a function of private employment, the capital stock (average of beginning and end-of-year figures), and time. In the employment variable the number of wage and salary earners is adjusted by multiplying it by an index of hours

---

[20] These errors are for the revised (1929–52) version. The 1929–50 version's errors are $5.4 and $3.8 billion respectively. See pp. 156–59.

[21] Again these errors are for the revised version; the 1929–50 version makes similar errors.

[22] P. 94. These graphs, showing the movements over time of each term in each equation, are very helpful.

worked per worker per year, but the number of farm and nonfarm entrepreneurs is not so adjusted, and I know of no suitable data for the purpose.

The production function's coefficients all have the expected algebraic signs, and all are significantly different from zero at the 1 percent level and beyond, except for the capital stock coefficient in the 1929–50 version. The capital coefficient is the only one to change much when 1951–52 are added to the sample; it nearly doubles. The function fits quite well in both versions. In each case only 4 residuals exceed 2 billion 1939 dollars; the largest absolute residuals are for 1947, being overestimates of $4.2 and $5.2 billion (about 4 percent) in the respective versions. Part of the reason for the good fits is the linear time-trend variable, which accounts for an output-increase of about 2 billion 1939 dollars per year; this is about 4 percent of the depression output and about 1½ percent of postwar outputs. The authors indicate (p. 69) that they would prefer a quadratic trend to a linear one, to reflect the rapid productivity rise, except that to use a quadratic trend makes other estimates in the equation "unstable." In my opinion even linear trend extrapolations should be used sparingly, for the very fact that we use a trend at all indicates that we do not understand the forces at work.

(4) The corporate saving equation is an innovation and a welcome one, for the variations of corporate saving are just as important as those of personal saving in transmitting the effects of exogenous tax and expenditure changes through the economy. This equation contains corporate profits after tax, lagged dividends, and corporate surplus at the start of the year, following Dobrovolsky. The fit is quite good for both the 1929–50 and 1929–52 versions, no residual exceeding 2 billion 1939 dollars and none exceeding $1 billion except for overestimates in 1936 by both versions and underestimates in 1948 and 1949 by the 1929–52 version. Of course these residuals must be viewed against the fact that corporate saving varied only between about −6 and +4 billion 1939 dollars over the whole period (p. 132). The coefficients of profits after tax in both versions are significantly different from zero at the 1 percent level and far beyond, but the coefficients of the other variables are not significant at the 10 percent level. The sign of the lagged dividends coefficient even changes from minus to plus (not an improvement!) when 1951 and 1952 are added to the sample, and the other coefficients change quite a bit in size.

(5) The corporate profits equation is a frankly empirical affair (p. 15), intended to bridge the gap between the corporate profits variable in the corporate saving equation and the property income variable in other equations. It simply says that corporate profits are a linear function of property income. The fit is quite good, no residuals exceeding 2 billion 1939 dollars and not many exceeding $1 billion. The coefficients are significant far beyond the 1 percent level. Nevertheless, like time trends, this equation leaves one with an uneasy feeling precisely because there is so little understanding behind it.

(6) The private wage-bill equation contains current and lagged gross business product and a time trend. All slope coefficients are significantly different

from zero at the 1 percent level except the trend. The fit is good; the only residual exceeding 2 billion 1939 dollars is an underestimate of $2.4 billion in 1938 in the revised (1929–52) version (this is an error of 7 percent) and most of the residuals are under $1 billion. The relative effects of current and lagged product appear quite different in the two versions, the coefficients being respectively 0.24 and 0.24 in 1929–50 version, and 0.36 and 0.14 in the 1929–52 version. The sum of the two coefficients is quite stable, changing only from 0.48 to 0.50. This of course is because current and lagged product are highly positively correlated, so that it is difficult to get reliable estimates of their separate effects.

The wage-bill equation is one of the easiest with which to get a good fit; even as a simple linear function of current gross business product alone, it would fit remarkably well. Its theoretical underpinnings are in the profit-maximizing behavior of entrepreneurs, and it may be regarded as a demand-for-labor equation (pp. 16–17).

(7) The wage-adjustment equation expresses the absolute change in the index of hourly money wage rates as a function of unemployment, lagged price-level change (*i.e.*, the change between last year and the year before), and a time trend. Its coefficients are virtually unaffected by the addition of 1951–52 to the sample, but none is significantly different from zero at the $2\frac{1}{2}$ percent level except trend, which is barely so. The fit is rather poor, especially in the 'thirties. For 1934 (the worst year) the equation (either version) underestimates the wage level by 10 index points, which is 10 percent of the 1934 level; the actual change from 1933 was +9 index points.[23] In the postwar period however the residuals have all been about 8 index points or less, which amounts to about 4 percent or less of the much higher postwar money wage level.

The seven equations just discussed are the most important stochastic equations in the model, either because they are theoretically central or because they concern big variables or both. The other eight stochastic equations (seven in model 1) concern imports, depreciation, the farm sector, interest rates, and holdings of liquid assets. In general their fits are not as good as those we have discussed, considering their residuals in relation to the size and variation of the variables being "explained."[24]

Several general comments on the equations occur to me. One of the purposes of these models, according to the authors (pp. vii–ix, 95–114), is to

---

[23] Albert Rees has pointed out to me that one would expect this equation to miss the substantial rise in wage rates between 1933 and 1934, because the equation does not reflect government policies set up under the National Recovery Administration. And also that one might expect it to underestimate wage rates in 1937 (as it actually does) because of its omission of the effects of the rapid growth of unions in that year.

[24] This is particularly true of the farm-income and short-term interest-rate equations. At the other extreme, the business liquid-assets and long-term interest-rate and farm-price equations fit quite well. It is unlikely that the latter would continue to fit well in 1953–55 for it makes farm prices a simple linear function of general prices.

provide a framework for forecasting one or two years in advance the broad changes in U.S. economic activity, under different assumptions about government policy. One would then expect that among the exogenous variables of the model there would be variables reflecting each of the important policy measures that are at the disposal of government. For fiscal policy this expectation is substantially met: government's total expenditures, wage and salary payments and employees are represented by exogenous variables, and there are five tax variables representing indirect tax payments less subsidies, and direct tax payments on account of farm income, labor income, property income, and corporate profits. This treatment of taxes is a notable advance. A further advance is that in making forecasts, the authors have regarded only the tax *rates* as exogenous, and have regarded the deflated amounts of taxes collected as being determined by the tax schedule, money incomes, and the price level (pp. 142–55). In the case of each type of income and tax schedule, they have fitted a linear equation to money tax receipts as a function of money income and then deflated the result to get real tax payments as a nonlinear function of real income and the price level.

However, in the field of monetary policy the above expectation about policy variables is not met. Excess bank reserves (as a percentage of total reserves) is an exogenous variable; but that is all. Reserve requirements, open-market operations, the Federal Reserve discount rates, and credit restrictions are ignored except to the limited extent that their full effects are reflected in the excess-reserve ratio. Presumably these variables are neglected because the authors believe that they are unimportant. But since this is an open issue among economists, it would be well to give monetary factors a chance to show up in a model of this kind.

The second comment concerns the treatment of prices and accounting definitions in the Klein-Goldberger models. Only the deflated values of the flows of goods and services appear; the money values do not. This creates certain difficulties, because the accounting definitions really apply to the *money* values. A model-builder has several options: (1) He can include both deflated and money values for each flow variable, along with a price index for each and an equation of the form $pq = v$. This would require a large number of variables and equations, and in particular it would require the equivalent of a price-adjustment equation for each flow variable, depending on supply and demand factors including inventories in the case of storable goods. In my opinion this is conceptually the best choice, as well as the most difficult one. (2) He can work with money values alone, ignoring deflated values. This is highly unsatisfactory for real relationships such as production functions. It is also unsatisfactory for demand functions, such as the consumption function, which are supposed to be homogeneous of degree zero in prices and the quantity of money.[25] (3) He can work with deflated values only, ignoring money

---

[25] One can argue that homogeneity requirements need not be taken seriously in a linear equation when the data cover only a small range of values far from zero, because the linear

values. This is essentially what all the models discussed in this article do, except Tinbergen's, which contains both deflated and money values of several variables.

If one uses deflated variables only, one must of course make the definitions hold in deflated terms. This could be done by deflating all variables by a general price index, but then all variations in relative prices would be ignored. Suppose each variable is to be deflated by a price index appropriate to it. Then little or no trouble arises with consumption, investment, and other similar items composed of flows of measurable quantities of goods and services. But trouble arises with disposable incomes, saving, taxes, transfers, and other items not composed of flows of measurable quantities of goods and services. These latter can be deflated by price indexes appropriate to the decisions of the payers or receivers, but then the definitions will usually not hold in real terms. Or they can be deflated by a general price index, so that the sum of all deflated income items is equal to deflated total output. This is what all the models discussed here (except Tinbergen's) did. It too can have strange results, as the Klein-Goldberger data illustrate. Their consumption expenditure is deflated by the Commerce Department's implicit deflator for consumer goods, and their disposable income variables are deflated by the Commerce Department's implicit deflator for GNP. Now the GNP deflator rose by about 8 percent relative to the consumption deflator over the sample period 1929–52.[26] This means that Klein and Goldberger give deflated disposable incomes a downward trend of 8 percent for the period relative to deflated consumption. The result is that their deflated personal saving, *i.e.*, the difference between their deflated disposable incomes and consumption, is too high at the beginning of the period and too low at the end—it is even negative in 1949![27] Thus their consumption function is fitted to a distorted set of data, from the point of view of consumption decisions.

---

equation may be only an approximation to a nonlinear function that is homogeneous even though the linear approximation is not.

[26] Survey of Current Business *National Income Supplement*, 1954 ed., Table 41, pp. 216–17.

[27] Klein and Goldberger do not present their saving or total disposable income figures, but one can calculate them from their income, tax, and consumption series (pp. 131–32). The table below shows a few values, together with the Commerce Department's undeflated data for comparison (*National Income Suppl.*, 1954, pp. 164–65).

Year	Disposable Income		Personal Saving		Saving Ratio	
	Dept. of Commerce (money)	Klein and Goldberger (deflated)	Dept. of Commerce (money)	Klein and Goldberger (deflated)	Dept. of Commerce (money)	Klein and Goldberger (deflated)
1929	83.1	67.2	4.2	5.0	5%	7%
1946	159.2	102.7	12.6	7.0	8%	7%
1949	188.2	102.6	7.6	−0.6	4%	−1%
1952	236.9	113.5	18.4	2.1	8%	2%

IV. ESTIMATING PARAMETERS

Let us now turn to some questions concerning the estimation of coefficients in the Klein-Goldberger models. The two estimation methods on which practical choice has centered in recent years are the familiar least-squares method and the less familiar limited-information method. The least-squares method chooses one variable in the equation as "dependent," concentrates on the deviations of the actual from the calculated values of this variable, and selects as its estimates the set of values of the parameters that minimizes the sum of the squares of these deviations. The results thus depend on one's choice of dependent variable. The limited-information method in effect adds together the endogenous terms in the equation to form a single new synthetic variable, and takes the least-squares regression of this new synthetic variable on a number of predetermined variables, including all those that appear in the equation and some others that do not; and then by imposing the condition that the coefficients of those predetermined variables that do not appear in the equation shall be zero in this regression, it unscrambles the synthetic variable into its components and obtains an estimate for the parameter of each endogenous variable, and for each predetermined variable in the equation too.[28]

The least-squares method is relatively easy computationally, and the estimates it yields have relatively small variances about their expected values. The trouble is that when it is applied to equations that are part of a simultaneous system, it typically yields biased estimates, that is, estimates whose expected values are different from the true values. Thus the least-squares method in a system of equations can be likened to a shotgun that scatters its shot (*i.e.*, its estimates) fairly close together, but not centered on the bullseye.

The limited-information method is relatively burdensome computationally,[29] and its estimates have larger variances about their expected values

---

[28] Another way to contrast the two methods is as follows. The least-squares method selects as its estimates the set of values of the parameters that makes the residuals (measured in the direction of the chosen "dependent" variable) sum algebraically to zero and be uncorrelated with each of the other variables in the equation. The limited-information method tries to select as its estimates the set of values of the parameters that makes the residuals (measured in the direction of any one of the endogenous variables) sum algebraically to zero and be uncorrelated with a number of predetermined variables, including all those that appear in the equation and some others. If the number of predetermined variables used is the same as the number of slope coefficients to be estimated the computations are relatively easy; if more, they are more cumbersome; if less, no unique estimates are possible. (These three cases are called the just-identified, over-identified, and unidentified cases.) The above descriptions of the limited-information method are not intended to convey a precise idea of it. For this, see Hood and Koopmans (eds.), *Studies in Econometric Method* (New York, 1953), Ch. 6, esp. pp. 143–78 or 162–78. A much more introductory presentation will be found in E. G. Bennion, "The Cowles Commission's 'Simultaneous Equations Approach,'" *Rev. Econ. and Stat.*, Vol. XXXIV (February, 1952), pp. 49–56, and in J. R. Meyer and H. L. Miller, Jr., "Some Comments on the 'Simultaneous Equations Approach,'" *Rev. Econ. and Stat.*, Vol. XXXVI (February, 1954), pp. 88–92.

[29] To obtain the estimates and their estimated standard errors, it requires inverting four matrices, instead of one as the least-squares method does; one of the four has at least

than do the least-squares estimates. Its estimates are biased too, except that under the typical assumptions made by model-builders, these biases become smaller and approach zero as the sample size (number of observations) approaches infinity. Thus the limited-information method can be likened to a shotgun that scatters its shot (*i.e.*, its estimates) less close together than the least-squares shotgun does, and not centered right on the bullseye either, but becoming better centered and approaching perfect centering as the sample size approaches infinity.

Thus the question of which method to use for any finite sample size is still open, for we do not know how to tell whether the bias of the limited-information method at a given sample size is smaller than that of the least-squares method by enough to compensate for its bigger variance.[30]

Empirical evidence of two types is slowly accumulating on this point. The first type is that obtained experimentally by the Monte Carlo method. This consists of taking a large number of samples of data from a synthetic real world that has been constructed in advance with known equations and parameters, and then computing from each sample an estimate of a certain known parameter. The large number of estimates of that parameter so obtained will give a pretty good empirical idea of the sampling distribution of the estimates. In an unpublished paper Wagner[31] has compared the least-squares and limited-information estimates of the marginal propensity to consume, based on 100 samples from one synthetic real world and another 100 samples from another. In each case his synthetic real world was a simple three-equation income-consumption-investment model; consumption was a linear function of income, the marginal propensity to consume was 0.5, and the predetermined variables in the model (used in the limited-information estimation process) were lagged income and time. The sample size in each case was 20. The distributions of the 100 estimates of the marginal propensity to consume in each synthetic real world are summarized in Table 2. Note that for each, the estimated bias of the least-squares estimates is greater than that of the limited-information estimates (line 3), but that the estimated standard deviation of the least-squares estimates is smaller than that of the limited-information estimates (line 4) by a margin great enough to bring the root mean square error of the least-squares estimates down slightly below that of the limited-information estimates (line 5). The differences are so small, however, less

---

as many rows and columns as the least-squares matrix (often more), and the other three have fewer.

[30] Let us accept the expected value of the squared error as the criterion of choice between the two methods. For either method, this is equal to the squared bias plus the variance of the estimate from its expected value. Thus to be better than least squares, the limited-information method must have a squared bias that is smaller than the squared least-squares bias by a margin greater than the difference between the two methods' variances.

[31] H. M. Wagner, "A Monte Carlo Study of Estimates of Simultaneous Linear Structural Equations," Technical Rept. No. 12, mimeo. (Stanford: Economics Department, 1954), esp. pp. 1–3, 6–8, 16–18, 22–23, and 54. [This paper has now appeared in *Econometrica*, Vol. XXVI (January, 1958), pp. 117–33.]

than 3 percent in fact, that this contest between the two methods ends in a standoff.[32]

TABLE 2

Summary of Wagner's Estimates of the Marginal Propensity to Consume Obtained by Two Estimation Methods

	Synthetic Real World I		Synthetic Real World II	
	Least-Squares Method	Limited-Information Method	Least-Squares Method	Limited-Information Method
1. True value	0.5000	0.5000	0.5000	0.5000
2. Average of 100 estimates	0.5137	0.4955	0.5087	0.5049
3. Estimated bias (100 estimates)	0.0137	−0.0055	0.0087	0.0049
4. Estimated standard deviation (100 estimates)	0.0107	0.0174	0.0453	0.0460
5. Root mean square error (100 estimates)	0.0174	0.0179	0.0462	0.0463

The second type of empirical evidence lies in the few real studies now available in which both the least-squares and limited-information methods have been used,[33] so that the results can be compared. In most of these the differences between the two sets of estimates are so small that it is difficult to say which set is better; that argues in favor of the least-squares estimates, which are simpler to compute. In the few cases I know of where the two sets of estimates do differ substantially, the least-squares estimates are nearly always more reasonable than the limited-information estimates, in the light of what can be expected theoretically about the parameters in question.[34]

Unfortunately for readers who want to face this issue, Klein and Goldberger do not present least-squares estimates of their models for comparison with their limited-information estimates. Fortunately, however, Karl Fox has computed and published least-squares estimates of their model 2 for 1929–52, using their data.[35] For most parameters, the least-squares and limited-information estimates are approximately equal, measured either by the percentage difference between the two or by the number of standard deviations by which

---

[32] See also A. L. Nagar, "A Monte Carlo Study of Alternative Simultaneous Equation Estimators," *Econometrica*, Vol. XXVIII (July, 1960), pp. 573–90.

[33] See Klein, *Economic Fluctuations in the United States 1921–1941*, pp. 108–13, and Christ, *op. cit.*, pp. 72–76 and 83–86.

[34] For example, see the investment and labor equations in Christ, *op. cit.*, pp. 72–73 and 85–86. For a possible explanation, see L. R. Klein and Mitsugu Nakamura, "Singularity in Equation Systems of Econometrics: Some Aspects of the Problem of Multicollinearity," *International Economic Review*, Vol. III (September, 1962), pp. 274–99.

[35] K. A. Fox, "Econometric Models of the U.S. Economy," *Jour. Pol. Econ.*, Vol. LXIV (April, 1956), pp. 135–36, Table III.

they differ. In only two cases are the algebraic signs different: (1) the least-squares version says plausibly (because of the relative stability of dividends) that high dividends last year contribute to low corporate saving this year, and the limited-information version says the opposite, but the coefficient is less than its standard error; and (2) the least-squares version says that high non-farm income last year contributes to high farm income this year, and the limited-information version says the opposite, but both coefficients are less than their standard errors. In only three other equations are there any coefficients whose least-squares estimates differ by as much as 20 percent from their limited-information estimates.[36] They are the business-liquidity equation and the rather unsatisfactory equations for imports and the wage rate. Of 32 limited-information estimates of slope coefficients,[37] 13 differ from their least-squares counterparts by no more than one standard error of the latter, 13 differ by more than one but not more than two, and 6 differ by more than two. These last 6 are in the equations for corporate saving, the wage bill, and household liquidity.

This comparison of least-squares and limited-information estimates, incomplete though it is because among other things it does not extend to their respective forecasts, confirms the impression that the issue between the two methods is still open, with perhaps an edge in favor of least-squares on grounds of simplicity.[38]

[36] This number would be four instead of three if I did not exclude the wage-bill equation. Its least-squares coefficients of current and lagged output differ by about 50 percent from its corresponding limited-information coefficients, but the *sum* of the two least-squares coefficients differs from the *sum* of the limited-information coefficients by only 6 percent. As noted in Section III, part (6), it is only the sum that is stable.

[37] I exclude the 6 slope coefficients in the three equations for which the limited-information method reduces to least-squares, namely the investment and short- and long-term interest-rate equations.

[38] To this discussion of estimation methods I must add brief mention of a third method, devised by my visiting colleague Henri Theil of the Netherlands School of Economics, and described in his forthcoming book. Theil's method consists essentially of replacing all but one of the current endogenous variables in the equation by their values as estimated by their reduced-form regressions on the predetermined variables, and then using least squares with the remaining current endogenous variable as the dependent variable. It yields consistent estimates but is considerably easier computationally than the limited-information method.

Some recent theoretical work on the relative merits of estimation methods suggests that simultaneous-equations methods may have the edge. See in particular R. L. Basmann's three articles in the *Journal of the American Statistical Association*, Nos. 292 (December, 1960), 295 (September, 1961), and 301 (March, 1963); Carl F. Christ, "Simultaneous Equation Estimation: Any Verdict Yet?" *Econometrica*, Vol. XXVIII (October, 1960), pp. 835–45; Lawrence R. Klein, "The Efficiency of Estimation in Econometric Models," in Ralph W. Pfouts (ed.), *Essays in Economics and Econometrics in Honor of Harold Hotelling, Studies in Economics and Business Administration* (Chapel Hill: Univ. of North Carolina Press, 1960), pp. 216–33; A. L. Nagar, "Double k-Class Estimators of Parameters in Simultaneous Equations and Their Small Sample Properties," *International Economic Review*, Vol. III (May, 1962), pp. 168–88.

See also Arnold Zellner and Henri Theil, "Three-Stage Least Squares: Simultaneous Estimation of Simultaneous Equations," *Econometrica*, Vol. XXX (January, 1962), pp. 54–78.

The meaning of the estimated standard deviations of the parameter-estimates deserves attention. It is common practice in constructing econometric equations and models to try several different theoretically plausible forms of each equation, estimating the parameters of each form, and then to choose the form that seems best in the light of several criteria such as the size and apparent randomness or nonrandomness of residuals, *a priori* expectations about the signs and sizes of parameters, the estimated variances of parameter estimates, etc. As far as I know everyone who estimates equations does some of this sort of experimenting. Indeed, I believe it is wise to do so, because in most problems the underlying theoretical analysis is not so exact as to be able to specify just what the form of the relationship is—linear, quadratic, linear in logarithms, or what—even when it can specify (as it sometimes cannot) just what variables enter and just what data are best suited to measure them. Hence if one does no experimenting of this sort, one often has to choose among several theoretically plausible forms of an equation without a basis for the choice.

The statistical theory, on which the least-squares and limited-information estimates and their estimated standard deviations are based, assumes that no experimenting of this sort has been done. It assumes that the form of each equation has been chosen before the data have been seen, so that the data have no chance to influence that choice. If this assumption is met (along with the others appropriate to the estimation method used) then the estimated standard deviations are what they seem to be, and can be used without adjustment in the usual tests of significance concerning parameters. But suppose that experimenting has been done, and the form of the equation has been chosen in the light of how well it fits the data in comparison with other forms. Then one is more likely to get a good fit simply as a matter of chance than if one tried only one equation-form, because one has several opportunities to choose from instead of just one. Hence the estimated standard deviations are spuriously small, and if they are used without adjustment in the usual significance tests, there will be a bias in favor of deciding that the parameters are significantly different from zero.

It is a difficult question how to make allowances for the fact that experimentation with different equation-forms has been done, especially if one does not know what different forms were tried. Klein and Goldberger give some information about what alternatives they tried,[39] but it would be more enlightening to readers if all the alternatives tried had been presented together with their estimates.[40]

It is a familiar fact of econometrics that the presence of serial correlation

---

[39] See Section III above, and pp. 50, 68, and 90 for general statements. Their specific remarks concern the equations for consumption (p. 65), investment (pp. 67–68), corporate profits (pp. 68–69), depreciation (p. 90), farm income (p. 69), household liquid assets (p. 70), long-term interest rate (pp. 28–29), and short-term interest rate (p. 30).

[40] Some further remarks related to this will be found at the beginning of Section V.

among the disturbances to a time-series equation decreases the reliability of the estimates of its parameters. Hence it is important to test for the presence of serial correlation. This Klein and Goldberger do, using a statistic known as δ^2/S^2, where δ^2 is the mean squared change in the value of the calculated residuals from year to year and S^2 is the variance of the same residuals. They conclude that disturbances in an equation are positively serially correlated if δ^2/S^2 is less than 1.25.[41] Four of the fourteen stochastic equations in model 1 (1929–50) show serial correlation of disturbances by this test, and so do seven of the fifteen stochastic equations in model 2 (1929–52). A widely used device that sometimes reduces positive serial correlation of disturbances (and sometimes produces negative serial correlation instead) is to fit the equations to first differences (year-to-year changes) of the data instead of to the raw data. Klein and Goldberger apparently did not try this.

V. PREDICTING ABILITY OF THE KLEIN-GOLDBERGER MODELS

This section deals with the performance of the Klein-Goldberger models in the "future," that is, in years following the periods whose data were used to decide on the form of their equations and to estimate their parameters. Before taking up numerical results, I want to offer some remarks on the nature and meaning of such extrapolations into the "future."

As decision-makers or advisers thereto, economists want to be able to fore-cast economic events for at least a short time ahead, and to forecast the consequences of alternative decisions. As seekers after truth and understanding, economists want to construct theories that will describe accurately a large part of economic experience. If we are to tell whether an econometric model will help in either quest, we must try it against data. I believe there is now fairly general agreement that more is required than simply choosing a model and fitting it to a set of data. It has been said by many—and I have been among the guilty—that the real test of a model lies in its ability to ex-plain or predict new data that were not used in estimating its parameters. There is a real and valid point involved here, but the statement is not quite correct as it stands. It suggests incorrectly that if one has data for a certain period, say 1929–1955, and one wants to obtain as reliable a model as possible with their aid, one must after choosing the model use only part of the data (say 1929–1950) to estimate the parameters, and must save the rest of the data (1951–55) to test the model. This is incorrect because the best one can accomplish is to devise a plausible model that explains well all the available relevant data, and it makes little difference whether this is done by fitting the model to all of the data, or by fitting it to part of them and discovering

---

[41] P. 52. This is a one-tail test at approximately the 5 percent level.

afterward that it explains the rest of them well.[42] In either case one has a good explainer of data to date, and one is uncertain about whether it will continue to explain future data.

What then is the real and valid point in the statement that the real test of a model lies in its ability to predict new data? It is the following: Since it is difficult (and even unwise, I argue above in Section IV) to avoid examining relevant data before choosing the form of the equation to be fitted, there is some danger of choosing an incorrect equation that for accidental reasons happens to fit the examined data well, in preference to a more nearly correct equation that for accidental reasons does not fit the examined data very well. It is this danger against which protection is needed. The protection is provided by new data, *i.e.*, data that were not examined in choosing the form of the equation. But it does not matter much whether these new data are incorporated into the sample used for fitting the equation, or are saved until after the fitting and used as a test. The important thing is that they were not examined while the form of the equation was being decided on. Thus if one chooses an equation now for use with data beginning with 1929, it makes little difference for the present purpose whether one now fits it to 1929–55 data and after 1960 tests it against 1956–60 data, or whether one now puts it on the shelf for five years and after 1960 fits it to 1929–60 data. For other purposes, of course, one prefers to fit it now instead of after 1960.[43]

Let us now turn to tests[44] based on the performances of the Klein-Goldberger models when faced with "future" data. It is possible to work either with the estimated structural equations, or with the reduced form obtained by solving them. To locate faulty structural equations one should examine them one by one. To evaluate the model's predictive ability one should work with the reduced form. It is possible to work either with *ex ante* or *ex post* predictions, as the authors use the terms. *Ex ante* predictions are real predictions, made in advance, for which it is necessary to guess the unknown values that the predetermined variables [45] will have. Errors in *ex ante* predictions may be due to faulty guesses about the predetermined variables, or to a faulty model, or to random disturbances. *Ex post* predictions are conditional, made after the event, by using the observed values of the predetermined variables. Their errors may be due to a faulty model or to random disturbances. I shall discuss tests based (1) on the *ex post* performances of the structural equations of both models, (2) on *ex post* predictions from the reduced form of model 1, and

---

[42] Indeed, in so far as there is a difference between these two alternatives, fitting the model to all the data is preferable, because it uses a larger sample and hence yields estimates with smaller variances.

[43] If one has a cross-section sample of several thousand observations, one can examine a hundred or so and devise a model to fit them, and then fairly safely test the model on the remaining unexamined part of the sample. This was pointed out to me by James Tobin.

[44] I use the word "test" very loosely here, not in the sense of statistical tests of hypotheses.

[45] The lagged variables may be unknown because of delay in measuring and reporting their values.

(3) on *ex ante* predictions from the reduced forms of both models. The tests are based on data for 1951–54. Unfortunately the Commerce Department's most recent revision of national income data came in the middle of this period, after the 1952 data were released. The revised data are available for all years from 1929 to 1954, but the unrevised data are not available for 1953 and 1954. Since Klein and Goldberger did nearly all of their work before the revision (which appeared late in 1954) it is necessary to use data for the 1953 and 1954 tests that are not strictly comparable with the data used in estimating the models. However, the revisions are not large enough to alter the quali-tative picture presented by the tests now to be discussed.[46]

1. The *ex post* structural tests consist of substituting into each estimated structural equation the observed values of the variables for the "future" year in question, and finding the calculated disturbance of the equation for that year. Klein and Goldberger give these calculated disturbances for 10 of the 14 stochastic equations of model 1 for the years 1951 and 1952.[47] In 4 of these 10 equations, either the 1951 or the 1952 residual is larger, or both are larger, than any of the sample-period residuals.[48] The authors also give calcu-lated disturbances for 11 of the 15 stochastic equations of model 2 based on preliminary data for the years 1953 and 1954.[49] In 5 of these 11 equations, either the 1953 or the 1954 residual is larger, or both are larger, than any of the sample-period residuals.[50] These results suggest that important parts of the models do not fit the postsample data as well as they do the sample data.

2. The *ex post* reduced-form tests consist of substituting into the estimated structural equations the observed values of predetermined variables for the "future" year in question, then solving the structural equations for the current endogenous variables, and comparing the results with the observed values of these variables. This requires data for all variables in the model. The authors give these data for 1951–52, so the reader can perform the test of model 1 based on those years. They also solve the 19 nonlinear structural equations and give the *ex post* reduced-form predictions, so the reader does not have to do all the arithmetic.[51] However, the reader cannot perform the test of either

---

[46] This is confirmed by preliminary tests of the 1954 forecasts given by the authors (p. ix).

[47] Recall that model 1 was estimated from 1929–50 data. For the residuals see pp. 86 and 156–57. The 4 omitted equations concern the money market.

[48] The equations are the production function and those for consumption, investment, and farm income.

[49] Recall that model 2 was estimated from 1929–52 data. For the residuals see pp. viii and 158–59. Again the 4 omitted equations concern the money market.

[50] The equations are those for consumption, the wage-bill, depreciation, corporate profits, and (especially bad) farm prices. The latter is because farm prices broke away from general prices in 1953–54, falling substantially.

[51] The authors say that the reduced form reduces to two nonlinear equations containing price level and national income as variables, and they reproduce these equations in general-ized form (p. 40). It would have been helpful to readers who wish to test the model's predic-tions of price level and income if they had given these two equations in a form showing

model based on 1953 or later years, even if he is willing to solve the equations for those years himself, because the book presents data only through 1952; and although the authors leave a quite detailed "trail" as to how they constructed their time series (pp. 118–41), it is not possible for the reader to follow it beyond 1952 on his own because so many of the sources are contained in private correspondence between the authors and government agencies.[52]

Ex post reduced-form predictions were made with model 1 for 1951 and 1952 for 14 of the 19 current endogenous variables. The results are shown in Table 3 together with the observed values.[53] Columns 4 and 9 show the errors as a percentage of the observed values, − 4 percent meaning that the prediction was 4 percent low, etc. Columns 5 and 10 show whether the predicted direction of change was right or wrong. Columns 6 and 11 show whether the predictions were better than those of the familiar no-change-from-last-year naive model. The comparison with the naive model is a rather severe test for variables that changed very little, such as consumption, but it is a correspondingly lax test for variables that changed a good deal, as GNP did from 1950 to 1951. Notice that in both years the predictions of real GNP were in error by 4 percent or less, showed the right direction of change, and were better than the naive model's predictions. The same is true of two other variables, the real private wage-bill and the money wage rate.

3. The *ex ante* reduced-form tests are a realistic rehearsal of a genuine forecasting effort. The authors estimated the values of the predetermined variables for the year in question before that year began, or only shortly after (pp. 82, 95), on the basis of their best guess about the government budget, etc. They then substituted these values into the structural equations, and solved for the predicted values of the jointly dependent variables.[54] They

---

explicitly how their parameters depend on the parameters of the original equations of the model.

[52] For this reason I present no tests based on predictions made by Fox's least-squares estimates of model 2 (1929–52), for such tests require data for 1953–54.

[53] Excluded were the four money-market variables and capital stock. See p. 81 for the figures.

[54] Klein and Goldberger say (p. 77) that they prefer not to make predictions by a mechanical use of the reduced form, but prefer instead to make certain adjustments in the structural equations, according to the following rule, before solving them: (a) If a structural equation in the preceding few years has errors all in the same direction and if there is independent evidence leading the authors to expect errors in that direction to continue, then they add to the constant term of that equation the error of that equation in the preceding year. (b) If either or both of the conditions under (a) is not met regarding a structural equation, they do not adjust the constant term of that equation. A rough check for 1951 and 1952, based on similar adjustments made in the reduced form predictions, suggests that such adjustments improve the predictions slightly in most of the cases where they are applicable. (This illustrates what I take to be a fact, that econometric models so far are sufficiently inaccurate and incomplete so that supplementary information applied with good judgment can improve their performance.) The 1953 and 1954 predictions referred to in the text above incorporate such adjustments (pp. 106–07).

TABLE 3

Ex Post Reduced-Form Predictions of Klein-Goldberger Model 1 for 1951 and 1952

Variable[a]	1950 Observed Value (1)	1951 Observed Value (2)	1951 Predicted Value (3)	1951 Error +high −low (4)	1951 Predicted Direction of Change (5)	1951 Prediction Better than Naive Model's (6)	1952 Observed Value (7)	1952 Predicted Value (8)	1952 Error +high −low (9)	1952 Predicted Direction of Change (10)	1952 Prediction Better than Naive Model's (11)
GNP	154.3	167.3	159.9	−4%	right	yes	170.8	169.9	−1%	right	yes
Consumption	108.7	108.4	108.7	+¼%	no change	tie	110.2	113.0	+3%	right	no
Gross investment	24.8	28.0	20.2	−28%	wrong	no	23.8	19.5	−18%	right	no
National income	126.1	135.9	130.9	−4%	right	yes	137.4	140.3	+2%	right	no
Private wage-bill	70.9	75.6	72.7	−4%	right	yes	77.2	77.3	0	right	yes
Farm income	7.5	8.0	9.3	+16%	right	no	7.7	10.3	+34%	wrong	no
Property income	34.9	37.0	33.6	−9%	wrong	no	35.5	35.7	+1%	right	yes
Depreciation	15.9	17.7	15.3	−10%	wrong	yes	20.6	16.6	−20%	wrong	no
Corporate profits	17.4	18.2	15.6	−14%	wrong	no	17.8	17.1	−4%	right	no
Corporate saving	2.3	1.4	−1.0	−170%	wrong	no	2.3	0.9	−61%	wrong	no
Imports	4.8	4.2	4.0	−5%	right	yes	4.6	4.0	−13%	wrong	no
No. of employees	50.7	54.3	53.6	−1%	right	yes	55.2	57.7	+5%	right	no
Money wage rate	287.1	309.9	304.1	−2%	right	yes	326.2	334.9	+3%	right	yes
Price level	183.2	196.8	196.8	0	right	yes	202.0	216.6	+7%	right	no

a All in billions of 1939 dollars, except employees in millions, and wage rate and price level in indexes 1939:100.

made *ex ante* predictions this way for 1953 with model 1, and for 1954 with model 2. Because of the difficulties over private sources of data referred to above, I was able to obtain observed 1953 and 1954 values of only a few of their predicted variables, even in the Commerce Department's new revised form; I concentrate on the following five as being most readily obtainable: real GNP, real consumption, real gross investment, the number of employees and the price level.

The results of the *ex ante* reduced-form predictions of these five variables for 1953 and 1954 are shown in Table 4.[55] Notice that in both years the predictions of real GNP were in error by $\frac{1}{2}$ percent or less, showed the right direction of change, and were better than the naive model's predictions. The same is true of real consumption and number of employees if the $\frac{1}{2}$ percent limit is amended to 1 percent. It is rather unusual for consumption to rise when GNP falls, as occurred between 1953 and 1954; the authors predicted this quite well. Presumably the reason is that income taxes were cut substantially at the beginning of 1954, and that it was known late in 1953 that they would be. The predictions of GNP, consumption, and employees for 1953 and 1954 are remarkably good, even if allowances are made for the fact that the observed values are based on the Commerce Department's 1954 revision of the national income data while the predictions are based on pre-revision data (for reasons discussed earlier).[56] In fact, they are so good that one might be pardoned for suspecting that the authors had a bit of good luck with these variables in 1953 and 1954. In any case, it would be exciting to see more results, with other variables and in other years.

A disturbing feature of the models is their tendency since 1951 to overestimate the price level by a substantial amount. This is especially bad for 1954, when model 2 predicts a decline of about 2 percent in real GNP and at the same time a rise of about 7 percent in prices.[57] Surely these two changes are unlikely to occur simultaneously in our economy as it has operated since the second world war. This suggests a fault in the models, which may be due to the way in which price changes are transmitted, mainly via the wage-adjustment equation.[58]

---

[55] Predictions are from Klein and Goldberger (pp. 83–84, 88, 99, and 111). Observations are calculated from the *Survey of Current Business*, July, 1955, pp. 8–9, 18, and 22–23, following the definitions in Klein and Goldberger, pp. 118–31.

[56] By comparing the 1952 values in Table 4 based on revised data with those in Table 3 based on unrevised data, one can get a sense of the magnitude of the revision. The approximate percentage differences between the revised and unrevised figures for 1952 are: GNP $\frac{1}{2}$ percent, consumption $\frac{1}{2}$ percent, investment 8 percent, employees 5 percent, and price level 1 percent. Thus the results in Table 4 stand, except that investment was predicted better and the number of employees was predicted worse than the table shows.

[57] According to the authors' preliminary figures (p. ix), these were 3 percent and 8 percent respectively.

[58] See pp. 37, 41, and Section III part (7) above.

TABLE 4

EX ANTE REDUCED-FORM PREDICTIONS OF KLEIN-GOLDBERGER MODELS 1 AND 2 FOR 1953 AND 1954

Variable[a]	1952	1953 (Model 1)					1954 (Model 2)				
	Observed Value (1)	Observed Value (2)	Predicted Value (3)	Error +high −low (4)	Predicted Direction of Change (5)	Prediction Better than Naive Model's (6)	Observed Value (7)	Predicted Value (8)	Error +high −low (9)	Predicted Direction of Change (10)	Prediction Better than Naive Model's (11)
GNP	169.8	177.5	177.4	0	right	yes	174.0	174.8	$+\frac{1}{2}\%$	right	yes
Consumption	109.9	114.7	114.4	$-\frac{1}{4}\%$	right	yes	116.6	117.3	$+1\%$	right	yes
Gross investment	21.7	21.9	24.2	$+11\%$	right	no	20.3	22.7	$+12\%$	wrong	no
No. of employees	56.4	57.5	57.1	-1%	right	yes	55.8	56.5	$+1\%$	right	yes
Price level	203.3	205.3	213.7	$+4\%$	right	no	207.2	220.5	$+6\%$	right	no

[a] All in billions of 1939 dollars, except employees in millions, and wage rate and price level in indexes 1939:100.

VI. CONCLUSION

By way of conclusion it is easy to say that the Klein-Goldberger models leave much to be desired. But who is to cast the first stone? Clearly, no other economist has done as well in the difficult business of making an aggregate econometric model for the U.S. economy. Their work would be even more useful to others had they presented all the equations with which they experimented and the estimates obtained for each, had they given least-squares estimates and the forecasts made with them, and were they now to extend their data to later years and show how the models perform in those years.

IV. STUDIES OF PARTICULAR VARIABLES

18

Introduction

UNIFIED THEORIES of the business cycle in the economy as a whole, and especially theories that are expressed in simultaneous mathematical equations, are constructed from well-defined building blocks, each block usually relating to the explanation of the behavior of some particular economic variable. In the mathematical models with several equations, each separate equation serves to elucidate some form of economic interrelationship that explains one of the particular variables of the model. Thus, dynamic versions of the Keynesian theory, which form the basis of many cyclical models, contain consumption functions, investment functions, liquidity-preference functions, and other aggregative functions to explain the behavior of employment, the labor force, the wage rate, or the price level.

Apart from the systematic attempts to build models of the whole economy, there have been numerous studies of these building blocks, both theoretical and empirical. It has been extremely difficult for us to choose among the many offerings that are available in the period since World War II. We have merely sampled among variables and authors in order to pick out some leading contributions.

Among many studies of the investment function, we have selected two, one by Kisselgoff and Modigliani and the other by Dale Jorgenson. The Kisselgoff-Modigliani paper deals with investment in a particular industry, but it is an important industry accounting for a significant portion of total investment. Reminiscent of the studies of Tinbergen, preparatory to his construction of the first large U.S. model, they test the acceleration principle of investment behavior. Their version of the accelerator is, however, more general and allows for excess capacity. This follows the improved generalizations of that theory studied by Hollis Chenery, L. Koyck, and Robert Eisner.[1] The extensive studies of investment behavior by John Meyer and Edwin Kuh are reported in their book on *The Investment Decision* and need not be

---

[1] Hollis Chenery, "Overcapacity and the Acceleration Principle," *Econometrica*, Vol. XX (January, 1952), pp. 1–28; L. M. Koyck, *Distributed Lags and Investment Analysis* (Amsterdam: North-Holland Publishing Co., 1954); and Robert Eisner, "A Distributed Lag Investment Function," *Econometrica*, Vol. XXVIII (January, 1960), pp. 1–29.

reproduced here.[2] Jorgenson's study of investment behavior is significant for giving a definitive statement in terms of received neoclassical theory of the firm and in generalizing Koyck's well-known methods of estimating the time shape of response to output movements. Jorgenson's study, being based on a large collection of quarterly statistics, provides useful information on the short-run lagged response that seems to be so important for business cycle movements.

Since Keynes's formulation of the basic relationship between aggregate consumption and aggregate income, there has been a veritable mountain of studies on the theory and measurement of the consumption function. The best that we can do here is to present two of the most recent contributions that have set the tone for the latest research in this area. These have to do with the dynamic planning of consumption (or saving) over the long term and the measured impact of this future planning on present aggregative behavior. The literature culminating in these new dynamic-planning theories is surveyed by Michael Farrell, who provides useful perspective on recent studies of the behavior of consumption. One of the proponents of these new theories has been Franco Modigliani, who first collaborated with the late Richard Brumberg on a paper that is already published in a collection.[3] We have selected a joint paper by Ando and Modigliani that reconsiders the theory in light of the relevant evidence.

The other major proponent of the new theories of dynamic consumer planning over a future horizon has been Milton Friedman.[4] His ideas are set forth in detail in *A Theory of the Consumption Function*. He has introduced the same types of arguments in his study of the demand for money, and we have selected that contribution for inclusion in the present volume as a means of illustrating his methods and throwing some light on the analysis of the money variable.[5] Friedman's theory and measurement of money demand follows the lines of the quantity theory of money. Other studies of money demand have been based on liquidity preference. The work of James Tobin is of particular significance, and evidence from many studies is summarized by Allan Meltzer.[6]

---

[2] J. R. Meyer and Edwin Kuh, *The Investment Decision* (Cambridge: Harvard University Press, 1957). See also J. R. Meyer and R. R. Glauber, *Investment Decisions, Economic Forecasting, and Public Policy* (Boston: Harvard Business School, 1964).

[3] R. Brumberg and F. Modigliani, "Utility Analysis and the Consumption Function: An Interpretation of Cross-Section Data," in K. Kurihara (ed.), *Post Keynesian Economics* (New Brunswick: Rutgers University Press, 1954), pp. 388–436.

[4] *A Theory of the Consumption Function* (Princeton: Princeton University Press, 1957).

[5] See also the more recent and longer paper by Milton Friedman and Anna J. Schwartz, "Money and Business Cycles," *Review of Economics and Statistics*, Vol. XLV (February, 1963, supplement), pp. 32–64.

[6] James Tobin, "Liquidity Preference and Monetary Policy," *Review of Economics and Statistics*, Vol. XXIX (May, 1947), pp. 124–31, and "The Interest-Elasticity of Transactions Demand for Cash," *Review of Economics and Statistics*, Vol. XXXVIII (August, 1956),

The relation between the wage level and employment or unemployment found early expression in the models of Tinbergen and Klein, but the whole question of the relationship between wage changes and unemployment was reopened in an interesting way by the study of A. W. Phillips.[7] At the same time, there were independent studies of postwar U.K. data by Leslie Dicks-Mireaux and Christopher Dow and by James Ball and Lawrence Klein.[8] Reexamination of the matter and testing of alternative formulations was carried out by Richard Lipsey in the paper reprinted here.

That the mathematical-statistical studies of particular variables mentioned above are only a sampling is indicated by a listing of some important variables whose separate study is not included in our volume. These include inventories, residential building, corporate finances, prices, profits, exports, and imports. In Part VI on International Aspects, some concrete evidence is given by Jacques Polak and Rudolf Rhomberg on propensities to import and export.

The cyclical behavior of a good many of the variables mentioned in the preceding paragraph (and others) has been studied intensively by the National Bureau of Economic Research. The work of the National Bureau has thrown new light on the cyclical behavior of particular variables both through intensive studies of these variables and through the Bureau's broader studies of the cyclical behavior of the economy as a whole. Geoffrey Moore's paper refers to both types of studies. The first would include, for example, studies of inventory behavior by Abramovitz and Stanback, of money by Friedman and Schwartz, of price-cost relationships and profits by Hultgren, as well as numerous others. The latter approach is reflected in the Bureau's work on leads and lags at the turning points and on the differences between mild and severe contractions, both of which are discussed in Moore's paper.

---

pp. 241–47; also, Allan Meltzer, "The Demand for Money: The Evidence from the Time Series," *Journal of Political Economy*, Vol. LXXI (June, 1963), pp. 219–46.

[7] A. W. Phillips, "The Relation between Unemployment and the Rate of Change of Money Wage Rates in the United Kingdom, 1861–1957," *Economica*, Vol. XXV (November, 1958), pp. 283–300.

[8] L. A. Dicks-Mireaux and J. C. R. Dow, "The Determinants of Wage Inflation: United Kingdom, 1946–1956," *Journal of the Royal Statistical Society*, A, Vol. CXXII (1959), pp. 145–84; and L. R. Klein and R. J. Ball, "Some Econometrics of the Determination of Absolute Prices and Wages," *Economic Journal*, Vol. LXIX (September, 1959), pp. 465–82.

19

Private Investment in the Electric Power Industry and the Acceleration Principle*

By AVRAM KISSELGOFF and FRANCO MODIGLIANI†

THIS INQUIRY is part of a more comprehensive investigation of investment behavior, carried out under a grant of the Merrill Foundation for Advancement of Financial Knowledge. In the companion studies of this investigation, extensive use was made of data on entrepreneurial expectations and plans.[1] Unfortunately, reliable and systematic information of this type is limited exclusively to the postwar period, relatively brief and abnormal in many respects. Thus it was thought desirable to supplement the studies based on business anticipations in the postwar period with an intensive analysis of historical data on investment in fixed capital in selected industries prior to the last war. In this analysis an attempt was made to isolate the causal factors underlying investment decisions without the benefit of the intermediate link represented by data on expectations and plans.

The present paper is concerned with the electric power industry only.[2] The most important considerations that led us to focus our attention on this industry are (a) its heavy capital requirements, (b) the homogeneous character of its physical output and productive capacity, (c) the availability of abundant economic accounting and operational data of a relatively high degree of uniformity.

---

* *The Review of Economics and Statistics*, Vol. XXXIX (November, 1957). Reprinted by courtesy of *The Review of Economics and Statistics* and the authors.

† Allied Chemical Corporation and Massachusetts Institute of Technology.

[1] See I. Friend and J. Bronfenbrenner, "Business Investment Programs and Their Realization," *Survey of Current Business*, December, 1950, and "Plant and Equipment Programs and Their Realization," *Studies in Income and Wealth, Vol. XVII*; F. Modigliani and O. H. Sauerlender, "Economic Expectations and Plans of Firms in Relation to Forecasting," *Studies in Income and Wealth, Vol. XVII*; R. Eisner, "Interview and Other Survey Techniques and the Study of Investment," *Studies in Income and Wealth, Vol. XIX*, and "Expectations, Plans and Capital Expenditures: A Synthesis of Ex Post and Ex Ante Data," *Proceedings of the Conference on Expectations, Uncertainty and Business Behavior*, sponsored by the Social Science Research Council.

[2] Another study on investment in the telephone industry is forthcoming.

The electric power industry can be divided into two segments: (1) privately owned utility companies which now provide about 80 percent of total public energy supply and (2) other electric power facilities mainly owned by the federal, state, and local governments which account for the remaining 20 percent.[3]

Since the primary objective of this study is to throw light on the behavior of private investment, the analysis will be restricted here to fluctuations in the capital expenditures of private electric utility companies. Because of the impossibility of separating new investments from reinvestments—a great many installations in the electric power industry being at the same time replacements, extensions, and improvements—gross expenditures on plant and equipment will be used in this paper as the variable to be explained.

The statistical analysis, unless otherwise indicated, is based on time series of industry aggregates for the period 1926–41.[4]

BASIC HYPOTHESES AND TESTS

It is a commonly accepted view in economic theory that the flow of capital expenditures depends on the relation between the anticipated productivity of money spent on additions to plant and equipment and the cost of funds, which is mostly identified with long-term interest rates after some allowance for risk. This view, however, is purely formal and is of doubtful value in a statistical analysis because of the lack of direct information on the anticipated productivity of capital. It has been frequently suggested that the productivity of capital can be approximated by the level of realized profits. This suggestion may have merits in dealing with competitive industries, although even in this case several assumptions must be made. In a competitive industry a shift to the right of the demand schedule or a reduction in costs should tend initially to increase profits. If the change in cost or demand conditions is regarded as permanent, the initial increase in profits (above the levels prevailing in other industries) would tend to bring about expansion of production and, therefore, investment by the existing firms and/or by new entrants. However, in monopolistic industries a high level of realized profits (i.e., a high *average* productivity of capital) need not be a reliable measure of the marginal productivity of investments, which presumably controls capital outlays; indeed the high level of profits may simply reflect the successful exploitation of the monopoly power which may be "spoiled" by an expansion. These considerations apply with particular force to regulated industries, such as electric utilities, where firms are usually without direct competition in their service areas and are subject to various controls which greatly affect, directly and indirectly, the level of their profits and the conditions under which the profits are obtained.

---

[3] The percentages mentioned above refer to the year 1953.

[4] A similar study for the electric power industry based on cross-section data will be published separately.

It is not surprising, therefore, to find that profits and interest rates alone completely fail to account for investment behavior of electrical utilities. This is shown by equations (1) and (2) based on data for 1924–41.

$$\left(\frac{I}{A}\right) = 18.9 - 0.162\left(\frac{\Pi'}{A}\right)_t + 62.9r_t \tag{1}$$

$$(\pm 0.805) \qquad (\pm 42.7)$$

$$\bar{R} = 0.22 \qquad \bar{S} = 122.0$$

$$\left(\frac{I}{A}\right)_t = 297 - 0.909\left(\frac{\Pi'}{A}\right)_{t-1} + 61.7r_{t-1} \tag{2}$$

$$(\pm 0.570) \qquad (\pm 35.0)$$

$$\bar{R} = 0.38 \qquad \bar{S} = 115.5$$

where

   $I=$ aggregate gross expenditures on plant and equipment in private electrical utilities, measured in millions of dollars;
   $A =$ construction costs for plant and equipment in the electric light and power industry, 1911: 1.00;
   $\Pi' =$ aggregate net income before interest deduction of private electrical utilities, measured in millions of dollars. Since the purpose of the present test is to determine the influence of the rate of interest on investment, interest charges were added to net income.[5]
   $r =$ annual yield averages of new bonds.

The numbers in parentheses below the regression coefficients are standard errors; $\bar{R}$ is the multiple correlation coefficient, and $\bar{S}$ is the standard error of estimate; both statistics are adjusted for degrees of freedom.

It can be seen from equation (1) that current profits and the cost of borrowed new money account for only a negligible proportion of the variation in investment; furthermore, the estimated coefficients of both variables have signs opposite from what would have been expected on *a priori* grounds, and they are not significantly different from zero at the 5 percent level.[6] Equally unsatisfactory results are obtained in equation (2), where lagged income and

---

[5] See T. Haavelmo, "The Effect of the Rate of Interest on Investment," this REVIEW, Vol. XXIII (February, 1941), pp. 49–52.

[6] It would have been interesting to repeat the test of equations (1) and (2) using as the dependent variable *net* investment (outlays for additions to capacity) instead of gross investment. Unfortunately data for such a test are not available. There are reasons to believe, however, that this substitution could not affect significantly the conclusions suggested by the test. In the first place the electric power industry is relatively young and the major types of plant and equipment it employs have a very long service life, ranging from twenty to fifty years. (Cf. Bulletin F, rev. ed. January, 1942, of the Bureau of Internal Revenue, U.S. Treasury Department.) Accordingly, in the period under consideration expenditures on replacements were relatively unimportant. This is precisely the finding of the investigation reported by Michael Gort in *Journal of Business of the University of*

interest rates were used in order to make some allowance for the time that may be required to carry out investment decisions.[7]

A major reason for these poor results is to be found in the influence of institutional factors. Because of their monopolistic character which may lead to abuses, electric utilities are subjected to various regulations. The most important among them, having a direct bearing on the problem under consideration, are controls over profits and rates. Generally, profits in the electric power industry are governed by the "cost plus" principle with the specific recognition that investors are entitled to a "fair return on a fair value." In practice the application of this principle is a complicated procedure which requires the determination of the utilities' operating expenses, taxes, depreciation, and the value of property, which is most frequently fixed by state commissions and courts. The rate of return, as a rule, is computed on the over-all rate base, and no increase in rates is granted on the basis of insufficient return on a part of investment. As a result, the return on new investments frequently is not estimated by utilities. Equally relevant in this connection is the fact that once capital expenditures are made, the commissions usually support the utilities' capitalization. However, when the demand for electrical power expands, no increase in the utilities' profits through an increase in rates is possible. The regulatory measures on the books will prevent electric utilities from exploiting this situation. On the contrary, since electric utilities are under obligation to meet the expanded demand, they can be expected to provide additional facilities which might result in reduced rates through reduced costs. But if a company, in its search for profit, decreases its costs to the extent that it obtains a considerable increment in earnings, the regulatory bodies can initiate an investigation and eliminate the whole increment. It may be observed here that the development of these practices applied by regulatory authorities in profit and rates determination have been greatly facilitated by a rather low price elasticity of demand for electrical energy.[8]

The protective as well as the restrictive nature of controls, as they are exercised in the electric power industry, greatly reduces the importance of past or current profits as a decision-making variable in planning investment. However, as a source of investible funds and as a factor reflecting short-run business expectations, profits probably are of some significance in the investment process and, therefore, should be considered in the analysis; their effect may be expected to become apparent only when other major investment determinants are taken into account.

In order to formulate a satisfactory hypothesis as to these other major

---

Chicago, Vol. XXIV (July, 1951), p. 188. According to Mr. Gort, "Of the six categories [of investment] the first, additional capacity for load growth, completely dominated all others in all the budgets seen."

[7] Poor results are also obtained when only current income, or income lagged one year, after deducting interest payments, is correlated with investment.

[8] See Emery Troxel, *Economics of Public Utilities* (New York, 1947), pp. 429–31.

determinants, one must take into account four essential characteristics of the industry which have been mentioned in the previous discussion: (a) the strong upward secular trend in the demand for electricity; (b) the legal obligation of the companies to satisfy the demand for electric power in the areas in which they have a franchise; (c) the expectation of the companies, founded on precedent and legal provisions, that the regulatory bodies will include the new investment in the rate base and will be willing to establish such rates as to insure an "adequate" return on the expanded property; (d) the confidence of the companies, justified by the growing demand and the monopolistic nature of the market, that such rates can be enforced.[9] These characteristics strongly suggest that the major determinant of investment in this industry is to be found along the lines indicated by the acceleration principle, i.e., in the relation between existing production, distribution, and transmission facilities and the facilities required to satisfy efficiently the current and prospective demand for electric power.

To translate this relation into a specific hypothesis capable of empirical testing, it will be useful to introduce the notions of "actual" and "optimum" annual rates of utilization of capacity.

The actual rate of utilization in a given year t is defined as the ratio of kilowatt-hours sold in that year, denoted by P, to kilowatts of installed capacity, S; it is, therefore, represented by $(P/S)_t$. The upper theoretical limit of this rate, is, of course, equal to the number of hours per year or 8,760. However, for a variety of reasons the technologically feasible and economically advantageous rate of utilization tends to be well below this ceiling.

First, the demand for electricity from a given source, like most other demands, exhibits characteristic and systematic patterns of daily and seasonal peaks and troughs. However, in contrast with many other commodities, electric power cannot, at present, be stored on a commercial basis and must, therefore, be produced at the instant it is demanded. Hence, facilities have to be geared to peak sales and generally cannot be utilized continuously and fully throughout the year. Moreover, in order to insure reliable and orderly service, suppliers must have enough reserve equipment for the replacement of any unit of equipment which becomes incapacitated for mechanical reasons. Finally, since this growing industry also enjoys economies of scale, when an expansion is undertaken, it is profitable (in the sense that it reduces costs over time) to add more capacity than is expected to be required in the immediate future. Hence, for this reason, too, it is generally advantageous for companies to carry *on the average* a certain margin of overcapacity.[10]

---

[9] It is this last characteristic together with the related characteristic (a) that sharply distinguishes the electric utilities from the other major regulated public utility, namely railroads. In the latter industry, because of the strong competition from other means of transportation, it may be impossible to enforce a system of rates insuring an "adequate" return.

[10] This idea has been aptly developed by H. B. Chenery in "Overcapacity and Acceleration Principle," *Econometrica*, Vol. XXII (January, 1952), pp. 1–28.

On the basis of these considerations, the optimum rate of utilization at a given point of time will be defined as the maximum number of kilowatt-hours per year which it is economically desirable to produce for sale per kilowatt of installed capacity, under the conditions (technology, pattern of demand, etc.) prevailing at that point of time. This optimum rate, varying over time, will be denoted by $\overline{(P/S)}_t$.

In terms of these concepts, we propose to test the hypothesis that the major factor controlling the rate of investment by private electric utilities is their endeavor to maintain the rate of utilization of capacity at the optimum level. It should be observed that capacity, as measured by kilowatts installed, does not include all the facilities of the industry. However, capacity so defined is a component which can be measured with a minimum of ambiguity and consti- tutes, in fact, the principal part of the facilities to which all other parts of the capital stock are largely geared.

Let us assume for the moment that additional capacity can be provided in about one year. Then, on the basis of the hypothesis put forth above, we should expect investment in a given year to be an increasing function of the difference between the ratio of demand anticipated a year hence to presently existing facilities, on the one hand, and the optimum rate of utilization of capacity, on the other. Neglecting other factors temporarily, this hypothesis can be approximated by a linear function as follows:

$$I_t = \alpha \left[\frac{AP_t^{t+1}}{S_{t-1}} - \overline{\left(\frac{P}{S}\right)_t} \right] \tag{3}$$

where I_t is investment, in real terms, in a given year t; AP_t^{t+1}, output antici- pated in the given year for the next year,[11] $t + 1$; S_{t-1}, the amount of capacity in existence in the previous year; and α, a proportionality constant, reflecting the intensity of response to the stimulus to invest as well as the cost of pro- viding additional capacity.

Since we have no direct information on anticipated output, AP_t^{t+1}, it is necessary to introduce some hypothesis as to how this variable might be approximated. Methods frequently used by electric utilities for estimating prospective demand are based on their past experience and amount roughly to an extrapolation of the sales trend. Since the latest information available on output is P_{t-1}, then, if demand is assumed to grow at a constant rate of i percent per year, we may write

$$AP_t^{t+1} = (1 + i)^2 P_{t-1} .$$

---

[11] In this study we shall consistently measure demand by output. Demand so defined exceeds sales by the loss of energy in the process of transmission and the use of energy by the utilities themselves; it may be regarded as the amount of production necessary to meet the given sales.

This leads by substitution in equation (3) to:

$$I_t = \alpha\left[\frac{(1+t)^2 P_{t-1}}{S_{t-1}} - \overline{\left(\frac{P}{S}\right)_t}\right] \tag{4}$$

$$= \alpha(1+i)^2\left[\frac{P_{t-1}}{S_{t-1}} - \frac{1}{(1+i)^2}\overline{\left(\frac{P}{S}\right)}\right]$$

$$= \alpha'\left[\frac{P_{t-1}}{S_{t-1}} - (1-\gamma)\overline{\left(\frac{P}{S}\right)_t}\right]$$

where $\qquad \alpha' = \alpha(1+i)^2 \qquad$ and $\qquad \gamma = 1 - \dfrac{1}{(1+i)^2}$.

Equation (4) is also consistent with another hypothesis on the formation of anticipations of future demand and the method of providing capacity to meet this demand. Instead of making explicit forecasts of future sales and deriving from them estimates of capital requirements, companies might adopt investment programs designed to provide a "normal" margin of reserve capacity over and above that needed for current demand. This idea can be formalized by introducing the notion of a "critical" rate of utilization of capacity, say $(P/S)_t^0$, some $\gamma\%$ below the optimum rate $\overline{(P/S)}_t$. Then whenever the current actual rate of utilization exceeds $\left(\dfrac{P}{S}\right)_t^0 = (1-\gamma)\overline{\left(\dfrac{P}{S}\right)}_t$, companies may be expected to invest in order to re-establish the proper cushion of excess capacity. For instance, if γ were 0.20 and $\overline{\left(\dfrac{P}{S}\right)}$ were 4,000 hours, an increase in the actual average rate of utilization of capacity beyond 3,200 hours would call for additional investment. The procedure described is a flexible way of allowing for the anticipated growth of demand, since the availability of reserve capacity permits the utility to meet increased demand while additional capacity is being provided. Clearly this type of behavior can be represented again by an equation of the form (4), and the expression $(1-\gamma)\left(\dfrac{P}{S}\right)_t^0$ in the bracket on the right-hand side can be regarded as the critical rate of utilization of capacity. Thus equation (4) is consistent with either approach to the determination of capital requirements, or with any mixtures of these two types or closely related ones.[12] While our equation need not describe accurately the behavior of any individual firm, it may be hoped to provide a reasonable approximation to aggregate behavior.

---

[12] Note that under the type of investment behavior implied by our second formulation, the actual rate of utilization would usually be above the critical rate, because of the growth of demand occurring during the gestation period. In fact, if demand were growing at a fairly steady rate, we might expect the coefficient γ to be such that the actual rate of utilization

In order to make our description of the investment process in the electric industry more realistic, we must, however, take into account the actual time period of planning, ordering, and installing of new generating capacity. According to information gathered directly from the industry, the length of this period under normal conditions can be estimated at about two years, on the average. Since the length of the gestation period plays an important role in our analysis, an attempt was made to test the reliability of this information by means of the following indirect test.

If about two years are required to complete an installation of new generating capacity, then part of investment expenditures in a given year, t, would represent outlays for the purpose of bringing to completion projects started in the year before. These outlays, which we shall call "completion expenditures" or simply "completions," should result in additions to generating capacity within year t itself, denoted by ΔS_t. Another part of current outlays would be generated by the initiation of new projects or "starts" and would result in additions to generating capacity in the following year, ΔS_{t+1}. Under these conditions total investment in year t should be closely correlated with, and largely accounted for by, ΔS_t and ΔS_{t+1}. Equation (5), based on these three variables for the period 1924–41, yields a confirmation of this expectation.

$$\left(\frac{I}{A}\right)_t = 101 + 0.057\Delta S_{t+1} + 0.074\Delta S_t \tag{5}$$

$$(\pm 0.015) \qquad (\pm 0.015)$$

$$\bar{R} = 0.935 \qquad \bar{S} = 46.3$$

where $\left(\frac{I}{A}\right)_t$ represents gross investment expenditure in year t in millions of deflated dollars; ΔS_t and ΔS_{t+1}, capacity installed in year t and $t+1$, respectively, in thousands of kilowatts.

It is hardly necessary to point out that this is essentially a "technical" and not a "behavior" equation. First, it relates investments in the year t to events occurring after that year, and second, it does not contain factors determining decisions to add to capacity. The fact that the coefficients of both variables are reliable statistically and their relative magnitude plausible, is, however, of significance. It confirms that it is both reasonable and useful to regard investment in year t as consisting of two major components, starts and completions, each of which must be taken into consideration.[13]

---

would tend, on the average, to be close to the optimum rate. The difference between the two alternative hypotheses leading up to equation (4) is, therefore, less significant than might appear at first sight, and it is quite conceivable that in many cases utilities might rely simultaneously on both approaches.

[13] A lack of data on replacements made it necessary to relate in equation (5) gross expenditures to net additions to capacity. Since, however, additional capacity for load growth was predominant during the period under consideration, the indicative value of the test is not greatly affected.

Since completion expenditures in year t are generated by starts of year $t-1$, we can account for this component by using equation (4), after replacing in it P_{t-1}/S_{t-1} by P_{t-2}/S_{t-2}. As for outlays on starts, we may measure the incentive to initiate new projects by means of the ratio P_{t-1}/S_{t-1}, corrected for the dampening influence of projects started in year $t-1$ which are not yet reflected in S_{t-1} but will shortly result in additional capacity. Since starts of year $t-1$ are assumed to depend on P_{t-2}/S_{t-2}, we propose to measure the net incentive in year t by means of the difference $\left(\dfrac{P_{t-1}}{S_{t-1}} - \dfrac{P_{t-2}}{S_{t-2}}\right)$. In so doing we recognize that P_{t-2}/S_{t-2} has the following double and partly offsetting effect on investment in year t: on the one hand, the larger the volume of projects in year $t-1$ the greater will be expenditures required for the completion of these projects in year t; on the other hand, the larger the volume of the projects started in year $t-1$, the smaller will be, *ceteris paribus*, the necessity to initiate new projects in year t. Thus when the lag between decisions to invest and the corresponding investment outlays is taken into account, our hypothesis becomes:

$$I_t = f\left\{\left(\frac{P}{S}\right)_{t-2}, \left[\left(\frac{P}{S}\right)_{t-1} - \left(\frac{P}{S}\right)_{t-2}\right], \overline{\left(\frac{P}{S}\right)_t}\right\}. \tag{6}$$

If $\overline{\left(\dfrac{P}{S}\right)_t}$ were constant, this relation would contain only two explanatory variables. However, we have evidence that the ratio $\overline{\left(\dfrac{P}{S}\right)_t}$ rose gradually over time, that is to say, an increasing flow of services was obtained from a given stock of capital. The main factors responsible for this increase are consolidation and integration of markets for electric energy, along with the development of new uses for such energy and incentive rates. As a result, coincidental peaks were greatly reduced and idle capacity and excess reserves were rendered more flexible in both space and time, a process that led to a gain in the average annual rate of utilization of capacity from 1926 to 1941 of a little more than 30 percent. Of course, it would have been ideal to know exactly the value of $\left(\dfrac{P}{S}\right)_t$ at each point of time. Unfortunately this information cannot be obtained directly from engineering data. One possible solution consists in approximating $\overline{\left(\dfrac{P}{S}\right)_t}$ by some function of time,[14] say,

$$\overline{\left(\frac{P}{S}\right)_t} = \phi(T). \tag{7}$$

---

[14] An alternative solution will be advanced later.

Substituting (7) into (6) we obtain:

$$I_t = F\left\{ \left(\frac{P}{S}\right)_{t-2}, \left[\left(\frac{P}{S}\right)_{t-1} - \left(\frac{P}{S}\right)_{t-2}\right], T \right\}. \tag{8}$$

We shall also add to this expression the variable, Π_t, representing net income plus depreciation in year t. This variable may be expected to play the role of an enabling factor, to the extent that it can be a source of funds from current operations for investment purposes, and of a controlling factor, to the extent that the net income component might reflect short-run business expectations and lead to the cancellation, postponement, or acceleration of investment plans. Thus, after adjustment of the variables I and Π for price changes, our basic hypothesis, when expressed in a linear form, becomes:

$$\left(\frac{I}{A}\right)_t = \delta_0 + \delta_1\left(\frac{\Pi}{A}\right)_t + \delta_2\left[\left(\frac{P}{S}\right)_{t-1} - \left(\frac{P}{S}\right)_{t-2}\right] + \delta_3\left(\frac{P}{S}\right)_{t-2} + \delta_4 T + E_t \tag{9}$$

where E is the random disturbance. The least-square estimates of the parameters are:

$$\left(\frac{I}{A}\right)_t = -495 + 0.661\left(\frac{\Pi}{A}\right)_t + 0.253\left[\left(\frac{P}{S}\right)_{t-1} - \left(\frac{P}{S}\right)_{t-2}\right]$$
$$(\pm 0.234) \quad (\pm 0.038) \tag{10}$$

$$+ 0.225\left(\frac{P}{S}\right)_{t-2} - 21.3T$$
$$(\pm 0.024) \qquad (\pm 2.4)$$

$$\bar{R} = 0.972 \qquad \bar{S} = 29.3 \qquad \bar{K} = 2.24.$$

Judged by statistical criteria, the parameters of equation (10) seem to be reliably estimated. The value of K, which is the measure of the autocorrelation of E, is high enough so that the hypothesis that the residual variation is random with respect to time cannot be rejected.[15] Taken together, the four explanatory variables account for about 95 percent of the annual variation in capital expenditures in the period under consideration. The most important of the variables are those representing the yearly rates of utilization of capacity and T, reflecting the gradual increase in the optimum rate of utilization of capacity and possibly also other influences.[16] The net income plus depreciation variable, $\left(\frac{\Pi}{A}\right)_t$, also was found significant. It may be observed, however, that when equation (10) is modified by replacing $\left(\frac{\Pi}{A}\right)_t$ with $\left(\frac{\Pi}{A}\right)_{t-1}$ the new

---

[15] K is the ratio of the mean-square successive differences to the variance of the residuals.
[16] See page 358 below.

estimates are:

$$\left(\frac{I}{A}\right)_t = -451 + 0.321\left(\frac{\Pi}{A}\right)_{t-1} + 0.261\left[\left(\frac{P}{S}\right)_{t-1} - \left(\frac{P}{S}\right)_{t-2}\right]$$
$$(\pm\,0.226)(\pm\,0.050)$$

$$+ 0.252\left(\frac{P}{S}\right)_{t-2} - 22.2\;T$$
$$(\pm\,0.026)(\pm\;\;2.4)$$

$$\bar{R} = 0.959 \quad ; \quad \bar{S} = 35.4$$

(11)

In this equation, the coefficient of regression of $\dfrac{\Pi}{A}$ decreases by a little more than 50 percent, becomes statistically less reliable, and the total correlation falls below that of equation (10).[17] On the contrary, the coefficients of regression of the other variables show a high degree of stability. Since at least one year is required to carry out large-scale investment programs, these results are not inconsistent with the hypothesis that profits are not a key variable in major investment decisions.

On the whole, our analysis so far indicates that the most satisfactory explanation of fluctuations in capital expenditures in the electric power industry for the period 1926–41 is provided by equation (10). It is not without interest, however, to review at this point some other hypotheses tested which throw additional light on the process of investment decisions.

FURTHER TESTS ON THE ROLE OF PROFITS, INTEREST RATES, OTHER VARIABLES

An attempt was made to take into account the structure of investment in the electric power industry. The available data allow the splitting of total investment into plant expenditures and equipment expenditures. This breakdown of total investment outlays, however, can be done only crudely and our estimates are subject to a very considerable margin of error. Yet the attempt appears worthwhile because the two components of investment may be expected to be affected by somewhat different influences.

Our hypothesis of a two-year gestation period appears acceptable in the case of investment in plant but probably is less reasonable for equipment expenditures. Accordingly, equation (9) can be used without further modification to explain outlays on plant.

The results are shown in equation (12).

---

[17] Unsatisfactory results are also observed when $\left(\dfrac{\Pi}{A}\right)_{t-2}$ is used in the similar test.

$$\left(\frac{I'}{B}\right)_t = -195 + 0.155\left(\frac{\Pi}{A}\right)_t + 0.123\left[\left(\frac{P}{S}\right)_{t-1} - \left(\frac{P}{S}\right)_{t-2}\right]$$
$$\quad\quad\quad (\pm 0.107) \quad\ (\pm 0.017)$$

$$+ 0.116\left(\frac{P}{S}\right)_{t-2} - 11.9\, T$$
$$(\pm 0.011) \quad\quad (\pm 0.82)$$

(12)

$$\bar{R} = 0.979 \quad\quad \bar{S} = 13.3 \quad\quad K = 2.43$$

where I' denotes plant expenditures in millions of dollars; and B, the plant construction cost index (1911 : 1.00).

These results are again quite favorable and are generally very similar to those of equation (10) both in form and interpretation. The only difference worth noting is that the coefficient of profits is considerably lower and its standard error is relatively greater. This indicates that the influence of profits, Π/A, on investment in plant is weak, a finding to be expected on *a priori* grounds. Once the construction of a plant is started, a utility might find it advantageous to carry it to completion regardless of current fluctuations in profits, rather than to incur losses from halting the construction. Such a situation seems to have existed, for instance, in 1930 when many companies, disregarding a decrease in their incomes, preferred to complete their plants under construction rather than to abandon them entirely.

In the case of equipment, the lag between decision and outlays is likely to be shorter. Hence spending, both for expansion and replacement, should be primarily influenced by the rate of utilization of capacity in the immediately preceding year, $(P/S)_{t-1}$. In addition, because of the complementarity between plant and equipment, we might expect equipment outlays to depend also on current expansion of plant, which can be approximated by plant expenditures, $(I'/B)_t$. Finally, because equipment can be procured, on the average, on relatively short notice, and previous commitments can be cancelled with smaller loss than in the case of construction under way, we should expect current profit to be of greater relevance than in equation (12). The resulting hypothesis explaining expenditures on equipment and its statistical test is as follows:

$$\left(\frac{I''}{C}\right)_t = -155 + 0.286\left(\frac{\Pi}{A}\right)_t + 0.034\left(\frac{P}{S}\right)_{t-1} + 0.802\left(\frac{I'}{B}\right)_t$$
$$\quad\quad\quad (\pm 0.082) \quad\ (\pm 0.009) \quad\quad (\pm 0.051)$$

(13)

$$\bar{R} = 0.985 \quad\quad \bar{S} = 11.0 \quad\quad K = 1.63$$

where I'' represents estimated equipment expenditures, and C is the price index of equipment (1911 : 1.00).

The data appear to support our hypothesis. This is evidenced by the very high multiple correlation coefficient and by the fact that the coefficients of all the variables have relatively small standard errors. In particular the coefficient of profits is larger than in equation (12) both in absolute terms and relative to its standard error. This suggests that the importance of the profit variable in equation (10), pertaining to total investment, can be attributed mainly to its significant role in the determination of equipment expenditures.

It may be noted that in equation (13) we have used as one of explanatory variables *current* expenditures on plant, $(I'/B)_t$. Since this variable is part of the total investment outlays that we are interested in explaining, it might appear that equation (13) could be of little use in forecasting. Such a conclusion would not be warranted, however, since for purposes of forecasting, the un-known value of $(I'/B)_t$ could be replaced by the known value computed from equation (12). This substitution in fact may be used also in estimating the coefficients of equation (13) and has some merit from the statistical point of view. It amounts to recognizing, in the estimating procedure, that equations (12) and (13) represent a system of simultaneous stochastic difference equa-tions in which (I'/B) and (I''/C) are jointly determined variables.[18] This procedure was, therefore, actually employed to obtain an alternative estimate of the coefficients of equation (13), and the results were found to be very nearly the same as those reported above.

It must be pointed out, however, that because of the crudeness of the estimates of the plant and equipment breakdown of total investment, great reliance cannot be placed on equations (12) and (13). The main reason for reporting the results, tentative as they are, is for the light they may throw on the behavior of the two components of investment and especially on the role of profits as a decision variable.

A full inquiry into the investment process should include an exploration of the effect of the rate of interest. While factual investigations in various indus-tries do not indicate that the interest rate has a marked influence on capital spending, there are theoretical reasons to believe that this variable might affect investments in long-lived assets, especially when financed with outside funds.[19]

Electric utilities have large capital investments of great longevity. Because they make capital commitments, on the average, of $5 to $7 in order to produce a yearly revenue of $1, the rate of utilities' capital turnover is low. This fact, as well as regulatory practices, makes it impossible for them to finance extensive construction programs by means of retained earnings and/or depreciation accruals alone. The available data indicate that during the second half of the 1920's approximately 75 percent of funds came from the capital market and the remaining 25 percent from internal sources.[20] During the

---

[18] This statement implies that $(\Pi/A)_t$ can be treated as an exogenous variable, an assumption which we regard as not too unrealistic for a single industry.

[19] See George W. Terborgh, *Dynamic Equipment Policy* (New York, 1949). Lawrence Klein found the effect of the rate of interest on investment decisions in the railroad industry to be significant. See his "Studies in Investment Behavior" (National Bureau of Economic Research). Although, from the viewpoint of "rational" behavior, the origin of funds should not affect investment decisions of management, it seems to be, empirically, a factor of importance.

[20] Eli Winston Clemens, *Economics and Public Utilities*, p. 119.

second half of the 1930's, the utilities had recourse to capital market funds for only about 20 percent of their total financial requirements. This lesser reliance on external financing is due partly to the lower level of their investments and partly to a shift from the retirement to the depreciation method of accounting which resulted in a greater availability of funds from internal sources.[21] In the postwar period when the utilities undertook a huge building program in order to meet the tremendously increased demand for electricity, the capital market again became the major source of their financing.

These observations suggest that, at least in the case of electric utilities, there might be some opportunity for interest rates to play a role in investment decisions. Yet there is surprisingly little evidence to support such a conclusion. While changes in interest rates may have had some influence on the form of financing, they do not appear to have exerted a significant stimulating or restraining effect on investments. In fact a cursory examination of the record shows that utilities (not unlike many other industries) usually drew heavily on external sources to finance their investments in periods when interest rates were high but reduced their demand for outside funds when interest was low.[22]

This lack of data supporting the proposition that interest rates influence investment decisions in the electric power industry may be due to the overshadowing influence of other variables whose importance was brought out by the earlier analysis. Therefore, in order to test the effect of interest rates on capital expenditures, we revised equation (10) by adding the variable r, annual yield average of new bonds lagged one year, and replacing $(\Pi/A)_t$ with $(\Pi'/A)_{t-1}$, the net operating income plus interest charges.[23] The statistical estimates of the parameters are:

$$\left(\frac{I}{A}\right)_t = -780 + \underset{(\pm 0.207)}{0.282}\left(\frac{\Pi'}{A}\right)_{t-1} + \underset{(\pm 0.060)}{0.300}\left[\left(\frac{P}{S}\right)_{t-1} - \left(\frac{P}{S}\right)_{t-2}\right]$$

$$+ \underset{(\pm 0.038)}{0.295}\left(\frac{P}{S}\right)_{t-2} + \underset{(\pm 35.1)}{33.3r_{t-1}} - \underset{(\pm 5.6)}{16.7\,T}$$

$$\bar{R} = 0.959 \qquad \bar{S} = 35.3.$$

(14)

In this equation the regression coefficient of r is smaller than its standard error and, furthermore, its sign is contrary to what would be expected on theoretical grounds.[24] This test also, therefore, fails to support the hypothesis that interest rates play a significant role in the investment process.[25]

---

[21] It may be observed that during the 1930's the utilities not only paid off large amounts of their notes payable and unsecured loans, but also accumulated large cash holdings.

[22] Huge utility borrowings during the 1930's represented to a great extent refunding operations for the purpose of reducing capital costs.

[23] See footnote 5.

[24] The large standard error and the positive sign of the coefficient of r may be partly due to a very high negative correlation between the variables r and T ($-.89$). While this intercorrelation reduces the reliability of our finding, it does not seem to affect the general nature of our conclusion.

This negative result may reflect, to a considerable extent, the regulatory bodies' policies and practices. When a company makes *bona fide* additions to plant and equipment, it is fairly confident that the state commissions will fix rates adequate to cover all the costs of the services and to yield an average return on the new investment.[26] Moreover, although the regulatory authorities can influence expenditures for capital additions through the control of security issues and capital ratios, it is not likely that a company with a balanced capital structure would be prevented from raising the necessary funds on the capital market for its legitimate investment, whatever is the level of the prevailing interest rates.[27] Under these practices the rate of interest as an element of cost does not seem to have much opportunity to influence investment decisions.

Another hypothesis considered in our investigation is that, in addition to variables contained in equation (10), the substitution of capital for labor may also affect investment expenditures of electric utilities. The ratio of A/W, where A is electric light and power construction cost index (1911 : 1.00), and W, average hourly wages measured in cents, may be used as an indicator of the incentive for such substitution. When this variable is added to equation (10) the following results are obtained:

Slightly better results are obtained when r and $\dfrac{\Pi r}{A}$ are related to the year of investment.

$$\left(\frac{I}{A}\right)_t = -493 + 0.580\left(\frac{\Pi r}{A}\right)_t + 0.261\left[\left(\frac{P}{S}\right)_{t-1} - \left(\frac{P}{S}\right)_{t-2}\right]$$
$$(\pm 0.213) \qquad (\pm 0.049)$$

$$+ 0.259\left(\frac{P}{S}\right)_{t-2} - 20.8r_t - 22.5\,T \qquad (14')$$
$$(\pm 0.025) \qquad (\pm 26.8)\ (\pm 4.3)$$

$$\bar{R} = 0.970 \qquad \bar{S} = 30.6.$$

Although the sign of the coefficient of r in this equation is correct the coefficient itself is still unreliable.

[25] This conclusion, however, is subject to a limitation which should be carefully noted. In our model the behavior of demand up to year t was taken as a datum; the only conclusion warranted by our test, therefore, is that, given the previous history of demand, interest rates are not an important factor. But this history of demand may depend on interest rates, since these certainly affect the price of electricity, which, in turn, may be expected to affect demand. A more comprehensive test of the effect of interest would require an analysis of the quantitative importance of this factor in the price of electric energy, as well as of the price elasticity of demand, which is beyond the scope of this study. If the demand for electricity is inelastic, as is frequently stated, then even the roundabout influence of interest may well be negligible.

[26] As already noted, this policy on the part of regulatory bodies is possible because the electric power industry is still growing and has a very great potential market for its output.

[27] Since 1930 there has been a tendency on the part of the state commissions to use more extensively their powers in the financial field. In 1935 the Public Utility Holding Company Act empowered the Securities Exchange Commission to prescribe capital ratios for corporations subject to its jurisdiction.

$$\left(\frac{I}{A}\right)_t = -799 + 0.626\left(\frac{\Pi}{A}\right)_t + 0.227\left[\left(\frac{P}{S}\right)_{t-1} - \left(\frac{P}{S}\right)_{t-2}\right]$$
$$(\pm 0.241) \quad (\pm 0.050)$$

$$+ 0.202\left(\frac{P}{S}\right)_{t-2} + 130\left(\frac{A}{W}\right)_{t-1} - 17.0\,T$$
$$(\pm 0.037) \qquad (\pm 157) \qquad (\pm 5.5)$$

$$\bar{R} = 0.971 \qquad \bar{S} = 29.8.$$

(15)

The coefficient of A/W is small relative to its standard error and it has the wrong sign. We can, therefore, find no evidence that the relation between capital goods prices and wage costs exerts a significant influence on investment in this industry.[28] The result is less surprising than the one relating to interest rates. The industry under consideration is highly mechanized with large physical assets in relation to the labor employed and its technology does not appear to offer much scope for substitution between capital and labor.[29]

REFORMULATION OF BASIC EQUATION, EXCLUDING TIME

The basic equation (10) was found to yield estimates in close agreement with investment experience in the years covered by the study. Yet the results obtained cannot be considered entirely satisfactory, either as an explanation of the past or as a tool for forecasting, without some exploration of the role and significance of the time trend used in the equation.

The time variable is introduced in empirical econometric analysis for reasons of expediency, as a convenient proxy for known or unknown influences. Obviously, more meaningful structural equations are obtained when proxy variables are replaced, whenever possible, by the specific factors which they are supposed to represent. Even if these factors can only be measured crudely, the equations which include them may be expected to provide a better description of the mechanism of economic decisions and to produce more accurate extrapolations to points of time considerably removed from the period of observation.

The major justification we have advanced for the inclusion of the time variable in equation (10) is the gradual increase in the optimum rate of utilization

---

[28] It may be argued that in this test one should consider not only the price of capital goods but also the cost of funds, which affects the carrying cost of the productive facilities. For this reason we considered using as a variable in this test rA/W instead of A/W (although this might exaggerate the role of interest). However, an inspection of the data suggested that the results would not be significantly different from those reported when A/W is used.

[29] It is interesting to note that Lawrence Klein did not find the substitution of capital for labor important in the investment process even in the railroad industry where there would appear to be more basis for substitution both because of the technology and because of the constant pressure to reduce costs in order to withstand the competition of other means of transportation.

of capacity from 1926 to 1941, made possible by the various developments discussed above. In order to attempt to measure this factor directly we shall have to recast our hypothesis.

We may assume that in any given year t, the investment program of the electric power industry will aim at providing a total capacity which will be denoted $(PS)_t^{t+1}$ with the superscript $t+1$ used as a reminder that the capacity resulting from capital expenditures in year t will be partly available only in the following year. The addition to capacity implied by the program is thus $(\Delta PS)_t^{t+1} = (PS)_t^{t+1} - S_{t-1}$ where S_{t-1} is actual capacity in the preceding year. Part of this increase in capacity will be caused within the year t by the current completion of previous starts and part by new projects with a short gestation period. Let us denote S_t' total capacity expected by the end of year t (after allowance for any reduction in the stock of capital goods due to retirements). Then the amount of additional capacity which must be started in year t for completion in year $t + 1$ will be $(PS)_t^{t+1} - S_t'$. On the assumption that investment expenditures in constant dollars required in the year $t + 1$ to complete such projects, denoted $(I^c/A)_{t+1}$, will be proportional to the added capacity we may write: $(I^c/A)_{t+1} = a_1[(PS)_t^{t+1} - S_t']$. It follows that completion expenditures in year t will be: $\left(\dfrac{I^c}{A}\right)_t = a_1[(PS)_{t-1}^t - S_{t-1}']$. In this equation the quantity S_{t-1}' is not directly observable but can be approximated by S_{t-1}. We therefore have:

$$\left(\frac{I^c}{A}\right)_t = {}_1a[(PS)_{t-1}^t - S_{t-1}]. \qquad (16)$$

Besides expenditures on completions, there will be in year t some expenditures on starts, i.e., new projects which will result partly in expansion of capacity in the same year t and partly in an increase in capacity in the following year. These expenditures will again be assumed proportional to the difference between the amount of capacity which appears desirable in year t, $(PS)_t^{t+1}$, and the amount of capacity which will be in existence in the year t upon the completion of projects carried over from the previous year. Since, by definition, the completion of the preceding year's investment program is supposed to produce a total capacity of $(PS)_{t-1}^t$, expenditures on starts, denoted by $(I^s/A)_t$, can be written:

$$\left(\frac{I^s}{A}\right)_t = a_2[(PS)_t^{t+1} - (PS)_{t-1}^t]. \qquad (17)$$

Total investment expenditures in year t thus will be:

$$\left(\frac{I}{A}\right)_t = \left(\frac{I^c}{A}\right)_t + \left(\frac{I^s}{A}\right)_t = a_1[(PS)_{t-1}^t - S_{t-1}] + a_2[(PS)_t^{t+1} - (PS)_{t-1}^t].^{30} \qquad (18)$$

---

[30] It should be noted that the two terms of equation (18) are not quite symmetrical. This is due to the fact that the first measures expenditures on projects carried over from the

In this equation $(PS)_t^{t+1}$ and $(PS)_{t-1}^t$ are variables on which we do not have direct information; they can, however, be readily expressed in terms of other variables by making use of the fundamental hypothesis underlying equation (10). According to this hypothesis, the investment policies of the electric utilities are directed toward the maintenance of a certain optimum ratio between the latest rate of production and capacity, denoted by $\overline{(P/S)}_t$. Hence the amount of capacity we should expect the industry to aim for in year t will be:

$$(PS)_t^{t+1} = \frac{P_{t-1}}{\overline{\left(\dfrac{P}{S}\right)}_t} = P_{t-1} \cdot \overline{\left(\frac{S}{P}\right)}_t \tag{19}$$

where $\overline{(S/P)}_t$ denotes the reciprocal of $\overline{(P/S)}_t$ and represents the desirable amount of capacity per unit of output. Substituting from (19) into (18) we now obtain:

$$\left(\frac{I}{A}\right)_t = a_1\left[P_{t-2}\overline{\left(\frac{S}{P}\right)}_t - S_{t-1}\right] + a_2\left[P_{t-1}\overline{\left(\frac{S}{P}\right)}_t - P_{t-2}\overline{\left(\frac{S}{P}\right)}_t\right]. \tag{20}$$

This equation, however, requires one important modification. In years when the demand for electricity falls below its previous peak, excess capacity may develop and the first term of equation (20) may become negative. In such cases the negative value should be replaced by zero, since it would be meaningless to assume that the existence of excess capacity in year $t - 1$ will lead to negative completion expenditures in year t. Or to formulate this more precisely, the quantity $(PS)_{t-1}^t$ of equation (18), the amount of capacity planned in year $t - 1$, can no longer be identified with the optimum amount of capacity $P_{t-2}\overline{\left(\dfrac{S}{P}\right)}_t$ as suggested by equation (19) and should instead be replaced by S_{t-1}. Thus when $P_{t-2}\overline{\left(\dfrac{S}{P}\right)}_t < S_{t-1}$, equation (20) becomes:

$$\left(\frac{I}{A}\right)_t = a_2\left[P_{t-1}\overline{\left(\frac{S}{P}\right)}_t - S_{t-1}\right]. \tag{20a}$$

The two special cases represented by equations (20) and (20a) may be consolidated in the following more general statement: our basic hypothesis is described by equation (18) with $(PS)_t^{t+1}$ defined by equation (19) and $(PS)_{t-1}^t$ defined as follows:

$$(PS)_{t-1}^t = \begin{cases} P_{t-2}\overline{\left(\dfrac{S}{P}\right)}_t, & \text{if larger than } S_{t-1} \\[2mm] S_{t-1}, & \text{otherwise.}^{31} \end{cases} \tag{19a}$$

The variable $\overline{\left(\dfrac{S}{P}\right)}_t$ appearing in the equations (19) and (19a) is not directly

previous year whereas the second measures spending on projects started in year t, part of which may be completed within year t.

observable. Its changing value over time, however, can be approximated. Since in the electrical utilities industry there is little incentive to cancel major projects once started because of the favorable long-term outlook and the high cost of cancellation, we may assume that $(PS)_t^{t+1}$ is equal to the actual amount of capacity in year $t + 1$, S_{t+1}. Then, on the basis of equation (19), we obtain:

$$(PS)_t^{t+1} = S_{t+1} = P_{t-1}\overline{\left(\frac{S}{P}\right)}_t. \tag{21}$$

This equation can be rewritten as follows:

$$\overline{\left(\frac{S}{P}\right)}_t = \frac{S_{t+1}}{P_{t-1}}. \tag{22}$$

In other words, the optimum rate of utilization in any given year may be measured by the ratio of actual capacity a year later to output lagged two years behind capacity. The lag reflects, of course, the interval between investment decisions and the capacity generated thereby. Since S_{t+1}, and hence the ratio S_{t+1}/P_{t-1} is not known in year t, it will be replaced in the statistical analysis by the latest known ratio, S_{t-1}/P_{t-3}. Because generating capacity was utilized with increasing intensity over the period under consideration, this ratio exhibited a declining trend. While there were occasional reversals in the direction of the ratio, these must be regarded as related chiefly to cyclical changes in demand and reflecting, therefore, temporary excess capacity.

It thus appears that the trend value of $\overline{\left(\frac{S}{P}\right)}_t$ in any given year t can be approximated best by the lowest previous ratio of capacity to lagged output, which we will denote by $(S_{t-1}/P_{t-3})^L$.

Substituting this term in equation (22) we have:[32]

$$\overline{\left(\frac{S}{P}\right)}_t = \left(\frac{S_{t-1}}{P_{t-3}}\right)^L. \tag{23}$$

------

[31] In this formulation, the second term of equation (18) is allowed to assume negative as well as positive values, in contrast with the first term which is allowed to assume only positive or zero values. This asymmetry is justified by the considerations mentioned in footnote 30 and by the additional assumption that only major expansion projects typically involve a long gestation period. A negative value for the second term indicates, of course, excess capacity in year t which may be expected to exert a depressing influence on capital outlays, tending to reduce expenditures below the level required to maintain capacity intact. It may be argued that we are not going far enough in recognizing the asymmetrical influence of under- as against over-capacity on investment expenditures. Positive and negative values of the second variable of equation (18) may well have a different quantitative effect, and one should, therefore, estimate two separate coefficients, one for positive and one for negative values. Whatever the theoretical merits of this argument, the number of years in which the second term of (18) is negative is so small in the period under observation that it would be impossible to secure a reliable estimate of the appropriate coefficient. Furthermore, the asymmetrical effect on investment of under- versus over-capacity is already recognized in our formulation through the definition (19a).

[32] We might also have measured $\overline{(S/P)}_t$ in terms of $(S_t/P_t)^L$, the ratio of capacity to output

Equation (23) represents the basic relation we have used in estimating the optimum amount of capacity per unit of output.[33]

In addition to the gradual increase in the optimum rate of utilization of capacity, another factor that appears to contribute to the downward trend in capital outlays in electrical utilities is a gradual decline in the ratio of plant to equipment expenditures, which prevailed through most of the period studied. This decline may be attributed to two major causes. In the 1920's when the industry was new and looking forward to an almost unlimited expansion, utilities tended to build a great deal of basic plant capacity in excess of immediate needs. As a result, although additions to plant facilities continued in subsequent years, relatively larger amounts were spent on equipment than on plant. It was not until 1940 and 1941, when the production of energy rose substantially above the 1929 level, that plant expenditures began once more to gain in relation to those on equipment. Another cause of the downward trend was found in the greater longevity of plant as compared with equipment, a factor of significance in the early stages of an industry's development when expenditures for replacement are concentrated mainly on equipment.

In order to take into account this last factor we shall incorporate in our equation the ratio of plant to equipment expenditures (both measured in constant dollars), namely $\left(\dfrac{I^P}{B}\Big/\dfrac{I^E}{C}\right)_t$.[34]

After the further inclusion of the profit variable $\left(\dfrac{\Pi}{A}\right)_t$, whose importance was suggested in previous sections, and with substitutions from (19), (19a), and (23), our equation becomes:

$$\left(\frac{I}{A}\right)_t = a_0 + a_1\left[P_{t-2}\left(\frac{S_{t-1}}{P_{t-3}}\right)^L - S_{t-1}\right] + a_2\left[(P_{t-1} - P_{t-2})\left(\frac{S_{t-1}}{P_{t-3}}\right)^L\right]$$

$$+ a_3\left[\frac{I^P}{B}\Big/\frac{I^E}{C}\right]_t + a_4\left(\frac{\Pi}{A}\right)_t + U_t \quad (24)$$

where U_t is a random term.

---

of the same year. If our model is substantially correct, however, the measure we have proposed should be more reliable, since, in contrast with the suggested alternative, it should not be significantly distorted by unforeseen short-run variations in demand. An examination of the data reveals considerably less pronounced short-run fluctuations around the falling trend of $(S_{t-1}/P_{t-3})^L$ than around that of $(S_t/P_t)^L$, thus confirming our expectations.

[33] Some further adjustment of the data was necessary for part of the decade of the 1930's. Because of the depressed conditions and the resulting widespread unintentional excess capacity, during this period $(S_{t-1}/P_{t-3})^L$ tends to overestimate the desirable amount of capacity per unit of output and therefore cannot be used as a direct measure of $\overline{(S/P)}_t$. Accordingly, from 1932 to 1940, $\overline{(S/P)}_t$ was approximated by interpolating linearly between the values of $(S_{t-1}/P_{t-3})^L$ in 1931 and 1939 and extrapolating to 1940. These adjustments, however, do not affect the basic logic of our approach.

[34] The value of this ratio is generally not known at the beginning of year t. Since the ratio changes very gradually over time, one can utilize for forecasting purposes, as a good first approximation, the actual ratio of the previous year.

When the hypothesis expressed in (24), an alternative to that in equation (10), is tested, the outcome is as follows:

$$\left(\frac{I}{A}\right)_t = -300 + 0.205\left[(P_{t-1} - P_{t-2})\left(\frac{S_{t-1}}{P_{t-3}}\right)^L\right] + 0.281\left[P_{t-2}\left(\frac{S_{t-1}}{P_{t-3}}\right)^L - S_{t-1}\right]$$
$$(\pm 0.045)(\pm 0.132)$$

$$+ 4.18\left[\frac{I^P}{B}\Big/\frac{I^E}{C}\right]_t + 0.441\left(\frac{\Pi}{A}\right)_t \qquad\qquad (25)$$
$$(\pm 0.98)(\pm 0.422)$$

$$\bar{R} = 0.935 \qquad \bar{S} = 43.0 \qquad K = 1.98$$

where the starts and completions variables are measured in ten thousand kilowatts and the ratio of plant to equipment expenditures is expressed in percentages.

Considering the nature of the approximations made in the process of reformulation of equation (10), these results appear quite satisfactory and are in agreement with our supposition that the time trend in equation (10) reflects primarily the two factors we have explicitly recognized in (24).

EXTRAPOLATION TESTS

A final test of the reliability of our results is provided by a check on the predicting ability of equations (10) and (25) outside the sample, 1926–41.

In the years preceding 1926 adequate information is available only for 1924 and 1925. In Table 1, actual values of investment (deflated) for these two years are compared with the values calculated by extrapolating our regression equations.

TABLE 1

ACTUAL AND COMPUTED EXPENDITURE ON PLANT AND EQUIPMENT, DEFLATED, 1924 AND 1925
($ million)

	1924	1925
Actual	426	397
Computed: Equation (10)	447	400
Computed: Equation (25)	437	416

It is apparent that the results of this test are quite favorable. For both equations the computed values are close to the actual experience both in terms of level and of year-to-year movements.

In attempting to carry out a similar test for years after 1941, several difficulties arise. For obvious reasons one cannot make use of the war years 1942–45. But even the years immediately following the war could not provide a satisfactory basis for a test, as there is reason to believe that, at least up to 1950, investment behavior was seriously disrupted by transitory conditions, reflecting the aftermath of the war and the effect of the Korean hostilities. There is, in particular, considerable evidence to suggest that throughout the above-mentioned years the electric power industry was unable to grow fast enough to bring capacity to desired levels, because of actual limitations on the supply of materials and equipment and probably also because of limitations on the rate at which firms can afford to grow. A meaningful extrapolation test can, therefore, be carried out at best beginning with 1951 and ending with 1955, the last year for which the required statistical information is presently available. Such a test is clearly a severe one since it involves extrapolating 10 to 15 years beyond the period underlying our equations.

An extrapolation over an interval of time as long as this raises serious questions particularly in connection with equation (10) because of the negative time trend appearing in it. From the previous analysis we have seen that this trend reflects in part a gradual increase in the efficiency with which capacity was being utilized during the period of observation. This trend appears to have considerably subsided if not altogether ceased in recent years, the major opportunities for more efficient utilization consistent with present technology having been largely tapped. The negative trend reflects also a gradual decline in the ratio of plant to equipment expenditures, occurring through most of the interwar period. Unfortunately, there exist no reliable estimates of the breakdown of total investment expenditures into plant and equipment for recent years, but there are indications that the declining trend in this ratio has actually been reversed in the course of the major expansion program of the postwar period. Thus, there seems to be no ground for extrapolating the negative time trend of equation (10), at least for the 1950's. Just how far (if at all) the trend should be extrapolated beyond 1941 is an issue which can not be precisely settled. It is worthy of note, however, that the answer to this question affects only the level of the "computed" series and not the direction of its yearly movements. Hence, even in the absence of a precise answer, we can still test how well equation (10) accounts for the year-to-year movement of investment in recent years. Accordingly, in Table 2 below, two sets of computed values are presented for equation (10), obtained respectively by extrapolating and not extrapolating the time trend beyond the period of observation.

It is apparent that a mechanical extrapolation of the time trend yields rather poor results: the computed values consistently underestimate investment with the discrepancy showing a systematic increase from year to year. When, however, the time trend is not extrapolated, the results are considerably improved. As noted above, the actual level around which the computed values fluctuate is not too important in this connection. However, the fact that, except for the minor dip in 1953, the year-to-year movements correspond fairly closely to those of actual investment is of some significance. It suggests that, while the

TABLE 2

ACTUAL AND COMPUTED EXPENDITURES ON PLANT AND EQUIPMENT,
DEFLATED, 1951–55
($ *million*)

	1951	1952	1953	1954	1955
Actual	464	551	579	555	514
Computed: Equation (10), time trend extrapolated	270	318	284	295	213
Computed: Equation (10), time trend not extrapolated	490	552	539	572	511
Computed: Equation (25)	445	553	597	563	488

negative time trend is no longer operating, the basic mechanism embodied in hypothesis (10) still provides a reasonably good explanation of the forces making for fluctuations in investment.

This conclusion is supported by the results of the extrapolation test for equation (25), given in the last row of the table. For the purpose of this test, in estimating the desired ratio of capacity to output through the lowest previous ratio $(S_{t-1}/P_{t-3})^L$, years preceding 1949 were disregarded. This procedure was dictated by the consideration that some of the extremely low ratios observed in the war years and the early postwar period reflected the inability of the industry to expand capacity as rapidly as demand was growing;[35] their use, therefore, would seriously underestimate the desired ratio. As a matter of fact, since 1949 the ratio has never fallen again to the low levels prevailing in some of the postwar years.[36] Another difficulty that had to be faced in extrapolating (25) is the absence of reliable estimates on the breakdown of total investment outlays into plant and equipment, to which reference has been made earlier. Lacking precise information, the extrapolation had to be based on an admittedly crude estimate of the average value of the ratio in the relevant years, a fact that reduces somewhat the conclusiveness of our

---

[35] The inability of the industry to expand its capacity is indicated, for instance, by the sharp decline in the margin of reserve capacity in the wartime and early postwar years. Only by about 1953 did the margin rise again to levels considered adequate to insure an uninterrupted flow of electrical energy.

[36] It is possible that the ratio remained somewhat abnormally low even after 1949—possibly as late as 1953. Beyond 1953 this phenomenon is unlikely to have been significant, as suggested by various considerations such as the abatement of investment outlays in 1954 and 1955. To the extent that $(S_{t-1}/P_{t-3})^L$ underestimates the desired ratio of capacity to output, the figures shown in the last row of the table would be unduly low. However, the error from this source cannot be substantial, since, between 1949 and 1955 the ratio (S_t/P_{t-2}) fluctuated within very narrow limits. Measured in kilowatts per 1,000 kilowatt hours of output, the ratio has a lowest value of 0.236 in 1953 as against a peak value of 0.246 in 1954, a fluctuation of only about 4 percent. See also footnote 37.

test.[37] Even if one keeps this qualification in mind, the results of the extrapolation test appear rather favorable. Considering the standard error of estimate of equation (25), there seems to be no ground for rejecting the hypothesis that the equation fits the recent postwar experience at least as well as it fitted the period of observation.

SUMMARY AND CONCLUSIONS

In this study we have developed and tested a model which appears to provide an acceptable explanation of investment decisions in the electric power industry. The main hypothesis of our model is that investment outlays are primarily determined by the relation between the demand for electricity and the amount of capacity required to satisfy this demand economically. This hypothesis, needless to say, is nothing else but the familiar acceleration principle. If properly understood, this "principle" is, of course, a broad concept which cannot be applied mechanically, as has sometimes been done in the past. In the present study the acceleration principle was adapted to our specific needs by taking into account a number of characteristics peculiar to the industry studied.

Of primary relevance among these characteristics are (a) the long planning and gestation period for investment; (b) the presence and quantitative importance of indivisibilities in fixed assets; (c) the rapid growth of the demand for electrical energy; (d) the impossibility of storing the product; and last but not least (e) the influence of institutional factors resulting from public regulation of the industry.

The first of these characteristics gives rise to a relatively long lag between capital spending and its principal determinants in our model and causes year-to-year fluctuations in investment to be influenced not only by the rate of change of demand (as in the classical interpretation of the acceleration principle) but also by the change in the rate of change. The next three characteristics, in conjunction with the first, make it advantageous for utilities to

---

[37] After extensive, though not very conclusive, consultations with experts and industry sources, the ratio of plant to equipment expenditure was estimated at 100 percent. This figure is roughly the same as the average value of the ratio in the period 1926–29 (namely 98 percent) in the course of which the industry underwent an expansion of dimension comparable to the postwar one. It is possible that the chosen figure is somewhat on the high side, which would tend to impart an upward bias to the computed values shown in the last row of Table 2. This bias is, however, unlikely to be too serious especially since it is in the direction opposite to the possible bias arising from the factors discussed in footnote 35. As a check, the figures of the last row of Table 2 were recomputed, assuming for the ratio of plant to equipment expenditure a value of 90 percent, and for the desired ratio of capacity to output a value of 0.245 which is the actual value of S_t/P_{t-2} in 1955. The following results are obtained for the years 1951 to 1955 respectively: 424, 535, 590, 609, 539. These figures do not agree with actual investment quite as closely as those obtained in Table 2; the average absolute error is somewhat higher (25 instead of 15) and the 1953 turning point is missed by one year. However, the differences are not too great, and the fit is actually improved in two years out of five. Furthermore, the average absolute error of 25 still compares favorably with a standard error of estimate of 40.

plan their investments so as to provide a normal margin of spare capacity over and above the capacity required to meet immediate needs; this margin in turn makes it possible to take care of the growth of demand which may, and normally does, occur during the long gestation period.

Over the years studied, we have also found a marked downward trend in the relation between investments and changes in demand. This trend appears to reflect primarily a gradually more effective utilization of capacity, technological progress (including, probably, improved marketing techniques), and a relative decrease in plant as compared with equipment expenditures. The latter development is likely to be an important feature of capital-intensive industries as they reach a more mature stage in their growth. In the electric power industry, however, this phenomenon reflected also the over-expansion of plant in the 1920's. Two alternative formulations of our basic hypothesis have been advanced to describe this downward trend. In the first, embodied in equation (10), we have introduced the time variable to represent this trend. The equation was found to give very satisfactory results in the period of observation and immediately neighboring years. It was also found to account rather well for year-to-year variations in investment in the long-run extrapolations when a proper adjustment is made for changes in the behavior of the factors underlying the time trend. In the second formulation—equation (25)— we have attempted to measure directly the factors for which the time variable was supposed to be a proxy. In spite of the crude nature of our measures the results were again quite satisfactory for the period of observation; furthermore, the model apparently stood the test of extrapolation to the postwar years well enough to suggest that its explanatory value is not merely historical.

The acceleration principle is also somewhat modified by the influence of profits—probably as a source of funds and a measure of the short-run business outlook. This influence is, however, not very pronounced; it manifests itself not in the planning but in the realization phase of the investment process, tending to stimulate capital expenditures in prosperity and retard them in depression. One may conjecture that the far greater role played by the accelerator mechanism as against profits in explaining investment behavior in the electric utilities industry reflects partly the institutional conditions under which firms operate—their obligation to meet the demand in the geographical regions in which they have a franchise and the customary support of their capitalization by the regulatory bodies whenever "legitimate" capital outlays are made. It would, therefore, be hazardous to extend our findings to industries having characteristics similar to those of the electric power industry but which are not in a sheltered position.

On the basis of our statistical analysis, we cannot reach a definite conclusion concerning the influence of interest rates on investment; however, the evidence strongly suggests that even in this industry, where fixed assets are of great longevity, the cost of borrowed funds was not an important factor. In general, cost considerations appeared to play a minor role in the decisions of the utilities—a finding which may again reflect the way the "fair return on the fair value" principle is applied in the industry.

APPENDIX

Symbols and Sources of Data

I = gross plant and equipment expenditures by privately owned electric utilities measured in millions of current dollars. George Terborgh, "Estimated Expenditures for New Durable Goods, 1919–1938," *Federal Reserve Bulletin*, September, 1939, p. 732, for 1924–36. J. B. Epstein, "Electric Power Output and Investment," *Survey of Current Business*, May, 1949, p. 23, for 1937–41. *Statistical Bulletin, 1955*, Edison Electric Institute, p. 55, for 1951–55.

I' = gross plant expenditures by privately owned electric utilities, measured in millions of current dollars. George Terborgh, "Estimated Expenditures for New Durable Goods, 1919–1938," *Federal Reserve Bulletin*, September, 1939, p. 732, for 1926–36. J. B. Epstein, "Electric Power Output and Investment," *Survey of Current Business*, May, 1949, p. 23, for 1937–41. For 1939, 1940, 1941, the estimates are obtained by splitting Epstein's aggregates into plant and equipment, on the basis of ratios of plant to equipment expenditures given by F. Dirks in "Durable Goods Expenditures in 1941," *Federal Reserve Bulletin*, April, 1942, p. 317.

I'' = gross equipment expenditures by privately owned electric utilities, measured in millions of current dollars. George Terborgh, "Estimated Expenditures for New Durable Goods, 1919–1938. *Federal Reserve Bulletin*, September, 1939, p. 733, for 1926–36. J. B. Epstein, "Electric Power Output and Investment," *Survey of Current Business*, May, 1949, p. 23, for 1937–41. For 1939, 1940, 1941, the estimates are obtained by splitting Epstein's aggregates into plant and equipment, on the basis of ratios of plant to equipment expenditures given by F. Dirks, in "Durable Goods Expenditures in 1941," *Federal Reserve Bulletin*, April, 1942, p. 317.

A = total electric light and power construction and equipment cost index, 1911: 1.00, *Engineering News—Record*, April 22, 1943, p. 100, for 1924–41. *Statistical Bulletin, 1955*, Edison Electric Institute, p. 69, for 1951–55. These data are given by region. The separate indexes are combined into a United States index by forming a weighted sum of the regional estimates with the weights proportional to regional population estimates from the nearest Census. The index is published for January and July of each year. An annual index is computed from a weighted sum of beginning of year, middle of year, and end of year figures. The weights are 0.25, 0.50 and 0.25 respectively.

B = electric light and power plant construction cost index, 1911 : 1.00. Source: *ibid.*

C = electric light and power equipment cost index, 1911 : 1.00. Source: *ibid.*

Π^r = electric utility companies' net income and interest payments, in millions of dollars. *Statistical Bulletin, 1942*, Edison Electric Institute, 39. *Statistical Bulletin, 1955*, Edison Electric Institute, p. 57, for 1951–55.

Π = electric utility companies' net income and depreciation, in millions of dollars. Same source as Π^r, for 1926–41. *Statistical Bulletin, 1955*, Edison Electric Institute, p. 57, for 1951 55.

r = yield averages on newly issued light, power, gas bonds. *Moody's Utilities*, 1947, p.a5.

P = output of electrical energy by private companies, in millions of kilowatt hours. *Statistical Bulletin, 1942*, Edison Electric Institute, p. 10, for 1924–41. *Statistical Bulletin, 1955*, Edison Electric Institute, p. 14, for 1951–55.

S = generating capacity of electric utility companies, in thousands of kilowatts. *Statistical Bulletin, 1942*, Edison Electric Institute, p. 5, for 1924–41. *Statistical Bulletin, 1955*, Edison Electric Institute, p. 6, for 1951–55.

W = average hourly earnings in the electric power industry, in cents. *Economic Almanac, 1941–42*, p. 306.

20

Capital Theory and Investment Behavior*

By DALE W. JORGENSON†

INTRODUCTION

THERE IS NO greater gap between economic theory and econometric practice than that which characterizes the literature on business investment in fixed capital. According to the neoclassical theory of capital, as expounded for example by Irving Fisher, a production plan for the firm is chosen so as to maximize utility over time. Under certain well-known conditions this leads to maximization of the net worth of the enterprise as the criterion for optimal capital accumulation. Capital is accumulated to provide capital services, which are inputs to the productive process. For convenience the relationship between inputs, including the input of capital services, and output is summarized in a production function. Although this theory has been known for at least fifty years, it is currently undergoing a great revival in interest. The theory appears to be gaining increasing currency and more widespread understanding.

By contrast, the econometric literature on business investment consists of *ad hoc* descriptive generalizations such as the "capacity principle," the "profit principle," and the like. Given sufficient imprecision, one can rationalize any generalization of this type by an appeal to "theory." However, even with the aid of much ambiguity, it is impossible to reconcile the theory of the econometric literature on investment with the neoclassical theory of optimal capital accumulation. The central feature of the neoclassical theory is the response of the demand for capital to changes in relative factor prices or the ratio of factor prices to the price of output. This feature is entirely absent from the econometric literature on investment.

* *American Economic Review: Papers and Proceedings*, Vol. LIII (May, 1963). Reprinted by courtesy of the American Economic Association and the author.

† University of California, Berkeley. The research for this paper was completed while the author was Ford Foundation Research Professor of Economics at the University of Chicago. The research was supported by the National Science Foundation.

It is difficult to reconcile the steady advance in the acceptance of the neoclassical theory of capital with the steady march of the econometric literature in a direction which appears to be diametrically opposite. It is true that there have been attempts to validate the theory. Both profits and capacity theorists have tried a rate of interest here or a price of investment goods there. By and large these efforts have been unsuccessful; the naïve positivist can only conclude, so much the worse for the theory. I believe that a case can be made that previous attempts to "test" the neoclassical theory of capital have fallen so far short of a correct formulation of this theory that the issue of the validity of the neoclassical theory remains undecided. There is not sufficient space to document this point in detail here; but I will try to illustrate what I would regard as a correct formulation of the theory in what follows.

Stated baldly, the purpose of this paper is to present a theory of investment behavior based on the neoclassical theory of optimal accumulation of capital. Of course, demand for capital is not demand for investment. The short-run determination of investment behavior depends on the time form of lagged response to changes in the demand for capital. For simplicity, the time form of lagged response will be assumed to be fixed. At the same time a more general hypothesis about the form of the lag is admitted than that customary in the literature. Finally, it will be assumed that replacement investment is proportional to capital stock. This assumption, while customary, has a deep justification which will be presented below. A number of empirical tests of the theory are presented, along with an analysis of new evidence on the time form of lagged response and changes in the long-run demand for capital resulting from changes in underlying market conditions and in the tax structure.

SUMMARY OF THE THEORY

Demand for capital stock is determined to maximize net worth. Net worth is defined as the integral of discounted net revenues; all prices, including the interest rate, are taken as fixed. Net revenue is defined as current revenue less expenditure on both current and capital account, including taxes. Let revenue before taxes at time t be $R(t)$, direct taxes, $D(t)$, and r the rate of interest. Net worth, say W, is

$$W = \int_0^\infty e^{-rt}[R(t) - D(t)]\, dt.$$

We will deduce necessary conditions for maximization of net worth for two inputs—one current and one capital—and one output. The approach is easily generalized to any number of inputs and outputs.

Let p be the price of output, s the wage rate, q the price of capital goods, Q the quantity of output, L the quantity of variable input, say labor, and I

the rate of investment; net revenue is

$$R = pQ - sL - qI.$$

Let u be the rate of direct taxation, v the proportion of replacement charge-able against income for tax purposes, w the proportion of interest, and x the proportion of capital losses chargeable against income; where K is capital stock and δ the rate of replacement, direct taxes are

$$D = u[pQ - sL - (v\delta q + wrq - x\dot{q})K].$$

Maximizing net worth subject to a standard neoclassical production function and the constraint that the rate of growth of capital stock is invest-ment less replacement, we obtain the marginal productivity conditions

$$\frac{\partial Q}{\partial L} = \frac{s}{p},$$

$$\frac{\partial Q}{\partial K} = \frac{q\left[\dfrac{1-uv}{1-u}\delta + \dfrac{1-uw}{1-u}r - \dfrac{1-ux}{1-u}\dfrac{\dot{q}}{q}\right]}{p}.$$

The numerator of the second fraction is the "shadow" price or implicit rental of one unit of capital service per period of time. We will call this price the user cost of capital. We assume that all capital gains are regarded as "transitory," so that the formula for user cost, say c, reduces to

$$c = q\left[\frac{1-uv}{1-u}\delta + \frac{1-uw}{1-u}r\right].$$

Second, we assume that output and employment on the one hand and capital stock on the other are determined by a kind of iterative process. In each period, production and employment are set at the levels given by the first marginal productivity condition and the production function with capital stock fixed at its current level; demand for capital is set at the level given by the second marginal productivity condition, given output and employment. With sta-tionary market conditions, such a process is easily seen to converge to the desired maximum of net worth. Let K^* represent the desired amount of capital stock. If the production function is Cobb-Douglas with elasticity of output with respect to capital, γ,

$$K^* = \gamma \frac{pQ}{c}.$$

We suppose that the distribution of times to completion of new investment projects is fixed. Let the proportion of projects completed in time τ be w_τ. If investment in new projects is I_t^E and the level of starts of new projects is

I_t^N, investment is a weighted average of past starts:

$$I_t^E = \sum_{\tau=0}^{\infty} w_\tau I_{t-\tau}^N = w(L)I_t^N \, ,$$

where $w(L)$ is a power series in the lag operator, L. We assume that in each period new projects are initiated until the backlog of uncompleted projects is equal to the difference between desired capital stock, K_t^*, and actual capital stock, K_t:

$$I_t^N = K_t^* - [K_t + (1 - w_0)I_{t-1}^N + \cdots] \, ,$$

which implies that:

$$I_t^E = w(L)[K_t^* - K_{t-1}^*] \, .$$

It is easy to incorporate intermediate stages of the investment process into the theory. For concreteness, we consider the case of two intermediate stages, which will turn out to be anticipated investment, two quarters hence, and anticipated investment, one quarter hence. A similar approach can be applied to additional intermediate stages such as appropriations or commitments. The distribution of completions of the first stage, given new project starts, may be described by a sequence, say $\{v_{0\tau}\}$; similarly, the distribution of completions of a second stage, given completion of the first stage, may be described by a sequence $\{v_{1\tau}\}$. Finally, the distribution of investment expenditures, given completion of a second intermediate stage, is described by a sequence $\{v_{2\tau}\}$. Where $I_t^{S_1 E}$ represents completions of the first stage, $I_t^{S_2 E}$ completions of the second stage, and I_t^E actual investment, as before, we have:

$$I_t^{S_1 E} = \sum_{\tau=0}^{\infty} v_{0\tau} I_{t-\tau}^N = v_0(L)I_t^N \, ,$$

$$I_t^{S_2 E} = \sum_{\tau=0}^{\infty} v_{1\tau} I_{t-\tau}^{S_1 E} = v_1(L)I_t^{S_1 E} \, ,$$

$$I_t^E = \sum_{\tau=0}^{\infty} v_{2\tau} I_{t-\tau}^{S_2 E} = v_2(L)I_t^{S_2 E} \, .$$

where $v_0(L)$, $v_1(L)$, and $v_2(L)$ are power series in the lag operator.

Up to this point we have discussed investment generated by an increase in desired capital stock. Total investment, say I_t, is the sum of investment for expansion and investment for replacement, say I_t^R:

$$I_t = I_t^E + I_t^R \, .$$

We assume that replacement investment is proportional to capital stock. The justification for this assumption is that the appropriate model for replacement is not the distribution of replacements for a single investment over time but rather the infinite stream of replacements generated by a single investment; in the language of probability theory, replacement is a recurrent event.

It is a fundamental result of renewal theory that replacements for such an infinite stream approach a constant proportion of capital stock for (almost) any distribution of replacements for a single investment and for any initial age distribution of capital stock. This is true for both constant and growing capital stocks. Representing the replacement proportion by δ, as before,

$$I_t^R = \delta K_t \, ;$$

combining this relationship with the corresponding relationship for investment in new projects, we have:

$$I_t = w(L)[K_t^* - K_{t-1}^*] + \delta K_t .$$

Using the assumption that capital stock is continued in use up to the point at which it is replaced, we obtain the corresponding relationships for gross investment at each of the intermediate stages, say $I_t^{S_1}$ and $I_t^{S_2}$:

$$I_t^{S_1} = v_0(L)[K_t^* - K_{t-1}^*] + \delta K_t ,$$

$$I_t^{S_2} = v_1(L)v_0(L)[K_t^* - K_{t-1}^*] + \delta K_t \, ;$$

we can also derive the following:

$$I_t^{S_2} = v_1(L)[I_t^{S_1} - \delta K_t] + \delta K_t ,$$

$$I_t = v_2(L)[I_t^{S_2} - \delta K_t] + \delta K_t ,$$

$$I_t = v_2(L)v_1(L)[I_t^{S_1} - \delta K_t] + \delta K_t .$$

For empirical implementation of the theory of investment behavior, it is essential that each of the power series—$v_0(L)$, $v_1(L)$, $v_2(L)$—have coefficients generated by a rational function; for example,

$$w(L) = v_2(L)v_1(L)v_0(L) = \frac{s(L)}{t(L)} ,$$

where $s(L)$ and $t(L)$ are polynomials. We will call the distribution corresponding to the coefficients of such a power series a rational power series distribution. The geometric and Pascal distributions are among the many special instances of the rational power series distribution.

EMPIRICAL RESULTS

To test the theory of investment behavior summarized in the preceding section, the corresponding stochastic equations have been fitted to quarterly data for U.S. manufacturing for the period 1948–60. The data on investment are taken from the OBE-SEC Survey; first and second anticipations of investment expenditure as reported in that Survey are taken as intermediate stages.[1] With two intermediate stages, six possible relationships may be fitted. First, for actual investment and both intermediate stages, the level of investment is determined by past changes in desired capital stock. Second, investment is determined by past values at each intermediate stage and the second anticipation is determined by past values of the first anticipation. The first test of the theory is the internal consistency of direct and derived estimates of the coefficients of each of the underlying power series in the lag operator.

The results of the fitting are given in Table 1. For each of the fitted relationships coefficients of the polynomials $s(L)$ and $t(L)$ in the expression for each power series as a rational function are given.[2] For example, the power series $v_2(L)v_1(L)v_0(L)$ is expressed as:

$$v_2(L)v_1(L)v_0(L) = \frac{0.00106L^2}{1 - 1.52387L + 0.63100L^2}.$$

The value of the replacement proportion δ estimated from data on capital stock is 0.025. Two sets of regressions were run, one with δ fitted from the data (unrestricted), the other with $\delta = 0.025$ (restricted). Throughout, the coefficient of multiple determination R^2, the standard error of estimate for the regression

---

[1] Data on capital stock were obtained by interpolating the capital stock series for total manufacturing given in the U.S. national accounts between 1949 and 1959, using the formula

$$K_{t+1} = I_t + (1 - \delta)K_t .$$

Given an investment series, a unique value of δ may be determined from the initial and terminal values of capital stock. Investment data from the OBE-SEC Survey were used for the interpolation. For desired capital stock, the quantity pQ was taken to be sales plus changes in inventories, both from the *Survey of Current Business*. User cost depends on a number of separate pieces of data. The quantity q is an investment deflator, δ is, of course, a fixed parameter (taken to be equal to 0.025), r is the U.S. government long-term bond rate. The tax functions vary with time; as an example, the tax rate u is the ratio between corporate income tax payments and corporate profits before taxes as reported in the U.S. national accounts. A detailed description of the data underlying this study will be reported elsewhere.

[2] To derive the form of the functions used in the actual fitting, we take $v_2(L)v_1(L)v_0(L)$ as an example. First:

$$I_t = \frac{s(L)}{t(L)} [K_t^* - K_{t-1}^*] + \delta K_t.$$

Secondly,

$$I_t = s(L)[K_t^* - K_{t-1}^*] + [1 - t(L)] [I_t - \delta K_t] + \delta K_t.$$

The coefficient t_0 may be normalized at unity so that:

$$1 - t(L) = - t_1 L - t_2 L^2 - \ldots$$

The *a priori* value $\delta = 0.025$ was used to compute $I_{t-\tau} - \delta K_{t-\tau}$. An estimate of δ is given by the coefficient of K_t. If δ is different from its *a priori* value, the process of estimation can be reiterated, using a second approximation to the value of δ.

The parameter γ is estimated using the constraint:

$$\sum_{\tau=0}^{\infty} w_\tau = 1.$$

TABLE 1

REGRESSION COEFFICIENTS AND GOODNESS OF FIT STATISTICS, UNRESTRICTED ESTIMATES

Regression	γ_{S0}	γ_{S1}	γ_{S2}	t_1	t_2	δ	R^2	s	Δ^2/s^2
$v_2v_1v_0$			0.00102 (0.00049)	−1.51911 (0.09945)	0.63560 (0.10098)	0.02556 (0.00163)	0.94265	0.10841	2.14039
v_1v_0		0.00132 (0.00073)		−1.25242 (0.12667)	0.36656 (0.12977)	0.02618 (0.00240)	0.89024	0.16229	2.00431
v_0	0.00109 (0.00085)			−1.26004 (0.13044)	0.37281 (0.13138)	0.02549 (0.00278)	0.87227	0.18974	2.37298
v_2v_1			0.81357 (0.03492)			0.01962 (0.00175)	0.92729	0.11955	1.16294
v_2		0.90024 (0.02722)				0.02295 (0.00127)	0.96234	0.08604	1.47693
v_1		0.89462 (0.03145)				0.02337 (0.00155)	0.95121	0.10597	1.70179

REGRESSION COEFFICIENTS AND GOODNESS OF FIT STATISTICS, RESTRICTED ESTIMATES

Regression	γ_{S0}	γ_{S1}	γ_{S2}	t_1	t_2	δ	R^2	s	Δ^2/s^2
$v_2v_1v_0$			0.00106 (0.00049)	−1.52387 (0.09925)	0.63100 (0.10074)		0.94156	0.10830	2.10778
v_1v_0		0.00133 (0.00073)		−1.25704 (0.12509)	0.36769 (0.12862)		0.88986	0.16087	2.00549
v_0	0.00109 (0.00084)			−1.26395 (0.12942)	0.37300 (0.13051)		0.87128	0.18848	2.53442
v_2v_1			0.82764 (0.04037)				0.89995	0.13883	0.87127
v_2		0.91545 (0.02933)					0.95406	0.09409	1.23560
v_1		0.90271 (0.03276)					0.94538	0.11100	1.53759

s, and the Von Neumann ratio Δ^2/s^2 are presented as measures of goodness of fit.

The first set of tests of the theory is the comparison of alternative estimates of each of the fundamental power series. As an example, one may take the hypothesis that the direct estimates of the power series $v_2(L)$ and $v_1(L)$, when combined, give an estimate of $v_2(L)v_1(L)$ which is close to that obtained by direct estimation. Using the unrestricted estimates, the result of this comparison is:

$$(0.91545L)(0.90271L) = 0.82639L^2 ;$$

the derived estimate, which may be compared with the direct estimate, $0.82764L^2$. The difference between the two estimates is slightly over 0.03 standard errors. A similar test of the hypothesis that the direct estimates of the power series $v_1(L)$ and $v_0(L)$, when combined, yield an estimate of $v_1(L)v_0(L)$ which is close to that obtained by direct estimation results in

$$0.00109 \frac{0.90271L}{1 - 1.26395L + 0.37300L^2} = \frac{0.00098L}{1 - 1.26395L + 0.37300L^2},$$

which may be compared with the direct estimate,

$$\frac{0.00133L}{1 - 1.25704L + 0.36769L^2}.$$

The coefficient of the numerator is within half a standard error of the derived estimate. The coefficients of the denominator are within 0.06 and 0.04 standard errors of the derived estimates. The similarity of derived and direct estimates for the power series $v_2(L)v_1(L)v_0(L)$ is less striking. The three possible derived estimates are extremely similar to each other, but they differ considerably from the direct estimate. Nevertheless, using any of the derived estimates as the null hypothesis for a test of the direct estimates would probably lead to acceptance of the null hypothesis. In general, the theory of investment behavior is strongly confirmed by the set of tests of internal consistency. Of course, given the internal consistency of the alternative estimates, it is possible to improve efficiency of estimation for the model as a whole by combining information from the various sources.

The tests of internal consistency just described are tests of the theory of investment in new projects. A test of the theory of replacement investment is a test of the consistency of the empirical results with the hypothesis $\delta = 0.025$. This hypothesis is borne out in two ways. First, for all but one of the regressions, the usual null hypothesis is accepted; a much stronger result is that for the first three regressions, estimates of the relationships under the restriction that $\delta = 0.025$ results in a reduction in the standard error of estimate for the regression. Finally, each of the standard errors of the estimates of δ is less than one-tenth the size of the corresponding regression coefficient. We conclude that the hypothesis that replacement is a constant fraction of capital stock, specifically, that $\delta = 0.025$, is strongly validated by the empirical results.

We turn now to comparisons of the fitted regressions with some simple alternatives. First, as alternatives for the first three regressions, we take the naïve models:

$$I_t = I_{t-1},$$

$$I_t^{S_2} = I_{t-1}^{S_2},$$

$$I_t^{S_1} = I_{t-1}^{S_1}.$$

Simple as these models may be, they are quite stringent standards for comparison for seasonally adjusted quarterly data, much more stringent, for example, than the corresponding models for annual data. The appropriate statistics for comparison are the standard errors of estimate and the Von Neumann ratios. Results of this comparison are given separately for the periods 1948–60 and second quarter 1955 to 1960 in Table 2.[3] For the period as a whole, each of the regression models has a standard error well below that for the corresponding naïve model. For the later subperiod the advantage of the regression models is even greater. Turning to the Von Neumann ratios, there is practically no evidence of autocorrelated errors for the fitted models and very clear evidence of autocorrelation for the naïve models. Of course, this test is biased in favor of the fitted regressions. Even with this qualification, the fitted regressions are clearly superior in every respect to the corresponding naïve models.

As a standard of comparison for the second three regressions, we take the forecasts actually used by the Department of Commerce in presenting the results of the OBE-SEC Survey. These alternative models take the form:

$$I_t = I_{t-2}^{S_1},$$

$$I_t = I_{t-1}^{S_1},$$

$$I_t^{S_2} = I_{t-1}^{S_1}.$$

Despite the high level of performance of the OBE-SEC anticipations data, the fitted regressions constitute a substantial improvement in both goodness of fit as measured by standard error of estimate and absence of autocorrelation of residuals. The test for autocorrelation is not biased in favor of the fitted regressions, so that the evidence is unequivocal; the fitted relationships are clearly superior to the corresponding forecasting models for the period as a whole and for the subperiod since second quarter 1955.

----

[3] Data for both anticipations and actual expenditures on a revised basis are available from the Department of Commerce only since the second quarter of 1955. Anticipations data for the earlier period were revised by multiplying each observation by the ratio of revised to unrevised actual investment for the period in which the observation was made.

TABLE 2

GOODNESS OF FIT STATISTICS: FITTED, NAÏVE, AND FORECASTING MODELS

Model	1948I–1960IV			1955II–1960IV			1948I–1960IV			1955II–1960IV		
	R^2	s	Δ^2/s^2	R^2	s	Δ^2/s^2	TP Error	Over-estimate	Under-estimate	TP Error	Over-estimate	Under-estimate
$I_t = f(\Delta K_t^*)$	.94156	.10830	2.10778	.94298	.11378	1.95800	29%	47%	24%	23%	41%	36%
$I_t^* = f(\Delta K_t^*)$	.88986	.16087	2.00549	.94757	.09368	1.84699	29	43	27	41	32	27
$I_t^* = f(\Delta K_t^*)$	.87128	.18848	2.53442	.91921	.14372	2.25394	39	33	27	41	27	32
$I_t = I_{t-1}$	.86193	.15950	.66900	.81929	.18410	.52078	22	39	39	23	32	45
$I_t^* = I_{t-1}^*$	.84966	.18058	1.04366	.81297	.19435	.94465	24	37	39	32	27	41
$I_t^* = I_{t-1}^*$	.83854	.20282	1.31901	.81161	.19947	.83580	35	25	39	32	27	41
$I_t = f(I_t')$	.92729	.11955	1.16294	.92169	.12996	1.09855	16	43	41	23	41	36
$I_t = f(I_t')$	.96234	.08604	1.47693	.95931	.09368	1.65030	14	45	41	18	45	36
$I_t^* = f(I_t')$	.95121	.10597	1.70179	.96477	.09045	2.26525	16	45	39	23	41	36
$I_t = I_t'$	.83673	.17391	.69933	.77138	.20707	.46505	25	47	27	27	50	23
$I_t = I_t'$	.93504	.10969	.99342	.91854	.12359	.91146	14	51	35	18	50	32
$I_t^* = I_{t-1}'$	.93380	.11983	1.45737	.92833	.12031	1.25062	20	49	31	18	45	36

NOTE: Total percentages may not add to 100% because of rounding error.

A further comparison of the fitted regressions with the corresponding naïve and forecasting models is given in the second half of Table 2, where an analysis of the conformity of turning points of each of the "forecasts" to the turning points of the actual data is presented. In general, the first set of fitted regressions is slightly inferior to the naïve models and the second set slightly superior to the forecasting models on the basis of this criterion. A final comparison is between the fitted regression of investment on changes in desired capital stock and the forecast of investment from its second anticipation. The comparison favors the fitted regression; however, the anticipations data used in a fitted relationship between investment and second anticipation provide a model which is superior to the simple forecasting model and to the fitted regression of investment on changes in desired capital stock.

STRUCTURE OF THE INVESTMENT PROCESS

In the preceding sections, only those aspects of the theory of investment behavior relevant to testing the theory were presented. In this section certain further implications of the theory are developed. Specifically, we will characterize the long-term response of investment to changes in the underlying market conditions and the tax structure and the time pattern of response of investment to changes in demand for capital.

First, using the facts that gross investment is determined by the relationship:

$$I_t = w(L)[K_t^* - K_{t-1}^*] + \delta K_t$$

and that capital stock is determined by past investments, we obtain:

$$I_t = [1 - (1 - \delta)L]w(L)K_t^*,$$

$$= y(L)K_t^*,$$

where $y(L)$ is a power series in the lag operator. We define the τ-period response of investment to a change in market conditions or tax structure as the change in gross investment resulting from a change in the underlying conditions which persists for τ periods. More precisely, suppose that desired capital remains at a fixed level for τ periods to the present; then,

$$K_t^* = K_{t-v}^*, \qquad (v = 1, 2 \dots \tau),$$

and

$$I_t = \sum_{v=0}^{\infty} y_v K_{t-v}^*,$$

$$= z_\tau K_t^* + \sum_{v-\tau+1}^{\infty} y_v K_{t-v}^*,$$

where $\{z_\tau\}$ is the sequence of cumulative sums of the coefficients of $y(L)$. As an example, the response of gross investment to a change in the rate of interest is:

$$\frac{\partial I}{\partial r} = z_\tau \frac{\partial K^*}{\partial r}.$$

The coefficients $\{z_\tau\}$ characterize the time pattern of response. Obviously,

$$\lim_{\tau \to \infty} z_\tau = \lim_{\tau \to \infty} \sum_{v=0}^{\tau} y_v = \delta,$$

so that the long-term response of gross investment to changes in, say, the rate of interest, is

$$\frac{\partial I}{\partial r} = \delta \frac{\partial K^*}{\partial r}.$$

Clearly, the short-term responses approach the long-term response as a limit; the approach is not necessarily monotone, since the coefficients of the power series $y(L)$ are not necessarily non-negative.

Long-term response and elasticities of gross investment with respect to the price of output, price of capital goods, and the rate of interest are given in the top half of Table 3. The corresponding responses and elasticities for

TABLE 3

RESPONSES AND ELASTICITIES OF INVESTMENT WITH RESPECT TO CHANGES IN MARKET CONDITIONS AND TAX STRUCTURE

	Response		Elasticity	
	Average	End of Period	Average	End of Period
Market Conditions				
Price of output	0.35830	0.35299	1.00000	1.00000
Price of capital goods	−0.35273	−0.32106	−1.00000	−1.00000
Rate of interest	−14.23653	−15.17789	−0.29143	−0.37866
Tax Structure				
Income tax rate	−0.37487	−0.33016	−0.50959	−0.42064
Proportion of replacement	0.18729	0.20502	0.39181	0.48565
Proportion of interest	0.55656	0.79840	0.19428	0.32659

the income tax rate, the proportion of replacement and the proportion of interest chargeable against income for tax purposes are given in the bottom half of Table 3. It should be noted that the rate of interest and the tax rate are measured as proportions, not percentages. For example, a decrease in the rate of interest by 1 percent increases manufacturing gross investment by $0.15178 billions per quarter in the long run, at least to a first approximation.

The time pattern of response is presented in Table 4, where the functions $w(L)$, $y(L)$, and $z(L)$ are derived from the fitted regressions. The average lag

TABLE 4

TIME FORM OF LAGGED RESPONSE

Lag	$w(L)$	$y(L)$	$z(L)$
0	0	0	0
1	0	0	0
2	0.11277	0.11277	0.11277
3	0.14209	0.03214	0.14491
4	0.13700	−0.00154	0.14337
5	0.11965	−0.01393	0.12944
6	0.09969	−0.01697	0.11247
7	0.08101	−0.01619	0.09628
8	0.06491	−0.01407	0.08221
9	0.05159	−0.01170	0.07051
10	0.04081	−0.00949	0.06102
11	0.03219	−0.00760	0.05342
12	0.02535	−0.00604	0.04738
13	0.01994	−0.00478	0.04260
14	0.01567	−0.00377	0.03883
15	0.01231	−0.00297	0.03586
16	0.00967	−0.00233	0.03353
17	0.00760	−0.00183	0.03170
18	0.00597	−0.00144	0.03026
19	0.00469	−0.00113	0.02913
20	0.00368	−0.00089	0.02824
Remaining	0.01346	−0.00325	
Rate of decline	0.78531	0.78531	

between change in demand for capital stock and the corresponding net investment is, roughly, 6.5 quarters or about a year and a half. Of course, this estimate is affected by the essentially arbitrary decision to set the proportion of the change invested in the same period and period immediately following the change at zero. The coefficients of the power series $z(L)$ are of interest for computation of short-period responses of investment to changes in the demand for capital stock. For example, the 2-period response of manufacturing gross investment to a change in the rate of interest of 1 percent is:

$$z_\tau \frac{\partial K^*}{\partial r} = \frac{0.11277}{0.02500} \, 0.15178 = 0.68465 \text{ billions/quarter.}$$

By comparison, the corresponding 10-period response is 0.37046 billions per quarter. The response dies out, almost to its long-term level of 0.15178 billions/quarter, by twenty periods from the initial change in demand for capital stock. Similar calculations of the response of gross investment to changes in market conditions or the tax structure may be made for any of the six determinants of demand for capital by combining the responses given in Table 3 with the time pattern presented in Table 4.

21

The New Theories of the Consumption Function*

By M. J. FARRELL†

I. INTRODUCTION

THERE HAVE recently been put forward—notably by Friedman (1957a) and Modigliani and Brumberg (1953 and 1954)[1]—new theories of the consumption function which have startling implications for a wide range of economic problems. It is my belief that the acceptance of these theories has been prejudiced, primarily by the conjunction of valuable and highly controversial hypotheses, and secondarily by certain flaws in exposition. I have, therefore, attempted an exposition of the essentials of these theories which, I hope, avoids these disadvantages.[2]

I distinguish sharply the different hypotheses involved, and consider separately the evidence for, and implications of, each of them. I must apologise to the reader for introducing a new terminology into a subject already overburdened with jargon. My excuse is that I felt it was essential.

---

* *Economic Journal*, Vol. LXIX (December, 1959). Reprinted by courtesy of the Royal Economic Society and the author.

† Gonville and Caius College, Cambridge University.

[1] The dates are misleading, as the theories were circulated in mimeograph and widely discussed as early as 1953. They had been partly anticipated by Harrod (1948) and Vickrey (1947), but these writers were interested primarily in other problems. The present paper owes a great deal to all three writers, and particularly to personal discussions with them during 1953–54. It has also benefited from the criticisms of Mr. J. S. Cramer and Dr. M. R. Fisher.

[2] The main ways in which my exposition differs from the original theories are as follows. First, I omit the utility theory, which is straightforward mathematics, and not really very illuminating, since uncertainty has to be introduced *after* the results have been derived. Secondly, I avoid Friedman's concept of "permanent income," which, although in some ways very attractive, involves considerable and unnecessary difficulties. In their treatment of the aggregate consumption function the New Theorists diverge sharply, and here I follow Modigliani and Brumberg.

379

II. NOTES ON DEFINITIONS

Initial assets are the individual's net worth at the beginning of the year. A point of minor interest is that, since this includes his holdings of consumer's durables, we are imputing to the individual as income the interest cost of these holdings.

Current income is the total of the individual's receipts (net of tax) during the year—including "earnings" in our sense and the interest yield of assets. The important point here is that contributions by employer or state to schemes for superannuation, health or unemployment insurance are clearly a part of the individual's income and must be included in computations of it.

Earnings differ from income in that (to avoid double-counting) they exclude the interest yield of assets.

Consumption would be perfectly straightforward were it not for the existence of consumers' durables. It has long been recognised (Hicks (1938), p. 176) in economic theory that purchases of consumers' durables are of the nature of capital expenditure, whereas the consumption of durables is the appropriate current cost—that is, depreciation plus interest costs. In the early work on the consumption function this was regarded (if at all) as a theoretical nicety, inappropriate to empirical work, and a great deal of the available empirical evidence is based on the assumption that purchases and consumption are equivalent, but in recent years the importance of the distinction has become quite widely appreciated, and not merely among the New Theorists.[3]

Savings are simply the accounting difference between current income and consumption. It should be noted that, as a result of their status as a residual, savings are particularly sensitive to any inaccuracies in the measurement of either income or consumption. In particular, any failure to impute employers' and state contributions to the individual's income is likely to produce a spectacular underestimate of his saving.

We may perhaps add that in *defining* savings as a residual we are not implying anything at all about the motives which lead a consumer to save.

III. THE NORMAL INCOME HYPOTHESIS

The basis of the new theories is the recognition that, if an individual plans rationally to maximise his utility over his lifetime, his consumption in any given year will depend, not on his income in that year, but on the resources of which he disposes during his lifetime. This is plausible but vague; we must first dispel the vagueness.

If an individual knows with certainty his future stream of earnings,[4] and

---

[3] For example, Morgan (1951), Goldsmith (1951), Boulding (1950).

[4] "Earnings" is slightly misleading, as we define it to include all receipts except the

faces a perfect capital market with a given rate of interest, it is possible to represent "the resources of which he disposes . . ." by the current value v of his current assets plus his expected future earnings, discounted at the rate of interest. The theory could be fully developed in terms of v, but it will assist the exposition if we convert v into an equivalent income stream. Consider a constant annual Y for the remainder of the individual's life-span; if Y is such that the current value of this income-stream is just equal to v, we shall call Y the individual's *normal income*.[5]

It is easy to show that if such an individual also knows his future tastes and the future course of prices, and plans his consumption so as to maximise his satisfaction over his lifetime, his planned consumption in each year will be uniquely determined by his normal income Y.

There is not, in practice, a perfect capital market, and this raises a number of theoretical difficulties—notably that it is not clear at what rate to discount future earnings. But these are complications that can easily be dealt with—the main practical difficulty lies in the penal interest rates attached to borrowing that reduces the individual's net worth below a certain level. This means that the above conclusion could not be expected to hold for income-and-consumption patterns that lead temporarily to excessive indebtedness: that is, for income streams that are, in relation to the optimal consumption pattern, unduly deferred. This qualification would probably not be very important, were it not for the problem of durable consumption goods, to which we shall return later.

The fact that we live in an uncertain world is a source of much greater difficulties. Rational behaviour in the face of uncertainty is a problem that has not yet been solved even in simple cases—it would be foolish to suppose that our simple theorem held precisely for so vast a problem as the individual's lifetime consumption plan. But in fact we need only a much more limited result, and one which is quite defensible. Let us now state

> *The Normal Income Hypothesis*: in any given period, an individual's current income y affects his consumption c only through its effect on his normal income Y. We may write $c = \beta(Y)$, where β is independent of current income and assets.

We are only concerned with consumption in the initial period (say, one year) of the plan, and it is reasonable to suppose that the individual's expectations remain stable long enough for him to carry out that part of the plan.

---

interest yield of assets. But the obvious alternatives—"income" or "receipts"—would be at least equally misleading.

We must also note that in point of pure theory, earnings are determined by the individual in his maximising calculations, and what is known is the function relating earnings to work done. But this point is not important in the present context.

[5] It should be noted that, given the rate of interest and the life-span, normal income is uniquely determined by v. In this (as well as other ways) it differs from Friedman's "permanent income," which seems a rather flexible concept. We shall argue later that the relevant life-span is not the actuarial expectation of life, but a slightly longer period, not directly measureable. This introduces a (relatively very small) element of flexibility into our concept.

Uncertainty about the future will undoubtedly affect his planned consumption in many and complex ways, but we must now consider whether it is likely to give current income any direct influence on current consumption.

One way in which this might happen is that uncertainty about the future might lead people to spend every penny they could lay hands on. Some people probably do this, but not those who have positive savings or assets. This effect seems to be confined to a small minority, and to be unimportant in the community as a whole.

A second possibility is that people's expectations of future earnings should be directly and stably related to their current earnings. This again may be true for a minority, but seems unlikely to be important in the aggregate. More likely is it that, although such a relationship does not hold for individuals, it does hold in the aggregate as a result of averaging out of deviations. This seems quite possible in any particular case, but one would doubt very much the *stability* of such a relationship.

The most important possibility is that uncertainty may lead people to abandon maximising calculations in favour of conventional rules of the Mrs. Beeton type. This is not unlikely—such rules are important in business behaviour and might be expected to be at least as popular with private individuals. Moreover, they are not necessarily inconsistent with rational behaviour; detailed planning may itself have a disutility, and a conventional rule that approximated the optimal spending pattern might well be most satisfactory to the individual. But just as the business-man adheres to his conventional prices only so long as they are roughly optimal, so we might expect consumers to stick to their conventional saving rule only so long as it gave roughly the right answer. For example, we might expect to find many of those with stable incomes following conventional rules, but we would be surprised if people with very variable incomes did so.

To sum up, for people with variable incomes, the *Normal Income Hypothesis* is roughly equivalent to postulating rational behaviour; but people habituated to stable incomes could rationally follow some such rule as "always save $\frac{1}{n}$th of your income"—which would quite invalidate the hypothesis.

IV. THE PROPORTIONALITY HYPOTHESIS

The second hypothesis of the new theories concerns the shape of the function β. They postulate that it shall be a straight line passing through the origin. Formally, this is

> *The Proportionality Hypothesis*: for any individual, the relationship between his consumption and his normal income is one of proportionality.

This was, I think, originally regarded by the New Theorists as purely a working hypothesis, but they may have given the impression that it is an integral part of their theories. At any rate, the attacks on the new theories have centred on this hypothesis.[6] I shall argue, first, that it is unnecessary, and secondly, that it is of doubtful validity.

It is unnecessary because, first and patently, the *Normal Income Hypothesis* is independent of it. More important, we shall see later that the *evidence* for the *Normal Income Hypothesis* is independent of the validity of the *Proportionality Hypothesis*.

I think it is a fair comment on the *a priori* arguments put forward by the New Theorists[7] for the *Proportionality Hypothesis* that they were never designed to do more than establish its plausibility as a working hypothesis; and certainly that they do no more than this. It is also, I think, fair to say (and I shall in part substantiate this comment in a later section) that neither Friedman (1957a) nor Fisher (1956) found any good evidence for the hypothesis. In contrast, Friend and Kravis (1957a) produce a cogent *a priori* argument as to why the proportional relationship should not hold exactly, although it might be argued that the deviations in question affect only the very rich, and are therefore negligible in the aggregate. They also produce (in Table 1) the only piece of (more or less) direct evidence that I have yet found. It concerns a sample of families who had had approximately the same income in the previous year and expected much the same income in the subsequent year. The regression of consumption on current income appears to be roughly

$$c = 900 + 0.68y.$$

There are four qualifications to be made. First, consumption is defined to include purchases of durables; but a similar relation holds for non-durable consumption, and there seems no reason why the case should be different for consumption correctly defined. Secondly, income is defined to exclude the value of employers' and state contributions to schemes for superannuation, health and unemployment insurance. The inclusion of these items would undoubtedly make the results more favourable to the *Proportionality Hypothesis*; but they would have to amount to over $1,300 per family to remove the whole discrepancy. Thirdly, the constancy of current income over three years does not imply logically that normal income must, in the sample, vary proportionately with current income; but I can think of no convincing reason why there should be a substantial and systematic deviation in the requisite direction, except for the possibility that the lower-income groups contain a higher proportion of retired people. Here we must rely on a remark by Friend and Kravis (p. 544) that "when the self-employed and not gainfully employed are eliminated . . . the results are only moderately improved from the viewpoint of the permanent income theories." Fourthly, it is

---

[6] For example, Friend and Kravis (1957a), Klein and Liviatan (1957).

[7] Modigliani and Brumberg (1954), Part I, Friedman (1957a), Chapter II.

possible that each individual's consumption varies proportionately with his income, but that the factor of proportionality is correlated, within the sample, with income. For instance, intelligent and responsible people might tend to have both higher propensities to save and higher incomes than the rest of the population. Such a correlation would, however, make the Proportionality Hypothesis useless for analysing cross-section data.

In the circumstances, and particularly in view of the hostility provoked by the *Proportionality Hypothesis*, it seems wise to keep an open mind about the shape of the function β.

V. THE SHORT-PERIOD MARGINAL PROPENSITY TO CONSUME

On the *Normal Income Hypothesis* the individual's consumption function is $\beta(Y)$ and his marginal propensity to consume out of normal income simply the slope β' at the appropriate point. We cannot, of course, say anything *a priori* about the magnitude of any individual β', but on the average we would expect β' to be equal to, or a little less than, unity.[8] But if we wish to calculate the marginal propensity to consume out of current income, we have also to analyse the response of normal income to a change in current income. Formally,

$$\frac{dc}{dy} = \beta' \frac{dY}{dy}.$$

We must now separate the direct and indirect effects on Y of a change in y. The direct effect of an increment Δy in y can be shown to be an increment in Y of the order of $\frac{2}{N}\Delta y$, where N is the life-span used in the individual's plan.[9] The indirect effect depends on his expectations. Suppose an increase Δy in current income leads him to expect an increase $\mu\Delta y$ in his earnings for n years; then it will produce an increase in normal income of approximately $\frac{n}{N}\mu\Delta y$.

---

[8] If all saving is consumption-spreading and the rate of interest is zero, the individual will plan to spend at some time or other any increment in his normal income. Hence the β''s will average to unity over his life-plan, and thus, too, they will average to unity if the averaging is performed over a "representative" group of individuals. The fact that individuals usually die before the completion of their life-plan (see footnote[9] below) will tend to lower β'.

Saving-for-its-own-sake would tend to lower β', but probably not very much in the aggregate; the effects of a positive rate of interest are difficult to determine (see Graaff (1951)), but are likely to be relatively small.

[9] Consider an income stream ΔY for N years. Its present value, discounted at 5% per annum, falls from $6\Delta Y$ at $N = 10$ to $10\Delta Y$ at $N = 40$, so that $\Delta Y \simeq \frac{1}{2}N\Delta Y$.

Since he is uncertain about how long he will live, and since great disutility attaches to exhausting one's assets before one's death, the individual will probably "play safe" by basing his plans on a life-span N considerably greater than his actual expectation of life.

Thus, adding the two effects,

$$\frac{dc}{dy} \simeq \beta' \left(\frac{2}{N} + \frac{n}{N} \mu \right)$$

$$\simeq \frac{2}{N} + \frac{n}{N} \mu.$$

Except for those nearing the retiring age, the first term will be small compared with the second, and the individual's marginal propensity to consume out of current income will be dominated by his elasticity of expectations. Table 1 gives a few illustrative examples, assuming that the individual bases his plans on retiring at 65 and living to 85.

TABLE 1

Age $\backslash$ μ	0	1	2
25	0.03	0.70	1.37
35	0.04	0.64	1.24
45	0.05	0.55	1.05
55	0.07	0.40	0.73

The short-period aggregate marginal propensity to consume is simply a weighted average of all the individual marginal propensities in the community—weighted, of course, by the increments of income received. The individual marginal propensities will vary not only with age, as shown in the table, but also with family responsibilities, social class, and so on. But speaking very roughly, and ignoring possible correlations between these factors and the elasticity of expectations, we may regard the aggregate marginal propensity as proportional to the weighted average of individual elasticities of expectations, the factor of proportionality being of the order of 0.5 or 0.6.

This short-period aggregate marginal propensity to consume is, of course, a relationship between hypothetical variations in income and the consequent changes in consumption, for a given group of people in a given year. It is not strictly applicable to year-to-year changes in income and consumption, as both the composition of the community and the individual β's will, in general, change from year to year. However, in the relatively short period the composition of the community will remain fairly constant and the changes in the β's may be assumed roughly to average out. Another complication is that the level of assets varies in time-series observations, but this can be neglected in the present rough calculations. (The marginal propensity to consume out of assets is of the order of $\frac{2}{N}$—roughly 0.1, allowing for weighting the individual marginal propensities by asset ownership, which is positively correlated with age.)

As the elasticity of expectations is not directly measurable, observations of the cyclical marginal propensity cannot be expected to provide any very satisfactory evidence for or against the hypothesis. However, the readily available data seem to imply an *average* (over time and the community) elasticity of about unity.[10] This cuts both ways. In so far as unity is a plausible value, the data are consistent with the *Normal Income Hypothesis*; but unit elasticity of expectations also suggests the possibility of a simple relationship between y and c, which would make the hypothesis redundant.

It should be emphasised that this section relates only to the *marginal* propensity to consume. The average propensity involves the complicating factors discussed in the next section.

VI. THE LONG-PERIOD CONSUMPTION FUNCTION

It is very tempting to argue that the long-period aggregate marginal propensity to consume is derived from the individual marginal propensities in the same way as the short-period one, save that in the long-period the elasticity of expectations will be greater, thus giving a greater marginal propensity. This is indeed the essence of much of Friedman's treatment of the time-series evidence (Friedman (1957a), Chapter V), but it is, unfortunately, illegitimate. The difficulty is that the composition of the community cannot be assumed constant in the long period; and further, that the changes in composition found in real life have a considerable effect on the consumption function.

If all saving is for the purpose of consumption-spreading, and if there is no uncertainty, each individual will, over his lifetime, exactly consume his total income—that is, his savings would sum to zero over his lifetime. In a community which was in all relevant respects stationary, this would imply that individual savings summed over the community would be zero in any year. On these assumptions, positive savings in an economy would be evidence that it was *not* stationary. If dis-saving is principally done after retirement, there are two obvious forms of change that can lead to positive aggregate savings.

First, a growing population will, in general, mean a disproportionately small number of retired people, and hence of dis-savers. Secondly, a rising level of real income per head will mean that the savers will, on the average, have larger lifetime incomes than the dis-savers. Modigliani and Brumberg (1953), in a most striking piece of research, investigated these effects in detail. They found that, on a number of simplifying assumptions, for rates of growth up to 5% per annum, each 1% per annum of growth in either real income

---

[10] Friedman (1957a), Table 12. Only lines 6–14 are based on a correct treatment of consumers' durables, and of these only lines 6–9 are for reasonably short periods. These give marginal propensities of 0.72, 0.65, 0.60 and 0.45.

per head or population would lead to 3–4 % of aggregate income being saved. Thus the saving-ratio is proportional to the rate-of-growth of aggregate real income, and is independent of how this growth is compounded of changes in population and in real income per head (so long as both change steadily). This suggests

The Rate-of-growth Hypothesis: In long-run equilibrium, aggregate saving is determined by changes in population structure and in real income per head. If these factors change steadily, the fraction of aggregate income saved is proportional to the rate of growth of aggregate real income.

The simplifying assumptions include a zero rate of interest, consumption spread evenly over the life-span and no bequests. There seems to be no reason why the calculations should be very sensitive to a positive rate of interest, or to plausible variations in the consumption pattern—so long as lifetime consumption equals lifetime income. But the assumption of no bequests seems crucial—and palpably false.

However, the hypothesis would still be valid if heirs planned to dis-save (the bulk of) their inheritances over their lifetime. They would do this on the *Normal Income Hypothesis* provided that saving-for-its-own-sake or for posterity was small; but they would also do so if they were "improvident," *i.e.*, deviated from the life-plan in the direction of shorter-run maximisation of utility. They would fail to dis-save adequately if for some reason they wished to maintain or increase their assets, or if they adopted some conventional rule (such as "never spend out of capital") which led them to do so. Such behaviour we may call "thrifty." The building-up of family fortunes over several generations is evidence of thrift, but the nineteenth-century saying, "From clogs to clogs in three generations," shows that even in the golden age of thrift, dis-saving by heirs was not uncommon.

It is obviously important to find out whether thrift generates a significant volume of saving, and Goldsmith (1955) gives estimates[11] of asset holdings by different age-groups which permit us to make a rough test. If the population is assumed to decline linearly after the age of 65 and if individuals are supposed to plan a linear running down of their assets over the same number of years, it is easy to show that average assets in the over-65 age-group will be $\frac{2}{3}$ of those at 65, assuming a history of stationary prices and incomes.

Goldsmith's Table XLII, Col. 1, shows observed net worth by age-groups, and estimating the 65 value by extrapolation, we get a ratio of 0.73. Goldsmith suggests (Vol. I, p. 217 n.) that this figure is too high, owing to the oldest age-group's having had a particularly favourable history of capital gains. In Col. 3 of the same table, Goldsmith gives estimates of accumulated life saving which yield a ratio of 0.52. (He regards these estimates as giving "the least distorted picture of life saving curves that can be fashioned out of the rough over-all data now available.") Unfortunately, the asset figures underlying

---

[11] Vol. I, pp. 214–25; Vol. III, pp. 102–35 and 284–381.

both estimates exclude consumers' durables other than motor cars, and so probably give a downward bias; but this should not be large.

These calculations suggest that the population as a whole is not thrifty.[12] However, figures based on estate-tax data (Vol. III, Table E-29) give ratios of approximately unity, which are presumably underestimates, as no allowance is made for gifts *inter vivos*. Thus, thrift is important among those subject to estate tax, and its absence from the aggregate results is due to the cancelling out of thrift among the wealthy and improvidence among the poor.

The direct evidence of Modigliani and Brumberg's calculations leads to much the same conclusion. Saving 12% of aggregate income would, on the *Rate-of-growth Hypothesis*, correspond to aggregate real income growing at 3–4% per annum. Thus the saving that would be generated by growth on the hypothesis is of approximately the same amount as that observed; but this could easily conceal substantial cancelling of errors, and in particular the balancing of thrift among the wealthy against improvidence among the poor.

We may conclude that the *Rate-of-growth Hypothesis* gives a good explanation of the long-period consumption function of the United States, but that this success depends partly on a balance of thrift and improvidence in different normal income groups. In applying the hypothesis to other economies, we must be prepared for the possibility that the balance will not hold there so that actual saving will differ from that predicted by the hypothesis. But however much thrift or improvidence may distort the picture, the rate of growth will remain the basic determinant of the aggregate savings/income ratio in the long run.

It is perhaps worth noting that the evidence considered in this section is quite unrelated to the *Normal Income Hypothesis*. Nor do Modigliani and Brumberg's calculations throw any light on the *Proportionality Hypothesis*—it is virtually impossible to make inferences from the observed long-run aggregate consumption function about the shape of the individual consumption functions. On the other hand, Goldsmith's data constitute some evidence against the *Proportionality Hypothesis*.

VII. THE FRIEDMAN EFFECT

If consumption depends on normal income, the interpretation of a sample survey which gives observations of consumption and current income must depend on the relationship in that sample between current and normal

---

[12] The data are approximate, and the theoretical figure of $\frac{2}{3}$ depends on linearity assumptions that may well not hold exactly. We must therefore allow for sizeable possible errors. Comparing an observed 0.52 with a theoretical 0.67, it seems reasonable to rule out the possibility that the observed value is really greater than the theoretical, but it would be risky to make any more precise inference.

income. Friedman (1957a, Chapter III) and Modigliani and Brumberg (1954, Part II) give *a priori* arguments that there will usually be a particular relationship between these quantities. We shall now attempt a brief summary of this argument. The brevity is achieved by sacrificing some detail and rigour, and also (I regret to say) by introducing a new notation.

Suppose that for a sample of families the elasticity of consumption with respect to normal income is E, and that the apparent elasticity with respect to current income, computed from survey data, is G. Suppose, too, that we can measure the relationship between normal income Y and current income y by the elasticity F of Y with respect to y. Then we can see at the intuitive level that $G = EF$, so that, for instance, if Y increases proportionately with y (that is, if $F = 1$) G is an estimate of E.

It is argued by the New Theorists that F is usually less than unity. Suppose that for the families in question year-to-year fluctuations in current income *which do not affect normal income* are important. Suppose further that in the particular period to which the survey refers the magnitude and direction of these fluctuations is not correlated with normal income. (This would clearly be true if we were considering the average over a number of years, but any particular year might, for example, be a good one for the rich and a bad one

TABLE 2

	A	B	C
Professional	1–5	61	60
	6–8	52	70
	9–10	69	53
Self-employed or Managerial	1–5	23	35
	6–8	38	51
	9–10	50	50
Clerical and Sales	1–3	65	58
	4–5	60	59
	6–8	62	58
	9–10	61	63
Skilled or Semi-skilled	1–3	40	50
	4–5	48	49
	6–8	63	54
	9–10	68	63
Unskilled	1–3	38	47
	4–5	43	53
	6–10	55	68
Farm Operator	1–3	26	40
	4–5	47	48
	6–10	58	53

A. Income group.
B. Percentage of those in that income group for 1947 who had an (appreciably) larger income than in 1946.
C. Percentage of those in that income group for 1948 who had an (appreciably) larger income than in 1947.
Data abstracted from Katona and Fisher (1951), Table 8.

for the poor.) Then, abstracting from possible complications through the correlation of normal income with age, the magnitude and direction of the temporary fluctuations will be positively correlated with current income. In other words, in the higher current income groups a larger proportion will be enjoying a "good year." This implies that Y increases less than proportionately with y, and thus that $F < 1$.

We shall find it convenient to call this phenomenon, of $F < 1$, the "Friedman Effect," and to speak of a smaller value of F as a larger Friedman Effect. The argument for the Friedman Effect is plausible, but equally it is clear that it may apply to some societies or social groups and not to others. As normal income is not directly measurable, we can make no direct tests, but there is a certain amount of indirect evidence.

Table 2, for example, shows for various American occupation groups the percentage of families in each current income group who were better off than they had been in the previous year. Where the Friedman Effect is present, this percentage will increase with income. Such a tendency is well marked among farm operators, manual workers and the self-employed and managerial groups. There is clearly no such effect in the "clerical and sales" group, while the professional group shows unsystematic movements.

TABLE 3

Income Group Fl. per Annum	Handarbeiders			Hoofdarbeiders		
	No. of Families	Average Current Income	Average Previous Income	No. of Families	Average Current Income	Average Previous Income
<1,600	72	1,144	1,183	34	1,136	1,110
1,600–2,000	33	1,740	1,623	21	1,745	1,672
2,000–2,600	18	2,215	2,073	36	2,287	2,151
2,600–3,400	8	2,950	2,460	31	2,983	2,739
3,400–4,500	1	4,140	3,855	22	3,847	3,503
4,500–6,700	1	4,832	4,111	12	5,094	5,034
>6,700	—	—	—	21	22,489	26,485

Taken from: "Resultaten von een inventarisonderzoeh in de Gemeente Rotterdam, ingesteld door de Schade Enquête Commissie aldaar, in 1941" in *Statistische en Econometrische Ondetzoekingen*, Maandschrift van het Centraal Bureau v.d. Statistiek 1943, nr. 4.

Mr. J. S. Cramer comments: "Not a very good sample, 'selected' by asking firms to ask for volunteers from among their employees." He quotes, "In several cases the current income could be ascertained with more accuracy than the 5 year average."

Some similar figures for Dutch families are given in Table 3. The occupation groups are *handarbeiders* (manual workers) and *hoofdarbeiders* (roughly, clerical workers). For each occupation the average current income of each current-income group is compared with its average income over the previous four years. If the latter is taken as a measure of normal income the manual workers display the Friedman Effect while the clerical workers do not.

This evidence, limited though it is, is enough to confirm our impression that the Friedman Effect may well be present in samples from some occupation groups—such as farmers, business-men and manual workers—and missing from other samples, such as professional men and salaried workers.

VIII. THE EVIDENCE FROM THE FRIEDMAN EFFECT

Friedman's analysis of the cross-section evidence for his theory (Friedman (1957a), Chapters IV, VI and VII) is a most brilliant and fascinating economic argument, and occupies 132 pages. The present short discussion cannot do justice to the rich detail of his analysis, but it will, I hope, serve to indicate both the strengths and the weaknesses of his arguments.

His analysis of the survey data is based on three assumptions:

(a) that $F < 1$, *i.e.*, that the Friedman Effect is present;
(b) the *Normal Income Hypothesis*;
(c) that $E = 1$, *i.e.*, the *Proportionality Hypothesis*.

He finds almost all the evidence he considers consistent with this set of assumptions. Unfortunately, since direct measurement of F is impossible, it is impossible to estimate accurately the value of F for any particular sample, so that this "consistency" does not go very far towards confirming the hypotheses.

But although the absolute magnitude of F is difficult to estimate, there may be good grounds for believing that F will be smaller in one group than another, and this will provide a test of the *Normal Income Hypothesis*. For suppose we have reason to believe that F is smaller in group A than in group B, and no reason to expect a significant difference in the values of E. Then we must expect to find a smaller G in group A on the *Normal Income Hypothesis*, and not otherwise. (Once again, the test is independent of the *Proportionality Hypothesis*.)

Friedman quotes a number of pieces of evidence of this type. In Table 1, for example, he gives the values of G computed from a number of surveys in the United States, Britain and Sweden. One would expect that, of these three countries, year-to-year fluctuations would be most important in the United States and least so in Sweden. This accords with the values of G, which are systematically larger in Sweden than in the United States, with Britain in an intermediate position.

It is a commonplace of economics that farm incomes are particularly subject to year-to-year fluctuations, and much the same is true of the business community. Friedman shows (Tables 1, 3, and 4) that the United States farm families exhibit smaller values of G than the rest of the community. In Table 5 he gives the results of a survey in which families are classified as "independent business," "farmers" and "others." The two former groups show values of G that are almost equal and much smaller than that of the "other." On the other hand, in Table 6 the G for independent businessmen is higher than for most other occupations; but Friedman attributes this to a faulty definition.

Fisher (1956) gives similar evidence from a British survey. He gives values of G (the figures called P_{ij} in columns (b) of Table 2.5) for four occupation groups—manual, clerical and sales, managerial and self-employed—broken down by age. If all ages are taken together, the self-employed have the lowest G, but this does not hold for all the individual age-groups. The number of observations in some of the cells is quite small, but even so, this unsystematic result may be a sign of the importance of factors that vary with age.

Perhaps a more important aspect of Fisher's results is that the manual workers have an unusually high G. In view of the low value of F in Table 2 above, this must suggest a breakdown of the *Normal Income Hypothesis*. Of course, the figures in Table 2 were for American workers, and their British counterparts may well have a much higher F; but, as we shall see later, this in itself suggests a limitation of the hypothesis.

Friedman bases a further test on the argument that classifying a group of families according to the difference between their current income and that of the previous (or subsequent) year will increase F. The results he quotes in Tables 10 (farm families) and 11 (mainly urban) appear to show that such classification produces a definite increase in G.

In those rare surveys that record the family's income for two consecutive years, it is possible to make rather more direct tests. Friedman develops a method of estimating F for a group of families from the regression of their current on their previous year's income (or vice versa). I am not convinced that F is more closely related to these estimates than to the correlation coefficient of the two years' incomes, but it is clear that all four quantities are likely to be fairly highly correlated.

In Table 20 Friedman gives these statistical measures and values of G for three occupational groups—independent non-farm business, farm operators, and clerical and sales. Although one should not attach undue significance to a correlation based on three observations, it is noteworthy that the values of G (line 4) are virtually identical with those of the correlation coefficient (line 5).

A more substantial piece of evidence of the same sort is quoted by Friedman from an unpublished paper by Margaret Reid. In Fig. 15, Panel 1, he shows estimates of F, similar to those discussed in the previous paragraph, plotted against values of G for 27 groups of families. The correlation is most impressive, although it must be said that all the groups but one are farm families, and that it is not clear whether all the points plotted represent different groups, as opposed to the same group at different times. There is also the possibility that these account-keeping families might be unusually sophisticated in their economic thinking, and perhaps therefore obey the *Normal Income Hypothesis* where others would not.

In any test where one uses the previous year's income as a proxy for normal income, it is always possible that the effects one attributes to the *Normal Income Hypothesis* are really due to a simple lag in the adjustment of consumption to income. This is, of course, not so where the *subsequent* year's income is the proxy, but it is fortunate that Friedman provides a further piece of evidence on this point. In Fig. 15, Panel 2, he again plots estimates of F against G, but here the estimates use the *penultimate* year's income as a proxy. Most forms of adjustment lag would imply a substantially lower correlation for Panel 2 than Panel 1, while the *Normal Income Hypothesis* suggests a roughly equal correlation. On inspection there appears to be a slight reduction, which may be partly explained by the fact that these calculations were possible for only some of the groups in Panel 1.

Individually, each of the pieces of evidence described above lacks the conclusiveness of a direct test. But together, I feel, they constitute a fairly strong confirmation that the effects predicted by the *Normal IncomeHypothesis* occur in real life. However, we must be careful not to overstate the case, for the fact that some people behave in a certain way does not mean that all do. In fact, if we look at the data with a view to determining what sort of people have gone into our tests, we find that the tests fall into three groups:

(*a*) tests based solely on figures for farmers and/or businessmen;
(*b*) tests based on contrasting the behaviour of farmers and businessmen with that of the rest of the community; and
(*c*) tests based on samples for the whole community, in which farmers and/or businessmen may be sufficiently important to account for the results we found.

Thus the evidence shows only that farmers and businessmen behave according to the *Normal Income Hypothesis*—it says nothing about the behaviour of the rest of the community. Now these two groups are those for whom year-to-year fluctuations in income are particularly important, and for whom therefore conventional saving rules are most obviously irrational. For a man with a secure job at a steady salary, on the other hand, a conventional rule might work very well. We must therefore be prepared to find that those with steady incomes do not obey the *Normal Income Hypothesis*.

We are not, then, surprised to find a negative result in the case of the British manual worker, habituated to over-full employment. The same might turn out to be true of clerical workers, who do not display the Friedman Effect either in Holland or the United States, but, on the other hand, American manual workers, a large group who show a substantial Friedman Effect, might prove to obey the hypothesis. However, this is conjecture. The fact is that there is strong evidence that the hypothesis holds for farmers and businessmen, and little or no evidence on the rest of the community.

We may note finally that since all the tests depend on relative magnitudes of F, their validity is independent of the *Proportionality Hypothesis*; and in so far as we have not felt able to provide estimates of the absolute magnitude of F, we have been unable to test the *Proportionality Hypothesis*.

IX. SOME FURTHER CONSIDERATIONS

Mr. H. W. Watts (1958, pp. 126–32) has recently produced evidence of a rather different sort for the *Normal Income Hypothesis*. He argues that a measure of the expected future income of a young man is given by the "cross-section income profile" of men with the same occupation, education and so on. (The "profile" is obtained by plotting average income against age for suitably qualified members of a cross-section survey.) He compares groups of men with different educational backgrounds, but otherwise similar, and finds that, for a given current income, the better educated have higher expected incomes and higher current spending.

The possible effects of education on spending behaviour are complex. Watts argues that it would promote rational rather than improvident behaviour, and thus lead, *ceteris paribus*, to higher saving; but it would also promote rational rather than thrifty behaviour. In addition, it might be argued that education develops a taste for the good things of life—books, foreign travel, winter sports, wine and food, and so on—and that this is only partly offset by the gambling and the television sets of the uneducated. However, Mr. Watts' results, so far as they go, favour the *Normal Income Hypothesis*.

"Contractual saving"[13]—for example, saving in the form of life-assurance premiums or annuity or mortgage payments—is a common phenomenon nowadays and is likely to work against the *Normal Income Hypothesis*. It is likely to make it more difficult for a man to reduce his net saving as much as would be rational during a temporary fall in income. However, one suspects that its popularity is largely confined to people with stable incomes—those with variable incomes are likely to have any contractual saving well-cushioned with liquid assets.

We have said little about saving for posterity. My own belief is that, while many parents give generously to their children during their own lifetime (and while the children are relatively young), few would deliberately reduce their own consumption in order to make a *post-mortem* gift to children who would by then be middle-aged. Bequests are certainly made, but these would be due to uncertainty as to the life-span, or to the need to maintain an equity in utility-yielding assets. However, it is possible that some people save in order to leave money to their children, and we must ask how this would affect our various hypotheses.

The phenomenon can best be represented by making the functions $\beta(Y)$ lower and less steep, on the average over a man's life, than they would otherwise have been. This will not affect the *Normal Income Hypothesis*, but will constitute an additional reason for doubting the *Proportionality Hypothesis*. So far as the *Rate-of-growth Hypothesis* is concerned, it will be just another factor making for thriftiness.

---

[13] See, for example, Klein (1954).

I am indebted to Mr. N. Kaldor for pointing out that, whereas capital gains are assumed by the New Theories to be included in current income, they are not so included in most of the data we have used. The cross-section data are the most important, and it is easy to show that here the exclusion of capital gains leads to over-estimates of both the marginal and average propensities to consume. However, we have worked in terms of the income-elasticity of consumption, and the effect here depends on the relative magnitude of these two biases. In fact, if any sample capital gains, on the average, increase more than proportionately with income—as I think we would expect —then the income-elasticity of consumption will be over-estimated. This tends to strengthen the evidence against the *Proportionality Hypothesis*, but its implications for the *Normal Income Hypothesis* are less clear. Our evidence there consisted in comparisons of income-elasticities for different groups, and would therefore be affected only by differential bias between groups—a subject on which *a priori* argument is rather hazardous, though one would expect such differential effects to be relatively small.

The omission of capital gains from aggregate time-series of personal disposable income will lead to an over-estimate of the short-period marginal propensity to consume if, as seems likely, capital gains are positively correlated with income. This means that the implied values for the elasticity of expectations, towards the end of Section V, will be somewhat too high; but it is doubtful whether this will make an appreciable difference to such rough calculations.

X. CONCLUSIONS

We have broken the New Theories down into three independent hypotheses. Of these, we have left on one side the *Proportionality Hypothesis*; it is unnecessary to the theories, and such evidence as we have found is against rather than for it. On the other hand, we found the *Rate-of-growth Hypothesis* to be substantially valid. Certainly, in the long-run the level of aggregate net saving is determined by balancing gross saving against dis-saving, and is therefore sensitive to changes in the structure of the economy that affect this balance. But it is also determined by the balancing of thrift and improvidence, and although in the United States these factors roughly cancel each other out, in other economies the balance might be different, with a consequent difference in the savings function.

It is thus an over-simplification to assert that, in the long-run, the proportion of aggregate income saved is proportional to the rate of growth of aggregate income; but it is much nearer the truth than the linear consumption functions so often postulated. It would be interesting to see the effect on the many "theories of economic growth" of substituting in them the *Rate-of-growth Hypothesis* for their present (usually linear) consumption functions.

Once the importance of structural factors is recognized, a vast new field of useful, scientific economic research is opened up. The effects of variations in the birth-rate, of emigration and of changes in the rate of change of productivity are all of great practical importance and open to relatively easy investigation.

The *Normal Income Hypothesis* we found to be well-substantiated for farmers and businessmen in the United States, but we kept an open mind as to how far it extends to other countries or occupations where incomes are more stable. However, even if the hypothesis were valid *only* for these groups (and there is no evidence for this) its importance is established. Friend and Kravis (1957b) estimate (p. 296) that these groups are responsible for 55–65% of personal saving in the United States, and (p. 278) that their marginal propensity to save is more than twice that of the rest of the community. As it is well known that their incomes are more variable, it is clear that their behaviour determines a very large proportion of the variation in personal savings.

This serves to put trade-cycle theory on what one might call "a fully expectational footing." The recent orthodoxy has been an expectational theory of investment *plus* a mechanistic consumption function—now consumers can have their expectations too! We must, however, enter a caution. Employment and trade-cycle theory depend, not on the marginal propensity to consume but on the marginal propensity to *spend*, which may be very much higher. A consumer may well use a temporary increase in his income to purchase some item of durable equipment, thus spending a large part while consuming only a small fraction of the increase. Another way of putting this might be to say that consumers' durables introduce a sort of accelerator effect on the consumer side.

The hypothesis also has implications for the use of budget studies to throw light on consumption behaviour. We have seen that where the Friedman Effect is present and the *Normal Income Hypothesis* holds, a simple regression analysis will give a biased estimate of the income elasticity of consumption. If a partial regression analysis of, say, consumption on current income and a third variable x is made in the same circumstances, even more misleading results can be produced. For a linear function of x and current income may well be significantly more closely correlated with normal income than is current income alone. In this case, x will appear to have a significant effect on consumption, even though there is no causal relation at all. Friedman (1957a, pp. 86–90) gives an excellent discussion of such possibilities.

It is clear that these phenomena make the interpretation of cross-section studies where only current income is recorded extremely hazardous. So far as existing data are concerned, it behooves the research worker to tread warily, with an eye constantly turned towards the possible effects of Normal Income. For future surveys, one hopes that, at the very least, income for several previous years and expected future income will be recorded; it is perhaps too much to hope that cross-section surveys will be replaced by the much more informative continuous budget studies.

REFERENCES

1. BOULDING, K. E. (1950). *A Reconstruction of Economics.*
2. BRADY, D. S., AND FRIEDMAN, R. D. (1947). "Savings and the Income Distribution," *National Bureau of Economic Research Studies in Income and Wealth,* Vol. X.
3. CRAMER, J. S. (1958). "Ownership Elasticities of Durable Consumer Goods," *Review of Economic Studies,* Vol. XXV.
4. FISHER, M. R. (1956). "Explorations in Savings Behaviour," *Bulletin of the Oxford Institute of Statistics,* 1956.
5. FRIEDMAN, M. (1957a). *A Theory of the Consumption Function.* Princeton University Press, 1957.
6. FRIEND, I., AND KRAVIS, I. B. (1957b). "Entrepreneurial Income, Saving and Investment," *American Economic Review,* June, 1957.
7. FRIEND, I., AND KRAVIS, I. B. (1957a). "Consumption Patterns and Permanent Income," *American Economic Review, Papers and Proceedings,* May, 1957.
8. GOLDSMITH, R. W. (1951). "Trends and Structural Changes in Saving in the Twentieth Century," *Conference on Savings, Inflation and Economic Progress,* University of Minnesota, 1951.
9. GOLDSMITH, R. W. (1955). *A Study of Saving in the United States,* Three volumes. Princeton University Press, 1955 and 1956.
10. GRAAFF, J. DE V. (1950). "Mr. Harrod on Hump Saving," *Economica,* 1950.
11. HARROD, R. F. (1948). "Lecture Two: The Supply of Saving," *Towards a Dynamic Economics.* London: Macmillan & Co., 1948.
12. KATONA, G., AND FISHER, J. A. (1951). "Post-war Changes in the Income of Identical Consumer Units," *N.B.E.R. Studies in Income and Wealth,* Vol. XIII.
13. KLEIN, L. R. (Ed.) (1954). *Contributions of Survey Methods to Economics.* New York: Columbia University Press, 1954.
14. KLEIN, L. R. AND LIVIATAN, N. (1957). "The Significance of Income Variability on Savings Behaviour," *Bulletin of the Oxford Institute of Statistics,* 1957.
15. KUZNETS, S. (1952). "Proportion of Capital Formation to National Product," *American Economic Review, Papers and Proceedings,* May, 1952.
16. MODIGLIANI, F. (1949). "Fluctuations in the Saving-Income Ratio: A Problem in Economic Forecasting," *N.B.E.R. Studies in Income and Wealth,* Vol. XI. 1949.
17. MODIGLIANI, F., AND BRUMBERG, R. E. (1953). *Utility Analysis and Aggregate Consumption Functions: An Attempt at Integration.*
18. MODIGLIANI, F., AND BRUMBERG, R. E. (1954). "Utility Analysis and the Consumption Function: An Interpretation of Cross-section Data," in K. K. Kurihara (ed.), *Post-Keynesian Economics.* Rutgers University Press, 1954.
19. MORGAN, J. N. (1951). "The Structure of Aggregate Personal Saving," *Journal of Political Economy,* 1951.
20. VICKREY, W. (1947). "Resource Distribution Patterns and the Classification of Families," *N.B.E.R. Studies in Income and Wealth,* Vol. X.
21. WATTS, H. W. (1958). *Long-run Income Expectations and Consumer Saving* (Cowles Foundation Paper No. 123).

22

The "Life Cycle" Hypothesis of Saving: Aggregate Implications and Tests*

By ALBERT ANDO AND FRANCO MODIGLIANI†

THE RECENT literature on the theory of the consumption function abounds with discussions of the permanent income hypothesis of Friedman and other related theories and attempts at their empirical verification. Friedman's formulation of the hypothesis is fairly well suited for testing against cross-section data, though numerous difficulties are associated with this task, and there is now a rapidly growing body of literature on this subject [5] [8] [11] [12] [14] [16] [17] [21] [25]. Friedman's model, on the other hand, does not generate the type of hypotheses that can be easily tested against time series data.

More or less contemporaneously with Friedman's work on the permanent income hypothesis, Modigliani and Brumberg developed a theory of consumer expenditure based on considerations relating to the life cycle of income and of consumption "needs" of households [34] [35]. Several tests of the Modigliani-Brumberg theory using cross-section data have been reported in the past including a comparative analysis of the cross-section implications of this hypothesis as against the Friedman model [8] [12] [32] [33].

Modigliani and Brumberg have also attempted to derive time series implications of their hypothesis in an as yet unpublished paper [34], and their theory appears to generate a more promising aggregative consumption function than does Friedman's. However, at the time of their writing the unavailability of data on net worth of consumers made empirical verification exceedingly difficult and indirect [6] [7] [20]. Since then, this difficulty has been partially eliminated as a result of the work of Goldsmith [18] [19].

* *American Economic Review*, Vol. LIII (March, 1963). Reprinted by courtesy of the American Economic Association and the authors. The latter have made some changes in the paper as originally published.

† Massachusetts Institute of Technology. The authors are indebted to a number of their colleagues and students for comments and suggestions, particularly to Robert Ferber of the University of Illinois, Fred Westfield of Northwestern University, Franklin M. Fisher, Ralph Beals, and Stephen Goldfeld of the Massachusetts Institute of Technology, who read an earlier draft of this paper and suggested a number of improvements. The final phase of the research for this paper was partially supported by a grant from the National Science Foundation.

In Part I of this paper, we give a brief summary of the major aggregative implications of the Modigliani-Brumberg life cycle hypothesis of saving. In Part II, we present the results of a number of empirical tests for the United States which appear to support the hypothesis.[1] The reader who is not interested in the derivation and statistical testing of the aggregate Modigliani-Brumberg consumption function may proceed directly to Part III, where we develop some features of the model which, in our view, make it particularly suitable for the analysis of economic growth and fluctuations, as indicated in our past and forthcoming contributions [1] [2] [3] [4] [29] [31].

I. THEORY

A. *Derivation of the Aggregate Consumption Function*[2]

The Modigliani and Brumberg model starts from the utility function of the individual consumer: his utility is assumed to be a function of his own aggregate consumption in current and future periods. The individual is then assumed to maximize his utility subject to the resources available to him, his resources being the sum of current and discounted future earnings over his lifetime and his current net worth. As a result of this maximization the current consumption of the individual can be expressed as a function of his resources and the rate of return on capital with parameters depending on age. The individual consumption functions thus obtained are then aggregated to arrive at the aggregate consumption function for the community.

From the above brief description, it is quite apparent that the most crucial assumptions in deriving the aggregate consumption function must be those relating to the characteristics of the individual's utility function, and the age structure of the population. The basic assumptions underlying the shape of the utility function are:

Assumption I: The utility function is homogeneous with respect to consumption at different points in time; or, equivalently, if the individual receives an additional dollar's worth of resources, he will allocate it to consumption at different times in the same proportion in which he had allocated his total resources prior to the addition.[3]

---

[1] Since this paper was submitted and accepted for publication, a model that bears some similarity to the one proposed here has been presented by Alan Spiro in "Wealth and Consumption Function," *Jour. Pol. Econ.*, Vol. 70 (August, 1962), pp. 339–54.

[2] The theory summarized here is essentially the same as that developed by Modigliani and Brumberg in [7] and [34]. Because of the untimely death of Richard Brumberg in August, 1954, the original paper by Modigliani and Brumberg [34] has never been published, and it is not likely to be published in the near future. Because of this, we present here a summary. However, the aggregation procedure developed here is different from that followed by Modigliani and Brumberg. This is because they are largely concerned with numerical prediction of parameters while we are interested only in exhibiting the conditions for existence of a particular form of the aggregate consumption function.

[3] This equivalence holds on the assumption that consumers deal in perfect markets.

Assumption II: The individual neither expects to receive nor desires to leave any inheritance. (This assumption can be relaxed in either of two ways. First, we may assume that the utility over life depends on planned bequests but assume that it is a homogeneous function of this variable as well as of planned consumption. Alternatively, we may assume that the resources an individual earmarks for bequests are an increasing function of the individual's resources relative to the average level of resources of his age group, and that the relative size distribution of resources within each age group is stable over time. It can be shown that either of these generalized assumptions implies an aggregate consumption function similar in all essential characteristics to the one obtained from the stricter assumption stated here.)

These two assumptions can be shown to imply (cf. [35, pp. 390 ff.]) that, in any given year t, total consumption of a person of age T (or, more generally, of a household headed by such a person) will be proportional to the present value of total resources accruing to him over the rest of his life, or:

$$c_t^T = \Omega_t^T v_t^T. \tag{1.1}$$

In this equation[4] Ω_t^T is a proportionality factor which will depend on the specific form of the utility function, the rate of return on assets, and the present age of the person, but not on total resources, v_t^T. The symbol c_t^T stands for total consumption (rather than for consumer's expenditure) in the year t. It consists of current outlays for nondurable goods and services (net of changes if any in the stock of nondurables) plus the rental value of the stock of service-yielding consumer durable goods. This rental value in turn can be equated with the loss in value of the stock in the course of the period plus the lost return on the capital tied up. Finally the present value of resources at age T, v_t^T, can be expressed as the sum of net worth carried over from the previous period, a_{t-1}^T, and the present value of nonproperty income the person expects to earn over the remainder of his earning life; i.e.,

$$v_t^T = a_{t-1}^T + y_t^T + \sum_{\tau=T+1}^{N} \frac{y_t^{eT\tau}}{(1 + r_t)^{\tau-T}} \tag{1.2}$$

where y_t^T denotes current nonproperty income; $y_t^{eT\tau}$ is the nonproperty income an individual of age T expects to earn in the τth year of his life; N stands for the earning span and r_t for the rate of return on assets.[5]

In order to proceed further, it is convenient to introduce the notion of "average annual expected income," y_t^{eT}, defined as follows:

---

[4] For the sake of simplicity, we shall not display the stochastic component of these relations explicitly in this section.

[5] To be precise $y_t^{eT\tau}$ is the income the person expects to earn at age τ, measured in prices prevailing in the year t, and r is the "real" rate of return on assets. In (1.2) the expected real rate is assumed to remain constant over time, but the formula can be generalized to allow for changing rate expectations.

$$y_t^{eT} = \frac{1}{N-T} \sum_{\tau=T+1}^{N} \frac{y_t^{eT\tau}}{(1+r_t)^{\tau-T}}. \tag{1.3}$$

Making use of this definition and of (1.2) we can rewrite equation (1.1) as:

$$c_t^T = \Omega_t^T y_t^T + \Omega_t^T (N-T) y_t^{eT} + \Omega_t^T a_{t-1}^T. \tag{1.4}$$

To obtain an expression for aggregate consumption we proceed to aggregate equation (1.4) in two steps, first within each age group and then over the age groups.

If the value of Ω_t^T is identical for all individuals in a given age group T, then it is a simple matter to aggregate equation (1.4) over an age group, obtaining:

$$C_t^T = \Omega_t^T Y_t^T + (N-T)\Omega_t^T Y_t^{eT} + \Omega_t^T A_{t-1}^T \tag{1.5}$$

where C_t^T, Y_t^T, Y^{eT}, and A_{t-1}^T are corresponding aggregates for the age group T of c_t^T, y_t^T, y_t^{eT}, and a_{t-1}^T. If Ω_t^T is not identical for all individuals in the age group, however, the meaning of the coefficients in equation (1.5) must be reinterpreted. It has been shown by Theil [41] that under a certain set of conditions the coefficients of (1.5) can be considered as weighted averages of the corresponding coefficients of (1.4).[6]

Next, taking equation (1.5) as a true representation of the relationship between consumption and total resources for various age groups, we wish to aggregate them over all age groups to get the consumption function for the whole community. Consider the equation:

$$C_t = \alpha_1' Y_t + \alpha_2' Y_t^e + \alpha_3' A_{t-1} \tag{1.6}$$

where C_t, Y_t, $Y_{t|}^e$ and A_{t-1} are obtained by summing respectively C_t^T, Y_t^T, Y_t^{eT} and A_{t-1}^T over all age groups T, and represent therefore aggregate consumption, current nonproperty income, "expected annual nonproperty income," and net worth.

The theorems given by Theil again specify the conditions under which the coefficients in equation (1.6) are weighted averages of the corresponding coefficients of equation (1.5). In this case, it is likely that the conditions specified by Theil are not satisfied, because both net worth and its coefficient in equation (1.5) are positively correlated with age up to the time of retirement. However, a much weaker set of conditions can be specified which are sufficient to insure stability over time of parameters in equation (1.6). In particular one such set of conditions is the constancy in time of (i) the parameters of

---

[6] See Theil [41, pp. 10–26]. More precisely, the least-squares estimates of the parameters of equation (1.5) will be weighted averages of the least-squares estimates of the corresponding parameters of equations (1.4) only if the set of conditions specified by Theil in the reference cited above is satisfied. Roughly speaking, these conditions require that there be no systematic relations between parameters and variables of equation (1.4) over individuals.

equation (1.5) for every age group, (ii) the age structure of population, and (iii) the relative distribution of income, of expected income, and of net worth over the age groups.

B. *A Priori Estimates of the Coefficients of the Aggregate Consumption Function*

Modigliani and Brumberg [34], in order to obtain *a priori* estimates of the order of the magnitude of the coefficients of equation (1.6) implied by their model, introduced a number of rather drastic simplifying assumptions about the form of the utility function and life pattern of earnings, to wit:

Assumption III: The consumer at any age plans to consume his total resources evenly over the remainder of his life span.

Assumption IV: (a) Every age group within the earning span has the same average income in any given year t. (b) In a given year t, the average income expected by any age group T for any later period τ, within their earning span, is the same. (c) Every household has the same (expected and actual) total life and earning spans, assumed to be 50 and 40 respectively for the purpose of numerical computation.

Assumption V: The rate of return on assets is constant and is expected to remain constant.

Under these assumptions, if aggregate real income follows an exponential growth trend—whether due to population or to productivity growth—the sufficient conditions for the constancy in time of the parameters of (1.6) are satisfied. The value of these parameters depends then only on the rate of return on assets and on the over-all rate of growth of income, which in turn is the sum of population growth and the rate of increase of productivity.[7]

TABLE 1

COEFFICIENTS OF THE CONSUMPTION FUNCTION (1.6) UNDER STATED ASSUMPTIONS[a]

Yield on Assets (percent)	0	0	0	3	5	5	5
Annual Rate of Growth of Aggregate Income (percent)	0	3	4	0	0	3	4
$\alpha_1 + \alpha_2$	0.61	0.64	—	0.69	0.73	—	—
α_3	0.08	0.07	0.07	0.11	0.13	0.12	0.12

[a]Missing values have not been computed because of the complexity of calculation.

---

[7] Strictly speaking the values of the parameters would vary somewhat depending on whether the growth of income results from population or from productivity growth. However, for rates of growth within the relevant range, say 0 to 4 percent per year, the variation turns out so small that it can be ignored for present purposes.

Table 1 gives some examples of the numerical value of the coefficients under the assumptions described above.

It should be emphasized that assumptions III to V have been introduced only for the sake of numerical estimation of the coefficients and are by no means necessary to insure the approximate constancy in time of the parameters in (1.6). A change in the assumptions would lead to somewhat different values of the parameters. But both *a priori* considerations and rough numerical calculations suggest that these values would not be drastically affected, and that it is generally possible to infer the direction in which these values would move when a specific assumption is changed. The recognition of the estate motive would tend to yield lower values for both coefficients, especially that of assets.[8]

On the whole, then, the values shown in Table 1 should be regarded as a rough guide to the order of magnitude of the coefficients consistent with the basic model; i.e., radically different values would cast serious doubts on the adequancy of the life cycle hypothesis.

C. *The Measurement of Expected Income*

The last point that must be clarified before we proceed to the discussion of the empirical tests is the measurement of expected nonproperty income, Y^e, which, at least at present, is not directly observable. A "naive" hypothesis is to assume that expected nonproperty income is the same as actual current income, except for a possible scale factor. Thus, we have:

$$Y_t^e = \beta' Y_t; \qquad \beta' \simeq 1.$$

Substituting the above expression into (1.6), we obtain the aggregate consumption function

$$C_t = (\alpha_1' + \beta'\alpha_2')Y_t + \alpha_3' A_{t-1} = \alpha_1 Y_t + \alpha_3 A_{t-1}$$

$$\alpha_1 = \alpha_1' + \beta'\alpha_2' \simeq \alpha_1' + \alpha_2'.$$

We designate this formulation as Hypothesis I.

A similar but somewhat more sophisticated formulation is to assume that expected income is an exponentially weighted average of past income, weights adding up to one, or slightly more than one in order to reflect the expected growth [15] [16]. But it is quite difficult to determine the weights from the data we have at our disposal, and Friedman, who favors this formulation, has acknowledged its shortcomings [15].

---

[8] On the other hand, if we assume (*i*) that the preferred pattern of allocation of consumption and the pattern of income over life are the type suggested by the available cross-section data, (*ii*) that income expectation is consistent with the prevailing pattern of income, again suggested by the cross-section data over age groups, then the resulting coefficients of income and assets in equation (1.6) would be somewhat higher than those reported in Table 1.

The third possible formulation is a slight modification of the first. Under our definitions, Y, and expected income, Y^e, are nonproperty or labor income, excluding, for instance, profits. We may hypothesize that for those currently employed, average expected income, y_t^e, is current income adjusted for a possible scale factor, i.e.,

$$y_t^e = \beta_1 \frac{Y_t}{E_t} \qquad (1.7)$$

where E_t is the number of persons engaged in production. We should expect β_1 to be quite close to unity.

For those individuals who are currently unemployed, we hypothesize that expected income is proportional to the average current income of those who are employed. The proportionality constant in this case represents three factors. First, as before, there may be some influence from expected growth. Second, and probably most important, the incidence of unemployment is likely to be smaller for higher-paid occupations than for lower-paid, less-skilled workers; hence, the average earnings the unemployed can look forward to, if reemployed, are likely to be lower than the average earnings of those currently employed. Third, it seems reasonable to suppose that some of the currently unemployed persons would expect their current unemployment status to continue for some time and, possibly, to recur. We shall therefore assume:

$$y_t^{eu} = \beta_2 \frac{Y_t}{E_t} \qquad (1.8)$$

where y_t^{eu} is the average expected income of unemployed persons; and, for the reasons given above, we expect the constant β_2 to be substantially smaller than β_1. The aggregate expected income is then given by:

$$Y_t^e = E_t y_t^e + (L_t - E_t) y_t^{eu} = E_t \beta_1 \frac{Y_t}{E_t} + (L_t - E_t) \beta_2 \frac{Y_t}{E_t} \qquad (1.9)$$

$$= (\beta_1 - \beta_2) Y_t + \beta_2 \frac{L_t}{E_t} Y_t$$

where L_t denotes the total labor force.[9]

Substituting (1.9) into (1.6), we obtain the following variant of Hypothesis I,

$$C_t = \alpha_1 Y_t + \alpha_2 \frac{L_t}{E_t} Y_t + \alpha_3 A_{t-1} \qquad (1.10)$$

where

$$\alpha_1 = \alpha_1' + \alpha_2'(\beta_1 - \beta_2)$$

$$\alpha_2 = \alpha_2' \beta_2 ; \qquad \alpha_3 = \alpha_3' .$$

---

[9] See Ando [1]. Mincer in [28] relied on a similar device, except that he used population in place of labor force.

We designate the formulation embodied in equation (1.10) above as Hypothesis II.

Since β_1 is thought to be close to unity, we have

$$\alpha_1 + \alpha_2 = \alpha_1' + \beta_1 \alpha_2' \simeq \alpha_1' + \alpha_2'. \tag{1.11}$$

The individual values of the observable coefficients α_1 and α_2 are, however, dependent on the nonobservable value of β_2, about which there is little we can say *a priori*.

II. EMPIRICAL VERIFICATION AND ESTIMATION

In this section we report results of a number of tests of our model for the United States.[10] Unless otherwise stated, the period of observation is 1929 through 1959 excluding the Second World War years 1941–46.[11] Consumption, C, labor income net of taxes, Y, and net worth, A, are all measured in billions of current dollars as called for by our hypothesis.[12]

In recent years, economists have become increasingly aware of the many sources of bias, inconsistency, and inefficiency that beset prevailing estimation procedures, e.g., the existence of simultaneous relations, errors of observations in the "independent" variables, spurious correlation, multicollinearity, and heteroscedascity.[13] As a result, the simple-minded and straightforward least-squares approach is being replaced by a host of alternative procedures. Unfortunately most of these alternative procedures are designed to cope with one specific source of difficulty, and they often do so at the cost of increasing the difficulties arising from other sources. Under these conditions, we feel that the best course is to utilize a variety of procedures, exploiting our knowledge of the structure of the model and the nature of data to devise methods whose biases are likely to go in opposite directions. By following such a procedure, we can at least have some confidence that the estimates obtained by different methods will bracket the value of the unknown parameters being estimated.

The main alternative procedures used and the estimates obtained are summarized in Table 2. Row (1) shows the results of a straightfoward least-squares fit of Hypothesis I.[14] The coefficients of both independent variables

---

[10] The data and the procedure by which they have been obtained will be found in Ando, Brown, Kareken, and Solow [3, Data App.]. The derivation of labor income after taxes is particularly troublesome and is based in part on methods suggested by [13] and [38].

[11] A few experiments were made using data including the Second World War years, and equation (1.6) appears to explain consumption behavior during these years better than any other consumption function to our knowledge. However, the fit is still not very good, and, at any rate, we do not feel that these years are relevant because of their obviously special characteristics.

[12] In this section, the time subscript will be omitted whenever there is no danger of confusion.

[13] See, for instance, Theil [40].

[14] In this section, we shall refer to equations by the rows in Table 2.

are highly significant and R^2 extremely high. But in other respects, the results are not altogether satisfactory. The coefficient of Y, which is an estimate of $\alpha_1 + \alpha_2$, is somewhat higher and that of A appreciably lower than our model would lead us to expect. Furthermore, the Durbin-Watson statistic [10] falls considerably short of 2, suggesting the presence of pronounced serial correlation in the residuals.

As can be seen from row (2), the results do not change appreciably if we replace Hypothesis I with II by introducing an additional variable $Y_{\bar{E}}^L$. Although the coefficient of $Y_{\bar{E}}^L$ has the right sign it does not appear to contribute significantly to the explanation of C. Meanwhile, it reduces still further the estimate of the coefficient of net worth, and increases the estimate of $\alpha_1 + \alpha_2$ which, it will be recalled, is approximately given by the sum of the coefficients of Y and $Y_{\bar{E}}^L$. Also, the serial correlation of the residuals does not change at all. As will soon become apparent, much of the difficulty with Hypothesis II can be traced back to multicollinearity, which makes it rather hard to obtain reliable estimates of the individual coefficients.

Note also that in both (1) and (2) the constant term is very significantly different from zero by customary standards, a result which would seem inconsistent with the hypothesis tested. In our view, however, this result is not as serious as might appear at first glance. The constant term is numerically rather small, amounting to only about 3 percent of the mean value of the dependent variable. Furthermore, we know that the least-squares estimate of the constant term is upward-biased in the present instance because of the simultaneous-equations bias as well as because of errors of measurement in the independent variables.[15] While the size of these biases cannot be directly estimated, we suspect it to be appreciable. Accordingly, on the basis of presently available evidence, we see no compelling reason to reject the hypothesis that consumption is in fact roughly homogeneous in income and assets. Under these circumstances, a more reliable estimate of the coefficients of these variables might be obtained by suppressing the constant term in accordance with the specification of our model.

The constrained estimation results in the equations reported in rows (3) and (5) of Table 2. A comparison of row (1) and row (3) shows that this procedure leads to estimates which are more nearly of the order of magnitude suggested by our model. Unfortunately the serial correlation is still so high that the reliability of the estimate is open to serious question. From row (5) it also appears that the addition of the variable $Y_{\bar{E}}^L$ is again not very helpful. Though its contribution is somewhat more significant, it again lowers the coefficient of A, and the serial correlation remains high.

A common procedure in time-series analysis when serial correlation of errors is high is to work with first differences. In the present instance this procedure also serves to reduce drastically the degree of multicollinearity and

---

[15] See footnote 17.

FIG. 1

TIME PROFILE OF (6) AND ITS COMPONENTS

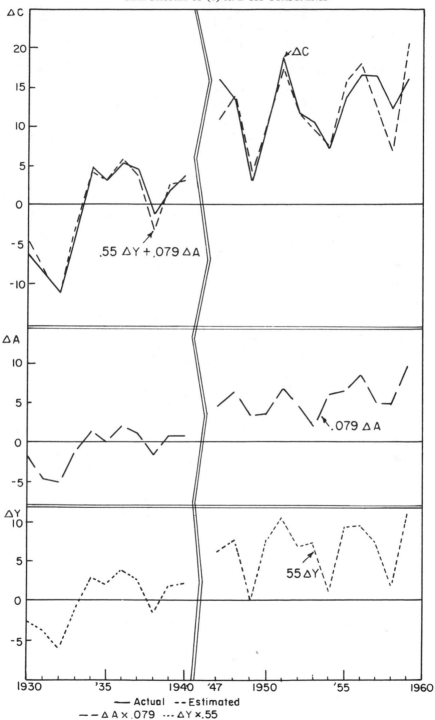

TABLE 2

Estimates of the Coefficients of the Consumption Function

Rows	Hypothesis Tested	Mode of Regression[a]	Constant	Y (α_1)	XY (α_{1x})	$Y\left(\frac{L}{E}\right)$ (α_2)	A (α_3)	XA (α_{3x})	$\alpha_1 + \alpha_2$	Standard Deviation of Dependent Variable	Standard Error of Estimate	R^2[c]	Durbin Watson Statistics
(1)	I	A	5.33 (1.46)	0.767 (0.047)			0.047 (0.010)		0.767	88.289	2.352	0.999	1.29
(2)	II	A	4.69 (1.51)	0.633 (0.112)		0.163 (0.124)	0.040 (0.012)		0.796	88.289	2.314	0.999	1.17
(3)	I	A		0.640 (0.039)			0.077 (0.008)		0.640	88.289	2.860	0.999	0.89
(4)	I	A		0.787 (0.086)			0.058 (0.013)	-0.010 (0.005)	0.787	88.289	2.756	0.999	1.17
(5)	II	A		0.430 (0.108)		0.287 (0.139)	0.058 (0.012)		0.717	88.289	2.690	0.999	0.85
(6)	I	B		0.550 (0.116)			0.079 (0.021)		0.55	8.292	2.335	0.921	2.01
(7)	I	B		0.577 (0.170)	-0.030 (0.138)		0.079 (0.022)		0.577[d]	8.292	2.385	0.918	2.03
(8)	I	B		0.550			0.082	-0.004	0.550	8.292	2.385	0.918	2.03

Coefficients and Their Standard Errors of Estimates[b]

Eq.	Form	Type	(1)	(2)	(3)	(4)	(5)	(6)	(7)	(8)	(9)	(10)
			(0.124)	(0.147)		(0.025)						
(10)	II	B	0.411 (0.127)	0.353 (0.163)		0.068 (0.029)	−0.028 (0.026)	0.764	8.292	2.211	0.929	1.97
(11)	I	C	0.634 (0.020)			0.080 (0.003)		0.634	0.092	0.018	0.962	1.00
(12)	I	C	0.644 (0.056)		−0.004 (0.018)	0.078 (0.008)		0.644[d]	0.092	0.019	0.958	1.02
(13)	I	C	0.654 (0.054)			0.077 (0.008)	−0.001 (0.004)	0.654	0.092	0.019	0.958	1.05
(14)	II	C	0.639 (0.081)		−0.003 (0.019)	0.077 (0.009)		0.646[d]	0.092	0.019	0.958	1.03
(15)	II	C	0.649 (0.079)	0.006 (0.070)		0.076 (0.009)	−0.001 (0.004)	0.655	0.092	0.019	0.958	1.05

[a] A: Regressions in which variables are used in the original form.
B: Regressions in which variables are used in the first-difference form.
C: Regressions in which variables are used in the form of ratios to labor income.

[b] Figures in parentheses underneath the estimates are estimated standard errors of respective estimates. Number of observations = 25. Where no estimate is shown, the variable is excluded from the equation.

[c] One minus the ratio of the variance of the residual to the variance of the dependent variable.

[d] Figures given do not include the coefficient of XY. In other words, the estimate of the coefficient pertains to the period 1929–40.

provides a more meaningful test for the adequacy of the hypothesis as a causal explanation of consumption. The results, reported in rows (6) and (9) and in Figure 1, appear quite favorable to the hypothesis. The multiple correlation remains quite high and the coefficient of net worth is highly significant. Also the Durbin-Watson statistic improves considerably and there is no longer any reason to suspect that the reliability of the estimate is seriously affected by serial correlation of residuals. A comparison of row (6) with row (3) reveals that the coefficient of A remains essentially unchanged, while the coefficient of Y is reduced from 0.64 to 0.55. On the other hand, comparison of rows (5) and (9) shows that, for Hypothesis II, estimates of all parameters remain essentially unchanged under the two estimation methods.

These results seem to be readily explainable. When we deal with actual values the movements of all variables are dominated by their trend. On the other hand, when dealing with first differences as in (6) and (9), we are primarily focusing on short-run cyclical variations. In this light, the results of row (6) suggest that consumption is less responsive to purely cyclical and temporary fluctuations in labor income than the estimate of row (3) would imply. The close agreement between (5) and (9) tends to support this interpretation, since the presence of the variable $Y(L/E)$ —which is cyclically more stable than Y— accounts for the relative stability of expected labor income over current labor income. It should be remembered in this connection that according to our model consumption depends largely on expected rather than current labor income. At the same time the fact that both $Y(L/E)$ and A perform a similar function in stabilizing consumption with respect to short-run variations in Y helps to explain why the addition of the latter variable generally tends to reduce not only the coefficient of Y but also that of A.[16]

All the estimates reported so far are based on the least-squares method applied to a single equation. As is well known this method leads to estimates which are biased, even in the limit, when one or more of the "independent" variables are related to the dependent variable by other simultaneous relations. In the present instance the variable A can be taken as predetermined, but the same is not true of labor income which is related to consumption via total income. That is, the true error component of the consumption function cannot be assumed to be uncorrelated with Y, and hence the least-squares estimates of its parameters are not consistent. Specifically, it can be shown that, asymptotically, the estimator of the coefficient of Y is upward-biased and that of the coefficient of A downward-biased.[17]

---

[16] The simple correlation between ΔA and $\Delta(Y\frac{L}{E})$ is 0.93, higher than that between ΔY and $\Delta(Y\frac{L}{E})$, 0.89.

[17] Let us denote the *true* error term in equation (1.6) by ϵ. Then, under the assumption that the correlation between Y and A and that between Y and ϵ are positive, while A and ϵ are uncorrelated with each other, it can be readily shown that

$$\text{plim } \hat{\alpha}_1 = \alpha_1 + \text{plim } \frac{\sum A^2 \sum Y\epsilon}{\sum A^2 \sum Y^2 - (\sum A Y)^2} \geq \alpha_1$$

The only really adequate way of resolving this difficulty would be to construct a complete model of the U.S. economy and then apply an appropriate simultaneous-equations estimation procedure. This approach would lead at least to consistent estimates, except to the extent that the model was incomplete or misspecified and the exogenous variables were subject to errors of measurement. Furthermore, the efficiency of the estimates might be reduced, particularly if the theory and data relating to other sectors of the economy were less reliable than those relating to the consumption sector. Whatever the merits of this approach, however, we regard the specification of a complete model beyond the scope of this paper.

A compromise followed by some authors is to introduce an accounting identity relating consumption, saving, and income, note that saving is equal to investment, assume that investment is autonomous, and estimate the parameters of the consumption function from the regression of consumption on saving [39] [43]. Now in our view this procedure is likely to lead to bias in the estimates of the parameters which is more serious than that resulting from the conventional regression on income. The arguments supporting this conclusion are developed formally in Appendix, section B and can be summarized here as follows:

1. When the "independent" variable is subject to errors of measurement, the resulting estimate of the regression coefficient is biased toward zero, the more so the greater the variance of the error of measurement of the independent variable relative to its true variance. Now since personal saving is in the order of one-tenth of disposable income, it is reasonable to suppose that the variance of true (as distinguished from measured) personal saving is a good deal smaller than the variance of disposable income. At the same time, personal saving, as actually measured in the national income accounts, represents the difference between largely independent estimates of disposable income and of personal consumption. Hence the error of measurement of personal saving is likely to be even larger than that of disposable income. We can therefore be rather confident that the bias toward

---

$$\text{plim } \hat{\alpha}_3 = \alpha_3 - \text{plim } \frac{\sum Y\epsilon \sum AY}{\sum A^2 \sum Y^2 - (\sum AY)^2} \leq \alpha_3$$

where $\hat{\alpha}_1$ and $\hat{\alpha}_3$ are the least-squares estimates of α_1 and α_3, respectively.

The above formulae are stated for the case in which the constant is suppressed, but for the case where the constant is not suppressed, it is only necessary to reinterpret the symbols as deviations from respective means. The asymptotic bias for the constant term can then be expressed in terms of the above limits and the means of the variables involved. Denoting the constant term and its least-squares estimate by γ and $\hat{\gamma}$ respectively, it can be shown that

$$\text{plim } (\hat{\gamma} - \gamma) = \text{plim } \frac{\sum Y'\epsilon}{\sum A'^2 \sum Y'^2 - (\sum A'Y')^2} (\bar{A}\sum A'Y' - \bar{Y}\sum A'^2)$$

where the primed symbols denote the deviations from the mean. The estimate from our data of the probability limit of the expression inside the parentheses is positive and fairly large, so that the asymptotic bias of the least-squares estimate of the constant term is most likely to be positive.

zero due to errors of measurement will be a good deal more serious when consumption is regressed on personal saving than when it is regressed on disposable income. Furthermore, given the estimating procedure, the error of measurement of consumption is likely to be negatively correlated with the error of measurement of saving, and this negative correlation will produce a further downward bias in the estimate of the true regression coefficient.

2. Personal saving is *not* identically equal to investment either conceptually or in terms of actual measurement, and investment is *not* exogenous, or independent of consumption, even in the short run, especially when account is taken of investment in inventories. At least over a very short period of time, such as a quarter or less, it is quite likely that random variations in consumption behavior will be accompanied by random variations in personal saving in the opposite direction, and, to the extent that this is true, an estimate of the propensity to consume based on the regression of consumption on saving will be seriously downward-biased, even in the absence of errors of measurement.

For the problem at hand, there exists an alternative and relatively simple way of securing consistent estimates of the parameters in Hypothesis I based essentially on the two stage least-squares method. Relying on the specification that the constant term is zero and that the true error is uncorrelated with A, this procedure consists in (i) regressing income on assets, and obtaining computed values of Y from this regression, say Y_c; (ii) then regressing C on Y_c and on A. The coefficients of Y_c and A so obtained can be shown to be consistent estimators of the coefficients of Y and A respectively.[18]

The application of this procedure to our problem yields estimates of 0.54 and 0.09 for α_1 and α_3, respectively. While these values are reasonably close

---

[18] Suppose that we estimate the parameters of the following equation by the method of least squares:

(a)
$$Y = b_y A + a_y + \eta_y$$

where η_y is the error term,

The substitution of the value of Y estimated by (a) into equation (1.6) yields

(b)
$$C = \alpha_1(b_y A + a_y) + \alpha_3 A + \epsilon = (\alpha_1 b_y + \alpha_3)A + \alpha_1 a_y + \epsilon.$$

Comparison of equation (b) with the regression of C on A

(c)
$$C = b_c A + a_c + \eta_c$$

results in

(d)
$$\alpha_1 b_y + \alpha_3 = b_c$$

(e)
$$\alpha_1 a_y = a_c$$

(d) and (e) can then be solved to give the estimated values of α_1 and α_3. These estimates are identical with those resulting from the two-stage least-squares procedure described in the text.

to those given in row (6) of Table 2, the loss of efficiency involved in this indirect procedure cautions us against attaching too much significance to these estimates.

Another possible way of coping with the problem of bias in the estimates resulting from a known cause but of unknown magnitude is to construct an alternative estimation procedure in which the same cause may be expected to produce a bias in the opposite direction. If this can be done, then the unknown parameters may be bracketed by the estimates generated by the two alternative procedures, and if they are close together, then we may conclude with some confidence that the bias in either procedure is not too serious. For this purpose, suppose that we divide both sides of equation (1.6) by Y, obtaining

$$\frac{C}{Y} = \alpha_1 + \alpha_3 \frac{A}{Y}$$

and then proceed to estimate the parameters of this equation by the conventional least-squares method. It can be shown that, in so far as the bias due to the positive correlation between Y and the true error of the consumption function is concerned, the least-squares estimate of α_3 will be upward-biased, and hence, that of α_1 will be downward-biased. Thus, for both coefficients, the bias is in the direction opposite to that resulting from other procedures reported so far. This approach has also other desirable properties: it eliminates the difficulties arising from the presence of strong multicollinearity, and the homoscedasticity condition is more likely to be satisfied. Furthermore, it eliminates altogether the common trend in the variables, thus providing a rather stringent test of the relevance of net worth as a determinant of consumption. Its main drawback is that the above-mentioned bias in the estimates may be appreciably reinforced by error of measurement in the variable Y, although error of measurement in A will tend to work in the opposite direction.[19]

The results of this test reported in row (11) are remarkably encouraging. As expected, this procedure yields a higher estimate of α_3 and a lower estimate of α_1 relative to corresponding estimates in row (3). But these estimates are so close to each other that, if our interpretation of these estimating procedures is correct, they provide very narrow limits within which the true values of these coefficients may be expected to lie. However, the very high serial correlation of errors in both (3) and (11) may cast some doubt on the reliability of the estimates.

----

[19] For possible problems arising from the use of ratios, see [26] and [37]. Note that the ratio estimates described above can be regarded as the Aitkin's generalized least-squares estimates of Hypothesis I and II under the assumption that the standard deviation of the residual errors is proportional to Y_t.

The high serial correlation in the estimated errors, in this and to a lesser extent in other procedures, suggests the desirability of testing for evidence of a significant change in the parameters of our consumption function as between the prewar and the postwar period. Individual tastes as well as the demographic structure and the rate of return on assets, on which the theoretical values of the coefficients depend, may have changed sufficiently over the two periods to cause a measurable change in the parameters. In addition, there exists a statistical problem arising from the fact that the data, particularly the net worth estimates, are based on somewhat different estimating procedures for the two periods. To test the hypothesis of a shift in parameters we have computed a number of regressions involving a "dummy" variable X, with value zero for the years 1929–40 and value one for the years 1947–59.

The results given in rows (4), (7), (8), (10), and (12) to (14), which constitute a representative sample of the tests we have carried out, show that the coefficient of the dummy variable is quite small in absolute value and statistically insignificant in all cases. Since its sign is consistently negative, we cannot rule out the possibility that there is very slight downward shift of the consumption function from the pre-war period to the postwar period.[20]

On the whole, known statistical properties of various estimation methods utilized appear to explain the pattern of most of the results reported in Table 2,[21] which we may now endeavor to summarize.

---

[20] Our model provides one possible clue to this apparent downward shift. An examination of the figures reported in [3] reveals a distinct decline in the ratio of nonlabor income to net worth, which can be taken as a measure of the rate of return on capital. This is presumably attributable in large measure to increases in corporate taxes and in the extent and progressiveness of personal income taxation. An examination of the values of the coefficients of income and net worth implied by our model, reported in Table 1, suggests that both coefficients should tend to decline as the rate of return on assets declines. However, we do not wish to press this point, especially since we cannot even be sure whether the apparent decline in the coefficients reflects anything more than error of measurement.

[21] One uncomfortable feature of Table 2 is the high serial correlation of residuals in a number of tests. One possible explanation for the high serial correlation in some of the tests is that consumption does not adjust fully to changes in income and assets within the arbitrary time unit of one year. To allow for this possibility Hypothesis I might be written as

$$C_t - C_{t-1} = \delta(\alpha_1 Y_t + \alpha_3 A_{t-1} - C_{t-1}), \text{ or } C_t = (1 - \delta)C_{t-1} + \delta\alpha_1 Y_t + \delta\alpha_3 A_{t-1},$$

where the constant δ, with the dimension $1/\text{time}$, measures the speed of adjustment of consumption and may be expected to approach unity as the time unit increases. This hypothesis was tested in ratio form (to avoid increasing further the already extremely high multicollinearity prevailing in the direct form) with the following results:

$$\frac{C_t}{Y_t} = 0.46 + \underset{(0.077)}{0.177} \frac{C_{t-1}}{Y_t} + \underset{(0.016)}{0.072} \frac{A_{t-1}}{Y_t}$$

implying $\delta = 0.82$, $\alpha_1 = 0.56$, $\alpha_3 = 0.087$.

The relatively low coefficient of C_{t-1} (which is only moderately significant) suggests that a span of one year is long enough for most of the adjustment to take place. Also the estimates of the remaining coefficients are not greatly affected and move closer to the first difference estimates. However, somewhat surprisingly, the serial correlation is increased still further.

In the first place, all of the tests seem, by and large, to support the basic hypothesis advanced in this paper, and in particular, the importance of net worth as a determinant of consumption. Unfortunately, some difficulties arise in the attempt to secure reliable estimates of the coefficients of the "independent" variables, although some tentative conclusions seem to stand out. First, the different estimation procedures when applied to Hypothesis I generally yield a similar estimate of the coefficient of net worth for the period as a whole, very close to 0.08. [Cf. rows (3), (6), (7), (11), and (12).]

At the same time, the estimate of the coefficients of income is somewhat unstable [see rows (3), (4), (6), (8), (10), and (12)]. This instability is appreciably reduced under Hypothesis II, where the third variable, $Y(L/E)$ apparently helps to disentangle the effect of purely cyclical and transitory changes in nonproperty income from that of long-run or permanent changes. The various estimates for the long-run marginal propensity, $\alpha_1 + \alpha_2$, are fairly consistent—0.72 for the first difference and straight estimates with constant suppressed [rows (5) and (9)] and moderately lower for the ratio estimate [row (15)]. There is however much less consistency in the values α_1 and α_2 separately and hence in the estimates of the short-run marginal propensity to consume with respect to labor income, α_1. While the ratio estimate yields the value of 0.65 [row (15)], all other methods produce much lower estimates, between 0.41 and 0.44 [rows (5), (9), (10)]. On the whole, we are inclined to regard the latter estimates as somewhat more reliable, in part because of the high serial correlation present in rows (5) and (15), but no firm conclusion seems warranted with the available data and methods. At the same time we observe that the introduction of the third variable, $Y(L/E)$ tends to reduce somewhat the estimate of the coefficient of net worth. It would appear that the value 0.08 obtained for Hypothesis I, where $Y(L/E)$ is not present, may be somewhat too high—since the cyclically sluggish variable A acts partly as a proxy for expected nonlabor income—and the true value may be closer to 0.06 or even somewhat lower.

As indicated earlier, a few tests of Hypothesis I have also been carried out for the period 1900–28. Because the data for this period are mostly obtained from different sources and are subject to very wide margin of error, we have seen little point in combining them with the series relating to the period since 1929. In fact, we are inclined to attach rather little significance to the results of these tests, which are accordingly confined to Appendix section A. For whatever they are worth, these results do not appear grossly inconsistent with those for the period after 1929, especially when account is taken of error of measurement and its likely effects on different estimation procedures. In particular, the contribution of net worth appears again to be significant, its coefficient being of the same order of magnitude as in the later period except in the first-difference test which is obviously most seriously affected by the error of measurement.

Finally, our empirical results are also roughly consistent with the *a priori* numerical predictions reported in Table 1. The fact that the coefficients of both variables, especially that of net worth, are on the low side may be accounted for by reference to the estate motive which was ignored in the numerical calculations for Table 1, while it probably plays a nonnegligible role at least for the high-income and/or self-employed groups.[22]

III. SOME IMPLICATIONS

A. *Relation to the Standard Keynesian Consumption Functions*

The standard Keynesian consumption function [23] is usually written in the form:

$$C = \gamma Y^* + \gamma_0 \qquad (3.1)$$

where Y^* denotes personal income net of taxes or disposable income and the γ's are constants.[23] A more sophisticated variant of this hypothesis, which has become quite popular of late, consists in separating income into two parts, disposable labor income Y, and disposable nonlabor or property income, which we shall denote by P. Thus,

$$C = \gamma_1 Y + \gamma_2 P + \gamma_0. \qquad (3.2)$$

This variant, which reduces to (3.1) when $\gamma_1 = \gamma_2$, is usually advocated on the ground that property income accrues mostly to higher-income and/or entrepreneurial groups who may be expected to have a lower marginal propensity to consume. Accordingly, γ_2 is supposed to be smaller than γ_1 and this supposition appears to be supported by empirical findings.

It is immediately apparent that (3.2) bears considerable similarity to Hypothesis I discussed in this paper, i.e.,

$$C = (\alpha_1 + \alpha_2)Y + \alpha_3 A. \qquad (3.3)$$

The main difference lies in the constant term which appears in (3.2) but not in (3.3), and in the fact that the wealth variable A in (3.3) is replaced in (3.2) by a closely related variable, income from wealth, P. We can avoid dealing with the first source of discrepancy by working with both hypotheses in first-difference form,

$$\Delta C = \gamma_1 \Delta Y + \gamma_2 \Delta P \qquad (3.2a)$$

$$\Delta C = (\alpha_1 + \alpha_2)\Delta Y + \alpha_3 \Delta A. \qquad (3.3a)$$

Equations (3.2a) and (3.3a) are quite useful since they allow a straightforward test of the usefulness of the Modigliani-Brumberg hypothesis as compared with the standard Keynesian one. We have already exhibited in Table 2,

---

[22] See for instance the results of cross-section studies reported in [24] and [32].

[23] Keynes' own formulation (See [23, Book 3]) was considerably more general than that contained in equation (3.1).

row (6), the results obtained by fitting (3.3a) to the data. In order to complete the test we need to estimate the parameters of (3.2a). If the standard Keynesian version is correct, the net worth variable in (3.3) and (3.3a) is merely a proxy variable for the return from wealth, P, and hence substitution of ΔP for ΔA should improve the fit. On the other hand, if (3.3) and (3.3a) are closer to the truth than (3.2), then the substitution of ΔA by a proxy variable ΔP should reduce the correlation.

The estimate of P needed for this test is given in [3].[24] The definition of consumption on which we rely, however, is somewhat different from that customarily used in the standard Keynesian formulation in that it includes the current consumption—depreciation—of the stock of consumer durables, while excluding expenditure for the purchase of such goods.[25] The results obtained for hypothesis (3.2a) are as follows:

$$\Delta C = 0.93\Delta Y + 0.07\Delta P \qquad R^2 = 0.86. \qquad (3.4)$$
$$\quad\; (0.07) \qquad (0.29)$$

Comparison of this result with those reported in Table 2, row (6), strongly suggests that net worth is definitely not a mere proxy for current property income. While the coefficient of P is positive and smaller than that of Y as expected, this variable is much less useful than A in explaining the behavior of consumption. In fact, its contribution is not significantly different from zero.[26]

These results, besides supporting our hypothesis, serve also to cast serious doubts on the conventional interpretation of the empirical coefficients of

---

[24] Our estimates of Y and P do not add up exactly to disposable personal income as usually defined because we include in disposable personal income contributions to, instead of benefits from, the social security system. However, this discrepency is quite minor.

[25] Also, our data are in current dollars, while the standard Keynesian version of the consumption function is usually stated in terms of constant dollars.

[26] For the sake of completeness several other variants of (3.2a) were tested by adding variables that were included in the test of our hypothesis and which are consistent with the spirit of the Keynesian model. The addition of the variable $\Delta(Y_{\frac{L}{E}})$, which might help to sort out the effect of long run from that of purely cyclical variations in income, yields

$$\Delta C = 0.47\Delta Y + 0.49\Delta (Y_{\frac{L}{E}}) + 0.17\Delta P \qquad R^2 = 0.921. \qquad (3.4a)$$
$$\quad\; (0.18) \qquad (0.13) \qquad\quad (0.23)$$

If we also include the dummy variable X to allow for possible shifts from the prewar to the postwar period, its coefficient is uniformly less than its standard error, and in general hypothesis (3.2) does not fare any better. This conclusion can be illustrated by the following result which is the most favorable to that hypothesis among the battery we have run:

$$\Delta C = 0.46\Delta Y + 0.51\Delta (Y_{\frac{L}{E}}) + 0.26\Delta P - 0.21X\Delta P \qquad R^2 = 0.921. \quad (3.4b.)$$
$$\quad\; (0.14) \qquad (0.14) \qquad\quad (0.28) \qquad (0.39)$$

The fact that in (3.4a) and (3.4b) the coefficient of the variable $\Delta(Y_{\frac{L}{E}})$ is a good deal higher and statistically more significant than in the corresponding tests reported in Table 2 is readily accounted for by the high correlation between this variable and A which, in the absence of A, makes this variable act partly as a proxy for A. (The correlation in question is 0.93. See also footnote 16.)

ΔY and ΔP in (3.2); namely, that incremental labor income is largely consumed while incremental property income is largely saved. For our tests of the Modigliani-Brumberg model indicate that consumption is quite responsive to variations in the market value of wealth, which, in turn, must largely reflect the capitalization of property income. Note, however, that the market valuation of assets will be controlled by expected long-run returns, say $\bar{P}$, which will tend to be a good deal more stable than *current* property income, P. We suggest therefore that the coefficient of P in (3.2) is small not because property income is largely saved but because short-run changes in P are dominated by transitory phenomena and hence are a poor measure of changes in the relevant long-run, or permanent, property income, which will be reflected far more reliably in the market valuation of assets. Put somewhat differently, the low coefficient of P does not imply a low marginal propensity to consume out of property income but merely a low propensity to consume out of transitory income. Correspondingly the extremely high coefficient of labor income in (3.3) is equally misleading, reflecting the fact that Y acts partly as a proxy for the permanent component of property income, $\bar{P}$.

One might be tempted to estimate the marginal propensity to consume with respect to permanent property income $\bar{P}$ by relying on the estimates of the coefficient of net worth in (3.3a) provided in Table 2, and on the relation

$$\bar{P} \simeq rA \quad \text{or} \quad A \simeq \frac{\bar{P}}{r}.$$

Following this reasoning, the coefficient of $\bar{P}$ in the consumption function would be given by $\dfrac{\alpha_3}{r}$, where r is the rate at which the market capitalizes the return from assets. If we are willing to approximate r with the average realized rate of return on assets, then, from the figures given in [3], we find that r was about 0.04 in the prewar period and somewhat lower (around 0.03) in more recent years.[27] Combining this estimate with our estimate of α_3, which is in the order of 0.06, we seem to be led to the conclusion that the marginal propensity to consume with respect to permanent property income $\dfrac{\alpha_3}{r}$, far from being low, is actually well above unity.

This result may appear preposterous if judged in terms of the standard Keynesian framework underlying (3.2), with its emphasis on the relation between flows. It is, however, possible to interpret this result in terms of the Modigliani-Brumberg framework. For, in this model, wealth affects consumption not only through the stream of income it generates but also directly through its market value which provides a source of purchasing power to iron out variations in income arising from transitory developments as well

---

[27] See, however, our comment below on the shortcomings of our estimate of P given in [3] as a measure of return on assets.

as from the normal life cycle. It is therefore not surprising that this model implies a marginal propensity to consume with respect to assets, α_3, larger than the rate of return r (cf. Table 1), an inference which, as we have just seen, is supported by empirical tests. It should be noted however that $\dfrac{\alpha_3}{r}$ should not be interpreted as the marginal propensity to consume with respect to permanent property income in the same sense in which $(\alpha_1 + \alpha_2)$ can be said to measure the propensity with respect to permanent nonproperty income, for it measures the *joint* effect on consumption of a change in property income, r constant, and of the accompanying change in assets. It is not possible to infer the two effects separately from knowledge of α_3 and of the average value of r. Although we cannot pursue this subject here, we wish to point out that the effect on C of a change in $\bar{P}$ will be quite different depending on the behavior of A and hence r, as $\bar{P}$ changes.

B. *Cyclical versus Long-Run Behavior of the Consumption-Income Ratio —Relation to the Duesenberry-Modigliani Consumption Function*

As is well known, one of the major difficulties encountered with the standard Keynesian consumption functions (3.1) or (3.2) lies in the constant term γ_0. This constant term is needed to account for the observed cyclical variability in the saving-income ratio, but it also implies a long-run tendency for the saving ratio to rise with income, which is contradicted by empirical findings. The lack of any positive association between income and the saving-income ratio in the long run, at least for the U.S. economy, was first uncovered by Kuznets, and has more recently been confirmed by the extensive investigation of Goldsmith [19], focusing on the years 1896–1949. In his summary recapitulation, he lists as the first item: "Long-term stability of aggregate personal saving at approximately one-eighth of income, and of national saving at approximately one-seventh."[28]

The consumption function proposed here is capable of accounting both for the long-run stability and the cyclical variability of the saving-income ratio. In order to exhibit its long-run properties, let us suppose that Y were to grow at a constant rate n, in which case Y^e can be taken as equal or proportional to Y. Suppose further that the rate of return on assets r is reasonably stable in time. Then the consumption function (1.6) implies that the income-net worth ratio, Y_t^*/A_{t-1} will tend to a constant h, related to the parameters of the consumption function by the equation:[29]

---

[28] Goldsmith [19, Vol. 1, p. 22.].

[29] Under the stated assumptions we have $Y_t^* = Y_t + P_t$, and $P_t = rA_{t-1}$. Hence, saving can be expressed as

(a) $$S_t = Y_t^* - C_t = Y_t + P_t - C_t = (1 - \alpha)Y_t^* - (\alpha_3 - \alpha r)A_{t-1}.$$

We also have $S_t = A_t - A_{t-1}$. (We disregard capital gains in this context, and in this context alone. This simplification seems to be justified for long-run analysis, but for a fuller

$$h = \frac{n + \alpha_3 - \alpha r}{1 - \alpha} \; ; \qquad \alpha = \alpha_1 + \alpha_2 . \qquad (3.5)$$

When the ratio $\dfrac{Y_t^*}{A_{t-1}}$ is in fact equal to h, then income and net worth grow at the same rate, n, and the saving-income ratio will be a constant given by:

$$\frac{S_t}{Y_t^*} = \frac{A_t - A_{t-1}}{A_{t-1}} \frac{A_{t-1}}{Y_t^*} = n \frac{1}{h} . \qquad (3.6)$$

Similarly, we find:

$$\frac{Y_t}{A_{t-1}} = \frac{Y_t^* - rA_{t-1}}{A_{t-1}} = h - r \qquad (3.7)$$

$$\frac{C_t}{Y_t} = \frac{Y_t^* - S_t}{A_{t-1}} \frac{A_{t-1}}{Y_t} = \frac{h - n}{h - r} . \qquad (3.8)$$

Thus the model implies that if income fluctuates around an exponential trend the income-net worth ratio will tend to fluctuate around a constant level h, and the saving-income ratio around a constant $\dfrac{n}{h}$.

The empirical estimates reported in Section II suggest that α is around 0.7, and α_3 close to 0.06. The average rate of return, r, is much more difficult to guess. If we are willing to rely on the ratio $\dfrac{P}{A_{t-1}}$ for this purpose, then r would be around or somewhat lower than 0.04. But this ratio is very likely to understate the true value for r, since the estimate of P given in [3] corresponds to the conventional definition of personal income and omits a number of items whose exclusion is appropriate for the standard Keynesian model but not for the Modigliani-Brumberg model. Among those items, the more important are imputed net rent on consumer durables and undistributed corporate profits.[30] These adjustments suggest an average value for r slightly over 0.04.

---

discussion of this problem, see Ando [2].) Substituting this definition for S_t in (a), dividing through by A_{t-1}, adding and subtracting n, and then rearranging terms, we obtain

$(b) \qquad \dfrac{A_t - A_{t-1}}{A_{t-1}} = n + (1 - \alpha)\left[\dfrac{Y_t^*}{A_{t-1}} - \dfrac{n + \alpha_3 - \alpha r}{1 - \alpha}\right].$

Comparison of (b) above with equation (3.5) shows that if Y_t^*/A_{t-1} were larger than h, the second term in the right-hand side would be positive, and hence net worth would grow at a rate larger than that of income, n, causing Y_t^*/A_{t-1} to fall toward h: and conversely if Y_t^*/A_{t-1} were smaller than h.

This argument is oversimplified and incomplete, particularly since it ignores the interaction between the behavior of consumers and the production process in the economy. A more complete analysis of this growth process is given in Ando [2].

[30] The rationale for including corporate saving in property income and personal saving is given in Modigliani and Miller [36].

If we further take for n, the rate of growth of income, a value in the order of 0.03, then from (3.6), (3.7), and (3.8) we obtain the following estimates for the various ratios under discussion: (*i*) total income to net worth, $h \simeq 0.2$; (*ii*) non-property income to net worth, $h - r \simeq 0.16$; (*iii*) saving to income, $\frac{n}{h} \simeq 0.15$.

It can be seen that the first two of the above figures are in fact close to the values around which the ratios

$$\frac{Y_t^*}{A_{t-1}} \quad \text{and} \quad \frac{Y_t}{A_{t-1}}$$

fluctuate according to the data given in [3] while the third, the saving-income ratio, is consistent with the findings of Goldsmith reported earlier.

Needless to say, these calculations are very crude and are given here primarily to bring out certain interesting testable implications of the consumption function discussed in this paper. Among these implications the long-run stability of the ratio of net worth to income is particularly significant, for it paves the way for an explanation of the historical stability of the capital-output ratio in terms of the supply of capital, thereby challenging the prevailing notion that the behavior of this ratio is explained by technological requirements [1] [2] [5] [29].

As for the cyclical implications of our model, we need only observe that at any given point in time net worth A_{t-1} is a given initial condition. Hence, retaining for the moment the assumption that $Y^e \simeq Y$, (1.6) implies that the aggregate consumption function for any given year is a straight line in the C-Y plane with slope α and intercept $\alpha_3 A_{t-1}$. It is shown in Figure 2 for the year 0 as the line labeled $\bar{C}_0$, and looks like the orthodox Keynesian version. Yet, it differs from the latter in one essential respect, namely, that its intercept will change in time as a result of the accumulation (or decumulation) of wealth through saving. As we have shown in preceding paragraphs, so long as income keeps rising on its exponential trend, the growth in net worth will shift the function in such a way that the observed consumption-income points will trace out the long-run consumption function (3.8) represented in our graph by the line $\bar{C}$ through the origin. This point is illustrated in Figure 2 for two years, 0 and 1. However, suppose that a cyclical disturbance caused income to fall short of Y_1, say to the level Y_1'. Then the consumption C_1' given by the short-run consumption function $\bar{C}_1$ implies a higher consumption-income ratio and a lower saving-income ratio.

Thus, cyclical swings in income from its long-run trend will cause swings in the saving-income ratio in the same direction,[31] especially since the

---

[31] This phenomenon will be further accentuated when we recognize the possibility that a cyclical fall in Y is likely to bring about a smaller change in Y^e. Also, because property income may be expected to fluctuate cyclically even more than labor income, the ratio of saving to total income will fluctuate even more than the ratio of saving to labor income. See footnote 30, equation (*a*).

position of the function will not change appreciably when income is cyclically depressed below its previous peak due to the small or negative saving that would prevail.[32] After income has recovered beyond the previous peak, it may for a while rise rapidly as it catches up with its trend, running ahead of the slowly adjusting wealth. In this phase we may observe points to the right of $\bar{C}$, and the corresponding high saving will tend to make A catch up with Y.

Fig. 2

CONSUMPTION INCOME RELATIONS: LONG-RUN AND SHORT-RUN

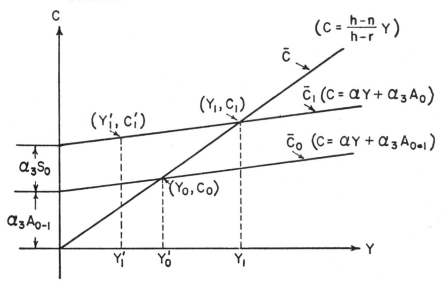

Thus the model advanced here may be expected to generate a behavior of consumption and saving which is very similar to that implied by the earlier Duesenberry-Modigliani type of hypothesis, in which consumption was expressed as a function of current income and the highest previous peak income (or consumption) [9] [30]. If we interpret the role of the highest previous income as that of a proxy for net worth, then the Duesenberry-Modigliani consumption function can be considered as providing a good empirical approximation to the consumption function discussed in this paper,

---

[32] Some downward shift of the consumption function might occur even in the absence of dissaving, if there is some downward revaluation of the market value of assets, as the depressed level of property income tends to bring about less favorable evaluation of the long-run prospects for return from assets.

Because of this dependence of the value of assets on property income, the statement made earlier to the effect that A_{t-1} can be taken as a given initial condition in the year t is only approximately true. Also the relation $\Delta A_t = S_t$ does not hold in the presence of capital gains and losses. Note however that what is relevant in the present connection is the change in the value of assets in terms of purchasing power over consumption goods and not the change in terms of money value, which may be considerably more severe.

and to this extent the empirical support provided for the Duesenberry-Modigliani type of hypothesis can also be considered as empirical support for the consumption function advanced here, and vice versa. At the same time the present model has the advantage that the hypotheses on which it rests are explicitly stated as specifications of the consumer's utility function. It is also analytically more convenient as a building block in models of economic growth and fluctuations, as we have endeavored to demonstrate in various contributions [1] [2] [3] [29] [31].[33]

APPENDIX

A. *Some Statistical Results for Earlier Years*

The following are the estimates obtained using data for 1900–28, excluding years 1917, 1918, and 1919. As stated in the text, the data used are very rough, and may not be compatible with the data for the period since 1929. The data and their derivation are described in Ando [2, App.], except for the adjustments needed for different treatments of the government sector. This adjustment is self-explanatory from the description given in [2]. The data presented in [2] are in turn based largely on [18] [19] [22] [27] and [42].

$$C = 0.755\,Y + 0.073A \qquad R^2 = 0.995 \qquad\qquad (a)$$
$$\quad (0.134) \quad (0.020) \qquad DW = 1.63$$

$$\Delta C = 0.731\Delta Y + 0.047\Delta A \qquad R^2 = 0.44 \qquad\qquad (b)$$
$$\quad (0.180) \quad\; (0.037) \qquad DW = 2.48$$

$$\frac{C}{Y} = 0.505 + 0.112\,\frac{A}{Y} \qquad R^2 = 0.51 \qquad\qquad (c)$$
$$\quad (0.144)\;\,(0.021) \qquad DW = 1.05$$

B. *Biases in Estimating the Consumption Function by Regression on Saving*

Suppose that true consumption c^* and true income y^* are related by a linear function (all variables being measured from their means),

$$c^* = \alpha y^* + \epsilon \qquad\qquad (a)$$

and measured income and measured consumption are related to their respective true values by

$$c = c^* + \eta \qquad\qquad (b)$$
$$y = y^* + \xi \qquad\qquad (c)$$

where ϵ, η, and ξ are random variables. For simplicity, let us assume that ϵ is

---

[33] On the other hand, because up-to-date estimates of wealth are not readily available, at least for the present, some variant of the Duesenberry-Modigliani model may well be more useful for short-run forecasting.

uncorrelated with η, and ξ; η and ξ are uncorrelated with c^* and y^*. We also have the definitions

$$s^* = y^* - c^* \tag{d}$$

$$s = y - c = y^* - c^* + \xi - \eta \tag{d'}$$

Using (a) and (d), we have

$$c^* = \frac{\alpha}{1 - \alpha} s^* + \frac{\epsilon}{1 - \alpha} \equiv \beta s^* + \epsilon'. \tag{e}$$

In order to concentrate first on the effect of errors of measurements, let us momentarily accept the unwarranted assumption that saving is equal to investment which in turn is truly exogenous. Under this assumption s^* can be taken as independent of ϵ' and therefore, if we could actually observe s^* and c^*, by regressing c^* on s^* we could secure an unbiased estimate of β from which we could in turn derive a consistent estimate of α. If, however, we estimate β by regressing c on s, then remembering that s is obtained as a residual from y and c, we obtain the estimate

$$\beta = \frac{\Sigma cs}{\Sigma s^2} = \frac{\Sigma (\beta s^* + \epsilon' + \eta)(s^* + \xi - \eta)}{\Sigma (s^* + \xi - \eta)^2} \tag{f}$$

$$= \frac{\beta \Sigma s^{*2} + \Sigma \eta(\xi - \eta)}{\Sigma s^{*2} + \Sigma (\xi - \eta)^2}.$$

The term $\Sigma \eta(\xi - \eta)$ arises from the fact that when there is a statistical error η in measuring consumption, there will be an error $-\eta$ in measuring saving, except in so far as this is offset by an error ξ in measuring income. This term will tend to be negative and introduces a downward bias into β. The term $\Sigma (\xi - \eta)^2$ in the denominator is the well-known result of an error of measurement of the independent variable, and it introduces an unambiguous bias towards zero into β.

However, as pointed out in the text, the assumption that personal saving is exogenous is completely unwarranted. In order to bring out the nature of the bias resulting from this misspecification, let us make the other extreme and equally unwarranted assumption that disposable income is truly exogenous. We can then regard y^* as independent of ϵ and by substituting (a) and (d) into (d') we find

$$s = s^* + \xi - \eta = (1 - \alpha)y^* - \epsilon + \xi - \eta. \tag{g}$$

Equation (f) is then replaced by

$$\beta = \frac{\alpha(1 - \alpha) \Sigma y^{*2} - \Sigma \epsilon^2 + \Sigma \eta(\xi - \eta)}{(1 - \alpha)^2 \Sigma y^{*2} + \Sigma \epsilon^2 + \Sigma (\xi - \eta)^2}. \tag{h}$$

The presence of the term $\Sigma \epsilon^2$ in both numerator and denominator is the result of the fact, discussed in the text, that when there is residual error ϵ in the consumption-income relationship, there will be residual error $-\epsilon$ in the saving-income relationship. Because of the signs, this effect, too, will bias β downward.

Since all the biases are downward and there is no offsetting upward bias of any significance, it is not surprising that recent applications of this approach [39] [43] lead in a number of cases to a negative estimate of the marginal propensity to consume.

REFERENCES

1. ANDO, A. *A Contribution to the Theory of Economic Fluctuations and Growth.* Unpublished doctoral dissertation, Carnegie Institute of Technology, 1959.

2. ———, "An Empirical Model of the U.S. Economic Growth: Exploratory Study in Applied Capital Theory," Conference on Income and Wealth, National Bureau of Economic Research (forthcoming).

3. ———, BROWN, E. C., KAREKEN, J., AND SOLOW, R. M. *Lags in Fiscal and Monetary Policy.* Monograph prepared for the Commission on Money and Credit (forthcoming).

4. ———, AND MODIGLIANI, F. "Growth, Fluctuations, and Stability," *Am. Econ. Rev., Proc.*, Vol. 49 (May, 1959), pp. 501–24.

5. BODKIN, R. "Windfall Income and Consumption," *Am. Econ. Rev.*, Vol. 49 (September, 1959), pp. 602–14.

6. BRUMBERG, R. E. "An Approximation to the Aggregate Saving Function," *Econ. Jour.*, Vol. 46 (March, 1956), pp. 66–72.

7. ———, *Utility Analysis and Aggregate Consumption Function: An Empirical Test and Its Meaning.* Unpublished doctoral dissertation, The Johns Hopkins University, 1953.

8. *Bulletin of the Oxford University Institute of Statistics*, Savings Behavior; A Symposium, Vol. 19 (2) (May, 1957), pp. 99–199.

9. DUESENBERRY, J. S. *Income, Savings, and the Theory of Consumer Behavior.* Cambridge: 1959.

10. DURBIN, J., AND WATSON, G. S. "Testing for Serial Correlation in Least Squares Regression, I and II," *Biometrika*, Vol. 37 (December, 1950), pp. 409–28; and *ibid.*, Vol. 38 (June, 1951), pp. 159–78.

11. EISNER, R. "The Permanent Income Hypothesis: Comment," *Am. Econ. Rev.*, Vol. 48 (December, 1958), pp. 972–89.

12. FISHER, M. R. "Exploration in Savings Behavior," *Bull. Oxford Univ. Inst. Stat.*, Vol. 18 (August, 1956), pp. 201–77.

13. FRANE, L., AND KLEIN, L. R. "The Estimation of Disposable Income by Distributive Shares," *Rev. Econ. Stat.*, Vol. 35 (November, 1943), pp. 333–37.

14. FRIEDMAN, M. "Comment on R. Bodkin's Windfall Income and Consumption,' in *Proceedings of the Conference on Consumption and Saving*, Vol. 2. Philadelphia: 1960.

15. ———, "The Concept of 'Horizon' in the Permanent Income Hypothesis," in *Proceedings of the Conference on Consumption and Saving*, Vol. 2. Philadelphia: 1960.

16. ———, *A Theory of the Consumption Function.* Princeton: 1957.

17. FRIEND, I, AND KRAVIS, I. "Consumption Patterns and Permanent Income," *Am. Econ. Rev. Proc.*, Vol. 47 (May, 1957), pp. 536–54.

18. GOLDSMITH, R. W. *The National Wealth of the United States in the Postwar Period*, National Bureau of Economic Research (forthcoming).

19. ———, *A Study of Saving in the United States.* Princeton: 1951.

20. HAMBURGER, W. "The Relation of Consumption to Wealth and the Wage Rate," *Econometrica*, Vol. 23 (January, 1955), pp. 1–17.

21. HOUTHAKKER, H. S. "The Permanent Income Hypothesis," *Am. Econ. Rev.*, Vol. 48 (June, 1958), pp. 396–404.

22. KENDRICK, M. S. *Productivity Trends in the United States.* London: 1960.

23. KEYNES, J. M. *General Theory of Employment, Interest, and Money.* London: 1937.

24. KLEIN, L. R. "Entrepreneurial Savings," in I. Friend and R. J. Jones (eds.), *Proceedings of the Conference on Consumption and Saving.* Philadephia: 1960.

25. KREININ, M. E. "Windfall Income and Consumption," *Am. Econ. Rev.*, Vol. 51 (June, 1961), pp. 310–24.

26. KUH, EDWIN, AND MEYER, J. R. "Correlation and Regression Estimates When the Data Are Ratios," *Econometrica*, Vol. 23 (October, 1955), pp, 400–16.

27. LEBERGOTT, S. "Earnings of Non-Farm Employees in the United States, 1890–1946," *Jour. Am. Stat. Assoc.*, Vol. 43 (March, 1948), pp. 74–93.

28. MINCER, J. "Employment and Consumption," *Rev. Econ. Stat.*, Vol. 42 (February, 1960), pp. 20–26.

29. MODIGLIANI, F. "Comment on 'A Survey of Some Theories of Income Distribution' by T. Scitovsky," in *Conference of Income and Wealth*, National Bureau of Economic Research (forthcoming).

30. ———, "Fluctuations in the Saving-Income Ratio: A Problem in Economic Forecasting," *Studies in Income and Wealth*, Vol. 11. National Bureau of Economic Research, New York: 1949.

31. ———, "Long-run Implications of Alternative Fiscal Policies and the Burden of the National Debt," *Econ. Jour.*, Vol. 71 (December, 1961), pp, 730–55.

32. ———, AND ANDO, A. "The 'Permanent Income' and the 'Life Cycle' Hypothesis of Saving Behavior: Comparison and Tests," in *Proceedings of the Conference on Consumption and Saving.* Vol. 2. Philadelphia: 1960.

33. ——— AND ———, "Test of the Life Cycle Hypothesis of Saving," *Bull. Oxford Univ. Inst. Stat.*, Vol. 19 (May, 1957), pp. 99–124.

34. ——— AND BRUMBERG, R. *Utility Analysis and Aggregate Consumption Functions: An Attempt at Integration*, unpublished.

35. ——— AND ———, "Utility Analysis and the Consumption Function: An Interpretation of Cross-section Data," in K. K. Kurihara (ed.), *Post-Keynesian Economics.* New Brunswick: 1954.

36. ——— AND MILLER, M. "Dividend Policy, Growth and the Valuation of Shares," *Jour. Bus.*, Vol. 34 (October, 1961), pp. 411–33.

37. PEARSON, K. "On a Form of Spurious Correlation Which May Arise When Indices Are Used in the Measurement of Organs," *Proc. Royal Soc. London*, 1897, Vol. 60, pp. 484–98.

38. SELTZER, L. H. *Interest as a Source of Personal Income and Tax Revenue*, National Bureau of Economic Research, New York: 1955.

39. SUITS, D. *The Determinants of Consumer Expenditure: A Review of Present Knowledge*, prepared for the Commission on Money and Credit (forthcoming).

40. THEIL, H. *Economic Forecasts and Policy.* Amsterdam: 1958.

41. ———, *Linear Aggregation of Economic Relations.* Amsterdam: 1954.

42. UNITED STATES BUREAU OF THE CENSUS, *Historical Statistics of the United States: Colonial Times to 1957.* Washington: 1960.

43. ZELLNER, A. "The Short-Run Consumption Function," *Econometrica*, Vol. 25 (October, 1957), pp. 552–67.

23

The Demand for Money: Some Theoretical and Empirical Results*[1]

By MILTON FRIEDMAN[†]

IN COUNTRIES experiencing a secular rise in real income per capita, the stock of money generally rises over long periods at a decidedly higher rate than does money income. Income velocity—the ratio of money income to the stock of money—therefore declines secularly as real income rises. During cycles, to judge from the United States, the only country for which a detailed analysis has been made, the stock of money generally rises during expansions at a lower rate than money income and either continues to rise during contractions or falls at a decidedly lower rate than money income. Income velocity therefore rises during cyclical expansions as real income rises and falls during cyclical contractions as real income falls—precisely the reverse of the secular relation between income and velocity.

These key facts about the secular and cyclical behavior of income velocity have been documented in a number of studies.[2] For the United States, Anna Schwartz and I have been able to document them more fully than has hitherto been possible, thanks to a new series on the stock of money that we have constructed which gives estimates at annual or semiannual dates from 1867 to 1907 and monthly thereafter. This fuller documentation does not, however, dispel the apparent contradiction between the secular and the cyclical behavior

* *Journal of Political Economy*, Vol. LXVII (August, 1959). Reprinted by courtesy of the *Journal of Political Economy*, the University of Chicago Press, and the author. Copyright 1959 by the University of Chicago.

† University of Chicago and National Bureau of Economic Research.

[1] This paper reports on part of a broader study being conducted at the National Bureau of Economic Research by Anna J. Schwartz and myself. I am indebted to Mrs. Schwartz for extensive assistance and numerous suggestions in connection with the present paper.

This paper has been approved for publication as a report of the National Bureau of Economic Research by the Director of Research and the Board of Directors of the National Bureau, in accordance with the resolution of the board governing National Bureau reports (see the *Annual Report of the National Bureau of Economic Research*). It is reprinted as No. 68 in the National Bureau's series of Occasional Papers.

[2] See in particular Richard T. Selden, "Monetary Velocity in the United States," in Milton Friedman (ed.), *Studies in the Quantity Theory of Money* (Chicago: University of Chicago Press, 1956), pp. 179–257; and Ernest Doblin, "The Ratio of Income to Money Supply: An International Survey," *Review of Economics and Statistics*, August, 1951, p. 201.

of income velocity. On the contrary, as the summary of our findings in the following section makes explicit, it reveals an additional contradiction or, rather, another aspect of the central contradiction.

Previous attempts to reconcile the secular and cyclical behavior of the velocity of circulation of money have concentrated on variables other than income, such as the rate of interest or the rate of change of prices. These attempts have been unsuccessful. While such other variables doubtless affect the quantity of money demanded and hence the velocity of circulation of money, most do not have a cyclical pattern that could explain the observed discrepancy. In any event, it seems dubious that their influence on velocity is sufficiently great to explain so large a discrepancy.

An alternative theoretical explanation of the discrepancy is suggested by the work I have done on consumption—a rather striking example of how work in one field can have important implications for work in another that has generally been regarded as only rather distantly related. This theoretical explanation, which concentrates on the meaning attached to "income" and to "prices," is presented in Sections II and III below and turns out to be susceptible of quantitative test. The quantitative evidence in Section IV is highly favorable. The result is both a fuller understanding of the observed behavior of velocity and a different emphasis in the theory of the demand for money.

One important feature of monetary behavior not accounted for by this explanation is the consistent tendency for actual cash balances, adjusted for trend, to lead at both peaks and troughs in general business. In Section V, a preliminary attempt is made to explore factors that might account for the discrepancy between desired cash balances as determined by income alone and actual cash balances. Finally, in Section VI, some broader implications of the results presented in this paper are explored.

I. A SUMMARY OF THE EMPIRICAL EVIDENCE FOR THE UNITED STATES

A full documentation of our findings about the secular and cyclical behavior of the stock of money and its relation to income and prices will be given in a nearly completed National Bureau of Economic Research monograph by Anna J. Schwartz and myself. For present purposes, a brief summary of a few of our findings will suffice.

A. Secular Behavior

1. Secular changes in the real stock of money per capita are highly correlated with secular changes in real income per capita. In order to study this relation, we have used average values over complete reference cycles as our elementary observations. For twenty cycles measured from trough to trough and covering the period from 1870 to 1954, the simple correlation between

the logarithm of the real stock of money per capita and the logarithm of real income per capita is 0.99, and the computed elasticity is 1.8.[3]

A 1 percent increase in real income per capita has therefore, on the average, been associated with a 1.8 percent increase in real cash balances per capita and hence with a 0.8 percent *decrease* in income velocity. If we interpret these results as reflecting movements along a stable demand relation, they imply that money is a "luxury" in the terminology of consumption theory. Because of the strong trend element in the two series correlated, the high correlation alone does not justify much confidence that the statistical regression is a valid estimate of a demand relation rather than the result of an accidental difference in trends. However, additional evidence from other sources leads us to believe that it can be so regarded.

We have investigated the influence of both rates of interest and rates of change of prices. In our experiments, the rate of interest had an effect in the direction to be expected from theoretical considerations but too small to be statistically significant. We have not as yet been able to isolate by correlation techniques any effect of the rate of change of prices, though a historical analysis persuades us that such an effect is present.

2. Over the nine decades that we have studied, there have been a number of long swings in money income. As a matter of arithmetic, these swings in money income can be attributed to movements in the nominal stock of money and in velocity. If this is done, it turns out that the swings in the stock of money are in the opposite direction from those in velocity and so much larger in amplitude that they dominate the movements in money income. As a result, the long swings in prices mirror faithfully the long swings in the stock of money per unit of output. These long swings are much more marked in money income and in the nominal stock of money than in real income and in the real stock of money, which is to say that the long swings are largely price swings.

B. Cyclical Behavior

1. The real stock of money, like real income, conforms positively to the cycle; that is, it tends to rise during expansions and to fall, or to rise at a less rapid rate, during contractions. However, the amplitude of the movement in the real stock of money is decidedly smaller than in real income. If we allow

---

[3] The corresponding figures for cycles measured from peak to peak are 0.99 and 1.7. In these and later correlations, "money" is defined as including currency held by the public, adjusted demand deposits, and time deposits in commercial banks. This total is available for the period from 1867 on, whereas the total exclusive of time deposits is not available until 1914. For other reasons supporting our definition see the NBER monograph now in preparation. For income, we have used Simon Kuznets' estimates of net national product adjusted for wartime periods to a concept approximating that underlying the current Department of Commerce estimates, and for prices, the deflator implicit in Kuznets' estimates of net national product in constant prices.

for secular trends, a 1 percent change in real income during a cycle is accompanied by a change in the real stock of money in the same direction of about one-fifth of 1 percent.

It follows that income velocity tends to rise during cyclical expansions when real income is rising and to fall during cyclical contractions when real income is falling—that is, to conform positively. So far as we can tell from data that are mostly annual, velocity reaches both its peak and its trough at roughly the same time as general economic activity does.

2. Cyclical movements in money income, like the long swings, can be attributed to movements in the nominal stock of money and in velocity. If this is done, it turns out that the movements in the stock of money and in velocity are in the same direction and of roughly equal magnitude, so that neither can be said to dominate the movements in money income.

3. Table 1 summarizes the size of the cyclical movements in the variables

TABLE 1*

CYCLICAL MOVEMENTS IN INCOME, MONEY STOCK, INCOME VELOCITY, AND PRICES: DIFFERENCE IN MONTHLY RATE OF CHANGE BETWEEN REFERENCE EXPANSION AND CONTRACTION, ANNUAL ANALYSIS, 1870–1954, EXCLUDING WAR CYCLES

| | Change per Month in Reference-Cycle Relatives during Reference | | Excess of Expansion over Contraction |
	Expansion (1)	Contraction (2)	Contraction (3)
Twelve mild depression cycles:			
Money income	0.64	−0.07	0.71
Money stock	0.55	0.28	0.27
Income velocity	0.08	−0.32	0.40
Implicit price deflator	0.12	−0.02	0.14
Real income	0.52	−0.05	0.57
Real stock of money	0.43	0.30	0.13
Six deep depression cycles:			
Money income	0.64	−0.97	1.61
Money stock	0.60	−0.28	0.88
Income velocity	0.02	−0.69	0.71
Implicit price deflator	0.16	−0.44	0.60
Real income	0.46	−0.53	0.99
Real stock of money	0.42	0.18	0.24

* The series were analyzed as described in A. F. Burns and W. C. Mitchell, *Measuring Business Cycles* (New York: National Bureau of Economic Research, 1947), pp. 197–202. Because of rounding, col. 3 sometimes disagrees with the difference between cols. 1 and 2. Deep depression cycles are 1870–78, 1891–94, 1904–8, 1919–21, 1927–32, and 1932–38. All others are mild depression cycles except for war cycles 1914–19 and 1938–46, which are excluded. The basis of classification is described in the NBER monograph on the money supply now in preparation. *Money income* is net national product at current prices, preliminary estimates by Simon Kuznets, prepared for use in the NBER study of long-term trends in capital formation and financing in the United States. Variant III (from 1929 based on estimates of commodity flow and services prepared by the Department of Commerce). *Money stock* is averaged to center on June 30 from data in the money monograph just mentioned. *Income velocity* is money income divided annually by money stock. *Implicit price deflator* is money income divided by real income. *Real income* is net national product, 1929 prices, Variant III from the same source as money income. *Real stock of money* is money stock divided by the implicit price deflator.

used in the analysis, where the size of cyclical movement is measured by the excess of the rate of change per month during cyclical expansions over that during cyclical contractions.

C. The Contrast

These findings are clearly in sharp contrast. Over long periods, *real* income and velocity tend to move in opposite directions; over reference cycles, in the same direction. Over long periods, changes in the nominal stock of money dominate, at least in a statistical sense, the swings in *money* income, and the inverse movements in velocity are of minor quantitative importance; over reference cycles, changes in velocity are in the same direction as changes in the nominal stock of money and are comparable in quantitative importance in accounting for changes in money income. I turn to an attempted reconciliation.

II. A SUGGESTED EXPLANATION

It is important to note at the outset an essential difference between the determinants of the nominal stock of money, on the one hand, and the real stock of money, on the other. The nominal stock of money is determined in the first instance by the monetary authorities or institutions and cannot be altered by the non-bank holders of money. The real stock of money is determined in the first instance by the holders of money.

This distinction is sharpest and least ambiguous in a hypothetical society in which money consists exclusively of a purely fiduciary currency issued by a single money-creating authority at its discretion. The nominal number of units of money is then whatever amount this authority creates. Holders of money cannot alter this amount directly. But they can make the real amount of money anything that in the aggregate they want to. If they want to hold a relatively small real quantity of money, they will individually seek to reduce their nominal cash balances by increasing expenditures. This will not alter the nominal stock of money to be held—if some individuals succeed in reducing their nominal cash balances, it will only be by transferring them to others. But it will raise the flow of expenditures and hence money income and prices and thereby reduce the real quantity of money to the desired level. Conversely, if they want to hold a relatively large real quantity of money, they will individually seek to increase their nominal cash balances. They cannot, in the aggregate, succeed in doing so. However, in the attempt; they will lower the nominal flow of expenditures, and hence money income and prices, and so raise the real quantity of money. Given the level of real income, the ratio of income to the stock of money, or income velocity, is uniquely determined by the real stock of money. Consequently, these comments apply also to income velocity. It, too, is determined by the holders of money, or, to put it differently, it is a reflection of their decisions about the real quantity of money that they desire to hold. We can therefore speak more or less interchangeably about decisions of holders of money to change their real stock of money or to change the ratio of the flow of income to the stock of money.

The situation is more complicated for the monetary arrangements that actually prevailed over the period which our data cover. During part of the period, when the United States was on an effective gold standard, an attempt by holders of money to reduce their cash balances relative to the flow of income raised domestic prices, thereby discouraging exports and encouraging imports, and so tended to increase the outflow of gold or reduce its inflow. In addition, the rise in domestic prices raised, among other things, the cost of producing gold and hence discouraged gold production. Both effects operated to reduce the nominal supply of money. Conversely, an attempt by holders of money to increase their cash balances relative to the flow of income tended to increase the nominal supply of money through the same channels. These effects still occur but can be and typically are offset by Federal Reserve action.

Throughout the period, more complicated reactions operated on the commercial banking system, sometimes in perverse fashion. For example, an attempt by holders of money to reduce cash balances relative to income tended to raise income and prices, thus promoting an expansionary atmosphere in which banks were generally willing to operate on a slenderer margin of liquidity. The result was an increase rather than a reduction in the nominal supply of money. Similarly, changes in the demand for money had effects on security prices and interest rates that affected the amount of money supplied by the banking system. And there were further effects on the actions of the Federal Reserve System for the period since 1914.

There were also indirect effects running in the opposite direction, from changes in the conditions of supply of money to the nominal quantity of money demanded. If, for whatever reason, money-creating institutions expanded the nominal quantity of money, this could have effects, at least in the first instance, on rates of interest and so on the quantity of money demanded, and perhaps also on money income and real income.

Despite these qualifications, all of which would have to be taken into account in a complete analysis, it seems useful to regard the nominal quantity of money as determined primarily by conditions of supply, and the real quantity of money and the income velocity of money as determined primarily by conditions of demand. This implies that we should examine the demand side for an initial interpretation of the observed behavior of velocity.

Along these lines, the changes in the real stock of money and in the income velocity of circulation reflect either (a) shifts along a relatively fixed demand schedule for money produced by changes in the variables entering into that schedule; (b) changes in the demand schedule itself; or (c) temporary departures from the schedule, that is, frictions that make the actual stock of money depart from the desired stock of money. The rest of this paper is an attempt to see to what extent we can reconcile the secular and cyclical behavior of velocity in terms of *a* alone without bringing in the more complicated phenomena that would be involved in *b* and *c*.

One way to do so would be to regard the cyclical changes in velocity as reflecting the influence of variables other than income. In order for this explanation to be satisfactory, these other variables would have to exert an influence opposite to that of income and also be sufficiently potent to dominate the movement of velocity. Our secular results render this implausible, for we there found that income appeared to be the dominant variable affecting the demand for real cash balances. Moreover, the other variables that come first to mind are interest rates, and these display cyclical patterns that seem most unlikely to account for the sizable, highly consistent, and roughly synchronous cyclical pattern in velocity. Long-term corporate interest rates fairly regularly reached their trough in mid-expansion and their peak in mid-contraction prior to World War I. Since then, the pattern is less regular and is characterized by shorter lags. Rates on short-term commercial paper also tend to lag at peaks and troughs, though by a briefer interval, and the lag has similarly shortened since 1921. Call-money rates come closer to being synchronous with the cycle, and this is true also of yields on long- and short-term government obligations for the six cycles for which they are available. Of the rates we have examined these are the only ones that have anything like the right timing pattern to account for the synchronous pattern in velocity. However, neither call-money rates nor government bond yields have been highly consistent in behavior from cycle to cycle. Even if they had been, it seems dubious that the effects of changes in these particular rates, or other unrecorded rates like them, would be sufficiently more important cyclically than secularly to offset the effects of countermovements both in other rates and in income. Furthermore, earlier studies that have attempted to explain velocity movements in these terms have had only limited success.[4]

A very different way to reconcile the cyclical and secular behavior of velocity is to regard the statistical magnitude called "real income" as corresponding to a different theoretical construct in the cyclical than in the secular analysis. This possibility was suggested by my work on consumption. In that field, too, it will be recalled, there is an apparent conflict between empirical findings for short periods and long periods: cross-section data for individual years suggest that the average propensity to consume is lower at high-income levels than at low-income levels; yet aggregate time-series data covering a long period reveal no secular decline in the average propensity to consume with a rise in income. It turned out that this conflict could be reconciled by distinguishing between "measured" income, the figure recorded by statisticians, and "permanent" income, a longer-term concept to which individuals are regarded as adjusting their consumption.[5]

---

[4] E.g., see Selden, *op. cit.*, pp. 195–202.

[5] See my *A Theory of the Consumption Function* (a publication of the National Bureau of Economic Research) (Princeton: Princeton University Press, 1957).

According to the permanent income hypothesis, when a consumer unit experiences a transitory increment of income, that is, when its measured income exceeds its permanent income, this transitory component is added to its assets (perhaps in the form of durable consumer goods) or used to reduce its liabilities rather than spent on consumption. Conversely, when it experiences a transitory decrement of income, it nonetheless adjusts consumption to permanent income, financing any excess over measured income by drawing down assets or increasing liabilities.

This theory of consumption behavior is directly applicable to that part of the stock of money held by consumer units rather than by business enterprises. The problem is how to interpret money holding. Much of the theoretical literature on "motives" for holding money suggests interpreting money holdings as one of the balance-sheet items that act as shock absorbers for transitory components of income; as an asset item that is increased temporarily when the transitory component is positive and that is drawn down, if necessary, to finance consumption when the transitory component is negative.

This interpretation may be valid for very short time periods. However, if it were valid for periods as long as a business cycle, it would produce a cyclical behavior of velocity precisely the opposite of the observed behavior. Measured income presumably exceeds permanent income at cyclical peaks and falls short of permanent income at cyclical troughs. Hence cash balances would be drawn down abnormally at troughs and built up abnormally at peaks. In consequence, cash balances would fluctuate more widely over the cycle than income, and velocity would conform inversely to the cycle, falling during expansions and rising during contractions, whereas in fact it conforms positively.

An alternative is to interpret money as a durable consumer good held for the services it renders and yielding a flow of services proportional to the stock, which implies that the shock-absorber function is performed by other items in the balance sheet, such as the stock of durable goods, consumer credit outstanding, personal debt, and perhaps securities held. On this interpretation, the quantity of money demanded, like the quantity of consumption services in general, is adapted not to measured income but to permanent income. This interpretation is consistent with our secular results. The income figure we used in obtaining these is an average value over a cycle, which may be regarded as a closer approximation to permanent income than an annual value. In any case, the long time period covered assures that the movements in money are dominated by the movements in the permanent component of income.[6] For the cyclical analysis, permanent income need not itself be stable over a cycle. It may well rise during expansions and fall during contractions. Presumably, however, it will rise less than measured income

---

[6] *Ibid.*, pp. 125–29.

during expansions and fall less during contractions. Hence, if money holdings were adapted to permanent income, they might rise and fall more than in proportion to permanent income, as is required by our secular results, yet less than in proportion to measured income, as is required by our cyclical results.

To put the matter differently, suppose that the demand for real cash balances were determined entirely by real permanent income according to the relation estimated in the secular analysis and that actual balances throughout equaled desired balances. Velocity would then fall during expansions and rise (or fall at a smaller rate) during contractions, *provided* that it was computed by dividing *permanent income* by the stock of money. But the numbers we have been calling "velocity" were not computed in this way; they were computed by dividing measured income by the stock of money. Such a *measured* velocity would tend to be lower than what we may call *permanent* velocity at troughs, because measured income is then lower than permanent income and would tend to be higher at peaks, because measured income is then higher than permanent income. Measured velocity might therefore conform positively to the cycle, even though permanent velocity conformed inversely.

These comments apply explicitly only to consumer cash balances. However, they can readily be extended to business cash balances. Businesses hold cash as a productive resource. The question is whether cash is a resource like inventories, in which case it might be expected to fluctuate more over the cycle than current production, or like fixed capital, in which case it might be expected to fluctuate less and to be adapted to the longer-term level of production at which a firm plans to operate. This latter possibility involves a concept analogous to that of permanent income. If the observed positive cyclical conformity of velocity reflects wider movements in income than in both business holdings and consumer holdings, as seems likely in view of the changing importance of these two components and the consistent behavior of velocity, the answer must be that cash balances are analogous to fixed capital rather than to inventories and that some other assets or liabilities serve as shock-absorbers for business as for consumers.

The distinction between permanent and measured income can rationalize the observed cyclical behavior of income velocity in terms of a movement along a stable demand curve. It cannot by itself easily rationalize the behavior of real cash balances. Our secular analysis implies that real cash balances should conform positively to the cycle with an amplitude nearly twice that of permanent real income. Observed real cash balances do conform positively, but their amplitude, at any rate for cycles containing mild contractions, is so small that it seems implausible to regard it as larger than that in permanent real income. Put differently, it would take only very moderate changes in the index of prices, well within the margin of error in such indexes, to convert the positive conformity into inverted conformity.

The resolution is straightforward. We have not yet carried our logic far enough. If applied to both money income and real income, the distinction between measured and permanent income implies a corresponding distinction for prices. To put the matter in terms of economics rather than arithmetic, our analysis suggests that holders of cash balances determine the amount to hold in light of their longer-term income position rather than their momentary receipts—this is the justification for distinguishing measured from permanent income. By the same token, they may be expected to determine the amount of cash balances to hold in light of longer-term price movements—permanent prices, as it were—rather than current or measured prices. Suppose, for example, prices were to double permanently or, alternatively, to double for day X only and then return to their initial level and that this behavior was correctly anticipated by holders of money. Holders of money would hardly want to hold the same nominal cash balances on day X in these two cases, even though prices were the same on that day. More generally, whatever the motives for holding cash balances, they are held and are expected to be held for a sizable and indefinite period of time. Holders of money presumably judge the "real" amount of cash balances in terms of the quantity of goods and services to which the balances are equivalent, not at any given moment of time, but over a sizable and indefinite period; that is, they evaluate them in terms of "expected" or "permanent" prices, not in terms of the current price level. This consideration does not, of course, rule out some adjustment to temporary movements in prices. Such movements offer opportunities of profit from shifting wealth from cash to other forms of assets and conversely, and they may affect people's expectations about future price levels. Like "permanent income," the "permanent" price level need not be—and presumably is not—constant over time; it departs from the current price level in having a smoother and less fluctuating pattern in time but need not go to the extreme of displaying no fluctuations.

On this view, the current price level would presumably fall short of the permanent price level at troughs and exceed it at peaks of cycles; hence measured real cash balances would tend to be larger than permanent real cash balances at troughs and smaller at peaks. It follows that measured real cash balances would show a smaller cyclical movement than permanent real cash balances and, indeed, might conform inversely to the cycle, even though permanent real cash balances conformed positively.

III. A SYMBOLIC RESTATEMENT

The distinction between permanent and measured magnitudes can thus reconcile the qualitative behavior during reference cycles of both measured velocity—its tendency to conform positively—and measured real cash balances—its tendency to show an exceedingly mild cyclical movement—with their behavior over secular periods. The crucial question remains whether it not only can reconcile the qualitative behavior but does in fact rationalize the quantitative behavior of these magnitudes. After all, an interpretation in terms of interest rates can also rationalize the qualitative results; we reject it because it appears likely to be contradicted on a more detailed quantitative level.

It will facilitate such a quantitative test to restate symbolically and more precisely the explanation just presented. Let

Y be measured aggregate income in nominal terms;

P be measured price level;

M be aggregate stock of money in nominal terms, measured and permanent being taken throughout as identical;

N be population, measured and permanent being taken as identical;

Y_p, P_p be permanent nominal aggregate income and permanent price level, respectively;

$y = \dfrac{Y}{P}$ be measured aggregate income in real terms;

$y_p = \dfrac{Y_p}{P_p}$ be permanent aggregate income in real terms;

$m = \dfrac{M}{P}$ be measured aggregate stock of money in real terms;

$m_p = \dfrac{M}{P_p}$ be permanent aggregate stock of money in real terms;

$V = \dfrac{Y}{M} = \dfrac{y}{m}$ be measured velocity;

$V_p = \dfrac{Y_p}{M} = \dfrac{y_p}{m_p}$ be permanent velocity.

In these symbols, the demand equation fitted to the secular data can be written thus:

$$\frac{M}{NP_p} = \gamma \left(\frac{Y_p}{NP_p} \right)^{\delta}, \qquad (1)$$

which expresses permanent real balances per capita as a function of permanent real income per capita, or in the equivalent form,

$$m_p = \gamma N \left(\frac{y_p}{N} \right)^{\delta} = \gamma N^{1-\delta} y_p^{\delta}, \qquad (2)$$

which expresses aggregate permanent real balances as a function of aggregate permanent real income and population, where γ and δ are parameters and δ was estimated to be approximately 1.8.[7]

By definition,

$$m = \frac{M}{P} = \frac{M}{P_p}\frac{P_p}{P} = \frac{P_p}{P}\,m_p,\tag{3}$$

so that still a third form of the demand equation is

$$m = \frac{P_p}{P}\,\gamma N^{1-\delta}y_p^{\delta},\tag{4}$$

which expresses aggregate measured real balances as a function of aggregate permanent real income, population, and permanent and measured prices.

This relation can also be expressed in terms of velocity. By definition, $V_p = y_p/m_p$. Divide y_p successively by the two sides of equation (2). This gives

$$V_p = \frac{y_p}{m_p} = \frac{1}{\gamma}\,N^{\delta-1}y_p^{1-\delta} = \frac{1}{\gamma}\left(\frac{y_p}{N}\right)^{1-\delta}\tag{5}$$

By definition,

$$V = \frac{Y}{M} = \frac{Y}{Y_p}\frac{Y_p}{M} = \frac{Y}{Y_p}\,V_p,\tag{6}$$

so that

$$V = \frac{Y}{Y_p}\frac{1}{\gamma}\left(\frac{y_p}{N}\right)^{1-\delta}\tag{7}$$

In interpreting equations (1), (2), (4), (5), and (7), it should be borne in mind that they will not, of course, be satisfied precisely by observed data. In consequence, at a later stage, I shall want to distinguish between observed values of, for example, measured velocity and the value estimated from, say, equation (7).

IV. TESTS OF THE EXPLANATION

It has so far been sufficient to suppose only that the permanent magnitudes introduced—permanent income and permanent prices—fluctuate less over the cycle than the corresponding measured magnitudes. We can clearly go farther and ask how much less the permanent magnitudes must fluctuate in order to account for the quantitative, as well as the qualitative, average behavior of velocity and real cash balances. The answer may provide some

---

[7] The basic analysis holds, of course, whatever the precise form of the demand equation for money. I use this particular form for simplicity and because it gave a satisfactory fit to the available evidence. The whole analysis could, however, be restated in terms of a generalized demand function whose form was unspecified.

internal evidence on the plausibility of the suggested explanation and will also provide a starting point for bringing external evidence to bear.

Consider the data for the mild depression cycles shown in Table 1 and neglect the mild cyclical movements in population, so that aggregate and per capita values can be regarded as interchangeable. If measured and permanent magnitudes were treated as identical, the income elasticity of 1.8 computed from the secular data would convert the 0.57 cyclical movement in real income into a movement of 1.03 in *real* cash balances demanded. The movement of 0.14 in the implicit price index would, in turn, convert this into a movement of 1.17 in *money* cash balances demanded. The actual movement in cash balances is 0.27, or 23 percent as large. Hence, to reconcile the secular and cyclical results, the cyclical movements in permanent income and permanent prices would each have to be 23 percent of those in measured income and measured prices—a result that seems not implausible. For deep depression cycles, the corresponding figure turns out to be 37 percent, which is equally plausible. Moreover, it seems eminently reasonable that this figure should be larger for deep, than for mild, depression cycles, since the deep depression cycles are longer on the average than the mild depression cycles.[8]

---

[8] Let $\dot{M}$ and $\dot{P}$ be the cyclical movements as measured in the final column of Table 1 in the nominal stock of money and in measured prices; let $\dot{m}_p$ and $\dot{P}_p$ be the cyclical movements in permanent real balances and permanent prices. Then, to a first approximation,

$$\dot{M} = \dot{m}_p + \dot{P}_p, \tag{i}$$

since the stock of money is the product of permanent real cash balances and the permanent price level. Using the demand equation (2), we get

$$\dot{m} = 1.8\dot{y}_p, \tag{ii}$$

where $\dot{y}_p$ is the cyclical movement in permanent real income (recall that we are neglecting any cyclical movement in population, so $\dot{y}_p$ also equals the movement in permanent real per capita income).
Let

$$\dot{y}_p = k\dot{y}, \tag{iii}$$

$$\dot{P}_p = k'\dot{P}, \tag{iv}$$

where $\dot{y}$ is the cyclical movement in measured real income and k and k' are unspecified constants to be determined. Substituting equations (ii), (iii), and (iv) in equation (i) gives

$$\dot{M} = 1.8k\dot{y} + k'\dot{P}. \tag{v}$$

At first glance, it seems possible to derive both k and k' from one set of data by deriving a similar equation starting with an identity like (i) expressing measured velocity in terms of permanent velocity. However, the resulting equation is identical with eq. (v), thanks to the definitional relations connecting velocity, money, and income.

The calculations in the text implicitly assume that $k = k'$ in eq. (v). Separate estimates for k and k' require two sets of data. One possibility is to assume that k and k' differ but that each is the same for mild and for deep depression cycles, an assumption that seems less plausible than the one made in the text that $k = k'$. This calculation yields an estimate of 0.11 for k and 1.15 for k'. The value for k' contradicts the concepts of permanent and measured prices that underlie the analysis.

Of course, this test of intuitive plausibility is a weak one. To get a stronger test, we must introduce some independent evidence on the relation of permanent to measured magnitudes. One source of such evidence is the work on consumption that suggested the explanation under test. In deriving a consumption function from aggregate time-series data, I concluded that an *estimate* of permanent income—which I called "expected" income to distinguish it from the theoretical concept—was given by

$$y_p(T) = \beta \int_{-\infty}^{T} e^{(\beta - \alpha)(t - T)} y(t)\, dt. \tag{8}$$

In words, an estimate of expected income at time T is given by a weighted average of past incomes, adjusted for secular growth at the rate of α percent per year, the weights declining exponentially and being equal to $e^{\beta(t - T)}$, where t is the time of the observation being weighted. The numerical value of β was estimated to be 0.4; of α, 0.02.[9] It is by no means necessary that the concept of permanent income that is relevant in determining total consumption expenditures should also be the one that is relevant in determining cash balances.[10] But it would not be at all surprising if it were. On the assumption that it is, we can get independent estimates of the percentages cited in the previous paragraph by computing estimates of permanent real income and permanent prices from the corresponding observed annual series, using the weighting pattern just described.

The results of these computations are summarized in columns 1, 2, and 3 of Table 2.[11] The agreement between the estimates in column 3 so obtained and the estimates constructed above from internal evidence alone is very good

---

[9] Friedman, *A Theory of the Consumption Function*, pp. 146–47.

[10] See *ibid.*, pp. 150–51.

[11] These results at first seemed to me relevant also to the choice between the two alternative assumptions used above—the one in the text that $k = k'$ and the one noted in footnote 8, that $k \neq k'$ but that k is the same for mild and deep depression cycles and so is k'. On this issue, the result is unambiguous. The entries in col. 3 clearly speak for the first assumption.

However, James Ford has pointed out to me that this result is largely a consequence of an assumption made in estimating permanent income and prices, namely, the use of the same value of β for both. There is no independent empirical evidence for this assumption, and hence results based on it can give no independent evidence for the essentially equivalent assumption that $k = k'$.

For the special case in which the measured magnitude is given by a sine curve, the relative amplitude of a permanent and a measured magnitude when the permanent is estimated by a weighted average of the measured is determined entirely by the value of β and the duration of the cycle. For $\beta = 0.4$ and a cycle 43 months in length, which is the average length of the mild depression cycles, the relative amplitude for the sine curve is 0.22. For $\beta = 0.4$ and a cycle 47.5 months in length, the average length of the deep depression cycles, the relative amplitude for the sine curve is 0.25. These results are fairly similar to the computed values in Table 2. They differ enough, however, to suggest that the departure from a sine curve affects the results appreciably.

I am indebted to James Ford for these calculations.

TABLE 2*

TWO ESTIMATES OF CYCLICAL MOVEMENTS OF PERMANENT REAL INCOME AND
PRICES AS PERCENTAGES OF THOSE OF MEASURED REAL INCOME AND
PRICES, REFERENCE CYCLES 1870–1954, EXCLUDING WAR CYCLES

	Excess of Change per Month in Reference-Cycle Relatives during Reference Expansion over That during Reference Contraction		Permanent as Percentage of Measured	
	Permanent Magnitude (1)	Measured Magnitude (2)	Permanent Estimated Separately (3)	Ratio Estimated from Money Equations (4)
Twelve mild depression cycles:				
Real income	0.11	0.57	19	23
Prices	0.02	0.14	16	23
Six deep depression cycles:				
Real income	0.29	0.99	29	37
Prices	0.18	0.60	30	37

* The sources for the columns are as follows (cycles grouped as in Table 1):
1. Permanent real income and permanent prices were estimated as described in the text, using Kuznets' data (see note to Table 1). These data begin in 1869. To obtain an estimate of the permanent magnitude in 1869, measured figures covering the years 1858–69 are required, the weights assigned declining exponentially. Measured figures were therefore extrapolated: for real income by assuming a constant rate of growth of 3.5 percent per year; for implicit prices by assuming that in each of the years 1858–68 they bore the same relation to the wholesale price index as in 1869.
2. Table 1, col. 3.
3. Column 1 divided by col. 2, the figures in each case being carried to an additional place.
4. Values from Table 1, col. 3, were substituted in the expression $M/(1.82\,\dot{y} + \dot{p})$, where M is money stock, y is real income, P is implicit price deflator, and the dot on top means "excess of change per month in reference-cycle relatives during reference expansion over that during reference contraction."

—the two differ by only 15–30 percent, even though they are based on independent bodies of data and even though the weights used in estimating the permanent magnitudes directly were derived for another purpose and rest on still other data. Moreover, the discrepancy is consistent; the difference between deep and mild depression cycles is in the same direction and of roughly the same magnitudes for both columns.

These results are sufficiently encouraging to justify going beyond this indirect test and seeing how far our interpretation is consistent not only with the size of the cyclical movement in cash balances and measured velocity but also with their entire cyclical patterns and not only on the average but also cycle by cycle.

In order to perform this test on a fully consistent basis, we first recomputed the secular demand equation, using as the independent variable the cycle averages of estimated permanent income rather than measured income. This substitution slightly raised the correlation coefficient, thus giving a minor bit of additional evidence in favor of the permanent income interpretation. It also raised slightly the estimated elasticity of demand, but not by enough to change the numerical value to the number of significant figures given above.

The resulting calculated equation for nominal cash balances is

$$M^* = (0.00323) \left(\frac{y_p}{N}\right)^{1.810} NP_p, \tag{9}$$

and, for measured velocity,

$$V^* = \frac{1}{0.00323} \left(\frac{y_p}{N}\right)^{-0.810} \frac{Y}{Y_p}, \tag{10}$$

where the asterisks are used to indicate values computed from the equation rather than directly observed. These equations, it will be recalled, were estimated from average values over whole reference cycles.[12]

From these equations, one can estimate for each year separately, from the corresponding annual data, desired cash balances and the value of measured velocity that would be observed if actual cash balances equaled desired balances as so estimated. I shall call these "computed cash balances" and "computed measured velocity."[13]

The estimates of computed measured velocity are plotted in Chart 1, along with observed measured velocity. In judging this figure, it should be borne in mind that the computed velocities were not obtained by trying to fit these observed velocities directly. They were obtained from a correlation for forty-one overlapping cycle bases—averages of groups of years varying in number from two to seven—plus a formula for estimating permanent income derived from an analysis of the relation of consumption expenditures to income plus a theoretical linkage between these two, summarized in equations (9) and (10). The high correlation between the cycle bases insures a close connection

---

[12] The numerical values given were computed from combined data for trough-to-trough and peak-to-peak averages. However, separate regressions for each set of averages are almost identical.

[13] To make these calculations, estimates of Y, Y_p, y_p, P_p and N are needed. Measured money income, Y, was taken to be Kuznets' annual net national product in current prices adjusted for war-time periods; Y_p was computed by applying eq. (8) to this same series, except for a minor adjustment in level; y_p, by applying eq. (8) to Kuznets' net national product in constant prices similarly adjusted, and again with a minor adjustment in level; P_p by applying eq. (8) to the price index implicit in computing net national product in constant prices; and N was taken as the mid-year population of the United States as estimated by the Census.

Equation (8) with $\beta = 0.40$ and $\alpha = 0.02$ implies that expected income is 1.05 times the weighted average of actual income, where the weights are the declining exponential weights inside the integral of eq. (8), adjusted to sum to unity. When permanent net national product per capita in constant prices was computed in this way, it turned out that the geometric mean of the ratios of the cycle bases of real measured net national product per capita to the cycle bases of permanent net national product in constant prices so computed was 1.057. This factor of 1.057 was used to adjust the level of the latter series rather than the 1.05 strictly called for by eq. (8) and was used also for permanent net national product in current prices. The logical implication of employing the same multiple for net national product in constant and current prices is that α was treated as zero for prices alone. None of these adjustments is of any moment for the present analysis, since they affect only the level of the series and hence all cancel out when cycle relatives are computed.

between the longer-term movements in computed and measured velocity; in this respect, Chart 1 is simply a repetition in a different form of the secular finding. What is added by this chart is the relation between year-to-year movements. The secular results in no way insure that these will correspond; still, if anything, the computed velocity series mirrors the year-to-year cycles in observed velocity even more faithfully than it does the longer-term changes.

In order to isolate the cyclical aspect of the analysis, we have computed reference-cycle patterns of computed measured velocity and computed cash balances, thereby eliminating entirely the part of Chart 1 that repeats the

CHART 1

OBSERVED AND COMPUTED MEASURED VELOCITY, ANNUALLY, 1869–1957

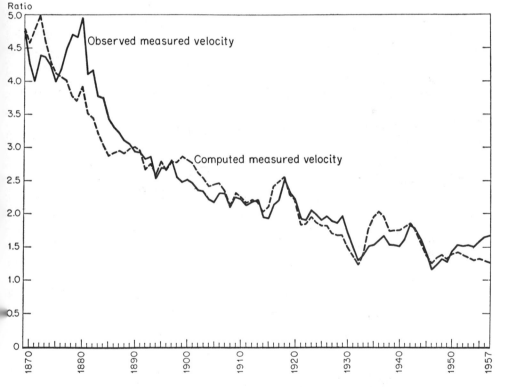

secular finding. Chart 2 gives the reference-cycle patterns of computed and observed measured velocity cycle by cycle, and Chart 3 gives average patterns for the mild and deep depression cycles, for both cash balances and measured velocity. It is clear from these that my interpretation accounts for the bulk of the fluctuations in observed measured velocity. The average pattern of computed measured velocity duplicates almost perfectly that for observed measured velocity for the mild depression cycles and corresponds very closely to that for the deep depression cycles. The cycle-by-cycle patterns demonstrate

CHART 2
Observed and Computed Measured Velocity, Reference-Cycle Patterns, 1870–1954

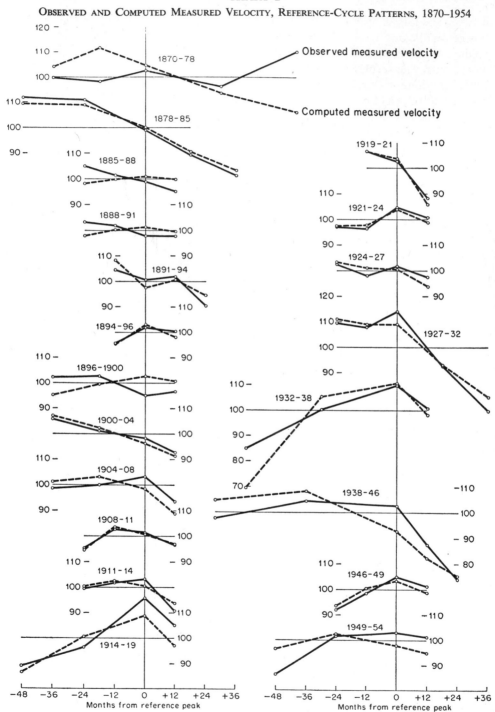

NOTE: These are reference-cycle relatives computed in the course of the cyclical analysis of the data shown in Chart 1 (see A. F. Burns and W. C. Mitchell, *Measuring Business Cycles* [New York: National Bureau of Economic Research, 1946], pp. 197–202).

that this coincidence is not simply in the averages. This closeness might reflect the use of the same values of measured income in both the observed and the computed velocities, in which case it could be regarded as largely spurious. The cash-balance patterns are included in Chart 3 to test this possibility. They demonstrate that this purely statistical interpretation of the findings is not valid. The cash-balance patterns agree about as closely as the velocity patterns.

CHART 3

OBSERVED AND COMPUTED MONEY STOCK AND MEASURED VELOCITY, AVERAGE REFERENCE-
CYCLE PATTERNS, MILD AND DEEP DEPRESSION CYCLES, 1870–1954

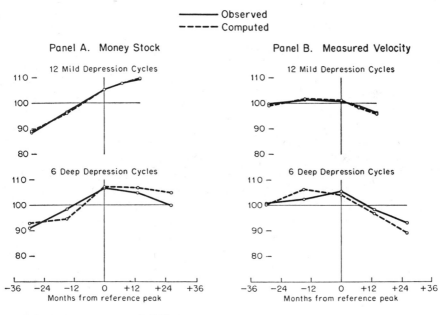

NOTE: Cycles are grouped as in Table 1.

These results give strong support to the view that cyclical movements in velocity largely reflect movements along a stable demand curve for money and that the apparent discrepancy between the secular and the cyclical results reflects a divergence between measures of income and of prices constructed by statisticians for short periods and the magnitudes to which holders of money adjust their cash balances.

V. LIMITATIONS OF THE EXPLANATION

Important though this explanation is, it cannot be the whole of the story, since it fails to account for some of the most important of our findings about the behavior of money balances. If the desired real stock of money were determined entirely by permanent real income and if the desired stock were always equal to the actual stock, then the actual real stock (computed in terms of permanent prices) would have a cyclical pattern that duplicated the pattern of permanent real income except for amplitude. Now our evidence suggests that permanent real income conforms positively to the cycle and is either synchronous or lags at the turning points. Hence real cash balances computed at permanent prices would do likewise. Nominal cash balances equal these real cash balances times permanent prices, and our evidence suggests equally that permanent prices conform positively to the cycle either synchronously or with a lag. This train of reasoning therefore implies that, under the supposed conditions, nominal cash balances would conform positively to the cycle and would be either synchronous or lag at the turning points. Yet one of the major findings of the broader study of which the results reported in this paper are a part is that the nominal stock of money, adjusted for trend, tends to lead at both peaks and troughs. Hence there is a residual element in the cyclical behavior of velocity that requires explanation.

A satisfactory analysis of this residual element requires the use of monthly rather than annual data. Annual data are unduly crude for studying timing relationships. For example, the cyclical patterns of the observed money stock in Chart 3, Panel *A*, reveal no average lead; yet our more detailed analysis of monthly money data establish such a lead, after adjustment for trend, beyond any reasonable doubt.

It may nevertheless be worth examining the residual element in the annual data as a first step. This residual element is approximated in Chart 4 by the ratio of the observed measured velocity to computed measured velocity. This ratio varies very much less over the cycle than measured velocity itself, and hence the movements it measures tend to be concealed by the movements in velocity arising out of the discrepancy between measured and permanent income. Yet our analysis of the stock of money suggests that this residual element may play a critical cyclical role. Indeed, perhaps the major significance of our analysis of velocity is that it enables us to extract this residual element, to eliminate the largely spurious movements of velocity that have hitherto masked the economically significant movements.

For deep depressions, the residual element has a clearly marked cyclical pattern. During expansion, the residual element at first falls, then rises, reaching a trough in mid-expansion. During contractions, the behavior is harder to determine, because one cycle—the earliest, from 1870 to 1878—has a major influence on the pattern for all cycles and the figures for this cycle are highly dubious.[14] If this cycle is omitted, the pattern for contractions is a mild fall from peak to mid-contraction and a sharper fall thereafter.

The residual element varies much less, on the average, for mild depression cycles than for deep depression cycles. Such cyclical movement as it does

[14] The problem is in the income estimates for the early period. These are characterized by an extraordinarily rapid rate of increase from 1869 to 1879. Other evidence suggests that this is at least partly a statistical artifact, reflecting the extreme paucity of reliable data for estimating income for this period.

show is similar to that for deep depression cycles during expansion and just the reverse of that for deep depression cycles during contraction. This residual element is the cyclical component in cash balances that cannot be explained simply by a movement along a univariate demand curve in response to a cyclical movement in permanent income. It is perhaps not surprising that this component should be so much larger for deep than for mild depression cycles. In the mild depression cycles, there is a relatively small cyclical movement in general, which presumably means that there are only relatively small movements in whatever other variables operate to produce a discrepancy between desired cash balances as judged from income alone and actual cash balances.

What are these other variables? The obvious candidates are measures of the return on other assets that could be held instead of money. One alternative to holding money is to hold securities; another, to hold physical goods. The return to the first is measured by the rate of return received on the securities. The return to the holding of physical goods is measured by the rate of change of prices minus storage costs; and either of these terms may be positive or negative—prices may rise or fall and storage of goods may yield a convenience return in excess of costs of handling and maintenance. In either case, these returns must be compared with those on money, which may be positive, as when interest is paid on deposits, or negative, as when service charges are incurred.

In our secular analysis, we have found that the yield on corporate bonds is correlated with the real stock of money and velocity in the expected direction: a rise in the bond yield tends to reduce the real stock of money demanded for a given real income—that is, to raise velocity—and conversely. Bond yields, however, play nothing like so important and regularly consistent a role in accounting for changes in velocity as does real income. The short-term interest rate was even less highly correlated with velocity than the yield on corporate bonds.

Chart 4 is designed to provide a rough test whether these secular results carry over to cyclical movements. In addition to the ratio of observed measured velocity to computed measured velocity, which is the residual element we are seeking to explain, Chart 4 also shows the average reference-cycle patterns of corporate bond yields as derived from annual data, of commercial paper rates as derived from monthly data (Panel *A*),[15] and of the yields on short- and

---

[15] The corporate bond yield data through 1900 are railroad bond yields from F. R. Macaulay, *Some Theoretical Problems Suggested by the Movements of Interest Rates, Bond Yields and Stock Prices in the United States since 1856*, a publication of the National Bureau of Economic Research (New York, 1938), pp. A145–A152, col. 5, with 0.114 percent arithmetic addition to raise them to the level of the following segment. After 1900 the data are "Basic Yields of Corporate Bonds to 50 Years Maturity," from *Historical Statistics of the United States, 1789–1945* (Bureau of the Census), p. 279; *Continuation to 1952 of Historical Statistics*, p. 36; *Statistical Abstract of the United States*, annually from 1953. Commercial paper rates in New York City, monthly, through January, 1937, are from Macaulay, *op. cit.*, pp. A145–A161; thereafter, monthly averages of weekly figures from

CHART 4

RATIO OF OBSERVED TO COMPUTED MEASURED VELOCITY, COMPARED WITH OTHER
ECONOMIC VARIABLES, AVERAGE REFERENCE-CYCLE PATTERNS,
MILD AND DEEP DEPRESSION CYCLES, 1870–1954

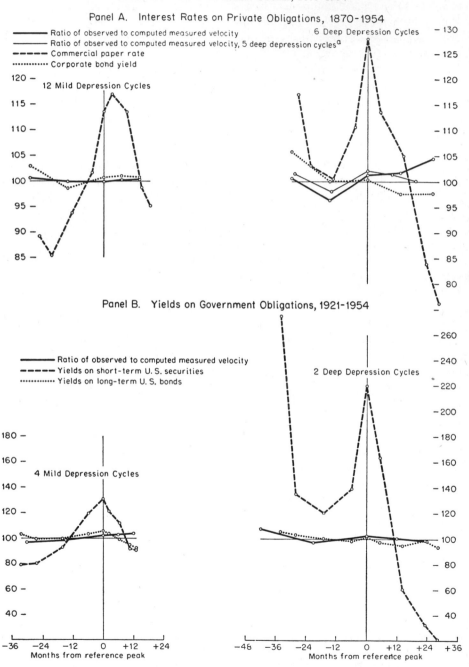

Panel A. Interest Rates on Private Obligations, 1870-1954

——— Ratio of observed to computed measured velocity
——— Ratio of observed to computed measured velocity, 5 deep depression cycles[a]
- - - - Commercial paper rate
·········· Corporate bond yield

6 Deep Depression Cycles

12 Mild Depression Cycles

Panel B. Yields on Government Obligations, 1921-1954

——— Ratio of observed to computed measured velocity
- - - - Yields on short-term U. S. securities
·········· Yields on long-term U. S. bonds

2 Deep Depression Cycles

4 Mild Depression Cycles

Months from reference peak

Months from reference peak

NOTE: Vertical scales are in reference-cycle relatives, except scale for prices in Panel C, which is in rate of change of reference-cycle relatives per month. The scale of reference-cycle relatives in Panel B is one-fourth that in Panel A, and the scale in Panel C is two and a half times that in Panel A.

[a] Excluding 1870–78.

CHART 4—*Continued*

Panel C. Rate of Change of Wholesale Prices, 1870–1954

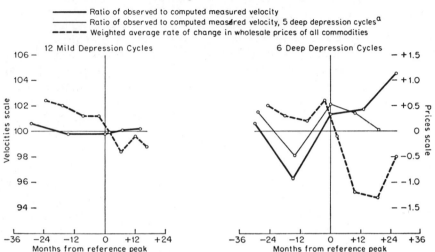

long-term United States securities, as derived from monthly data (Panel *B*).[16] Panel *A* covers the whole period 1870–1954, excluding only war cycles; Panel *B* covers only the six non-war cycles after 1921, since yields on United States securities are not readily available for the earlier cycles.

Short-term rates have, of course, a much larger cyclical amplitude than long-term rates, which in turn have roughly the same amplitude as the residual element in velocity. These differences in amplitude are of no special significance for our purpose except as they reflect the consistency of the cyclical pattern, since the effect of a change in interest rates depends not only on the size of the change but also on the elasticity of the response of cash balances to a change. Volatility of rate can be offset by a small elasticity of response and vice versa. The differences in amplitude do, however, make it more difficult to read the chart and tend somewhat to obscure the similarity or divergence in pattern that is of major interest.

The most striking feature of the charts is the high degree of similarity between the pattern of interest rates and that of the residual element of velocity during the expansion phase of deep depression cycles. Long and short rates and rates on private and public obligations all show much the same pattern for this phase, and the pattern of all four is similar to the pattern in the residual element in velocity: interest rates are high at the initial stage of expansion, and so is velocity, which is an appropriate response to a high rate of

---

Bank and Quotation Record of the Commercial and Financial Chronicle. This series was seasonally adjusted through December, 1933. No seasonal adjustment has been necessary since.

[16] Yields on short-term United States securities are from *Banking and Monetary Statistics*, p. 460, and *Federal Reserve Bulletin*, monthly issues, May, 1945, to May, 1948, and September, 1950, to December, 1954. This series was seasonally adjusted, 1920–30, 1951–54. Yields on long-term United States securities are from the same sources and are unadjusted.

return on non-cash assets; interest rates then decline to mid-expansion, and so does velocity; interest rates then rise to the peak of the cycle, and so does velocity.

There is no such unanimity of movement for the remaining phase of the deep depression cycles or for the mild depression cycles. For these phases, there is, at best, a family similarity between the movements in rates and those in the residual element in velocity. During the contraction phase of deep depression cycles, short and long rates diverge, short rates declining throughout, long rates leveling off or recovering in mid-contraction. The residual element behaves rather more like short rates, if we abstract from the unusual behavior during the 1870–78 cycle, but the similarity is not close in detail. For mild depression cycles, the cyclical movements in short and long rates are fairly similar, the main differences being a shorter lag in commercial paper rates at peaks and troughs than in the corporate bond yield. For the period as a whole (Panel *A*), the cyclical movement in the residual element, though fairly clear, is so small that no very precise comparison is justified; for the period since 1921 (Panel *B*), it is almost non-existent, the average reference-cycle pattern being dominated by an intracycle trend.

A number of empirical studies have demonstrated that the rate of change of prices has an important effect on the quantity of money demanded during periods of considerable instability of prices—as during hyperinflations or major and long-continued inflations.[17] These studies suggest, further, that the expected rate of change of prices, which is the variable that directly influences the demand for money, can be regarded as derived largely from past experience with the actual movement of prices and that it changes more smoothly than actual prices; it is something like the rate of change in what I earlier designated "permanent" prices. These findings imply that any changes in the expected rate of change of prices during periods of relative price stability will be small, perhaps too small to have any appreciable effect. And this is, indeed, the conclusion reached by Richard Selden in his study of the behavior of velocity.[18]

As a further check on this conclusion, we have plotted in Chart 4, Panel *C*, the rate of change of prices from reference stage to reference stage. This is derived from the nine-stage reference-cycle patterns of the monthly wholesale price index,[19] by dividing the difference between successive average standings by the average time interval between them. The resulting eight rates of change

---

[17] See Phillip Cagan, "The Monetary Dynamics of Hyperinflation," in Milton Friedman (ed.), *Studies in the Quantity Theory of Money*, pp. 25–117. The same relation has been documented for other countries and episodes in a number of unpublished studies done in the Workshop on Money and Banking of the University of Chicago.

[18] Selden, *op. cit.*, p. 202.

[19] *Historical Statistics of the United States, 1789–1945* (Warren-Pearson series, 1870–89; B.L.S. series, 1890–1945 [Bureau of the Census]), p. 344; *Continuation to 1952 of Historical Statistics*, p. 47; thereafter, U.S. Department of Labor, Bureau of Labor Statistics, *Wholesale (Primary Market) Price Index*, monthly issues.

per month are plotted at the mid-points of the corresponding intervals. Since these are the actual rates of change, they presumably vary more than expected rates of change and, in addition, may lead the latter in time. However, one might expect enough similarity between the actual rates of change and the expected rates of change to permit the detection of any moderately close relation between expected rate of change and the residual element in velocity.

Interestingly enough, the results largely duplicate those for interest rates. For the expansion phase of the deep depression cycles, there is the same striking agreement in pattern between the rate of change of prices and the residual element in velocity as there is between interest rates and the residual element. There is only slightly less similarity in pattern for the expansion phase of mild depression cycles. There is no systematic relation for the contraction phase of either group of cycles.

This analysis, based as it is on annual velocity data and on a comparison solely of average reference-cycle patterns, is too crude to be at all decisive. Yet the results are most suggestive. If the cyclical patterns of interest rates and the rate of change in prices are compared with the pattern of measured velocity itself (Chart 3, Panel *B*), there is no clear relation—as we noted at the outset in explaining why an alternative reconcilation of the secular and cyclical behavior of velocity is required. When the comparison is made instead with the residual element of velocity—that part of the movement in measured velocity that is accounted for neither by the effect of changes in permanent income on desired cash balances nor by the discrepancy between measured and permanent income—there is a striking consistency for one phase of one set of cycles, and at least a family resemblance elsewhere, though, of course, not without considerable irregularity. These results are of the kind that might be expected if the returns on alternative ways of holding assets were the chief factor other than permanent income affecting desired cash balances. Of course, they do not demonstrate that this is so. They might, for example, reflect accidental concurrence of movement in just a few cycles. And they do not provide any estimate of the quantitative strength of the connection. But they certainly justify further research in this direction. The main requirements for such research are the use of monthly data on velocity or indicators of velocity and the examination of cycle-by-cycle relations and not simply relations between average patterns.

VI. CONCLUSION

The results summarized in this paper have implications for the theory of money, the study of business cycles, and the conduct and possibilities of monetary policy.

In the theory of money, much emphasis has been placed on different "motives" for holding money—the "transactions" motive, the "speculative" motive, and the "assets" or "precautionary" motive being the three commonly distinguished. The transactions motive is often regarded as implying something of a quasi-mechanical relation between cash balances and the flow of payments and is frequently given priority of importance as well as place. Our results cast serious doubt on the acceptability of this emphasis. In the first place, the cyclical results make it clear that changes in cash balances over short periods are adapted to magnitudes less volatile than the volume of transactions. In the second place, the secular decline in income velocity is hard to explain in terms of transactions. It is dubious that there has been any secular increase in the ratio of transactions to income large enough to explain the growth in the ratio of money balances to income that has occurred. Further, improvements in transportation and communication, let alone in financial organization, have almost surely reduced any mechanical requirement for cash balances per unit of transactions—indeed, it was on these grounds that Irving Fisher implied nearly half-a-century ago that velocity was likely to increase secularly and that others have since expressed similar views.[20]

Our findings equally cast doubt on the importance of the so-called speculative motive. One would expect this motive to be subject to wide cyclical variations and hence, if it dominated the demand for money, to lead to correspondingly wide cyclical variations in desired cash balances, whereas we observe the reverse.

The assets or "precautionary" motive is in a different state. Permanent income can be regarded as a concept closely allied to wealth and indeed as an index of wealth, provided that we count both human and non-human sources of income as components of total wealth. Along these lines, our results can be interpreted in either of two ways. One is that the relevant asset motive is equivalent to a consumption or income motive. As permanent income, which is to say, total wealth, rises, consumer units expand their expenditures on some items disproportionately—we term these items "luxuries." On this interpretation, the services rendered by money can be included among these luxuries. The other interpretation is more nearly an asset motive proper. It is that the holdings of cash are linked not to total wealth but primarily to non-human wealth and that, as permanent income rises, the total value of non-human wealth rises more rapidly than permanent income, either because such a more rapid rise is a necessary condition for a rise in income or because it corresponds to the preferences of individuals as their total wealth rises. Unfortunately, the available evidence on the secular or cyclical behavior of the ratio of non-human wealth to income is inadequate to provide a test of this explanation.[21] On either interpretation, however, our results suggest that motivations and variables linked with assets are the most fruitful category to explore—that the most fruitful approach is to regard money as one of a

---

[20] Irving Fisher, *The Purchasing Power of Money* (rev. ed.; New York, 1913), pp. 79–88.
[21] Raymond Goldsmith's estimates in *A Study of Savings* (Princeton, N.J., 1955) suggest that, if anything, the ratio of non-human wealth to income has declined secularly rather than risen.

sequence of assets, on a par with bonds, equities, houses, consumer durable goods, and the like.

Our results have a bearing on another aspect of the so-called precautionary motive, namely, the view that the amount of cash balances held is highly sensitive to "the" or "a" rate of interest, at least for some range of rates of interest. If this were so for rates of interest within the range observed during the period our data cover, it would imply that real cash balances and the ratio of income to money would be highly variable, both secularly and cyclically, since small movements in interest rates would be accompanied by large movements in desired cash balances. The highly stable secular behavior of velocity is evidence against this view. So is our inability to find any close connection between changes in velocity from cycle to cycle and any of a number of interest rates. So also is our finding that most of the cyclical movement in income velocity as ordinarily measured can be accounted for by the use of measured rather than permanent income in the numerator. The remaining movement in velocity, though characterized by a consistent cyclical pattern and though, on the basis of our tentative explorations, it may well be accounted for by movements in interest rates, is much too small to reflect any very sensitive adjustment of cash balances to interest rates.

Some of these comments about the implications of our results for the theory of money have their direct and obvious counterparts for the empirical study of business cycles. The most important additional implications are two that have to do with the interpretation of cyclical movements in velocity. The fact that velocity changes have been about as important as changes in the stock of money in accounting, in an arithmetic sense, for the movements in money income, together with the small amplitude of cyclical movements in the stock of money, has fostered the view that changes in the stock of money cannot be the prime mover, or even of major independent importance, in cyclical change. This view may of course be correct, but it needs re-examination in light of our finding that most of the velocity movement is, from one point of view, "spurious," as well as a possible consequence of this finding, discussed more fully below, that measured income may be highly sensitive to changes in the stock of money. The other important implication for the study of cycles is that the cyclical pattern of velocity changes that needs study and explanation is very different from what it has been supposed to be. Measured velocity has a cyclical pattern roughly synchronous with that in general business, tending to rise relative to its trend from reference trough to reference peak and to fall from reference peak to reference trough. But when this pattern is corrected for the deviation of measured income from permanent income, the residual movement is very different, and it is the residual movement that needs explanation.

The most interesting implication of our analysis for monetary policy is highly speculative and involves taking our findings more seriously in detail than I can fully justify. It may nonetheless be worth recording if only in the hope of stimulating further work. Suppose one accepts fully both the reasonably well-supported finding that money holdings are adapted to permanent magnitudes and also the much more questionable and tentative suggestion that the economic actors derive their estimates of permanent magnitudes from prior measured magnitudes by implicitly constructing some kind of weighted average of them. It will then follow that, given a stable demand function for money, measured income will be highly sensitive in short periods to changes in the nominal stock of money—the short-run money multiplier will be large and decidedly higher than the long-run money multiplier.[22] To illustrate with some figures based on our tentative results: In the long run, if we take real income as given, a $1 increase in the stock of money would imply an annual level of money income higher than otherwise by $1 times the velocity of circulation, or, at current levels of velocity, about $1.50 higher—the long-run money multiplier equals the velocity of circulation. In the short run, however, an increase of $1.50 in measured income would be inadequate, since that much of a rise in measured income would raise permanent money income by decidedly less than $1.50 and hence desired cash balances by less than $1. If we take a year as our unit and accept the numerical weights we have used in estimating permanent income from measured income, measured income would have to rise by roughly $4.50 for estimated permanent income to rise by $1.50, the rise required to raise desired cash balances by $1 for given real income—the short-run money multiplier is thus triple the long-run multiplier.

The story does not, of course, end here. There would be carry-over effects into future years, as estimated permanent income continued to be revised in the light of measured income. These would make the initially assumed rise in money income not sustainable without further rises in the stock of money and hence would give rise to a cyclical reaction in measured income. Further, the assumed change in money income would presumably be associated with changes in output and in prices that would affect the relation of desired cash balances to the change in measured money income. These further complications require much more study than I have given them. They do not, however, affect the main point—the sensitivity of measured income to changes in the stock of money that is implied by our results if they are accepted at face value.

It is interesting that the permanent-income hypothesis should have such contrasting implications for the sensitivity of the economy to changes in the stock of money and to changes in investment—the major other factor regarded as a prime mover in cyclical change. The permanent-income hypothesis implies that the economy is much less sensitive to changes in investment than it would be if consumption were adapted to measured rather than permanent income— the short-run investment multiplier is decidedly smaller than the long-run multiplier.[23] On the other hand, we have just seen that the economy is much

---

[22] This point was first suggested to me by Gary S. Becker.
[23] See *A Theory of the Consumption Function*, p. 238.

more sensitive to changes in the stock of money than it would be if money balances were adapted to measured rather than permanent income.

A corollary for policy is that the effects of monetary policy may be expected to operate rather more than would otherwise be supposed through the direct effects of changes in the stock of money on spending, and rather less through indirect effects on rates of interest, thence on investment, and thence on income. Another corollary is to emphasize the potency of relatively small changes in the stock of money—a potency, needless to say, for good or evil. Relatively small changes in the stock of money, properly timed and correct in magnitude, may be adequate to offset other changes making for instability. On the other hand, relatively small changes in the stock of money, random in timing and size, may equally be an important source of instability. If the reaction mechanism I have described is in any substantial measure valid, the system may not have a large tolerance for mistakes in monetary management.

24

The Relation between Unemployment and the Rate of Change of Money Wage Rates in the United Kingdom, 1862-1957: A Further Analysis*[1]

By RICHAR D G. LIPSEY†

IN AN EARLIER paper in this journal, Professor Phillips[2] has advanced the hypothesis that the percentage rate of change of money wage rates in the United Kingdom ($\dot{W}$) can be explained to a very large extent by: (i) the percentage of the labour force unemployed (U), and (ii) the *rate of change* of unemployment ($\dot{U}$). After an inspection of the data, Phillips concluded not only that there is a clearly observable relationship between these variables, but that the form of the relationship has been remarkably stable over a period of almost one hundred years. The purpose of the present paper is to reconsider Phillips' work in some detail. In particular it seemed necessary: (i) to consider the general theoretical model that is being tested; (ii) to quantify Phillips' results, determining, if possible, the proportion of the variance in money wage rates that is associated with the two variables, level of unemployment (U) and rate of change of unemployment ($\dot{U}$); (iii) to provide systematic tests of the various subsidiary hypotheses framed by Phillips during the course of his analysis; and (iv) to test hypotheses that follow from possible alternative models. The logical order in which to deal with these topics, in the

 ---

* *Economica*, Vol. XXVII (February, 1960). Reprinted by courtesy of *Economica* and the author.

† The University of Essex, Colchester.

[1] The present paper, like Professor Phillips', is a part of a wider research project financed by the Ford Foundation. The writer was assisted by Mr. Peter Lantos and Mrs. June Wickins. This paper was the subject of extended discussion at the LSE Staff Seminar on Methodology and Testing in Economics and I am indebted to all the members for many comments and suggestions; I also benefited from the discussion at the University of Manchester Advanced Economics Seminar where some of the material embodied in this paper was first presented. Mr. F. Brechling and Dr. S. F. Kaliski have given valuable criticisms and I am particularly indebted to Professor Phillips for his constant aid and encouragement.

[2] A. W. Phillips, "The Relation Between Unemployment and the Rate of Change of Money Wage Rates in the United Kingdom, 1861–1957," *Economica*, November, 1958.

absence of Phillips' paper, would be, first, to outline the phenomena which require explanation, then to develop a model which will explain the phenomena, and, finally, to test further implications of the model. Given Phillips' paper, however, a slight change of approach seems to be desirable. In the first section of this paper a report is given of the statistical analysis carried out on data for the period 1862–1913. Although the main purpose is to discover what phenomena require explanation, a rather elaborate treatment is required in order to test the hypotheses about these phenomena framed by Phillips. This is necessary in order to build up a clear picture of our explicanda. Although many of Phillips' subsidiary hypotheses are rejected, the data are shown to support Phillips' main contention that there is a significant relation between the rate of change of money wage rates and the level and the rate of change of unemployment. Having established the evidence for these relations, the second section is devoted to the construction of a theoretical model which adequately accounts for them. Phillips had given very little indication of the sort of model of market behaviour which would produce his postulated relations. The third section is devoted to an analysis of the data for the post-1918 period. The theory developed in Section II is particularly useful in interpreting the differences which occur between the relations existing in the nineteenth century and in the twentieth century.

I. THE PERIOD 1862–1913

1. *The Relation between the Rate of Change of Money Wage Rates* $(\dot{W})$ *and the Level of Unemployment* (U)[3]

The unemployment figures used by Phillips showed the percentage of the unionized labour force unemployed, while the figures for the rate of change of wage rates were calculated[4] from the Phelps Brown-Hopkins index.[5]

---

[3] Since the *level* of unemployment is uncorrelated with the *rate of change* of unemployment, as is any trend-free variable with its own rate of change, the relation between the rate of change of money wages and each of the independent variables, U and $\dot{U}$, can be considered separately. The actual r^2 for U and $\dot{U}$ is 0.0002.

[4] Phillips, *ibid.*, p. 290, n. 1, took half the first central differences $(W_{t+1} - W_{t-1}) \div 2$ as the best approximation to the absolute rate of change of wages. The argument for approximating a continuous derivative by this method rather than by the more intuitively plausible method of taking the difference between this year's wage index and last year's $(W_t - W_{t-1})$ can best be explained by reference to the diagram. Fig. 1 shows a continuous time series (say one for the rate of change of wages). Only a discrete number of regularly-spaced observations are available, say those at 1, 2, and 3, and it is desired to approximate the derivative at 2 (the true value being given by the slope of the broken line tangent to the curve at 2). Taking the rate of change to be equal to the difference between the values of the function at 2 and at 1 is equivalent to estimating the derivative at 2 to be equal to the slope of the line joining 1 and 2. But the slope of this line is typical of the value of the derivative somewhere *between* 1 and 2, so that this method gives the derivative somewhere *between* the two points of time and is thus equivalent to introducing a time lag of approximately six months into the rate-of-change series. On the other hand, taking half the first central

Fig. 3 shows the data for $\dot{W}$ and U for the period under consideration. Phillips elected to describe the data by a curve of the type

$$\dot{W} = \alpha + \beta U^{\gamma} \tag{1a}$$

or
$$\log(\dot{W} - \alpha) = \log \beta + \gamma \log U \tag{1b}$$

where $\dot{W}$ is the rate of change of money wage rates $\left(\dot{W}_t \equiv \dfrac{W_{t+1} - W_{t-1}}{2W_t} \right)$, and U is the percentage of the labour force unemployed. This curve could not be fitted to all 52 observations because points below the asymptote

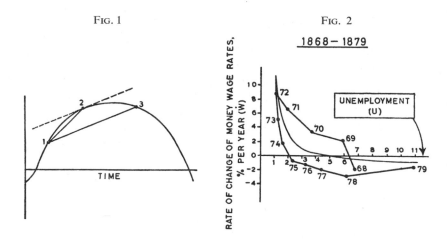

FIG. 1   FIG. 2

difference is equivalent to estimating the derivative to be equal to the slope of the line joining 1 and 3. In a regular curve this latter value is likely to be closer to the true value of the derivative at 2 than is the former value. In a recent article criticising Phillips' work, Mr. Routh has argued that the actual wage rate series is too crude to make the difference between the two methods of calculating $\dot{W}$ significant. (Guy Routh, "The Relation Between Unemployment and the Rate of Change of Money Wage Rates: A Comment," *Economica*, November, 1959.)

[5] E. H. Phelps Brown and Sheila Hopkins, "The Course of Wage Rates in Five Countries, 1860–1939," *Oxford Economic Papers*, June, 1950. Mr. Routh (*loc. cit.*, pp. 299–305) gives a detailed study of the coverage of the wage rate and the unemployment series and argues that " . . . in the two series used by Professor Phillips, neither the weights, occupations nor the industries are a good match (p. 303)." Routh argues, for example, that any fixed weighted index of rates will not allow for movements between areas and occupations. This is undoubtedly correct. It is, however, always possible to show that any set of statistics are not perfect or even, by some absolute standard, that they are downright bad. The relevant question is not whether the figures are perfect, but whether they are good enough for the purposes at hand. The question of whether or not the postulated relation is strong enough to show up in spite of imperfections in the data, can only be answered by the empirical results: in this case the postulated relation is strong enough. Another criticism of Phillips' article is to be found in K. G. J. C. Knowles and C. B. Winsten, "Can the Level of Unemployment Explain Changes in Wages?" *Bulletin of the Oxford Institute of Statistics*, May, 1959.

($\dot{W} < \alpha$) would require negative logarithms. Hence Phillips grouped his observations into six class intervals based on the level of unemployment[6] and found the mean values of $\dot{W}$ and U for each of the six groups. Having thus

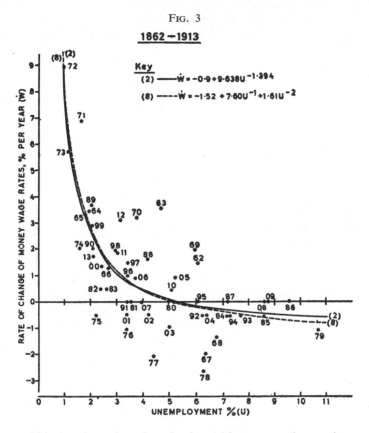

FIG. 3

1862—1913

Key

(2) ——— $\dot{W} = -0.9 + 9.638U^{-1.394}$

(8) ----- $\dot{W} = -1.52 + 7.60U^{-1} + 1.61U^{-2}$

compressed his data into six points, he fitted his curve to these points, using a trial-and-error procedure, and obtained the following equation:

$$\dot{W} = -0.9 + 9.638U^{-1.394}, \qquad (2)$$

which is plotted as curve (2) in Fig. 3.

Since, for purposes of the present study, it seemed desirable to treat the data by standard statistical methods if at all possible, a new equation was adopted which could be fitted to all the 52 original observations:[7]

$$\dot{W} = a + bU^{-1} + cU^{-2} + \varepsilon \qquad (3)$$

---

[6] The class intervals (percentage unemployment) with the number of items contained in each class given in parentheses are: 0–2 (6), 2–3 (10), 3–4 (12), 4–5 (5), 5–7 (11), 7–11 (9) (the upper limit is included in each class).

[7] For purposes of the present section the shape of the relation assumed by Phillips

It was found that, by suitable choice of the constants b and c, this curve could be made to take up a position virtually indistinguishable from that taken up by curve (1) for any value of γ between -1 and -2. Thus choosing between the two curves does not necessitate choosing between different hypotheses about the nature of the relation between $\dot{W}$ and U.[8]

The curve was first fitted to Phillips' six points of averages and gave the equation

$$\dot{W} = -0.44 + 0.023U^{-1} + 12.52U^{-2}. \tag{4}$$

The difference[9] between equations (2) and (4) results from the procedure of minimising the squares of the differences between the actual and the estimated values expressed in logarithms for (2) and in natural numbers for (4).[10] Next the curve was fitted to Phillips' original 52 observations for the years 1862–1913 which resulted in the following equation:

$$\dot{W} = -1.14 + 5.53U^{-1} + 3.68U^{-2}. \tag{5}$$

The difference between (4) and (5) indicates the distorting effect caused by fitting to points of averages rather than to the original observations.[11]

Next the Phelps Brown-Hopkins series for wage rate changes in 1881 to 1885 was replaced by the Bowley series for the same years.[12] The fitted equation then became

$$\dot{W} = -1.42 + 7.06U^{-1} + 2.31U^{-2} \tag{6}$$

There is a noticeable shift in the relationship when equation (5) is replaced by equation (6) and there is room for debate as to which series for the disputed years, and thus which equation, should be used. The Bowley series conforms with the pattern seen in the other eight cycles which cover the period

is accepted so that the problem is merely to find an equation which takes the same shape as equation (1) but which can be fitted by least squares. In Section II the general form of the relationship between $\dot{W}$ and U is considered in some detail.

[8] When (1) and (3) are fitted to the same data, normal least squares fitting does, however, result in slightly different shapes to the two curves because in one case the sum of the squares of the residuals expressed in logarithms is minimised while, in the second case, it is the sum of the squared residuals expressed in natural numbers that is minimised.

[9] The different fitted relationships may be at least roughly compared by comparing the values of the asymptotes.

[10] Some of the difference is accounted for by the fact that Phillips did not fit to all six points by least squares but rather made his curve go as closely as possible to the two points representing the highest levels of unemployment and then minimised squares on the other four points.

[11] When fitting to points of averages each of the six points is given equal weight although there are considerable differences between the number of items within each class interval.

[12] The Phelps Brown-Hopkins series shows a suspicious stability in wage rates over the period 1881–85 in spite of wide variations in employment, while the Bowley series shows the usual relation with wage rates rising when unemployment falls and then falling as unemployment rises. See Phillips, *loc. cit.*, pp. 287 and 291. Routh (*loc. cit.*, p. 313) has given reasons for the stability in the Phelps Brown-Hopkins index and has argued that this index should *not* be replaced by the Bowley series for these years.

under consideration and thus seems to be the more plausible of the two. In the absence of any evidence favouring one series rather than the other, we cannot eliminate one merely because it does not conform with our hypothesis. Therefore, although the Bowley substitution for the years 1881–85 is used on the subjective grounds that it seems more plausible, all relations have been recalculated using the Phelps Brown-Hopkins series for the disputed years, the values for the latter being given in footnotes.

The relation specified in equation (6) gives an r^2 of 0.64, indicating that, over the period 1862–1913, 64 percent of the variance in money wage rates is associated with variations in the level of unemployment.[13]

2. The Relation between the Rate of Change of Wages ($\dot{W}$) and the Rate of Change of Unemployment ($\dot{U}$)

After an inspection of his graphs Phillips noted that the relationship between $\dot{W}$ and $\dot{U}$ appeared to be important; he observed that, compared to the value predicted by the relation between $\dot{W}$ and U, $\dot{W}$ tended to be high when unemployment was falling ($\dot{U} < O$) and low when unemployment was rising ($\dot{U} > O$). In other words, the change in money wage rates is greater than would otherwise be expected when unemployment is *falling* and less than would otherwise be expected when unemployment is *rising*. He did not, however, attempt to determine either the precise form of the relationship between $\dot{W}$ and $\dot{U}$ or its quantitative significance. Fig. 2 shows the relation between $\dot{W}$ and U for the years 1868–79 together with the curve described by equation (2). This general picture is typical of the nineteenth century cycles. The "loop" is clearly observable with the actual $\dot{W}$ being above the fitted curve when unemployment is falling and below the curve when it is rising.

It was now desired to measure this relationship which was very strongly suggested by inspection. Half the first central difference was taken as the best approximation to the rate of change of unemployment in any year.[14] Thus, a new variable was defined, $\dot{U}_t \equiv \dfrac{U_{t+1} - U_{t-1}}{2U_t}$. 100, and the new regression equation became

$$\dot{W} = a + bU^{-1} + cU^{-2} + d\dot{U} + \varepsilon \tag{7}$$

which, when fitted to the original observations, gave

$$\dot{W} = -1.52 + 7.60U^{-1} + 1.61U^{-2} - 0.023\dot{U} \tag{8}$$

Curve (8) in Fig. 3 shows this relation when $\dot{U} = O$. R^2 for this relationship is

---

[13] Equation (5) which shows the comparable relation determined without the substitution of Bowley's index for 1881–85 gives $r^2 = 0.64$.

[14] See p. 457, n. 4.

0.82 while the squared partial correlation coefficients are 0.78 for U and 0.50 for $\dot{U}$. This indicates that 82 percent of the variance in $\dot{W}$ can be associated with variations in U and $\dot{U}$, and that $\dot{U}$ can remove 50 percent of the variance not already associated with U while, if U is considered first, U is associated with 78 percent of the residual variation in $\dot{W}$.[15]

Now that the influence of $\dot{U}$ has been measured it is possible to check quantitatively on Phillips' observation that " . . . it appears that the width of the loops obtained in each trade cycle has tended to narrow, suggesting *a reduction in the dependence of the rate of change of wage rates on the rate of change of unemployment.*"[16] This statement is taken to mean that, throughout the period, any given rate of change of unemployment was associated with a progressively diminishing rate of change of money wages (i.e., that, if it were fitted separately for each cycle, the parameter d in equation (7) would diminish from cycle to cycle). In order to check this statement equation (6) was used to predict values for $\dot{W}$ and the differences between these predicted values and the observed values were plotted on a scatter diagram against $\dot{U}$.[17] A separate diagram was drawn and a straight line (i.e. $R_{(6)} = a + b\dot{U}$) was fitted for each cycle. The slope of the line is an index of the width of Phillips' loops. The values in Table 1 show that, in the cycle of 1893–1904, for example, a 100 percent increase in the percentage of the working force unemployed

---

[15] The relations without the Bowley substitutions 1881–85 are as follows:
$\dot{W} = -1.23 + 6.00U^{-1} + 3.05U^{-2} - 0.021\dot{U}$, $r^2 = 0.79$. The squared partial correlation coefficient for $\dot{U}$ of 0.41 is smaller than the one quoted in the text. As would be expected the substitution of a series without a loop for a series with a loop results in a reduction of the explanatory power of $\dot{U}$.

[16] Phillips, *loc. cit.*, p. 292, italics added. After making this observation, Phillips offers two possible explanations to account for the supposed change.

[17] Since the units in which all the variables are expressed are percentage points there is the possibility of confusion when residuals are calculated. To avoid such confusion it may be worthwhile defining all the variables and the residuals at this point:

(i)   the rate of change of money wage rates at time $t \equiv$

$$\dot{W}_t \equiv \frac{W_{t+1} - W_{t-1}}{2W_t} \cdot 100 \; ;$$

(ii)   the percentage of the labour force unemployed at time $t \equiv U_t$;
(iii)   the rate of change of unemployment at time $_t \equiv$

$$\dot{U}_t \equiv \frac{U_{t+1} - U_{t-1}}{2U_t} \cdot 100 \; ;$$

where W_t is the index of money wage rates. Since lagged variables are not used in this section, the time subscript t is dropped from all the variables in the equations.

(iv)   the deviation of the observed value of $\dot{W}$ from the value predicted from equation $n \equiv R_n \equiv \dot{W}_o - \dot{W}_{en}$ where o stands for observed, and en for estimated, from equation n. R_n is always expressed in original units which, in the case of $\dot{W}$, are percentage points. Thus a residual of $+1$ percent might mean that the actual $\dot{W}$ was 3 percent while the estimated value was 2 percent. R_n is always used as defined above and *never* as a proportional residual (i.e. R_n percent $\equiv \dfrac{\dot{W}_o - \dot{W}_{en}}{\dot{W}_{en}}$ is never used).

(e.g. from 3 percent unemployment to 6 percent) was associated with an observed figure for the rate of change of wage rates 2.2 percent below the value predicted by equation (6). The value of the r^2 indicates the importance of $\dot{U}$ as an additional explanatory variable in each cycle. An inspection of Table 1 reveals that there is considerable variation in the value of the coefficient "b" from cycle to cycle but that there is no clear evidence that it becomes progressively smaller cycle by cycle. The cycle 1868–79 is unusual in

TABLE 1

STRAIGHT LINES RELATING RESIDUALS FROM
EQUATION (6) TO THE RATE OF CHANGE OF
UNEMPLOYMENT $R_6 = a + b\dot{U}$

Period[18]	b	r^2
1862–68	0.017	0.25
1868–79	0.046	0.91
1879–86	0.015	0.56
1886–93	0.016	0.91
1893–1904	0.022	0.59
1904–09	0.011	0.49

that the deviations of the observed from the predicted values of $\dot{W}$ associated with any given level of $\dot{U}$ are three times as large as those associated with most other cycles. At the 5 percent probability level there is a significant difference between the coefficient b for the cycle 1868–79 and those for all other cycles, while the coefficients for the other cycles do not differ significantly from one another. Thus there is some evidence that the loop for 1868–79 is significantly wider than all the other loops, while there is no evidence of significant variations in widths of loop between the other cycles. A hasty comparison of the loop for the period 1868–79 with those that came afterwards may have led Phillips to the erroneous conclusion that the loops were getting progressively narrower.[19]

We must conclude therefore that there is no clear evidence in favour of the hypothesis that $\dot{U}$ is a variable whose importance was diminishing over the period. There is thus no need to attempt the sort of explanation given by Phillips.

---

[18] To make the figures comparable with those of Phillips, the last year of each cycle has also been included as the first year of the subsequent cycle. The years 1910–13 are excluded because they do not constitute a complete cycle.

[19] The same experiment was made relating $\dot{U}$ to the residuals from Phillips' own equation ($R_{(2)}$) with similar results to those given in the text. Thus the rejection of Phillips' hypothesis is not the result of the adoption of a new equation.

3. *Consideration of Effects of Changes in the Cost of Living as an Additional Explanatory Variable*

Phillips advanced the hypothesis that cost of living adjustments affect money wage rates with a threshold effect. If wage rates would have risen by X percent in the absence of any changes in the cost of living, then an increase of up to X percent in the cost of living will have no effect on wages " . . . for employers will merely be giving under the name of cost of living adjustments part of the wage increases which *they would in any case have given as a result of their competitive bidding for labour.*"[20] If, however, the cost of living rises by *more than X percent*, then this will also cause wages to rise by more than X percent, i.e., by more than they otherwise would have done. This implies that the outcome of the wage bargain is unaffected by any change in the cost of living unless it actually threatens to reduce real wages, so that active and at least partially successful attempts must be made to push up money wage rates in response to price level changes that actually threaten to lower real wages. It also implies, however, either that unions passively accept any change in the price level which threatens to take away anything less than 100 percent of the increase in real wages that could have resulted from a rise in money wages, or that any attempts to resist such losses are totally frustrated by employers. This behaviour may seem intuitively implausible but it is necessary to see if the data provide any evidence for it.

In order to test Phillips' hypothesis two series were computed. First, the residuals R_8 were calculated. This series showed whether actual money wage rates had risen by more or by less than the amount associated with the existing levels of U and $\dot{U}$. The second series was the change in the real wage rate which was computed by adjusting the change in the money wage rate for the change in the retail price index.[21] A scatter diagram was then drawn relating the residuals, R_8, to the change in the real wage rate. The Phillips hypothesis predicts that when the real wage actually fell, the observed rise in money wage rates would be greater than the predicted rise, but it says nothing about what happens when the real wage rate rises.

In the period under consideration there were fifteen years in which the real wage fell (i.e. when the cost of living increase from the previous year to the present one was more than the increase in money wage rates). In only five of these years was the increase in money wage rates more than that predicted from the equation relating $\dot{W}$ to U and $\dot{U}$, and in none of these years was the deviation more than one half of 1 percent.[22] In other words, of those years in which the real wage fell there was not one in which the money wage rate rose

---

[20] Phillips, *loc. cit.*, p. 284, italics added. Phillips gives no reason for believing that cost-of-living adjustments operate in this manner.

[21] The index used was the retail price index taken from Phelps Brown-Hopkins, *loc. cit.*

[22] The same experiment was made, using Phillips' equation (2), to estimate the values of $\dot{W}$, and the results were substantially the same as those reported in the text.

by more than one half of 1 percent more than was predicted by equation (8). In ten of the years in which the real wage fell the rise in money wage rates was *less* than that predicted by equation (8). Thus we must conclude that the evidence does not support Phillips' hypothesis that the cost of living affects wage rates only with a threshold effect.[23]

The rejection of Phillips' hypothesis suggests that it may be desirable to consider a simpler cost of living hypothesis. This hypothesis is that the outcome of the wage bargain is affected simply by the *change* in the cost of living, that an increase in the cost of living makes trade unions more aggressive in demanding increases and employers and arbitrators more willing to grant them, while a decrease in the cost of living acts in the reverse direction. This hypothesis predicts simply that deviations of actual wage increases from those predicted by equation (8) would be associated with the change in the cost of living index, increases in the cost of living being associated with positive deviations and decreases with negative deviations.

As a first check on this hypothesis the residuals from equation (8) were plotted against the percentage change in the cost of living index. In 37 of the 52 years under consideration the residual, R_8, was not more than 1 percent ($-1 < R_8 < +1$). Of the eight years in which there was a positive residual of more than 1 percent ($R_8 > +1$), six were years in which the cost of living rose. Of the eight years in which there was a negative residual greater than 1 percent ($R_8 < -1$), seven were years in which the cost of living fell while only one was a year in which the cost of living rose. This suggested that, if there was any relation between cost of living changes and wage rate changes, it was a simple one, $\dot{W}$ being related in a straightforward manner to changes in the cost of living. The degree of scatter was, however, very large; there were, for example, eight years in which the cost of living changed by more than 2 percent while the actual wage rate change was within half of 1 percent of the value predicted by equation (8).

In order to check further on the quantitative significance of cost of living changes as an additional explanatory variable, equation (8) was amended by adding a term for the percentage change in the cost of living index. The equation then became

$$\dot{W} = a + bU^{-1} + cU^{-2} + d\dot{U} + e\dot{P} + \varepsilon \qquad (9)$$

where $\dot{P}$ is the percentage change in the cost of living index,[24]

---

[23] One other possibility is that there might be a time lag in this process so that decreases in the real wage rate at year t would be followed by abnormally high increases in money wage rates in year $t + 1$. The one year lag, however, produces results comparable to those quoted in the text.

[24] $\dot{P}_t \equiv \dfrac{P_t - P_{t-1}}{\frac{1}{2}(P_t + P_{t-1})}$ was tried as an alternative cost of living variable thus introducing a six-months' time lag on cost of living adjustments. The results were broadly similar, but the correlations slightly lower.

$\dot{P}_t \equiv \dfrac{P_{t+1} - P_{t-1}}{2P_t}$. 100. When fitted to the data for the years 1862 to 1913 this becomes:

$$\dot{W} = -1.21 + 6.45U^{-1} + 2.26U^{-2} - 0.019\dot{U} + 0.21\dot{P} \qquad (10)$$

A comparison of equations (8) and (10) shows that the addition of a cost of living variable causes the curve relating $\dot{W}$ to U (when $\dot{U} = \dot{P} = O$) to shift upwards for levels of U greater than 3 percent and less than 1 percent, while, between 1 and 3 percent, the curve shifts slightly downwards. The (small) coefficient of $\dot{P}$ indicates that an increase of almost 5 percent in the cost of living is associated with an increase in money wage rates of only 1 percent. Finally, the R^2 for this relation is 0.85 while the squared partial correlation coefficient for $\dot{P}$ is 0.17, indicating that 17 percent of the variance in $\dot{W}$ which remains after allowing for U and $\dot{U}$ can be removed by associating $\dot{W}$ with $\dot{P}$.[25]

Finally, it was desired to see if $\dot{P}$ could be an alternative explanatory variable to either U or $\dot{U}$. The most plausible hypothesis here seemed to be that $\dot{U}$ and $\dot{P}$ might be very highly correlated since retail prices would tend to rise on the upswing of a trade cycle and fall on the downswing. Thus the loops relating $\dot{W}$ to $\dot{U}$ might be merely a reflection of cost of living changes over the cycle. There is in fact very little relation between $\dot{U}$ and $\dot{P}$; the squared coefficient of correlation between $\dot{U}$ and $\dot{P}$ is only 0.19. In order to see which is the better explanatory variable, $\dot{U}$ or $\dot{P}$, equation (9) was amended by dropping the term for $\dot{U}$, thus producing:

$$\dot{W} = -0.90 + 5.23U^{-1} + 3.20U^{-2} + 0.37\dot{P} \qquad (11)$$

R^2 for this relation is 0.76. The squared partial correlation coefficient for $\dot{P}$ is 0.33, which compares with 0.50 for $\dot{U}$ when the effect of U is already allowed for. This indicates that $\dot{P}$ has only about two-thirds the explanatory value of $\dot{U}$ when they are considered as alternative variables to be added to the effect of U. The other possible situation would be to use $\dot{P}$ as the sole explanatory variable so that $\dot{P}$ would be an alternative for U. A linear relation between $\dot{W}$ and $\dot{P}$ produced the equation $\dot{W} = 1.14 + 0.55\dot{P}$ and $r^2 = 0.27$.

---

[25] The standard error of estimate of $\dot{W} = 0.86$, while standard errors for the regression coefficients are $b = 2.12$, $c = 2.13$, $d = 0.004$, $e = 0.07$. All of the partial correlation coefficients are significant at the 5 percent level and there is no evidence of significant autocorrelation in the $\dot{W}$ residuals for time lags of one to four periods at the 5 percent probability level. The size of the standard errors for b and c may be misleading because quite large changes can be made in these coefficients without causing large shifts in the curve relating $\dot{W}$ to U.

The comparable relations without the Bowley substitution for 1881–85 are as follows:

$$\dot{W} = -0.94 + 4.92U^{-1} + 3.66U^{-2} - 0.016\dot{U} + 0.20\dot{P},$$

$r^2 = 0.82$.

4. *The Special Explanation of 1893–96*

Phillips singled these years out for a special *ad hoc* explanation, apparently believing that the residuals were especially large or particularly significant in these years. He suggested that this could be accounted for by the growth of employers' federations in the 1890's and resistance to trade union demands from 1895 to 1897. Whatever may have been the industrial history of the period, there is no empirical evidence of *exceptional* downward pressure on wages. Estimated values for the change in money wage rates were calculated from equation (10) for the period 1894–96. The wage rate change in 1894 was actually one-third of 1 percent higher than the change predicted from equation (10); in 1895 it was only one-third of 1 percent less than that predicted by the equation, while in 1896 the actual rise (1 percent) was only eight-tenths of 1 percent less than the predicted rise (1.87 percent). Such very small deviations of the actual from the predicted values can hardly be regarded as significant; larger deviations than that occurring in 1896 were observed in no less than 21 of the 52 years under consideration. We must conclude, therefore, that there is no need for a special explanation of the observed events of 1893–96 which in fact conformed quite closely to the general pattern of the whole period.

5. *Conclusions*

(i) There is a significant relation between the rate of change of money wage rates on the one hand and the level of unemployment and its rate of change on the other. Over 80 percent of the variance in money wage rates over the period 1862–1913 can be associated with these two variables, U and $\dot{U}$. (ii) The Phillips hypothesis that the influence of the rate of change of unemployment has diminished over the period is rejected. (iii) The Phillips hypothesis that the cost of living enters with a threshold effect is rejected. There seems to be some evidence in favour of a simple (but rather weak) relation between changes in the cost of living and changes in money wage rates. (iv) There is no evidence of a *need* for any special explanation of the years 1893–96.

II. THE MODEL[26]

The analysis reported in Section I shows that there is a significant relation between $\dot{W}$, U, and $\dot{U}$, and it is now necessary to construct a theoretical model that will satisfactorily account for the relationship. It is necessary to take this

---

[26] I am particularly indebted to Mr. G. C. Archibald whose persistent criticisms of measurement without adequate theory have been to a very great extent responsible for the whole of Section II. He should in fact be regarded as joint author of part (1) of this section.

step for at least three reasons. First, the relation between $\dot{W}$, U, and $\dot{U}$ is open to serious misinterpretation, and such misinterpretations can be prevented only when the model which underlies the relation is fully specified. Second, if the relation ceases to hold, or changes, and we have no model to explain it, we can only say "the relation has ceased to hold" or "the relation has changed" and we will have learned nothing more than this. If we have a model explaining the relationship, we will know the conditions under which the relation is expected to remain unchanged. Then, if a change occurs, the model will predict *why* this has happened and this prediction will give rise to further tests from which we can learn. Third, unless it is a very *ad hoc* one, the model will give rise to further testable predictions in addition to the relation between the three variables $\dot{W}$, U, and $\dot{U}$, and from the testing of these we will gain further relevant information.[27]

1. *The Relation between* $\dot{W}$ *and* U

We shall consider this relationship, first, for a single market, and then for the whole economy, using lower-case letters to refer to the single market variables and capitals to refer to the corresponding macro-variables.

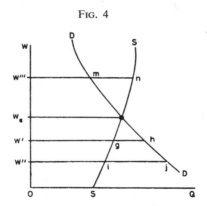

Fig. 4

We might analyse the market for any commodity since the argument at this stage is quite general. Since, however, the subject of the present article is the labour market we shall use the terminology appropriate to that market. The usual argument merely states that when there is excess demand, for example *ij* in Fig. 4, wage rates will rise, while, when there is excess supply, for example *mn* in Fig. 4, wage rates will fall. Nothing is said about the speed at which the adjustment takes place. We now introduce the dynamic hypothesis

---

[27] The relation between $\dot{W}$, U, and $\dot{U}$ is already known and the model will be specifically constructed to account for it. Thus to *test* the model against the existing observations of these variables is to conduct a "sun-rise test," that is, to test the theory by checking some prediction which has a zero chance of being found wrong.

that the rate at which w changes is related to the excess demand, and specifically, the greater is the proportionate disequilibrium, the more rapidly will wages be changing.[28] Thus the hypothesis is $\dot{w} = f\left(\dfrac{d-s}{s}\right)$ which says that the speed at which wages change depends on the excess demand as a proportion of the labour force.[29] Fig. 5 illustrates a simple form of this relation, $\dot{w} = \alpha\left(\dfrac{d-s}{s}.100\right)$ according to which if we start with excess demand of, for

FIG. 5

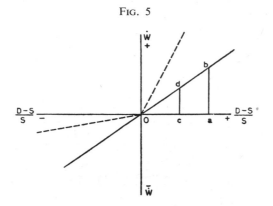

example, Oc, $\left(=\dfrac{gh}{w'g}\text{ in Fig. 4}\right)$, wages will be rising at the rate cd, but, if the excess demand increases to Oa, $\left(=\dfrac{ij}{w''i}\text{ in Fig. 4}\right)$, wages will be rising at the rate ab.[30]

There are a number of advantages in including the relations illustrated in Fig. 5 in one's theory rather than having only the ones illustrated in Fig. 4. If it is known that both of the curves of Fig. 4 are shifting continuously (e.g. the demand curve due to cyclical variations in income, and the supply curve due to exogenous changes in the labour force), then no two price-quantity observations will lie on the same curve. It will then be difficult to discover by observation the *ceteris paribus* relations either between supply and price or between demand and price. For the relation in Fig. 5 to be observed it is necessary only that there be an unchanging *adjustment mechanism*

---

[28] This is Phillips' hypothesis, *loc. cit.*, p. 283. It is also used extensively, for example, by Bent Hansen, *The Theory of Inflation*, London, 1951.

[29] If we were only concerned with a single market, the hypothesis could be expressed either in absolute or in proportional terms. Inter-market comparisons, however, require a proportionate measure. Consider the elasticity analogy.

[30] The relationship might of course be non-linear, indicating that $\dot{w}$ increased at either an increasing or a decreasing rate as excess demand increased. The simpler linear relationship is, however, capable of explaining all of the observed phenomena and, in the absence of empirical evidence about the second derivative of $\dot{w}$, the simpler relationship is assumed.

in the market, i.e., that a given excess demand should cause a given rate of change of price *whatever the reason for the excess demand*—whether demand shift, a supply shift, or a combination of both. The rate of change of price can be observed directly and, to obtain the relation shown in Fig. 5, it is only necessary to know demand and supply *at the existing market price*; it is not necessary to know what would be demanded and supplied at other prices.

Now if excess demand for labour were directly observable there would be no need to go any further. Unfortunately, this is not the case, at least over a large part of the period under consideration,[31] and it is necessary to relate excess demand to something that is directly observable, in this case the percentage of the labour force unemployed.

Fig. 6 shows the relation between $\dfrac{d-s}{s}$ and the percentage of the

FIG. 6

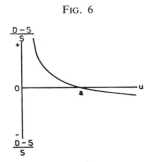

labour force unemployed, u. When demand is equal to supply (wage rate Ow_e in Fig. 4), there will be jobs available for all those who wish to work at the going wage rate. This is *not* equivalent to saying that there will be no one unemployed, but rather that the number of unemployed will be matched by an equal number of unfilled vacancies. Given that workers change jobs for any reason whatever, and that a finite time is taken to change, zero excess demand must be accompanied by some positive amount of *frictional unemployment*. From this it follows that, when the wage rate is stable (at Ow_e in Fig. 4), there will be some quantity of unemployment (Oa in Fig. 6), the exact quantity being determined by the amount of movement and the time taken to move. Now consider points to the left of a in Fig. 6. The larger is the excess demand the easier will it be to find jobs, and the less will be the time taken in moving between jobs. Thus, unless there is a completely offsetting increase in numbers of persons moving between jobs, an increase in excess demand will cause a reduction in u. It is, however, impossible that u

---

[31] The difference between unfilled vacancies and unemployed workers might provide a reasonable direct measure of excess demand; but such data are not available for most of the period under consideration.

could be reduced below zero so that as $\dfrac{d-s}{s}$ approaches infinity, u must approach zero (or some small value >0) asymptotically.[32] Now consider points to the right of a. Any increase in excess supply brings an equal increase in the number of persons unemployed. Therefore, to the right of point a, there will be a linear relation between $\dfrac{d-s}{s}$ and u.[33]

Now in order to obtain the relation between the two observable quantities, $\dot{w}$ and u, we need merely combine Figs. 5 and 6 to obtain the relation illustrated in Fig. 7. The relation between $\dot{w}$ and $\dfrac{d-s}{s}$ (Fig. 5) is assumed to be linear throughout. The relationship between $\dot{w}$ and u, however, is non-linear to the left of the point a because of the non-linear relation over that range

---

[32] The following is a simple model which will produce the postulated relationship:

Symbols: $L \equiv$ labour force $\equiv S$ in Fig. 4, $E \equiv$ number employed, $V \equiv$ number unemployed, $J \equiv$ total jobs available $\equiv D$ in Fig. 4, $N \equiv$ number of unemployed finding jobs, $X \equiv$ proportionate excess demand $\equiv \dfrac{J-L}{L} \equiv \dfrac{d-s}{s}$, α and β are two constants.

Assumptions: A constant proportion of those employed, αE, leave employment per unit of time; the number of unemployed who find jobs depends on the number looking for jobs and the number of jobs available: $N = \beta V(J - E)$.

A constant level of V requires: $\alpha E = \beta V(J - E)$.

But $E = L - V$, so $\alpha(L - V) = \beta V(J - L + V)$.

Expanding: $J = \dfrac{\alpha L}{\beta V} - V + L - \dfrac{\alpha}{\beta}$. But $X = \dfrac{J-L}{L}$.

Eliminating J: $X = \dfrac{\alpha}{\beta V} - \dfrac{V}{L} - \dfrac{\alpha}{\beta L}$. ...(1)

Differentiating: $\dfrac{\partial X}{\partial V} = -\dfrac{\alpha}{\beta V^2} - \dfrac{1}{L} < 0,\ \dfrac{\partial^2 X}{\partial V^2} = \dfrac{2\alpha}{\beta V^3} > 0$.

Therefore an increase in X is associated with a decrease in V but as X increases V falls at a decreasing rate and, from (1) above, as $X \to \infty$, $V \to 0$.

[33] There are some reasons for believing that to the right of a the relation might have a slight curvature which would *increase* as u increased (i.e., $\dfrac{\partial w}{\partial u} < 0$ *and* $\dfrac{\partial^2 w}{\partial u^2} < 0$). The excess supply of labour is $\dfrac{d-s}{s}$. 100 while u is $\dfrac{d-s}{s}$. $100 + F$, where F is the proportion of the labour force frictionally unemployed. If F remains constant as excess supply increases, the relationship between $\dfrac{d-s}{s}$ and u will be linear. If, on the other hand, $F \to 0$ as $u \to 100$, then the line relating u to $\dfrac{d-s}{s}$ will *curve* slightly downwards, starting at $u = F$ when $\dfrac{d-s}{s} = 0$ and reaching $u = \dfrac{d-s}{s}$ when excess supply is 100 percent. If F is small (say 5 percent), this curvature will be very slight. A second reason is that people in excess supply may not register as unemployed so that recorded u may not increase as fast as real excess supply. With the data used in this study it is impossible to distinguish between $\dfrac{\partial^2 \dot{w}}{\partial u^2} \lessgtr 0$ for high values of u. If, however, it were possible to demonstrate that $\dfrac{\partial^2 w}{\partial u^2} > 0$, we should have to abandon the linear hypothesis illustrated in Fig. 5, at least for situations of excess supply.

between u and $\dfrac{d-s}{s}$ (Fig. 6) while the relation between $\dot{w}$ and u is linear to

the right of a because of the assumed linear relation over that range between

u and $\dfrac{d-s}{s}$ (Fig. 6). The relation illustrated in Fig. 7 shows the *speed at*

which prices adjust to a disequilibrium and we shall call it an *adjustment*
function.

FIG. 7

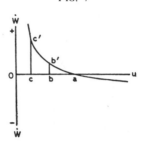

This relationship between $\dot{w}$ and u is an extremely simple one, and it holds considerable promise for empirical testing. The relation is, however, easily misinterpreted, and it may be worth considering some examples. Consider, first, a case in which a market is observed over three successive time periods at the points a, b' and c' in Fig. 7. This means that the demand and/or the supply curves have shifted over the period in such a way as to increase the disequilibrium in spite of the increase in wage rates. For example, the demand curve may have shifted so quickly to the right that the equilibrating movements in w were more than offset. Now consider a case in which the market is observed first at c', then at b' and finally at a. This is consistent with many market changes, two of which will be mentioned by way of illustration. First, both the demand and supply curves might be stable while the increase in wages restores equilibrium. Second, even though the demand curve is shifting to the right, the rate of increase in wages is fast enough to reduce the excess demand. When we observe either of these time sequences (a to b' to c' or c' to b' to a) we do not know what shifts in the curves have occurred but only that, in the first case, the shifts were such as to increase the disequilibrium in spite of equilibrating movements in w while, in the second case, any shifts that did occur either were not sufficient to offset the equilibrating changes in w or actually helped to remove the disequilibrium. If, to take a final example, the market is observed at b' over several successive periods, then we know that rightward shifts in demand and/or leftward shifts in supply were sufficient just to offset the equilibrating effects of changes in w, leaving excess demand constant.

It must be emphasised that knowledge of the shape of the adjustment function does not allow one to distinguish between *causes* of disequilibrium.

Consider a market that is observed at a at time 0, at b' at $t = 1$, at c' at $t = 2$, at b' at $t = 3$, and finally at a at $t = 4$. All we know is that there was an increasing disequilibrium associated with ever faster increases in w, but that after a while the disequilibrium lessened until, at $t = 4$, it is completely eliminated. Now these observations are consistent with either a rightwards shift in the demand curve, first at an increasing rate and then at a decreasing rate, or with a leftwards shift in the supply curve, indicating first a rapid withdrawal of labour supplies and then a slower withdrawal.

The relation also raises the problem of the influence of unions, but, in fact, tells us very little about their influence on the market processes. There are a number of points to notice here. First, the observation of the postulated relation is quite consistent with changes in wages caused by union-induced shifts in the labour supply curve. For, as illustrated in the previous paragraph, shifts in the supply curve would give rise to observations lying on the adjustment function. Second, unions might influence the speed of the dynamic adjustment illustrated in Fig. 5. They might, for example, cause a faster increase of wages in response to excess demand and a slower fall in response to excess supply than would otherwise occur. In other words, they might shift the adjustment function to the shape illustrated by the dotted line in Fig. 5.[34] If a completely stable relation between $\dot{w}$ and u is observed over time, all that can be said is that, whatever is the influence of the union on the market, this influence has remained *relatively stable* over that time period.

We must now consider the effect of aggregating a number of markets each with the same relation between $\dot{w}$ and u in order to obtain a relation between $\dot{W}$ (the rate of change of a national index of wage rates) and U (the percentage of the whole labour force unemployed). The main problems can be illustrated in the case of two markets, α and β, *with identical reaction functions* of the sort illustrated in Fig. 7. We assume for simplicity in exposition that the labour force is divided equally between the two markets so that

$$U = \frac{u_\alpha + u_\beta}{2} \quad \text{and} \quad \dot{W} = \frac{\dot{w}_\alpha + \dot{w}_\beta}{2}.$$

Consider, first, what would happen if both markets always had identical levels of unemployment. Since the percentage of the labour force unemployed would be the same in both markets, the national index of percentage unemployment would be the same as the figure for the two markets ($u_\alpha = u_\beta = U$). Also, since both markets would be showing identical rates of change of money wage rates, the national index would show the same rate of change

---

[34] It is worth noting that, if they were successful in shifting the reaction function, they could be affecting the distribution of the national product even though they were completely unable to shift either the demand or supply curve and thus were unable to affect the position of *equilibrium*. By increasing the *speed of adjustment* when there is excess demand and by slowing it down when there is excess supply, they would ensure that, over any finite time period, the average wage rate would be higher than it would otherwise be.

($\dot{w}_\alpha = \dot{w}_\beta = \dot{W}$). If the level of unemployment then were allowed to vary in exactly the same way in both markets (so that $u_\alpha = u_\beta$ and $\dot{w}_\alpha = \dot{w}_\beta$), it follows that the observed relation between $\dot{W}$ and U would be identical with the relation between $\dot{w}$ and u in each of the individual markets.

Consider, second, what would be observed if aggregate unemployment were held constant at say $0a$ percent $\left(\dfrac{u_\alpha + u_\beta}{2} = 0a\right)$, while the distribution of this unemployment were varied as between markets (say $u_\alpha < u_\beta$). Since the relation between $\dot{w}$ and u is non-linear to the left of the point a, wages will be increasing faster in the market with excess demand (α) than they will be falling in the market with excess supply (β). Therefore the national index of wage rates will be rising $\left(\dot{W} = \dfrac{\dot{w}_\alpha + \dot{w}_\beta}{2} > 0\right)$ in spite of the fact that the over-all unemployment percentage remains unchanged at $0a$. Furthermore, as the distribution of U between the two markets is made less equal, $\dot{W}$ will take on larger and larger values since, when u_α is reduced by the same amount by which u_β is increased, $\dot{w}_\alpha$ will be increased by more than the amount by which $\dot{w}_\beta$ will be decreased.

Finally, consider what would happen if the two markets were kept in the same relation to each other (e.g. $u_\alpha = k \cdot u_\beta$, where $k < 1$) while the total level of employment $\left(\dfrac{u_\alpha + u_\beta}{2} = U\right)$ were allowed to vary. As U varies, a relation between U and $\dot{W}$ will be traced out. We will call this curve A_m for *macro-adjustment curve* and distinguish it from the curves a_i for *individual market adjustment curves*. By the reasoning in the last paragraph, this relation between $\dot{W}$ and U will lie above the individual market adjustment curves. Now consider increasing the degree of inequality between two markets (i.e. reduce the value of k). Because of the non-linearity in the individual market relations between $\dot{w}$ and u, this will increase $\dot{w}_\alpha$ by more than it will reduce $\dot{w}_\beta$. Therefore $\dot{W}$ for the whole economy will be increased. It should be noted, however, that because of the linear relation to the right of a, this upward displacement will not occur if there is excess supply in both markets (u_α and $u_\beta > 0a$).

This analysis leads to a number of important conclusions about the relation between the individual adjustment functions (the a_i's) and the macro-curve (A_m). (1) The macro-function can never lie below the individual market functions.[35] (2) The macro-function will coincide with the individual (identical) a_i's only if there is an identical percentage of the labour force unemployed in each market at all levels of aggregate unemployment. (3) Whenever there is any degree of inequality in the distribution of unemployment combined with excess demand in at least one market ($u < 0a$ for some markets), the macro-observations will lie above the individual market curves

---

[35] If the a_i curves are not identical this conclusion reads: "The curve A_m can never lie below the "average" or typical curve a_i ."

for corresponding levels of unemployment. (4) The greater is the degree of inequality between markets, the further will the macro-observations be above the individual market curves, and thus the greater will be the degree of upward displacement of the observed macro-function.[36] The macro-function relating $\dot{W}$ and U will be *linear* only if there is excess supply in all markets (i.e. if *all* markets are in the range where the relation between $\dot{w}$ and u is linear). In all other cases it will be non-linear.[37]

These conclusions have a number of interesting real-world implications: (1) If one wishes to predict the rate of change of money wage rates ($\dot{W}$), it is necessary to know not only the level of unemployment but also *its distribution between the various markets of the economy*. It follows immediately that the observed macro-function need not be accepted as immutable even if the individual functions are. The macro-relation may be shifted by a policy designed to change the degree of inequality existing between the individual markets; if the distribution of U were made more even the macro-curve would shift downwards, thus increasing the downward flexibility of the overall wage level. (2) Because of the upward displacement of the macro-observations, the observed macro-relation between $\dot{W}$ and U will always tend to overstate the upward flexibility and to understate the downward flexibility of wage rates to be found in a typical individual market. (3) Thus, given non-linear a_i's, if a stable macro-relation between $\dot{W}$ and U is observed over a large number of cycles, it is implied that in both the upswing and the downswing roughly the same degree of inequality of unemployment has existed as between cycles.[38] (4) Finally, great caution must be exercised in trying to infer from a statistically fitted relation between $\dot{W}$ and U what would happen to wage rates if unemployment were held constant at any level for a long time. If unemployment were held constant, we would expect the degree of inequality in its distribution between markets to change substantially. We would thus expect the macro-adjustment function to shift.[39]

---

[36] This conclusion can be upset only if the rate of response of wages to excess demand is slower than the rate of response to excess supply so that the a_i curves are kinked in the opposite way to the dotted function in Fig. 5.

[37] Thus the form of the function actually used (see equation 3) is to be understood as an approximation to the "true" curve which becomes linear (but with a negative slope) when there is excess supply in all markets. The difference between the $\frac{\partial^2 \dot{w}}{\partial u^2} = 0$ of the theory and the $\frac{\partial^2 \dot{w}}{\partial u^2} > 0$ of the fitted curve is slight over the range of u's studied, and the data are too crude to allow us to distinguish between the two.

[38] We would expect this to be true at least in some rough sense since certain sectors of the economy, e.g. the capital goods sectors, are typically hit much harder by fluctuations in the level of activity than are other sectors, e.g. the non-durable consumer goods sectors.

[39] It is an open question which way the curve would shift. It might be expected that a stable period would give time for the classical adjustment mechanism—movements of labour between markets and changes in relative prices—to reduce the degree of sectoral inequality. On the other hand, it might well be that cyclical fluctuations in employment aided the markets in adjusting to changes in demand and in techniques, and that the removal of these fluctuations would increase the average degree of inequality existing between markets.

2. The Relation between $\dot{W}$ and $\dot{U}$

Phillips noted that the actual values for $\dot{W}$ tended to be above the curve relating $\dot{W}$ to U when U was falling, and below the curve when U was rising. He therefore postulated a relation between the rate of change of wages, $\dot{W}$, and the rate of change of unemployment, $\dot{U}$, according to which $\dot{W}$ will be higher, for any given level of U, the larger is $\dot{U}$. The statistical analysis reported in Section I of this paper shows that a linear relation between $\dot{W}$ and $\dot{U}$ is capable of explaining about half of the variation in $\dot{W}$ not already associated with U alone. In the present section we must attempt a theoretical explanation of this relation.

Phillips argued that this relation was the result of a direct reaction of employers and workers to *changes* in the level of unemployment. He would seem to have had two possible reactions in mind. The first is that there will be more competitive bidding when $\dot{u}$ is negative than when it is positive, because in the former case there will be *net* hiring of labour while in the latter case there will be *net* dismissals. The second effect is the reaction of *expectations*, and hence of competitive bidding, to changes in u. Both of these explanations lead us to expect to find loops in a single labour market. It is most important to note that, to obtain a loop, it is necessary that something affect $\dot{w}$ without simultaneously affecting u. It is quite possible, however, that the factors mentioned by Phillips are unsatisfactory because they will produce changes in both $\dot{w}$ and u. We must, therefore, consider these factors carefully. Consider the first effect. When there is significant excess supply, more labour can be obtained at the going wage rate. As long as there is excess supply in a particular market throughout the period, there would seem to be no reason to expect there to be more competitive bidding on the average if excess supply falls from, say, 10 percent to 6 percent, than if it rises, say, from 6 percent to 10 percent. When there is significant excess demand, employers will be prepared to take on workers at the going wage rate if the labour were forthcoming. Assume that in January they are prepared to take on 10 percent more workers than they are employing at present but that demand steadily falls so that by December they are only prepared to take on 5 percent more than they are employing. There seems to be no reason to expect the situation just described to cause less competitive bidding than would occur when employers start by wanting 5 percent more labour in January and end by wanting 10 percent more in December. The second reason which Phillips apparently had in mind is that the loops might be the result of an expectation effect which makes employers bid harder when $\dot{U}$ is negative than when it is positive. Employers might vary the strength of their bidding not merely in response to present need but because of what they expect to need in the future. Assume a given demand for final goods and that the amount of labour required to produce these goods is such that 6 percent of the labour force would be unemployed and wages would be falling at 1 percent per annum.

Assume, however, that the demand for goods is rising, and that employers increase their demands for labour in the expectation of needing more in the future. As a result of this change, unemployment will be lower than it otherwise would have been (say 4 percent) and the rate of fall of wages will be less than it otherwise would have been (say -0.25 percent). There is, however, no loop; all that happens is that the point attained on the adjustment curve is different than would have been predicted solely on the basis of current demand for final goods; u is lower and $\dot{w}$ is higher than they otherwise would have been.

The difficulties encountered with these explanations in terms of a single market suggested that the origin of the loops might lie in the aggregation of the u's and the $\dot{w}$'s for a number of different labour markets each affected differently by fluctuations in the level of aggregate demand for final goods.[40]

Fig. 2 shows the observations of $\dot{W}$ and U for the twelve years 1868–79. The fitted relation between $\dot{W}$ and U lies in the middle of the observations, and this invites an interpretation of the "loops" as consisting of both positive and negative deviations from the relation $\dot{W} = f(U)$.[41] The theoretical argument of the present paper suggests, however, that this interpretation may be seriously misleading. The stable behavioural relation that we have postulated is the one between $\dot{w}$ and u in individual markets (see Fig. 7). The analysis of the previous section suggests that the macro-relation between $\dot{W}$ and U will *always be displaced upwards* from the individual market relation. The degree of upward displacement will be a function of the degree of inequality in the distribution of U between the various markets. This invites interpretation of the "loops" not as positive and negative deviations from a stable macro-relation between $\dot{W}$ and U, but as upward displacements from the stable single-market relations between $\dot{w}$ and u, the loops being produced by systematic variations in the degree of upward displacement.

In order to see how macro-observations of the type illustrated in Fig. 2 might arise, we may follow out the course of a hypothetical cycle in an economy with two imperfectly linked labour markets. Fig. 8 shows the (identical) relation between $\dot{w}$ and u in the two labour markets;[42] Arabic numerals refer to the positions at successive time periods in the two markets, while the crosses with Roman numerals show the corresponding aggregate observations that will be generated.

Assume that the economy begins in a period of depression with heavy

---

[40] The hypothesis actually offered is by no means an untestable alibi. On the contrary, it leads to a number of testable hypotheses, other than the relation between $\dot{W}$ and $\dot{U}$, that are of considerable interest. If the hypothesis stands up to these further tests it may be regarded as an interesting one. If it is refuted by these tests we shall learn from *the way in which it is refuted* much more about the conditions which must be fulfilled by its successor.

[41] Cf. Phillips, *loc. cit.*, p. 290.

[42] The assumption that the relations between $\dot{w}$ and u are identical in the two markets is relaxed later in the analysis.

unemployment in one market (*a*) and lighter unemployment in the second market (*b*). The cross I indicates the percentage of the total labour force unemployed and the rate of change in a national index of wage rates that will be observed. Now assume that a recovery starts, and that it is at first mainly

FIG. 8

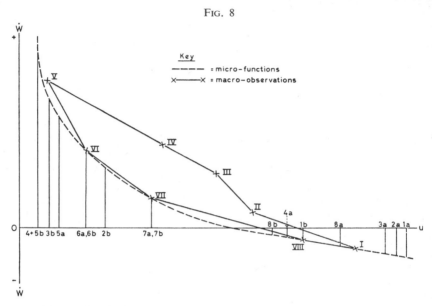

centred in market *b*. As soon as excess demand occurs in market *b*, wage rates will begin to rise, although *U* for the whole economy is still high as a result of the heavy unemployment in market *a* (periods 2 and 3). As the excess demand in market *b* grows, the macro-observations will trace out a relation similar to that of the curve for market *b* but displaced to the right because of the influence of the heavy unemployment in market *a*. When market *a* begins to recover rapidly, *U* for the whole economy will fall rapidly but there will not be a further large increase in $\dot{W}$ until serious excess demand develops in market *a*. If both markets should reach the same level of excess demand, the macro-observations will lie on the micro-curve. Now assume a fall in activity in both markets. If *U* rises more or less uniformly in both markets, the observations of $\dot{W}$ in the downswing will lie near the micro-curves and, therefore, well below those for corresponding *U*'s on the upswing. If the downswing comes before the same degree of excess demand is achieved in both markets, then the macro-observations for the downswing will lie above what they would be if the equality of excess demand had been achieved.

The "loops" can thus be accounted for on the hypothesis that the recovery affects different markets at different times while the fall in effective demand is, at least during the early stage of the recession, more evenly distributed.[43]

---

[43] This would be true if, for example, the consumer-goods industries recovered first

Another way of making the same point is to say that the hypothesis requires that time lags are greater in the upswing than in the downswing. If a fall in demand in one market causes a fall in demand in other markets with a time lag of only a few months, then all markets will be observed to decline more or less together. If, on the other hand, there is a longer time lag before an increase in demand in one market is transmitted to other markets then all markets will not recover together and there will be a greater degree of sectoral inequality in unemployment in the early upswing than in the early downswing.[44]

This analysis points a general warning against the procedure of accepting statistically fitted relations without relating them to models of *market behaviour*. We have already seen that the data are consistent with the hypothesis that there is an association between $\dot{W}$ and $\dot{U}$ but it will be noted that, if a relation $\dot{W} = f(U)$ were fitted to the macro-observations of Fig. 8, the curve would go through the centre of the loop and thus be displaced upwards from the stable micro-adjustment functions. The observed macro-curve relating $\dot{W}$ and U goes through the centre of most of the "loops" and therefore gives the average relation between $\dot{W}$ and U, *given the degrees of inequality in excess demand that have in fact been experienced*. The macro-curve will thus be useful for prediction providing that the same sort of inter-market inequalities continue to occur. Great care must be taken in using the curve to predict what would happen if the level of U were held constant for some itme for, if this were done, the degree of inter-market inequality in excess demand would be expected to change considerably.[45]

III. THE PERIOD 1919–1957

Phillips' scatter diagram relating $\dot{W}$ to U for the period 1919–57 is reproduced here as Fig. 9.[46] The diagram reveals very little relation between the

---

while the capital-goods sector did not recover until significant excess demand had developed in the consumer industries; while, on the other hand, when demand fell in one sector demand also fell in the other with less than a one year time lag.

[44] It may be objected that the assumption of identical relations between $\dot{w}$ and u greatly restricts the applicability of the model. This is not so. It has been shown in the text that varying degrees of sectoral inequalities in the distribution of unemployment (for which there is some empirical evidence) is a *sufficient* condition for the generation of the loops. If the loops are explained as a phenomena of aggregation then inequality in distribution is also a *necessary* condition. If for any level of U, u_α and u_β always bear the same relation to each other there will be a unique relation between $\dot{W}$ and U for any relations: $\dot{w}_\alpha = f_1(u_\alpha)$ and $\dot{w}_\beta = f_2(u_\beta)$. If different reaction functions (about which we have little empirical evidence) were superimposed onto the model in the text the only difference would be a change in the *shape of the macro-loop*.

[45] This would be particularly important in the middle range of U values, where all experience has been of rapidly changing level of U, and less important at extreme values where U has more often been stable at least for two or three years at a time.

[46] The figures for the years after 1945 have been amended in an attempt to make them comparable with the earlier figures. See section (5) below. The extreme values for 1919–22 are not included as the scale would have to be drastically reduced if they were. The $\dot{W}$ values are as follows: 1919 (+28.6), 1920 (+2.5), 1921 (−25.0), 1922 (−19.1).

level of unemployment and the rate of change of wages. Phillips argued, however, that there was evidence of a close relation between the two variables in
certain periods. He also argued that, in the period following the second world
war, the relation between $\dot{W}$ and U was substantially the same as it had been
in the period 1861–1913. In the present section we will first consider the years
1919–58 as a single period and then consider the various sub-periods dealt with
by Phillips.

FIG. 9

1923–1957

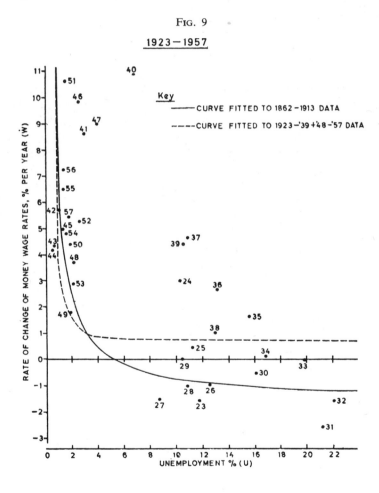

When considering this period there are three major hypotheses that may
be worth testing: (i) that the changes in money wage rates continue to be
explained mainly by changes in U, $\dot{U}$, and $\dot{P}$; (ii) that the relative explanatory
power of these three independent variables is unchanged; and (iii) that the
exact relation between $\dot{W}$, U, $\dot{U}$, and $\dot{P}$ is unchanged so that equation (10)
which was fitted to the years 1862–1913, predicts accurately the experience of

this period. The first hypothesis is in fact borne out by the data but the second and third are refuted.[47]

1. *The Years 1920–39 and 1947–57*[48]

The curvilinear relation between $\dot{W}$ and U described by equation (3) was first fitted to the data for this period. R^2 for this relation is 0.28, which indicates that only a low proportion of the variance in $\dot{W}$ can be accounted for by variations in U. Next the variables $\dot{U}$ and $\dot{P}$ were added (i.e., equation 9 was fitted to this data) and the R^2 increased to 0.88. The squared partial correlation coefficients for this relation are $U = 0.06$, $\dot{U} = 0.05$, and $\dot{P} = 0.83$ which indicate that $\dot{P}$ is the most important of the three explanatory variables while U and $\dot{U}$ add practically nothing to the explanation of $\dot{W}$. Even more startling than the high partial correlation between $\dot{W}$ and $\dot{P}$ is the magnitude of the regression coefficient for $\dot{P}$. This has a value of 1.28, indicating that on the experience of the whole period a 1 percent rise in prices is associated with a rise in wages of more than 1 percent.

There are, however, a few very extreme values for $\dot{W}$ in this period and their existence poses some serious problems. The variance in $\dot{W}$ over the period under consideration is 47.2 while, if the four years 1920, 1921, 1922, and 1947 are eliminated, the variance drops to 10.2.[49] Thus 13 percent of the years account for 78 percent of the variance in $\dot{W}$, and any explanatory variable which accounts for $\dot{W}$ in these four years will necessarily produce a high R^2 for the whole period *irrespective of its ability to account for variations in $\dot{W}$ over the remaining years.* It is also true that the regression coefficient associated with this variable will mainly reflect the relation between it and $\dot{W}$ over these four years. There is therefore good reason to mistrust the regression coefficients calculated from a series containing a few such very extreme values which must dominate the whole estimation procedure. For this reason the four extreme years were dropped from the series and the various relations recalculated.

---

[47] The model used throughout the present paper is the simplest sort of "single-equation model." This report is a part of a larger study in which simultaneous relations will be used. The single-equation model is probably justified as a first approximation especially where it is desired to try alternative explanatory variables, alternate specification of the lags, and alternative functional forms. The single-equation model does, however, introduce some serious biases into the estimates. The most serious error is likely to be on $\dot{P}$ which is the main variable affected by other parts of the system. It is easily shown, however, that the regression coefficient of $\dot{P}$ is biased upwards. Calculations taking what appear to be reasonable specification of the dependence of prices on wages, suggest that the bias may be of the order of 0.2 to 0.3 (so that the subsequent estimate of 0.69 for the coefficient of $\dot{P}$ should probably be more like 0.40 to 0.50).

[48] The periods of the two world wars plus the first postwar year (1914–19 and 1940–46) were omitted on the argument that a period of heavy war-time controls is not an appropriate period from which to infer the relations being studied.

[49] It is probably reasonable enough to eliminate 1920 and 1947 on the argument of the previous footnote. One is less certain about the years 1921 and 1922.

2. The Years 1923–39 and 1948–57

The curve fitted to this period was of the form:[50]

$$\dot{W} = a + bU^{-1} + cU^{-4} + d\dot{U} + e\dot{P} + \varepsilon \tag{12}$$

which, when fitted to the data, gives

$$\dot{W} = +0.74 + 0.43U^{-1} + 11.18U^{-4} + 0.038\dot{U} + 0.69\dot{P} \tag{13}$$

R^2 for this relation is 0.91, while the squared partial correlation coefficients are $U = 0.38$, $\dot{U} = 0.30$, and $\dot{P} = 0.76$.[51]

There are a number of interesting things to note about these results.

(i) *The General Relation:* A very high proportion of the variance in $\dot{W}$ can be associated with these variables.[52] Thus the hypothesis that about the same proportion of the variance in $\dot{W}$ can be associated with U, $\dot{U}$, and $\dot{P}$ as in the earlier period is consistent with the facts.

(ii) *The Variable $\dot{P}$:* The importance of $\dot{P}$ as an explanatory variable has greatly increased compared with the pre-war period (a squared partial correlation coefficient of 0.76 compared to 0.17). The regression coefficient for $\dot{P}$ has also increased greatly (0.69 compared to 0.21). This indicates a substantial movement in the direction of a one-one relation between changes in prices and changes in wages. This is an extremely interesting change. The face-value interpretation is that the demand and supply model of Section II accounts for less of the variations in wage rates in the twentieth century than it did in the nineteenth, while more of the twentieth-century variations can be explained in terms of wages "chasing" prices or of prices chasing wages.

(iii) *The Variable U:* The fitted relation between $\dot{W}$ and U has changed substantially compared with the earlier period. The curve relating these variables has pivoted about the 3 percent unemployment level (see Fig. 9). The new curve lies above the old one for levels of U greater than 3 percent and below the old one for levels of U less than 3.[53] This indicates that the post-1922 experience was of less flexibility of wages in response to excess demand, whether positive or negative, than occurred in the pre-1914 period. It will also

---

[50] The curvature became much sharper in this period than it was in the nineteenth century. If Phillips' curve (2) were fitted to the data the coefficient γ would have been less than minus two. Thus the fixed coefficients on U had to be changed. The relationship described by equation (12) is the same as that described by (10) only the curvature is more marked.

[51] The standard error of estimate for $\dot{W}$ is 0.97; standard errors for the regression coefficients are: $b = 2.10$, $c = 6.00$, $d = 0.012$, $e = 0.08$. There is no evidence of significant auto-correlation of the residuals for lags of one to three periods at the 5 percent probability level. Correlation of the "independent variables" is as follows:

$$r^2\,(U, U) = 0.003;\ r^2\,(U, \dot{P}) = 0.47;\ r^2\,(\dot{U}, \dot{P}) = 0.09$$

[52] Corrected for degrees of freedom, the R^2 is 0.89.

[53] When the curve is fitted without a cost of living variable $[\dot{W} = f(U, \dot{U})]$, it shifts upwards from its pre-1914 position over its whole range, but when $\dot{P}$ is added the curve is found to pivot as described in the text.

be noted that the asymptote in equation (13) is positive. This indicates that, on the *average experience* of the 1920's and the 1930's, high levels of unemployment are not in themselves associated with a reduction in wages. Here again the theory of Section II must be recalled and the qualification "given the degree of sectoral inequality in unemployment that then existed" be emphasised.

(iv) *The Variable* $\dot{U}$: Finally, we must note the interesting changes in the relation between $\dot{W}$ and $\dot{U}$. Comparing equations (13) and (10), we see that the regression coefficient for $\dot{U}$ has changed signs. This reveals that, on the average experience of the post-1922 period, other things being equal, times of falling unemployment were associated with lower $\dot{W}$'s than were times of rising unemployment. It would appear then that Phillips' loops have changed directions. Before considering a theoretical explanation of this experience, it is necessary to check the relation between $\dot{W}$ and $\dot{U}$ in various sub-periods in order to determine exactly what it is that has to be explained. The data were broken up into three time periods and the following equation was fitted to each period.[54]

$$\dot{W} = a + bU + c\dot{U} + d\dot{P} + \varepsilon \qquad (14)$$

The coefficients for $\dot{U}$ were as follows:

$$1923\text{--}29 = +1.91, \qquad 1929\text{--}39 = -6.25, \qquad 1948\text{--}57 = +3.28$$

Thus we see that, taken period by period, the experience of the 1930's agreed with that of the nineteenth century while that of the 1920's and 1950's did not.

We must now ask if this experience can be explained by our theory. Feeding these data into the theory, we obtain the testable predictions that in the 1930's the upswing was associated with increasing degrees of sectoral inequalities in unemployment as some markets recovered very much more rapidly than did others. On the other hand, in the 1920's and the 1950's, downswings in activity were accompanied by increases in sectoral inequalities, while upswings were associated with decreases. Here again the theory accounts for the observations by producing hypotheses that are clearly testable. These tests, which are being conducted, are beyond the scope of the present paper.

These considerations point to the rejection of hypotheses (ii) and (iii) listed above. Hypothesis (ii), that the variables have had the same relative importance in explaining $\dot{W}$ in the periods before and since the first world war, is refuted by the fact that the partial correlation coefficients relating $\dot{W}$ to each of the independent variables have changed considerably. Hypothesis (iii) is refuted by the fact that the regression coefficients have changed markedly.

---

[54] The range of variations in U within each of the three periods is such that a linear approximation to the relation between $\dot{W}$ and U is quite adequate. A similar disaggregation for the nineteenth century is summarised in Table 1.

In the following sections the period under consideration is broken up into three sub-periods. By comparing the predictions of equation (10) fitted to the period 1862–1913 with those of equation (13) fitted to the present period, we seek to determine how and when these relationships have shifted.

3. *The Period 1920–29*

In the years 1920 and 1921, very large decreases in both the cost of living and money wage rates were experienced. When $\dot{W}$ for these years is predicted from equation (13) the errors are extremely large (a residual of 16.8 percent for 1921 and of 9.8 percent for 1922). This shows that the relation describing the remainder of the period (equation 13) is not a good description of these two years. This is mainly because the relation between $\dot{W}$ and $\dot{P}$ seems to be stronger in these two years than it is over the rest of the period.[55] In the years 1925 to 1929 the government attempted to check aggregate demand in order to reduce the price level. Unemployment stayed at about 10 percent, while wage rates fell on the average less than 1 percent per year. Phillips makes the point that the results of this experiment could have been predicted quite accurately on the basis of the experience for 1861–1913. The average annual reduction in wage rates that in fact occurred over the five years 1925–29 was 0.60 percent. The prediction for the annual average reduction made from the equation fitted to the 1862–1913 experience (equation 10) is 1.00 percent. We must conclude, therefore, that there was no reason to be surprised at the very slow reduction in wage rates that actually occurred, and that the experience of the late 1920's seems to provide little evidence of diminished downward flexibility of wage rates. The measurements give strong support to Phillips' statement (*loc. cit.*, p. 295) that: "The actual results obtained, given the levels of unemployment which were held, could have been predicted fairly accurately from a study of the pre-war data, if anyone had felt inclined to carry out the necessary analysis."

4. *The Period 1930–39*

The equation fitted to the pre-1914 data consistently underestimates the changes in wage rates over this period. In only three years, 1936, 1937, and 1939, does equation (10) not predict a fall in wage rates. The average annual predicted fall over the whole period is 0.54 percent, while the average annual error $\sum /R_{10}/ \div n$ was 1.67 percent. In fact, money wage rates rose from 1934 onwards and the average annual change in wage rates over the ten-year period was +0.99 percent. Equation (13), on the other hand, predicts this result quite accurately at 0.89 percent. Some of the errors in individual

---

[55] When $\dot{W}$ is estimated from the equation fitted to the years 1920–39 and 1947–57, the residuals are only 6.8 percent for 1921 and 1.8 percent for 1922. This shows how much the estimated relation is influenced by these extreme years.

years are, however, quite large and the average annual error over the period is 0.74 percent. We must conclude that there is evidence that $\dot{W}$ increased faster in the 1930's than in the pre-1914 period for comparable levels of U, $\dot{U}$, and $\dot{P}$.

It should also be noted that wages rose from 1934 onwards in spite of very high levels of unemployment (never less than 10 percent over the entire period). There are two probable causes of this experience. First, if we accept the results of the statistical analysis as showing an increased response of wages to changes in the cost of living, much of the rise in wages in the 1930's can be explained as a response to such changes (the average annual increase in the cost of living between 1934 and 1939 was 3.15 percent). If, however, the increase in wages due to cost of living changes is estimated from equation (13) and this amount deducted from the actual increase, the result is still positive.[56] Something further, then, is required to explain that part of the increase in wage rates not associated with $\dot{P}$. A second reason may be found in the degree of sectoral inequality in unemployment rates. The theory produces the testable hypothesis that from 1935 onwards there was sufficient excess demand in some markets to cause an increase in the national index of wage rates in spite of extremely large excess supplies in other markets.

5. *The Period 1948–57*[57]

Table 2 shows the observed and the predicted changes in wage rates over the period.[58]

It will be noted that the average annual increase predicted from equation (13) agrees very closely with the observed annual average, while the average predicted from equation (10) considerably underestimates the observed figure. Considering the predictions from equation (13), the large errors occur in the years 1949, 1950, and 1954. 1949–50 were the years of wage restraint, and the large errors shown in Table 2 indicate that over the two years wages rose much less than would have been expected from the experience of the rest of the period 1923–57. These large errors provide a measure of the effectiveness of the wage policy. In 1954, on the other hand, the increase in wage

---

[56] These corrected figures for $\dot{W}$ 1934 to 1939 are:

$$-0.62, \ +0.22, \ +0.13, \ +2.68, \ +0.13, \ -0.98.$$

[57] A detailed study of this period is to be found in L. A. Dicks-Mireaux and J. C. R. Dow, "The Determinants of Wage Inflation: United Kingdom, 1946–56," *The Journal of the Royal Statistical Society*, 1959. These authors obtain a coefficient of wages on prices of approximately 0.50.

[58] The figures have been changed to make them comparable with the earlier ones. The increase in coverage after the second war has been mainly in groups with very low unemployment percentages. Thus the post-war figures are not comparable with the pre-war ones. Mr. Routh (*loc. cit.*, p. 367) estimates that the figures for U must be raised by a minimum of $12\frac{1}{2}$ percent in order to make them comparable with the earlier figures. In the present study the figure has been increased by 20 percent. The most accurate adjustment probably lies somewhere between these two figures.

TABLE 2

Year	Observed $\dot{W}$	Estimated $\dot{W}$ Equation 13	Error	Estimated $\dot{W}$ Equation 10	Error
1948	3.73	2.89	0.85	4.28	−0.54
1949	1.82	3.58	−1.76	3.51	−1.69
1950	4.40	5.71	−1.31	4.29	0.11
1951	10.61	9.95	0.66	5.57	5.04
1952	5.28	5.49	−0.21	2.76	2.52
1953	2.90	2.49	0.41	3.37	−0.47
1954	4.88	3.76	1.12	4.53	0.35
1955	6.58	7.32	−0.74	5.92	0.66
1956	7.31	6.87	0.44	4.80	2.51
1957	5.50	5.19	0.31	3.09	2.41
Mean	5.30	5.33	0.78[59]	4.21	1.63[59]

rates was more than 1 percent in excess of the value predicted from equation (13). We must conclude, therefore, that, except for 1949 and 1950, there is evidence of a more rapid increase in wages in response to demand and prices in the period since the second world war than in the period prior to the first world war.

. . . .

Phillips used his curve relating $\dot{W}$ to U to predict the level of unemployment that would be compatible with stable prices and a 2 percent annual increase in productivity (a little under $2\frac{1}{2}$ percent according to Phillips). There are at least three very serious problems involved here. (i) The estimated value can be shifted a great deal by fitting curves of different types, by including additional variables, and by excluding particular years. *Thus, although it might be held with a high degree of confidence that a significant and very interesting relation had been discovered, a very low degree of confidence might be attached at this stage to a particular estimate of the parameters.*[60] (ii) The

---

[59] Ignoring signs.

[60] Mr. Routh in the article already cited has constructed some alternative series to the ones used by Phillips and has done some alternative correlations. He concludes (p. 314): "I have shown that there are other equations, in some ways more valid, that would give different results." To my mind, the remarkable thing is not that Mr. Routh is able to get different results, but that the differences are so slight for all the possible variations that he suggests (see, for example, his Diagram I, p. 311). He also appears to be rather uncritical in assessing the significance of his possible variations. For example, he suggests a possible alternative to the series used by Phillips for 1948–57 and concludes "The points in Professor Phillips' Fig. ii, if row 2 (Routh's series) were substituted for row 1 (Phillips' series), would no longer 'lie closely along a smooth curve which coincides almost exactly with the curve fitted to the 1861–1913 data' (p. 306)." This is just not correct. Consider the deviations of the two series from Phillips' curve. The standard deviation of the residuals for Routh's series are 1.6 and for Phillips 1.9, while the mean deviations are 1.4 for Routh and 1.1 for Phillips. We must conclude therefore that there is very little difference between the two series as far as lying on the curve is concerned.

theory outlined in Section II suggests that the fitted relation may not be a very good guide to the relation between $\dot{W}$ and U if U were to remain substantially unchanged for a long time. (iii) A satisfactory theoretical explanation (together with independent tests) would be needed of the high correlation between $\dot{W}$ and $\dot{P}$. Until more is known about the causal links between $\dot{W}$ and $\dot{P}$ it is very dangerous to argue as if either of these variables were independent of the other.[61]

The analysis given in this paper has considerable bearing on the controversy about the causes of inflation. There are a number of points to be noted here. Phillips clearly considered a high correlation between $\dot{W}$ and U as evidence in favour of a demand-pull as against a cost-push hypothesis. This is not the occasion to state these hypotheses in sufficient detail to make them testable. However, the theory outlined in Section II suggests that there are versions of the cost-push hypothesis which are compatible with this relation. The present study does, however, seem to refute the extreme version of the cost-push *spiral* which envisages as unstable a situation in which wages and prices chase each other in a non-convergent cycle. This theory predicts a one-one relation between changes in prices and changes in wages, and the present coefficient of 0.69 would, if correct, refute the theory. On the other hand, it must be noted that the considerable increase in the coefficient attached to $\dot{P}$ indicates a very much closer association between changes in prices and changes in wages after the first world war than before it. Only a very much more detailed analysis than that conducted here could attempt to sort out the direction of the causation between $\dot{P}$ and $\dot{W}$. The analysis so far conducted is, however, not inconsistent with the hypothesis that there is a strong feed-back from price changes to wage changes with a great deal *but not all* of the rise in wages being attributed to wages chasing prices.

In my opinion it would be a serious mistake to try to judge between cost-push and demand-pull hypotheses solely, or even mainly, on the basis of the present paper although the material presented here is relevant evidence. The conclusions of this analysis would seem to be much more important for economic theory than for *immediate* policy issues. At this stage the numerical values of any of the parameters is not so important; what is important is the possibility of measuring and testing the type of dynamic relation used here, and of building up a theory that will, as ours already has done, suggest further hypotheses, the testing of which will in turn suggest further improvements in the theory.

---

[61] When policy decisions must be made they have, of course, to be based on the best evidence available at the moment. A premature application to policy can, however, easily discredit a hypothesis that is potentially very fruitful.

25

Tested Knowledge of Business Cycles*

By GEOFFREY H. MOORE†

A DOZEN YEARS have passed since Arthur Burns wrote the National Bureau's Thirtieth Annual Report, *New Facts on Business Cycles.*[1] Three business cycles have come and gone. In the interim more new facts have been uncovered and many earlier findings have been tested, modified, and clarified. Such a process of discovery, testing, modification, and explanation is the essence of the National Bureau's research program, as of any scientific effort. In this way knowledge cumulates. It may be well to take stock once again of our work on business cycles. I shall concentrate on the contributions that have been made since Burns' report was written, note their practical use, and discuss some directions that future work might take. Such a review will demonstrate, I think, the unique value of continuity in our research program.

1. THE POSTWAR SETTING

The postwar period has testified to the continued potency of the forces that cause business cycles. At the outset it was uncertain whether the business cycle, as it had been known in the past, would continue to exist. The Great Depression and World War II had stimulated an enormous growth in governmental activity relative to private enterprise; new governmental functions, such as insuring of bank deposits and mortgages, provision of social insurance, and regulation of stock market trading, had been developed to prevent some of the serious consequences of depressions; and there was a new determination, epitomized in the Employment Act of 1946, to use governmental power when necessary to curb cyclical fluctuations. In the sequel, it is clear that these developments and some others have indeed

* National Bureau of Economic Research, Inc., *Forty-Second Annual Report*, June, 1962. Reprinted by courtesy of the National Bureau of Economic Research and the author.

† Associate Director of Research, National Bureau of Economic Research. I am indebted to Arthur F. Burns, Solomon Fabricant, and other colleagues for their suggestions on this report. Sophie Sakowitz and Alexander Pitts were responsible for the statistical work.

[1] Reprinted in *Business Cycle Indicators*, Princeton University Press for National Bureau of Economic Research, 1961, Vol. I, Chap. 2.

helped to reduce the severity of cyclical declines.[2] On the other hand, it is equally clear that the business cycle has not been eliminated.

Indeed, it is fair to say that the recessions since 1945 have stimulated much greater public interest in the problem of business cycles. Each of these recessions has also led to a variety of governmental actions for dealing with the problem. All this has made it easier for the student of business cycles to justify his work, and has whetted his appetite to pursue it. Besides, the business cycle policies of government have given rise to new questions for study. For example, what were the effects of these policies? How timely were they? How could they have been made more effective? What opportunities were missed and why?

Partly as a result of this interest and activity, the postwar student of business cycles has had at his command a greater wealth of current economic statistics than before. The figures are more frequent and timely—witness the replacement of annual by quarterly estimates of gross national product and its components; they are more appropriately designed—witness the publication nowadays of numerous economic indicators in seasonally adjusted form; and they cover some new dimensions of economic activity—witness the proliferation of data on businessmen's intentions to invest and consumers' intentions to spend.

In this setting, the National Bureau's research on business cycles has come to be used widely, not only in this country but also abroad. One evidence of this was the publication last autumn, following a protracted period of experimentation and testing in which Julius Shiskin played a primary role, of *Business Cycle Developments*, a monthly report of the United States Department of Commerce. This report, to which I shall refer frequently, contains a broad collection of economic indicators selected and classified by the National Bureau, relies upon the business cycle peak and trough dates established in the course of our researches, and includes a number of analytical measures largely developed in our studies.[3] Basically it owes its existence to the postwar developments I have mentioned—the continued occurrence of recessions, the great public interest in dealing with them, and the new emphasis on economic statistics. All this has stimulated both our own work and its application and testing by others, and has fostered the accumulation of knowledge of business cycles during the period since Burns wrote his *New Facts*.

Burns formulated four chief propositions in his report. I shall consider each of them in turn, describing some of the applications and tests that have

---

[2] See Arthur F. Burns, "Progress Towards Economic Stability," *American Economic Review*, March, 1960, pp. 1–19.

[3] Shiskin described the background and rationale of the new monthly report in *Signals of Recession and Recovery: An Experiment with Monthly Reporting*, Occasional Paper 77, New York, NBER, 1961.

since been made, and the additional knowledge we now have concerning them.

2. BURNS' "UNSEEN CYCLE"

A business cycle, according to the definition adopted by Burns and Mitchell,[4] not only is "a fluctuation in aggregate economic activity" but also consists of "expansions occurring at about the same time in many economic activities, followed by similarly general recessions, contractions, and revivals which merge into the expansion phase of the next cycle." Mitchell later elaborated one aspect of this definition: "Business cycles consist not only of roughly synchronous expansions in many activities, followed by roughly synchronous contractions in a slightly smaller number; they consist also of numerous contractions while expansion is dominant, and numerous expansions while contraction is dominant."[5] That is to say, it is characteristic of business cycles that they are widely diffused, but it is also characteristic that they are imperfectly diffused.

In his 1950 annual report Burns observed that this phenomenon of diffusion constitutes an "unseen cycle" that lies hidden within the movements of economic aggregates. During each expansion in total activity there is first a rise and then a fall in the scope of the expansion, and during each contraction in total activity there is first a rise and then a fall in the scope of contraction. Expansionary movements, which begin during a contraction in aggregate activity, spread from firm to firm, industry to industry, region to region, and from one aspect of economic activity to another, and this cumulative process takes time. Contractions in their turn spread in a similar way, beginning while aggregate activity is still rising, but engulfing more and more enterprises and processes until the tide turns and activity as a whole begins to decline. In this sense, recession begins while expansion is still dominant, and recovery begins while recession is still dominant.

This process is evident in every business cycle of which we have a record. Though it may have been "unseen" before Burns wrote, it has been "seen" ever since, both historically and currently. Before 1950 the only statistical evidence on this point—in the form of what has come to be known as a "diffusion index"—was historical in nature. These indexes showed what percentage of a group of activities had undergone expansion at different stages of past business cycles, but not what percentage was currently expanding. Since then many current diffusion indexes have been constructed, and a number are regularly published in *Business Cycle Developments*. From these one can determine quickly, for example, what proportion of companies in a large sample have recently experienced rising profits, or what proportion have recently increased their appropriations for new investment projects.

---

[4] *Measuring Business Cycles*, New York, NBER, 1946, p. 3.
[5] *What Happens during Business Cycles*, New York, NBER, 1950, p. 79.

Although the date when a business cycle expansion reaches its widest scope depends on how it is measured, diffusion indexes of a broadly representative sort have invariably reached their highest values some months before the peak in aggregate economic activity. Burns observed that this was true of all the prewar cycles, and it has continued to be true. The expansion of 1945–48 reached its widest scope in the fourth quarter of 1947, about a year before the business cycle peak. The next expansion (1949–53) reached its widest scope in the third quarter of 1950, narrowed, and then became fairly widespread again in the third quarter of 1952, about nine months before the business cycle peak. The 1954–57 expansion reached its maximum diffusion in the second quarter of 1955; aggregate activity continued to expand for two years more. The scope of the 1958–60 expansion was greatest in the second quarter of 1959, about a year before the cyclical peak.[6]

If there is not much uniformity in these intervals, this was also true of the prewar record. The "unseen cycle" casts a shadow of varying length before it. This limits, but does not destroy, its value. No one landmark on the road of business cycles seems to hold an absolutely fixed position; yet all together they can help us chart a sounder course.

The diffusion indexes that Burns examined in 1950 were not only historical in nature; they were limited in their coverage to the United States. Later research carried out in Canada, Japan, and Italy demonstrates that the diffusion phenomenon is characteristic of those economies as well, and resembles that of the United States (Chart 1). In these countries, too, business cycles are widely but imperfectly diffused, and the degree of diffusion has the property of waxing and waning in a cycle that precedes the cycle in aggregate activity.

Ise Mintz has extended diffusion analysis to world trade. Since cyclical movements in the imports of different countries are neither perfectly synchronized nor scattered at random, they form both a cycle in aggregate world trade and a diffusion cycle that precedes it (Chart 2). Her diffusion index shows that in most of the postwar period most countries have expanded their imports, but it also brings out the less well-known fact that at times very widespread reductions have occurred. At these times, or shortly afterward, our own exports have declined, and they have not begun to rise again until rising imports have become rather general in the rest of the world. The diffusion index is an indicator of demand for our exports, and they have been highly responsive to it. In these days, when the balance of payments is a matter of national concern, it is well to keep an eye on such clues as this index may give to the prospects for exports.[7]

---

[6] The dates of maximum diffusion are based on a monthly index covering employment in thirty-two and production in twenty-five nonfarm industries (see Shiskin, *Signals of Recession and Recovery*, p. 183). Other broadly based diffusion indexes reached peaks at about the same dates.

[7] Another type of clue is provided by statistics on orders of goods for export. See NBER, *Forty-Second Annual Report*, June, 1962, pp. 96–99.

Discerning the process of cyclical diffusion long after the fact is easy; recognizing what is going on currently is far more difficult, as the indexes in Chart 1 demonstrate. Numerous devices to accomplish this have been tested, both at the National Bureau and elsewhere, and more no doubt will

CHART 1

DIFFUSION INDEXES FOR SEVERAL COUNTRIES, 1919–61

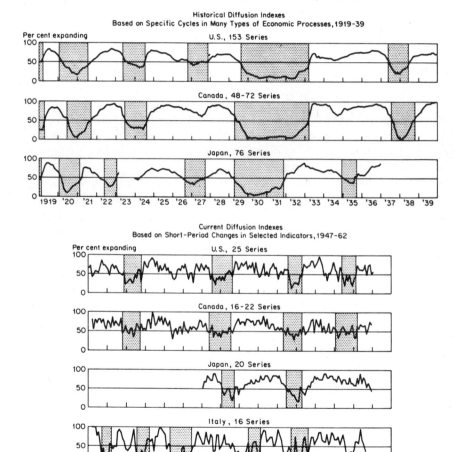

NOTE: Shaded areas represent business cycle contractions in each country; unshaded areas, expansions.
SOURCE: National Bureau of Economic Research, *Forty-Second Annual Report*, pp. 24–25.

be. Eventually it may become no more difficult to date a "reference peak" in diffusion indexes—representing the point at which the business cycle expansion reached its widest scope—than to date a business cycle peak, and likewise for troughs. If this could be done not too long after the event, it would improve our capacity to identify the current stage of the business cycle and to envisage the next stage.

The matter is important, for one of the findings to which the study of diffusion indexes has led is that the change in scope of an expansion or contraction during a business cycle has a great deal to do with the rate at which aggregate activity expands or contracts. Expansions do not proceed

CHART 2

UNITED STATES EXPORTS, WORLD IMPORTS, AND PERCENTAGE
OF COUNTRIES WITH RISING IMPORTS, 1947–61

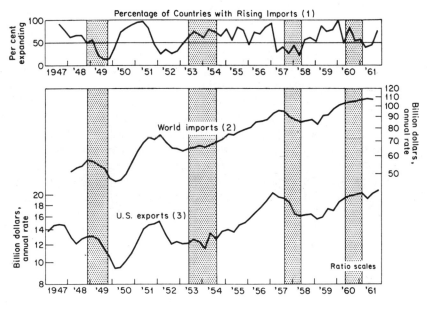

NOTE: Shaded areas represent U.S. business cycle contractions; unshaded areas, expansions.
SOURCE: Same as Chart 1.

at a constant pace. Some expansions are vigorous, others lethargic. There is much evidence to show that the variations both within and between expansions are attributable in large part to differences in the number of firms or industries that are expanding. Hence it would seem to be desirable, if we are concerned with preserving and extending the rate of growth of the economy, that we also be concerned with making expansion as general as is practicable. By this criterion, policies that have widespread stimulative effects are better, other things being equal, than those with narrow effects. Choices cannot, of course, always be made along these lines, but our studies of diffusion suggest that it may be an important consideration.

To illustrate the relation between diffusion and rate of expansion, consider the dates mentioned earlier, when the postwar expansions reached their widest scope. On the first occasion, the fourth quarter of 1947, gross national product in constant prices was currently rising at an annual rate of 6 percent. On the succeeding dates of maximum diffusion, the annual percentage rates of expansion in GNP were 19, 4, 8, and 12. So far the current expansion was most widespread in the second quarter of 1961, at which time the rate of expansion in GNP again was 12 percent per year. These rates are, of course, exceedingly high, far greater than those sustained over each expansion as a whole.[8] Except perhaps for the last, they occurred when each expansion was as widespread as it ever got to be.

3. LEADS AND LAGS

After commenting on the reasonableness of the proposition that cyclical movements spread gradually through the economy in the manner described by diffusion indexes, Burns lifted "the veil of anonymity" clothing these indexes and developed the proposition that this cumulative movement contains sequences that persist in some degree from one cycle to the next. A diffusion index based on a range of economic activities may tell us that the proportion undergoing expansion first rises and then falls during a business cycle upswing, but it does not tell which activities came first in the procession, or whether any of them came first in every cycle or most cycles.

Since these sequences may contain clues to the causal process of business cycles, it is important to look for them. One of the strongest conclusions that emerged from our studies of business cycles before World War II, Burns observed, was that "the check to the dominant movement of business activity, whether it be expansion or contraction, is typically felt especially early in financial processes and activities preparatory to investment expenditure." By this he meant that such indexes as new orders for investment goods, construction contracts and building permits, stock prices and market activity, new security issues, and starts of business enterprises typically turn down before aggregate production, employment, income, or sales, and that they typically turn up earlier also. Note that these activities are *preparatory* to investment expenditure, representing an early, decision-making stage of the process of investment, not the actual expenditure or final, installation stage.

This finding has been confirmed in the postwar period. Moreover, we now have some valuable new statistical series with which to observe the process. For example, one of the products of Zarnowitz' study of the cyclical behavior of new orders was a series that combined orders for machinery

---

[8] The rates cited are based on changes from the preceding quarter, converted to annual equivalents. The annual rates for the entire expansion from business cycle trough to business cycle peak are: IV 1945–IV 1948, 1.1 percent; IV 1949–II 1953, 7.2 percent; III 1945–III 1957, 4.3 percent; II 1958–II 1960, 5.9 percent. The rate for the first expansion is low, partly because GNP had, by the fourth quarter of 1945, not yet reached its lowest point. If the period I 1947–IV 1948 is used instead, the rate is 3.8 percent.

and equipment with contracts for construction of commercial and industrial buildings and utility plants. This monthly series, a direct descendant of Burns' compilation for 1919–39, is currently published in *Business Cycle Developments*. Burns' index reached cyclical highs and lows in advance of every business cycle peak and trough but one in the interwar period, with an average (median) lead of four months. The new series has led at every business cycle peak and trough of the postwar period, with an average (median) lead of five months. There can be no question that decisions to invest, in the aggregate, typically take an unfavorable turn well before there is any decline in aggregate output, sales, or income, and that they usually begin to improve before there is any improvement in these basic factors.

We shall return to this matter later. Meantime, note that there are other persistent sequences in business cycles. Some pertain to the labor market. For example, Bry has shown that in virtually all industries cyclical adjustments in the workweek take place prior to adjustments in employment, on the average about four months earlier. This comes about as enterprises seek to achieve a prompt and efficient balance of labor and other resources devoted to production. Other repetitive sequences are found among different types of inventories, as shown by Abramovitz' and Stanback's studies; in the markets for stocks and bonds, as Macaulay's and Hickman's work demonstrated; and in the behavior of prices, costs, and profits, as Hultgren has shown. Sequences in the cyclical movements of these diverse elements have different though related causes, and the authors of the studies mentioned have taken great care in working out the explanations and testing their hypotheses and findings. All of these types of sequence, and others, were mentioned in Burns' report, although additional work has been done since then.

One way in which we have sought to make the results available for practical use is to compile lists of indicators, classified according to their typical timing in business cycles. Three such lists have been constructed, one in 1938 by Mitchell and Burns, the other two by me in 1950 and 1960. Each of these lists has drawn on the studies that had previously been made, and each has been tested against subsequent data. One of them (the 1950 list) has also been tested on data for another country, Canada. The results reveal a substantial degree of persistence in the characteristic timing of the selected series.[9] The successive revisions in the lists reflect largely the expanding scope of our studies and the improvements in available data; changes in cyclical behavior account for only a small fraction of the revisions. For practical reasons the lists have been restricted to a modest number of indicators—twenty-one in the first two and twenty-six in the third. However, the publication of *Business Cycle Developments* has made it feasible to use a much larger list, which we

---

[9] See *Business Cycle Indicators*, Vol. I, Chaps. 1–4, 7, 10. For a test of the 1960 list, see NBER, *Forty-Second Annual Report*, June, 1962, pp. 65–66.

therefore supplied for the purpose. It also will make it convenient to revise the list more frequently and therefore to incorporate more promptly the results of new research and new statistical compilations.

Studies of leads and lags can, as I have said, contribute to understanding of the causal processes involved in business cycles. By helping us to recognize the interconnections among current developments, and to distinguish the more significant and meaningful from the less, they enhance our ability to forecast. As a result, although many uncertainties remain, a turn in the business cycle can now be recognized more promptly and with greater confidence than was the case twenty or even ten years ago.

4. THE ROLE OF PROFITS

The subject of price-cost-profit relations in business cycles has had a long history. Wesley Mitchell gave it much attention in his *Business Cycles* (1913). He viewed the encroachment of unit costs on prices as one of the critical factors that brought a boom to an end, just as he viewed the reduction of costs relative to prices as a significant factor in the revival in business that followed depression. There the matter was virtually left, as far as empirical research was concerned, until Hultgren took it up in his *American Transportation in Prosperity and Depression* (1948). The result left Mitchell doubtful about the validity of his original formulation,[10] but Hultgren's later work on other industries than railroads put a different face on the matter, as Burns observed in *New Facts*. In support of Mitchell's propositions, Burns cited the evidence contained in Hultgren's analysis of the diffusion of profits.[11]

Since then, Hultgren's further work on costs, prices, and profits, part of which was published in 1960, and Kendrick's study of productivity, published last year, have provided much new evidence.[12] Now, with the publication of *Business Cycle Developments*, one can trace currently, for the first time, many of the important links among the processes that center around the cyclical behavior of profits.

Let me state the salient findings on this subject as they now appear to stand, particularly for manufacturing industries. A collection of relevant series is shown in Charts 3 and 4. Table 1 summarizes the timing of these series at business cycle peaks and troughs since 1919.

---

[10] See Arthur F. Burns (ed.), *Wesley Clair Mitchell: The Economic Scientist*, New York, NBER, 1952, p. 53.

[11] *Cyclical Diversities in the Fortunes of Industrial Corporations*, Occasional Paper 32, New York, NBER, 1950; reprinted in *Business Cycle Indicators*, Vol. I, Chap. 11.

[12] Thor Hultgren, *Changes in Labor Cost During Cycles in Production and Business*, Occasional Paper 74, New York, NBER, 1960; John W. Kendrick, *Productivity Trends in the United States*, Princeton for NBER, 1961. See also Edwin Kuh, "Profits, Profit Markups, and Productivity," Study Paper 15, *Employment, Growth, and Price Levels*, Joint Economic Committee, 86th Congress, 1st Session, 1960. Canadian economists have cultivated this area, too, and their analysis of an independent body of information provides a valuable check on our own.

CHART 3

MANUFACTURING PRICES, COSTS, AND RELATED VARIABLES

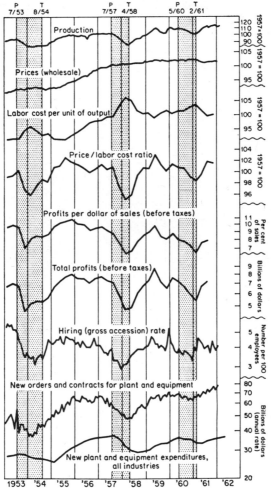

NOTE: All series are adjusted for seasonal variations. Shaded areas are business cycle contractions; unshaded areas, expansions. Prices, labor cost, and price/labor cost ratio are on arithmetic scales, all others on ratio scales.

SOURCE: Same as Chart 1.

1. Price-cost ratios and profit margins (profits per dollar of sales) undergo sharp fluctuations in general conformity with business cycles but with significant leads at both peaks and troughs.[13] The movements are so sharp that they

CHART 4

OUTPUT PER MAN-HOUR, HOURLY COMPENSATION, AND LABOR COST PER UNIT
OF OUTPUT, MANUFACTURING (ALL EMPLOYEES), 1947–61

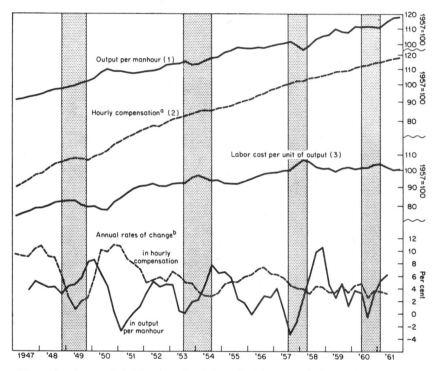

NOTE: All series are adjusted for seasonal variations. Shaded areas are business cycle contractions; unshaded areas, expansions (monthly chronology). The top three series are on ratio scales.
SOURCE: Same as Chart 1.
ᵃ Including wages, salaries, and supplements.
ᵇ Percentage changes between quarterly averages, one year apart, centered at midyear.

often dominate those in aggregate profits, even though the latter are sustained by rising sales while margins are declining toward the end of expansions, and are depressed by falling sales while margins are improving near the end of

---

[13] If the data on costs, prices, profits, and sales were comprehensive and comparable, the profit margin would be equal to one minus the reciprocal of the price-cost ratio. Hence the movements in the margin and the ratio would always be in the same direction and their turning points would coincide. The series used in Chart 1 and Table 1 do not possess this elegant relationship, but since 1947 (when the margin data begin) their movements have been closely correlated.

TABLE 1

COSTS, PROFITS, AND RELATED VARIABLES: NUMBER OF LEADS AND LAGS AND THEIR MEDIAN AT BUSINESS CYCLE PEAKS AND TROUGHS, 1919–61

	Manufacturing Production (1)	Wholesale Prices, Mfd. Goods (2)	Labor Cost per Unit of Output, Mfg. Positive (3)	Labor Cost per Unit of Output, Mfg. Inverted (4)	Ratio, Price to Unit Labor Cost, Mfg. (5)	Corp. Profits after Taxes, Mfg. (6)	Gross Access. Rate, Mfg. (7)	Orders and Contracts for Investment Goods (8)	Plant and Equipment Expenditures (9)
Leads exceeding 12 mos.	..	..	..	3	2	..	4	1	..
Leads of 7–12 mos.	1	2	..	5	4	4	4	2	..
Leads of 1–6 mos.	6	4	..	3	10	7	9	14	2
Coincidences	7	2	..	1	1	4	2	1	4
Lags of 1–6 mos.	3	4	6	1	2	2	..	..	13
Lags of 7–12 mos.	..	..	6	..	..	..	..	..	..
Lags exceeding 12 mos.	..	1	3	..	..	..	..	..	..
Total Comparisons	17	13	15	13	19	17	19	18	19
Bus. Cycle Turns Skipped									
Number	2	6	4	5	..	..	..	..	..
Years when they occurred	'26–7	'53–61	'24–9	'26–33, '48	..	..	..	..	..
Bus. Cycle Turns Not Covered									
Number	..	..	..	1	..	2	..	1	..
Years when they occurred	..	..	..	'19	..	'19–20	..	'48	..
Extra Specific Cycle Turns									
Number	..	2	2	2	2	4	4	..	..
Years when they occurred	..	'51–2	'34–6	'33–4	'33–4	'33–4, '50–1	'33–6, '51	..	..
Median lead (−) or lag (+), in mos.	0	0	+9	−8	−4	−2	−4	−5	+1

NOTE: Leads or lags at the wartime peak, February, 1945, and postwar trough, October, 1945, are omitted. When unit labor cost is treated invertedly (col. 4), peaks are matched with business cycle troughs and troughs with business cycle peaks.

SOURCE: Same as Chart 1.

contractions. As a result of the sharp movements in the ratio of prices to costs, the average (median) lead of aggregate profits at business cycle turns since 1919 has been only slightly shorter than the average lead of the price-cost ratio: two months in the one case, four months in the other (Table 1, cols. 5 and 6). Turns in both the price-cost ratio and in total profits have usually preceded the corresponding turns in production, although the tendency is clearer in the ratio than in total profits, and the evidence of a lead in profits is stronger for the postwar than for the prewar period.

2. The cyclical leads of profit margins cannot be attributed to early downturns or upturns in the prices of manufactured goods. This price level has usually risen throughout business cycle expansions and stabilized or fallen throughout contractions. The price-cost ratio and the profit margin have usually turned before prices, and in recent cycles have undergone sharp cyclical contractions even while the price level was rising.

3. The timing of profit margins is primarily determined by the movements of unit costs, particularly unit-labor costs. These costs have usually declined during the initial stages of business cycle expansions, but have begun to rise before the end of expansion (that is, while output was still rising), and the upturn has been accompanied or soon followed by a downturn in profit margins. Unit costs have continued to rise during the early months of business contractions, but have turned down usually a few months before the end, reversing the decline in margins. Of course, like the two blades of the proverbial scissors, both prices and costs determine margins, but costs have generally been the widely moving element accounting for the leads in margins.[14]

4. Unit-labor costs tend to move inversely with output because of the overhead nature of certain types of jobs, contractual commitments, and so on, but at the same time other factors cause them to move in a significantly different way from output.[15] Were it not for these differences, profit margins and price-cost ratios might be expected to duplicate the movements of production rather than to lead them.

5. Some of the factors that bring about the distinctive behavior of unit-labor costs can be seen when cost is subdivided into its two components, average hourly compensation and output per man-hour. The early stages of a

---

[14] This result for manufacturing is confirmed by economy-wide data for all corporations developed by Kuh in the study cited in footnote 12. He defines the profit markup as the ratio of the value of net output to wages, with the value of net output being equal to profits plus wages. Hence the markup is equal to the ratio of prices to labor cost per unit of output; in terms of the profit margin, it is the reciprocal of one minus the margin (see footnote 13). Kuh divides the quarterly percentage change in markup into a price component and three other components: net output, man-hours, and hourly wage rate (see his Table 8, p. 107), which we have combined to form a unit labor cost component. We find that in 34 out of 49 quarters, 1947–59, the cost effect on the profit markup exceeded the price effect. On the average, it was twice as large. In addition, the cost effect was highly correlated over time with the change in the markup, whereas the price effect was not.

[15] Compare the inverted timing comparisons for labor costs with the (positive) comparisons for production in Table 1, cols 4 and 1.

business cycle expansion usually witness a rapid rise in output per man-hour and a slower rise in hourly compensation; hence unit costs decline. In the later stages, output per man-hour rises less rapidly than before, and hourly compensation more rapidly. When the advance in compensation exceeds that in output per man-hour, unit costs rise. This happened, for example, in 1950, 1955, and again in 1959, as Chart 4 shows. When business contracts, a brief decline usually occurs in man-hour output while compensation rates continue to rise, lifting unit costs. Later in the contraction the rate of increase in output per man-hour picks up while the advance in hourly compensation weakens; and when the former exceeds the latter, unit costs begin to decline. As the chart shows, this occurred in manufacturing industry as a whole in 1949, 1954, 1958, and 1961. Thus the wide swings in the rate of change in output per man-hour and in hourly compensation have pursued very different courses during business cycles, and their systematic failure to synchronize has been responsible for the cyclical swings in unit-labor costs and, ultimately, for those in profit margins.[16]

In this account, I have traced only the proximate factors determining the cyclical behavior of costs and profits. A full account would, of course, deal with the effect on prices and sales of changes in demand by business enterprises, consumers, and government; with the effect on output per man-hour of changes in the level of output, in the efficiency of workers and management, and in the utilization of capacity; with the effect on hourly compensation of changes in overtime earnings, in the relative number of employees at various wage levels, and in wage and salary rates as affected by escalation clauses and the negotiation of new contracts; and with the effect on costs of such factors as materials prices, interest payments, and maintenance. A full account would also tell what diffusion indexes of prices, profits, costs, and output contribute to our knowledge of the way these developments spread from industry to industry and from firm to firm. Finally, it would consider whether my sketch applies to industries outside of manufacturing, as well as to what extent it is representative of individual manufacturing industries.[17] Many of these matters are covered in Hultgren's investigation.

---

[16] Kendrick's recent study of productivity provides some interesting information on cyclical patterns of change in output per man-hour in manufacturing, although his data are annual. In the first year of each of the nineteen business cycle expansions from 1888 to 1960, output per man-hour rose, and the average change was +7.2 percent. Sixteen of these expansions lasted at least two years; the average change in the first year was +7.7 percent; in the second, +2.6 percent. For the eight expansions that lasted at least three years, the average change in the first year was +7.1 percent; in the second, +3.3 percent; and in the final year of expansion, −0.6 percent. Output per man-hour declined in the final year of six of these eight expansions. In the first year of the eighteen business cycle contractions, the average change in output per man-hour was +0.3 percent. In eight instances it fell; in ten it rose. Since only three contractions lasted more than a year, on an annual basis, the data provide virtually no information on the characteristic pattern of change during contractions.

[17] In addition, there are important technical questions having to do with the measurement of output per man-hour, prices, costs, and profits. For example, the series on output

If costs do have a dominant influence on the cyclical behavior of profit margins, which in turn dominate the swings in total profits, they must play an important role in the generation of business cycles, as Mitchell long ago suspected. For along with other developments they affect the prospect of profit, which remains one of the strongest incentives in a private enterprise economy. How far does the upturn in costs and the ensuing downturn in margins that takes place while sales and output are still expanding explain the downturn in orders for equipment and contracts for plant construction, which also occurs while business is expanding? Does the price-cost squeeze, and its reversal, help to explain the leads in the hiring rate and in the layoff rate? Is it a factor in the early turns in the number of new enterprises established and in the bankruptcies of larger-size businesses, which have been a regular feature of business cycles for nearly a hundred years, as Zarnowitz and Lerner have shown? These apparent links between costs, prices, profits, and decisions by business enterprises to expand or contract operations need to be carefully checked and worked out. With the data now available we are in a good position to carry out such a study.

5. MILD AND SEVERE DEPRESSIONS

Burns concluded his report on *New Facts* with the proposition that there are systematic differences between mild and severe depressions, and that the elucidation of these differences is a crucially important line of research, because severe depressions must be prevented. As an indication of the way in which developments during a boom may increase the severity of a subsequent depression, he cited the work of Mintz and of Saulnier, which disclosed that the quality of new issues of foreign government bonds and of urban mortgages deteriorated as the boom of the 1920's progressed. This deterioration contributed, through its impact on default rates, to the severity of the depression of the thirties. He thought that further research would be fruitful on this and on other clues to the problem why some business contractions remain mild while others become extremely serious.

Although each of the five contractions since World War II has, by comparison with the more severe prewar contractions, been mild or moderate, the problem is still an important one. Closely related to it, and no less important,

---

per man-hour used in Chart 4 is based on an index of output constructed, in part, with the aid of interpolated and extrapolated measures of output per man-hour; hence it reflects, in part, these interpolations and extrapolations rather than actually recorded levels. It is also based on an estimate of man-hours that assumes, for lack of information, that so-called nonproduction workers were employed for a forty-hour week throughout the period. These assumptions can be, and to some extent have been, tested and the results compared with alternative methods of estimation. One of the critical tests is the comparison of the price-labor cost ratio with the independently derived profit per dollar of sales (see Chart 3). The broad conclusions are supported by these tests, but the figures cannot be regarded as precise.

is the problem of ensuring the vigor of expansions. Of the advances in our understanding of these matters that have been made in recent years, I shall discuss two in some detail and briefly mention others.

The method of cyclical analysis described by Burns and Mitchell in *Measuring Business Cycles* (1946) involved the computation of patterns showing in skeleton form the behavior of a given statistical series during each business cycle that it covered. From these patterns the characteristic behavior of production, prices, and other activities could be discerned, and the patterns could be used to reveal the cyclical interrelationships among different economic variables. In recent years we have given attention to the adaptation of these patterns to current business cycle analysis, and in particular to the problem of distinguishing, as promptly as possible, severe contractions and vigorous expansions from their milder counterparts.

Some examples of the results are shown in Chart 5. Consider the second panel, industrial production. The numbered points represent the course of production during each business cycle recovery since 1920. Points numbered (1) refer to the recovery that began in November 1927, following the mildest contraction of the entire period. Points numbered (10) refer to the recovery beginning March 1933, following the severe contraction of 1929–33. The other recoveries are arrayed similarly, the current recovery (solid line) being (3) since the 1960–61 contraction is the third mildest in the list. Except for the current recovery the levels are shown only every six months in order to simplify the chart. The dashed line is an average (median) pattern based on the six recoveries that followed mild or moderate contractions, this range of experience being most nearly pertinent to the current situation.

Historical analysis of the type described by Burns and Mitchell led to certain findings concerning the behavior of industrial production during business cycles. One was that rates of increase during the initial stages of recovery were generally larger following severe contractions than following mild ones. Another was that initial rates of increase (during, say, the first six to twelve months) usually exceeded those at any subsequent time during the business expansion, although the retardation that occurred after the initial spurt was often succeeded by some reacceleration toward the end of expansion.[18]

The production patterns serve both to demonstrate these findings and to relate them to recent experience. The fact that in each column of dots the higher numerals are generally at the top demonstrates the first finding, since the high numerals identify recoveries following severe contractions.

---

[18] A deficiency of Chart 5 is that it does not clearly depict events at the end of expansion, since expansions have lasted various lengths of time, often more than the twenty-four months covered by the chart. Hence the protracted slowing down in the growth of industrial production shown by the median (dashed) line on the chart does not properly characterize what happens toward the end of a business cycle expansion, although the rate of growth in, say, the last twelve months of expansion has, as a rule, been smaller than in the first twelve.

CHART 5

A Sample of Business Recovery Patterns

1. GROSS NATIONAL PRODUCT, IN CURRENT PRICES

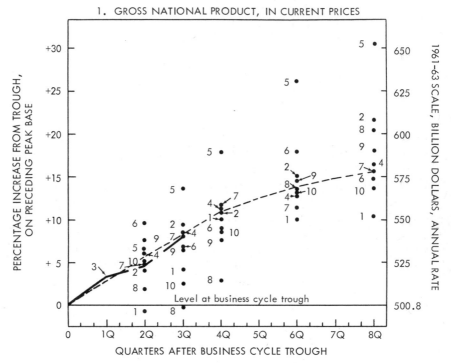

QUARTERS AFTER BUSINESS CYCLE TROUGH

1Q61   2Q61   3Q61   4Q61   1Q62   2Q62   3Q62   4Q62   1Q63

Standing at II Q 1960 business cycle peak: 506.4; at I Q 1961 trough: 500.8.

———————— Recovery beginning Feb. (IQ) 1961.

— — — — Median of previous recoveries that followed mild or moderate recessions (nos. 1, 2, 4, 5, 6, 7).

Arabic numerals identify recovery periods arrayed according to severity of the
preceding recession, beginning with the mildest. The periods start with the
business cycle trough, as follows:

1. Nov. (IVQ) 1927   4. Aug.(IIIQ)1954   7. Apr.(IIQ) 1958   10. Mar.(IQ) 1933
2. Oct. (IVQ) 1945   5. Oct.(IVQ)1949   8. July(IIIQ) 1921
3. Feb. (IQ) 1961 6. July(IIIQ) 1924 9. June(IIQ) 1938

SOURCE: Same as Chart 1

The greater rate of increase in production during the first six months of
recovery than later is apparent, too. Although many factors affect the pace
of a recovery and cause the variations that are evident in the chart, it also
reveals some—although not a high—degree of stability in the relative positions of the several recoveries after the first six months.

CHART 5 (*continued*)

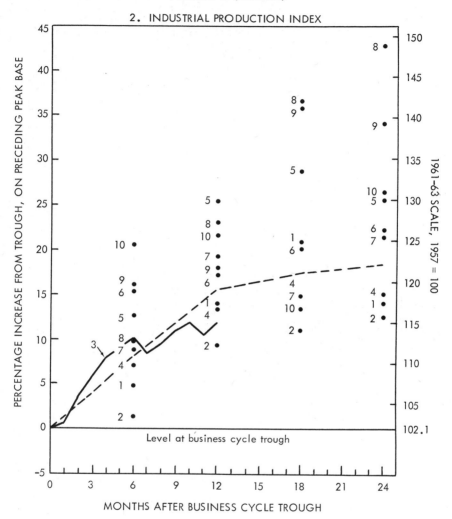

2. INDUSTRIAL PRODUCTION INDEX

PERCENTAGE INCREASE FROM TROUGH, ON PRECEDING PEAK BASE

1961-63 SCALE, 1957 = 100

Level at business cycle trough

MONTHS AFTER BUSINESS CYCLE TROUGH

Feb.61 May 61 Aug.61 Nov.61 Feb.62 May 62 Aug.62 Nov.62 Feb.63

Standing at May 1960 business cycle peak: 190.3 (3 mo. av.); at February 1961 trough: 102.1.

A broad collection of such patterns, covering various aspects of economic activity, such as employment, income, sales, prices, costs, profits, and investment, can, I think, bring into useful focus a large portion of the histori- cal experience garnered in our business cycle studies, demonstrating the variations that have occurred from cycle to cycle as well as the consensus,

CHART 5 (*continued*)

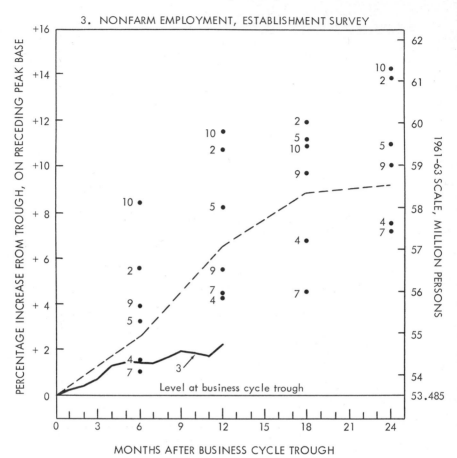

3. NONFARM EMPLOYMENT, ESTABLISHMENT SURVEY

MONTHS AFTER BUSINESS CYCLE TROUGH

Feb.61   May 61   Aug.61   Nov.61   Feb.62   May 62   Aug.62   Nov.62   Feb.63

Standing at May 1960 business cycle peak: 54.608 (3 mo. av.); at February 1961 trough: 53.485.

revealing relationships between unusual developments in one sector and those in another, and helping distinguish the economy's larger swings from its more ephemeral twists and turns. Some charts of this sort are provided each month in *Business Cycle Developments*. By such means any current expansion can be compared with its predecessors as it proceeds, its vigor can be assessed, forecasts of its future course appraised, and unusual aspects noted. Similar charts can be constructed for recessions, and appear to be helpful in distinguishing the more severe of these episodes from the less.

CHART 5 (*continued*)

4. PERSONAL INCOME

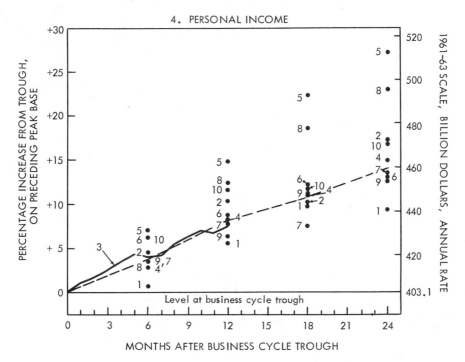

Feb.61 May 61 Aug.61 Nov.61 Feb.62 May 62 Aug.62 Nov.62 Feb.63

Standing at May 1960 business cycle peak: 403.1 (3 mo. av.); at February 1961 trough: 403.1.

During the 1957–58 recession we conducted an experiment designed to facilitate a series of judgments on its ultimate severity. Historical evidence had suggested that, about four months after a downturn began, features that would distinguish a severe contraction from a mild one could begin to be discerned in early-moving indicators. As the contraction proceeded, more evidence would accumulate month by month, providing a basis for revising or retaining the initial judgment and reducing the uncertainty surrounding it, although no more than a rough ranking of the current contraction relative to earlier ones was envisaged. The method also provided an approximate estimate of how long economic activity would remain depressed, based essentially on an estimate of how long it would take, after recovery started, to regain the prerecession level. The latter intervals are generally shorter, the milder the contraction.

The preliminary results for 1957–58 were published in *Measuring Recessions* (Occasional Paper 61, 1958), and a supplement showing how the

CHART 5 *(continued)*

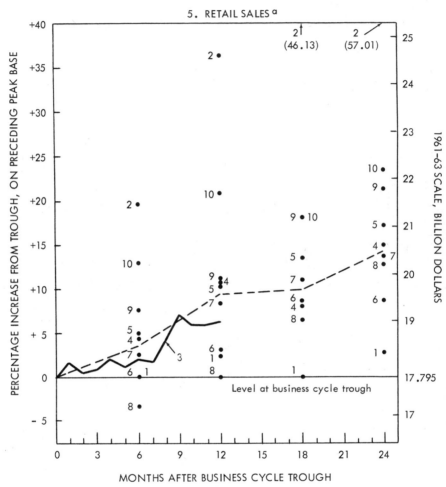

5. RETAIL SALES ᵃ

MONTHS AFTER BUSINESS CYCLE TROUGH

Feb.61 May 61 Aug.61 Nov.61 Feb.62 May 62 Aug.62 Nov.62 Feb.63

Standing at May 1960 business cycle peak: 18.585 (3 mo. av.); at February 1961 trough: 17.795.

ᵃDepartment store sales for 1, 6, 8, 10.

experiment ultimately turned out was included in *Business Cycle Indicators.* The 1957–58 contraction ranked fifth in ultimate severity among the eight that had occurred since 1920[19] and the period of "depressed activity" lasted

_____

[19] Omitting the contraction of February–October, 1945 because of its anomalous character.

CHART 5 *(concluded)*

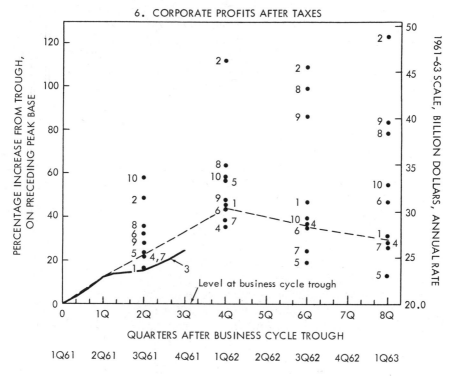

6. CORPORATE PROFITS AFTER TAXES

QUARTERS AFTER BUSINESS CYCLE TROUGH

1Q61   2Q61   3Q61   4Q61   1Q62   2Q62   3Q62   4Q62   1Q63

Standing at II Q 1960 business cycle peak: 23.3; at I Q 1961 trough: 20.0.

nineteen months according to the industrial production index. This ranking was initially indicated by data covering the first four months of the contraction, i.e., July–November, 1957, and was substantially confirmed in each succeeding month thereafter. The period of "depressed activity" was considered likely, on the basis of historical experience, to fall within a range of eighteen to thirty months, and the actual interval turned out to be at the lower end of this range.

A similar experiment was carried out during the 1960–61 recession. In this case, data covering the first four months (May–September, 1960) suggested that the contraction would rank close to the mildest of the eight since 1920, and this ranking was substantially supported in each succeeding month.[20] The total decline from the business cycle peak, May, 1960, to the

---

[20] See my testimony at the hearings on the *Current Economic Situation and Short-Run Outlook* before the Joint Economic Committee, 86th Congress, 2nd Session, December 7 and 8, 1960, pp. 92–107.

trough, February, 1961, turned out to be, by most measures, somewhat larger than the 1926–27 contraction, but smaller than any of the other seven. The period of "depressed activity," thirteen months as measured by the industrial production index, was correspondingly brief.

These experiments are an example of efforts to take account of the fact that the amplitude of each business cycle varies from its fellows, to understand the variations that have occurred, and to utilize that understanding in appraising the current cycle. Let me now turn to another illustration, prompted by the recent publication by the Joint Economic Committee of Thomas Stanback's *Postwar Cycles in Manufacturers' Inventories.*[21] This monograph has also been published by the National Bureau as No. 11 in Studies in Business Cycles.

In his basic study, *Inventories and Business Cycles* (1950), Abramovitz observed that changes in the rate of accumulation of inventories are related to the cyclical swings in business activity in a highly important and systematic way; their contribution to an upswing or downswing is likely to be large initially, but to dwindle as the expansion or contraction lengthens. Consequently, in short business cycle phases the change in inventory investment is apt to have a dominating influence, whereas in longer swings other factors take on the chief role.

Stanback shows that this pattern has continued to be true of the postwar period. Reductions in inventory investment have been a prime factor in each of the postwar business contractions, which have been relatively short. On the other hand, increases in inventory investment have been of primary significance only in the early stages of the expansions, which have been relatively long. For example, in the four expansions between 1946 and 1960, gross national product (in 1954 prices) rose by $20 billion in the first year and by $14 billion in the second, on the average. The rise in inventory investment contributed $4 billion to the advance in the first year, less than half a billion in the second. Not only did the contribution of inventory investment to the rate of expansion in GNP become smaller as the expansions proceeded, but it accounted for a large part of the reduction in the rate of expansion itself.

Hence there is a systematic shift in the effect of inventory investment on economic activity during a business cycle. There is also a shift in its composition. The initial impact during an expansion, Stanback shows, is largely attributable to a rise in investment in purchased materials and goods-in-process inventories. Later on the rise in investment in finished-goods inventories typically becomes the dominant factor. Similar statements apply to contractions.

Stanback probes further into the behavior of purchased materials by

---

[21] Printed in *Inventory Fluctuations and Economic Stabilization*, 87th Congress, 1st Session, 1961.

examining the level of unfilled orders, which provides a motive for accumulating materials for future use, and the availability of materials, which also can stimulate or inhibit accumulation. Ruth Mack has been investigating a new concept in this connection, one that combines stocks of materials on hand with those that are on order. Since purchasing decisions are made with an eye on both quantities, and unforeseen changes in the one can be offset quickly by deliberate changes in the other, this idea is surely worth pursuing. A preliminary draft of her analysis appeared in the Joint Committee print referred to above; a final version will, we expect, be completed shortly.

These investigations have an important bearing on the brief and relatively mild business cycle contractions that have characterized the postwar economy. Substantial progress has been made, also, on other research on the severity of depressions and the vigor of expansions. Earley and his associates have followed up the findings of Mintz and Saulnier on the quality of credit with an extensive investigation designed to produce means of detecting signs of deterioration at an early stage. The studies of Friedman and Schwartz have revealed that sharp contractions in the money supply have occurred only in severe depressions. Abramovitz' study of long waves suggests that during the long upswings in construction, business cycle expansions have usually been long and vigorous and contractions brief and mild; while during the long downswings, the reverse has generally been the case. All these studies are nearing completion.

* * *

6. CONTINUITY

In May, 1938 the National Bureau published its first report on business cycle indicators; in October, 1961, some twenty-three years later, a federal agency began publishing a monthly statistical report based on our most recent selection and classification of indicators. This experience is not unique. Many of the results of National Bureau studies have eventually been incorporated in the regular statistical work of government agencies—the estimates of national income, of productivity, of consumer credit, of the flow of funds, for example. This outcome, fostered by the cooperation and initiative of many government economists and other officials, has made our research more broadly useful. But it would not have come about unless the research itself commanded confidence, and confidence is not attained overnight.

The scientific integrity of the individual who is responsible for the research—the author—is one basic ingredient upon which this confidence depends. There are also other vital ingredients, not the least of which is the careful review of each of our studies by the research staff, by the Board, and often by outside experts. This reviewing process virtually always brings out points that require revision or clarification before final publication.

Another factor, and one that I wish to stress, is the continuity in our research program itself. Continuity and responsibility go together. If mistakes have, despite all precautions, been made, it is our duty to correct them; if new data suggest that earlier results are no longer valid, it is our duty to set them straight. In this way confidence in the dependability of research is built up and preserved.

Continuity in a research program also helps to ensure that the results of research will cumulate, producing a growing body of tested knowledge. *Ad hoc* projects are much less likely to have this effect. All research generates questions as well as answers. In a continuing program the questions can be picked up and new studies planned to deal with them. New ideas generated in the course of research become the focus of new work, and the interest and experience of those engaged is enlisted to the full.

Finally, continuity in a research program fosters thoroughness. Investigations of this type take a great deal of time—time to collect the evidence, time to think through its implications, time to recover from false starts, time to consider the views of one's colleagues, time to write and rewrite the results and to document them so that others can verify the work and extend it. The problems we select must be worth the time—and the money that it costs. If we choose our research wisely, we shall anticipate many of the problems of the day and make it easier to reach sound conclusions.

The history of the National Bureau's research has demonstrated this truth over and over again. When Mitchell and Burns were requested by the Secretary of the Treasury, in the fall of 1937 as the economy was undergoing a sharp contraction, to tell him what statistical series would give the earliest reliable indication that the contraction was coming to an end, they were able to give him a prompt answer. The answer was not only essentially valid for that contraction but for every one since. This accomplishment was made possible by the basic studies of business cycles that they could draw upon, which had been under way for many years before 1937. Last summer, when the Joint Economic Committee requested the National Bureau for a report that would contribute to their investigation of inventory fluctuations and economic stabilization, we were able within a short time to provide them with the results of Stanback's work, the culmination of several years of methodical research. His work in turn depended heavily upon Abramovitz' study, which was begun in 1938, just as Abramovitz had depended upon other studies of the National Bureau. The confidence that Stanback's report justifies is a product of the continuing program of basic research of which it was a part.

"The ultimate goal of science in any field," Milton Friedman[22] once wrote, "is a theory—an integrated 'explanation' of observed phenomena that can be used to make valid predictions about phenomena not yet observed.

---

[22] *Wesley Clair Mitchell, The Economic Scientist*, p. 237.

Many kinds of work can contribute to this ultimate goal and are essential for its attainment: the collection of observations about the phenomena in question; the organization and arrangement of observations and the extraction of empirical generalizations from them; the development of improved methods of measuring or analyzing observations; the formulation of partial or complete theories to integrate existing evidence."

We have not reached this ultimate goal, but we are striving toward it—in our business cycle studies as in our other major investigations.

V. LONG CYCLES

26

Introduction

THE SUBJECT of "long waves" has interested economists and economic historians for a good many years. Largely due to the work of Kondratieff, attention was initially directed to the possible existence of long swings of 50 to 60 years; and the "Kondratieff cycle" played an essential role in, for example, Schumpeter's interpretation of business cycle history.[1] Evidence in favor of such a long swing in real variables, as distinct from price and value series, has not accumulated,[2] and interest in the Kondratieff swing has tended to wane since World War II.[3]

Instead, attention has increasingly turned toward the possible existence of a cycle in economic growth of some 15 to 20 years in duration. The pioneering studies that first suggested the existence of these intermediate swings were made in the early 1930's by Simon Kuznets and Arthur F. Burns.[4] Following the suggestion first made in the article by O'Leary and Lewis reprinted here, these swings have come to be called "Kuznets cycles."

The paper by Moses Abramovitz reprinted here first appeared, appropriately enough, in a collection of essays in honor of Kuznets. This article is particularly interesting because of its attempt to explore the types of interrelationships which might generate these long swings. For a more detailed presentation of the statistical evidence which Abramovitz has compiled, the reader should consult the source cited in footnote 16 of his paper in this volume. Mention should also be made of the interesting recent paper by

---

[1] See N. D. Kondratieff, "The Long Waves in Economic Life," *Review of Economic Statistics*, Vol. XVII (November, 1935), pp. 105–15, and J. A. Schumpeter, "The Analysis of Economic Change," *Review of Economic Statistics*, Vol. XVII (May, 1935), pp. 1–10. Both of these were reprinted in the *A.E.A.* volume of *Readings in Business Cycle Theory* (1944). See also J. A. Schumpeter, *Business Cycles* (New York: McGraw Hill, 1939).

[2] See, for example, George Garvy, "Kondratieff's Theory of Long Cycles," *Review of Economic Statistics*, Vol. XXV (November, 1943), pp. 203–20.

[3] See, however, L. H. Dupriez, *Des Mouvements Economiques Généraux* (Louvain, 1947), and *Philosophie des Conjonctures Economiques* (Louvain, 1959).

[4] Simon Kuznets, *Secular Movements in Production and Prices* (New York: Houghton Mifflin, 1930), and Arthur F. Burns, *Production Trends in the United States Since 1870* (New York: National Bureau of Economic Research, 1934). Abramovitz, in the paper reprinted here, refers also to the slightly earlier work of C. A. R. Wardwell.

Bert G. Hickman which interprets postwar American experience in terms of Kuznets cycles.[5]

The paper by O'Leary and Lewis probably represents the most systematic and inclusive attempt so far made to ascertain whether these long swings have occurred in countries other than the United States. Additional evidence has been supplied by Kuznets in his recent comparative work on economic growth.[6]

The Kuznets swings obviously bear a close relationship to the long building cycle, on which there is considerable literature that goes back a good many years. Unfortunately, no examples of that literature are included in the present volume. The reader interested in these long swings should also have his attention called to a series of articles by Walter Isard on the "transport-building cycle," one of which is mentioned by Abramovitz.

---

[5] B. G. Hickman, "The Postwar Retardation: Another Long Swing in the Rate of Growth?" *American Economic Review: Papers and Proceedings*, Vol. LIII (May, 1963), pp. 490–507.

[6] See "Quantitative Aspects of the Economic Growth of Nations: I. The Levels and Variability of Rates of Growth," *Economic Development and Cultural Change*, Vol. V (October, 1956), esp. pp. 44–51. Mention should also be made of the studies by Brinley Thomas and A. K. Cairncross, both of which are referred to by Abramovitz.

27

The Nature and Significance of
Kuznets Cycles*

By MOSES ABRAMOVITZ†

TWO FORMS of general economic change have long been accepted by most economists as systematic features of industrialized economies organized under capitalist institutions. One is persistent long-term growth; the other is the business cycle.

Both are generalizations of apparently irregular behavior. Total output rarely rises or falls at the same rate for two consecutive months, and it seldom moves in the same direction for many months together. These irregular movements, however, are not without pattern. The month-to-month movements are, for periods of time, predominantly upward, and these periods of expansion are succeeded by other periods in which movements are predominantly downward. These are the *business cycles* of capitalist economic life. They are fluctuations of aggregate output in which other aspects of economic activity join; they are widely diffused through the many sectors of the economy; and they recur at intervals which are as long as ten to twelve years but are normally less than five or six. And when we consider periods longer than those of business cycles, there emerges a persistent underlying tendency for output to rise. Although the rate of growth is not constant, the average level of output during any business-cycle period is normally higher than that attained during the preceding cycle period. The persistence of growth is one characteristic of the *primary secular trend* of output in capitalist countries in the era of industrialization.

The existence of business cycles and of irreversible primary trends is supported by considerable bodies of evidence. Both types of movement are widely regarded as at least partly, perhaps chiefly, systematic in nature, and both are the subject of intensive investigation.

Economists, however, are not generally agreed that these are the only

* *Economic Development and Cultural Change*, Vol. IX (April, 1961). Reprinted by courtesy of *Economic Development and Cultural Change*, the University of Chicago Press and the author. Copyright 1961 by the University of Chicago.
† Stanford University.

systematic, or quasi-systematic, movements which the record of economic change presents. There are recurrent suggestions of waves, of reversals in levels or rates of change of output, with durations longer than business cycles. As regards duration, these suggestions essentially span the spectrum of possibilities. They include a relatively short wave of eight to eleven years, the so-called Juglar cycle, a very long wave of 40 to 60 years, the so-called Kondratieff cycle, and a wave of intermediate length, between 15 and 25 years in duration.

Considering the span of years for which output records are available, it is hard to see how waves longer than the Kondratieff could be at all separated, however tentatively, from the primary trend itself. And considering the admitted variability of the shorter movements, it is hard to see how more than two, if even two, other systematic waves could be fitted between the business cycles at the short end and the Kondratieff at the long end of the spectrum.

Useful discussion of the relative validity of these several hypotheses is beyond the scope of this article. It must suffice to start from the assertion that continuing study has tended to cast doubt on the usefulness of the Kondratieff and Juglar hypotheses and has concentrated attention on the postulated wave of intermediate length.[1] For this reason, the present article proposes to give some account of the chief features of these intermediate waves, and to discuss their probable nature and significance.[2]

This subject is especially appropriate for treatment in the present volume because Simon Kuznets was one of the discoverers of this wave. Kuznets, no doubt, must share honors with others whose pioneering work helped to establish the general importance of the wave. More than others, however, Kuznets has continued to investigate its properties and to defend its significance. W. A. Lewis has suggested that we recognize this long record of work by referring to the 15–25 year general waves in economic changes as *Kuznets cycles*, and I propose to accept this suggestion with the understanding that the use of the term "cycles" is not meant to prejudge the question whether these waves are significantly self-generating, a matter about which Kuznets is dubious and which the present writer regards as unsettled.[3] Following Kuznets' own practice in recent writings, it may be better to substitute "swings" or "waves" for "cycles."

---

[1] For critical appraisal of Kondratieff cycles, see G. Garvy, "Kondratieff's Theory of Long Cycles," *Review of Economic Statistics*, Vol. XXV, No. 4 (November, 1943), pp. 203–20; also A. F. Burns and W. C. Mitchell, *Measuring Business Cycles* (New York, 1946), Ch. 11. On the Juglar movements, see *ibid.*, Ch. 11, and R. C. O. Matthews, *The Business Cycle* (Chicago, 1959), Ch. 12. Representative literature on the intermediate wave is cited below.

[2] Readers will, I hope, understand that what I propose is in the nature of a preliminary rather than a definitive discussion.

[3] W. A. Lewis and P. J. O'Leary, "Secular Swings in Production and Trade, 1870–1913," *The Manchester School of Economic and Social Studies*, Vol. XIII, No. 2 (May, 1955), pp. 113–52. [Reprinted in the present volume.]

I

Kuznets first encountered his cycles in the course of his early work on long term trends which he published in 1930.[4] Here Kuznets showed that production and price series, with primary trends eliminated and the influences of business cycles attenuated or smoothed by moving averages, exhibited pronounced wave-like undulations. He called them "secondary secular movements."[5] Kuznets' measurements suggested that the average duration of the cycles had been about 22 years in the production series and 23 years in the price series.

Although Kuznets apparently believed that the swings he observed in the output and prices of individual commodities appeared at about the same time in many different activities, he made no systematic attempt in his early work to establish the existence of long swings in aggregate economic activity. This matter was settled, at least for the United States, by Arthur F. Burns. Burns studied a large sample of United States production series for the years 1870–1930. From his original data, he calculated rates of growth during successive overlapping decades displaced five years. These he expressed as deviations from the trend rate of growth. He called the fluctuations of the corrected decade rates of growth "trend-cycles."[6] Burns argued that "if a set of common causes, variable in time, operate uniformly through the trend-cycles of individual industries, their effects will be registered in the movements of the averages of the trend-cycles, even though random factors operate simultaneously with the set of common causes."[7] Burns' findings left little doubt that a set of common causes had been operating. He found that the median rates of growth of the industries in his sample traced out definite oscillatory

---

[4] Simon Kuznets, *Secular Movements in Production and Prices* (New York, 1930) Ch. III–VI.

[5] Kuznets was not the first to publish empirical evidence suggesting the existence of general long swings of 15–25 years duration. Three years before Kuznets' book appeared, C. A. R. Wardwell announced the discovery of fluctuations in economic time series with a duration longer than business cycles but definitely shorter than the alleged Kondratieff cycles. Apparently Kuznets' work was already fairly far advanced when Wardwell published. Indeed, Wardwell and Kuznets studied each others' unfinished manuscripts. Both were aware of having turned up evidence of the same new type of fluctuation, and Wardwell, though taking cognizance of Kuznets' work then in progress, did not claim priority on account of his earlier publication (C. A. R. Wardwell, *An Investigation of Economic Data for Major Cycles* [Philadelphia, 1927], pp. 14–15). Wardwell's evidence was less elaborate than Kuznets' in that it included fewer time series, a much shorter time period, and fewer countries. In at least one respect, however, Wardwell went further than Kuznets. He asserted that the major peaks and troughs of his American series appeared in well-defined clusters suggesting that long swings were characteristic of the economy at large as well as of individual activities.

[6] A. F. Burns, *Production Trends in the United States Since 1870* (New York, 1934), Ch. V. Burns' procedures were somewhat more complicated than this statement suggests. Interested readers should consult Burns' book for details of his methods and for the size and composition of his sample of production series.

[7] *Ibid.*, pp. 179–80.

movements, that the pattern of these movements ran through the entire system of series, that irregularities were confined chiefly to the agricultural sector, that the waves in the median rates of growth were matched by the trend-cycles of indexes of total industrial production and of major industrial groups and that the same was true of trend-cycles in other aspects of the economy—prices, money in circulation, the monetary stock of gold, real earnings, business failures, and patents issued. Burns felt able to conclude that the concurrence of trend-cycles in the various branches of non-agricultural production and their consilience with trend-cycles in other aspects of economic life created "a strong presumption that a long-term rhythm has been pervasive in the American economy since the Civil War. . . ."[8]

These indications have been bolstered in more recent years by the appearance of Kuznets' long-term estimates of national product. Kuznets first published his extended estimates in the form of averages for overlapping decades displaced five years (1869–78, 1874–83, etc.). Since such decade averages may be presumed to accomplish a substantial smoothing of business cycles, rates of change between overlapping decade averages may be thought to constitute approximations to rates of secular growth. Such rates display wave-like fluctuations which succeed each other at intervals of about twenty years. Their maxima and minima correspond sufficiently closely with those previously determined by Burns and, still earlier, by Wardwell so that there can be little doubt that all three were revealing the same phenomenon.[9]

Kuznets cycles in the rate of growth of output have been found in a number of countries besides the United States.[10] Kuznets cycles, moreover, are not confined to output growth. In addition to the various facets of economic life already mentioned above, they are particularly prominent in building and other forms of construction. Kuznets cycles, therefore, can be thought of as the more general manifestation of the well-known long cycles in building and of the "transport-building cycle" revealed by Isard.[11] Such cycles are, further,

---

[8] *Ibid.*, pp. 174–75.

[9] Simon Kuznets, "Long Term Changes in National Income of the United States since 1870," in Simon Kuznets (ed.), *Income and Wealth, Series II* (Cambridge, 1952), Tables 3 and 4; also M. Abramovitz, "Resource and Output Trends in the United States since 1870," *American Economic Review*, Vol. XLVI, No. 2 (May, 1956), Chart I, p. 16. There are differences in the dates of the peaks and troughs determined by each writer and even an "extra" cycle in Burns' waves, but there is little doubt that these differences can be traced to differences in the data they used and the manner in which they treated them.

[10] See W. A. Lewis and P. J. O'Leary, *op. cit.*; also Simon Kuznets, "Quantitative Aspects of the Economic Growth of Nations, I, Levels and Variability of Rates of Growth," *Economic Development and Cultural Change*, Vol. V, No. 1 (October, 1956).

[11] See W. Isard, "A Neglected Cycle: The Transport-Building Cycle," *Review of Economic Statistics*, Vol. XXIV, No. 4 (November, 1942), pp. 149–58. Burns' measures (in *op. cit.*) seem to suggest that the trend cycles of building activity did not have a regular connection with his more general trend cycle in output. The tables in Kuznets' forthcoming book (Simon Kuznets, *Capital in the American Economy: Its Formation and Financing*) carry the same suggestion. The irregularity, however, is only apparent: It stems in part from

clearly apparent in the great waves of immigration before the 1930's. These were naturally accompanied by similar, though smaller, swings in the rate of growth of the labor force and population. The long swings in population and labor force growth, however, were never wholly the result of immigration waves, and since World War I, their chief source has been in the fluctuations of marriage and birth rates, and, in the case of labor force growth, in those of participation rates. The illumination of the demographic aspects of Kuznets cycles has, indeed, been one of Simon Kuznets' more important contributions to the subject.[12]

The participation of immigration waves in the Kuznets cycles of the USA and of other "new" migrant-receiving countries in the 19th and early 20th centuries suggests that Kuznets cycles in the new countries may have had an inverted relation to Kuznets cycles in the "old" countries of emigration. Such inversion was established, so far as Great Britain is concerned, by the work of Brinley Thomas, Cairncross, and others.[13] Thomas also showed that the waves of British population migration were accompanied by similar waves of capital exports,[14] and it can now be added that the Kuznets cycles in British capital exports are matched by similar waves in U.S. capital imports and by inverse swings in the U.S. balance of payments.[15]

Finally, the present writer[16] has shown that at least in the United States, Kuznets cycles in output growth have arisen from swings in almost all the elements into which output growth can be resolved. Waves in the rate of change in output have been accompanied—with certain characteristic differences in timing—not only by swings in additions to the labor force, but also by fluctuations in additions to the capital stock, in the rate of increase of

---

the fact that the rate of change of building activity from the Civil War to World War I tended to lag behind that of output at large in the course of Kuznets cycles and in part from the fact that, in the special circumstances of World War I, the pace of total output growth accelerated while building activity was understandably depressed.

[12] Simon Kuznets, "Long Swings in the Growth of Population and in Related Economic Variables," Proceedings of the American Philosophical Society, Vol. CII, No. 1 (February, 1958), pp. 25–52.

[13] B. Thomas, Migration and Economic Growth (Cambridge, 1954); also A. Cairncross, Home and Foreign Investment, 1870–1914 (Cambridge, 1953).

[14] Cairncross, Thomas, and others have also shown that Kuznets cycles in British foreign investment were accompanied by inverse, but not completely synchronous, waves in British home investment. The partially compensating character of these two investment waves apparently masked the Kuznets cycle in over-all British activity, while their incomplete compensation caused total investment to move in a wave with a period of about ten years. It appears, therefore, that while Juglar cycles dominate U.K. statistics on a superficial view, the underlying movements are connected with Kuznets cycles. Cf. Matthews, op. cit.

[15] I base this statement on an investigation now being conducted by Jeffrey G. Williamson at Stanford University.

[16] Moses Abramovitz, Statement in United States Congress, Joint Economic Committee, Employment, Growth and Price Levels, Hearings (86th Congress, 1st Session), Part II (Washington, 1959), pp. 411–66. (This paper will be cited hereinafter as "Joint Economic Committee Statement.")

output per unit of resources employed, and in indicators of the intensity of resource-utilization. Such waves were not confined to the period since 1870 to which the studies by Burns, Kuznets, and Lewis and O'Leary were restricted. For the United States, at any rate, there is evidence of general Kuznets fluctuations going back at least to the 1830's and perhaps earlier and suggesting, therefore, the presence of a phenomenon which persisted over a very considerable period of time.

This review of earlier work leads me to the following general conclusion. In the United States and in at least some other growing economies, development during the nineteenth and early twentieth centuries took the form of a series of surges in the growth of output and in capital and labor resources followed by periods of retarded growth. The duration of these waves in the United States was roughly 15–20 years.[17] These waves in the growth of physical resources and activity were accompanied by generally similar swings in other aspects of economic life—in gold movements, in the growth of money supply and in the rate of change in prices, and in the balance of payments and in international capital flows, to mention only some of the more prominent features of the movements. Whatever their underlying nature, therefore, the Kuznets swings represent pulses of economic life which ramified widely through the developing economies of the past century or more and, on that account alone, they deserve close study.

II

What kind of phenomena are these swings? In particular, do they reflect principally a fluctuation in the rate of growth of the economy's capacity to produce as determined by the rate of growth of labor and capital resources and by the productivity of resources optimally employed, or do they also, and perhaps chiefly, reflect a fluctuation in the intensity with which resources are utilized? When one considers the primary trend of aggregate output, one thinks chiefly of the factors that control the growth of capacity to produce. When one considers business cycles, one thinks chiefly of factors that control the intensity of resource utilization and one is concerned principally with fluctuations in the determinants of effective demand. Have the Kuznets cycles been capacity or demand phenomena, or have they partaken of the nature of both?

One might suppose that, if one proceeds by applying moving averages or other smoothing devices to crude data with the purpose of eliminating the

---

[17] In making this statement about duration, I assume that it is appropriate to neglect two short and mild movements which appear in some indicators of activity, one, running from roughly 1914–21, associated with World War I, and one in the middle eighties associated with a serious decline in railroad construction and the accompanying business contraction of 1882–85. But see also the table below and accompanying text.

fluctuations associated with ordinary business cycles, and if one defines Kuznets cycles, in a rough fashion, as the fluctuations in the level or rate of growth of data so smoothed, one has eliminated the effects of fluctuations in the intensity of resource utilization. This, however, would be an unjustified inference, and this section argues, first, that Kuznets cycles have been compounded of fluctuations in the rate of growth of resources and productivity and of fluctuations in the intensity with which resources are used, and, secondly, that the fluctuations in resource growth and in utilization rates have been interconnected causally. A long swing in the volume of additions, perhaps even in the rate of growth of additions, to the stock of capital, that is, in capital formation, is likely to involve a fluctuation in effective demand and thus to generate an alternation between states of relatively full and relatively slack employment. A long swing in unemployment rates in turn appears to have been among the chief causes of Kuznets cycles in the volume of additions to the labor force and, perhaps, in capital formation. It has also shaped the patterns formed by the waves in measured productivity growth so that it becomes difficult to say whether a wave in output per unit of resources employed at standard rates of utilization has actually been present. The evidence on which I base these conclusions is drawn from a study of long swings in U.S. development.

To help establish these points, I present a table of figures derived from data presented on an earlier occasion.[18] The table purports to show the peaks and troughs of Kuznets cycles in output growth and in some of the major elements into which output growth can be resolved: productivity growth, additions to labor force and capital stock, growth in the input of resources, and an indicator of the intensity of resource utilization. The sources of the data on which the table is based are described in source notes attached to the article in which the data originally appeared. Kuznets cycles in such series as additions to the labor force and additions to capital stock (i.e., capital formation) were isolated by calculating averages of annual data for periods bounded by successive pairs of ordinary business-cycle peaks and then for periods bounded by pairs of troughs. These two sets of averages were then intermixed to form a series of averages for overlapping business-cycle periods. We may think of the result as indicating how these series would have stood in the absence of ordinary business cycles (but not, according to the argument below, as the series would have stood in the absence of extraordinarily long or severe business-cycle movements). The Kuznets cycles in such series as the rate of growth of output or of productivity were isolated by calculating average rates of change between average standings for business-cycle periods.[19] Again the resulting series of rates of growth are to be interpreted as indicating

---

[18] See my Joint Economic Committee Statement, Tables 9 and 11.

[19] The rates of change were calculated between average standings for non-overlapping cycle periods and then intermingled to form a series of rates of change during overlapping inter-cycle intervals.

A Chronology of the Peaks and Troughs of Kuznets Cycles in Selected Aspects of the U.S. Economy*

	Rates of Change in:						Volume of Additions to		
GNP per Member of Labor Force	Gross Physical Output per Unit of Input	Gross Physical Output	Economic Activity or Gross National Product	Industrial and Commercial Production	Total Input of Labor and Capital	Labor Force	Capital Stock (= Capital Formation)	Years Preceding the Beginning or End of Protracted Depression or "Stagnation"
Long Swing Peaks								
(1)	(1)		1814	(1)	(1)	(1)	1815–18	1815
(1)	(1)		1834	(1)	(1)	(1)	1836–37	1836
(1)	(1)		1846	(1)	(1)	1851.5	1854–55	1853
(1)	(1)		1864.25	1864.25	(1)	1871	1871	1873
(2)	(1)		1881	1881	(1)	1884.5	(2)	1882
1890	(1)		1889.75	1888	(1)	1893.5	1892–93	1892
1899.75	1896.5	1899	1899	1899	1900	1906.5	1906	1907
(3)	(3)	(3)	1914.5	1913.25	(3)	(2)	1919	1920
1923.25[a]	1923	1923	1923	1923	1923	1924.5	1927–28	1929
1943.75	1938.5	1936.75	1938.5	1938.5	1938.5	(2)	(2)	(2)
Long Swing Troughs								
(1)	(1)	(1)	1819	(1)	(1)		1821–4	1821
(1)	(1)	(1)	1840	(1)	(1)		1842–4	1843
(1)	(1)	(1)	1858	(1)	(1)	1859.5	1862–4	1858
(1)	(1)	(1)	1874.25	1874.25	(1)	1874.25	1877–8	1878
1886.5	(1)	(1)	1886.5	1884	(1)	1886.5	(2)	1885
1893	1892.25(t)	1892.25(t)	1892.25	1892.25	1893.75	1896.5	1895	1896
1906.75	1913.5	(3)	1911	1906.75	(3)	1919.5	1912–13	1914
(3)	(3)	1920.25	1920.25	1920.25	1920.25	(2)	1921–2	1921
1930.25	1927.5	1930.25	1930.25	1930.25	1930.25	1935.5	1933	1932

* Dates expressed in whole years refer to years with midpoints at June 30. Dates expressed in whole years plus fractions have midpoints later than June 30 by the specified fraction of a year.   (1) Not available.   (2) Turning point skipped or, at end of table, not yet reached.   (3) Extra movement makes comparison with GNP impossible.   (t) Tentative selection; earlier data if available might suggest that the turning point was reached at an earlier date.
[a] Value at this date was the same as that at 1921.75.

how the series would have grown in the absence of normal, but not abnormal, business cycles.

We have no way of measuring the intensity of resource utilization or its changes that is even roughly reliable before 1900. Even after that date such figures are confined to joblessness and do not touch fluctuations in the utilization of employed workers and of the stock of capital. To help show that there were changes in the intensity of resource utilization in the course of Kuznets cycles and to help indicate the phases of such cycles in which the turning points of changes in the rate of utilization probably occurred, we simply list the peaks preceding the beginning of protracted depressions and the troughs preceding the beginning of sustained recoveries from such depression. By protracted depressions we mean deep contractions of general business activity sustained over periods longer than ordinary recessions, or periods in which recoveries, if they occur, do not bring the economy back to full employment or do so only transiently. In the latter event, *stagnation* may be the better term to employ. The periods so selected will be seen to include the classic periods of deep depression or stagnation in the United States. Some question, no doubt, may be raised about the periods 1853–58 and 1907–14, but I believe the weight of the evidence justifies my treatment.[20]

There are a number of uncertainties about the table of which the reader ought to be aware. First, the swing in the rate of growth of output, 1911–21, was a movement connected with World War I in which the normal relations between swings in the rate of growth of output and those in other aspects of the economy were upset. War demand caused output growth to speed up and unemployment to drop, but these conditions, which in peacetime normally saw a rise in immigration, labor force growth, and in residential and other civilian construction, were accompanied by a drop in all these variables under the unusual strains and restrictions of war. It was a short and peculiar Kuznets cycle, if indeed it should be thought one at all, and it ended in a depression in 1920–21 which, while severe, was hardly protracted. Secondly, there is a peculiarly short period of alternation between acceleration and retardation in the late eighties and early nineties. The very short duration of this swing and some of its internal characteristics[21] make it questionable whether it is useful to recognize the acceleration 1886–1890 as more than a cyclical interruption of the retardation which began in the early 1880's. The use of ten-year moving averages, rather than the shorter business-cycle averages, as a device

---

[20] The factual material underlying the selection is described in my Joint Economic Committee Statement, especially Table 10 and its notes and pp. 427–28.

[21] The acceleration of 1886–1890 represents a recovery from a very low rate of growth associated with the unusually long and somewhat severe contraction of 1882–85 in which railroad building declined sharply while urban residential construction continued to rise. This was the only notable instance in which these two great sectors of construction parted company for very long during the nearly three-quarters of a century in which railroad building was important.

for smoothing out business cycles would wash out both the short movement in the late 80's and the short and mild movement connected with World War I. There may well be grounds for using the more radical smoothing provided by decade averages, but no substantial point in the argument that follows turns on the choice of smoothing methods or on such difference in chronologies as would flow from that choice. It may be of interest to note, however, that the two movements referred to immediately above are the only "extra" movements which turn up as a result of using our less radical smoothing device. Including these two short movements in our chronology makes the average durations of Kuznets cycles in this country slightly under 14 years while their elimination would make their average duration almost exactly 18 years, a figure long associated with building cycles and closer to the durations of Kuznets' earlier "secondary secular movements" and Burns' "trend-cycles." There is, however, no one right method of smoothing to eliminate business-cycle fluctuations, and we can only try to remain aware of the differences which variant smoothings can make in our results.

While a mere chronology of turning points cannot persuasively establish the relations among time series, our table suggests a far-reaching and interesting conclusion, namely, that the long waves in the rate of growth of output[22] are the reflection of underlying long waves in almost all the measurable elements into which output growth can be resolved. Our table suggests, first, that there were long waves in additions to resources, both labor force and capital stock. However, since the long waves in resource growth lag far behind those in output growth, it appears that the earlier turning points in output growth must be traced in the first instance to a concomitant or still earlier change in the rate of growth of output per unit of resources available. So far as concerns labor, we have direct evidence of this connection in the turning points of output per member of the labor force.[23]

The growth of output per unit of resources can itself be resolved into two

---

[22] Readers may be puzzled by at least some of the dates assigned to peaks and troughs in output growth. They may, for example, resist the suggestion that the rate of growth of output was at a low point in 1930–31 (1930.25) and at a high point in 1938–39 (1938.5). They should, however, remember two points. First, the dates are themselves merely the midpoints of the interval between the midpoints of two business-cycle periods and are a short-hand device to refer to the interval between the two periods. To say that the rate of growth was at a trough at 1930.25 is a short-hand device for saying that the output change between the level reached during the business-cycle period 1926–29 and that reached during the period 1929–37 was lower than that in the intervals between the two preceding and following business-cycle periods. Similarly, the high rate of output growth at 1938.5 refers to the change between the output level of the period 1932–38 and that of the period 1938–45. Secondly, while the fluctuations in rates of growth during Kuznets cycles may be supposed to be free of the influence of business cycles of ordinary duration and amplitude, they do reflect changes in the severity of business cycles, as the argument below suggests at greater length.

[23] It is not, however, a very satisfactory measure since the underlying annual data of labor force are based in part on interpolations of participation rates for which there was evidence only at 10-year intervals.

elements. One is the part contributed by changes in output per unit of input used at standard intensity, or, for short, per intensity unit. We may think of this part as the growth of "true" productivity. The other is the part contributed by changes in the number of intensity units employed per unit of resources available, that is, by changes in the rate of employment, or more generally, the rate of utilization of available resources. Changes in the utilization rate will occur not only because of changes in the unemployment rate for labor or because of changes in the number of hours worked, but also because of change in the intensity with which employed labor and available capital are used.

There is no completely satisfactory measure of either true productivity change or of changes in utilization rates. There is, however, a substantial quantity of evidence that changes in utilization rates have been a regular concomitant of Kuznets cycles and that they probably account for a considerable share in the apparent changes in the growth of output per unit of available resources.

We begin with the observation, documented elsewhere by the present writer, that each period of retardation in the rate of growth of output has culminated in a protracted depression or in a period of stagnation in which business cycle recoveries were disappointing, failing to lift the economy to a condition of full employment or doing so only transiently.[24] Because such protracted depressions or stagnation periods have occurred only once in each of the long swings or Kuznets cycles and always at the same phase of each successive swing, their effects cannot be smoothed out or eliminated completely by moving averages with a period substantially less than that of the Kuznets cycles themselves, say, fifteen to twenty years. And since averages with such a long period would presumably smooth out the Kuznets cycles also, it is not practicable to aim at eliminating, at least by moving averages, the extraordinary depressions or stagnations which have marked the boundaries

---

[24] Abramovitz, Joint Economic Committee Statement, pp. 427–28. Cf. the somewhat similar statement by Burns, *op. cit.*, p. 251: "We may therefore conclude from our analysis of American experience since 1870: first, that periods of sharp advance in the trend of general production, which are characterized invariably by considerable divergence in production trends, have been followed invariably by severe depressions; second, that most of the business depressions of marked severity have been preceded by a sharp advance in the trend of general production and considerable divergence in the trends of individual industries."

The present writer's statement is based upon experience running back to 1816, while Burns' is based on experience since the 1870's. The difference in the form of the statements, however, is due chiefly to the difference in the methods by which Burns and the present writer treated their data to smooth out business cycles—Burns by computing decade rates of growth for decades displaced five years, the present writer by computing rates of growth between the average standings of series during periods bounded by business-cycle turning points, both peak-to-peak and trough-to-trough. At the time of writing, Burns considered his trend-cycles to be substantially free of changes in rates of unemployment and thought of the observed serious depressions as phenomena substantially separate from his measures of cycles in "secular" rates of growth. He subsequently altered his view.

between successive long swings. Not only is it impracticable to smooth away these episodes fully, it would be wrong to do so because, as the argument below suggests, the occurrence of protracted periods of abnormally high rates of unemployment and underemployment of labor and capital probably forms an essential part of the Kuznets-cycle mechanism.[25]

That the behavior of important economic indicators which display Kuznets cycles still reflects the effects of a long swing in unemployment and, presumably, underemployment is attested by evidence both direct and indirect. The direct evidence consists of the time-patterns formed by annual estimates of the percentage of the labor force unemployed, after smoothing to eliminate ordinary business cycles. For the limited time such data are available, they give a clear picture of a Kuznets cycle in unemployment rates for non-farm workers. Thus, the percent of the non-farm employees out of work stands at around 12 percent in the mid-1890's. From this high level, the percentage falls to around five percent in the middle of the next decade, then rises again to approximately 10 percent in the period 1907–1915. By the early 1920's, the rate is down again to about 6 percent. The curves then display the huge rise of unemployment associated with the Great Depression. In the smoothed data, the peak level for this last swing is reached in the mid-1930's, and, there-after, unemployment rates fall until the late 1940's with some indications of a very mild rise since that time.[26]

In addition to these more or less direct evidences of Kuznets cycles in utilization rates, we must interpret the behavior of the series representing the growth of output, input, and output per unit of input, the turning points of whose Kuznets cycles are shown in our table. Note, first, that in every case in a line going back to the early part of the 19th century, the trough in output growth occurred during a period of sustained depression or stagnation. We note, secondly, that in most cases, the peak of output growth occurred within a few years after the beginning of sustained recovery from depression or

---

[25] This view seems to be accepted also by Lewis and O'Leary, *op. cit.* Noting that the high phase of Kuznets cycles (as they measure them, in trend-adjusted but otherwise unsmoothed, form) lasted longer than the low phase, they write: "The fact that prosperity outlasts depression is not without significance. One may be tempted to deny that there is fundamentally a Kuznets cycle, and may prefer to say that all that happens is that once every twenty years one of the Juglar depressions gets out of hand, and lasts six to eight years, instead of lasting one or two years only. Even such regularity as this, however, deserves the name of cycle: there is no reason why the number of years of prosperity and of depression in a cycle should be equal to one another."

[26] The estimates in question are those presented by Stanley Lebergott, "Annual Esti-mates of Unemployment in the United States, 1900–1954," in *The Measurement and Be-havior of Unemployment* (A Conference of the Universities–National Bureau for Economic Research) (Princeton, 1957), p. 215, from 1900 on, pieced out by figures collected by Kuznets for the 1890's, and published in *Capital in the American Economy*, Chart VII-8. Essentially the same results, aside from some differences in the timing of peaks and troughs, are ob-tained whether the annual data are smoothed by a ten-year moving average or by averages for successive periods bounded by the peaks and troughs of the National Bureau chron-ology of business-cycle turning points.

stagnation. The three exceptional cases, when the peak in output growth did not occur until some years after the beginning of recovery, fell in 1834, when the basis for an estimate of output growth is most unreliable, in 1864, when the economy operated under the strain of war production and disturbance, and in 1889, during a movement whose qualifications for inclusion in a list of Kuznets cycles is doubtful. In five other cases, the peak in output growth appears to have fallen no more than three years after the beginning of sustained recovery.[27] In one other case, 1938–39, the peak growth rate comes 6 or 7 years after the beginning of sustained recovery, dating the latter from 1933. There can be no doubt, however, that in this case, the peak in the rate of growth of output was associated with the reemployment of idle resources, which, as I shall now argue, is the moral of these figures.

I have already argued that the substantial lead of the turning points in output growth relative to those in additions to labor force and capital stock implies that the former must be associated with turning points in growth of output per unit of available resources. Now, the fact that the turning points in output growth occur in association with sustained depressions and stagnations and with recovery therefrom strongly suggests that the turning points in growth of output per resource unit are to be associated with turning points in the rate of change of resource utilization.

This interpretation is supported by consideration of the behavior of Kuznets cycles in three comparable series provided by Fabricant on the basis of Kendrick's estimates.[28] The series refer to gross physical output, to the associated total input of labor and capital, and to output per unit of total input. To interpret these series, we should remember that the input series does not represent the number of intensity units utilized. It makes no allowance for changes in the utilization rate of plant and equipment. Moreover, although the input of labor is measured in manhours, it is doubtful whether the hours estimates Kendrick had to use fluctuate as widely as hours actually do. Finally, the input estimates make no allowance for changes in the flow of work per hour to either production workers or salaried employees, many of whom obviously are kept on the job through both slack and busy periods. It follows that output per unit of measured input can vary either because of changes in output per intensity unit or because of changes in the intensity of utilization.

Allowing for some differences in amplitude (input and output per unit of input fluctuate less widely than their product, gross physical output), the Kuznets cycles in the growth of all three series resemble one another closely, and all three resemble closely the Kuznets cycles in gross national product.[29] The only serious divergence occurred during World War I, when input growth

---

[27] This statement is, of course, subject to the inaccuracy unavoidable when crude smoothing procedures have been applied to data.

[28] Solomon Fabricant, *Basic Facts on Productivity Change* (National Bureau of Economic Research, Occasional Paper 63) (New York, 1959), Table A.

[29] See my Joint Economic Committee Statement, Chart 7.

slowed down, but output per unit of input accelerated while output growth itself followed an intermediate course. For the time the series are available, however, (since 1890) the turning points in the rates of growth of the three series bear the same relation to the development of, or recovery from, protracted depression or stagnation as those in the rate of growth of total output for a longer period. This association suggests that turning points of Kuznets cycles in input growth are connected with fluctuations in the growth or decline of unemployment. We may surely assume, further, that the intensity of utilization of capital and employed labor will move inversely with unemployment. Recalling now that the movements of output per unit of measured input will reflect the effects of variations in the utilization rate for employed resources, it is plausible to think that the conjunction of the turns of Kuznets cycles in output per unit of input with those in input itself and of both series with the onset of depression and recovery is due to changes in rates of utilization.

We turn now to several other features of the Kuznets swings which seem to be most easily explained if we may assume that there is a Kuznets swing in the level of unemployment. The first is the Kuznets swing in immigration. Kuznets and Rubin have shown that the waves in aggregate immigration were formed from generally similar waves of migration from many different countries of origin. The considerable degree of international diffusion in immigration waves points clearly to some variation in conditions in the United States as the common cause influencing movements from different countries.[30] Granted this inference, it seems plausible to point to the ease or difficulty of finding employment as the specific common cause directly responsible.

This hypothesis is quite consistent with Jerome's well-known observation of a correlation between migration and business cycles.[31] It is also consistent with the relation between the Kuznets swings in the volume of immigration and long swings in unemployment rates for the period since 1890 when estimates of unemployment begin.[32] Finally, the troughs and peaks in the Kuznets swings in immigration are consistent in their timing with the occurrence of the periods of protracted depression or stagnation which punctuated U.S. development. The troughs of the Kuznets swings in immigration regularly occurred toward the end of periods of depression or stagnation, while the peaks in immigration occurred toward the close of periods of sustained

---

[30] Cf. Simon Kuznets and Ernest Rubin, *Immigration and the Foreign Born* (National Bureau of Economic Research, Occasional Paper No. 46) (New York, 1954); also Richard A. Easterlin's study of European overseas emigration in *Economic Development and Cultural Change*, Vol. IX (April, 1961), pp. 331–51, for additional evidence supporting the same conclusion.

[31] See Harry Jerome, *Migration and Business Cycles* (New York, 1926). A high inverse correlation between migration and unemployment was also found by Mr. Belton Fleisher in his still unpublished study of Puerto Rican migration to the United States since World War II. I am grateful to Mr. Fleisher for making his early results available to me.

[32] The worth of this evidence is, of course, qualified by the fact that unemployment figures are not very dependable before quite recent years.

growth. From all this, I infer that the very large Kuznets waves in the level of immigration are evidence supporting the belief that there were Kuznets waves in the rate of unemployment.

If this be accepted, then one may add, parenthetically, that a considerable portion of the responsibility for the pre-World War I swings in the growth of the labor force and of population are also to be attributed to the occurrence of protracted periods of unemployment and of recovery therefrom. For a large part of these fluctuations consisted precisely in fluctuations in the volume of immigrants. One should also note that immigration is not the only demographic variable that displays Kuznets swings. They are to be found in marriage and birth rates, in rates of household formation, and in the labor-force participation rates of various native-born groups. Fragmentary data suggest that at least a partial explanation of these waves may also be found in the postulated long swing in unemployment rates.[33]

Finally, we must consider the fact that, among the several elements of the general Kuznets swing is a long wave in capital formation. This wave derives in part, though not entirely, from the well-known long cycles in railroad construction, in residential building, and in construction of associated community facilities and consequently is associated with the wave in population growth and household formation just noticed. The wave in total capital formation manifestly has implications for the hypothesis that the general Kuznets swing involves a fluctuation in effective demand. In some cases, the down phase of these waves has consisted only in a marked retardation— lasting longer than an ordinary business cycle—in the rate of growth of capital expenditures. In other cases, there is evidence of a protracted period of at least mild decline between one business-cycle period and another.[34] In either event, we should expect such behavior to be accompanied by abnormally high unemployment rates for periods longer than ordinary business cycles.

---

[33] Space does not permit review of the evidence here, but see R. A. Easterlin's forthcoming report for the National Bureau of Economic Research on "Long Swings in Labor Force Growth."

[34] By way of support for this assertion, I cite the following figures calculated from Kuznets' estimates of gross capital formation:

A. Rates of growth between averages of annual data in successive business-cycle periods.

(Dates refer to midpoints of intervals between the midpoints of successive non-overlapping business cycles measured alternatively from trough-to-trough and peak-to-peak.)

	Percent		Percent		Percent		Percent		Percent
1874.25	6.94	1891	6.83	1903	3.16	1914.5	3.65	1926	2.27
1877.75	6.34	1892.25	−0.60	1904	3.01	1917.25	6.00	1927.5	−5.46
1881	4.71	1893.75	−1.35	1906.75	1.13	1918.25	2.00	1930.25	−10.56
1884	3.91	1895.25	1.87	1907.75	0.82	1920.25	−6.21	1932.25	−6.72
1886.5	4.27	1896.5	3.93	1910	2.57	1921.25	−1.24	1936.75	8.64
1888.75	6.13	1899	5.89	1911	2.17	1923	8.75	1938.5	10.16
1889.75	11.74	1900	5.53	1913.5	2.24	1924	8.10		

B. Rates of growth (exponential) between peaks of successive short cycles in gross

And if as they do, these protracted periods of slow growth or decline in capital expenditures coincide with periods which have, on other grounds, been identified as periods of depression or stagnation, we may take the observation of a Kuznets cycle in total investment as another piece of indirect evidence that the general Kuznets wave has been characterized by a fluctuation in effective demand which expresses itself in a swing in the rate of unemployment of labor and in the utilization of resources generally.

The evidence and its implications run to the conclusion that general Kuznets swings have regularly involved alternations in effective demand and in the rate of resource utilization. Before going on, however, a short digression may be desirable to deal with a scruple, or qualm, which readers may harbor. If our own observations of the long swings still manifest fluctuations in the intensity of resource utilization, does this not mean simply that we have not "smoothed-out" business cycles successfully, so that to isolate long swings in economic growth from business cycles, we ought to employ a more radical smoothing technique? This question may occur to readers with especial force in connection with the technique which lies back of our table, a technique designed to smooth out "ordinary" business cycles (that is, those identified by the National Bureau of Economic Research), but which does not pretend to smooth out completely the alleged "major" or "Juglar" cycles.

To this question, there are two answers. First, no reasonable smoothing technique which depends essentially on some variant of the moving average device will eliminate employment fluctuations or their effects. For example, the use of ten-year moving averages and decade rates of growth leaves unchanged the observations and argument made above in every essential point except one. Specifically, a fluctuation of significant size still appears in a ten-year

capital formation.

	Percent		*Percent*		*Percent*
1873–81	6.37				
1881–87	3.49	1899–03	6.03	1913–16	6.21
1887–90	9.07	1903–06	6.10	1916–19	2.23
1890–92	10.40				
1881–92	6.23	1899–06	6.06	1913–19	4.20
1892–95	−4.09	1906–09	−0.54	1919–23	0.91
1895–99	2.40	1909–13	3.39	1923–26	3.76
1892–99	−0.43	1906–13	1.69	1926–29	0.32
				1919–29	1.58
				1929–37	−0.10

Both sets of calculations tell substantially the same story. They reveal the relatively high rate of growth of investment in the 1880's; the decline and slow growth rate in the middle nineties; the rapid growth of the early 1900's; the slow growth of the period between 1907 and the beginning of the war; then after the rapid rise in the war and the collapse in 1920–21, the relatively rapid rise in the early and mid-twenties and finally the collapse and recovery of the thirties. Only the figures for the 1870's seem inconsistent with the view that this decade witnessed a very serious depression. Kuznets' gross national product estimates in general seem to belie this view, and they call for closer examination.

moving average of unemployment rates running back to the 1890's. Moreover, we may take it as probable that such a moving average of unemployment rates would stand at lower levels in the mid-eighties than in the mid-nineties and at higher levels in the mid-seventies than in the mid-eighties. Further, the timing of peaks and troughs in the decade rates of growth of output, input, and productivity bear the same relation to one another and to the onset and end of periods of depression or stagnation as do the turning points revealed by the less radical smoothing technique that underlies our table.[35] Troughs in the decade rates of growth of these series occur in the early part of depression periods or in years just preceding depression, which indicates that they rest on a comparison between years when employment rates were high with years when they were low. Peaks in years marking recovery from protracted depression or recovery suggest that they rest on a comparison between years with opposite characteristics. A fluctuation in unemployment, finally, still remains the most plausible explanation for the long waves in immigration.

The one important difference which the use of ten-year moving averages makes in our picture of Kuznets swings is that there is no longer a clear and pronounced long swing in gross capital formation in the period between 1870 and 1914. One may still find a fluctuation in the rate of growth of investment, but it is less pronounced than that revealed by the less radical smoothing, the results of which were cited in footnote 34. I interpret this difference to be an example of the vagaries of moving averages. The behavior of the crude data, of business-cycle averages, and of measures taken from one business-cycle peak to the next seem to me to be persuasive evidence of long periods when gross capital formation alternately grew at a rapid rate and then grew at a very low rate or actually declined.

If decade averages and rates of growth will not eliminate completely the effects of fluctuation in unemployment, it is plausible to think that no reasonable smoothing technique would do so. Moving averages of longer period would presumably remove a portion, perhaps a considerable portion, of the phenomenon we want to observe, particularly if some examples of long swings are shorter than the 17 or 18 years which represented their average duration in the past. Given all the data and experience needed it would, ideally, be

---

[35] If one defines Kuznets swings as the fluctuation in a ten-year moving average of annual data or in decade rates of growth, it is, of course, true that the chronology of the peaks and troughs of Kuznets swings is altered. In particular, two movements displayed in our table are eliminated, viz., the period of acceleration in the late eighties and early nineties and the period of retardation associated with the depression of 1920–21. With these movements removed, our table would show seven instead of nine swings from peak to peak. Their average duration would be between 17 and 18 years corresponding closely to the duration of the familiar building cycles. There may be some reason to work with the more radical smoothing and the chronology it yields. But there are also losses, and one is unlikely to remain satisfied with the results obtained from any smoothing technique so crude as a moving average.

possible to eliminate the effects of unemployment by direct measurement. A fully adequate study of Kuznets cycles would certainly employ such measures. But they could only be a part of the investigation since the full story of long swings appears to include a fluctuation in employment and utilization rates as both the effect and the cause of other prominent features of the general Kuznets cycle. As pointed out, a long swing in unemployment is at least a likely accompaniment of a pronounced wave in the rate of growth—still more in that of the level—of gross capital formation. It is the most plausible explanation of the observed long waves in the level of immigration, and it contributes to an explanation of waves in certain other demographic variables and of those in still other features of long swings not noticed in this paper.

The stress we place on the existence of a wave in unemployment and utilization rates as an integral feature of the general Kuznets cycle should not, of course, cause us to lose sight of the fact that such waves involve much more than an alternation in the intensity of resource use. They also involve waves in the growth of the supply of resources. And while the argument above suggests that the swings in the growth rate of resource supply stem at least in part from the occurrence of protracted periods of unemployment and partial failure of effective demand, it remains true that the growth of resources was alternately rapid and slow. In addition, there may have been waves in the growth of "true," as distinct from measured, productivity. While it seems clear that the waves in measured productivity growth take their form in part from a fluctuation in utilization ratios, it is an open question whether there may not have been underlying waves in the growth of output per intensity unit of input, that is, in true productivity. Since capital equipment is the material embodiment of technique, we expect each year's gross addition to the stock of capital to carry with it an advance in technology. It follows, then, that the rate of growth of true productivity depends in part on the ratio of gross capital formation to the existing stock of capital. Waves in gross capital formation should, then, tend to produce waves in true productivity growth. This is an expectation qualified by the fact that the Kuznets waves in the level of gross capital formation, as distinct from rate of change, were usually very mild. It is an expectation which, however, is to some degree heightened by Kuznets' observation[36] that, at least before World War I, the wave in total gross capital formation was the net result of two more pronounced, but partly offsetting, waves in what he calls "population-sensitive" capital formation (railroad investment plus urban residential building) and "other" capital formation. Kuznets argues, plausibly, that since the contribution of residential building to productivity growth is dubious and that of railroad building long-deferred, it is the wave in the residual which counts for productivity change in the context of the long swings. As stated, this is a more pronounced wave than that in total gross capital formation.

---

[36] *Capital in the American Economy, op. cit.*

III

The general view of the long swings to which this argument leads is that they have a two-sided character. They involve first, an ebb and flow in the pace of economic growth in the basic sense that the development of our capacity to produce, of our supplies of labor and capital and, perhaps, of their productivity at optimum rates of utilization, has alternately proceeded faster and slower in waves that, in the past, have been longer than ordinary business cycles. Secondly, they involve swings in the intensity of resource use in which periods of relatively high unemployment, or low intensity of use, alternate with periods in which the labor market is tighter and capital is used more intensively. The two sides of the phenomenon interact and each stands in relation to the other both as cause and effect.

Granted the validity of this view, I should like to take a few pages simply to notice the variety of these interactions as they appear in the context of the long swings experienced in the United States. These examples of interaction between resource growth and intensity of resource use are also present in the more common business-cycle process, and some attention has been given to them in that connection. But chiefly because of the shorter duration of such movements, they are probably of lesser importance in business cycles. They appear in their full stature only in the longer movements. From the fact that there are interactions, we may anticipate that disturbances or movements in either direction will for a time, gain strength cumulatively, while the important and moot question whether the Kuznets cycles are in any significant sense self-generating may, of course, also turn on the nature of the interactions.

A. *Interactions Via the Relation between Capital Stock and Income Flow*

For a number of reasons, the simpler capital-stock adjustment models with their implied requirements for balanced growth take on heightened interest when considered in the context of long swings rather than in that of shorter business cycles. First, insofar as these models treat investment as dependent in part on current or past changes in the demand for finished goods, there has always been justifiable skepticism about their applicability to durable equipment and structures, so long as the theory was supposed to illuminate investment movements in short cycles. Since investment in durables is made for long periods of time, it is doubtful whether it would respond readily to income change over short periods. This difficulty disappears, however, when we consider expansions lasting 8 to 12 years or more.

In the same way, we are unlikely to explain much of the fluctuations of investment in durables during short business cycles by appealing to fluctuations in the growth of capital stock. A. F. Burns has pointed out that in such cycles, there is little regularity in the relation between the growth of installed capital stock and business activity.[37] Because the lag between investment expenditure and the installation of equipment and structures is of the same order of magnitude as a business-cycle phase, because the lag may vary depending on the mix of investment, and because the heights of peaks and troughs in investment vary widely, the curve of capital stock during business cycles when measured in physical units appears to follow a rising trend with random variations. The duration of the phases of long swings, however, overshadows the expenditure-delivery lag, and there is less reason to doubt that if there is a long swing in the level or rate of growth of capital formation, there will be an associated long swing in the rate of growth of capital stock or in the rate of change in such growth. In business cycles, the observed fluctuation in the ratio of capital stock to income would appear to arise systematically from the fluctuation in income. In long swings, however, it presumably arises both from income and capital stock movements.

Finally, the capital stock adjustment models stress the requirement that income and, therefore, investment, should grow at some critical rate in order to avoid the accumulation of excess capacity. So far as concerns fixed capital, however, it is no more than an implication of the argument above that the consequences of failure to meet this requirement is unlikely to be an important feature of short cycles. Given the lag between investment and installation, business cycle expansions reach peaks before excess capacity could seriously cumulate as a result of the investments made during the same cyclical phase. By contrast, the duration of long-swing expansions makes such cumulation, with its implications for protracted depression or stagnation, at least an interesting possibility.

B. *Interactions Through Growth of Population and Labor Force*

Kuznets has taught us that long swings in the rate of economic growth are associated with long swings in additions to the population.[38] Before World War I, these population waves reflected principally the large waves in immigration. Since then, they have turned far more on a fluctuation in marriage and birth rates. As pointed out above, the most plausible explanation of these waves, apart from the effects of wars, is that they were responses to the occurrences of protracted periods of abnormally high unemployment and to the recovery from such periods. The long waves in population growth in turn operated through several mechanisms to aggravate and prolong periods of depression or stagnation and the periods of recovery and growth that followed.

---

[37] A. F. Burns, "Keynesian Economics Once Again," reprinted in *The Frontiers of Economic Knowledge* (Princeton, 1954), p. 234, fn. 13.

[38] Kuznets, "Long Swings in the Growth of Population . . . ," *op. cit.*

In the first place, the long waves in population growth acted on the demand for residential housing and, presumably on that for related commercial, public utility, and community facilities. The mechanism is not altogether simple because there is not a rigid proportional relation between population growth and household formation. The latter depends also on age composition and on changes in headship rates in each age group. Until the 1930's, however, headship rates remained relatively steady. The fluctuations in household formation were determined chiefly by the waves of immigration which accounted for most of the swings in population growth and at the same time so altered age composition as to cause household formation to increase and decline with the level of immigration.[39]

It is chiefly, though not entirely, to this fact that the well-known long waves in the national aggregate of urban residential building are to be attributed. We may, indeed, explain long cycles in local building activity on the basis of a cobweb process arising from long lags of building supply to changes in demand. In the absence of some common cause acting on all urban communities at about the same time, however, it is hardly likely that the local waves so engendered would run together to form national waves. Such a common cause is the long wave in population growth, which is widely diffused geographically because of its dependence on the state of the national labor market. In addition to unifying the local building waves, moreover, the swing in population growth must have acted to prolong them. A wave in building activity, once set in motion, must have tended to keep rising not only because of the lagged response of housing supply to the initial excess in demand, but also because of the further increase in demand caused by population growth so long as that kept rising.

The demographic response to change in the level of unemployment acts on the volume of capital formation not only through an associated wave in household formation, but also through an associated swing in labor force growth. As Easterlin has shown, in his monograph on *Long Swings in Labor Force Growth* (forthcoming), swings in labor force growth are connected with the state of the labor market not only through the response of immigration, but also through changes in the participation rates of marginal groups (women, racial minorities, and older workers), who enter or withdraw from the labor force in response to employment opportunities. An upswing in growth of capital formation which led to a tighter labor market was, therefore, strengthened and prolonged by the labor-force response to rising employment opportunities. For the rise in labor-force growth must have helped maintain the marginal productivity of capital and, therefore, the marginal efficiency of investment, in the face of an upsurge of investment.

---

[39] In this connection, see a forthcoming Stanford dissertation prepared by Burnham Campbell.

C. *Interactions Through Change in the Composition of Capital Formation*

Having divided total gross capital formation into "population-sensitive" (railroad capital expenditures plus residential building) and "other" investment, Kuznets[40] found in the period between the Civil War and World War I, that these two categories of investment tended to move inversely to one another, at least with respect to their rates of change, sometimes with respect to their levels. The result was a regular wave in the share of each category in total capital formation.

The observed alternation in the shares of "population-sensitive" and "other" investment is presumably not a perfectly satisfactory characterization of the fluctuations in the composition of capital formation since the "other" category is a heterogeneous grouping whose components did not always behave uniformly. For this reason alone, it is impossible to account briefly for the causes of the swing in the composition of investment. Part of the explanation, however, is probably to be traced to the wave in the level of unemployment and capacity utilization. If, as we suspect, the onset of a tight labor market and of near-capacity utilization of plant helps account for retardation in the growth of output, it can also help explain retardation in the growth, perhaps even a decline of those parts of "other" gross capital formation the demand for which is linked to output growth—for example, inventory investment and some branches of producer durables and non-residential construction. By contrast, a tight labor market stimulates immigration and otherwise encourages household formation and, therefore, the demand for residential building. To say this much is not to explain the observed shift in the composition of investment satisfactorily, but it is, perhaps, enough to identify another important connection between the intensity of utilization and the character of economic growth.

Granted that there was a characteristic change in the composition of capital formation of the general nature described by Kuznets, we may look for its significance in at least two directions. In the first place, it presumably influences the growth of productivity in the fashion alluded to above. Kuznets, indeed, suggests that the shift in the composition of capital formation may be the chief reason for the observed wave in productivity growth.[41]

The shift in the composition of investment is also connected with the question of financial ease or stringency. The argument is, briefly, as follows. Each category of real investment generates its own characteristic types of financial assets. These differ from one another in liquidity, risk, maturity, and other qualities which reflect the type of issuer and the kind of liabilities he feels able to undertake, given the nature of his business and the durability and liquidity

-----

[40] *Capital in the American Economy, op. cit.,* Ch. VII.
[41] *Ibid.*

of the real assets in which he is sinking his capital. The terms on which business can obtain finance, therefore, depend in part on how readily the public is willing to change the composition of the financial assets they absorb along with the change in the composition of real investment, or on the willingness and ability of intermediate financial institutions to absorb the changing mix of securities offered by the "real" investors and to issue to the public a more attractive mix. Unpublished historical analyses by John Gurley and Edward S. Shaw indicate that at least on some occasions before World War I, the shift of real investment demand to Kuznets' "population-sensitive" types generated a mixture of financial assets which did not easily satisfy the public's desire for liquidity. The result was a hardening of the financial markets which helped to check the growth of total investment and to bring on a period of under-employment.

The swing in the composition of investment has still another special aspect which I note below.

D. *Interactions Via the Foreign Balance, International Capital Movements, and the Supply of Money*[42]

From the early part of the 19th century until World War I, each general Kuznets cycle was accompanied by an inverse movement in the current balance of payments. This, in turn, reflected chiefly, but not exclusively, a positive wave in merchandise imports. In the early part of this era, the swing in the balance of payments alternately aggravated and then alleviated a chronically negative current balance. In later decades, the level of the balance gradually rose, so that the wave produced an alternation between times when the balance was positive and those when it was negative.

Given a specie standard, such as obtained during most of the era, the prolongation of a period of rapid growth manifestly depended then on the country's ability to finance a rising payments deficit either by gold shipments or capital imports. Except in the unusual circumstances of the years following the California discoveries, however, continued gold shipments in the size of the deficits would have brought rapid growth to a halt through monetary stringency and associated unemployment. Protracted periods of rapid development, therefore, implied rising capital imports such as did in fact accompany the rising phases of the Kuznets cycles. Finally, since these phases lasted for a number of years, sale of long-term securities was required and not merely the accumulation by foreigners of short-term claims. In short, foreigners, more particularly British investors, had to be offered securities they were willing to hold for some time. The question, therefore, is, what kinds of securities could foreigners be induced to accept as each upsurge of

---

[42] I base this section chiefly on the results of research now being carried on at Stanford University by Jeffery G. Williamson.

development generated its payments deficit. In the 19th and early 20th centuries the answer is clear. Only the securities of the railroads or those of the states (which were in turn issued in good part to finance railroad and canal building) were available. Throughout the century, these, in fact, constituted the bulk of the securities purchased by foreigners. The finance of the payments deficits, and, to that extent, the prolongation of general development, therefore, depended on recurrent upsurges of transport development.[43] It was, therefore, associated with the shift in the composition of capital formation to which Kuznets points.

Transport development, therefore, appears to have played three roles in the drama of United States development. First, the expansion of transport facilities enlarged our productive capacity. Secondly, the expenditures made in the course of railroad development, together with associated expenditures for farm and urban building, sustained the growth of demand during the upswings of Kuznets cycles. When the pace of railroad development declined, this contributed to retardation in the growth of total investment and so to the onset of protracted periods of unemployment and slow growth. Finally, the upsurges of transport development generated a flow of securities abroad which offset the accompanying rise in our payments deficit. When, however, the prospects for railroad profits became dimmer, this not only discouraged capital expenditures, it made for balance of payments difficulties. Manifestly, the competing pressures for finance of British home investment and of demands in other areas of the world played their parts in determining whether the United States could continue to finance a large deficit.

The mechanism by which the Kuznets swings in our payments deficit, together with those in the railroad industry, influenced our capacity to sustain rapid growth cannot be presented fully here. It may be interesting to point out, however, that waves in the rate of growth of the money supply and in the rate of change of prices accompanied the general Kuznets cycle, that during most of the period before 1914, the growth of the money supply depended on the expansion of the domestic stock of specie, and that changes in that stock depended on the relation between the level of our current balance of international payments and that of capital imports.[44] In the context of nineteenth century institutions, therefore, the swings in the profits prospects and in the rate of expansion of the transport system played a peculiarly important part in determining whether our international accounts and our monetary position would favor slow or rapid growth.

---

[43] I do not mean to say that foreigners necessarily had to buy the new issues of expanding railroads. This was doubtless the case in early decades when the float of outstanding securities was small. Later, the capital imports might be covered by sale of old securities. In either case, however, financing the deficit implied a period when prospects for railroad (or canal) profits were bright and seemed to justify expansion.

[44] Domestic gold production was, of course, another important element—in some years a dominant one.

IV

The last two sections have argued and illustrated the thesis that the long swings were the outcome of interactions between the pace at which resources were developed, the generation of effective demand, and the intensity of resource use. If we accept this view, then one may contend that, at least for the United States and possibly also for other countries, they are the most useful historical experiences available in terms of which the problems of maintaining balanced growth and of the relations between growth and business cycles may be studied realistically. While the standard business cycles involve some of the interesting interchanges between resource growth and effective demand, particularly as regards inventories, such cycles run their course in too short a time to display the full range of response. The various interactions sketched in Section III manifestly do not constitute a model which displays the essentials of these problems in a comprehensive and systematic way. They do, however, suggest the range of interrelations which such a model would have to encompass. It would necessarily include not only the direct relations between capital stock and income flow normally built into such models but also the repercussions via growth of population and labor force, the composition of capital formation, the terms of finance, the balance of international payments, and the supply of, and demand for, money.

The various interactions sketched above are also relevant to a question which must lie at the heart of all work on long swings, the question whether the observed long swings are to be regarded as systematic self-generating movements or as the outcome of episodic shocks. Again, the considerations set forth above do not and cannot settle the question. They do, however, suggest that there are a variety of cumulative responses set off by recovery from a protracted depression and that these responses are of a type that do not exhaust themselves in a single standard business-cycle expansion. As a result, we may well consider that there were systematic reasons for the fact that the periods of protracted depression or stagnation which punctuate the successive Kuznets cycles do not follow one another as frequently as do minor recessions.[45]

In addition, there is reason to think that some of the responses to recovery from protracted depression are of a type likely to push activity in some directions to unsustainable levels or rates of growth. This is true in part because recovery goes forward at first with the help of a general inventory build-up and without the restraints imposed by capacity ceilings. As full employment and capacity are approached, however, such restraints gradually force a reduction in the pace of output growth; and this also serves to dampen the pace of inventory accumulation and perhaps that of other kinds of investment

---

[45] There are, indeed, more reasons than the processes touched on in Section III can suggest.

which may be closely tied to output growth. The same sort of difficulty will arise in part because periods of protracted depression or stagnation are years in which the fulfillment of normal aspirations or plans is blocked, plans, for example, to immigrate, to marry, to establish separate households, or to undertake far-reaching industrial ventures. Recovery, when it comes, is sustained by the renewed opportunity it affords to carry out such deferred intentions. When, however, the various backlogs have been worked down, investment demand is likely to decline or to grow less rapidly. Further, the kinds of investment important in the long swings—notably construction, including railroad and public utilities construction—are notorious examples of sectors in which supply responds only slowly to change in demand and often only in large, indivisible lumps. There is, therefore, ample opportunity for investment to be overdone and for supply of capital to overshoot requirements. Finally—at least as a matter of history—our surges of growth involved deterioration in our current balance of payments, while the finance of that balance depended largely on the sale to foreigners of securities whose attractiveness rested on the profits prospects of a comparatively narrow sector of the economy, viz., railroads. As with any single sector, it is hard to imagine that those profits prospects should advance in even a roughly steady fashion.

It is, therefore, not difficult to find reasons for believing that the progress of a developing economy, particularly one in which spurts of growth have their beginnings in periods of underemployment, should develop hindrances and obstructions. We do not know, however, how powerful these checks are or what offsetting and stabilizing forces they may release. At the present time, therefore, we may be justified in contending no more than that the long swings are quasi-self-generating, in the limited, but important, senses that:

1. They involve certain forces which operate cumulatively for a time to strengthen a surge of development following a protracted period of relatively high unemployment and so to prevent the early recurrence of another such period.
2. They generate checks and obstacles which, after a time, generally longer than a single business cycle, render the economy more vulnerable to another period of depression or stagnation.

To say this much is, of course, not to say that episodic factors were not important, nor is it to say that the cumulative and self-reversing tendencies, such as they are, have remained generally constant. Episodic factors were clearly important in determining the course of the successive surges of development. Financial panics have aggravated depressions. Accumulations of deferred demands have arisen during wars as well as in depressions. Monetary policy and gold discoveries as well as capital imports and the current balance of payments have influenced the supply of money. Capital imports have been affected by events in Europe as well as by profits prospects in this country. However important their systematic mechanism, the course of Kuznets cycles in the United States has clearly been disturbed by extraneous influences to a very considerable degree.

Moreover, the systematic mechanism has clearly changed during the last century and a quarter in which the swings can be observed. The character of capital formation has changed from investment chiefly designed to extend the settled and cultivated area of the country to investment designed chiefly to extend capacity to provide manufactured goods and services. The speed with which capacity responds to demand must have altered a great deal in consequence. Residential construction has declined in importance. Decision-making units, which were chiefly farm households 125 years ago, are now giant corporations. Immigration is now a minor factor in the growth of population and labor force, but this change has apparently been accompanied by an increased sensitivity of our native-born elements to influences affecting internal migration, marriage, household formation, and labor-force participation. The country now stands on a capital-exporting rather than a capital-importing basis, and the supply of money is now at least partially managed. In a variety of ways the sensitivity of income to declines in investment has been dulled.

These changes and many others will, no doubt, have altered the relations between economic development and intensity of resource use. If, however, this problem, which is the same problem as that of maintaining balance between capacity and effective demand, is to be studied empirically over a reasonably long stretch of history, these difficulties must be accepted. The Kuznets long swings appear to have been the phenomena in terms of which this problem manifested itself in the United States and, indeed, in several other countries in the past. Historical and analytical studies of these swings in a number of countries should, therefore, enrich and test the models designed to help us understand the problem of maintaining balance in growth as this old problem is faced both by advanced and backward countries in a modern setting.

28

Secular Swings in Production and Trade, 1870–1913*

By P. J. O'LEARY and W. ARTHUR LEWIS†

EVER SINCE Professor Simon Kuznets published his *Secular Movements in Production and Prices* in 1930 we have known that a great many statistical series relating to the volume of economic activity (*i.e.* excluding price effects) show a secular fluctuation, of about 16 to 22 years duration, which is so pronounced that it dwarfs the 7 to 11 year cycle into relative insignificance. Professor Kuznets dealt with many industries and many countries, but somehow this secular fluctuation has become identified in most people's minds with the building industry. Professor A. F. Burns[1] reiterated the point in 1934, drawing on a very wide range of industries in the United States, and the point was made again by Professors Warren and Pearson[2] in 1937; but it was not until Professor Kuznets published his estimates[3] of real income in the United States since 1869, and drew attention once more to the secular swing in output as a whole, that the importance of this fluctuation in the American economy was generally recognised.

On this side of the Atlantic, the existence of a similar secular fluctuation in the British building industry was first pointed out by Professor A. K. Cairncross, in a series of studies culminating recently in the publication of his great work on British capital formation.[4] From this work it also emerged that home investment other than in residential building had the same pronounced secular fluctuation as residential building; and that foreign investment had a secular fluctuation in the reverse directions. Next, Mr. E. W. Cooney demonstrated[5] that the U.S. and the U.K. building cycles fluctuated in opposite directions to each other, thus raising the question how these

* *The Manchester School*, Vol. XXIII (May, 1955). Reprinted by courtesy of *The Manchester School* and the authors.

† University of Bristol and Princeton University.

[1] *Production Trends in the United States since 1870*, New York, 1934.

[2] *World Prices and the Building Industry*, New York, 1937.

[3] *National Product since 1869*, New York, 1946.

[4] *Home and Foreign Investment, 1870–1913*, Cambridge, 1953.

[5] "Capital Exports and Investment in Building in Britain and the U.S.A., 1856–1914." *Economica*, November, 1949.

two great economies, with investment cycles in opposite directions, reacted upon each other, and upon the rest of the world. This was the question to which Professor Brinley Thomas addressed himself,[6] starting from the angle of international migration, and he showed that the effect was an enormous secular fluctuation in the movement of people across the water, with the same duration, timing and direction as is found in the U.S. building cycle, and in the U.K. export of capital.

The purpose of this article is to explore further the effect of these countries' swings upon each other and upon the rest of the world. The article begins with the U.S. fluctuation, but does not linger with this fluctuation, since it is well known. The U.K.'s position is less certain; if foreign investment and home investment alternated with each other, did this keep the economy as a whole stable, or was there a secular swing, and if so, in which direction? Next the article considers the position of France and of Germany. From these it turns to the agricultural countries, considering both the statistics of world production and trade, and also series relating to individual countries. A picture thus emerges of inter-related secular fluctuations in the world economy in the forty years before the first world war. The purpose of the article is not mainly theoretical, but rather to see what the relevant statistics show, and to make a few comments on the results.

It is convenient to have a name to distinguish a secular swing from the other cycles in economic activity. Following the precedent of naming each cycle after the person who first focussed attention upon it—cf. the Kitchin 40-month cycle, the Juglar 9-year cycle, and the Kondratieff 50-year cycle—we suggest calling this the "Kuznets" cycle, hoping that Professor Kuznets will not take amiss this tribute to his pioneering work.

The series used are described in Appendix I.[7] They are all "volume" series, i.e. physical series, or financial series deflated by price indices. The method used is the same in all cases: the series has been reduced to logarithms, and a straight line trend fitted by the method of least squares.[8] This trend shows what the series would have been if it had grown at a constant rate throughout the period. The percentage deviations of the actual series from the trend are plotted, and are shown in the charts. The chart shows us simultaneously the level of the series and its rate of growth. For example, at any time the series may be above trend but stagnating, or below trend but showing vigorous growth. The rate of growth is deduced from the chart from the slope of the line, and not from its position above or below the trend.

Treating a series in this way gives queer results if the average rate of growth is not in fact about the same in the first half of the period as it is in

---

[6] *Migration and Economic Growth*, Cambridge, 1954.

[7] Not reproduced here. See the article as originally published in *The Manchester School*, May, 1955, pp. 147–51.

[8] There is one exception: the trend has not been removed from the series showing the percentage of unemployment in the U.K.

the second half of the period. For example, if there is no growth in the first half, and rapid growth in the second half, the deviations when plotted assume the shape of a 'V.' Fortunately, most of the series in which we were interested show uniform growth; the only series which we have had to discard as unsuitable for this treatment are those relating to New Zealand and to Canada.[9] Fitting a straight line trend is also misleading if there is constant

CHART 1

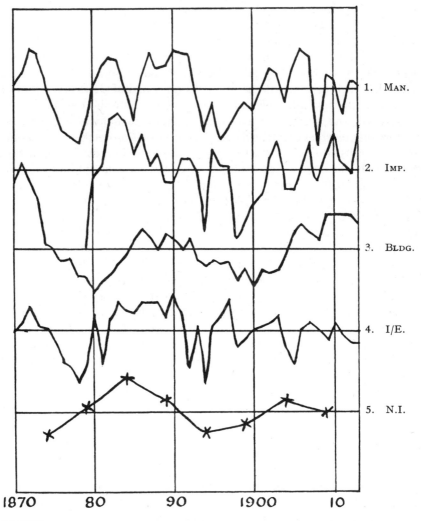

1. MAN.

2. IMP.

3. BLDG.

4. I/E.

5. N.I.

1870   80   90   1900   10

[9] The volume of Canada's exports (for example) was the same in 1889 as in 1873; then from 1890 to 1913 the average annual increase was 5.5 percent per annum. See K. W. Taylor, "Statistics of Foreign Trade" in C. A. Curtis and others, *Statistical Contributions to Canadian Economic History*, Vol. I, Toronto, 1931.

retardation (or acceleration) in the rate of growth; it may then be more appropriate to fit a parabola of second or higher orders. One disadvantage of fitting a second order parabola is that the chart of the deviations is no longer sufficient to tell us what is happening to the series; when comparing different charts we have then to bear in mind that the trend of some may be subject to a sharp retardation (or acceleration) which is not present in others. Fortunately, most of the series in which we are interested show no retardation between 1870 and 1913, or such slight retardation that the difference between a first order and a second order parabola is negligible.

I. THE U.S.A.

We need not spend long with the U.S.A., since the general pattern of the economy's behaviour is well known, and easily described: decades of prosperity alternate with decades of relative depression. Peaks of prosperity were reached in 1873, in 1892 and 1913 and troughs of depression occurred in 1878 and in 1896. Kuznets, Warren and Pearson, and Brinley Thomas have produced an enormous number of series which show this fluctuation, ranging from railway traffic and the production of pig iron to the number of patents registered and the number of marriages, so we may confine ourselves here to a few series which relate to the economy as a whole.

Series 1 in Chart 1 is Frickey's index of manufacturing production (from which the dates in the preceding paragraph were derived). It shows how marked is the secular swing, compared with all other fluctuations. Series 2 shows the volume of imports. This has the same swing, but gives rather a sharp drop in imports in the later 1880's. U.S. series differ as to the state of prosperity in the second half of the '80's, compared with the first half. Building activity (series 3) and the percentage of imports into the U.S. coming from Europe (series 4) testify to great activity, but a number of other series, such as coal output, suggest that though the second half of the '80's was above trend, it was not as prosperous as the first half. National income (series 5) cannot resolve the difficulty, since the series consists of averages for overlapping decades. However, all the important annual series, including agriculture,[10] but with the single exception of exports,[11] confirm that there was a marked secular fluctuation in the U.S. economy, with 1880–92 and 1901–13 above trend, and 1874–79 and 1893–1900 below trend.[12]

---

[10] The position of U.S. agriculture is discussed in Section IV below, and shown in Chart 8, series 36. It was influenced as much by U.K. as by U.S. prosperity.

[11] Exports in the first half of this period were mainly agricultural, so discussion is reserved to Section IV below. See series 35 in Chart 8. Exports have a marked secular swing which is the reverse of the swing in the rest of the economy. This represents the effect of the U.K. secular swing.

[12] The reader should note that in the charts each series has its own vertical scale, so the vertical distances of different series must not be compared directly. Information is given in the Appendix about each series from which the vertical scale can be computed.

The fact that prosperity outlasts depression is not without significance. One may be tempted to deny that there is fundamentally a Kuznets cycle, and may prefer to say that all that happens is that once every twenty years one of the Juglar depressions gets out of hand, and lasts for 6 to 8 years, instead of lasting for 1 or 2 years only. Even such regularity as this, however, deserves the name of cycle: there is no reason why the number of years of prosperity and of depression in a cycle should be equal to each other.

The causes of this secular fluctuation—or this propensity to have a runaway Juglar depression every twenty years—are not yet definitely established, and it is not the purpose of this article to establish them. Following Schumpeter's lead, one may pick on the fact that railway construction and immigration show exactly the same periodicity, and may develop the thesis that the economy needs a digestion period to cope with major innovations of these types. Or again, following in the same footsteps, one may pick out the industries which show greatest growth during the upswings, and name each upswing for its major industrial innovation.[13] On the other hand, perhaps the whole thing can be attributed to the building cycle. Since residential building amounts to as much as 20 to 30 percent of gross investment in the U.S.A., it would not be surprising that wide secular fluctuations in residential building should produce corresponding fluctuations in the rest of the economy, including other forms of investment. As for the building cycle itself, it is not difficult to explain without resort to the study of innovations. One has only to postulate some stickiness of rents, combined with cobweb-like behaviour on the part of speculative builders, in order to obtain this kind of model.

II. THE U.K.

The U.K. economy did not fluctuate as widely as the U.S. economy because U.K. exports and U.K. home investment moved in the opposite directions. U.K. exports were large, relatively to the economy as a whole, both because the U.K.'s imports were large, and also because the U.K. was a great exporter of capital. In the U.S.A., on the contrary, exports were too small to offset home investment, so the economy had no such stabiliser.

There was a marked secular swing in U.K. exports, which at least in the first half of the period, virtually coincided with the swing in U.S. manufacturing production.[14] This can be seen by comparing series 6 in Chart 2 with series 1 in Chart 1. That a contributory cause of this U.K. swing was the swing in the U.S. economy is demonstrated by the next two series. Series 7

---

[13] This is the line taken by B. Weber and S. J. Handfield-Jones in "Variations in the Rate of Economic Growth in the U.S.A., 1869–1939," *Oxford Economic Papers*, June, 1954.

[14] The low level of U.K. exports in 1900 and immediately after, which is the main difference between series 6 and series 1, was attributed at the time to the effects of the Boer War, which made shipping scarce and reduced foreign borrowing.

CHART 2

U.K.

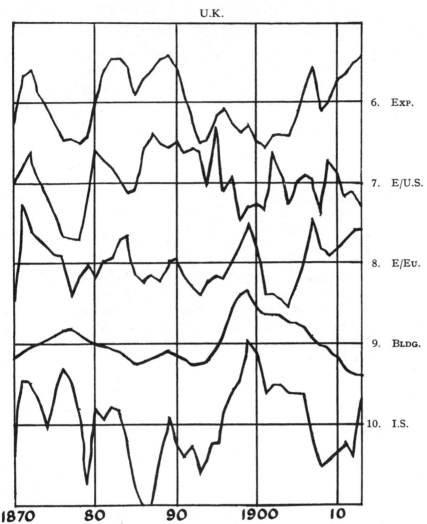

6. Exp.

7. E/U.S.

8. E/Eu.

9. Bldg.

10. I.S.

|1870   80   90   1900   10

shows the percentage of U.K. exports going to the U.S.A. (trend removed).
(The low level after 1900 is probably due to the effects of the U.S. tariff.)
Series 8 shows U.K. exports to Europe; this series does not have the same
pattern; it parallels instead the behaviour of German exports (series 20 in
Chart 5), which also went chiefly to Europe. On the other hand, since the
U.S.A. was taking only 12 percent of the U.K.'s exports in the 1880's, its
purchases from the U.K. were not enough to produce such a decisive swing.
As we shall see in the next section, Germany was prosperous at the same time
as the U.S., and though agricultural Europe and France were depressed in
the second half of the '80's, German prosperity will have helped to keep up

READINGS IN BUSINESS CYCLES

British exports. Exports to Australia and to Latin America were also above trend in the second half of the '80's, because of the investment boom in those countries, and a similar boom, again financed by capital export, also contributes to the 1905–13 boom in exports.

Series 9 is Cairncross's index of building, and series 10 is his series for home consumption of iron and steel. As in the United States, building and other domestic investment (of which iron and steel consumption is an excellent reflection) go together. Both swing in the opposite direction to exports.

This divergent movement of exports and of investment raises interesting questions. It has often been assumed that fluctuations in exports produced corresponding fluctuations in investment, if only because exports were at this time about one-fifth of the national income, and probably one-third of industrial production. Here the distinction between Juglar and Kuznets cycles is significant. If we were to take a nine-year moving average through the original series, we should find that home investment shows the same Juglar fluctuations as exports; it is only the Kuznets fluctuation that is different. Again, if one takes a still longer view, the fact that the rate of growth of exports of manufactures dropped from 5.6 per cent per annum (1820–60) to 2.1 percent per annum after 1870 (1870–1913) is probably causally associated with a similar fall in the rate of growth of industrial production, and with the fall in the proportion of savings invested at home.

Now, although exports were larger than home investment, the secular fluctuations in gross investment were so much wider than those in exports that they offset the fluctuations in exports. The mean deviation of exports from trend was 6.6 percent, whereas the mean deviation of gross investment from trend was 9.4 percent. Series 11 in Chart 3 is the result of adding exports at constant prices and gross investment at constant prices together. It will be observed that the Kuznets swing disappears.

Three other series confirm that exports and home investment offset each other. Series 12 is Hoffman's index of industrial production (without building); series 13 is the index of retained imports of industrial raw materials; and series 14 is an index of domestic consumption of coal (production minus exports and bunkers). All these demonstrate that the wide secular fluctuation in the U.S. economy found no parallel in industrial production in Great Britain.

This is not the same as saying that there was no secular fluctuation in consumption. On the contrary, if production was constant, and there was a secular swing in the terms of trade, this would produce a secular swing in consumption. More important, if industrial production was constant, but there was a Kuznets swing in building, again there would be a Kuznets swing in total output and consumption.[15]

---

[15] We do not use a deflated national income series because we do not have an appropriate

CHART 3

U.K.

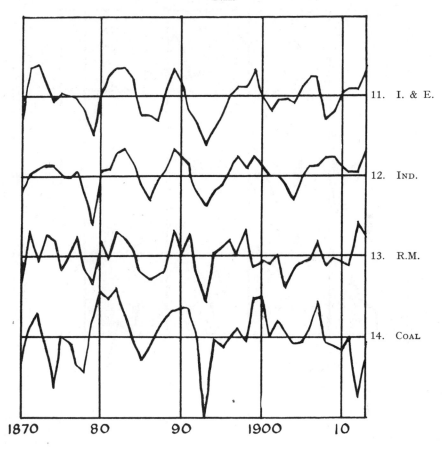

11. I. & E.

12. IND.

13. R.M.

14. COAL

1870   80   90   1900   10

That there was a Kuznets swing in consumption can be seen from the series in Chart 4. Series 15 is Tinbergen's index of real consumption of commodities, excluding services (production plus imports minus exports). The swing can be seen more clearly in the nine-year moving average, which is plotted as a dotted line through the series. It is not a wide swing; the nine-year moving average swings from 2.5 percent below to 3.3 percent above the trend. Exactly the same rather narrow swing can be seen in the trade

series for the price of British output with which to deflate it. The prices used by other authors are heavily weighted by the price of imported food, and the secular swing which then results merely reflects the behaviour of the terms of trade. An appropriate price series should have as its largest constituent the price of services, on which information is scanty. It seems also very likely that Mr. A. R. Prest's pioneer national income estimate (*Economic Journal*, March, 1948) seriously underestimates the national income in the early part of the period, since its rate of growth exceeds that of the physical indices which we possess.

CHART 4

U.K.

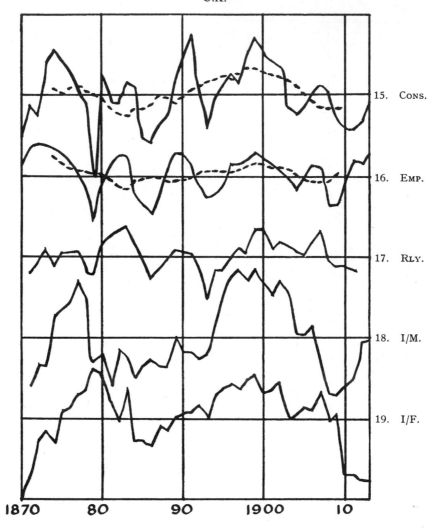

15. Cons.

16. Emp.

17. Rly.

18. I/M.

19. I/F.

1870   80   90   1900   10

union index of employment, series 16 (the unemployment percentage reversed; the trend has *not* been removed). But the unemployment percentage is not a good index of secular fluctuations in employment since the percentage of people belonging to trade unions rises in prosperity and falls in depression. There is even clearer evidence of the swing in series 17, which shows the weight of goods carried by the railways.[16]

---

[16] On closer examination, domestic consumption of coal (series 14 in Chart 3) also gives slight supporting evidence of a Kuznets cycle in consumption, with peaks at 1883 and 1899.

Since industrial production for home consumption was steady,[17] the swing in consumption has to be accounted for by imports. Imports did in fact have a wide swing; series 18 shows retained imports of manufactures and series 19 retained imports of food. Their swings cannot be explained mainly by the terms of trade. In the first place, if the terms of trade were the explanation, manufactures and food would swing in opposite directions, whereas they swing together. And in the second place, the terms of trade do not swing in this way; for example, they were deteriorating in the second half of the '90's, when these series, on the contrary, were rising rapidly above trend. The obvious explanation is the building cycle (series 9), whose pattern is basically similar. Food imports rise sharply at the end of the '70's despite declining building, because of a succession of bad harvests; and fall more sharply than building in the 1900's, because of deteriorating terms of trade, coupled with a shift from wages to profits. Otherwise, the situation is adequately described by saying that while during these forty years industrial production grew without a secular swing, nevertheless, imports and building swing together, and exports swing in the opposite direction.[18] From the point of view of the rest of the world, to whom U.K. imports were the decisive factor, the periods of Kuznets prosperity (*i.e.* above trend) ran from 1875 to 1883, and from 1894 to 1906.

Writers have sought to explain why investment in the U.S. and the U.K. should have fluctuated in opposite directions.[19] The decades of depression for the U.K. were decades when home investment was low, when the U.S. was booming, and when U.K. foreign investment was high; home investment and foreign investment alternated with each other. Since the U.S.A. was importing capital, it is tempting to argue that the U.S.A. had to fit itself into the U.K. home investment cycle; that is to say, to wait until the U.K. had had a surfeit of home investment, and could spare capital for investment overseas. This line of argument is not very plausible if it is applied

---

[17] This is deduced from the steadiness of industrial production (series 12) and of home investment plus exports (series 11).

[18] There is no support in this material for Professor Phelps-Brown's "Climacteric of the 1890's," *Oxford Economic Papers*, October, 1952. He bases much of his conclusion on statistics which reflect consumption rather than production (real wages and national income deflated by price series reflecting mainly the cost of living). Series 11, 12 and 13 in Chart 3 show that industrial production grew as rapidly after 1900 as before. Phelps-Brown's data are per capita, but there was no climacteric in the growth of the industrial population. Anyway, changes in the rate of growth of population at this time were insignificant—fractions of one percent per annum—and in the wrong direction from his point of view (steadily growing output divided by decelerating population growth is favourable to calculations of productivity). The series Phelps-Brown presents for individual industries show divergent trends, as we would expect. The fall in the rate of growth of consumption per head after 1900 was due to the building cycle, reinforced by deteriorating terms of trade, and by a shift from wages to profits. There is no need to introduce speculations about the changing nature of innovations. In any case, no explanation of the phenomenon is convincing which assumes that it is unique, and does not take account of similar features twenty years earlier.

[19] Especially Cairncross, *op. cit.*, and Thomas, *op. cit.*

to the period from 1870, for while it is true that the U.S.A. was importing capital, its capital imports were so small in relation to its own savings—averaging between 1874 and 1895 less than a half of one percent of gross national product[20]—that it is impossible to hold that capital formation in the U.S. was at this time dependent on U.K. lending, even when allowance is made for the fact that much of the U.K. capital went into such strategic investments as railway building. The argument is a bit more plausible if it is taken back earlier into the century, say to the thirties and forties. British capital was then perhaps more necessary to U.S. development, and the alternation of the British and U.S. cycles then established may have continued automatically for the rest of the century. Even then it is not very plausible, however, if the U.S. Secretary of the Treasury of the day was right in thinking that foreign investments in the U.S.A. were worth only 222 million dollars in 1853. We have probably to conclude that the U.S. governed its own fortunes in the nineteenth century, and if any adjustment had to be made it was made on the other side of the Atlantic.

May it then be that it was the U.K. which timed its building cycle to fit in with the American? The mechanism in this case would be that British capitalists would invest abroad when the U.S. was prosperous, and return to home investment when the U.S. market slumped. This mechanism is plausible for the period after 1870; but the alternation of the two building cycles goes back much earlier in the century, and it is much less easy to apply this explanation to the earlier period, because of the much smaller importance of foreign investment at that time. If the two economies were linked in this way, the link was not direct but indirect, since most of the British foreign investment did not go to the U.S.A.[21] There is also the possible link through migration, since presumably fewer houses were needed in the U.K when the U.S. was booming and migration heavy, than when the U.S. was depressed and migration small. But differences in emigration rates made less than a quarter of one percent difference to the annual rate of growth of population, so one treats this explanation with suspicion. Besides migration was even less important earlier in the century, when the alternation was already well established (the U.K. building cycle reached peaks in 1825 and 1847, the American in 1836 and 1853). Also, emigration from Germany coincided with emigration from Britain, but, as we shall see in a moment, Germany's investment cycle seems to have *coincided* with the U.S. cycle.

We cannot even rule out the possibility that the alternation of the U.S. and U.K. building cycles was a sheer accident, springing perhaps from the

---

[20] U.S. Bureau of the Census, *Historical Statistics of the United States*, p. 242, relying on C. J. Bullock, J. H. Williams, and R. S. Tucker, "The Balance of Trade of the United States," *The Review of Economic Statistics*, July, 1919.

[21] According to Bullock, Williams and Tucker, the U.S.A. imported £200 million of capital from all foreign sources between 1874 and 1895. In this period British capital export amounted to £800 million.

different effects which the Napoleonic Wars may have had upon the progress of residential building in the two countries. The case for thinking that it may have been an accident lies in the fact that if the two cycles had coincided, there would have been no mechanism to make them alternate. It would then have been the case that British imports and British exports would have boomed together, and been depressed together. British capital exports would then have been steady, instead of fluctuating widely as a result of booming exports and depressed imports alternating with depressed exports and booming imports. On the other hand, the economy as a whole would have fluctuated more widely. The U.S. economy fluctuated more widely than the British economy because the fluctuations of home investment were not offset by opposite fluctuations of foreign investment, as in the British case. If the two building cycles had coincided, the British economy would have fluctuated as widely as the U.S. economy, in the same direction, and at the same time, and there is no mechanism which would automatically have set to work to counter this, by bringing about opposite fluctuations of the two building cycles. This is what happened in Germany, where capital exports and home investment coincided.

Perhaps this problem will yield to further analysis if we get better figures for foreign investment in the first half of the nineteenth century, and better information on its geographical division. Until we know more precisely to which countries British capital went, and why, we cannot offer definitive explanations of the timing of foreign investment.

III. GERMANY AND FRANCE

The two economies we have just considered, the U.S. and the U.K., are remarkable for the fact that their internal prosperity fluctuated in the reverse direction to their exports; this indicating that their prosperity was not dictated by the level of their export trade—at any rate, over the period of the Kuznets cycle. Germany and France, it turns out, were also in this category, so we must deal with them separately before turning to countries whose prosperity depended upon events elsewhere.

The German statistics are presented in Chart 5. Before proceeding, we must draw attention to an adjustment we have had to make before using the existing indices. This arises out of the fact that the area covered by German trade statistics was changed in 1872, in 1879, in 1889 and in 1906. The German Empire came into existence in 1872. The Hanse towns, however, did not join the customs union until 1889. From 1872 to 1879 the published totals for German trade involve double counting; from 1880 they exclude the trade of the Hanse towns; then when in 1889 the Hanse towns join the union, recorded imports rise sharply, and recorded exports drop sharply. There still remained certain free port areas, which were not brought into the statistics until 1906, but these affected the position by less than 1 percent,

and can be ignored. We explain in Appendix I [not reproduced here] how
we have overcome these breaks in the statistics (which affect the existing index
of industrial production also, in so far as it is based upon import statistics).

CHART 5

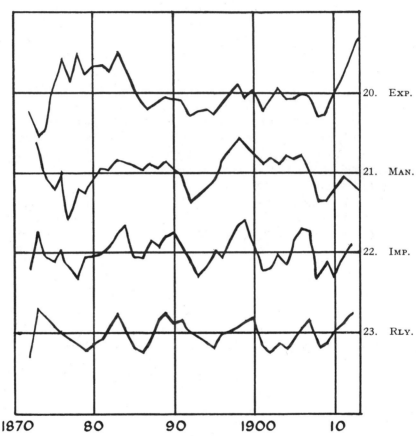

Since there can be no precision in the methods used, it is fortunate that none
of the conclusions which follow depends upon what is assumed to be the
correct movement of the figures for 1879 to 1880, and from 1888 to 1889,
provided the assumptions are kept within reasonable limits.

  Germany's exports depended upon the prosperity of Europe, and thus
to some extent of the U.K., but not on the prosperity of the U.S.A. This
can be seen by studying the matrix of world trade in 1887 which is presented
as Table 1. In 1887 the U.S.A. was mainly an importer of manufactures
and an exporter of agricultural products. She did little trade with continental
Europe. Her European trade was mainly with the U.K., and as the U.K.'s

imports did not fluctuate in line with the U.K.'s exports, prosperity in the U.S.A. had little effect on continental Europe.

Continental Europe, excluding France and Germany, exported mainly foodstuffs, and its prosperity was therefore very dependent on the volume of British, French, and German imports, and on the terms of trade. Both Britain and France were booming up to 1883, and then depressed for a decade;

TABLE 1

PERCENTAGE DISTRIBUTION OF WORLD EXPORTS, 1887

From: To:	U.K.	Germany	U.S.A.	France	Australasia	Other Europe	Asia	Other America	Africa	Unclassified	Total
U.K.	..	1.2	2.2	1.0	1.5	3.6	3.6	2.5	0.8	0.1	16.5
Germany	2.3	..	1.1	1.0	..	6.9	0.1	0.3	..	..	11.7
U.S.A.	5.6	0.9	..	0.9	0.1	1.4	0.4	1.5	..	0.1	10.9
France	2.4	1.0	0.8	..	..	3.6	..	1.1	0.6	0.2	9.7
Australasia	1.7	0.1	0.1	0.1	..	..	0.1	..	0.1	..	2.2
Other Europe	6.8	7.9	1.1	4.6	..	7.1	0.4	0.7	0.1	1.6	30.3
Asia*	3.3	0.1	1.0	1.0	0.2	1.3	†	†	†	2.4	9.3
Other America*	1.9	0.3	2.9	1.3	..	0.8	†	†	†	0.2	7.4
Africa*	1.0	..	..	0.6	..	0.3	†	†	†	0.1	2.0
Total	25.0	11.5	9.2	10.5	1.8	25.0	4.6	6.1	1.6	4.7	100.0

.. = less than 0.05.   * The figures in italics are based on import statistics.
† = not known.
SOURCE: See Appendix II of the original article in *The Manchester School*, May, 1955, p. 152.

during which decade the terms of trade were also very unfavourable to agriculture. Recovery began in the middle '90's, and though British imports were again below trend from 1906 to 1913, the terms of trade were on this occasion favourable, so agricultural Europe remained prosperous until the war.

This is the picture shown by series 20, Germany's exports of industrial products. The great boom in British imports from 1875 to 1883 stands out clearly. Then there is stagnation from 1884 to 1895, followed by prosperity up to the war. U.K. exports to Europe (series 8 in Chart 2) followed more or less the same course; the Juglar boom of 1889 is low in both cases, but series 8 shows a bigger Juglar depression after 1900 than does series 20.

The series representing internal conditions give a somewhat different picture. Series 21 is manufacturing industry, series 22 is imports, and series 23 is railway traffic. They do not agree completely, yet they support each other. They agree that the boom of the second half of the '80's was as powerful as that of the first half of the '80's, despite the depression of exports. The manufacturing series virtually denies that there was a Juglar depression in the middle of the '80's; and though the other two series both show such a depression, they agree that it was mild and short. Imports and manufacturing agree on the super-boom of the late '90's. Then manufacturing again asserts that the following Juglar depression was mild, and though the other two series do not agree, the imports series at least supports the contention that the year 1906 saw a major break in prosperity.[22]

We can justifiably say of the German economy that it was above trend from 1881 to 1890, and again from 1896 to 1907. These are also the dates of the heaviest capital export, except that the capital export boom continued until 1913. This is a remarkable mixture of the British and the American dates; from 1870 to 1892 the German economy behaves like the American, after which it behaves like the British. The resemblance to the American economy before 1892 is coincidental, but the resemblance to the British economy thereafter has a causal link.

The main explanation of the German Kuznets fluctuation is the German building cycle, which seems virtually to have coincided with the U.S. building cycle, at least between 1870 and 1900. We have not been able to find a series covering the whole period from 1870, but Warren and Pearson[23] present a number of charts which suggest peaks in 1873 and 1890, and Wagenfuhr's figures[24] show another peak in 1904–6 (rather earlier than the U.S.A.). This latter series, which begins in 1890, is specially interesting.

1896	88	1902	115	1908	100
7	95	3	140	9	93
8	103	4	147	10	124
9	115	5	143	1	139
1900	110	6	146	2	125
1	106	7	125	3	100

It shows that if the building cycle had been the only factor, the super-boom would have come not in 1898–99, but in 1906–7. The boom of 1898–99 probably owed something to the super-boom in the British economy, produced by the U.K. home investment cycle, which in turn reflected itself in the super-boom in British imports of food and manufactures (series 18 and 19), and in the resulting prosperity of continental Europe. But it must be admitted that the German export series does not give enthusiastic support to this thesis.

The French picture is again different. French trade statistics for the period before 1914 are notoriously unreliable,[25] because of lack of care in compiling them. The series for exports, series 24 in Chart 6, should be dominated by U.K. imports, and by the prosperity of agricultural Europe, since,

---

[22] Estimates of German national income exist, but in the absence of prices for services we are unable to present a real income series.

[23] *Op. cit.*, p. 123.

[24] *Die Industriewirtschaft*, p. 61.

[25] See the discussion in H. D. White, *The French International Accounts*, Cambridge, Mass., 1933.

CHART 6

FRANCE

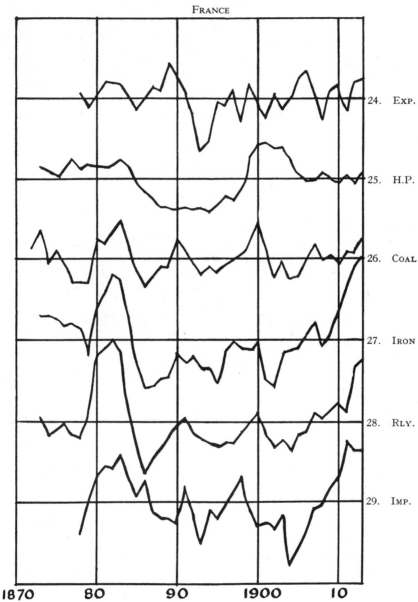

as the matrix shows, these were her chief customers. This would give a super-boom up to 1883, followed by a great depression to 1895, then a super-boom centred on 1899–1900, followed by a tug-of-war between European prosperity and U.K. depression. Instead one gets super-booms in 1889 and 1907, coinciding with super-booms in French capital exports.

In France, as in the three preceding cases, exports and the internal economy do not move together. The internal series show that France had a secular Kuznets fluctuation, with its super-booms in 1883 and 1900. The movement comes out very clearly in a unique French series, showing the horse-power of steam engines installed in industry (stock, not annual additions). This is series 25. Confirmation is supplied by series 26, French coal consumption (production plus imports minus exports and additions to stocks), which also makes France the only country so far where the depression of 1908 does not bring the series below trend, and is followed by accelerated growth to 1913. Series 27, pig iron production, does not conform quite so markedly. The downturn of 1900 is indeed sharper than that of 1890, but is swiftly reversed by a powerful upswing to a new super-boom in 1913; and the same upswing dominates series 28, railway traffic, and series 29, imports. Additionally, all these series emphasise the fact that in France the Kuznets picture is one of sharp peaks, separated by irregular country, rather than the flat plateaus separated by deep gorges which we associate with Germany and the U.S.A.

Alas there is no series for residential building before 1901. The best series we can find is an index number of the output of cement, starting in 1896 which runs as follows:[26]

1896	48	1902	50	1908	70
7	51	3	47	9	71
8	56	4	47	10	79
9	59	5	48	1	93
1900	59	6	65	2	100
1	58	7	65	3	100

This shows peaks in 1900 and 1913, and is confirmed after 1900 by the official index of building. It also corresponds well with series 27, 28 and 29. This correspondence in turn throws some doubt on the behaviour of series 25, the horsepower series, after about 1904. It looks as if the French economy was working up to a new super-boom when the war broke out. We cannot say whether France had the normal building cycle, or what its timing was, but if there was such a cycle it was probably not as important as other constituents of the investment cycle. Since population grew only by 7 percent in the 35 years from 1876 to 1911, the annual investment in buildings must have been small in relation to national income, and fluctuations in its size cannot have had much effect upon the rest of the economy.

We cannot offer any explanation of the French Kuznets cycle in industrial investment.[27] Like the British cycle, it alternated to some extent with a cycle in foreign investment, but the fit is not very good—which is the reason why French output shows a secular fluctuation which does not appear in British industrial production.

---

[26] *Annuaire Statistique*, 1945, p. 105.

[27] The depth of the depression of 1884–95 may have owed something to the *phylloxera*, which was at its worst in those years.

IV. AGRICULTURE

The outcome of the analysis so far is three Kuznets cycles in industrial production in the U.S.A., Germany and France, with corresponding cycles in imports; and a fourth Kuznets cycle in the U.K., not in industrial production, or in imports of raw materials, but in other production and in other imports. How was the rest of the world affected?

We note first that these fluctuations could not exactly offset each other, both because their timings did not alternate precisely, and also because the economies differed in size and importance.

The U.S.A. was above trend in the years 1880–92 and 1901–13; the U.K. in the years 1875–83 and 1894–1906; Germany in the years 1881–90 and 1896–1907; and France had its super-peaks in 1883 and 1900. These dates overlap to give the greatest years of prosperity as 1880–83 and 1900–06; with the worst period of depression as 1892–96. What is usually called "The Great Depression 1873 to 1896" should be "The Great Depression 1883 to 1896." The phrase then has meaning for world production as a whole; but even then it is inapplicable to the U.S.A. and to Germany, and is only of strictly limited application to the U.K.

In Chart 7 these dates are confirmed by series 30, world production of raw materials, and by series 31, world production of foodstuffs, both of which have a marked secular fluctuation, with roughly the same timing. Exactly the same phenomenon is revealed by the terms of trade between primary products and manufactures, series 32, which when the trend has been removed, reiterates that the great depression began not in 1873 but in 1883, and which remains continuously below trend until 1899.

When we turn from world production to world trade, we cannot expect quite the same picture. The U.S. demand for primary products was small; she was a net exporter. The U.K. had no secular movement in its imports of raw materials; here Germany's dates would be dominant, to give a prosperity plateau from 1881 to 1890 and from 1896 to 1907. Whereas, in foodstuffs British imports would set the dominant dates on either side of 1879 and of 1899. We do not have separate series for world trade in food and in raw materials. Primary products together are shown in series 33 (quinquennial averages), which alas starts only in 1876. The influence of Germany and the U.K. is very plain. World trade in manufactures is compounded of the terms of trade and of the volume of trade in primary products;[28] series 34 therefore behaves exactly as we would expect it to behave, in the light of series 32 and 33.

When we turn to the agricultural statistics of individual countries, what pattern do we expect to find? First, we must distinguish exporters of raw

---

[28] The relationship is demonstrated statistically in W. A. Lewis, "World Production, Prices and Trade, 1870–1960," *The Manchester School*, May, 1952.

CHART 7

WORLD PRODUCTION AND TRADE

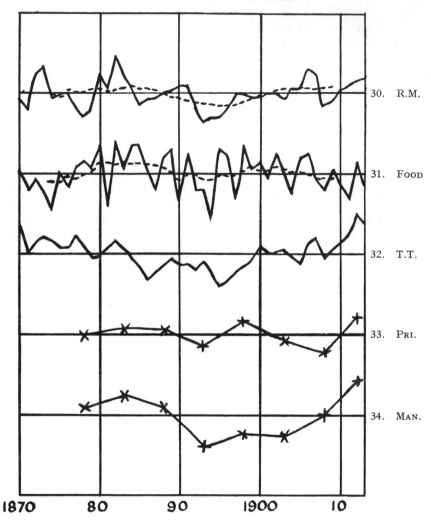

materials from exporters of foodstuffs; the former should have the German-American pattern, with prosperity continuing throughout the '80's, and depression lasting far into the '90's, whereas the latter should have the U.K. pattern, with prosperity disappearing in the middle '80's, and reaching a new peak around 1900.

Secondly, we must distinguish exporters to the U.S.A. from exporters to the U.K. This distinction is not the same as the previous distinction for it applies equally to foodstuffs. For example, exports of tea and exports of coffee should have different secular fluctuations.

Thirdly, we must distinguish exporters sensitive to fluctuations in demand from those who are not. In some countries agricultural output has a very low elasticity of supply; whether world demand is high or low, roughly the same amount reaches the market from these countries. Others are more sensitive, and so bear the major part of the fluctuations in output corresponding to the fluctuations in demand. As we shall see in a moment, there was a pronounced contrast in this respect between Russia and the U.S.A.

Fourthly, in any country where the elasticity of supply was low, production would be affected more by changes in supply conditions than by changes in demand. The most important change in supply conditions was brought about by the building of railways, which increased the areas supplying the world market. Now in the overseas countries the timing of railway building was decided by the timing of capital exports from the U.K. This timing did not coincide with the peaks in the U.K.'s demand for primary products; on the contrary, it was in the reverse direction. Hence we must not be surprised if we find some countries increasing their agricultural exports most rapidly just when world demand was growing most slowly. This in turn would put a greater strain on those countries whose exports were more sensitive to demand.

We have agricultural series for 9 countries. Of these, two show a Kuznets fluctuation related to demand; five show Kuznets fluctuations more probably related to the availability of capital imports;[29] and two show no secular fluctuation.

We begin in Chart 8 with the U.S.A. Series 35 shows U.S. exports, which at this time were more than half agricultural, and which, in so far as they were agricultural were predominantly to the U.K. The secular fluctuation is extremely wide, and is clearly parallel to that of U.K. imports. It does not correspond to U.S. farm output, shown in series 36. This also was governed by demand, but it was a joint U.S.–U.K. demand. It was the U.K. influence that raised the series above trend as early as 1877, but the U.S. influence that kept it there till 1891. Again it was the U.K. influence that produced the super-peak of 1899, and that then brought the series so low just before the war.

The next two series relate to Sweden. We have neither agricultural output nor exports, but we presume that general indexes for an agricultural country reflect mainly agricultural output. Series 37 shows railway traffic in Sweden, and series 38 shows annual investment. Sweden's chief export was timber, and the two pronounced peaks in these series show clearly the influence of the British building cycle. No other external factor could explain the super-peak of 1875.

---

[29] This excludes the Canadian and New Zealand series, which are also closely correlated with capital imports. As is explained in our introduction, these series cannot usefully be treated by the technique we are using because their average rate of growth differs between the first half and the second half of the period.

CHART 8

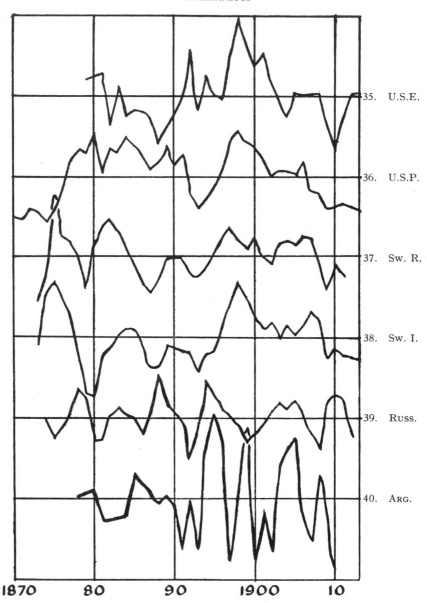

35. U.S.E.

36. U.S.P.

37. Sw. R.

38. Sw. I.

39. Russ.

40. Arg.

1870   80   90   1900   10

Then we come to two series which show no secular fluctuation. Series 39, grain exports from Russia, seems to have fluctuated only with the weather. Series 40 covers most of the exports from Argentina, including livestock products as well as grain. The peculiar behaviour in the middle of the series

CHART 9

MISCELLANEOUS

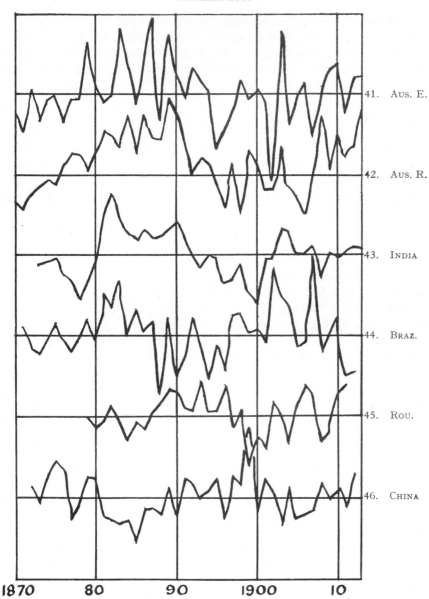

41. AUS. E.

42. AUS. R.

43. INDIA

44. BRAZ.

45. ROU.

46. CHINA

1870   80   90   1900   10

is due to the growth and decline of the importance of grain exports which fluctuate more widely than wool and hides, which are the important exports when the series starts, and more widely than meat, which comes into increasing prominence at the end. There is no correlation with any Kuznets fluctuation in demand. Neither does the series correlate with railway building, in which there were great bursts of activity from 1883 to 1893, and from 1899 to 1912.

The influence of railway building upon exports can be seen in Australia. Series 41 in Chart 9 shows agricultural exports from Australia (excluding animal products), and series 42 shows railway miles added in each year. These two series have the same secular fluctuation, corresponding with U.K. capital exports, and running contrary to the U.K. demand for food. A similar explanation probably accounts for the secular fluctuations in agricultural exports from India, series 43, and in coffee exports from Brazil, series 43, which have much the same pattern, though in the case of Brazil the U.S. demand may already have been the decisive factor. But we do not know why the exports of grain from Roumania, series 44, were so high in the 1890's, or why the exports of silk from China, series 45, grew more rapidly than their trend from 1884 to 1895; in neither case can railway extension be the explanation.

V. REFLECTIONS

In this concluding section we list a few features which have impressed themselves upon us in the course of this study.

1. First, we have been surprised to discover how widespread the Kuznets cycle is, not only in industrial countries, but in the agricultural countries as well. In the light of this, the fact that there was no Kuznets cycle in U.K. manufacturing output stands out as an oddity; the fact that home and foreign investment alternated so closely with each other looks more than ever like a coincidence. The theory that it was produced by some automatic stabilising mechanism is hard to credit in the absence of such a mechanism in the U.S., the German, and other economies which have a marked secular swing.

2. Secondly, the depth and protraction of the Kuznets depressions in Germany starting in 1872, 1890, and 1906 stand out, especially as the phenomenon was repeated again in 1929, when the German depression was worse than that of any other country except the U.S.A. Economists have known for some time about the propensity of the U.S.A. to have these deep Kuznets depressions about once every twenty years[30]—1873, 1892, and signs of a new one just before the first world war—but the existence of the same phenomenon in Germany has not been emphasised before. The German economy had even more reason to fluctuate than the American since—in contrast with the U.K. and the U.S.A., at any rate up to 1906—the periods

---

[30] The point was emphasised by Warren and Pearson, *op. cit.*, p. 150, who showed that throughout the nineteenth century protracted depressions came in the U.S.A. regularly about three years after the downturn of the building cycle.

of heaviest capital export coincided with the periods of heaviest home investment, if the building cycle is a good guide. The coincidence of the U.S.–German timing was not complete—Germany slumped in 1906, while the U.S. continued above trend until the war—and there was probably no causal link, since at this time Germany and the U.S.A. did little business with each other, either in trade, or in international investment.

3. In fact, our third impression is how remarkably independent of each other the four great industrial countries were. Even the dating of their Juglars was not the same. The United States and Germany slumped in 1872 or 1873, but the big slide did not occur in France until 1875, or in Britain until 1877. The slump of 1883 occurred more or less simultaneously. The next slump, however, dates variously from 1889 to 1892; and the slump after that, in 1899, is barely traceable in U.S. statistics. Neither is there continuous leadership; Germany slumped first in 1872, Britain first in 1889, and Germany again first in 1906. The theory that "all slumps come from the United States" cannot be applied before the first world war. The Juglar troughs also do not coincide. Germany and the U.S.A. favour 1878, the U.K. and France 1879. The U.S. favours 1885, the U.K., Germany and France 1886. Germany and the U.K. turn up in 1893, France in 1895, and the U.S.A. in 1896. Germany has her next trough in 1903, the others in 1904. If there were a candidate for leadership into and out of Juglar slumps, it would have to be Germany. But the evidence suggests independence, except perhaps for the great boom of 1899–1900, which seems to have been associated with the high level of British home investment at that date.[31]

The most important evidence that these four economies were independent lies in the fact that in each of them the behaviour of the economy as a whole is quite different from the behaviour of exports, on the level of secular fluctuations. In the U.K. and the U.S., exports and the rest of the economy behave in diametrical opposition to each other. The divergence is not so marked in the two other cases; but Germany continues to be depressed in the second half of the '70's, although exports are booming, continues to be prosperous in the second half of the '80's although exports are depressed, and continues to be depressed after 1910 although exports are booming; and France shows a similar divergence in the second half of the '80's. The correct conclusion seems to be that each of these four economies was in the grip of a powerful autonomous investment cycle of its own, which outweighed all external influences.

---

[31] Some observers were puzzled by the fact that the U.S. recessions of 1949 and of 1953–54 did not coincide with recession in Europe (1952–53). As the above paragraph shows, coincidence of Juglar depressions in the four big industrial countries is the exception rather than the rule. A Kuznets depression in the U.S.A. is bound to cause a draught in Europe, especially when it coincides with a Kuznets depression in Germany (1873, 1892, 1929); but Europe can take a Kitchin in its stride, and may not respond immediately even to a Juglar. Much depends on the share of U.S. imports and U.S. capital exports in world trade, which is of course much greater than it was before 1913.

4. The failure of these four autonomous cycles to offset each other completely was of great importance to the rest of the world, and particularly to the terms of trade between industrial and agricultural countries. The timing was good in the '70's; the peak of the British building cycle coincided with the trough of the American, and prevented the deep U.S. and German depression of most of the years from 1873 to 1880 from destroying prosperity everywhere else. The timing was also pretty good in the '80's; German and U.S. prosperity in the second half did not completely offset the depressions of British and French imports; but the result was at least better than what followed. For what followed was that the recovery of British home investment was delayed. If the peak of 1877 had been succeeded by another peak in 1895, or even in 1897, the world would have escaped both the great depression of the first half of the '90's, and also the great boom terminating in 1907; agricultural prices would neither have fallen so low, nor risen again so high. If there was an automatic mechanism for fitting the investment cycles together, it seems to have broken down after 1890.

5. The relationship between U.S. agriculture and that of the rest of the world seems to have been based upon an interesting automatism. We have seen that, because of the failure of the investment cycles of the great powers to offset each other, there was a pronounced Kuznets fluctuation in world demand and supply of agricultural commodities. We have also seen that individual agricultural countries did not respond to this cycle. Their output grew steadily, like that of Russia, or at a rate determined by the spread of railways, like that of Australia, or in cycles determined by other factors not related to demand. U.S. agricultural output, on the other hand, fluctuated closely with demand, and the deficiency between world demand and supplies from other sources seems to have been made good by a pronounced secular swing in exports from the U.S.A. For example, whereas in the boom period 1896–1900 world trade in primary products averaged only 1.7 percent above trend, and U.K. imports averaged only 7.8 percent above trend, U.S. exports averaged 19.8 percent above trend. U.S. agriculture has continued right down to our own day to play this widely fluctuating role of residual supplier. Its corollary, presumably, is a willingness to carry over long periods much larger stocks of agricultural commodities than any other nation would carry.

6. The fact that railway building was not timed to fit demand is another of the puzzles. The depression of the agricultural countries began at least as early as 1883: this can be seen from British exports to Europe (series 8) or German exports (series 20), or from the terms of trade (series 32). But the export of capital from Britain did not rise above trend until 1881, and stayed there until 1890; and the same is true of French and German capital exports. In the light of this (and of the coincidence of German home and foreign investment) it is not very plausible to argue that the British and the French invested abroad when overseas investment was profitable, and cut their home investment for the purpose. The supposed link between the terms

of trade and foreign investment does not hold for the 1880's, and may therefore have been a mere coincidence in the 1900's. Alternatively, one may argue that foreign investment was a *pis aller*, occurring whenever the home investment cycle was in the trough. This would fit French and British behaviour, both in the 1880's and the 1900's, but it would be hard to square with capital export from Germany, which on this thesis should have been (but was not) larger in the '90's than in the '80's. Again it is plausible to argue that it was the existence of a balance of payments surplus that gave rise to foreign investment, rather than the desire for foreign investment that produced a balance of payments surplus. There was a balance of payments surplus in the U.K. and in France in the '80's, perhaps because American and German prosperity raised their exports, while the downturn of their own domestic investment cycles reduced their imports. Since 1945 we have had plenty of evidence of the fact that the behaviour of the balance of payments may be residual rather than planned. However, the "residual" explanation cannot be exclusive, since the high level of British and French exports in the '80's cannot be explained exclusively in terms of U.S. and German prosperity. In the last analysis one may have to fall back on a psychological argument. Prosperity in the U.S. having started a migration and foreign investment boom, it became fashionable to emigrate to or invest in other overseas countries at the same time, even though these other countries were then depressed. Mob psychology explains the timing of foreign investment better than the terms of trade.

7. Whatever may have been the cause of the secular fluctuation in the export of capital, its effect on the dependent overseas economies was deplorable from their point of view, since it transmitted to them a secular fluctuation in investment and output which was not necessarily even related to demand: on the contrary, their capacity to produce built up most during the prolonged slump in prices from 1883 to 1896. It is not surprising, in view of this, that most of these countries entered the twentieth century determined to become independent of the great powers for money and for markets as rapidly as they could. If there was an automatic mechanism for stabilising the U.K. economy, by its very nature this was a mechanism for destabilising the rest of the world.

8. Finally, it is disturbing to note that the alternation of building cycles which existed throughout the nineteenth century has probably now ended. The U.S., the U.K., Germany and France are all four currently involved in great building booms and great home investment programmes. (Correspondingly the export of capital, excluding U.S. aid, is very small when compared with 1910–13 or 1926–28.) Presumably all four will therefore have building slumps at about the same time. This has never happened in the past century. At the time of the great U.S.–German slump of 1873, U.K. home investment was just working up to a peak; in 1892 again the U.K. and France were just about to turn upwards as Germany and the U.S.A. turned downwards; in

1907 Germany and the U.K. paired in falling low, but France and the U.S. kept well above trend; in 1929 there were three against one: Germany, France and the U.S.A. had just completed great investment booms, but the U.K. building boom was only just about to begin. What will happen round about 1960 (plus or minus one or two years) if the U.S.A., the U.K., Germany and France then all enter upon building downswings at the same time?

VI. INTERNATIONAL ASPECTS

29

Introduction

THE INTERNATIONAL transmission of economic fluctuations from one country to another has long been a subject of interest to economists, although that interest seems to have abated somewhat during the period of rapid but reasonably stable growth in the advanced countries during the last 15 years or so. The theory of income and employment was long ago applied to the case of open economies, and in recent years there has been a good deal of debate regarding the potential conflict between the goals of full employment and equilibrium in the balance of payments.

A modest number of journal articles have been published since the war on such topics as the cyclical experience of various countries in relation to what was happening in the rest of the world, the international impact of American recessions, and the theory of international transmission of cyclical disturbances.[1] There have also been an increasing number of econometric studies of the process of international economic adjustment.

We have decided to limit this section to one of the best of these econometric studies. Jacques Polak and Rudolf Rhomberg analyze the international stability problem in terms of a world model. Using an econometric model as a basic framework for a world divided into three great trading blocs (North America, other industrialized areas, and underdeveloped countries), they take into account both incomes and relative price effects in international trade. Their system has some implict dynamic elements, and they are able to approximate the actual transmission process that seems to occur.

---

[1] The following may be offered as samples: Angus Maddison, "The Postwar Business Cycle in Western Europe and the Role of Government Policy," *Banca Nazionale del Lavoro Quarterly Review*, No. 53, (June, 1960), pp. 99–148; symposium on "Problems of Economic Instability in Other Countries," *American Economic Review: Papers and Proceedings*, Vol. LI (May, 1961), pp. 378–416; Ilse Mintz, *Trade Balances During Business Cycles: U.S. and Britain Since 1880*, National Bureau of Economic Research Occasional Paper 67 (1959); Hans Neisser, "The International Propagation of Income Changes," *Metroeconomica*, Vol. II (April, 1950), pp. 1–19; Edward Marcus, "Countercyclical Weapons for the Open Economy," *Journal of Political Economy*, Vol. LXII (December, 1954), pp. 479–93; papers by J. J. Polak and Nicholas Kaldor in Erik Lundberg (ed.), *The Business Cycle in the Post-War World* (London: Macmillan, 1955), pp. 246–65 and 266–82; J. H. Furth, "The United States Balance of Payments in the Recession," *Quarterly Journal of Economics*, Vol. LXXIII (May, 1959), pp. 197–206.

30

Economic Instability in an International Setting*

By *JACQUES J. POLAK* and *RUDOLF R. RHOMBERG*†

DURING THE PAST decade the world economy has shown remarkable stability. Broadly speaking, unemployment was a minor problem during the fifties and, apart from the consequences of the Korean war, price fluctuations have also been relatively small, although it is true that the general upward drift of price levels in the industrial countries has not been fully arrested, and that the terms of trade of many primary-producing countries have tended to decline during the second half of the decade. It is an indication of the success already achieved that in addressing oneself to the question of measures to improve the stability of the world economy in the years to come, one is speaking in large part of effects which twenty-five years ago would have been considered to be of the second order of smallness.

The fact that we have enjoyed this degree of stability is no ground for complacency. It would seem definitely too early to say that we have mastered the control of the business cycle. New problems are, moreover, arising. Perhaps the most important of these follows from the increasing international mobility of capital which, in a world of many convertible currencies, is creating a new environment for the conduct of domestic stabilization policy in the industrial countries. New forms of international co-operation may be required for the realization of the potential benefits and for the suppression of the harmful side effects of such institutional changes.

The problem of economic stability may be approached in a number of ways. Perhaps the most important point to remember is that the approach should not be too narrow. It is easy to slip into the error of discussing *one* aspect of instability and, having found reasons for dismissing it, to think that one has covered the subject as a whole. In this presentation we shall deal with three aspects of the problem of short-run international instability: (1) the trade propagation or transmission mechanism, by which shocks that originate

---

* *American Economic Review: Papers and Proceedings*, Vol. LII (May, 1962). Reprinted by courtesy of the American Economic Association and the authors.
† International Monetary Fund.

somewhere in the system are passed on through the international economy; (2) the cyclical and other short-run variations in domestic aggregate demand in the industrial countries; and (3) the international movements of short-term capital. We do not discuss a possible fourth subject, supply-fluctuations in the output of primary products, because their destabilizing impact falls mainly on the countries concerned rather than on the world economy.

I. THE TRANSMISSION MECHANISM

Our study of the transmission mechanism is intended to assess the impact of economic fluctuations in one region on the remainder of the world economy. To do this we need a manageable set of estimates of the quantitative income-trade relations as they seem to have operated in recent years. With respect to the construction of what is in effect a world economic model we are, however, still in the impasse about which one of us complained ten years ago in connection with an earlier attempt to build a world model: we lack the national economic models that could be hooked together into a world model by linking their international trade connections.[1] Since then even less progress has been made than might have been hoped in the construction of national models, and it is just as necessary now as it was then to proceed directly to the construction of a broad international model. In doing so we have been even more boldly aggregative than on the earlier occasion, conceiving the world in terms of only three regions: the United States and Canada, the other industrial countries, i.e., Western Europe and Japan, and the primary-producing countries, and we have made certain very broad assumptions about the behavior of the economies of these regions.[2]

One of the difficulties in any attempt to summarize the world economy in a small number of relationships is its rapidly changing nature. It is true that we now have statistics for something like fifteen postwar years; but for the industrial countries outside of North America this period is not homogeneous in the characteristic of greatest importance in our present context: the determination of imports. It is only in the last few years that these countries generally have convertible currencies, a minimum reliance on import restrictions, virtually no discrimination in their imports, and adequate reserves. While these changes in behavior do not necessarily present insurmountable obstacles to the statistician, they call for great caution in the interpretation of the results.

The first two groups of countries have many characteristics in common. They are similar in size with gross national products in 1960 of about 540 billion and 340 billion dollars, respectively, as well as in behavior. The

---

[1] J. J. Polak, *An International Economic System* (Univ. of Chicago Press, 1953), p. 14.
[2] The model is described in the Appendix to this paper. This appendix was not included in the paper as originally published.

estimates of their short-run marginal propensities to consume out of real GNP are both equal to about one-third. Both areas have strong built-in stabilizers which would give them small "international reflection ratios"; that is, changes in imports induced by unit changes in exports. They have sufficiently large reserves to ride out changes in their exports; in other words, they do not normally have to upset the functioning of their built-in stabilizers by sudden governmental policies to rescue the balance of payments. This is not to say that some of these countries did not occasionally have to take emergency balance-of-payments action; but such action had to be taken to correct troubles of domestic, not of foreign, origin.

For our world model we require estimates of the marginal propensities to import of each region. In making these estimates we have made allowance for the fact that import fluctuations, especially in Europe, are closely related to inventory changes, by using deviations of GNP from trend plus a separate trend term in the import functions. The resulting marginal propensities to import reflect the cyclical rather than the longer run dependence of imports on income. North American imports tend to rise by about 5 percent of an increase in GNP relative to its trend value, compared to an average propensity to import of about 3 percent. By contrast, the imports into Western Europe and Japan are found to rise by about 22 percent of an increase in GNP relative to the trend, compared to an average propensity to import of about 10 percent. For both areas the induced increases in imports are about equally distributed between goods and services coming from the other industrial region and those bought from the primary producers. As we have seen in the preceding paper, the fluctuations in income and output in postwar Western Europe were so minute that these estimates of a cyclical marginal propensity to import must be interpreted with caution. Nevertheless, these figures fit the past data quite well. They help explain, for instance, why North American imports have fluctuated much less than European imports, despite the fact that European business conditions have fluctuated much less than those prevailing in North America. They also provide a partial explanation of the fact that the U.S. trade balance deteriorated during the 1958 recession although the European decline was far milder than the American contraction.

With respect to price elasticities of demand the two industrial regions are found to be quite similar. For instance, their short-run price elasticities of demand for one another's commodities are estimated to be between -1 and -2, and their elasticities of demand for the products of third countries seem to lie around -0.5.

The third area is quite different in its economic behavior. Most of the countries in this area do not have strong built-in stabilizers. Quite apart from this, however, almost none of these countries has adequate reserves to be able to afford such stabilizers even if they could be fitted into its social and economic structure. The postwar history of this group has been—after some of the high reserves left over from the war had been used up—that the aggregate reserves of these countries have remained roughly stable at a level of around 12 billion dollars over the last decade. As a group these countries have had to adjust their foreign exchange outgo, mostly for imports, to their foreign exchange receipts on account of exports, inflow of private capital, and aid. Individual countries have been able at times to delay the reduction of their imports in response to a decline in exports by drawing on their reserves or on credits; but at the same time other countries have had to reconstitute their reserves or to repay credits even at a time when their exports were declining. Broadly speaking, therefore, it is not an inaccurate description of the behavior of these countries as a group to say that they have had to adjust their imports to their exports; i.e., that they should be considered to have an international reflection ratio of the order of magnitude of unity.

Mention must still be made of the role of price fluctuations in the international model. In this connection, particular attention has to be paid to the prices of primary products, which have shown large fluctuations in response both to industrial demand and to supply conditions. Since the demand for primary commodities in the industrial areas is fairly inelastic, the export value of the less developed countries, and thus their imports, will generally fluctuate more than the volume of their exports in response to changes in world demand. This indirect influence of demand variations in the industrial countries, via changes in primary product prices, on their own exports to the less developed areas is only to a small extent offset by changes in domestic expenditures due to the real income effect of these price changes, since the short-run marginal propensity to spend in the industrial countries is quite low. In other words, a decline in primary product prices amounts to a redistribution of purchasing power from high marginal spenders to high marginal savers and, therefore, to a net decline in world aggregate demand.

Leaving out refinements, the description of the transmission mechanism implied in the model may be summarized by referring to some of the key multipliers of the system. Assuming consumption and imports of the industrial areas to be the only variables directly dependent on GNP, changes in domestic investment and government expenditures on goods and services in North America affect the GNP of this region by a multiple of about 1.4, and the GNP of Western Europe and Japan by one of less than 0.1. On the other hand, the internal multiplier of Europe and Japan is smaller, perhaps 1.2, because of this region's larger marginal propensities to import, and for the same reason the multiplier effect of variations in autonomous expenditures in this region on North America's GNP is considerably larger, around 0.3, than the corresponding effect in the opposite direction. That is to say, a fall in North American investment by 10 billion dollars would reduce the GNP of the other industrial countries by less than 1 billion, while a similar decline of investment in Europe and Japan would reduce North America's GNP by 3 billion. This last effect would, of course, still be very small in relation to the size of North America's GNP. A substantial decline in European economic activity would, therefore, be a matter of concern to North America for its balance-of-payments effect rather than for its impact on income and employment.

The substantial damping in the mechanism by which fluctuations in economic activity are transmitted between the two industrial regions is fully in accordance with the observations made during the last decade about the virtual independence of cyclical developments in Europe and in the United States. The mild movements in economic activity in either one of these areas— and it is important to stress that the autonomous movements since the war have always been mild—transmitted by a heavily damped mechanism, produced very little effect in the other area. As far as the primary-producing countries are concerned, their main difficulty during the decade would seem to have been attributable to changes on the supply side in conjunction with low price elasticities of demand rather than to demand fluctuations.

Stabilization Measures.   The preceding discussion would seem to indicate that there is little scope for bringing greater stability to the world economy as a whole by increasing even further the shock absorbing nature of the transmission mechanism. Whatever can be done in this respect concerns chiefly the primary-producing countries. In this connection one could think in the first place of measures to stabilize the exchange receipts of these countries, and thus their imports, by stabilizing prices and production of primary commodities—a subject that can only be mentioned here.

Slightly more should be said of measures of the general character of providing for the primary-producing countries' access to supplementary international resources that would permit them to stabilize their import level in the face of fluctuations in their foreign exchange receipts. Because of the well-known tendency of the less developed countries to use up their own reserves under the pressures of internal demand, these supplementary resources would preferably have to be made available on a loan basis, to be drawn upon in periods of difficulty and to be repaid subsequently in periods, if not of ease, at least of less extreme difficulty. Resources for these purposes are available to countries through their membership in the Fund. Quite a number of countries have used the Fund for just this purpose by drawing on it to provide compensatory financing in cases of export declines. It has recently been suggested, both in a report by a group of UN experts and at the Punta del Este meeting of the countries of the Western Hemisphere, that additional funds be lined up internationally, on a partly contributory basis, to compensate export fluctuations of primary-producing countries on a more automatic basis.

It is, of course, difficult to estimate the stabilizing effect of measures of the types just discussed, since the extent to which they would lower the reflection ratio of the underdeveloped region would depend, among other things, on the manner in which the compensatory funds are made available. In the limiting case in which the imports of the primary producers would remain constant in the face of fluctuations in the demand for their exports, the internal multipliers in the two industrial regions would be very slightly reduced, but the cross-effects of expenditure variations in one of the industrial areas on the other, that is, the transmission effects, would be reduced by about one-half. In reality the stabilizing effect would probably be smaller. The reflection ratio of the underdeveloped region is, of course, not precisely unity at present, nor is it likely to fall to zero as a result of any program of compensatory financing of fluctuations in export receipts. On the other hand, we have not taken account of the influence of demand fluctuations in the industrial countries on primary product prices. Had we done so, the original multipliers would have been larger and the reduction in the size of these multipliers due to the stabilization of the imports of primary producers would also have been larger.

The limiting case in which the imports of the primary producers do not change at all may be used to compute the order of magnitude of the resources necessary to carry out a program of full compensatory financing. If a recession were to reduce the GNP of each of the two industrial areas by 5 percent, or by 25 billion dollars in North America and by 15 billion in Europe and Japan, the compensatory financing necessary to offset the induced balance-of-payments deficit of the primary producers, apart from the effect of a likely fall in their export prices and a very probable reduction in their receipts of private foreign capital, would be of the order of magnitude of 2.5 to 3 billion dollars. What proportion of such an amount would be actually used, if available on a short-term credit basis, would depend on the attitude of the primary producers toward such a program.

II. AUTONOMOUS FLUCTUATIONS IN AGGREGATE DEMAND

During the postwar period the fluctuations in aggregate demand in the industrial countries have been very mild. The model which has been used as the background for this paper is, in fact, one which applies chiefly to such mild fluctuations. There can be little doubt that in the case of a sustained decline in income of the sort experienced during the early thirties the marginal propensity to consume would tend to increase and induced changes in invest-ment would also take place. While we have estimated certain constant coefficients from the postwar data, we must expect to encounter a number of important nonlinearities outside the range of economic fluctuations actually observed during this period. Some of these nonlinearities are related to cumulative effects on the levels of certain stocks. Just as the exhaustion of the stock of past personal savings during a period of progressive decline in income will lead to an increase in the marginal propensity to consume, so will the exhaustion of foreign exchange reserves during a period of persistent balance-of-payments deficits lead to government policies which adjust imports more quickly to a falling level of exports and which thus amount to an increase in the international reflection ratio. It is not necessary to describe in detail how this principle applies to the cases of unemployment insurance and welfare funds, corporate savings, and other exhaustible stocks whose variation normally provides part of the built-in stabilization which we have found implicit in the low estimates of the marginal consumption-GNP ratios.

As a result of these considerations, a system describing a world economy subject to severe autonomous shocks would also be inherently more unstable in its response mechanism. The avoidance of such severe shocks is chiefly a matter of the pursuit of the proper national policies in the industrial countries, under which heading we should also admit a large and growing role for the influence on national policies of direct consultations among countries and of international agencies acting in the pursuit of their assigned functions. It is national action that attacks the problem of world-wide fluctuations at its root: in the generation of the level of over-all demand. National policies ought to see to it that this demand is neither excessive nor insufficient.

Among the policies determining aggregate demand in the industrial countries are those relating to foreign investment in the less developed countries and to foreign aid. Since it is assumed that primary producers spend their entire foreign exchange receipts on imports, variations in private foreign investment in these countries and in foreign aid grants and loans to their governments have an indirect employment effect in the industrial regions. The size of this effect reflects the over-all multiplier of the system, which gives the ratio of the change in real income in the two industrial areas combined to the originating change in autonomous expenditure, wherever it may have occurred, as about 1.5. Ignoring price effects, output in the industrial countries will thus tend to rise by 1.5 times an increase in foreign aid or in other capital receipts by the underdeveloped countries, and (disregarding the possible distributional effects of the "tying" of aid) this increase will be equally distributed between North America and the other industrial countries. Stability of the annual outlays under these programs is, of course, desirable for a number of reasons other than that of employment stability in the industrial regions.

Action by individual countries to maintain a stable level of aggregate demand can be supported by proper management of international liquidity. There has been a great deal of discussion on this topic in recent years, particularly on the extent to which a lack of international liquidity would cause world deflation or a reversal of the movement towards freer trade and exchange policies, and the extent to which an excess of liquidity would produce world inflation. These important questions cannot be dealt with further in this context. It would, however, be a mistake to look to the management of international liquidity as the cure for cyclical instability of the world economy. The primary responsibility for keeping the world economy on an even keel inevitably rests with the main industrial countries. The regulation of international liquidity could help only to a limited extent to stave off the consequences of any failure on the part of these countries to perform this task.

III. INTERNATIONAL MOVEMENTS OF SHORT-TERM CAPITAL

One of the important characteristics of the model that has been described is the assumption that the industrial countries have adequate reserves to let their built-in stabilizers do their shock absorbing work. This assumption seems to be quite reasonable as far as fluctuations in the exports of the industrial countries are concerned. It is not, however, fully justified without qualification with respect to changes in reserves that may arise as a result of large movements of short-term capital. These movements have become far more important in the last few years as a result of the restoration of convertibility. These new developments have brought with them a potential threat to international economic stability, arising this time from the capital account rather than from the trade account of the balance of payments, and new policy approaches are emerging to meet this threat. The problem is that the effect of capital outflows on foreign exchange reserves may at times preclude desirable domestic expansionary measures, while capital inflows may sometimes make it more difficult to contain inflationary pressures.

Insofar as the movements of capital are attributable to differences in interest rates, one approach to the problem lies in the co-ordination of interest rate policies. This is without doubt a most important field for the further extension of international co-operation. Before much advance in this field can be expected, it will be necessary, however, to clarify what is meant by "co-ordination" of interest rate policies. On the one hand, the aim of such policies could be to ensure that national interest rates are sufficiently different so as to reflect adequately the different cyclical positions among countries; on the other hand, the objective could be to make interest rates in different countries sufficiently alike so as to minimize the international movements of short-term capital. It would appear that in the long run the closer integration of the industrial countries will tend to lead to a similarity in interest rates—somewhat on the pattern, if perhaps not to the extent, of the development in the United States over the last fifty years. This may entail that monetary policy in the industrial countries would have to be more uniform than it has been in the past. To the extent that individual countries find themselves in different phases of the business cycle, their stabilization policies would have to rely to a larger extent on fiscal and other nonmonetary measures, while the objective of a co-ordinated monetary policy would be to assist in the attainment of the appropriate international average levels of employment and prices.

Interest rate differentials are, of course, not the only determinants of capital movements. Whatever is done, therefore, in the field of interest rate policy, it is clear that adequate reserves must be available to deal with international movements of capital among the industrial countries. The provision of these financial resources is the cornerstone of the policies to ensure international financial stability. This problem was brought into international discussion about a year ago in terms of strengthening the resources of the International Monetary Fund. As a result of the discussions that took place before and at the last Annual Meeting of the Fund in Vienna, attention has been focused more specifically, not on an increase in the general resources of the Fund, but on lining up supplementary resources that could be used in special situations to forestall, or to cope with, an impairment of the international monetary system as such. The importance of this change in focus is that both the International Monetary Fund and the main industrial countries that are expected to make credit arrangements with the Fund for the lending of their currencies have undertaken the responsibility to see to it that the international economy is not endangered by a collapse of the international monetary system.

APPENDIX*

The Structural Equations

The model consists of 29 structural equations of which 3 are identities. The coefficients of the equations have been estimated from annual data for the 13-year period 1948–60. The classical least-squares method of estimation has been applied. At this stage of the investigation no attempt has been made to select an estimation technique appropriate for simultaneous relationships, except that the propensity to consume out of GNP has been estimated from a relation between consumption and GNP excluding consumption. The least-squares bias in the other equations is not expected to be appreciable.

In the presentation below, the standard errors of the coefficients are given in parentheses below the point estimates. $\bar{R}^2$ denotes the coefficient of determination adjusted for degrees of freedom and d denotes the Durbin-Watson test statistic for serial correlation.

List of Variables

Note: Subscripts ($i = 1, 2, 3$) refer to the three regions: North America $= 1$; other industrial countries $= 2$; rest of the world $= 3$.

Jointly dependent variables:

Y_i = GNP, in current prices and 1954 exchange rates, in billion U.S. dollars
C_i = Consumption, in current prices and 1954 exchange rates, in billion U.S. dollars
P_{xi} = Export price index in U.S. dollars, 1954 = 1.0
M_{ij} = Value of merchandise imports into region j from region i, in billion U.S. dollars
F_{ij} = Payments for transportation services by region j to region i, in billion U.S. dollars
V_{ij} = Payments for tourist travel services by region j to region i, in billion U.S. dollars
D_{ij} = Payments of interest and dividends by region j to region i, in billion U.S. dollars

---

* This appendix was not included in the paper as originally published.

O_{ij} = Payments for all other services by region j to region i, in billion U.S. dollars

$S_{ij} = F_{ij} + V_{ij} + D_{ij} + O_{ij}$

Exogenous variables:

A_i = Fixed investment plus government expenditures on goods and services, in current prices and 1954 exchange rates, in billion U.S. dollars

H_i = Change in inventories, in current prices and 1954 exchange rates, in billion U.S. dollars

P_i = Implicit GNP price deflator, 1954 = 1.0

r_2 = Implicit exchange rate of OEEC countries vis-à-vis U.S. dollar, 1954 = 1.0; i.e., OEEC countries' GNP in current U.S. dollars and 1954 exchange rates divided by GNP in current U.S. dollars and current exchange rates; (a rise in r_2 signifies a depreciation by the OEEC countries)

K_3 = Net capital imports into the underdeveloped region, in billion U.S. dollars

B_i = Adjustment item: discrepancy between current account balance in the national income accounts and in the balance of payments accounts

t = Calendar year minus 1947

W_c = Korean-war dummy variable for consumption function: takes the value 1.0 in 1951, 1952, and 1953, otherwise 0

W_p = Korean-war dummy variable for primary product export price equation: takes the value 1.0 in 1951, otherwise 0

Equations

A. Region 1, North America

(1) Income identity

$$Y_1 = C_1 + M_{12} + M_{13} + F_{12} + F_{13} + V_{12} + V_{13} + D_{12} + D_{13} + O_{12} + O_{13}$$
$$- M_{21} - M_{31} - F_{21} - F_{31} - V_{21} - V_{31} - D_{21} - D_{31} - O_{21} - O_{31}$$
$$+ B_1 + H_1 + A_1$$

(2) Consumption function

a. Estimated:

$$\Delta \frac{C_1}{P_1} = 0.487 \; \Delta \frac{Y_1 - C_1}{P_1} - 9.94 \; \Delta W_c + 5.12$$
$$\quad\quad (0.179) \quad\quad\quad\quad (4.32) \quad\quad (1.57)$$

$$\bar{R}^2 = 0.34 \quad\quad\quad d = 2.76$$

b. Transformed:

$$\Delta \frac{C_1}{P_1} = 0.328 \, \Delta \frac{Y_1}{P_1} - 6.68 \, \Delta W_c + 3.44$$

Comment: The two consumption functions (equations 2 and 15) have been estimated from first differences, since estimates from the original data give a marginal propensity to consume which is distorted by the common trend in both series. The estimated marginal propensities to consume out of GNP of about one-third may appear low, but these values explain cyclical variations in consumption much better than the somewhat higher (one-half) apparent marginal propensities estimated from the original data.

(3) Merchandise imports from other industrial countries

$$\frac{M_{21}}{P_{x2}} = 0.0189 \; \frac{Y_1 - H_1}{P_1} + 0.0483 \; \frac{H_1}{P_1} + 8.34 \; \frac{P_1}{P_{x2}} - 12.5$$
$$\quad\quad (0.0043) \quad\quad\quad\quad (0.0328) \quad\quad (2.89) \quad\quad (1.9)$$

$$\bar{R}^2 = 0.91 \quad\quad d = 1.24$$

Comment: The price elasticity of import demand at the mean of the variables equals -2.4.

(4) Merchandise imports from underdeveloped countries

$$\frac{M_{31}}{P_{z3}} = \underset{(0.0027)}{0.0126} \frac{Y_1 - H_1}{P_1} + \underset{(0.0187)}{0.0557} \frac{H_1}{P_1} + \underset{(1.21)}{2.14} \frac{P_1}{P_{z3}} - \underset{(0.667)}{0.706}$$

$$\bar{R}^2 = 0.92 \qquad d = 1.57$$

Comment: The price elasticity of import demand at the mean of the variables equals -0.3.

(5) Payments to other industrial countries for transportation services

$$F_{21} = \underset{(0.0194)}{0.0627} \ M_{21} + \underset{(0.0084)}{0.0379t} + \underset{(0.021)}{0.205}$$

$$\bar{R}^2 = 0.99 \qquad d = 2.12$$

Comment: Apart from a trend term the value of these services depends on the value of merchandise imports.

(6) Payments to underdeveloped countries for transportation services

$$F_{31} = \underset{(0.0144)}{0.0396} \ M_{31} + \underset{(0.00023)}{0.00332t^2} + \underset{(0.0844)}{0.0712}$$

$$\bar{R}^2 = 0.98 \qquad d = 1.43$$

(7) Payments to other industrial countries for tourist travel

$$V_{21} = \underset{(0.00017)}{0.00387} \ C_1 - \underset{(0.045)}{0.590}$$

$$\bar{R}^2 = 0.98 \qquad d = 1.78$$

(8) Payments to underdeveloped countries for tourist travel

$$V_{31} = \underset{(0.00042)}{0.00142} \ C_1 + \underset{(0.00041)}{0.00181t^2} - \underset{(0.0852)}{0.0515}$$

$$\bar{R}^2 = 0.99 \qquad d = 1.18$$

(9) Interest and dividend payments to other industrial countries

$$D_{21} = \underset{(0.00102)}{0.00015 Y_1} - \underset{(0.027)}{0.007t} + \underset{(0.00086)}{0.00261t^2} + \underset{(0.250)}{0.263}$$

$$\bar{R}^2 = 0.92 \qquad d = 1.70$$

Comment: The hypothesis, not convincingly borne out by the data, was that these payments vary with deviations of income from its trend.

(10) Interest and dividend payments to underdeveloped countries

$$D_{31} = \underset{(0.000254)}{0.000436 Y_1} - \underset{(0.0068)}{0.0243t} + \underset{(0.00021)}{0.00182t^2} - \underset{(0.0623)}{0.0443}$$

$$\bar{R}^2 = 0.96 \qquad d = 0.86$$

(11) Other current-account payments to other industrial countries

$$O_{21} = \underset{(0.0016)}{0.0377t} + 0.149$$

$$\bar{R}^2 = 0.98 \qquad d = 1.02$$

(12) Other current-account payments to underdeveloped countries

$$O_{31} = 0.0222t + 0.0027$$
$$(0.0023) \quad (0.0186)$$

$$\bar{R}^2 = 0.88 \qquad d = 1.05$$

(13) Export supply price

$$P_{x1} = 1.81P_1 + 0.00668 \, \frac{M_{12} + M_{13}}{P_{x1}} - 0.0203t - 0.000615t^2 - 0.726$$
$$(0.23) \quad (0.00280) \qquad \qquad (0.0060) \quad (0.000229) \quad (0.186)$$

$$\bar{R}^2 = 0.98 \qquad d = 1.92$$

Comment: The price elasticity of supply at the mean of the variables equals $+10.5$.

B. Region 2, other industrial countries

(14) Income identity

$$Y_2 = C_2 + M_{21} + M_{23} + F_{21} + V_{21} + D_{21} + O_{21} - M_{12} - M_{32} - F_{12}$$
$$- V_{12} - D_{12} - O_{12} + B_2 + H_2 + A_2$$

Comment: Data on gross payments for services between the other industrial countries and the underdeveloped countries are not available. The net amount of these payments is included in B_2.

(15) Consumption function
    a. Estimated:

$$\Delta \frac{C_2}{P_2} = 0.574 \, \Delta \, \frac{Y_2 - C_2}{P_2} - 3.62 \, \Delta W_c - 3.04$$
$$(0.259) \qquad \qquad (1.33) \qquad (1.57)$$

$$\bar{R}^2 = 0.42 \qquad d = 1.73$$

    b. Transformed

$$\Delta \frac{C_2}{P_2} = 0.365 \, \Delta \frac{Y_2}{P_2} - 2.30 \, \Delta W_c + 1.93$$

(16) Merchandise imports from North America

$$\frac{M_{12}}{P_{x1}} = 0.00790 \, \frac{Y_2 - H_2}{P_2} + 0.381 \, \frac{H_2}{P_2} + 12.8 \, \frac{P_2}{r_2 P_{x1}} - 10.3$$
$$(0.00306) \qquad \qquad (0.090) \qquad (2.7) \qquad \quad (2.7)$$

$$\bar{R}^2 = 0.82 \qquad d = 0.93$$

Comment: The price elasticity of import demand at the mean of the variables is -2.2. (The residuals from this equation appear to be serially correlated; the coefficient of the price variable and its reliability are, however, approximately the same when the equation is estimated in first differences.)

(17) Merchandise imports from underdeveloped countries

$$\frac{M_{32}}{P_{x3}} = 0.0630 \, \frac{Y_2 - H_2}{P_2} + 0.371 \, \frac{H_2}{P_2} + 5.25 \, \frac{P_2}{r_2 P_{x3}} - 5.05$$
$$(0.0047) \qquad \qquad (0.090) \qquad (1.65) \qquad \quad (1.18)$$

$$\bar{R}^2 = 0.99 \qquad d = 1.97$$

Comment: The price elasticity of import demand at the mean of the variables is -0.3.

(18) Payments to North America for transportation services

$$F_{12} = 0.101\ M_{12} + 0.172$$
$$\phantom{F_{12} = }(0.015)\phantom{M_{12} + }(0.087)$$
$$\bar{R}^2 = 0.80 \qquad d = 1.72$$

(19) Payments to North America for tourist travel

$$V_{12} = 0.000637\ C_2 - 0.0163$$
$$\phantom{V_{12} = }(0.000083)(0.0135)$$
$$\bar{R}^2 = 0.83 \qquad d = 0.53$$

(20) Interest and dividend payments to North America

$$D_{12} = 0.00237\ Y_2 - 0.0894$$
$$\phantom{D_{12} = }(0.00017)(0.0427)$$
$$\bar{R}^2 = 0.94 \qquad d = 1.90$$

(21) Other current-account payments to North America

$$O_{12} = 0.00201\ Y_2 - 0.0333$$
$$\phantom{O_{12} = }(0.00011)(0.0281)$$
$$\bar{R}^2 = 0.96 \qquad d = 1.03$$

Comment: In equations (19), (20), and (21) the coefficients of C_2 or Y_2 are approximately the same when the equations are estimated in first differences.

(22) Export supply price

$$P_{x2} \cdot r_2 = 2.56 P_2 + 0.0679\ \frac{M_{21} + M_{23}}{P_{x2}} - 0.108t - 0.00354t^2 - 1.72$$
$$\phantom{P_{x2} \cdot r_2 = }(0.40)(0.0225)\phantom{\frac{M_{21}+M}{P}}(0.030)\ (0.00116)(0.39)$$
$$\bar{R}^2 = 0.95 \qquad d = 2.58$$

Comment: It should be remembered that P_{x2} is a U.S. dollar price index of the exports of other industrial countries. The "local currency" equivalent is, therefore, P_{x2} multiplied by r_2. But since M_{21} and M_{23} are expressed in U.S. dollars their proper price deflator is P_{x2}. The price elasticity of supply at the mean of the variables is 0.9.

C. Region 3, Underdeveloped Countries

(23) Determination of current-account payments

$$M_{13} + M_{23} + F_{13} + V_{13} + D_{13} + O_{13} = M_{31} + M_{32} + F_{31} + V_{31} + D_{31}$$
$$+ O_{31} - B_1 - B_2 + K_3$$

Comment: Merchandise imports plus service payments to North America equal merchandise exports plus service receipts from North America plus net service receipts from the other industrial countries (included in B_2) plus net capital inflows. The adjustment item B_1 also appears in (23) since the consolidated current-account balance of all three regions must equal zero.

(24) Share of merchandise imports from North America

$$M_{13} = 0.394(M_{13} + M_{23}) - 13.6\ \frac{P_{x1}}{P_{x2}} + 13.6$$
$$\phantom{M_{13} = }(0.037)\phantom{(M_{13} + M_{23}) - }(4.2)\phantom{\frac{P_{x1}}{P_{x2}}}(3.7)$$
$$\bar{R}^2 = 0.92 \qquad d = 2.05$$

Comment: From this equation (and a similar one in which the share in real imports, rather than money imports, coming from North America is determined) the elasticity of North America's share in the imports of underdeveloped countries with respect to the ratio of North American export prices to the export prices of other industrial countries appears to be in the range of -1.5 to -2. This is to say that an increase by one per cent in North American export prices relative to Western European export prices would lower North America's share in Region 3 imports by 1.5 to 2 per cent, i.e., since this share is normally slightly below 40 per cent, by between 0.6 and 1 percentage point.

(25) Payments to North America for transportation services

$$F_{13} = 0.0453 \, M_{13} + 0.00147t^2 + 0.283$$
$$(0.0225) \qquad (0.00070) \quad (0.170)$$
$$\bar{R}^2 = 0.71 \qquad d = 1.15$$

(26) Payments to North America for tourist travel

$$V_{13} = 0.0204t + 0.0974$$
$$(0.0016) \quad (0.0125)$$
$$\bar{R}^2 = 0.93 \qquad d = 0.71$$

(27) Interest and dividend payments to North America

$$D_{13} = 0.0430 \, (M_{31} + M_{32}) + 0.0498t + 0.130$$
$$(0.0145) \qquad\qquad (0.0150) \quad (0.229)$$
$$\bar{R}^2 = 0.96 \qquad d = 2.01$$

Comment: Interest and dividend payments are taken to depend, apart from a trend term, on the value of total merchandise exports which reflect the prosperity of domestic business and the need for, and ability to obtain, foreign financing.

(28) Other current-account payments to North America

$$O_{13} = 0.0137 \, \frac{M_{31} + M_{32}}{P_{x3}} + 0.00151t^2 + 0.00605$$
$$(0.0087) \qquad\qquad (0.00069) \quad (0.15680)$$
$$\bar{R}^2 = 0.96 \qquad d = 2.40$$

Comment: These miscellaneous service payments are assumed to depend on the volume (rather than the value) of export business.

(29) Export supply price

$$P_{x3} = 0.0296 \, \frac{M_{31} + M_{32}}{P_{x3}} + 0.160W_p - 0.00252t^2 + 0.453$$
$$(0.0114) \qquad\qquad (0.039) \qquad (0.00091) \quad (0.204)$$
$$\bar{R}^2 = 0.73 \qquad d = 2.20$$

Comment: The price elasticity of supply at the mean of the variables is 1.5. The effect of the dummy variable W_p is to eliminate the observation for 1951.

* * *

Two general comments should be made about the propensities to import in the two industrial regions. First, when industrial Europe plus Japan is considered as a region (whose economic size is of the same order of magnitude as that of North America), the marginal propensities to import from outside of the region are seen to be of the same low order of magnitude as those found, say, for the United States. Second, in all four import demand equations of the industrial regions (equations 3, 4, 16, and 17) the change in inventories plays an appreciable role. This is especially true of imports by the other industrial countries (Region 2), for which charts show a striking correlation between imports and inventory changes. The coefficients do not, however, necessarily reflect the import content of inventory investment. Particularly in OEEC Europe, GNP has shown mainly a rising trend and very little cyclical variation in annual data. In this case changes in inventories stand partly as a proxy for changes in business activity which affect marginal imports although they are not pronounced enough to show up as fluctuations of annual GNP in the national accounts.

The table below summarizes the marginal propensities and price elasticities (evaluated at the mean of the respective variables) found in the model.

TABLE 1

MARGINAL PROPENSITIES TO IMPORT AND PRICE ELASTICITIES

	Demand for Imports		
	Marginal Ratio of		
	Imports to GNP Ex. Inventories	Imports to Inventories	Price Elasticity of Demand
1. *North America's Imports*			
a. from Other Industrial	0.019	0.048	—2.4
b. from Underdeveloped	0.013	0.056	—0.3
2. *Other Industrial Countries' Imports*			
a. from North America	0.008	0.38	—2.2
b. from Underdeveloped	0.063	0.37	—0.3
3. *Underdeveloped Countries* Price Elasticity of North America's Share in Imports	..	..	—2.0

	Supply of Exports	
	Marginal Ratio of Export Prices to GNP Price Deflator	Price Elasticity of Supply
1. North America	1.81	10.5
2. Other Industrial Countries	2.56	0.9
3. Underdeveloped Countries	..	1.5

Multipliers of the Model

For the purpose of further analysis the size of the model was reduced by combining each set of four equations for the payments for imported services (transportation, tourist travel, interest and dividends, and other services) into one equation by adding the linear terms. These combined service payments from region j to region i are designated by S_{ij}. Furthermore, the model was linearized by expansion around the mean of the nonlinear variable combinations involving unlagged dependent variables. The multipliers of the model were computed by post-multiplying the

TABLE 2

Selected Multipliers of the Linearized Model

(Multiplier effects of unit changes in the variables appearing in the column heads on the variables appearing in the row stubs.)

	A_1	A_2	H_1	H_2	P_1	P_2	r_2	K_3	t	t^2
1. Y_1	1.45	0.12	1.41	0.91	151.	29.	−30.	0.89	−0.48	0.0061
2. Y_2	0.040	1.45	0.087	0.61	40.	78.	32.	0.63	0.51	−0.0064
3. P_{x1}	0.00013	0.00042	0.00035	0.0035	1.51	0.091	−0.11	0.0032	−0.019	−0.00086
4. P_{x2}	0.00092	0.0016	0.0022	0.0067	0.51	0.71	−0.40	0.014	−0.037	−0.0024
5. P_{x3}	0.00049	0.0022	0.0015	0.0084	0.033	−0.13	−0.091	0.0012	0.00061	−0.0020
6. M_{12}	−0.00056	0.0086	−0.0017	0.36	−10.	9.5	−12.	−0.018	0.14	0.0060
7. M_{13}	0.021	0.061	0.059	0.22	−12.	5.5	−5.8	0.55	−0.23	−0.056
8. M_{21}	0.023	−0.0054	0.045	−0.015	1.0	−2.9	1.4	−0.051	0.17	0.012
9. M_{23}	0.0059	0.055	0.026	0.23	15.	−13.	1.1	0.49	0.27	−0.034
10. M_{31}	0.020	0.011	0.066	0.048	−0.92	−0.22	−0.76	0.016	−0.0032	−0.0088
11. M_{32}	0.0076	0.11	0.022	0.43	2.8	−7.2	−4.4	0.052	0.038	−0.022
12. S_{12}	0.00013	0.0076	0.00023	0.039	−0.86	1.4	−1.1	0.0011	0.016	0.00058
13. S_{13}	0.0024	0.0091	0.0072	0.034	−0.47	−0.13	−0.52	0.029	−0.0084	0.067
14. S_{21}	0.0035	−0.00017	0.0048	0.00033	0.77	−0.14	0.044	−0.0019	0.079	0.0034
15. S_{31}	0.0021	0.00055	0.0039	0.0027	0.28	0.017	−0.057	0.0014	−0.0027	0.0066

inverted coefficient matrix of the dependent variables by the coefficient matrix of the predetermined variables. Table 2 gives a selection from the table of multipliers. It should be noted that the dollar-value variables are all in current prices rather than in real terms. The table shows the effects of a unit change in the exogenous variables on GNP in the two industrial regions, on export prices, and on all international trade and service flows. These values are to be interpreted in terms of the original units of the variables. For instance, since the price variables are expressed in terms of 1954 $= 1.0$, the multiplier value in a price column gives the effect of a doubling of that price; division by 100 will give the effect of a price change by 1 per cent.

A second table of multipliers has been derived on the assumption that under-developed countries are provided the financial means to stabilize their imports and do in fact stabilize them completely. This is, of course, an extreme assumption made here to show the results of a limiting case. The question is: to what extent would such a stabilization measure reduce the intensity with which cyclical fluctuations in economic activity in one of the industrial regions is transmitted to the

TABLE 3

MULTIPLIERS WITH AND WITHOUT STABILIZATION OF
IMPORTS OF UNDERDEVELOPED COUNTRIES

		A_1	A_2	H_1	H_2
Y_1	without	1.45	0.12	1.41	0.91
	with	1.43	0.015	1.33	0.51
Y_2	without	0.040	1.45	0.087	0.61
	with	0.022	1.38	0.033	0.33

other industrial region? Table 3 compares some of the multipliers from both systems.[1] It is found that this stabilization measure would tend to reduce the internal multipliers somewhat (for instance A_1 on Y_1, etc.), particularly the effect of inventory changes on GNP in the other industrial countries. But much more striking is the reduction in the transmission effects (for instance A_1 on Y_2, etc.). It is seen, for example, that a reduction in fixed investment and government expenditures in industrial Europe (A_2) by, say, $10 billion would reduce North America's GNP by $1.2 billion without the stabilization of underdeveloped countries' imports, but by only $0.15 billion with such stabilization. With stabilization in effect all the multipliers in Table 3 are reduced. Although the transmission effects are relatively small to begin with, efforts to stabilize primary producers' foreign exchange receipts may contribute in some measure to economic stability in the industrial countries, too. Such stabilization measures have, of course, their chief beneficial results in the underdeveloped countries themselves and their adoption does not depend on the ancillary effect discussed in this paper.

---

[1] The second system is characterized by the replacement of the original equation (23) by
$$(23^1) \quad M_{13} + M_{23} + F_{13} + V_{13} + D_{13} + S_{13} = \text{constant}$$

VII. FORECASTING

31

Introduction

THE THREE articles reproduced here reflect three of the main lines of development in economic forecasting during the last twenty years. It is fair to say that all three, in different ways and to different degrees, have contributed to our ability to make short-term predictions of economic activity.

Daniel Suits' paper reports on one of the longest experiences that we have in the continuous testing of an econometric model, a direct descendant of the original Klein-Goldberger model, for forecasting purposes. The paper also serves as an excellent introduction to the nature of aggregative econometric models, their stability properties, and the way in which they can be used also for policy purposes. Suits' paper is a valuable supplement—and indeed can serve as an introduction—to the separate section on econometric models included in this volume.

A considerable number of other econometric models have been constructed and used for forecasting purposes. One, which has been revised and used over a period dating back to 1947, is for the Canadian economy; another is the quarterly model for the American economy on which Lawrence Klein and his associates have been working at the University of Pennsylvania. Both have been described in a recent volume of *Studies in Income and Wealth*.[1] Models have also been constructed for a number of other countries. Undoubtedly the most ambitious project to date is the large-scale quarterly model of the United States, on which some dozen and a half economists have collaborated, which was originally sponsored by the Social Science Research Council. A preliminary report on this project has recently been completed and is now being published.[2] Experimentation with the model is continuing at the Brookings Institution.

The paper by Sidney Alexander serves to introduce, albeit in a somewhat critical tone, a second major line of development in economic forecasting

---

[1] T. M. Brown, "A Forecast Determination of National Product, Employment, and Price Level in Canada from an Econometric Model," and Lawrence R. Klein, "A Postwar Quarterly Model: Description and Applications," both in Conference on Research in Income and Wealth, *Models of Income Determination, Studies in Income and Wealth*, Vol. 28 (Princeton: Princeton University Press, 1964), pp. 11–96.

[2] James Duesenberry, Gary Fromm, Lawrence Klein, and Edwin Kuh (eds.), *The Brookings-Quarterly Econometric Model of the United States* (Chicago and Amsterdam: Rand McNally and North-Holland Publishing Co., 1965).

—namely, the work of the National Bureau of Economic Research on statistical indicators and diffusion indices. Here pioneering work has been done by Geoffrey Moore, and a number of his important papers in this field have already been republished by the National Bureau.[3] His work on statistical indicators has been taken up and continued on a current basis by the United States Bureau of the Census under the leadership of Julius Shiskin.[4] Lists of cyclical indicators have also been prepared for some other countries.

In his paper reprinted earlier in this volume, Moore refers to the "unseen cycle" revealed by diffusion indices. An array of such indices for the United States is published currently in *Business Cycle Developments*. Sidney Alexander, in the paper reprinted here, critically examines the value of current diffusion indices and compares their performance with measures derived from simple first differences (appropriately smoothed) of aggregative measures.

Relatively little has been published in English on the so-called Munich Business Test, developed by the Ifo-Institut für Wirtschaftsforschung, in Munich. The English version of the article by Theil and Jochems, originally published in German, helps to fill the gap. Another interesting paper on the uses and analytical implications of the Munich Test was published in English by O. Anderson, Jr., a dozen years ago.[5] Considerable experimentation with Business-Test data has gone on in Europe, particularly in Munich and Rotterdam.

The Munich Test essentially combines two elements: first, a variant of the notion underlying the diffusion index (that is, counting the number of zero, plus, and minus changes occurring in a given period in the components of an aggregate) and, second, data on anticipations (as well as realizations) gathered from many firms. Some of the uses to which such data can be put are illustrated in the paper by Theil and Jochems, as well as in the other publications cited in their bibliography.

It might be added at this point that increasing emphasis has come to be put on anticipations data in making forecasts, and such data are frequently introduced into econometric models, for example, as described in Section I.B. of Suits' paper on the Michigan model. Useful evaluations of anticipations data, particularly those on investment plans, have been made by Foss and Natrella and by Modigliani and Weingartner.[6]

---

[3] Geoffrey H. Moore (ed.), *Business Cycle Indicators*, Vol. I (Princeton: Princeton University Press, 1961). Moore, in turn, built on the prewar study by W. C. Mitchell and A. F. Burns, *Statistical Indicators of Cyclical Revivals*, N.B.E.R. Bulletin 69 (May, 1938).

[4] See the monthly issues of *Business Cycle Developments*, published by the United States Department of Commerce.

[5] Oskar Anderson, Jr., "The Business Test of the IFO-Institute for Economic Research, Munich, and Its Theoretical Model," *Revue de l'Institut Internationale de Statistique*, Vol. XX (1952), pp. 1–17.

[6] M. F. Foss and Vito Natrella, two articles in *Survey of Current Business*, Vol. XXXVII (January, 1957), pp. 16–24, and June, 1957, pp. 12–18; F. Modigliani and H. M. Weingartner, "Forecasting Uses of Anticipatory Data on Investment and Sales," *Quarterly Journal of Economics*, Vol. LXXII (February, 1958), pp. 23–54.

32

Forecasting and Analysis with an Econometric Model*

By *DANIEL B. SUITS*†

ALTHOUGH AN econometric model is the statistical embodiment of theoretical relationships that are every economist's stock in trade, its discussion has largely been kept on a specialized level and confined to the more mathematical journals. Models are rarely explored from the point of view of their usefulness to the profession at large; yet there is nothing about their nature or their application—aside, again, from a solid grasp of economic theory—that requires anything more than an elementary knowledge of school algebra. The compilation of an econometric model requires a certain degree of technical specialization, but once constructed, any competent economist can apply it to policy analysis and economic forecasting.

The purpose of this article is to present an actual econometric model of the U.S. economy, to demonstrate its use as a forecasting instrument, and to explore its implications for policy analysis. To minimize the technical background required, the presentation is divided into two main parts. Part I deals with the general nature of econometric models, and, using a highly simplified schematic example, illustrates how forecasts are made with a model, how a model can be modified to permit the introduction of additional information and judgment, and how short-run and long-run policy multipliers are derived from the inverse of the model. Part II presents the 32-equation econometric model of the U.S. economy compiled by the Research Seminar in Quantitative Economics. This model is the most recent product of a research project whose initial output was the well-known Klein-Goldberger model [1] [3]. In Part III the outlook for 1962, as calculated and published in November, 1961, is studied as an example of an actual forecast; and earlier forecasts of

* *American Economic Review*, Vol. LII (March, 1962). Reprinted by courtesy of the American Economic Association and the author. (This is the report of a continuing project of the Research Seminar in Quantitative Economics at the University of Michigan, sponsored by National Science Foundation grant G-13423.)

† University of Michigan.

this kind that have been prepared by the Research Seminar annually since 1953 are compared with actual events as a demonstration of the potential of the method.

In Part III the inverse of the model is also presented and its application to policy evaluation is reviewed. Short-run and long-run multipliers are calculated for selected policy variables. Part III also includes a digression on deficit financing, covering an interesting and important theoretical implication of the model.

I. ECONOMETRIC MODELS AND THEIR APPLICATIONS

The science of economics can be variously defined, but for the present purpose it is useful to think of it as the study of the relationships among a system of observable and essentially measureable variables: prices, costs, outputs, incomes, savings, employment, etc. These relationships derive from the complex behavior and interaction of millions of households, millions of firms, and thousands of governmental units, producing and exchanging millions of products. The relationships can be represented by a system of mathematical equations, but unfortunately a theoretically complete representation (e.g. a Walrasian system) would involve trillions of equations—surely millions for each household and firm. Moreover these equations would be individually as complex as human behavior, and involve the elaborate interaction of numberless variables.

We have neither the time nor the resources to deal with such a vast system of equations; to proceed at all we must simplify and condense. Millions of individual households become a single "household sector," millions of products become a single item of expenditure, e.g. "durable goods." Moreover, complex mathematical relationships among thousands of variables become simple linear approximations involving two or three aggregates. An econometric model of the economy is obtained by confronting these highly simplified equations with data arising from the historical operation of the economic system and, by appropriate statistical techniques, obtaining numerical estimates for their parameters.

The minimum number of equations necessary for an adequate representation of the economic system depends on a number of considerations, but clearly the fewer the equations the greater must be the level of aggregation and the less accurate and useful the result. On the other hand, the larger the number of equations and the greater the detail shown in the variables, the more complicated it is to derive the individual equations, to manipulate the resulting system, and to see the implications of the model. Where modern computing facilities can be used the mere size of the model is no longer a serious barrier to its effective application, but for purposes of exposition the smaller and simpler the model the better.

A. *A Simple Illustrative Example*

To illustrate the principles of application, let us suppose that the statistical procedure gave rise to the following, purely schematic, model of four equations.

$$C = 20 + 0.7(Y - T) \tag{1}$$

$$I = 2 + 0.1 Y_{-1} \tag{2}$$

$$T = 0.2Y \tag{3}$$

$$Y = C + I + G \tag{4}$$

According to equation (1), consumption (C) depends on current disposable income ($Y - T$). In equation (2), investment (I) depends on income lagged one period. The third equation relates taxes (T) to income, while the last defines income as the sum of consumption, investment and government expenditure G.

While this model is small, it illustrates most of the properties of the larger model. The single consumption function in equation (1) corresponds to the set of four equations (01), (02), (03), and (04) that describe the behavior of the consumer sector in Part II. The investment behavior represented in (2) corresponds to equations (05), through (10). The single tax equation (3) corresponds to a combination of the eleven tax and transfer equations, while the relationship of production to income embodied in equation (4) is indicated in much greater detail by equations (11) through (20).

This econometric model approximates the economy by a system of equations in which the unknowns are those variables—income, consumption, investment, and tax yield—whose behavior is to be analyzed. The "knowns" are government expenditure and lagged income. When projected values for the "knowns" are inserted in the equations, the system can be solved to forecast the values of the unknowns.

Quotation marks are used advisedly on the word "knowns." For, while some economic variables move so slowly along secular trends that their future values can be projected with considerable accuracy, others—for example new government expenditures—are unknown in advance of their occurrence, even in principle. Moreover, even the values of lagged variables are unknown at the time of the forecast, since a useful forecast must be made some months before the end of the preceding year. For example, each of the forecasts shown in Table 3 (p. 614) was made during the first week of November of the preceding year. To make such forecasts, lagged variables are estimated from data for the first three quarters of the year, with the third quarter given double weight.

At any rate, suppose we expect next year's government expenditure to be 20, and the preliminary estimate of this year's income is, say, 100. Substituting $G = 20$ and $Y_{-1} = 100$ into the equations above and solving gives $C = 86.2$, $I = 12$, $T = 23.7$, $Y = 118.2$.

B. *Introducing Outside Information*

It may appear from the foregoing that this kind of forecasting is a blind, automatic procedure; but while an econometric model looks like a rigid analytical tool, it is actually a highly flexible device, readily modifiable to bring to bear additional information and judgment. For example, the investment equation in our little model is surely an unreliable predictor of capital formation. If no other information were available the equation would have to serve the purpose. But suppose we have available a survey of investment intentions reported by business. An estimate derived from such a survey is clearly superior to any that equation (2) could produce. To introduce the information into the forecast we simply remove equation (2) from the model and, in the remaining equations, set I equal to the survey value. Forecasts made from the Research Seminar model have frequently involved use of a figure for gross investment in plant and equipment derived from the McGraw-Hill Survey of Investment Intentions rather than from equation (05) of the model.[1]

Information can also be used to modify individual relationships short of replacing them entirely. For example a prospective improvement in consumer credit terms—a variable that does not appear in our schematic model—would be expected to stimulate consumption expenditure. It is often possible to set an upper limit to this stimulating effect, and by increasing the constant term in the consumption function by this amount, to set an upper limit to the forecast economic outlook. An adjustment of this kind was applied to equation (01) to allow for the probable influence of the compact car on the outlook for automobile sales during 1960. For the same forecast, a similar modification of the housing starts equation (06) was made in anticipation of activity of the Federal National Mortgage Association.

Using the flexibility to full advantage permits the forecaster to explore any desired number of alternative sets of projections and modifications, and to bring to bear all information and judgment he possesses. The econometric model is not, therefore, a substitute for judgment, but rather serves to focus attention on the factors about which judgment must be exercised, and to impose an objective discipline whereby judgment about these factors is translated into an economic outlook that is consistent both internally, and with the past observed behavior of the economic system.

---

[1] The McGraw-Hill Survey of Investment Intentions is conducted annually in the fall. It becomes available just in time to be incorporated in the forecast presented before the Conference on the Economic Outlook, held annually during the first week of November at the University of Michigan. For several years the Conference has been the occasion for the release of the data by *Business Week*.

C. *The Inverse Matrix*

In principle, the exploration of a range of alternative projections and other modifications of the model consists of inserting each set of alternatives in turn as "knowns" in the equations and solving for the resulting forecast. The process is greatly expedited by further simplifying the model and by the use of the inverse matrix. Simplification of the model is made possible by the fact that one of the unknowns, I, depends only on knowns. I helps to determine the current values of C, T, and Y, but the latter do not, in turn, feed back into the determination of the current value of I. As a result, once the knowns are given, I can be directly calculated from (2) without reference to any other part of the model, and hence, as far as the remaining equations are concerned, I can be treated as a known in the sense used above. (Indeed it is this fact that enables us to replace equation (2) with survey values for I.)

The process of solving the system of equations can then be divided into two parts. First: using the values of the knowns, calculate the value of I. Second: substitute the knowns (now including I) into the remaining equations, and solve for the other unknowns.

The inverse matrix facilitates the second step. For those unfamiliar with matrix manipulations the following will help clarify the nature and use of this table. Since I is now considered as known, the model is reduced to the system of three equations (1), (3) and (4) above. By transferring all unknowns to the left side, and representing the right sides by P_1, P_3, and P_4, these equations can be expressed as:

$$C - 0.7Y + 0.7T = 20 = P_1 \tag{1}$$

$$-0.2Y + 1.0T = 0 = P_3 \tag{2}$$

$$-C + Y = I + G = P_4 \tag{3}$$

Now using any convenient method to solve this system for C, Y, and T in terms of P_1, P_3, and P_4 will yield:

$$C = 2.273P_1 - 1.591P_3 + 1.273P_4$$

$$T = 0.445P_1 + 0.682P_3 + 0.455P_4$$

$$Y = 2.273P_1 - 1.591P_3 + 2.273P_4$$

That is, the value of each unknown is obtained as a specified weighted total of P_1, P_3, and P_4. Where a large number of equations is used, and a lot of calculating is to be done, it is convenient to display the weights used for each unknown as a column of numbers in a table, with the detail of the P's shown in a separate column at the right:

Equation No.	C	T	Y	P
(1)	2.273	0.455	2.273	20
(3)	-1.591	0.682	-1.591	0
(4)	1.273	0.455	2.273	$I + G$

To make a forecast we first substitute Y_{-1} into equation (2) and solve for I. Then I and G are substituted in the P column of the table and the values of P_1, P_3, and P_4 calculated. These values, weighted by the numbers shown in the C column of the inverse and summed, give the forecast value of consumption; use of the weights in column Y gives the forecast for income, etc.[2] For example if we set $Y_{-1} = 100$ and $G = 20$, we first find from (2) $I = 12$. Substituting these values in column P of the table gives the forecast values: $C = 86.2$, $T = 23.7$, $Y = 118.2$.

D. *Short-Run Policy Multipliers*

It is an obvious step from economic forecasting to short-run policy analysis. To investigate any specified set of prospective government actions, we insert them in the proper place in column P and solve for the forecast implied by these assumptions. The analysis is expedited if we first calculate short-run multipliers for the individual components of government action. These can then be applied in any desired policy mixture.

Short-run multipliers for any policy variable are readily calculated by inserting $+1$ for the variable everywhere it appears in column P, and then (ignoring all terms that do not contain the variable in question) extending a forecast using the columns of the inverse. For example, to calculate the government expenditure multiplier, set $G = 1$ in row (4) of column P. This makes $P_4 = 1$. To find the effect of this value of G on, say, income, multiply this value of P_4 by the weight in row (4) of the Y column to get $Y = 1 \times 2.273 = 2.273$. That is, the income multiplier on government expenditure is 2.273. Likewise, $T = 1 \times 0.455 = 0.455$. That is, the tax-yield multiplier on government expenditure is 0.455. In other words, for every dollar of additional government expenditure, tax receipts rise by nearly 46 cents. A corollary is that—according to our schematic model—an increase in government expenditure of 1 with no change in tax legislation will generate an increase in deficit of only:

$$G - T = 1 - 0.46 = 0.54$$

In addition to changing the value of exogenous variables like government expenditure, government policy can produce changes in the equations themselves. An extensive change—e.g. a substantial alteration in tax rates— can only be studied by replacing the old tax equation by a new one, but less extensive changes can be studied as shifts in the levels of existing equations, the coefficients being unaltered.

Multipliers for such shifts are easily determined by placing $+1$ in the row of column P that corresponds to the equation being shifted. The extensions are then made as before. For example, to calculate the multipliers on a $+1$ shift in the level of the tax equation, we put $+1$ in the row marked (3) of column P, since the tax equation is (3). The multiplier effect of this shift is

---

[2] As those familiar with matrix algebra will recognize, the inverse matrix is tabulated here in its transposed form, and goes into the P vector at the right column by column.

then calculated by multiplying this 1 by the weight in the corresponding row of the appropriate column, as shown above. For example for income:

$$Y = 1 \times (-1.591) = -1.591$$

For consumption:

$$C = 1 \times (-1.591) = -1.591$$

In other words, the multipliers associated with the shift of any equation are merely the weights in the row of the inverse corresponding to that equation.

Note that according to our simplified model, the tax-yield multiplier is 0.682. That is, an upward shift of $1 billion in the tax *schedule* actually increases *yield* by only $682 million. The difference is due to the decline in income arising from the shift in the tax schedule.

The small size of our illustrative model limits the policy variables to government expenditure and the level of taxes. In the more extensive model below, policy is given considerably more scope; a number of individual tax and transfer equations can be shifted, and a number of different kinds of expenditure altered. The number of possible combinations of action is correspondingly very large; but one important advantage to a linear system lies in the fact that once multipliers for the individual components have been calculated, the economic implications of a complete policy "package" can be estimated by summing the effects of the individual components.

For example, an increase of $1 in government expenditure coupled with an upward shift of $1 in the tax schedule would generate a change in income given by the sum of the two individual multipliers:

$$Y = 2.273 - 1.591 = 0.682$$

This is what might be called an *"ex-ante*-balanced" government expenditure multiplier. That is, the change in the law is such as to increase tax yield at the *existing* level of income by enough to balance the planned expenditure, but the budget will not necessarily be balanced *ex post*. The tax and expenditure program will alter income, and hence will change tax yields. Analysis of the complete fiscal impact of the operation requires the examination of all revenue and outlay items combined. Adding together the two tax-yield multipliers we find that the additional expenditure of $1 is offset by a tax yield of:

$$0.682 + 0.455 = 1.137$$

That is, the *ex-ante*-balanced expenditure of $1 billion would, in our example, be accompanied by an increase of $1.137 billion in tax yield and give rise to an *ex-post* surplus of $137 million.

E. *Dynamics and Long-Run Multipliers*

An increase in government expenditure of 1.0 will increase income by 2.273 the same year. But the long-run effect of expenditure sustained at this level will differ from this. According to equation (2), an increase in income this year will generate an increase in investment next year. This will again raise income and add further stimulus the following year, etc. Once the inverse has been tabulated, however, the sequence can easily be calculated by inserting the forecast values of one year as the "knowns" of the next. Thus an initial increase in G of 1 will raise Y by 2.273. This will raise I by $0.1 \times 2.273 = 0.227$ the following year. The value of P_4 is then $G + I = 1.227$ and the second year income rises to 2.790 above its initial value, etc. The five-year sequence of values would be:

Year	1	2	3	4	5
Income	2.273	2.790	2.907	2.933	2.934

This means, for example, that if government expenditure is increased by 1 in 1961, and sustained at that new level, the level of income in 1965 will—other things equal—be 2.934 higher than it was in 1960.

Similar sequences can be worked out for other policy variables. For example a shift of 1 in the tax schedule in year 1 would imply the following sequence of anual income values:

Year	1	2	3	4	5
Income	-1.591	-1.953	-2.035	-2.055	-2.060

Like short-run multipliers, these long-run multipliers can be combined by simple addition. For example, a permanent rise of 1 in government expenditure coupled with an *ex-ante* shift of 1 in the tax schedule would raise income by $2.273 - 1.591 = 0.682$ the first year. After 5 years, however, income would be $2.934 - 2.060 = 0.874$ higher than its initial level.

Although the discussion has been focused on a highly simplified example, the principles developed apply equally to any linear econometric model. The presentation of the actual Research Seminar model in Part II will follow the same pattern as the illustration of Part I.

. II. THE MODEL OF THE U.S. ECONOMY

The model developed by the Research Seminar in Quantitative Economics consists of 32 equations, most of them least-squares linear regressions fitted to annual first differences in the variables.[3]

Five advantages are gained by the use of first differences. In the first place, the autocorrelation of residuals from time series regressions causes a downward bias in calculated standard errors, giving an exaggerated appearance of precision to the result. The use of first differences serves to reduce this bias. Secondly, many of the equations—e.g. the demand for consumer durables— involve stocks for which data are not currently available. The increase in a

---

[3] The exceptions are definitional equations, and those approximating tax laws. Use of least squares is unnecessary for the former, and inappropriate to the latter. The frequency of change in tax laws makes past data irrelevant to their current analysis. Tax equations were fitted by eye through a few relevant points.

stock is composed of current acquisitions less retirements. Since the latter tends to be a smooth series, exhibiting little year-to-year variation, the first difference in stock is well represented by acquisitions, a figure readily available on a current basis. Thirdly, in short-run analysis and forecasting, the present position is known, and *ceteris paribus* will continue. The important question is what change from that position will result from projected changes in other factors. The use of first differences serves to focus the power of the analysis on these changes. Fourthly, the use of first differences minimizes the effect of slowly moving variables such as population, tastes, technical change, etc., without explicitly introducing them into the analysis. The net effect of changes in these factors is represented in the constant term of the equation. Finally, use of first differences minimizes the complications produced by data revision when the model is applied. Revisions usually alter the level at which variables are measured, rather than their year-to-year variation.

In calculating the equations, the prewar and postwar periods were explored separately to determine whether there was any indication of a change in the coefficients. Except for institutional relationships—tax laws, transfers, etc.— no important shifts were discovered. Nevertheless the final equations are fitted only to data drawn from the period 1947–60 to maximize their applicability to current problems.

The equations of the model are presented and discussed below by sectors, and the symbol for each variable is explained the first time it appears. In general the variables correspond to the magnitudes as given in the national accounts, measured in billions of 1954 dollars. In calculating the equations however, all imputations were removed from the Department of Commerce figures for consumer expenditure and disposable income. These imputations, mainly associated with services rendered by financial institutions and by owner-occupied dwellings, are added back in after a forecast is made to maintain comparability with the national accounts. First differences are indicated throughout by prefixing Δ to the symbol of the variable. Note, however, that lagged undifferenced values of certain variables appear at some points (e.g. in the automobile demand equation (01) below). These undifferenced values serve as proxy variables for first differences in stocks as explained above. Figures in parentheses are the standard errors of the regression coefficients.

A. *Aggregate Demand*

1. Consumption
(01) Automobiles and Parts:

$$\Delta A = 0.177\ \Delta(Y - X_u - X_f - X_s) - 0.495\ A_{-1}$$
$$\quad(0.086)\qquad\qquad\qquad\qquad(0.168)$$

$$+\ 0.260\ \Delta L_{-1} + 4.710$$
$$\quad(0.082)$$

Consumer expenditure for new and net used automobiles and parts (ΔA) depends on disposable income (Y), net of transfers for unemployment compensation (X_u), and other federal (X_f) and state (X_s) transfers. These transfers are deducted on the ground that they are unlikely to find their way into the automobile market. Servicemen's insurance dividends (X_{GI}) are not deducted from disposable income. In addition, automobile demand depends on the stock of cars on the road (A_{-1}) and on the real value of consumer liquid assets at the end of the preceding year (ΔL_{-1}). For this purpose liquid assets are defined as household holdings of currency and demand deposits plus fixed-value redeemable claims as estimated by the Federal Reserve Board. The sizeable constant term in the equation probably reflects replacement demand.[4]

(02) Demand for Other Durables:

$$\Delta D = 0.176\ \Delta Y - 0.0694\ D_{-1} + 0.0784\ \Delta L_{-1} + 0.262$$
$$\quad\ (0.015)\qquad (0.029)\qquad\ \ (0.016)$$

This equation relates ΔD, consumer expenditure for durables (other than automobiles and parts) to disposable income (ΔY), the accumulating stock of durables (D_{-1}) and liquid assets.

(03) Demand for Nondurable Goods:

$$\Delta ND = 0.224\ \Delta Y + 0.205\ \Delta ND_{-1} + 0.143\ \Delta L_{-1} - 0.149$$
$$\quad\ \ (0.060)\qquad (0.135)\qquad\quad\ (0.059)$$

Nondurable expenditure depends on disposable income, liquid assets, and last year's nondurable expenditure (ΔND_{-1}). Notice the difference between this and the foregoing equations. In (01) and (02) the lagged values were undifferenced representing accumulation of stock. In this equation the difference itself is lagged, representing a dynamic adjustment in nondurable expenditure: an initial rise in level is followed by a subsequent secondary rise.

(04) Demand for Services:

$$\Delta S = 0.0906\ \Delta Y + 0.530 \Delta S_{-1} + 0.0381\ \Delta L_{-1} + 0.363$$
$$\quad\ \ (0.029)\qquad (0.170)\qquad\ (0.029)$$

This equation is similar to (03) and relates expenditure for services (ΔS) to disposable income, liquid assets, and lagged service expenditure. It should be remembered that service expenditure is here defined to exclude imputed items.

These four equations constitute the demand sector. Note that the aggregate marginal propensity to consume can be estimated by summing the income coefficients in the four equations. The sum, 0.67, is an estimate of the marginal propensity to consume, at least as an initial impact. The lagged terms in the

---

[4] This equation is a simplified version of that given in [5].

individual equations, however, generate a dynamic response of consumption to income. As the equations show, the long-run response of nondurables and services tends to be greater, and that of automobile and durables less, than the initial impact. The implications of this fact for the calculation of multipliers will appear below.

2. Gross Capital Expenditure

(05) Plant and Equipment Expenditure:

$$\Delta PE = 0.605 \, \Delta(P^*_{-1} - T_{fc-1} - T_{sc-1}) - 0.124 \, PE_{-1} + 4.509$$
$$\quad\quad (0.238) \quad\quad\quad\quad\quad\quad\quad\quad\quad\quad (0.216)$$

ΔPE, expenditure for new plant and equipment, includes producers' durables, nonfarm nonresidential construction, and all farm construction. It is related to the preceding year's corporate profits (P^*_{-1}) after federal (T_{fc}) and state (T_{sc}) corporate income taxes and to its own lagged, undifferenced value (PE_{-1}). The latter represents growth in the stock of plant and equipment. As in (01) above, the large constant term probably represents replacement.

(06) Housing Starts:

$$\Delta HS = 19.636 \, \Delta\left(\frac{FHA + VA}{2} - Aaa\right) - 0.702 \, HS_{-1} + 66.147$$
$$\quad\quad (17.0) \quad\quad\quad\quad\quad\quad\quad\quad\quad\quad\quad (0.312)$$

This equation, which applies only to the postwar period, relates the number of nonfarm residential housing starts (ΔHS), measured in thousand of units per month, to the gap between the simple average of the FHA and VA ceiling interest rates on the one hand, and the *Aaa* bond yield on the other (both expressed in percentage points). This interest rate differential reflects the substantial influence of credit availability on the volume of FHA and VA financed residential construction.[5] It can function, however, only in the presence of a strong underlying housing demand. With the accumulation of a large stock as a consequence of construction in recent years, this interest rate differential may lose its role in the model.[6] The term HS_{-1}, the lagged undifferenced value of housing starts, only partially represents the effect of this accumulation, and equation (06) is probably due for revision.

(07) Housing Expenditure:

$$\Delta H = 0.125 \, \Delta HS + 0.024 \, \Delta HS_{-1} + 6.580 \, \Delta C + 0.083$$
$$\quad\quad (0.013) \quad\quad\quad (0.012) \quad\quad\quad (5.42)$$

Expenditure on housing, (ΔH), depends on the rate at which residential construction is carried forward, and thus on current and lagged starts. In

---

[5] This aspect of credit availability has been recently discussed by J. M. Guttentag [2]. Guttentag is skeptical of the influence of the ceiling rates. Our equation was, of course, developed independently of his work, and was first introduced into the model in the fall of 1959 in making the forecast for 1960.

[6] Guttentag argues that this is not necessarily the case [2, p. 297].

addition it depends on construction costs. The term ΔC is the ratio of the index of construction costs to the GNP deflator.

(08) Durable Goods Inventory:

$$\Delta ID = 0.291\ \Delta(A + D) + 0.591\ \Delta PD + 0.305\ \Delta M_{+1} - 0.669\ ID_{-1}$$
$$\quad\ (0.100) \qquad\qquad (0.157) \qquad\ (0.085) \qquad\quad (0.109)$$

Accumulation of durable inventories, ΔID, depends on sales of consumer durables, producers durables ΔPD, and the stock of inventory already accumulated ID_{-1}. In addition an important component of inventory is associated with government military orders. Production on such orders appears in the national accounts as goods in process, and exerts a strong impact on the economy long before delivery of the finished product material-izes as government expenditure. A wide variety of arrangements and lead times are involved in this process.[7] As a proxy for such orders in any given year, we use ΔM_{+1}, federal military purchases from private industry the following year.

The equilibrium sales-inventory ratio implied by this equation compares favorably with that observed from other data.

(09) Nondurable Goods Inventory:

$$\Delta IND = 0.427\ \Delta ND - 1.121\ IND_{-1}$$
$$\qquad\ (0.111) \qquad\quad (0.248)$$

Accumulation of nondurable inventory, ΔIND, depends on consumer sales of nondurables and the stock already on hand, IND_{-1}.

(10) Imports:

$$\Delta R = 0.0602\ \Delta G^{*} + 0.369$$
$$\quad\ (0.03)$$

This relates the aggregate level of imports to the private GNP (G^{*}).

3. Private Gross National Product

(11) $\Delta G^{*} = \Delta(A + D + ND + S) + (\Delta F - \Delta R) + \Delta ID + \Delta IND$
$\qquad\quad + \Delta PE + \Delta H + \Delta g$

Private GNP is defined as the sum of its parts including net exports ($\Delta F - \Delta R$) and government purchases from private firms (Δg).

B. *Income and Employment*

(12) Wage and Salary Workers, Private Sector:

$$\Delta E = 0.068 \Delta G^{*}$$

This production function, relating ΔE, the number of full-time equivalent

---

[7] For an excellent study of these see [6].

employees in the private sector (measured in millions of persons) to the private GNP, applies specifically to the forecast of 1962 and is based on the first three quarters recovery experience during 1961.

(13) Unemployment:

$$\Delta U = \Delta LF - \Delta E_0 - \Delta E_G - \Delta E$$

Unemployment is the difference between labor force (ΔLF) on the one hand, and the number of self-employed and unpaid family workers, (ΔE_0), government workers, including armed services (ΔE_G) and employees of private industry (ΔE).

(14) Average Annual Earnings:

$$\Delta w = - 0.0216 \, \Delta U + 0.00436 \, P^*_{-1} - 0.0743$$
$$\quad\quad (0.0076) \quad\quad (0.0025)$$

Δw, average annual earnings (including wages and salaries plus "other labor income," and measured in thousands of dollars) is related to unemployment and last year's profits. This relationship reflects two facts. First and probably more important, annual earnings are heavily influenced by overtime pay which varies inversely with the level of unemployment. Secondly, pressure of union demands varies directly with profits and inversely with the level of unemployment. The undifferenced level of profits is used since the *existence* of profits acts as a target for wage demands.

(15) Private Wage Bill:

$$\Delta W = \Delta(wE) = w_{-1}\Delta E + E_{-1}\Delta w$$

By definition the wage bill is the product of average earnings and employment. To keep the model linear, this nonlinear relationship is replaced by the linear approximation shown.

(16) Depreciation:

$$\Delta Dep = 0.0456 \, \Delta G^* + 0.763$$

(17) Property Income:

$$\Delta P = \Delta G^* - \Delta W - \Delta Dep - \Delta T_{fe} - \Delta T_{cd} - \Delta T_{bp}$$
$$- \Delta T_{ss} - \Delta T_{os} - \Delta SI_r$$

Property income (ΔP) is a residual from the GNP after deducting wage costs, depreciation (ΔDep), employer contributions for social insurance (ΔSI_r), and indirect business taxes: federal excises (ΔT_{fe}), customs duties (ΔT_{cd}), business property (ΔT_{bp}), state sales (ΔT_{ss}), and other state taxes on business (ΔT_{os}).

(18) Corporate Profits:

$$\Delta P^* = 0.902 \, (\Delta P - \Delta P_f) - 1.027$$

This relates profits (ΔP^*) to total property income net of farm income (ΔP_f). There is, of course, no strong theoretical basis for the particular distribution of corporate business found in the U.S. economy. This equation is an empirical representation of the distribution of property income under existing institutional arrangements.

(19) Dividends:

$$\Delta Div = 0.229\Delta(P^* - T_{fc} - T_{sc})$$
$$(0.064)$$

$$+ 0.0198 \, (P^* - T_{fc} - T_{sc} - Div)_{-1} - 0.0191$$
$$(0.052)$$

Current dividends (ΔDiv) depend on current profits after federal (T_{fc}) and state (T_{sc}) corporate profits taxes, and on last year's level of undistributed profits.

(20) Disposable Income:

$$\Delta Y = \Delta W + \Delta W_G + (\Delta P - \Delta P^*) + \Delta Div + \Delta i_G + \Delta X_u + \Delta X_f + \Delta X_s$$

$$+ \Delta X_{GI} - \Delta T_{fy} - \Delta T_{sy} - \Delta T_{eg} - \Delta T_{op} - \Delta SI_e + \Delta T_{ref}$$

Disposable income is the sum of wages, including government wages (W_G), noncorporate property income ($\Delta P - \Delta P^*$), dividends, government interest payments (i_G), plus transfers, less personal taxes: federal (ΔT_{fy}), and state (ΔT_{sy}) income, estate and gift (ΔT_{eg}), other personal taxes (ΔT_{cp}) and personal contributions for social insurance ΔSI_e, all net of tax refunds ΔT_{ref}.

C. Taxes and Government Transfers

1. Federal Taxes
(21) Federal Corporate Profits Tax:

$$\Delta T_{fc} = 0.500\Delta P^*$$

(22) Federal Personal Income Tax Receipts:

$$\Delta T_{fy} = 0.111(\Delta W + \Delta W_G) + 0.150(\Delta P - \Delta P^* + \Delta i_G) + 0.195\Delta Div$$

This equation relates income tax receipts in the form of withholding, quarterly payments on estimated tax, and final tax payment to the several income components. The coefficients reflect both variation in income shares by tax bracket and the effect of the dividend tax credit.

(23) Federal Personal Income Tax Liability:

$$\Delta T^*_{fy} = 0.100(\Delta W + \Delta W_G) + 0.114(\Delta P - \Delta P^* + \Delta i_G) + 0.154\Delta Div$$

Tax receipts commonly exceed liability. The difference (ΔT_{ref}) appears as a tax refund the following year.

(24) Federal Excise Taxes:

$$\Delta T_{fe} = 0.099\Delta A + 0.011\Delta D + 0.003\Delta ND + 0.010\Delta G^* + 0.015\Delta Y$$

(25) Customs Duties:

$$\Delta T_{cd} = 0.083\Delta R + 0.012$$

2. State and Local Taxes
(26) State Corporate Income Taxes:

$$\Delta T_{sc} = 0.019\Delta P^*$$

(27) State and Local Sales Taxes:

$$\Delta T_{ss} = 0.033(\Delta A + \Delta D + \Delta ND + \Delta S)$$

(28) State and Local Personal Income Taxes:

$$\Delta T_{sy} = 0.010(\Delta W + \Delta W_G + \Delta P - \Delta P^* + \Delta Div + \Delta i_G)$$

3. Social Insurance Programs
(29) Private Employer Contributions for Social Insurance:

$$\Delta SI_r = 0.149\Delta E$$

(30) Personal Contributions for Social Insurance:

$$\Delta SI_e = 0.129(\Delta E + \Delta E_G) + 0.050(\Delta P - \Delta P^*)$$

(31) Covered Unemployment:

$$\Delta U_c = 0.675\Delta U - 0.140(\Delta LF - \Delta LF_{-1})$$

The relationship of unemployment covered by compensation programs (ΔU_c) to total unemployment varies with the rate of increase in the labor force. When the labor force is growing rapidly, new entrants, not yet covered, make up a larger proportion of total unemployment.
(32) Unemployment Compensation:

$$\Delta X_u = 1.77 \Delta U_c + 0.101$$

III. THE MODEL AS A FORECASTING INSTRUMENT

A. *The Forecast of 1962*

The unknowns of the model are the 32 variables like automobile demand, disposable income, private GNP, etc. that stand on the left side of the equations. The knowns are variables like government purchases from private firms, labor force, household liquid assets, etc. that appear only on the right side of the equations, and whose values must be projected or assigned before the unknowns can be forecast.

TABLE 1

PROJECTIONS UNDERLYING FORECAST OF 1962

Equation

(01) $A_{-1} = 14.3$ $\Delta L_{-1} = 16.9$ $X_f = \Delta X_s = 0$
(02) $D_{-1} = 27.3$ $\Delta L_{-1} = 16.9$
(03) $\Delta ND_{-1} = 1.2$ $\Delta L_{-1} = 16.9$
(04) $\Delta S_{-1} = 3.4$ $\Delta L_{-1} = 16.9$
(05) $\Delta PE = 1.3^a$

(06) $\Delta Aaa = +0.02$ $\Delta\left(\dfrac{FHA + VA}{2}\right) = -0.06^b$ $HS_{-1} = 93.1$

(07) $\Delta HS_{-1} = 3.2$ $\Delta C = 0$
(08) $\Delta PD = 0.7^a$ $\Delta M_{+1} = 1.0$ $ID_{-1} = 0.0$
(09) $IND_{-1} = 1.7$
(10) —
(11) $\Delta F = 0$ $\Delta PE = 1.3^a$ $\Delta g = 6.9$
(12) —
(13) $\Delta LF = 1.2$ $\Delta E_0 = 0.2$ $\Delta E_G = 0.6$
(14) $P^*_{-1} = 39.6$
(15) $w_{-1} = 4.38$ $E_{-1} = 46.9$
(16) —
(17) $\Delta T_{bp} = 0.730$ $\Delta T_{os} = 0.087$
(18) $\Delta P_f = 0$
(19) —
(20) $\Delta X_f = \Delta X_s = \Delta X_{GI} = 0$ $\Delta W_G = 1.5$ $\Delta i_G = 0.1$ $\Delta T_{op} = 0.35$ $\Delta T_{eg} = 0.08$
          $\Delta T_{ref} = 0$
(21) —
(22) $\Delta W_G = 1.5$ $\Delta i_G = 0.1$
(23) $\Delta W_G = 1.5$ $\Delta i_G = 0.1$
(24) —
(25) —
(26) —
(27) —
(28) $\Delta W_G = 1.5$ $\Delta i_G = 0.1$
(29) —
(30) $\Delta E_G = 0.6$
(31) $\Delta LF = 1.2$ $\Delta LF_{-1} = 1.0$
(32) —
(Addendum) Δ Imputed Services $= 1.5$

---

a Based on McGraw-Hill survey showing 4 per cent increase in plant and equipment expenditure.
b FHA ceiling rates are projected at their present level throughout 1962. The projected decline reflects the fact that they were above this level in early 1961.

The forecast of 1962, calculated and presented in November, 1961, employed the projected values shown in Table 1. The most important single item was the $16.9 billion increase in consumer holdings of liquid assets. A few of the other key items were: a $6.9 billion projected increase in government purchases from private firms; an increase of 0.6 million in government employment; increase in government wage payments of $1.5 billion; and a $1 billion rise in military orders. Note that investment in plant and equipment is projected directly on the basis of the McGraw-Hill survey rather than from equation (05). All monetary values are in 1954 dollars.

TABLE 2

REVIEW OF 1961 AND OUTLOOK FOR 1962

(Monetary figures, except column 5, are billions of 1954 dollars)

	1961		Forecast Increase	Forecast 1962 (1954 Prices)	(1962 Prices)
	Forecast	Actual[p]			
Gross National Product	450.1	446.8	27.5[a]	474.3	559.9
Consumption Expenditures					
Automobiles and Parts	14.6	14.3	4.5	18.8	21.2
Other Durables	25.1	24.8	1.9	26.7	28.7
Nondurables	144.7	142.7	5.3	148.0	163.6
Services	119.9	119.6	5.5[a]	125.1	147.9
Private Gross Capital Expenditure					
Plant and Equipment	39.0	37.3	1.3	38.6	48.1
Residential Construction	19.9	17.7	0.1	17.8	21.4
Inventory Investment					
Durables	} 2.4	0.0	2.6	2.6	2.8
Nondurables		1.7	0.4	2.1	2.3
Imports	24.8	22.2	1.9	24.1	24.8
Exports	24.6	26.4	—	26.4	28.7
Government Expenditure on					
Goods and Services	84.7	84.5	7.8	92.3	120.0
Corporate Profits	40.3	39.6	5.1	44.7	52.5
Dividends	12.4	12.3	0.7	13.0	15.3
Civilian Labor Force[b]					
(millions of persons)	71.3	71.6	0.9	72.5	
Private Wage and Salary					
Workers	} 67.0	46.9	1.7	48.6	
Govt. Employees (Civilian)		8.8	0.3	9.1	
Self-employed		11.0	0.2	11.2	
Unemployed[b]					
Number (millions)	4.3	4.9	−1.3	3.6	
Percent of Civilian Labor Force	6.0	6.8	—	5.0	

[p] Preliminary.
[a] Includes imputed services.
[b] Annual average.

When the projections of Table 1 were inserted in the equations, the solution gave the outlook for 1962 shown in Table 2. The first two columns contain a detailed comparison of the forecast of 1961 with the preliminary actual values. The middle column contains the solutions obtained from the equations. These are in first differences and are expressed as increases over 1961. When the forecast increase is added to the preliminary actual level for 1961 the result is the forecast level of 1962 shown in the fourth column. In the last column this forecast has been translated into approximate 1962 prices.[8]

_____

[8] To convert the values from 1954 to 1962 prices they were multiplied by deflators obtained by raising 1961 deflators 1½ percent across the board. The result serves to put the forecast in proper perspective, but should not be thought of as part of the forecast itself.

TABLE 3
Review of Past Forecasts

	1953[a]		1954[a]		1955[a]		1956[a]		1957[b]	
	Forecast	Actual	Forecast	Actual	Forecast	Actual	Forecast	Actual	Forecast	Actual
Gross National Product	177.4	178.6	174.8	173.9	176.4	188.5	191.6	191.2	337.0	335.2
Consumption Expenditure	114.4	115.9	117.3	116.7	118.6	125.1	127.4	128.5	226.2	226.1
Private Gross Capital Formation	24.2	24.9	22.7	23.6	25.2	25.9	28.7	26.3	47.2	44.4
Employee Compensation	80.4[f]	79.8[f]	82.3[f]	83.0[f]	81.2[f]	89.5[f]	107.1	104.3	196.5	196.3

	1958[c]		1959[d]		1960[e]	
	Forecast	Actual	Forecast	Actual	Forecast	Actual
Gross National Product	432.7	432.5	456.7	475.7	432.0	439.2
Consumption Expenditure	282.1	287.3	295.4	310.7	287.1	296.8
Automobiles	—	—	—	—	16.7	15.6
Other Durables	—	—	—	—	25.2	25.2
Non Durables	—	—	—	—	138.9	141.9
Services	—	—	—	—	106.3	113.7
Private Gross Capital Expenditure	61.9	53.7	61.2	70.4	62.4	60.5
Plant and Equipment	—	—	44.0	43.0	40.5	39.3
Residential Construction	—	—	17.8	21.6	19.7	18.0
Inventory	—	—	-.6	5.8	2.2	3.2
Government Purchase of Goods and Services	88.8	90.5	100.1	94.6	83.7	80.3
Net Exports					-1.3	1.6
Employee Compensation	254.3	251.8	261.0	273.4	236.3	257.1
Corporate Profits	39.5	36.5	47.7	45.8	42.7	38.7
Dividends	—	—	—	—	12.2	12.2
Civilian Employment	66.4	66.5	66.0	65.6	65.5[g]	66.7[h]
Unemployment	4.8	4.7	3.4	3.8	4.4[g]	3.9[h]

[a] 1939 prices [c] 1954 prices [e] 1957 prices [a] excludes Alaska and Hawaii [g] excludes Alaska and Hawaii

The forecast entails substantial increases in consumption expenditure, especially for automobiles. The forecast level of $18.8 billion for this sector constitutes a record level of automobile sales, exceeding the $17.9 billion reached in 1955. This large increase derives primarily from the high level of consumer liquidity and the small addition to stocks of cars during 1961.

Aside from the consumer sector the main stimulus to the economy derives from projected increases in government outlays, associated with the trend of state and local expenditures and federal defense expenditure. In preparing the forecast no allowance was made for the possible effect of a steel strike during 1962. Inventory accumulation in anticipation of interruption of steel supplies will probably accelerate inventory accumulation in the first half of the year and depress it in the second half. There is no indication that this will alter the over-all level for the year.

The forecast increase in production is adequate to absorb more than the growth of the labor force, and the outlook concludes by showing a reduction of 1.3 million in unemployment, reducing the average for the year to 3.6 million or 5 percent of the civilian labor force.

B. *Review of Past Forecasts*

The Research Seminar in Quantitative Economics has been making annual forecasts since 1953, each a matter of record published in advance of the year forecast. The econometric model has been revised and improved several times over this period (the version presented here was first used for the 1962 forecast), but the review of past forecasting performance in Table 3 will illustrate the general reliability of the method.[9] Each forecast is shown as it was presented, and compared with the actual outcome.[10] Note that from 1953 to 1956 the figures are given in 1939 dollars; thereafter the price level employed was changed almost every year. The increasing elaboration of the model is evident in the table.

As plotted in Figure 1, the general accuracy of these forecasts speaks for itself. The direction of movement was correctly forecast each year, and the levels were generally well predicted. The recession of 1954 was forecast with considerable precision. The recovery of 1955 was likewise forecast, but the magnitude of the boom that developed was grossly underestimated. The fact that the error of the 1955 forecast is concentrated in the consumer sector lends support to the idea that this was a consumer-generated movement.

---

[9] The review of the 1961 forecast, compared with the actual outcome, is provided in Table 2.

[10] Since data revisions occur frequently, there is some question as to what figures should be taken as "actual." Since we want the "actual" figures as close as possible in definition and economic context to the data on which the forecast was based, they are taken from the issue of the *Survey of Current Business* appearing in the February following the forecast year. E.g., the "actual" GNP for 1954 is the value for 1954 published February, 1955.

The recession of 1958 was well predicted. The recovery of 1959 was somewhat underestimated.

In many respects the forecast of 1960 was the most interesting of all. Made in November 1959 at the height of business optimism, and amidst

FIG. 1

COMPARISON OF FORECAST WITH ACTUAL CHANGES IN GNP (1953–61)
(Billions of 1954 Dollars)

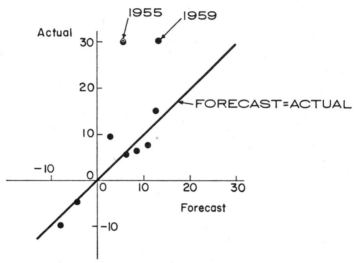

general anticipation of the "soaring 'sixties," its pessimistic outlook for 1960 was greeted with almost complete skepticism, but it proved to be more exact than any other forecast placed on record in advance.

C. *Short-Run Policy Multipliers*

Simplification of the model is carried out as illustrated in Part I. Inspection shows that in equation (05), plant and equipment expenditure (ΔPE) depends only on "known" values: last year's profits after taxes, and the stock of plant and equipment available at the beginning of the year. Similarly in equations (06) and (07), housing starts (ΔHS) and expenditure for nonfarm residential construction (ΔH) depend only on credit availability, construction costs, last year's starts, and the stock of houses at the beginning of the year. To make a forecast, therefore, we use the knowns to estimate ΔPE, ΔHS, and ΔH via equations (05), (06), and (07), and then use these values, together with the other knowns, to solve the remaining equations. The inverse of the model is shown in Table 4. This is merely an enlarged version of the little table shown earlier for the illustrative model of Part I, and is used in the same way. For example, if the projected values of Table 1 are inserted in column P of Table 4, multiplied by the weights in the Automobile column and summed, the result is 4.5, the forecast increase in automobile demand shown in Table 2.[11] Short-run multipliers for any policy variable are readily calculated as before by inserting 1 for the variable everywhere it appears in column P and then (ignoring all terms that do not contain the variable in question) extending a forecast using the columns of Table 4.

For example, to find the multiplier on government purchases from private firms, set $\Delta g = +1$ everywhere it appears in column P. The term Δg is found in only one place: in row (11) it is multiplied by 1. To find the effect of $\Delta g = \$1$ on, say, private GNP, we multiply the weight in row (11) of the GNP column by 1:

$$\Delta G^* = 1 \times 1.304 = 1.304$$

That is to say, the short-run multiplier on government purchases is about 1.3. Similarly, the effect on, say, automobile demand is given by

$$\Delta A = 1 \times 0.092 = 0.092$$

i.e. the short-run "automobile demand multiplier" on government purchases from the private sector is 0.092.

In working out a policy multiplier, care must be taken to include changes in *all* exogenous variables affected by the policy action. For example, an increase in government employment involves hiring additional people [ΔE_G in rows (13) and (30)] and paying them wages [ΔW_G in rows (20), (22), and (28)]. At an average annual wage of $5000, an addition of $1 billion to the government wage bill will hire 0.2 million additional employees. To find the multipliers on government wages, therefore, we set $\Delta E_G = 0.2$. This gives -0.2 in row (13) and 0.0258 in row (30) of column P. We also set $\Delta W_G = \$1$ to get 1 in row (20), 0.111 in (22) and 0.010 in row (28) of column P. The impact of additional government employment on private GNP is then found by extending these figures by the weights in the corresponding rows of the GNP column:

$$\begin{aligned}\Delta G^* &= -0.2 \times 0.167 + 1 \times 1.119 - 0.111 \times 1.119 - 0.010 \times 1.119 \\ &\quad - 0.0258 \times 1.119 \\ &= 0.921\end{aligned}$$

To find the effect of the action on total GNP, we must add in the additional value added by government (i.e. government wages and salaries). Thus:

$$\text{Total GNP} = 0.921 + 1 = 1.921$$

---

[11] To save space some of the less interesting columns of the matrix have been omitted from Table 4. Moreover the tax and transfer equations have been consolidated to show only totals for federal taxes, state and local taxes, and social insurance contributions. If values of any omitted variable are required, they can be calculated from the others. For example, to calculate the federal corporate profits tax yield, use the inverse to calculate ΔP^* and substitute this value in equation (21).

TABLE 4

INVERSE MATRIX

Equation No.	ΔA	ΔD	ΔND	ΔS	ΔID	ΔIND	ΔR	ΔG^*	ΔE
01	1.113	.089	.113	.046	.350	.048	.100	1.660	.113
02	.117	1.092	.118	.048	.351	.050	.101	1.676	.114
03	.130	.103	1.130	.053	.068	.483	.112	1.854	.126
04	.091	.072	.091	1.037	.047	.039	.078	1.298	.088
08	.092	.073	.093	.037	1.048	.040	.078	1.304	.089
09	.092	.073	.093	.037	.048	1.040	.078	1.304	.089
10	− .095	− .076	− .097	− .040	− .050	− .041	.921	−1.318	− .089
11	.092	.073	.093	.037	.048	.042	.078	1.304	.089
12	.884	.623	.793	.321	.439	.339	.192	3.205	1.218
13	− .118	.091	.116	.047	− .008	.049	.010	.167	.011
14	8.621	8.030	10.220	4.133	4.845	4.364	2.283	37.929	2.579
15	.184	.171	.218	.088	.103	.093	.049	.809	.055
16	− .040	− .037	− .047	− .019	− .022	− .020	− .012	− .175	− .012
17	.040	.037	.047	.019	.022	.020	.012	.175	.012
18	− .179	− .166	− .212	− .086	− .100	− .090	− .047	− .786	− .053
19	.202	.188	.240	.097	.114	.102	.054	.890	.061
20	.254	.237	.302	.122	.143	.129	.067	1.119	.076
21	− .046	− .043	− .055	− .022	− .026	− .024	− .012	− .204	− .014
22	− .254	− .237	− .302	− .122	− .143	− .129	− .067	−1.119	− .076
24	− .040	− .037	− .047	− .019	− .022	− .020	− .012	− .175	− .012
25	− .040	− .037	− .047	− .019	− .022	− .020	− .012	− .175	− .012
26	− .046	− .043	− .055	− .022	− .026	− .024	− .012	− .204	− .014
27	− .040	− .037	− .047	− .019	− .022	− .020	− .012	− .175	− .012
28	− .254	− .237	− .302	− .122	− .143	− .129	− .067	−1.119	− .076
29	− .040	− .037	− .047	− .019	− .022	− .020	− .012	− .175	− .012
30	− .254	− .237	− .302	− .122	− .143	,− .129	− .067	−1.119	− .076
31	.101	.391	.498	.201	.143	.213	.088	1.461	.099
32	.058	.221	.281	.114	.081	.120	.050	.825	.056

Projections

01	$4.710 - .495A_{-1} + .260\Delta L_{-1} - .177\Delta X_f - .177\Delta X_s$
02	$.262 - .0694D_{-1} + .0784\Delta L_{-1}$
03	$- .149 + .205\Delta ND_{-1} + .143\Delta L_{-1}$
04	$.363 + .530\Delta S_{-1} + .0381\Delta L_{-1}$
08	$0 + .591\Delta PD + .305\Delta M_{+1} - .669ID_{-1}$
09	$0 - 1.121IND_{-1}$
10	$.369$
11	$0 + \Delta F + \Delta PE + \Delta H + \Delta g$
12	0
13	$0 + \Delta LF - \Delta E_0 - \Delta E_G$
14	$- .0743 + .00436P^*_{-1}$
15	0
16	$.763$
17	$0 - \Delta T_{bp} - \Delta T_{os}$

TABLE 4—(Continued)

Equa-tion No.	ΔW	ΔP^*	ΔDiv	$\Delta(P-P^*)$	Federal Tax Receipts	State and Local Tax Receipts	Social Ins. Contr.	ΔX_u	ΔY
01	.609	.694	.076	.076	.585	.066	.035	−.135	.506
02	.615	.780	.085	.084	.545	.068	.036	−.136	.525
03	.680	.875	.096	.096	.600	.072	.040	−.151	.583
04	.476	.606	.066	.066	.414	.060	.028	−.105	.407
08	.478	.638	.070	.069	.432	.028	.028	−.106	.414
09	.478	.638	.070	.069	.432	.028	.028	−.106	.414
10	−.483	−.719	−.079	−.078	−.546	−.030	−.029	.107	−.431
11	.478	.638	.074	.069	.458	.030	.030	−.106	.438
12	6.568	−3.586	−.395	−.390	−1.002	.076	.319	−1.455	3.539
13	−.952	.997	.109	.109	.430	.016	.009	1.181	.516
14	60.808	−25.478	−2.806	−2.767	−4.726	1.091	.579	−3.082	45.619
15	1.297	−.543	−.059	−.060	−.101	.023	.012	−.066	.973
16	−.064	−.980	−.107	−.107	−.544	−.026	−.009	.014	−.211
17	−.064	.980	.107	.107	.544	.026	.009	−.014	.211
18	−.288	.651	.075	−1.038	.106	−.021	−.067	.064	−.946
19	.326	.395	1.040	.043	.497	.045	.019	−.072	1.070
20	.410	.496	.040	.054	.378	.045	.024	−.091	1.346
21	−.075	−.090	−.238	−.010	.886	−.010	−.004	.017	−.245
22	−.410	−.496	−.040	−.054	.622	−.045	−.024	.091	−1.346
24	−.064	−.980	−.107	−.107	.456	−.026	−.009	.014	−.211
25	−.064	−.980	−.107	−.107	.456	−.026	−.009	.014	−.211
26	−.075	−.090	−.238	−.010	−.114	.990	−.004	.017	−.245
27	−.064	−.980	−.107	−.107	−.544	.974	−.009	.014	−.211
28	−.410	−.497	−.040	−.054	−.378	.955	−.024	.091	−1.346
29	−.064	−.980	−.107	−.107	−.544	−.026	.991	.014	−.211
30	−.410	−.497	−.040	−.054	−.378	−.045	.976	.091	−1.346
31	.535	.661	.072	.072	.486	.059	.031	1.651	2.224
32	.303	.374	.041	.041	.274	.033	.018	.932	1.256

Projections—Continued

18	$-1.027-.902\Delta P_f$
19	$-.0191+.0198(P^*-T_{fc}-T_{sc}-Div)_{-1}$
20	$0+\Delta W_G+\Delta i_G+\Delta X_f+\Delta X_s+\Delta X_{GI}-\Delta T_{op}-\Delta T_{sg}+\Delta T_{ref}$
21	0
22	$0+.111\Delta W_G+.150\Delta i_G$
24	0
25	$.012$
26	0
27	0
28	$0+.010(\Delta W_G+\Delta i_G)$
29	0
30	$0+.129\Delta E_G$
31	$0-.140(\Delta LF-\Delta LF_{-1})$
32	$.101$

TABLE 5

Selected Multipliers

Multiplicand	GNP		Employment		Tax Receipts		Social Insurance		Government Surplus or Deficit (−)			
	Private	Total	Private	Total	Federal	State and Local	Contributions	Transfers	Federal	State and Local	Social Insurance	Total
Plant & Equipment[a]	1.690	1.690	0.115	0.115	0.586	0.058	0.038	−0.137	0.586	0.058	0.175	0.819
Federal Purchases from Firms	1.304	1.304	0.089	0.089	0.458	0.030	0.030	−0.106	−0.542	0.030	0.136	−0.376
Federal Employment[b]	0.921	1.921	0.063	0.263	0.348	0.037	0.044	−0.314	−0.652	0.036	0.358	−0.258
Federal Personal Income Tax Shift	−1.119	−1.119	−0.076	−0.076	0.622	−0.045	−0.024	0.091	0.622	−0.045	−0.115	0.462

a Additional expenditure of $1 billion of which half is spent for producers' durable equipment.
b Additional expenditure of $1 billion in government wages to hire 0.2 million new workers.

We also recall that government tax policy can be expressed by shifts in the equations themselves. As shown in Part I, these shift multipliers are equal to the weights found in the row of the inverse matrix that corresponds to the equation being shifted. Thus we see from the -1.119 in row (22) of the GNP column that a $1 billion shift in the federal personal tax function will reduce private GNP by $1.1 billion, etc. Note again [row (22) of the federal tax column] that an upward shift of $1 billion in the federal income tax *schedule* increases federal tax *yield* by only $622 million due to the decline in personal income and expenditure associated with the rise in taxes.

Some multiplier effects of a selection of government actions are given in Table 5. As before, once the multipliers are worked out they can be combined in any desired proportions. Thus an increase in government purchases of $2 billion coupled with additional government wages of $0.5 billion and an upward shift of the personal tax schedule of $1.3 billion would produce a total change in GNP of $(2 \times 1.304) + (0.5 \times 1.921) + (1.3 \times -1.119) = \$2.1$ billion. The same program would raise total employment by 0.211 million, and add $0.60 billion to the federal deficit.

D. *A Digression on Deficit Financing*

An interesting and important conclusion to be drawn from Table 5 is that the impact of a government action cannot be measured by merely the existence, or even the size of a surplus or deficit. In the first place it makes a great deal of difference whose deficit is under discussion, and it is not always clear whether deficit "multipliers" are supposed to be applied to the federal deficit or to the consolidated government sector. In what follows we confine ourselves to the latter. In the second place, surpluses and deficits result from courses of action; they are the difference between certain expenditures and receipts. While it is elementary that expenditures promote and taxes retard economic activity, the net result depends not only on the amounts of expenditures and tax yields, but also on the kinds, and we cannot speak unqualifiedly of a deficit multiplier.

Although this point can be made from purely theoretical considerations [4, pp. 133–55], the econometric model shows the substantial order of magnitudes involved. We see from Table 5, for example, that a $1 billion consolidated deficit will result from either $\$1 \div 0.376 = \$2.66$ billion of federal government purchases or, say a cut of $\$1 \div 0.462 = \$2.16$ billion in the federal income tax schedule. Yet the former action raises total GNP by $1.304 \times 2.66 = \$3.47$ billion, while the latter generates an increase of only $1.119 \times \$2.16 = \$2.42$ billion.

This result can be generalized. According to the multipliers in the last column of Table 5, the consolidated balance (surplus or deficit) is given by

$$\Delta b = -0.376\Delta g + 0.462\Delta a$$

where Δb is the change in the balance and Δa is the shift in the federal income tax schedule. A wide range of combinations of expenditures and taxes will produce the same budgetary balance. In fact, if we set Δb at some fixed value, say $\Delta b = 2$, then

$$2 = -0.376\Delta g + 0.462\Delta a$$

is the equation of an "isobalance" locus. That is, every combination of expenditures and taxation that satisfies this equation produces a $2 billion increase in consolidated surplus. Three isobalance lines—corresponding to a $1 billion surplus, a balanced budget and a $1 billion deficit—are plotted as solid lines in Figure 2.

Fig. 2

RELATIONSHIP OF GNP AND DEFICIT TO GOVERNMENT PURCHASES AND
LEVEL OF PERSONAL TAXES

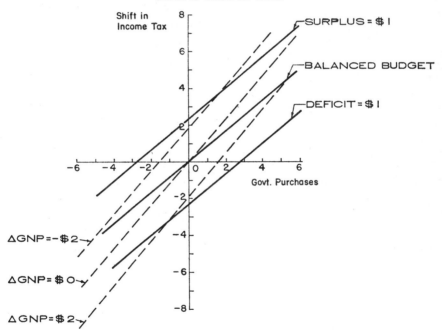

By the same token, the increase in total GNP is given by:

$$\Delta GNP = 1.304\Delta g - 1.119\Delta a,$$

and if we assign, say $\Delta GNP = 5$, then

$$5 = 1.304\Delta g - 1.119\Delta a$$

is the equation of an "iso-GNP" locus. Three of these are plotted as broken lines in Figure 2.

Inspection of the figure immediately shows that any specified increase in GNP can be attained in association with a wide range of balances and that any deficit or surplus may be associated with a wide range of impacts on GNP. In fact, a government program can simultaneously generate a substantial deficit and a sharp deflation, or a substantial surplus and general expansion. Since transfers, corporate profits taxes, defense orders, and government employment will have still other isobalance and iso-GNP lines, this merely scratches the surface of the possibilities.

E. *Dynamic Responses and Long-Run Multipliers*

As shown in Part I, dynamic responses are studied by iteration. Among the initial impacts of any program, we must find the effects on automobile demand, inventory accumulation, plant and equipment, and other variables whose values re-enter the system with a lag. These form a set of additional knowns for the next year. Using these values, in turn, gives rise to another set, etc. Repeating this operation enables us to follow the implications of a given program over as long a period as desired. It appears, however, that the dynamic elements stabilize by the end of the fifth year, and the system can be treated as in equilibrium after five iterations.

A complete study of the dynamic behavior of each variable in response to each possible policy action cannot be presented here, but Table 6 shows the response of the GNP and its components to a permanent increase of $1 billion in government expenditure. The tabulated figures are the values of the variables measured as deviations from their levels as of year 0 before the shift in expenditure policy.

TABLE 6

DYNAMIC RESPONSES TO A PERMANENT INCREASE OF $1 BILLION IN
GOVERNMENT EXPENDITURE

(Tabulated figures are deviations from initial levels)

	Year				
	1	2	3	4	5
Gross National Product[a]	1.304	1.619	1.582	1.545	1.335
Automobiles and Parts	0.092	0.088	0.050	0.042	0.014
Other Durables	0.073	0.104	0.113	0.117	0.104
Nondurables	0.093	0.159	0.193	0.215	0.213
Services	0.037	0.075	0.104	0.126	0.134
Plant and Equipment	0.	0.186	0.173	0.133	0.082
Inventory					
Durable Goods	0.048	0.079	0.017	−0.010	−0.031
Nondurable Goods	0.040	0.023	0.012	0.008	−0.002
Net Foreign Investment	−0.078	−0.101	−0.103	−0.103	−0.098
Government Purchases	1.	1.	1.	1.	1.

[a] Detail may not add to total because of rounding.

In response to increased government expenditure, the GNP rises by $1.3 billion the first year and under the stimulation of the dynamic factors climbs to a maximum of $1.6 billion over its initial level. It declines thereafter under the backpressure of accumulating stocks. The behavior of the individual components is in keeping with their respective natures. Automobile demand rises immediately to its maximum and declines slowly as the stock of cars on the road accumulates. Consumer expenditure for durables rises sharply and levels off, while outlays on nondurable goods and services continue to rise throughout the period, although at declining rates.

Investment in plant and equipment spurts in response to the immediate improvement in corporate profits and tapers off as the new plant becomes available. Inventory accumulation occurs at a high rate, but durable inventory overshoots and the rate of accumulation is forced somewhat below the year 0 level.

IV. CONCLUSION

To approximate the behavior of a complex economy by a set of 32 linear approximations is a heroic simplification. Yet experience has shown the statistical model to be a useful and flexible device for economic forecasting. Moreover, while the system of equations is small in relation to the vast structure of pure theory, it is considerably more elaborate than other devices that can be brought to bear on a practical level. Indeed, if an econometric model is nothing else, it is a highly sophisticated method of observing the past operation of the economy and systematizing the information obtained.

Yet, once the technical work of constructing the model is completed, a competent economist needs little more than a knowledge of elementary algebra to understand its nature, or to apply it to a wide range of analytical problems. Properly used, the model provides quantitative estimates of economic responses to specified changes in conditions. It goes without saying that the accuracy of these estimates is below the level that might be inferred from the precision of their statement in the text. But they show the proper order of magnitude involved and fall well within the practical tolerances required for effective policy evaluation.

REFERENCES

1. GOLDBERGER, A. S., *Impact Multipliers and Dynamic Properties of the Klein-Goldberger Model*. Amsterdam, 1959.
2. GUTTENTAG, J. M., "The Short Cycle in Residential Construction," *Am. Econ. Rev.*, Vol. 31 (June, 1961), pp. 275–98.
3. KLEIN, L. R., AND GOLDBERGER, A. S., *An Econometric Model of the United States, 1929–1952*. Amsterdam, 1955.

4. SAMUELSON, P. A., "The Simple Mathematics of Income Determination," in *Income, Employment and Public Policy*: *Essays in Honor of Alvin Hansen*, New York, 1948.

5. SUITS, D. B., "The Demand for New Automobiles in the United States *1929–1956*," *Rev. Econ. Stat.*, Vol. 40 (August, 1958), pp. 273–80.

6. WEIDENBAUM, M. L., *Government Spending*: *Process and Measurement*. Seattle: The Boeing Co., 1958.

33

Rate of Change Approaches to Forecasting—Diffusion Indexes and First Differences*[1]

By SIDNEY S. ALEXANDER†

A DIFFUSION INDEX for any time period and for any group of time series is simply the number of series in the group that are rising in that time period expressed as a percentage of the total number of series in the group. An *historical* diffusion index is one in which a series is classed as rising or falling by reference to its own peaks and troughs, identified well after the event. Consequently, even though a series is rising from month to month over a certain period, it may still be classed as falling if the period is part of a downswing as identified subsequently.

Historical diffusion indexes have been shown by Geoffrey Moore[2] consistently to lead the turning points of the general business cycle, typically by eight months or so in the case of peaks, 1919–37. This lead holds in the post-war period also.

---

* *Economic Journal*, Vol. LXVIII (June, 1958). Reprinted by courtesy of the Royal Economic Society and the author.

† Massachusetts Institute of Technology.

[1] The statistical work underlying this paper was supported by the Sloan Research Fund of the School of Industrial Management at M.I.T.

[2] *Statistical Indicators of Cyclical Revivals and Recessions* (Occasional Paper 31), National Bureau of Economic Research, 1950, henceforth referred to as *S.I.*; "Analyzing Business Cycles," *American Statistician*, April–May, 1954, "The Diffusion of Business Cycles," in R. A. Solo (ed.), *Economics and the Public Interest* (Rutgers University Press, 1955); *Twenty-sixth, Thirtieth, Thirty-third*, and *Thirty-seventh Annual Reports of the National Bureau of Economic Research*; Thor Hultgren, *Cyclical Diversities in the Fortunes of Industrial Corporations* (Occasional Paper 32), National Bureau of Economic Research, 1950; Milton Lipton, National Industrial Conference Board, *Business Record*, June, 1954, pp. 227–33, and June, 1955, pp. 212–17; and NICB Technical Paper No. 5, *Cyclical Diffusion: A New Tool for Business Analysis*, 1956. For more critical approaches see Arthur L. Broida, "Diffusion Indexes," *American Statistician*, June, 1955, pp. 7–16, and reply by Moore, *American Statistician*, October, 1955, pp. 13–18, and John E. Maher, "Forecasting Industrial Production," *Journal of Political Economy*, Vol. LXV, No. 2 (April, 1957), pp. 158–65. Broida anticipated many of the negative findings of this paper, and Maher's findings with respect to the leading-series approach closely parallel those of this paper with respect to the diffusion-index approach.

The object of the present inquiry is to find whether a similar *current* measure can be constructed which also displays a long and unambiguous lead over business-cycle turning points. To this end we may ask which of the operations involved in the construction of a diffusion index are critically important for the forecasting value of a diffusion index, and which are irrelevant. Can the important ones successfully be performed currently, that is, with a lag that is small relative to the lead time of the diffusion index over business-cycle turns?

A diffusion index is constructed by the following operations:

1. A *smoothing* operation, either on the individual series or on the final index, to iron out fluctuations which are not cyclical in the business-cycle sense.
2. A *differencing* operation on the individual series.
3. A *transformation* of the differences to a two-valued system of attributes: rising and falling.
4. An *equally weighted count* of the number of series rising, expressed as a percentage of the total number of series in the group.

A test of the predictive power of a current diffusion index based on fifteen to twenty-six of the components of the Federal Reserve Board Index of Industrial Production, as compared with the first differences of the F.R.B. Index itself, leads to the following conclusions:

1. The *smoothing* operation is necessary, but it may be performed currently with a loss in lead time that is small compared to the length of lead time involved. A currently smoothed diffusion index of the F.R.B. Index components led business-cycle peaks, in the inter-war and post-war period, by six to twelve months.
2. The *differencing* operation is also fundamental, but it may be performed currently on an aggregate, such as the F.R.B. Index, about as effectively as on the components.
3. The *transformation* of the quantitative differences to a two-valued system of attributes, rising and falling, is not essential to the lead over turning points. The first difference of the F.R.B. Index, which preserves quantitative relations, leads turning points just about as well as does the corresponding current diffusion index. A diffusion index based on a large number of series may be somewhat smoother than the first difference of the corresponding aggregate, however.
4. Nor is the *weighting* operation fundamental, since the equally weighted diffusion index and the unequally weighted first difference of the F.R.B. Index behave similarly with respect to their leads over business-cycle turning points.
5. While the use of *hindsight* is not fundamental to the lead over business-cycle turns, hindsight *is* of fundamental importance in avoiding false forecasts, or more accurately, in distinguishing forecasts of minor fluctuations from those of fluctuations large enough to be called business cycles.

In short, a currently smoothed first difference of the F.R.B. Index has about the same predictive value as a currently smoothed diffusion index based on the components of the F.R.B. Index. Both lead all recognised business-cycle peaks in the F.R.B. Index (1919–37 and 1947–56) by six to twelve months, but both also reflect numerous minor intermediate fluctuations with a lead close to zero. The signals for a minor fluctuation do not seem to be contemporaneously distinguishable from those for a "real" business-cycle turning point.

A current rate of change measure, either first difference or diffusion, does, nevertheless, have a genuine predictive value, even though it falls far short of an historical diffusion index. First, it has the negative predictive value that unless a slow down of the rate of growth has taken place, no business-cycle downturn is to be expected. Second, there appears to be sufficient stability in the sign, the level and possibly in the direction of movement of the smoothed rate of change to make it a useful short-term predictor of itself, and hence of the short-term future movements of the smoothed aggregate index. There is hope, therefore, of predicting, from the trend of first differences or of diffusion measures, the ups and downs of a smooth curve through the F.R.B. Index, but not of distinguishing, at the outset of a change of direction, whether it is a major or minor swing.

Whatever its limitations in forecasting what is going to happen, a diffusion index, particularly when cumulated, does furnish a valuable measure of what *is* happening. Because a current cumulated diffusion index can probably be made available some weeks earlier than the corresponding weighted aggregate index, and because it appears to be slightly smoother and to have substantially better defined turning points, it may be found to be a most valuable tool for the interpretation of current developments, possibly superior even to the F.R.B. Index.

THE NATIONAL BUREAU APPROACH TO FORECASTING

In *Statistical Indicators of Cyclical Revivals and Recessions* Moore explored two approaches to business-cycle forecasting arising out of the work of the National Bureau of Economic Research. One, the leading series approach, an extension of the work of Burns and Mitchell,[3] consists of a search for series which characteristically lead turning points of the business cycle, as clouds precede a storm.[4] A second approach, similar in spirit to a forecasting technique developed by C. Ashley Wright,[5] depends on the assumption, not that a particular series or set of series will characteristically lead business-cycle turning points, but that some series will always lead. That is, the leading series, or Burns and Mitchell, approach always looks to the same series to lead; the diffusion index, or Ashley Wright approach, depends on the empirical observation that all series do not turn simultaneously at a cyclical turning point, but there is a gradual build-up of the number of series that have

---

[3] Wesley C. Mitchell and Arthur F. Burns, *Statistical Indicators of Cyclical Revivals* (Bulletin 69), National Bureau of Economic Research, 1938.

[4] For a constructively critical contribution to the leading series approach, see Maher, *op. cit.*

[5] "Business Cycle Research and Business Policy," *Conference on Business Cycles*, National Bureau of Economic Research (New York, 1951), pp. 339–74.

turned as a turning point is approached, a build-up that reaches a peak at the turning point itself. It may accordingly be possible to predict the imminence of a turning point, and its timing as well, by a projection of the rate of build-up of a cluster of turning points in individual series in the early stage of the build-up.

Wright actually fitted the tail of a normal curve to the build-up in its early stages and predicted the turning point as the central point of the curve so fitted. Moore's approach is to construct a diffusion index, a measure of the percentage of a specified group of economic series that is rising at any time. A broadly based diffusion index will characteristically reach a peak well before the peak of the business cycle, and will cross the 50% line in the neighbourhood of a business-cycle turning point.

One such diffusion index (based on 404 economic time series with "acceptable conformity") was found to lead peaks and troughs of the general business cycle, in different periods, on the average by eight to thirteen months, and others behaved similarly.[6] This historical diffusion index led every business cycle by a substantial lead time, it skipped none, and it indicated no turning points (except 1933–35) that did not occur. "Hence the intriguing possibility presents itself that we may be able to recognise the clusters [of turning points] well before the peak or trough in aggregate economic activity."[7]

CURRENT SMOOTHING

One major hurdle must be leaped over, or cleared away, before this technique can be used for forecasting, however. The diffusion indexes which give such early and unambiguous forecasts of business-cycle turning points are *historical* diffusion indexes. A component series is counted as rising in any month, irrespective of whether it is moving up or down in that month, so long as it follows a trough and precedes a peak, as determined many months, or even years, later. It is very hard, currently, to say whether a series is rising or falling in this historical sense. That is itself a forecast.

Of course, a diffusion index can be constructed on the basis of current month-to-month movements. Such an index is shown as the thin line fluctuating around curve *B* in Chart 1. It is based on fifteen to twenty-six components of the Federal Reserve Board Index of Industrial Production.[8] It clearly does not exhibit the one-to-one relation of its own turning points with those of business cycles that is characteristic of Moore's historical diffusion indexes. The use of the historical definition of rising or falling involves, obviously, an heroic act of smoothing.

Smoothing introduces a lag. Thus, if either the individual series or the diffusion index itself is smoothed by a twelve-month equally weighted moving

---

[6] *S.I.*, Table 10, pp. 46–47.
[7] *S.I.*, p. 45.
[8] Kindly furnished by Moore, whose splendid co-operation should not go unmentioned.

CHART 1

FRB INDEX OF INDUSTRIAL PRODUCTION AND ASSOCIATED RATE OF CHANGE
MEASURES

(Solid vertical lines indicate peaks, broken vertical lines, troughs, of FRB index)

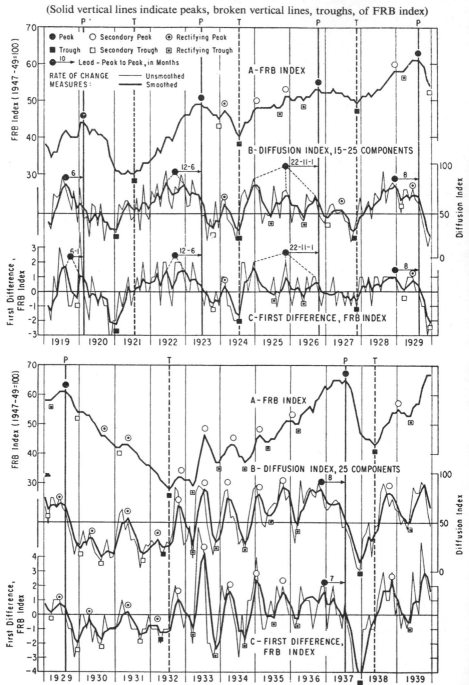

CHART 1—(*Continued*)

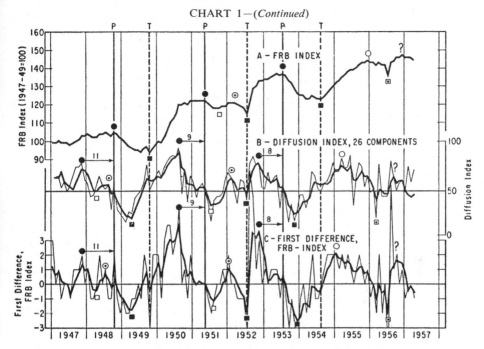

average, a five-and-a-half-month lag will be introduced. Moore has experimented in this manner, and his conclusion is that even with this reduction in lead time the results are still useful in forecasting. He also uses shorter moving averages and tries to interpret the rather erratic results. But cannot a smoothing be achieved that gets rid of most of the erratic fluctuation in the current month-to-month diffusion index and still leaves a substantial lead time?

The answer seems to be yes. Curve *B* in the chart shows a currently smoothed version of the diffusion index based on fifteen to twenty-six components of the F.R.B. Index, plotted contemporaneously.[9] That is, the smoothed value plotted for June, 1935 is the value that can be computed the day that the F.R.B. Index for June, 1935 becomes available. From an historical point of view it would be more appropriate to center this smoothed curve one month earlier, but that is not done in the present forecasting context because it is not actually available one month earlier. The turning points of the smoothed curve may accordingly lag about a month or so

---

[9] The smoothing formula used was: $14Y_t = 5x_t + 4x_{t-1} + 3x_{t-2} + 2x_{t-3} + x_{t-4} - x_{t-6}$, where Y_t is the smoothed value and x_t the original observation. This corresponds to fitting a second-degree polynomial to each set of seven successive observations and reading off the value corresponding to the next to the last observation. The value corresponding to the last observation was not chosen because it would involve greater computational complexity. This general type of smoothing was chosen because, based on a second-degree parabola, it would preserve curvilinearity that an equally weighted moving average would iron out. Secondly, the steadily declining weights give this smoothing formula the advantage of a substantially shorter lag at the turning points than that of an equally weighted moving average of comparable smoothing power.

behind the turning-point dates of the unsmoothed series that can be identified by hindsight. Of course, if greater smoothness is required a longer lag must be accepted.

The currently smoothed diffusion index has quite definite peaks and troughs, although there are frequent one- and two-month interruptions of the main fluctuations. A little more smoothing, certainly introducing no more than another month's lag, would eliminate most of these interruptions. And the peaks and troughs of the smoothed contemporaneous diffusion index certainly lead the corresponding peaks and troughs of the general business cycle.

For simplicity, let us confine our attention to the peaks. Similar findings also apply to the troughs, with some qualifications, principally that the leads are shorter.

TABLE 1

LEADS OF PREDICTING SERIES OVER BUSINESS-CYCLE PEAKS 1919–39 AND 1947–55

Year of Peak	Predicted Series Peak		Lead of Predictor (Months)			Drop in (2) up to Predicted Peak (Points)
	N.B.E.R. Reference Cycle	F.R.B. Index	(1) Moore's Diffusion Index[a]	(2) Current Diffusion Index[b]	(3) First Difference[c]	
1920	January	February	6	6	6–1[d]	24
1923	May	June	9	6–12[d]	6–12[d]	16–19[d]
1926	October	October	21	22–11–1[d]	22–11–1[d]	17–6–3[d]
1929	June	August	8	8[f]	8[f]	11
1937	May	July	8	8	7	29
1948	November	October		11[f]	11[f]	24
1951[e]	—	May		9	9	37
1953	July	July		8	8	25

   [a] 404 series with acceptable conformity; S.I., Table 10, pp. 46–47.
   [b] 1919–22, 15 components F.R.B. Index; 1923–40, 25 components; 1947–56, 26 components; smoothed by formula of footnote 9. Curve B on chart.
   [c] First difference of F.R.B. Index, smoothed by formula of footnote 9. Curve C.
   [d] Multiple peaks in predicting series.
   [e] Possibly should not be considered a "real" business-cycle peak, cf. footnote 21.
   [f] This prediction impaired by a false trough in the predictor before the predicted series actually peaked.

Table 1 shows the leads of the relevant peaks of this contemporaneously smoothed diffusion index of the fifteen to twenty-six components of the F.R.B. Index over the peaks of the Index itself, 1919–39 and 1947–56. The corresponding leads of Moore's historical diffusion index of 403 conforming series over the National Bureau's turning points, 1919–37, are shown in Table 1. The difference in peak dates reflects principally the difference in timing of the F.R.B. Index peaks from those of the general business cycle as dated by the National Bureau, since the National Bureau's general criteria for dating peaks and troughs were followed in both cases.[10] The National Bureau's measures indicate a one-month average lag of the F.R.B. Index behind general business-cycle peaks, 1919–38.[11]

The smoothed-current diffusion index had substantially the same leads over cycle peaks in the F.R.B. Index as Moore's historical diffusion index had over peaks in the general business cycle.[12] It must certainly be considered a highly satisfactory forecasting device if it is not vitiated by disadvantages in other respects. It may accordingly be concluded that the current smoothing problem is surmountable, at least in the sense that a turning point in the predicting series can be recognised some six months to a year before the corresponding turning point can be recognised in the predicted series.[13]

IS THE DIFFUSION INDEX NECESSARY?

But is the diffusion index necessary, or is there a more easily obtained measure that will forecast as satisfactorily? Aside from the smoothing operation, the three characteristic operations involved in a diffusion index are:

1. *Differencing* the individual series.
2. *Transforming* the differences into a two-valued system: rising or falling.
3. *Weighting* the resulting binary values equally as among series.

Differencing the Aggregate versus Differencing the Components

Broida[14] has pointed out that a measure of the rate of change in an aggregate would often lead turning points just as a diffusion index does.

---

[10] Arthur F. Burns and Wesley C. Mitchell, *Measuring Business Cycles*, National Bureau of Economic Research (New York, 1947), p. 58. Substantially, the peak month is the last month before lower levels are encountered.

[11] *S.I.*, Table 2, p. 7.

[12] The only conspicuous difference is possibly with respect to the 1926 peak. There are three peaks in each predicting series, each of which might be matched with the peak in the predicted series. Their leads are twenty-two, eleven and one months, respectively. The predicting peak with the largest lead corresponds almost exactly to Moore's lead of 21 months. (Actually, the predicting peak being almost flat, its lead could be dated 21 months as appropriately as twenty-two months.) The predicting peak with the shortest lead leads the predicted peak by only one month, although the flat predicted peak might reasonably be dated five months later, so that the shortest lead would then be six months.

[13] It might be argued, in view of the lag of the availability of the data behind the months to which they refer, and the fact that it takes at least one and possibly two or three months beyond the turning point to identify it, that the forecasting lead of the currently smoothed diffusion index is too short to be useful. But whatever lag in the appearance of the data or in the interpretation thereof applies to the predictor series also applies to the predicted series. Thus, if the peak, clearly defined, of the predictor series leads the peak, equally well defined, of the predicted series by six months, and if there is a lag of two months in the availability of the data and another two months are required to recognise a turning point clearly, the corresponding total four-month lag applies to both predictor and predicted, and it will still be true that the turning point can be recognised six months earlier from the predictor series than from the predicted series. In short, the peak-to-peak lead is an appropriate measure of the effective lead for forecasting purposes if the two series are equally smooth.

[14] *Op. cit.*, p. 13.

"In periods of expansion, for example, the rate of increase in industrial production frequently would decline before the peak is reached, and be near zero around the peak. In periods of contraction, as the trough is approached, the rate of decline would tend to fall off and be near zero around the trough." Moore agrees "that certain types of diffusion indexes, namely those computed by taking directions of change over identical intervals in the components of economic aggregates, are closely correlated with the rates of change in the corresponding aggregate."[15] But he claims that there is a fundamental difference in that the diffusion index focuses attention on the components of the aggregate rather than on the aggregate itself.

It is hard to see why a diffusion index, a count of the relative frequency of positive first differences of the components, should put a stronger focus on the components than a conventional index which is a weighted average of the quantitative levels of the components. In either case the final index depends upon a weighted sum of the movements of individual components and has lost sight of the individuality of those components. The fact is that the diffusion index will differ from the first difference of a corresponding aggregate only because of the transformation and weighting operations. Broida doubts that anything is gained by the transformation of quantitative information into the two-valued attributes of rising and falling. He also argues that equal weighting is likely to be inferior to weighting by importance.

A comparison of the smoothed current diffusion index based on fifteen to twenty-six components of the F.R.B. Index (curve *B*) with a comparably smoothed first difference of the F.R.B. Index (curve *C*) indicates that little is lost by the two-valued transformation and equal weighting, but little is gained either. Nothing can be inferred from either of the curves *B* and *C* that cannot be inferred from the other. The only substantial difference is the superior performance of the diffusion index in 1919–20, when some ambiguity arose in the direction of movement of the first difference just before the downturn. Otherwise, the two curves are closely comparable, with the leads evenly balanced (see Table 1).

The choice between a diffusion index and the first difference of the aggregate, therefore, is almost purely one of convenience, so far as predicting turning points is concerned.

Weighting and Transformation Effects

The practical equivalence of curves *B* and *C*, for forecasting business-cycle turning points of curve *A*, also resolves the weighting and transformation problems. Obviously, neither the weighting nor the transformation makes critical difference, since the equally weighted and two-valued transformed diffusion index yields substantially the same information as the first

---

[15] *American Statistician*, October, 1955, p. 13.

difference of the carefully weighted F.R.B. Index with the quantitative differences preserved.

We may conclude, then, that the smoothing and the differencing are essential to the forecasting value of these predictors, while the weighting and the transformation are not.

The Agreement Is Empirical

A diffusion index and the first difference of a weighted aggregate index do not necessarily have to agree in their turning points. They will agree in certain circumstances, but not in others.

They can generally be expected to agree, however. When an increasing number of series is rising the average rise will usually also be increasing, and the two measures will move together. This should be our normal expectation, and it is, in fact, found to be the usual case in the data here under review.

But it is possible for the diffusion index to rise while the first difference falls. If, as the number of series rising increases, the rising series rise by declining amounts and the falling series fall by increasing amounts, the two measures may diverge. In this case the peak of the first difference can lead that of the diffusion index.

Of more interest to those who favour the use of the diffusion index is the possibility that the diffusion index may lead the first difference of the aggregate index. If, as the number of series rising decreases, the series still rising increase their rates of rise, the first difference may continue to rise even though the diffusion index is falling.

These theoretically possible differences in behaviour of the two measures do not seem to be encountered in practice, except in the form of occasional month-to-month divergences that must be considered erratic fluctuations.

Another type of divergence occurs when there is a highly intense disturbance localised in a single sector of the economy, such as a steel strike. In such cases the first difference of the aggregate is more severely affected than is the diffusion index.

In view of the high frequency of extreme items in economic time series, a diffusion index, taken over a very large number of components, can be expected to be smoother than the corresponding first difference of aggregates. The transformation operation, which cuts all quantitative variations down to the same size, can produce a smoother movement, especially when a very large number of components enter into the diffusion index, than that of the first difference of the weighted aggregate. The latter is more strongly affected by large disturbances in a small number of series, especially if they are heavily weighted.

It does appear that the same smoothing operator applied to the two predictors yields a slightly smoother curve for the diffusion index than for the first difference, especially over that period when the diffusion index is based on twenty-five or twenty-six components rather than fifteen. (Compare curves *B* and *C* from 1923 on.) It can be inferred that, were the diffusion index based on many more series, say the 175 monthly series underlying the F.R.B. Index, it would have a substantial advantage in smoothness.[16]

A simple, early and relatively smooth approximation to the F.R.B. Index can be made by cumulating an unweighted diffusion index. It should be possible, even before the end of each month, to get for many of the 175 component activities underlying the F.R.B. Index a judgment as to whether they are moving up or down for the month. The resulting diffusion index, cumulated, will closely agree with the F.R.B. Index itself, which would become available only several weeks later. Such differences as may be observed in the two measures, and they are slight, give the advantage, for forecasting purposes, to the cumulated diffusion index.[17] The latter's small advantage in smoothness is particularly evident in the neighbourhood of turning points, so that its turning points are more sharply defined. Whatever the forecasting value of a diffusion index may be, a cumulated diffusion index clearly has a substantial value as a smooth and prompt measure of current developments, a value possibly superior to the best measures now in general use, such as the F.R.B. Index.

While the diffusion index is somewhat smoother than the first difference of an aggregate, this advantage is insignificant, so far as forecasting turning points is concerned, compared to a disadvantage common to both predictors, a tendency to produce false leads.[18]

FALSE LEADS

Moore's historical diffusion index not only called all the cyclical turning points correctly and with a substantial lead, it never called a wrong turn, except in 1933–35. The current diffusion index, and the first differences, as shown in the chart, unfortunately call a large number of wrong turns. More accurately, there are a number of peaks and troughs in the two smoothed current predictors that do not correspond to the conventionally recognised turning points in the business cycle. Each false lead is given by both predictors, which agree as well on the false peaks and troughs as on the true ones.

As shown in Table 2 there were eleven "false peaks"[19] indicated on

---

[16] See Moore, *American Statistician*, October, 1955, Chart 1, p. 15, for a dramatic illustration of the smoothing power of the diffusion index based on 225 new orders series, National Association of Purchasing Agents, as compared with the corresponding aggregate. That chart also compares the F.B.R. Index with a cumulated diffusion index based on twenty-six components of the F.R.B. Index.

[17] As can be inferred from reference of preceding footnote.

[18] The leading series approach is also subject to the same major shortcoming. See Maher, *op. cit.*

[19] Very short false leads of one to three months' duration were not counted, since they could presumably be smoothed away without introducing a lag that is long relative to the true leads. A subjective element enters into this count of false leads which could be removed

TABLE 2

Secondary Peaks or Plateaus Associated with "False Leads" in
Current Diffusion Index

F.R.B. Index components[a]

Date of Secondary Peak or Plateau[b]	Lead of Current Diffusion Index, Months	Length of Secondary Half-cycle Plateau, Months[c]	Drop in F.R.B. Index, %	Drop in Current Diffusion Index, Points
Plateau 1/25	1[d]	8	0	32
Peak 11/25	—1[d]	6	2	23
Peak 10/32	0	7	10	41
Peak 7/33	0	24	20	53
Peak 4/34	1	9	14	46
Peak 2/35	0	6	2	22
Peak 11/35	1	5	2	38
Peak 1/39	3	5	4	30
Peak 11/39	1	10	9	35
Peak 1/52	—1	7	2–4[e]	15
Peak 12/55	6–9	9	3–6[e]	35

[a] Cf. footnote *a*, Table 1.
[b] Dated as first month high is reached, not last as in Table 1.
[c] Number of months before high is surpassed.
[d] Can also be interpreted as a longer lead over true peak.
[e] Lesser figure implies rough adjustment to eliminate effect of steel strike.

upswings[20] in the period 1919–39 and 1947–56, in addition to the eight true peaks.[21] Ten of them were related to short downswings, and one to a flattening out in the rate of increase. The ten secondary half-cycles and one plateau lasted from one to ten months, except for one which lasted twenty-four months. The predicting series did not lead these downturns by more than three months, except in one recent case, and the median lead was only one month.

A comparison of the drops in the currently smoothed diffusion index that are associated with the false leads (final column, Table 2) with the drops associated with the true business-cycle peaks up to the point where

---

only by precisely specifying the smoothing to be applied and the criteria of peak identification to be used. That is, more false leads could be identified, but not fewer, unless true leads are also to be destroyed.

[20] False peaks indicated on downswings are not counted here because they would be relevant to the preceding false troughs. They occur when one is looking for a trough, and so are merely corrections of false indications of a trough. Such peaks are indicated as "rectifying peaks" in the chart, and similarly, false troughs on upswings are called "rectifying troughs."

[21] Assuming that May, 1951 was a genuine business-cycle peak. Even under the contrary assumption, the corresponding peak in the predicting series should not be counted as a false lead because the decline in the rate of increase was clearly related to governmental measures, and would not have been contemporaneously interpreted as a prediction of a recession. By the same token, 1951 might be deleted from the list of successfully predicted peaks in Table 1.

the peak appears (final column, Table 1) suggests that any smoothing which could eliminate the false leads would be likely also to eliminate the leads over the true business-cycle peaks. It is true that the potentialities for smoothing depend not only on the size of the drop but also on the entire configuration of the series in the neighbourhood of the false peak. But there is no clear difference in configuration of the predictors as between true and false peaks such as to suggest the possibility of currently smoothing out the false peaks without destroying the lead of the predictors over true peaks.

The "false leads" shown by the two predictors reflect more than merely random fluctuations in the data. They are related to genuine hesitations in the upward movements of the F.R.B. Index, hesitations which usually reflect developments that pervade the entire economy. Similar false leads are also shown by many other current diffusion indexes. Thus, Lipton's diffusion index based upon twelve statistical indicators, only five or six of which relate directly to industrial production, shows a pattern of false leads over the period 1921–39 almost identical with that shown by curves B and C.[22] An average duration of run measure applied to fifteen broadly heterogeneous statistical indicators also shows identical false leads.[23] This measure is based on month-to-month changes, and so behaves like a current, rather than an historical, diffusion index. Maher's regression of the F.R.B. Index on various leading series demonstrates not only a similar tendency to generate false leads but also a substantially similar pattern of the occurrence of the false leads.[24]

The one feature of the historical diffusion index that cannot be satisfactorily matched in a current diffusion index is, therefore, the smoothing out of false leads. Because these false leads cannot be eliminated in a current measure, the current predictors fall far short of the forecasting potential suggested by the crisp one-to-one leads of the historical diffusion indexes over business-cycle turning points.

The simple fact of the matter is that there are frequent hesitations in business-cycle upswings and downswings. A broad class of statistical indicators, which are either measures of rates of change or activities which are sensitive to rates of change, reflect these hesitations. It is not a mathematically necessary condition that every business-cycle turning point be preceded by a turning point in the rate of change, but empirically it seems to be so. Consequently, these indicators, sensitive to rates of change, generally lead business-cycle turning points; the ones considered in this paper do so without exception.

But not every hesitation *need* be followed by a business-cycle turning point, so many false leads are given. Consequently, a peak in one of these indicators

[22] N.I.C.B., *Business Record*, June, 1955, pp. 214–15.
[23] *S.I.*, Chart 7, p. 84.
[24] *Op. cit.*, especially Chart 1. Maher's regression, being less smooth, gives many more false leads, but it is clear that after some smoothing it would show many of the false leads shown by curves *B* and *C*.

can tell us that we *may* be heading into a downturn, but the chances, derived from the inter-war and post-war period, are about three to two that any particular hesitation will furnish a false rather than a true lead.[25] That is, the chances are three to two that a peak in the smoothed predicting series will be associated with a secondary peak or plateau in the predicted series rather than a "real" business-cycle peak.

LENGTH OF LEAD AS A DISCRIMINANT

Some forecasting value can possibly be derived from the fact that the predictors led the predicted series by six months or more in all cases of genuine business-cycle peaks, while, with only one exception, they had substantially zero lead over the downswings and plateau which must be regarded as false peaks. If, then, three months after a peak in the predictors no peak appears in the predicted series, the probability would seem to be high that the predicted downturn will actually turn out to be a significant business cycle and not a secondary peak or plateau.

The outstanding failure of this criterion in the period under review is, unfortunately, the most recent "false peak," that of December, 1955 (see Table 2). This "false peak" was predicted from six to nine months in advance by the smoothed current-diffusion index, and eleven months in advance by the first difference.

Even if we are prepared to dismiss this one exception as not disproving a rule which seems to apply to the ten other cases of false peaks, and to all eight cases of true peaks listed in Table 1, further scrutiny reveals that the proposed discriminant would have little value in practical operation. While, as indicated in Table 1, the peaks of the predictors led those of the predicted series by six to twelve months, they would not have been recognised contemporaneously as leading by so long a time. In all of the cases of true turning points listed in Table 1, with the possible exception of 1953, there was, within a month or two of the peak of the predicting series, a preliminary small downturn, or at least a short plateau, in the predicted series, which was soon thereafter surpassed.

Consequently, a contemporaneous attempt to apply the proposed discriminant would have led, in at least seven out of the eight cases of true peaks, to the matching of the peak in the predicting series with preliminary false peaks which were practically simultaneous with the peaks in the predictors. It would then be concluded, erroneously, that a secondary or false peak was being forecast. The difference in lead time that we are considering as a potential contemporaneous discriminant between true and false leads

---

[25] The chances are three to two on the assumption that the predictions are based on data smoothed to an extent consistent with the determination of the eleven false peaks of Table 2. A lesser degree of smoothing would yield more false peaks.

turns out, therefore, to be one that can be established, in all but one case, only by hindsight.

We cannot get away from the fact that while peaks are always led by slowdowns, slowdowns do not always lead to a business-cycle peak.

34

A Survey of Studies in the Analysis of Business Test Data*

By H. THEIL and D. B. JOCHEMS†

1. INTRODUCTORY

THE MUNICH BUSINESS TEST, which was devised by the *IFO-Institut für Wirtschaftsforschung* at Munich, is a survey with the following characteristics. It is based on monthly written questionnaires in which selected entrepreneurs of various branches of industry and trade are asked to state the direction of change of certain variables compared with the previous month, as well as the anticipated direction of change in the next month compared with the present. For example, a number of (individual) shoe manufacturers receive a questionnaire at the end of May, in which they are asked whether they raised or lowered or kept unchanged the rate of their production, their selling prices, etc. in that month compared with the April level; whether the number of orders received, their stocks of unfinished products, etc., increased or decreased or remained constant compared with the April level; also whether they plan to raise or to lower or to keep unchanged their production in June; and whether they expect that the number of orders received in June will be larger or smaller than or the same as the number received in May. These questionnaires are sent out regularly to the same firms, month after month, so that a multidimensional[1] time series of answers results. The number of possible answers is only three (increase, no change, or decrease, either realized or anticipated); it is up to the respondent how to interpret "no change"—no indications like percentage intervals are given. This general set-up has been

---

* Originally published in German under the title, "Ein Überblick über einige Studien zur Analyse von Konjunkturtestdaten," in *IFO-Studien: Zeitschrift des IFO Institut für Wirtschaftsforschung*, 1960, Vol. VI. Reprinted by courtesy of the publisher, Duncker und Humblot, the IFO Institut für Wirtschaftsforschung, and the authors.
† Netherlands School of Economics, Rotterdam; State Mines, Heerlen, Netherlands, formerly of the Netherlands School of Economics.
[1] This time series is multidimensional because it contains for each month specifications of changes in several variables, both realized and anticipated.

followed by a number of institutions outside Germany, sometimes with minor modifications.

The primary purpose of the Munich Business Test was and still is to supply detailed information on short-term economic changes on short notice. However, after a number of surveys were completed, it became clear that the resulting data are also very useful in providing a new source of information in economic statistics, which could be used to test the validity of economic theories on realized and planned or expected changes. In this connection we should mention in particular the name of Dr. O. Anderson, Jr., who was the first in analyzing these data. The purpose of the present paper is to give a summarizing picture of the work that has been carried out in this field by the Econometric Institute of the Netherlands School of Economics. In the first part (Sections 2 and 3) we shall consider the interrelationships among Business Test data themselves; in the second (Section 4) we consider the relations between these data and conventional statistical data. We start with the problem of the accuracy of the entrepreneurial forecasts as measured by their correspondence with the data on actual developments reported by the forecasters themselves (Section 2). Next, we consider (in Section 3) the "causal" problem of the development of such variables over time: how are expectations determined by observed facts and possibly by other expectations; how are plans determined by observations and expectations; and how is behavior determined by observations, expectations, and previous plans? After this, we consider the relationship between price, volume, and value data according to the Business Test, and the corresponding data of the more traditional statistical type; this takes place at the microlevel first (Sections 4.1 and 4.2), and then at a more aggregative level (Section 4.3).

2. MEASURING THE ACCURACY OF ENTREPRENEURIAL FORECASTS

2.1 *Accuracy Analysis at the Microlevel*

As stated in the Introduction, an entrepreneur who participates in the Business Test will report that he expects his sales to increase, say, in the next month; and one month later he will report whether he really observed this increase, or perhaps a decrease, or no change. It will be clear that data of this kind provide an opportunity to analyze the predictive power of firms of various types with respect to various types of variables. It is true that we have no guarantee that the participating entrepreneurs answer to the best of their knowledge, so that an accuracy analysis of this kind is open to the risk of certain spurious results. Even so, one may be of the opinion that it remains interesting to analyze the accuracy of the participants' statements in terms of a comparison with their own reports on actual facts afterwards.

The simplest type of comparison is that of a 3×3 table, which can be explained as follows. Suppose a firm or a group of firms answers the questions on anticipations and realizations in a series of successive months. Then we can count the number of cases in which an entrepreneur predicts an increase for the next month and reports an increase afterwards; and the number of cases in which he predicts an increase but reports no change, or a decrease. These frequencies will be denoted by f_{11}, f_{12}, f_{13}, respectively, where the first index refers to predictions, the second to corresponding realizations, and where 1 stands for increase, 2 for no change, 3 for decrease. The sum of these three f's is denoted by P_1, which is the total frequency of predicted increases. A similar notation is adopted if no change is predicted (f_{21}, f_{22}, f_{23}) and when a decrease is forecast. As a whole, these frequencies can be arranged as in Table 1.

TABLE 1

GENERAL FORM OF A PREDICTION-REALIZATION TABLE

Predictions	Realizations			Marginal Total
	Increase	No Change	Decrease	
Increase	f_{11}	f_{12}	f_{13}	P_1
No Change	f_{21}	f_{22}	f_{23}	P_2
Decrease	f_{31}	f_{32}	f_{33}	P_3
Marginal Total	A_1	A_2	A_3	N

Tables of this kind were analyzed in great detail by Jochems and Boot [12].[2] A summarizing picture is presented in Table 2, which contains the total frequencies of the aggregate material which they had at their disposal. This material includes data of the German textile trade and industry, of the German paper trade and industry, of the Dutch shoe industry, and of the Swedish engineering and textile industry.[3] It is seen from Table 2 that in each of the three columns and each of the three rows the diagonal element (f_{11}, f_{22}, f_{33}) exceeds the other two, which implies that the forecasts have at least some merits, although they are evidently far from being perfect.

Various breakdowns of this table were made, viz., according to country, industry, size of the firm, and type of variable; as a whole, 179 prediction-realization tables were considered in [12], N being about 400 on the average with a minimum of 150. We confine ourselves to the following. A useful measure for the quality of the forecasts is the fraction of the forecasts that

---

[2] A similar analysis was carried out by Anderson *et al.* [3].

[3] It is to be noted that the Swedish Business Test is on a quarterly, not on a monthly basis; also, that the questionnaire for the Swedish textile industry refers to comparisons with the same quarter of the preceding year, not the preceding quarter. Further, the halves of Table 2 are all due to the Swedish data, some of the participants' answers having been interpreted as lying halfway between increase and no change, or between no change and decrease.

TABLE 2

PREDICTION-REALIZATION TABLE OF JOCHEMS AND BOOT'S
AGGREGATE DATA

Predictions	Realizations			Marginal Total
	Increase	No Change	Decrease	
Increase	$7393\frac{1}{2}$	$4813\frac{1}{2}$	$1253\frac{1}{2}$	$13460\frac{1}{2}$
No Change	6052	36035	7718	49805
Decrease	$1000\frac{1}{2}$	4296	7874	$13170\frac{1}{2}$
Marginal Total	14446	$45144\frac{1}{2}$	$16845\frac{1}{2}$	76436

turned out to be correct:

$$V_1 = \frac{f_{11} + f_{22} + f_{33}}{N}. \tag{2.1}$$

This measure was computed for each of the 179 tables. A summarizing picture is given in Table 3, which contains in its first column the average of the V_1's for different variables. Thus, there are 8 tables available for buying prices, and the mean of their V_1's equals 0.78. It is seen that for the material as a whole V_1 is about two thirds, but that the range is from slightly more than 0.5 to almost 0.8. Another interesting measure is the degree to which changes are underestimated (viz., when no change is predicted while either increase or decrease is reported afterwards). For this we use

$$V_2 = \frac{f_{21} + f_{23}}{N}. \tag{2.2}$$

TABLE 3

AVERAGE V'S AS DEFINED IN (2.1)–(2.4) FOR 179 PREDICTION-REALIZATION
TABLES, ACCORDING TO SEPARATE VARIABLES

Variable	V_1	V_2	V_3	V_4	Number of Tables
Buying Price	0.78	0.11	0.12	0.00	8
Selling Price	0.74	0.13	0.12	0.01	36
Employment	0.73	0.16	0.10	0.01	21
Production	0.68	0.18	0.13	0.01	24
Rentability	0.66	0.19	0.14	0.01	6
Investment	0.64	0.19	0.14	0.03	12
Raw Materials Bought	0.60	0.23	0.14	0.04	17
Stocks	0.60	0.23	0.13	0.04	26
Orders	0.57	0.25	0.14	0.04	21
Sales	0.55	0.26	0.11	0.09	8
Total	0.67	0.18	0.12	0.03	179

Table 3 shows that V_2 ranges from 0.1 to about 0.25; it is larger when V_1 is smaller, which seems rather obvious because a small V_1 implies that there is more "room" for V_2.

Third, we have the degree to which changes are overestimated (viz., when either increase or decrease is predicted while no change is reported afterwards). This is measured by

$$V_3 = \frac{f_{12} + f_{32}}{N}, \qquad (2.3)$$

which is shown in the third column. Two things are remarkable: we have $V_3 < V_2$ except for the most successfully predicted variables (for which $V_3 \approx V_2$), which implies a bias towards underestimation of changes; and V_3 is approximately constant (between 0.10 and 0.14), there being no negative association between V_1 and V_3 in spite of the fact that a small V_1-value provides for more "room" for V_3. Finally, we have the cases of very bad forecasting in which increases are predicted as decreases and *vice versa*. It is easily seen that forecasts of this kind necessarily imply turning point errors.[4] The frequency of these cases is measured by

$$V_4 = \frac{f_{13} + f_{31}}{N}, \qquad (2.4)$$

which, when added to the sum of V_1, V_2, V_3, always gives 1. Table 3 shows that the V_4's are generally very small except when a variable is badly forecast according to V_1.[5]

2.2. *Accuracy Analysis at an Aggregative Level*

In Section 2.1 we were concerned with an analysis carried out at an extremely microeconomic level: we considered forecasts of individual firms of changes in separate variables in separate months. It is also possible to proceed at a more aggregative level, which can be described as follows. Consider all firms of a certain branch of industry or trade which participate in the survey, and consider also one particular variable (e.g., the production of

---

[4] There are turning point errors of two distinct kinds. First, there may be an actual turning point which is not predicted (e.g., if the variable increased last month and decreases in the present, while the prediction for this month was a further increase). Second, there may be no actual turning point at all but only a predicted turning point (e.g., if the variable continues to increase, both in the last month and in the present, while this month's forecast was a decline). For more details, cf. Theil [21, pp. 27–31, 112–18].

[5] It is perhaps useful to note that the figures which are presented in Table 3 are not to be interpreted as stable parameters. This will be particularly clear when it is realized that the bias towards underestimation of changes implies that V_1 must be relatively large in times when the actual development is such that no change has to be reported frequently. In fact, the correlation between V_1 and the frequency of realized no change (A_2/N) over the set of all 179 tables is substantial, viz., 0.88.

the respondent) in one month. A certain percentage of these firms will report an increase in that variable in that month, a certain percentage will report no change, and another percentage a decrease. Suppose then that we weight the answers proportionally to the size of the responding firm;[6] then the answers of this branch of industry or trade regarding this particular variable can be arranged in a column vector of "test variates,"

$$x = \begin{bmatrix} x^1 \\ x^2 \\ x^3 \end{bmatrix}, \tag{2.5}$$

where x^1 stands for the (weighted) fraction of firms responding an increase, and x^2 and x^3 for no change and decrease respectively; their sum is of course unity. A similar procedure can be applied to planned and expected changes.

The macroeconomic procedure amounts to a comparison of a time series of test variates on actual development with the corresponding time series of test variates of the predicted variable. Of course, this procedure suppresses a great deal of information compared with that of Section 2.1; it is nevertheless appropriate to mention it here, however, first because it can be carried out on the basis of information which is easily available,[7] and, second, because it deals with aggregates of a kind that will be used rather frequently in the remainder of this paper. In fact, it is useful to define another aggregate based on test variates, viz.,

$$b(x) = x^1 - x^3, \tag{2.6}$$

which is the "balance" of the test variates.[8] It is a measure for the degree to which increases or decreases dominate in the group of firms as a whole. Its limits are ± 1, the upper (lower) limit being attained when all firms respond "increase" ("decrease").

Table 4 gives a picture of the forecasting quality of four groups of firms in the German leather and shoe industry with respect to their buying prices. It contains the correlation coefficients of the time series of the fractions x^1 of reported increases and the corresponding time series for expected increases, as well as similar correlations for the fractions of decreases (x^3) and the

---

[6] For purposes of weighting, the *IFO-Institut* uses the number of employees in the case of manufacturing firms, and the value of sales in the case of traders. In some cases different weights are applied for different variables of the same set of firms.

[7] The survey results are disclosed to the participants in the form of weighted percentages of firms reporting (or planning or expecting) an increase or no change or a decrease in some variable in some month. The publication takes usually a graphical rather than a numerical form.

[8] A similar concept is the "diffusion index" which was introduced by the National Bureau of Economic Research in New York. This is an aggregate based on monthly time series; for each month it is defined as the number of series that go up minus the number of series that go down. Cf. [7, 8].

balances (*b*). The results show that the correlations tend to be larger for those groups of firms that are closer to the ultimate consumer, thus implying that these firms are more successful in forecasting the changes in their buying prices than the other firms are.[9] It is also seen that the correlations of the

TABLE 4

CORRELATIONS BETWEEN THE FRACTIONS OF PREDICTED AND REALIZED
INCREASES (DECREASES, BALANCES) FOR BUYING PRICES: GERMAN
LEATHER AND SHOE INDUSTRY, 1951–1953

	Increases (x^1)	Decreases (x^3)	Balances (*b*)
Traders in Hides	0.63	0.54	0.65
Wholesalers in Leather	0.74	0.77	0.78
Wholesalers in Shoes	0.96	0.77	0.90
Retailers in Shoes	0.92	0.96	0.95

balances are higher on the average than the corresponding correlations of the fractions of increases and those of the fractions of decreases. The phenomenon of underestimation of changes can also be analyzed in terms of the present data: Table 5 shows that the average fraction of predicted no-change

TABLE 5

AVERAGES (OVER TIME) OF THE FRACTIONS OF PRE-
DICTED AND REALIZED NO-CHANGE FOR BUYING PRICES:
GERMAN LEATHER AND SHOE INDUSTRY, 1951–1953

	Predicted	Realized
Traders in Hides	0.49	0.30
Traders in Leather	0.68	0.53
Wholesalers in Shoes	0.75	0.75
Retailers in Shoes	0.67	0.66

exceeds the average fraction of realized no-change. The latter statement does not apply to the firms that are close to the consumer; however, this is not at all different from our findings of Section 2.1, where we observed similar effects for the group of 8 prediction-realization tables on buying prices which we considered there.

---

[9] Certain qualifications must be made, of course. First, the correlation coefficient is not a fully adequate indicator of forecasting quality, because it is only an indicator of linearity; second, the aggregation procedure may conceal prediction imperfections of the microsphere. For more details, cf. [21, Chap. IV], which contains also the underlying data for the tables of this section and Section 3.

3. INTERRELATIONSHIPS OF EXPECTED, PLANNED, AND ACTUAL DATA FOR DIFFERENT VARIABLES

3.1. *The Matrix Method*

The problem of how anticipations and realizations as measured by Business Test data are determined numerically by other anticipations and realizations can be attacked by means of a microeconomic approach as well as a macroeconomic approach. So far, however, we did not use the former approach, although we plan to do so for manufacturing firms and wholesalers in the German paper industry in the near future.[10]

The first macroeconomic procedure which we shall consider is the so-called matrix method, which can be described as follows. Suppose there is some variable which depends on one other variable; for example, a selling price depending on a buying price. Suppose also that we have time series of test variates of these two variables at our disposal; we denote the test variates of the dependent variable (selling price in the example given above) by y^1, y^2, y^3, and those of the independent variable (buying price) by x^1, x^2, x^3. Then we postulate that each of the three test variates of the independent variable depends linearly on the three test variates of the dependent variable:

$$y^1 = \alpha_{11}x^1 + \alpha_{12}x^2 + \alpha_{13}x^3$$
$$y^2 = \alpha_{21}x^1 + \alpha_{22}x^2 + \alpha_{23}x^3 \qquad (3.1)$$
$$y^3 = \alpha_{31}x^1 + \alpha_{32}x^2 + \alpha_{33}x^3$$

Hence α_{12} can be interpreted as the fraction of those firms that report no-change in their x-variable which raise their y-variable; and similarly for the other α's. It is easily seen that, when all firms which report a particular change in their x-variable (increase, no change, or decrease) report the same change-type in their y-variable, we have $\alpha_{rr} = 1$ and $\alpha_{rs} = 0$ if $r \neq s$ ($r, s = 1, 2, 3$). Employing the matrix notation (2.5), we can write (3.1) in the simple form

$$y = Ax, \qquad (3.2)$$

where A is the 3×3 matrix $[\alpha_{rs}]$ (hence the term "matrix method"); it is easily seen that the special case just mentioned implies $A = I$, I being the unit matrix of order 3.

Two examples of this matrix method are given in Tables 6 and 7. Table 6 deals with selling price plans of the German traders in hides, the test variates of which are described in terms of the test variates of the expected buying prices of these firms. Table 7 is concerned with the realized buying prices of the traders in leather, their test variates being described in terms of those of

---

[10] Some work in this microeconomic field has been done by Anderson and others, [2, 5, 6].

the realized selling prices of the tanners, which are the suppliers of the leather traders. The figures in parentheses are least-squares standard errors;[11] they show that in neither case does the estimated A-matrix differ significantly from

TABLE 6

THE MATRIX METHOD APPLIED TO THE PLANNED SELLING PRICES
OF THE TRADERS IN HIDES AS DETERMINED BY THEIR EXPECTED
BUYING PRICES: GERMAN LEATHER AND SHOE INDUSTRY,
1951–1953

	x^1	x^2	x^3
y^1	0.98 (0.02)	0.01 (0.02)	−0.01 (0.02)
y^2	0.03 (0.03)	0.95 (0.04)	−0.01 (0.03)
y^3	−0.01 (0.02)	0.04 (0.03)	1.02 (0.02)

TABLE 7

THE MATRIX METHOD APPLIED TO THE BUYING PRICES OF THE
TRADERS IN LEATHER AS DETERMINED BY THE SELLING PRICES
OF THE TANNERS: GERMAN LEATHER AND SHOE INDUSTRY,
1951–1953

	x^1	x^2	x^3
y^1	1.19 (0.12)	0.01 (0.05)	−0.00 (0.07)
y^2	−0.12 (0.17)	1.01 (0.07)	−0.08 (0.09)
y^3	−0.07 (0.13)	−0.03 (0.06)	1.08 (0.07)

the unit matrix, although the point estimates of Table 7 show larger discrepancies from the unit form than those of Table 6. But such a difference must be expected in view of the fact that the two variables with which Table 7 is concerned refer to different sets of firms (viz., tanners and leather traders).

It is of some interest to add that in some cases certain slight modifications of the matrix method have been found appropriate. Thus it appeared that the matrix method applied to the planned selling prices of other sets of firms than the traders in hides gave rise to a matrix A of which the leading element is

---

[11] It is to be doubted whether the classical least-squares standard errors are valid in this case, because they are based on the assumptions of fixed—though unknown—coefficients (the α's) and of additive disturbances which are uncorrelated and have constant variance. An alternative approach which seems worthwhile (but which has not yet been explored) is based on the assumption that there are certain parent coefficients α_{rs} ($r, s = 1, 2, 3$) and that the actual coefficients in the separate months are subject to sampling fluctuations. This procedure seems appropriate when the α's are interpreted as proportions (cf. the preceding paragraph in the text); it implies that the randomness in the equations is of the multiplicative rather than the additive type. In this connection, cf. Rubin [20], Hurwicz [9], and Theil and Mennes [23].

significantly smaller than unity ($\alpha_{11} < 1$), and the element below it is significantly positive ($\alpha_{21} > 0$).[12] This is in contradiction with the simple assumption $A = I$; it implies that only part of the firms expecting an increase in their buying prices plan to raise their selling prices, the other firms being inclined to keep their selling prices unchanged. A closer inspection revealed, however, that the former part tends to increase when the number of firms expecting buying price increases is larger. This points to a curvilinear relationship and, in fact, the following pair proved to be adequate:

$$y^1 = (x^1)^2 \qquad \text{and} \qquad y^3 = x^3, \tag{3.3}$$

where x^1 (x^3) is the fraction of firms expecting an increase (decrease) in their buying price, and similarly y^1 and y^3 for selling price plans. It is easily seen that according to (3.3) the fraction of those firms that expect buying price increases and which plan to raise their selling prices, y^1/x^1, increases with the size of the group of firms that expect an increase in their buying prices.[13]

3.2 *The Balance Method*

The matrix method is inapplicable as soon as there is more than one explanatory variable.[14] Another method is then useful, viz., the balance method, which can be explained conveniently by means of the following example:

$$b(\bar{p}_b)^{\text{III}} = 0.3b(p_b)^{\text{III}}_{-1} - 0.1b(p_b)^{\text{III}}_{-2} + 0.25b(p_s)^{\text{I}}_{-1}, \tag{3.4}$$

where $b(\bar{p}_b)^{\text{III}}$ stands for the balance of expected buying prices of the traders in leather (indicated by the superscript III), $b(p_b)^{\text{III}}_{-1}$ for the balance of the actual buying prices of the same group of firms lagged one month, $b(p_b)^{\text{III}}_{-2}$ for the same variable lagged two months, and $b(p_s)^{\text{I}}_{-1}$ for the balance of the actual selling prices of the traders in hides (indicated by the superscript I) lagged one month. The general idea behind relationships in balances of the type (3.4) is that a balance can be regarded as a measure of central tendency of microchanges in the same way as the change in a macrovariable can be regarded as a measure of central tendency of such changes; i.e., that a balance of production (say) of 0.5 (implying that the percentage of respondents of "increase" exceeds the percentage of "decrease" by 50 percent) can be compared with a rise of the traditional production index of, e.g., 2 percent. We shall go deeper into this problem in Section 4; we note here that, insofar as this idea is

---

[12] It can be easily shown that the sum of the three α's in each column of A is necessarily unity. Hence, if some α deviates from the value implied by the unit form of the matrix (like α_{11} in this case), this must be "compensated" by another α in the same column.

[13] For more details, cf. [21, pp. 266–71].

[14] The reason is that matrix relations of the type $y = A_1x_1 + A_2x_2$ are characterized by complete multicollinearity due to the fact that the sums of the test variates of both x_1 and x_2 are 1.

tenable, we may consider relations like (3.4) in a way similar to regressions on traditional data. If we do so, the interpretation of (3.4) is as follows: the changes in buying prices expected by the traders in leather for next month are positively affected by the realized changes in the present month, negatively by the realized changes in the month before, and positively by the realized changes in the selling prices of the traders in hides in this month. The interpretation of the last of these explanatory variables is obvious, since leather traders have good reasons to expect higher buying prices when the traders in hides raise their selling prices. To interpret the first two explanatory variables, we write their linear combination in (3.4) in the following form:

$$0.2b(p_b)^{III}_{-1} + 0.1\{b(p_b)^{III}_{-1} - b(p_b)^{III}_{-2}\}.$$

The first term implies that, when buying prices increased in the present month, this is a stimulus for the traders to expect further increases in the next month. The second term implies a similar stimulus when buying prices increased more generally in the present month than in the month before.

It was noticed in the preceding paragraph that a certain relationship may be supposed to exist between balances and conventional statistical data. This is of special importance when certain data of either type are lacking, because the other type can then be used as a substitute. An interesting example is the following:

$$b(p_b)^I = 5I(p_H) + 1.2b(T)^I - 0.4b(T)^I_{-1}, \tag{3.5}$$

where $b(p_b)^I$ stands for the balance of (realized) buying prices of the traders in hides, $I(p_H)$ for the relative change in the index of import prices of hides in Western Germany in the same month, $b(T)^I$ for the balance of sales of the traders in hides, and $b(T)^I_{-1}$ the same variable lagged one month. This relation implies that there are domestic as well as foreign factors which affect the traders' buying prices. For the latter factors no test variate information is available; so a "conventional" index is used as a substitute. In the same way, it is conceivable that one introduces variables that have the form of test variates in a relation which otherwise contains mainly "conventional" variables; for example, when an expectation variable is needed which is not available in conventional form.

4. THE EMPIRICAL RELATION BETWEEN BUSINESS TEST AND CONVENTIONAL DATA

4.1. *The Indifference Interval Approach*

In the preceding sections we accepted the Business Test data as they are. Although the results obtained do not suggest that this attitude is wholly unrealistic, it is nevertheless of considerable interest to analyze their merits in a more straightforward way. A convenient approach is that of a comparison of these data with corresponding numerical data of the more traditional statistical type. Of course, it is in general never quite certain whether such data are really "corresponding"—we shall consider this in more detail in Section 4.3—but even so, such a comparison is interesting.

The simplest approach is as follows. It will seem self-evident that, in general, no entrepreneur will regard a very small positive change (say, a production increase of 1 percent) as an increase. Instead, he will consider it as a case of no change, and the same applies to small decreases. So let us assume that an interval (a, b) exists, to be called the *indifference interval*,[15] with the following property: if an entrepreneur is confronted with a numerical increase δ which exceeds b, he reports an increase; if $\delta < a$, he reports a decrease; and if $a \leqq \delta \leqq b$, he reports no change. The next problem is to estimate a and b from observable data, which was attacked by Jochems [10] in the following manner. He considered the case in which N firms report on a certain variable in a certain month, and arranged their numerical percentage changes in increasing order:

$$\delta_1 \leqq \delta_2 \leqq \ldots \leqq \delta_N. \tag{4.1}$$

Suppose further that N^1 firms report an increase, N^2 no change, and N^3 a decrease; hence $N^1 + N^2 + N^3 = N$. Then, for the purpose of estimating a and b, the N^1 firms reporting an increase were identified with the N^1 largest δ's of the ranking (4.1); similarly, the N^3 firms reporting decreases were identified with the N^3 smallest δ's of this ranking. It is then evident that b must lie between the $(N - N^1 - 1)$-st and the $(N - N^1)$-th δ of (4.1), and a between the N^3-th and the $(N^3 + 1)$-st.

This idea has been applied to two variables (production and stocks) of the Dutch shoe industry, for which both "conventional" and Business Test data were available. For each of 35 months in the period 1954–56 the coefficients a and b were calculated in the way explained above. The results are presented in Table 8 in summarized form; the table contains, both for production and for stocks, the medians of the 35 lower and upper limits of the indifference intervals (a and b), as well as the medians of the lengths of these intervals $(b - a)$ and of their midpoints $[\frac{1}{2}(a + b)]$. It is seen that the intervals are quite large—of the order of 30–40 percent—and that, surprisingly enough, the indifference intervals for stocks are so far on the positive side.

4.2. *The Response Function Approach*

The results of Table 8 are somewhat surprising, in particular when they are compared with data given by Lönnqvist [18] for firms participating in the Swedish Business Test. The Swedish *Konjunkturinstitutet* sent a special questionnaire to these firms in which it asked for the smallest percentage

---

[15] This concept was introduced by Theil and Cramer [22].

change that was considered as increase or decrease. The answers obtained imply indifference intervals of the order of 10 percent, which suggests a much greater sensitivity of the respondents than we found in Section 4.1. This difference can perhaps be partly explained by the fact that the Swedish Business Test refers to quarterly changes,[16] partly by the way in which the special

TABLE 8

MEDIAN VALUES OF ESTIMATED INDIFFERENCE INTERVALS FOR
PRODUCTION AND STOCKS OF THE DUTCH SHOE INDUSTRY,
1954–1956

Variable	a	b	$b - a$	$\frac{1}{2}(a + b)$
Production	$-24\frac{1}{2}$	15	$38\frac{1}{2}$	$-3\frac{1}{2}$
Stocks	$\frac{1}{2}$	$40\frac{1}{2}$	32	22

questionnaire was interpreted by the respondents. For, if the interpretation was in the sense of the smallest change that was *ever* considered as an increase or a decrease, this may easily lead to a downward bias of the implied indifference interval.

More serious, however, is the fact that the estimation procedure of Section 4.1 is based on a wholly unrealistic assumption. It is simply not true that the N^1 firms reporting increases are those which have the largest δ's in the ranking (4.1), nor that the N^3 firms reporting decreases correspond with the smallest δ's of this ranking. The following approach, originally due to Pfanzagl [19] and further developed by Theil [21], is then of some interest. We introduce the probability p that an entrepreneur, when confronted with a given numerical percentage change δ, reports an increase; and similarly, the probability q that he reports a decrease, given δ. Hence both p and q are functions of δ; they are called *response functions*. It seems rather obvious that $p(\delta)$ should be zero when δ is sufficiently negative, and that it increases with increasing δ; similarly, that $q(\delta)$ is a monotonically decreasing function until it vanishes for sufficiently positive δ. Evidently, this assumption is much weaker than the indifference interval hypothesis of Section 4.1.

Response functions for production and stocks of the German shoe industry were estimated by Jochems and Neudecker [13, 14]. For this purpose they calculated the fractions of reported increase and reported decrease for various percentage intervals of the numerical changes. The results, which are summarized in Table 9, are far from being perfect. The best thing that can be said is that the p-fractions tend to increase from left to right, and the q-fractions to decrease, in spite of the fact that these fractions must be disturbed due to the rather small numbers on which they are based.[17] But otherwise it is clear,

---

[16] Cf. footnote 3 above.
[17] The total number of reports for production and stocks is about 1400 and 700 respectively.

TABLE 9

ESTIMATED RESPONSE FUNCTIONS FOR THE SAME DATA AS TABLE 8

A. Probability of Reporting an Increase p (δ)

Variable	Percentage Intervals of Numerical Changes (δ)								
	Less than −29	−29 to −10	−9 to 0	1 to 5	6 to 10	11 to 20	21 to 40	41 to 80	Over 80
Production	0.09	0.14	0.12	0.17	0.22	0.21	0.28	0.22	0.27
Stocks	0.00	0.03	0.09	0.14	0.16	0.33	0.34	0.32	0.34

B. Probability of Reporting a Decrease q (δ)

Variable	Percentage Intervals of Numerical Changes (δ)								
	Less than −45	−45 to −30	−29 to −18	−17 to −10	−9 to −6	−5 to −1	0 to 10	11 to 40	Over 40
Production	0.35	0.13	0.11	0.16	0.13	0.04	0.03	0.04	0.04
Stocks	0.64	0.67	0.65	0.70	0.47	0.47	0.41	0.35	0.34

first, that only in a minority of cases an increase is reported even when the numerical change is positive and large; second, that for stocks a decrease is reported in as much as one third of the cases in which there is a large numerical increase; third, that for production no change is reported in more than 50 percent of all cases even when the numerical change is a large increase or a large decrease.

4.3. *An Aggregative Approach*

The results obtained in Section 4.2 are not very promising, which may be due to a variety of causes. It may be that the respondents handle the questionnaire in a careless manner; it may be that the data on numerical changes are of unsatisfactory quality; it may also be that the two kinds of data refer to different variables even if they bear the same name. We feel that all three error sources must play some role, although we are unable to specify their relative importance. The organizers of the survey pointed out that several of the participating entrepreneurs may have interpreted "production" as "sales" when informing the Central Bureau of Statistics on numerical changes. Clearly, this can lead to sizable errors when monthly changes are analyzed.[18]

However, modest and even poor results at the microeconomic level are not at all unknown. For example, when analyzing household data for individual families and individual commodities, one usually finds relatively substantial deviations from the Engel curves. But after a suitable aggregation—either over families or over commodities—one finds that the correlations of the Engel regressions increase substantially, thus pointing to a reduction of discrepancies after aggregation. In the same way, one may hope that a more aggregative approach to the problem of correspondence between Business Test and conventional data leads to better results. In fact, this approach was applied by Anderson several years ago;[19] it can be described as follows. Suppose that, in a certain month and with respect to a certain variable, the percentage of firms reporting an increase is large while the percentage of those reporting a decrease is small. Suppose also that an index number of the conventional type is available for this variable. Then it seems plausible that the overall tendency of reported increase will be accompanied by a large rise of the index number in

---

[18] Alternative approaches in terms of "productive activity" instead of production were also considered, productive activity being defined as a moving average of production. This did not lead to substantial improvements, however. It is of some interest to note that much more success was obtained with respect to response functions of football predictions and realizations. There it appeared that a close relation exists between the ranking of teams according to previous successes and failures in the season, on the one hand, and the realized and predicted outcomes of matches (especially the latter) on the other hand. For more details, cf. Jochems [11].

[19] Cf. Anderson [1, 4]. The problem described here is known in the German literature as the "quantification problem"; i.e., that of transforming qualitative information (increase. no change, decrease) into quantitative information in the form of index numbers

the same month. So we may assume that the relative change in the index (y) is associated positively with the fraction of reported increase (x^1) and negatively with the fraction of reported decrease (x^3). If we make the further assumption that the two types of association are of equal strength, we may employ the

Fig. 1

INDEX-BALANCE RELATION:

SALES OF ALL RETAILERS

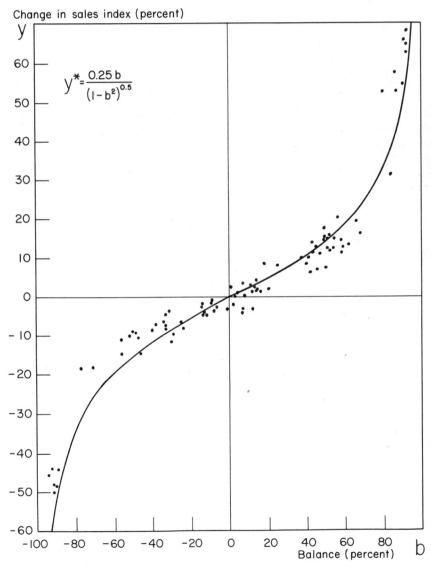

Change in sales index (percent)

$$y^* = \frac{0.25\,b}{\left(1 - b^2\right)^{0.5}}$$

Balance (percent)

TABLE 10

ESTIMATES OF THE PARAMETERS α AND ϵ OF THE INDEX-BALANCE RELATION (4.2), AND OF RESIDUAL STANDARD DEVIATIONS:

GERMAN RETAIL TRADE, 1950–1957

	Sales				Purchases				Stocks				Prices			
	α	ϵ	σ_1	σ_2	α	ϵ	σ_1	σ_2	α	ϵ	σ_1	σ_2	α	ϵ	σ_1	σ_2
All Retailers	0.25	0.50	0.03	0.06	0.30	0.50	0.05	*	0.20	0.25	0.03	*	0.025	0	0.006	*
Textiles	0.20	0.50	0.04	0.09	0.35	0.25	0.06	0.06	0.15	0.25	0.02	0.04	0.025	0	0.005	0.008
Shoes	0.25	0.25	0.07	0.13	0.25	0.25	0.10	0.09	0.15	0.25	0.04	0.04	0.020	0	0.003	0.010
Ironware	0.25	0.50	0.05	0.08	0.30	0.25	0.06	0.08	0.15	0	0.05	0.05	0.020	0	0.005	0.013
Foods	0.15	0.25	0.03	0.05	0.10	1.00	0.05	0.06	0.15	0	0.05	0.05	0.020	0	0.008	*

* The number of observations is insufficient for the calculation of a standard deviation.

balance (2.6), which leads to a relation of the form $y = f(b)$, $b = b(x) = x^1 - x^3$ being the balance of the test variates. Some examples are given in the attached chart, which is derived from Jochems and De Wit [15]. They used the relation

$$y = \frac{\alpha b}{(1 - b^2)^\varepsilon},$$ (4.2)

where α and ε are (positive) parameters to be estimated. The specification (4.2) implies that the relative change in the index is approximately proportional to the balance as long as the latter is small. However, when the balance is large—either positively or negatively—the curve becomes much steeper. This is in accordance with the scatter of the chart and also rather obvious, since the balance is confined to the interval $(-1, 1)$ while no such limits exist for the change in the index.[20]

Jochems and De Wit applied the specification (4.2) to five groups of German retailers (all retailers, retailers in textiles, shoes, ironware, and foods) and four variables (sales, purchases, stocks, selling prices), the period considered being 1950–57. Estimates of α and ε are given in Table 10 for each of the twenty combinations, together with estimates of the residual standard deviations for $|b| \leq \frac{1}{2}$ and $|b| > \frac{1}{2}$, which are denoted by σ_1 and σ_2 respectively.[21] It is seen that, for most of the cases considered, a balance of 0.1 corresponds approximately with a relative change in the index of 0.02 (an increase of 2 percent), except for the prices which show a much greater sensitivity in the survey. The parameter ε is of the order of $\frac{1}{2}$, except again for the prices, the balances of which did not show sufficient variation for a specification of this parameter. As to the residual standard deviations, they are generally larger for large balances than for small ones, which is rather obvious after inspecting the chart. They are certainly not very small (of the order of 5 or 10 percent, except for the prices), but on the other hand not such as to make the relations useless for a prediction of the change in the index, given the balance. We plan to carry out predictive tests in the near future.

REFERENCES

1. ANDERSON, O., JR. "The Business Test of the IFO-Institute for Economic Research, Munich, and Its Theoretical Model," *Review of the International Statistical Institute*, Vol. 20 (1952), pp. 1–17.

---

[20] Except that the latter change cannot be below -1 as long as the index is to be non-negative. This feature introduces some spurious kind of asymmetry which can be handled by a logarithmic transformation proposed by Kaptein and Jochems [16, 17], but this has not been done in [15].

[21] More precisely, σ_1 and σ_2 are standard deviations of the points (b, y) around the curve (4.2), and σ_1 refers to the points (b, y) for which $|b| \leq \frac{1}{2}$, σ_2 to those for which $|b| > \frac{1}{2}$. These standard deviations were derived after the application of certain seasonal corrections. For more details, cf. Jochems and De Wit [15].

2. ANDERSON, O., JR. *Das Konjunkturtestverfahren und sein Beitrag zur empirischen Untersuchung der ex ante- ex post-Problematik.* Munich, 1957.

3. ANDERSON, O., JR., BAUER, R. K., AND FELS, E. "Zur Treffsicherheit kürzfristiger Unternehmererwartungen." IFO-Institute, Munich, 1954.

4. ANDERSON, O., JR., BAUER, R. K., AND GIEHL, R. "Zur Theorie des Konjunkturtestes," *IFO-Studien,* Vol. 1 (1955), pp. 159–204.

5. ANDERSON, O., JR., BAUER, R. K., FÜHRER, H., AND PETERSEN, J. P. "On Short-Term Entrepreneurial Reaction Patterns," *Weltwirtschaftliches Archiv,* Vol. 81 (1958), pp. 243–64.

6. ANDERSON, O., JR., FÜRST, H., AND SCHULTE, W. "Zur Analyse der unternehmerischen Reaktionsweise," *IFO-Studien,* Vol. 2 (1956), pp. 129–54.

7. HASTAY, M. "The Dun and Bradstreet Surveys of Businessmen's Expectations," *Proceedings of the Business and Economic Statistics Section of the American Statistical Association.* Washington, 1955, pp. 93–123.

8. HASTAY, M. "The Role of Business Expectations in the Operating Behavior of the Firm." Paper presented at the Conference on the Quality and Economic Significance of Anticipations Data, Princeton, 1957.

9. HURWICZ, L. "Systems with Nonadditive Disturbances," *Statistical Inference in Dynamic Economic Models* (ed. T. C. Koopmans), Chapter 18. New York–London, 1950.

10. JOCHEMS, D. B. "A Micro-Analysis of the Indifference Intervals of Entrepreneurs Participating in Business Tendency Surveys." Report 5815 (1958).[22]

11. JOCHEMS, D. B. "Responsie-functies en voetbaluitslagen." Report 5902 (1959).[22]

12. JOCHEMS, D. B., AND BOOT, J. C. G. "Prediction-Realization Tables of Business Test Data." (Forthcoming.)[22]

13. JOCHEMS, D. B., AND NEUDECKER, H. "Micro-Economic Business Test Data Compared with Traditional Statistics." Report 5818 (1958);[22] to be published in *Metrika.*

14. JOCHEMS, D. B., AND NEUDECKER, H. "An Application of Wilcoxon's Test to Numerical and Survey Data of the Dutch Shoe Industry, 1954–1956." Report 5822 (1958).[22]

15. JOCHEMS, D. B., AND DE WIT, G. M. "The Macro-Economic Relationship Between Business Tendency Surveys and Numerical Data." Report 5904 (1959).[22]

16. KAPTEIN, E. "Fluctuations in Inventories of Dutch Shoe Factories, 1954–56." Report 5814 (1958).[22]

17. KAPTEIN, E., AND JOCHEMS, D. B. "The Analysis of Frequency Distributions of Changes in Economic Microvariables Applied to the Dutch Shoe Industry, 1954–56," Report 5808 (1958).[22]

18. LÖNNQVIST, Å. "Ueber die Beziehungen zwischen ex ante- und ex post-Daten in Schwedischen Konjunkturtest," *IFO-Studien,* Vol. 4 (1958), pp. 35–56.

19. PFANZAGL, J. "Zur Methodik des Konjunkturtest-Verfahrens," *Statistische Vierteljahresschrift,* Vol. 52 (1962), pp. 161–73.

20. RUBIN, H. "Note on Random Coefficients," *Statistical Inference in Dynamic Economic Models* (ed. T. C. Koopmans), Chapter 19. New York–London, 1950.

21. THEIL, H. *Economic Forecasts and Policy.* Amsterdam, 1958.

---

[22] Report of the Econometric Institute of the Netherlands School of Economics.

22. THEIL, H., AND CRAMER, J. S. "On the Utilization of a New Source of Economic Information: An Econometric Analysis of the Munich Business Test." Paper presented at the 16th European Meeting of the Econometric Society, Uppsala, 1954.

23. THEIL, H., AND MENNES, L. B. M. "Multiplicative Randomness in Time Series Regression Analysis." Report 5901 (1959).[22]

---

[22] Report of the Econometric Institute of the Netherlands School of Economics.

VIII. POLICY

35

Introduction

THE JOURNAL literature on stabilization policy since the war would fill a good many volumes. For a number of reasons, however, it has not been easy to select a few articles for inclusion in this section. For one thing, some of the most useful papers have already been reprinted in other volumes of this series of *A.E.A. Readings* or in other published collections. These include the series of papers on national debt and fiscal policy in *Readings in Fiscal Policy*, of which one is the excellent report on "The Problem of Economic Instability" by a committee of the American Economic Association.[1] Similarly, *Readings in Monetary Theory* includes a number of papers on monetary policy, of which the two best known are probably Henry Simons' "Rules Versus Authorities in Monetary Policy" (1936) and Milton Friedman's "A Monetary and Fiscal Framework for Economic Stability" (1948).

Another difficulty lies in the ephemeral nature of a good deal of the literature that deals with questions of current economic policy. Even though directed toward current issues, however, this literature does provide a useful backdrop against which to review some of the more important policy debates of the postwar period. The frequent symposia in the *Review of Economics and Statistics* are good examples.

By the nature of the case, some of the most important literature on stabilization policy in the postwar period emerged as a result of the work of government committees or formal commissions under private auspices. One can cite the reports of the United Nations experts (1949), the Douglas subcommittee (1950), the Radcliffe Committee (1959), and the Commission on Money and Credit (1961). The publications of the Joint Economic Committee should also be mentioned, particularly the Staff Report and Study Papers prepared for the Committee's study of *Employment, Growth, and Price Levels*.[2] Reference might also be made to the useful collection of papers on monetary policy published by the American Assembly.[3]

We have chosen to reproduce four papers here. The first is one of two

---

[1] Originally published in *American Economic Review*, Vol. XL (September, 1950), pp. 501–38.

[2] See particularly *Staff Report on Employment, Growth, and Price Levels*, prepared for the Joint Economic Committee, 86th Congress, 1st sess. (Washington: Government Printing Office, 1959).

[3] American Assembly, *United States Monetary Policy* (New York: 1958).

pioneering articles by A. W. Phillips on the relationship between the dynamic properties of an economic system and the effectiveness of stabilization policy. The earlier of these two papers is the more fundamental one,[4] but because of its length we have chosen to reprint the shorter, second article. Clearly the author has opened up an important area of research which, as he suggests, now needs to be directed toward the study of more realistic models.

The income effects of a balanced government budget first aroused the interest of economists during World War II. Among the pioneers in exploring the relative multiplier effects of taxes and government expenditures were William Salant, Samuelson, Hansen and Perloff, Kaldor, Wallich, and Haavelmo, and later contributions were made by Baumol, Peston, and Turvey.[5] Broadly speaking, this literature has been concerned primarily with two questions: the income-generating effects of tax changes and the complications introduced by including, in addition to consumption, other variables (such as imports) that are related to income. This literature has been neatly integrated and put into appropriate perspective by William Salant in his paper reprinted here.

In the field of fiscal policy, a great deal has been written about the automatic stabilizers; and in the last few years a number of economists have stressed the need for some degree of "formula flexibility." Perhaps the most prominent and persistent advocate of automatic flexibility in the United States has been the Committee for Economic Development.[6] It has seemed to us useful to reproduce Walter Heller's critical evaluation of thus assigning to fiscal policy what he terms "an inherently passive role." We presume that his emphasis would be much the same were he writing the paper today, after four years as Chairman of the Council of Economic Advisers.

Howard Ellis has referred to the "Rediscovery of Money" which occurred at the beginning of the 1950's,[7] and Heller, in his paper, protests against the "unleashing" of monetary policy that then occurred. During the preceding 15 years or so, economists' concern with the stabilizing role of monetary policy had been held in check by several factors: the influence of the Great Depression, neo-Keynesian minimizing of the role of monetary variables (and neglect of price-level changes), and the subordination of monetary policy to the needs of war finance and debt management. In the last 15 years, money has truly been rediscovered, and the ensuing debate regarding the desirability and effectiveness of an active monetary policy shows no signs of ending. Among the issues that have been debated and the topics on which useful work has been

---

[4] "Stabilisation Policy in a Closed Economy," *Economic Journal*, Vol. LXIV (June, 1954), pp. 290–323.

[5] References to this literature will be found in the paper by Salant included in this section.

[6] See, for example, *Fiscal and Monetary Policy for High Employment* (New York: Committee for Economic Development, 1962).

[7] In *Money, Trade, and Economic Growth: In Honor of John Henry Williams* (New York: Macmillan, 1951), p. 253.

done, one might mention the question of lags, potential conflicts in policy goals, the role of financial intermediaries and of holdings of financial assets other than currency and demand deposits, the increased emphasis on credit availability and not merely the interest rate, the interrelations of monetary and debt policy, and, of course, the influence of interest-rate changes on different kinds of investment.

James Schlesinger, in the paper included here, offers both a useful survey of some of this recent literature and a judicious defense of the use of monetary policy within appropriate limits. For a more recent and extensive attempt to evaluate the role of money and monetary policy, the reader is referred to the special supplement of the *Review of Economics and Statistics* in February, 1963, on "The State of Monetary Economics."[8] This issue of the *Review* also contains extensive references to the research papers prepared for the Commission on Money and Credit.[9]

---

[8] Presenting the papers and discussion at a Conference on Monetary Economics arranged by the Universities–National Bureau Committee for Economic Research and held in April, 1962.

[9] See particularly Martin Bronfenbrenner, "A Sample Survey of the Commission on Money and Credit Research Papers," *Review of Economics and Statistics*, Vol. XLV (February, 1963, supplement), pp. 111–28.

36

Stabilisation Policy and the Time-Forms of Lagged Responses*[1]

By A. W. PHILLIPS[†]

IN AN EARLIER article[2] I used a number of dynamic process models to illustrate the operation of certain types of stabilisation policy. In setting up the models I assumed that each lagged response was of the particular time-form known as an exponential lag. I pointed out[3] that other time-forms would probably give better representations of the real responses in an economic system, but did not introduce these more realistic lag forms into the models owing to the difficulty of solving the high-order differential equations to which they would have led.

Since then the National Physical Laboratory and Short Brothers and Harland, Ltd., have allowed me to use their electronic simulators, by means of which the time responses of quite complex systems with a variety of lag forms can be found very rapidly.[4] In addition, I have become more familiar with the frequency-response method of analysis based on the Nyquist stability criterion. This is a graphical method which not only enables considerable information to be obtained about the dynamic properties of a system without solving the differential equation of the system, but also gives valuable insight

---

* *Economic Journal*, Vol. LXVII (June, 1957). Reprinted by courtesy of the Royal Economic Society and the author.

† London School of Economics.

[1] I wish to thank Professor R. G. D. Allen, Professor J. E. Meade, Professor Lionel Robbins and Mr. R. H. Tizard for helpful comments on an earlier draft of this paper.

[2] " Stabilisation Policy in a Closed Economy," *Economic Journal*, June, 1954, pp. 290–323.

[3] *Ibid.*, p. 292.

[4] I am indebted to the Director of the National Physical Laboratory and to Short Brothers and Harland, Ltd., for permission to use the simulators. At the National Physical Laboratory, where most of the work was carried out, Mr. D. V. Blake operated the simulator and gave invaluable help and advice. I benefited greatly from discussions with him and am most grateful to him for his willing co-operation. I also wish to thank Mr. E. Lloyd Thomas, Mr. R. J. A. Paul and Mr. P. A. R. Wright of Short Brothers and Harland, Ltd., for their assistance. The possibility of using electronic simulators for studying problems of economic regulation was suggested to me by Mr. R. H. Tizard.

into the ways in which the dynamic properties would be altered if the relationships and lag forms in the system were modified or additional relationships included.[5]

A study, using frequency-response analysis and electronic simulators, of the properties of models in which the lags are given more realistic time-forms has shown that the problem of stabilization is more complex than appeared to be the case when attention was confined to the simpler lag forms used in my earlier article. In this study a number of alternative models were first analysed by the frequency-response method, and the effects of variations in the lag forms and the values of the parameters on the stability of the models were investigated. Some of the models were then set up on the electronic simulators, disturbances were applied and the resulting time paths of the variables were found. In the present article two of the models which were studied are described and their dynamic properties illustrated by recordings from the electronic simulators.

I. A MULTIPLIER MODEL WITH ERROR CORRECTION

The first model is shown diagrammatically in Fig. 1, which is similar to Fig. 10 of my earlier article[6] except that the accelerator relationship has been omitted. The lines in the diagram represent the variables of the system, measured as deviations from initial equilibrium values. Relationships between variables are indicated by the symbols in the squares, the arrows showing the causal direction of the relationships. The lower closed loop in the diagram represents a simple multiplier model. It is assumed that aggregate real income or production, P, responds to changes in aggregate real demand, E, through the lag relationship L_P. Changes in aggregate demand are analysed into three components, E_Y, E_π and u. E_Y denotes those changes in demand which are related to changes in income through the marginal propensity to spend $1 - l$. We shall give l, the "marginal leakage" from the circular flow of income, the value 0.25, so that the multiplier is 4.0. E_π is the policy demand, *i.e.*, it is the amount by which aggregate demand is increased or decreased as a direct result of action taken by the regulating authorities for the purpose of stabilising the system. All changes in aggregate demand caused by changes in factors other than income and stabilisation policy are included in the variable u.

---

[5] There is an extensive literature on the use of frequency-response methods in the analysis and synthesis of engineering systems. See, for example, H. M. James, N. B. Nichols and R. S. Phillips, *Theory of Servomechanisms* (New York: McGraw-Hill Book Co., 1947) and G. S. Brown and D. P. Campbell, *Principles of Servomechanisms* (New York: John Wiley and Sons, 1948). For a brief description of the methods with some applications to economic problems see A. Tustin, *The Mechanism of Economic Systems* (London: William Heinemann, Ltd., 1954), especially Chapter III. See also R. G. D. Allen, "The Engineers' Approach to Economic Models," *Economica*, May, 1955, and R. G. D. Allen, *Mathematical Economics* (London: Macmillan and Co., Ltd., 1956), Chapters 8 and 9.

[6] *Op. cit.*, p. 306.

The relationships shown at the top of the diagram represent an error-correction type of stabilisation policy. The actual level of production is subtracted from the desired level of production, P_d, giving the error in production,[7] ε. It is assumed that the regulating authorities are able to make

FIG. 1

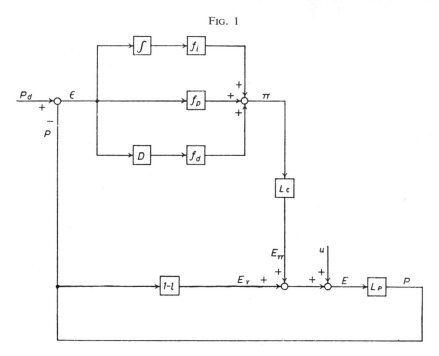

continuous adjustments in the strength of the correcting action they take but that there is a distributed time lag, L_c, between changes in the strength of the correcting action and the resulting changes in policy demand. The amount by which policy demand would be changed as a direct result of the policy measures if they operated without time lag will be called the potential policy demand, π; the amount by which it is in fact changed as a direct result of policy measures is the actual policy demand E_π.

The basic problem in stabilising production is to relate the actual policy demand to the error in production in such a way that errors caused by unpredicted disturbances are corrected as quickly and smoothly as possible.[8]

---

[7] The error is here defined to be $P_d - P$ rather than $P - P_d$ as in my earlier article. In the literature on regulating systems the error in a variable is usually defined as the desired value minus the actual value.

[8] If reliable and frequent measurements of aggregate demand were available the potential policy demand could also be related to the error in demand. This would permit a more rapid correction of errors in production caused by shifts in aggregate demand.

For a given correction lag the problem reduces to that of finding the most suitable way of relating the potential policy demand to the error in production. In my earlier article[9] I argued that to obtain satisfactory regulation of a system it is usually necessary for the potential policy demand to be made the sum of three components, one component depending on the error itself, one depending on the time integral of the error and the third depending on the time derivative (or rate of change) of the error. That is, the relationship should be of the form $\pi = f_p \varepsilon + f_i \int \varepsilon dt + f_d \dfrac{d\varepsilon}{dt}$, where f_p, f_i and f_d are parameters which I called respectively the proportional, integral and derivative correction factors. This relationship is represented by the three loops at the top of Fig. 1, the symbol $\int$ indicating integration with respect to time and D indicating differentiation with respect to time.

We shall consider three different forms of the production lag L_p. These are illustrated by curves (a), (b) and (c) of Fig. 2, which show hypothetical time

FIG. 2

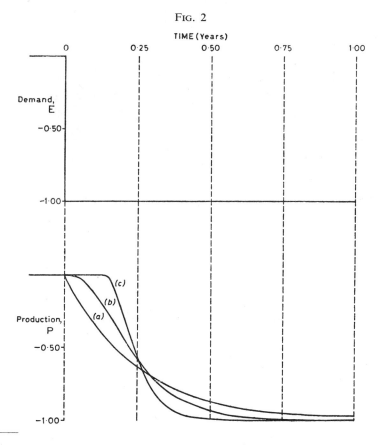

TIME (Years)

[9] *Op. cit.*, pp. 293–303.

paths of the response of production to a unit step fall in demand occurring at time $t = 0$. With lag form (a) the rate of change of production at any time is proportional to the difference between demand and production at that time. We call this an exponential lag and define the time constant of the lag as the reciprocal of the factor of proportionality; for the response shown in curve (a) the time constant is 0.25 year. The exponential lag form is very convenient for mathematical treatment, but it implies a more rapid response in the early stages of an adjustment than is likely to be typical of economic behaviour. The time path of adjustment shown in curve (b) of Fig. 2 is probably more realistic. This time path is obtained if the lag is equivalent to three shorter exponential lags operating in sequence, the time constants of the individual lags being 0.0833 year, so that the total time constant of the composite lag is again 0.25 year. This triple exponential form of lag is probably a fairly good representation of many economic relationships. In some cases, however, we should expect that there would be no response at all until some considerable time after a change had occurred, the time path of the adjustment being somewhat like that shown in curve (c) of Fig. 2. We shall call an interval during which there is no response at all a time delay, to distinguish it from the exponential type of lag in which a continuous gradual adjustment takes place. The adjustment path in curve (c) results from a lag which is equivalent to a sequence consisting of a time delay of 0.125 year and three exponential lags each with a time constant of 0.0417 year, the total time constant of the composite lag again being 0.25 year.

The time forms which we shall use for the correction lag will be similar to those shown in Fig. 2, except that the time scale will be doubled. Thus lag form (a) for the correction lag will be a single exponential lag with a time constant of 0.50 year, lag form (b) will be a sequence of three exponential lags, each with a time constant of 0.167 year, and lag form (c) will be a sequence consisting of a time delay of 0.25 year and three exponential lags, each with a time constant of 0.0833 year.

Figs. 3, 4, and 5 reproduce recordings from the electronic simulators showing the response of production to a unit step change in the variable u applied negatively at time $t = 0$, for different combinations of correction factors and lag forms. The responses shown in Fig. 3 are obtained when the proportional correction factor f_p is 0.5, the integral correction factor f_i is 0.5 and the derivative correction factor f_d is zero. When both the production and the correction lags are of form (a) the response is that shown in curve (a).[10] When the lags are changed to form (b), the rest of the system remaining the same, the response is that shown in curve (b). When the lags are of form (c) the response shown in curve (c) is obtained. In the case now being considered, with proportional and integral correction factors of 0.5, the "overshoot" which occurs in the response

---

[10] This response was obtained mathematically in my earlier article and was shown as curve (b) of Fig. 7, p. 300 (see p. 676, this text).

when the lags are of form (*b*) or (*c*) can be eliminated by introducing a small amount of derivative correction. When the lags are of form (*b*) the overshoot is eliminated if the derivative correction factor is raised from zero to about 0.06; when they are of form (*c*) a derivative correction factor of about 0.09 is required to prevent overshoot in the response.

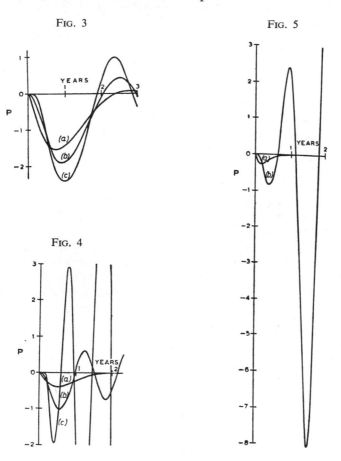

FIG. 3

FIG. 5

FIG. 4

Curves (*a*), (*b*) and (*c*) of Fig. 4 show the responses obtained with lag forms (*a*), (*b*) and (*c*) respectively when both the proportional and the integral correction factors are 2.0 and the derivative correction factor is 0.5. With the higher values of the proportional and integral correction factors the system has become less stable, and even when the lags are of form (*a*) some derivative correction is needed to prevent an oscillatory response. When the lags are of form (*b*) the system is on the verge of instability. Nor can the response be improved by adjustment of the derivative correction factor. Any appreciable increase or decrease in its value makes the system completely unstable. When the corrective action has some effect fairly quickly, as is the case when the lags are of form (*a*), the use of derivative correction is a powerful method of reducing or eliminating fluctuations. But when the corrective action does not have much effect until some considerable time after it is applied, as is the case when the lags are of form (*b*) and still more when they are of form (*c*), derivative correction is less effective in reducing oscillations, and indeed if used excessively it will introduce an additional cycle of high frequency. When the proportional and integral correction factors are 2.0 and the lags are of form (*c*) the system is unstable for all values of the derivative correction factor.

Curve (*a*) of Fig. 5 shows the response when both the proportional and integral correction factors are raised to 8.0 and the derivative correction factor is 1.0, the lags being of form (*a*).[11] With lags of form (*b*) the response becomes that shown in curve (*b*). With lags of form (*c*) the system is so violently unstable that it proved impossible to obtain a satisfactory recording of the response given by the electronic simulator. Adjustment of the derivative correction factor again fails to stabilise the system in this case when the lags are of form (*b*) or (*c*).

Figs. 3, 4, and 5 show that a comparatively small change in the time-forms of the lags may have a great effect on the stability of a closed-loop control system, especially if the values of the correction factors are high. It is in fact only in the simplest systems in which there are not more than two lags, each of single exponential form, that it is possible to give any value, no matter how large, to one correction factor and then to find values for the other correction factors such that the system is stable and non-oscillatory. Any system in which there is time delay or a sequence of more than two lags of single exponential form, or in which any lag is equivalent to a sequence which includes a time delay or more than two single exponential lags, as is the case with lags of form (*b*) or (*c*), will be stable and non-oscillatory only if the values of the correction factors are kept sufficiently low. This limitation of permissible values of the correction factors implies a corresponding limit to the speed with which it is possible to correct an error caused by a disturbance.

It is not possible to make any completely general statement about the effect on the response of a closed-loop system of an alteration to one part of the system unless the remainder of the system is fully specified. It will, however, be found that except in very special cases which are most unlikely to occur in practice a reduction in the length of the correction lag brought about by a reduction in the time scale, the form of the lag remaining unchanged, increases the maximum values of the correction factors that can be used without causing instability, and so permits a more rapid correction of errors. A similar effect is produced, again except in very special cases, if the form of the correction lag is altered from form (*c*) through form (*b*) to form (*a*). As can be seen from Fig. 2, this implies that the maximum values of the correction factors that can be

---

[11] This response was also obtained mathematically in my earlier article and was shown as curve (*e*) of Fig. 7.

used without causing instability are increased if the interval between the time when an error occurs and the time when the corrective action *begins* to take effect is reduced, even if the time required for the full effect of the corrective action to be obtained is simultaneously increased. Thus it is important, both for obtaining rapid correction and for avoiding instability, that the corrective action should be adjusted continuously and quickly to changes in the error and that it should have some initial effect quickly; whether its full effect is obtained quickly or slowly is comparatively unimportant.[12]

We have seen from Fig. 3 that a cycle with a period of about three years occurs if the lags in our system are of form (*b*) or (*c*) and if the proportional and integral correction factors are 0.5 (which may perhaps be about the order of magnitude of these correction factors that can be attained in actual economic regulation) unless a small amount of derivative correction is also applied. Since the basic multiplier model which has been used so far is non-oscillatory, this may properly be called a control cycle. A more adequate model of an economy might itself have cyclical properties, for example, inventory adjustments are likely to cause cycles with a period of three or four years. The question immediately arises whether the maximum values of the correction factors that can be used without causing instability are not further reduced when the system being controlled has oscillatory tendencies. This question is examined briefly in the next section.

II. AN INVENTORY MODEL WITH ERROR CORRECTION

A model with inventory adjustments is shown in Fig. 6. An "inventory demand," E_V, is now distinguished as an additional component of aggregate demand, total demand for purposes other than inventory adjustment being E_N. Thus $E = E_N + E_V$ and $E_N = E_Y + E_\pi + u$. We assume that any excess of the "non-inventory demand" E_N over aggregate production P is met by drawing on inventories, and any excess of production over non-inventory demand is added to inventories. Then the rate of change of inventories, $\dfrac{dV}{dt}$, is equal to $P - E_N$. Integration of $\dfrac{dV}{dt}$ with respect to time gives total inventories, V. Some part of the total inventories will be locked up in work in progress and essential stocks closely related to the level of production. These "minimum working inventories," which we shall call V_1, are assumed to be a constant proportion, w, of production. We shall give w the value 0.2, *i.e.*, we shall assume that minimum working inventories are equal to one-fifth of a year's production.

---

[12] Justification of the above statements would require an extensive use of the frequency-response method of analysis and cannot be given here. The reader who wishes to acquire sufficient familiarity with the method to convince himself of their truth will find the necessary material in the works cited in footnote 5.

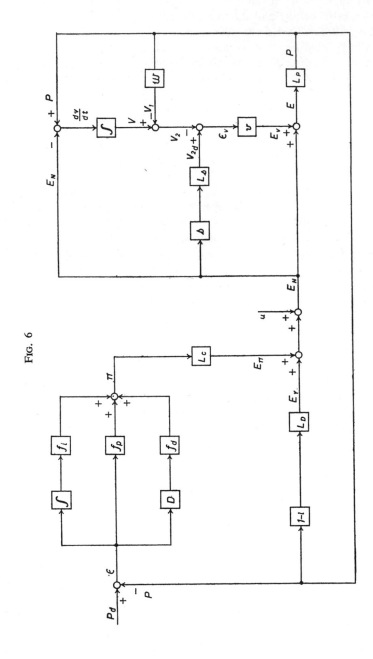

Fig. 6

Inventories held in excess of minimum working inventories will be called V_2, so that $V_2 = V - V_1$.[13] From precautionary and speculative motives businesses will wish to hold some inventories in excess of minimum working inventories, but the amount they wish to hold, which we shall call V_{2_d} or the desired value of V_2, will not always be equal to the amount they are holding. In this simplified model we shall assume that V_{2_d} is a lagged function of non-inventory demand and we shall give the magnitude of this dependence, s, the value 0.125 and assume that the lag, L_s, is of form (b) with a time constant of 0.75 year. (In fact, of course, V_{2_d} will also be influenced by other factors, in particular by interest rates and expected rates of change of prices.) Subtracting V_2 from V_{2_d} gives the "error in inventories," ε_V. We shall assume that the inventory demand, E_V, is a constant proportion, v, of the error in inventories and shall give v the value 2.0.

The only other change from the model shown in Fig. 1 is the addition of the demand lag, L_D, which, because of the fairly rapid adjustment of expenditure by wage-earners when their incomes change, we shall assume to be of form (a) with a time constant of 0.125 year. We shall, however, give the marginal leakage, l, the value 0.4 instead of its previous value 0.25. This reduces the multiplier from 4.0 to 2.5, which is probably a more realistic value, and makes the system more stable. We assume a correction lag of form (c) with a total time constant of 0.5 year and a production lag of form (b) with a total time constant of 0.25 year.

When all three correction factors are zero the response of production to a unit step change in the variable u, applied negatively at time $t = 0$, is the damped inventory cycle shown in curve (a) of Fig. 7. If derivative correction only is applied the equilibrium position of the system is unchanged, so the error in production persists. With low values of the derivative correction factor the fluctuations in the response are reduced, but with higher values another cycle appears with a period of just over one year, and if the derivative correction factor is raised above 0.38 this cycle becomes explosive. Curve (b) of Fig. 7 shows the response when the derivative correction factor is 0.25.

If proportional correction only is applied, the fluctuations in the response are slightly reduced when the value of the proportional correction factor is very low, but if it is raised above 0.1 the fluctuations become worse again and the system becomes unstable when the proportional correction factor is raised above about 0.28. If any integral correction at all is applied alone the amplitudes of the fluctuations increase and the system becomes unstable if the integral correction factor is raised above about 0.08. Similarly, any combination of proportional and integral correction without the addition of derivative correction reduces the stability of the system and increases the magnitudes of

---

[13] It will be noticed that the distinction made here between V_1 and V_2 corresponds closely to the distinction between working capital and liquid capital made by Keynes in Chapters 28 and 29 of the *Treatise on Money*. It is also analogous to his later distinction between M_1 and M_2 in monetary theory.

the fluctuations unless the two correction factors have extremely low values, while if the values are extremely low the improvement in the response is negligible.

FIG. 7

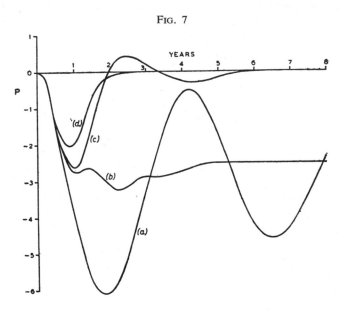

Even if derivative correction is included in the stabilisation policy, the speed with which an error can be corrected is rather limited. About the best response that can be obtained is that shown in curve (c) of Fig. 7. This response results when $f_p = 0.3$, $f_i = 0.4$ and $f_d = 0.2$. Higher values of the correction factors worsen the response by reducing the stability of the system. If the correction lag is changed from form (c) to form (b), the time constant remaining at 0.5 years, the correction factors can be increased a little. The best response is then that shown in curve (d) of Fig. 7, the correction factors being $f_p = 0.4$, $f_i = 0.5$ and $f_d = 0.3$.

FIG. 8

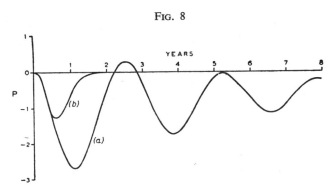

If the correction lag is of form (b) with a total time constant of 0.25 year the best response is obtained when $f_p = 0.9$, $f_i = 0.9$ and $f_d = 0.25$. It is shown as curve (b) of Fig. 8. It is of interest to note that even with this correction lag the stabilisation policy is not satisfactory unless it includes an element of derivative correction. If $f_d = 0$ about the best response that can be obtained is that shown in curve (a) of Fig. 8, the proportional and integral correction factors being 0.4 and 0.1 respectively. With either higher or lower values of f_p and f_i the fluctuations are of greater amplitude.

III. CONCLUSIONS

Because of the simplified nature of the models considered in this paper the results that have been obtained cannot be applied directly to the interpretation of actual economic situations. Indeed, one of the first lessons one learns from studying a variety of hypothetical models is that the problem of economic stabilisation is, even in principle, an extremely intricate one, and that a much more thorough investigation of both theoretical principles and empirical relationships would be needed before detailed policy recommendations could be justified. A few very elementary conclusions can, however, be drawn with some confidence.

The first is that the regulation of a system can be improved if the lengths of the time delays operating around the main control loop are reduced. The distinction between delays and lags should here be noticed. What is of primary importance is that the correcting action should be adjusted continuously and with the minimum possible delay to changes in the error and that the adjustments should quickly produce some initial effect. It does not matter very much if it takes a long time for the policy changes to have their full effect. In fact, it can be shown that if there is a long delay before corrective action is taken or before it begins to have an appreciable effect it is better that the effect, when it does come, should be gradual rather than sudden. The worst possible condition for regulating purposes is one in which the adjustment of policy demand to a change in the error is delayed for a considerable time and then effected quickly and abruptly.

A second conclusion is that it is usually necessary to include an element of derivative correction in a stabilisation policy if regulation is to be satisfactory. In other words, the potential policy demand should be made to depend not only on the magnitude of the current error and on the sum of the past errors,[14] but also on the rate of change of the error, or when observations are at discrete intervals on the difference between the last two observed values of the error.

---

[14] The quantity to which integral correction is related is the integral, or sum, of all past errors. In practice a good approximation to integral correction would be obtained if the integral component of potential policy demand was made to depend on the sum of the errors over the past four or five years or on a weighted sum of these errors, the earlier errors being given less weight than the later ones.

The longer the time delays in the responses around the main control loop, the less effective is derivative correction in reducing fluctuations. Nevertheless, the longer the delays, the more desirable it is that some derivative correction be used, since the delays reduce the stability of the system and so make it more important that whatever stabilising effect can still be obtained by derivative correction should not be foregone.

A third conclusion is that if the lags in the real economic system are at all similar to those we have used in the models it is unlikely that the period needed to restore any desired equilibrium conditions after an economy has experienced a severe disturbance could be much less than two years, even assuming that the regulating authorities use the policy which is most appropriate to the real system of relationships existing in the economy. As these relationships are not known quantitatively, it is unlikely that the policy applied will be the most appropriate one; it may well cause cyclical fluctuations rather than eliminate them.

It is true that many relationships inherent in the real economic system have been omitted from our models and that some of the omitted relationships seem intuitively to be of a stabilising type. But intuitions about dynamic processes may be dangerously misleading and need to be carefully tested. Most of the inherent relationships which at first sight would seem to have stabilising effects can be expressed in forms similar to the policy relationships in the models we have been using. If the lengths and forms of the time lags of these inherent relationships are also similar to those which we have assumed for the correction lag the effects of the inherent relationships will be similar to the effects of the policy relationships which we have already considered. The existence of inherent relationships which appear intuitively to be of a stabilising type may therefore reduce the amount of correction that needs to be applied deliberately by regulating authorities (particularly the proportional and integral elements of correction; it is difficult to think of any inherent relationship which is equivalent to the derivative element of a correction policy), but will not reduce the time required to restore equilibrium after a disturbance unless these relationships operate with shorter time lags and delays than we have been assuming. Nor do the additional inherent relationships make it more likely that cyclical fluctuations will be avoided. In fact, they make it less likely, since it becomes very difficult to judge what quantitative values should be given to the deliberate policy relationships when the system already contains numerous inherent relationships whose magnitudes and speeds of operation are unknown.

The main conclusion that must be drawn from this investigation is that much more research is needed in the general field of economic regulation. To throw light on the practical problems involved in regulating complex economic systems it is necessary to study the properties of more realistic models in which non-linear relationships, growth trends, multiple objectives and multiple disturbances are incorporated. The means for carrying out such studies are now becoming available and should be fully exploited. It is equally important that improved methods should be developed for estimating quantitatively the magnitudes and time-forms of economic relationships in order that the range of permissible hypotheses may be restricted more closely than is at present possible.

37

Taxes, Income Determination, and the Balanced Budget Theorem*

By WILLIAM A. SALANT†

THE PROPOSITION THAT a tax-financed change in expenditure will lead to an equal change in income has been subjected to critical examination in two recent articles.[1] Both emphasize that the proposition, which has been christened the "balanced budget theorem," applies only when certain conditions are fulfilled, and they dismiss it as a special case of little interest because of the restrictive character of these conditions.

There is undoubtedly a danger that conclusions drawn from simplified models will be applied beyond the context in which they are valid and will be invested with the aura of universal truths. By defining and calling attention to the limitations on the validity of the balanced budget theorem, the articles cited serve as a useful corrective against this danger in this case. There is, however, some danger that in two respects they may be the source of confusion rather than clarification. In the first place, they concentrate attention on the limitations of the balanced budget theorem in such a way that the reader may easily lose sight of its essential core of truth. Second, they may create a somewhat inaccurate impression as to the exact location of those limits. The first danger is discussed in the succeeding paragraphs; the second in the later portions of the present paper.

---

* The Review of Economics and Statistics, Vol. XXXIX (May, 1957). Reprinted by courtesy of the Review of Economics and Statistics and the author.

† Chico, California. The writer is indebted to Walter S. Salant for a number of helpful suggestions and to Seymour Harris for improving the readability of this article by suggesting that some of the duller algebra be relegated to footnotes. He was saved from becoming bogged down in unmanageable multiplier formulas by Paul Samuelson's observation, in his article on "The Simple Mathematics of Income Determination," cited below, that it is much easier to work with the underlying equations expressing equilibrium conditions than with the multiplier formulas derived from them.

[1] Ralph Turvey, "Some Notes on Multiplier Theory," American Economic Review, Vol. XLIII (June, 1953), pp. 282–86; and W. J. Baumol and M. H. Peston, "More on the Multiplier Effects of a Balanced Budget," American Economic Review, Vol. XLV (March, 1955), p. 140.

It may well be that the balanced budget theorem has little direct application to the world of reality because the necessary pre-conditions to its validity are rarely fulfilled in that world. Nevertheless, it does not follow that the theorem is completely uninteresting and that it provides no insight whatever into the real world. In order to recognize its role in the evolution of income theory, it is only necessary to recall that, until the balanced budget theorem was advanced, it was generally believed that, under exactly the same general conditions that are assumed in the development of the theorem, a change in expenditures balanced by a change in taxes had no effect on income whatever. That is, it was believed that the multiplier for a balanced budget was zero. Whatever its limitations, the balanced budget theorem represents an important refinement of this earlier view.

That view followed from the assumption (or impression) that taxes could be treated simply as deductions from expenditure. In the balanced budget analysis, it was recognized that, while expenditures (on currently produced domestic goods and services) generate income directly, taxes do not directly reduce expenditure and income. Instead, they reduce the flow of funds available either for spending *or nonspending*. If this flow is subject to further leakages (after the taxes have been paid), such as through saving, the distinction becomes significant.

The balanced budget theorem can best be regarded as a corollary of this treatment of taxes. In a still more refined analysis, it is true, the effect upon spending of different kinds of taxes would be distinguished (and the substitution effect as well as the income effects of taxes might be considered, as Baumol and Peston have suggested). Nevertheless, it remains true that the first step was to introduce taxes explicitly as a distinct entity in the analysis and to formulate some hypothesis, however simple, as to their effect on the flow of income.

Turvey has pointed out that, in his model, the balanced budget multiplier is unity when household saving is the only leakage.[2] Does this mean, as he seems to imply, that the balanced budget multiplier will *not* be unity if there are any other leakages, or, to put it more precisely, if there are any dependent variables other than household saving and consumption? Here we must distinguish between taxes themselves and other variables. The case in which taxes are a dependent variable, assumed to be a function of income, is considered in section III below. In section IV, new dependent variables, such as induced investment, imports, and business savings are introduced, and the effect of tax changes and balanced budget changes is considered in these enlarged systems. We shall find that the application of the balanced budget theorem is not limited to the simple model for which it was first developed.

Before we proceed to these enlarged systems, it will be useful to place the balanced budget analysis in perspective by reviewing briefly, in section I,

---

[2] Turvey, *loc. cit.*, pp. 285–86.

the earlier treatment of taxes in the theory of income determination. In section II, the model from which the balanced budget theorem was originally deduced is presented.[3]

I. BACKGROUND

It is a paradoxical fact that, although Keynes's *General Theory* was highly influential in directing attention to the role of governmental fiscal operations in determining the level of income, government as such plays no explicit part in the formal Keynesian model. That model divides the economy into two sectors, firms and households. Expenditures of households (consumption) are regarded as a function of income, while net expenditures of firms for goods and services (i.e., output less sales to households, or investment) are taken to be determined by other factors. Thus, given the consumption function, income is determined by investment.

In discussions based on this formulation, deficit spending by the government was considered equivalent, in its effect on income, to investment.[4] Tax-financed expenditure was assumed by implication to have no effect on income. It was sometimes mentioned, perhaps as an afterthought, that tax remission was equivalent in its effect to deficit spending. Thus taxes were treated, again by implication, as equivalent to negative investment (or to saving).[5]

Subsequent refinement of the theory brought about two major changes in the treatment of taxes.

---

[3] It may be noted at this point that Baumol and Peston characterize the balanced budget analysis as "misleading in that it appears by a feat of magic to be able to determine an empirical magnitude (the value of the multiplier) without the use of any empirical material" (*loc. cit.*, p. 140). This complaint is difficult to understand. The balanced budget theorem is, in this respect, formally equivalent to (a) the proposition that *if* the numerator and denominator of a fraction are equal, the value of that fraction will be 1, regardless of the magnitude of numerator and denominator; or (b) the proposition that *if* the elasticity of demand for a commodity is unity, a change in supply will cause no change in the value of sales regardless of the magnitude of the shift in the supply function or the elasticity of supply. The validity of these statements is a matter of logic, not of fact. Whether either proposition is applicable to a particular situation, however, cannot be determined without the empirical knowledge, in the case of proposition (a), that the numerator and denominator of the fraction are in fact equal or unequal, or, in the case of proposition (b), that the demand function does or does not have unit elasticity. See also Prof. Alvin Hansen's comment on the Baumol and Peston paper in "More on the Multiplier Effects of a Balanced Budget: Comment," *American Economic Review*, Vol. XLVI (March, 1956), p. 157; and the "Reply" by Baumol and Peston, *ibid.*, p. 160.

[4] In D. H. Robertson's phrase, the government deficit was regarded as "honorary investment." See "Mr. Clark and the Foreign Trade Multiplier," *Economic Journal*, Vol. XLIX (June, 1939), p. 354.

[5] The only explicit reference to taxes in the *General Theory* is the observation that they might influence the aggregate consumption function by redistributing income among individuals or by affecting the net return on savings. See *General Theory of Employment, Interest and Money* (New York, 1936), pp. 94–95.

1. It was recognized quite early that it is unrealistic to treat tax receipts or collections as an autonomous or exogenous variable, since, with a given structure of tax rates, tax collections tend to vary with income. Consequently, tax receipts were treated as a function of income.

2. It was recognized, though considerably later, that taxes cannot correctly be treated as equivalent to negative spending (or to saving) in their effect on income. Tax remission does not in itself involve any change in income or expenditure. It merely reduces the receipts of government and puts additional disposable income into the hands of the private sectors, income which they are free to save or to spend. If government expenditure and investment are considered autonomous, tax remission can raise income only by inducing an increase in consumption. As a first approximation, particularly appropriate in the case of income taxes, it seemed reasonable to assume that decisions about the division of income between consumption and saving are based on income after taxes, that is, to retard consumption as a function of *disposable* income.

These two refinements meant the introduction into the Keynesian model of one new equation, the tax-income function, and the modification of an old one, the consumption equation, to make consumption a function of disposable income instead of national income. These changes in the model altered the conclusions that it yields as to (1) the effect on income of changes in investment, government, or consumption expenditure with a *given* set of tax rates, and (2) the effect of changes in the tax structure itself.

With respect to the effect of changes in investment or government expenditure, or shifts in the consumption function, the recognition of tax receipts as a function of income meant that an autonomous change in spending would cause an income-induced change in taxes. Thus an increase in government spending would cause taxes to rise, and the resulting deficit would be smaller than the spending itself.[6]

Moreover, the increase in tax receipts would be a leakage that would reduce the multiplier effect of the spending. The multiplier adjusted to allow for the marginal tax-income ratio is smaller than the simple Keynesian multiplier which allowed only for the leakage into saving.[7]

When we consider the effect on income of autonomous changes in taxes themselves, we find that much of the discussion does not appear to incorporate the second refinement mentioned above, the treatment of tax receipts as a function of income. For example, the two most explicit algebraic statements of the balanced budget theorem treat taxes as an independent variable.[8]

---

[6] While this point was frequently mentioned in the late 1930's, especially by advocates of expansionist fiscal policies, it is interesting to note that it was also recognized in Kahn's original formulation of the theory of the multiplier. See R. F. Kahn, "The Relation of Home Investment to Unemployment," *Economic Journal*, Vol. XLI (June, 1931), p. 171.

[7] See Paul A. Samuelson, "Fiscal Policy and Income Determination," *Quarterly Journal of Economics*, Vol. LVI (August, 1942), p. 581.

[8] See Trygve Haavelmo, "Multiplier Effects of a Balanced Budget," *Econometrica*, Vol. XIII (October, 1945), p. 311, reprinted in Smithies and Butters (eds.), *Readings in*

On that assumption, it was concluded that:

1. Dollar for dollar, changes in taxes have a weaker income-generating effect than changes in expenditures (for currently-produced goods and services). Specifically, if the multiplier applicable to expenditures is k, the (negative) tax multiplier is $(k - 1)$.
2. As a corollary of (1) it follows that changes in expenditure balanced by an equal change in taxes will have a multiplier of 1.[9]

Whether these conclusions apply when tax receipts are assumed to vary with income is, as indicated above, one of the questions raised by Turvey's discussion and is considered in section III below.

While the treatment of taxes in the Keynesian system was refined along

---

Fiscal Policy (Homewood, Ill.: Richard D. Irwin, Inc., 1955), and Samuelson, "The Simple Mathematics of Income Determination," in Lloyd Metzler et al., *Income, Employment, and Public Policy, Essays in Honor of Alvin H. Hansen* (New York, 1948), p. 138.

[9] Among the early statements of the balanced budget theorem, the point that the (negative) tax multiplier is smaller than the (positive) expenditure multiplier was made first, and the balanced budget multiplier developed as a corollary, in the present writer's privately circulated paper of July, 1942 on "Taxes, the Multiplier, and the Inflationary Gap," in Richard A. Musgrave, "Alternative Budget Policies for Full Employment," *American Economic Review*, Vol. XXXV (June, 1945), p. 387, and in Samuelson, "Simple Mathematics of Income Determination," cited above. Nicholas Kaldor discussed tax-financed expenditure first, and tax remission alone in the succeeding paragraph, in his Appendix C to William H. Beveridge, *Full Employment in a Free Society* (London, 1944), pp. 346–7. Henry C. Wallich mentioned in passing that the tax multiplier is smaller than the expenditure multiplier in "Income-Generating Effects of a Balanced Budget," *Quarterly Journal of Economics*, Vol. LIX (November, 1944), p. 78. Trygve Haavelmo, however, confined himself to the balanced budget case, *loc. cit.*, as did Alvin Hansen and Harvey Perloff in *State and Local Finance in the National Economy* (New York, 1944), pp. 245–46.

Most discussions of the balanced budget theorem consider the situation of underemployment equilibrium, in which an increase in effective demand will raise output and employment, and is therefore considered desirable. The reasoning, of course, applies also to full employment situations, in which the objective of policy is to prevent effective demand from rising. Thus, in order to prevent an increase in government expenditure (or in other forms of demand) from causing an inflationary gap, it is not sufficient for taxes to rise in step with expenditure. Such a balanced increase in expenditures and taxes would leave disposable income and private expenditure unchanged. What is needed, however, is a reduction in private expenditure in order to free resources for the additional government expenditure; this requires that tax receipts increase more than expenditures.

This point was clearly recognized in such wartime studies of the inflation problem as the articles by Walter S. Salant and Milton Friedman on "The Inflationary Gap," *American Economic Review*, Vol. XXXII (June, 1942), pp. 309 and 318, respectively. It did not appear to be recognized in the British budget address of 1941, which introduced the inflationary gap, which has been described as the cornerstone of British wartime fiscal policy (see R. S. Sayers, *Financial Policy*, 1939–1945 [London, 1956]), and in which Keynes had a guiding hand. The language of that address seemed to imply that a rise in taxes equal to additional expenditure would be sufficient to forestall an inflationary gap. In his detailed account of the evolution of the 1941 budget, however, Sayers quotes an internal memorandum written by Keynes in September, 1940, which stated that extra taxes of £300 million might reduce consumption by only £150–200 million, the remainder of the taxation falling on saving (*op. cit.*, p. 71). To effect a £300 million cut in consumption, the additional taxes needed were of the order of £400 million. This is, of course, as clear a statement as could be asked of the principle underlying the balanced budget theorem. Evidently the point was regarded as a refinement which could be dropped in the budget address itself, since that address stated that taxes of £500 million would reduce consumption by the same amount (*op. cit.*, p. 72].

the lines just described, it was shown that the original simple model could be developed and enlarged in numerous other ways, by the addition of new variables, the disaggregation of old ones, and the introduction of new behavior hypotheses. For example, exports, imports, and induced investment could be introduced, or saving could be divided into a business and a household component.[10] What is the effect of these developments on the conclusions as to the income effects of tax changes? In particular, does the balanced budget theorem apply to such enlarged systems? Section IV is addressed to these questions.

II. CONSUMPTION THE ONLY DEPENDENT VARIABLE

The simple model from which the balanced budget theorem was derived contains only the definitional identities:

$$Y = C + I + G \tag{1}$$

$$X = Y - W \tag{2}$$

and the single behavior equation

$$C = a + bX \tag{3}$$

where Y denotes income, C consumption, I investment, G government expenditure on currently produced goods and services, X disposable income (income less taxes plus government transfer payments), and W tax receipts less government transfer payments,[11] all in real terms. Equation (3) is an aggregate consumption function, assumed to be linear.[12] Investment, government expenditures, and taxes less transfer payments are all assumed to be autonomous.[13]

---

[10] For an excellent summary of these developments, see Samuelson's article on "The Simple Mathematics of Income Determination," cited above.

[11] It will be noted that transfer payments are treated as negative taxes. This treatment implies that the income effect of transfer payments is equal and opposite to that of taxes. Specifically, it is assumed that, although transfer payments do not themselves represent income, they do add to the disposable income available for consumption or saving. On this assumption, which is reasonable for simple models, it is easier to treat transfer payments as negative taxes than as a special category of expenditure. In the text below, we shall, for the sake of brevity, refer to tax receipts less transfer payments of government simply as "taxes" or "tax receipts." Similarly, G, government expenditures, always denotes expenditures for currently-produced goods and services. Thus it excludes transfer payments, purchases of existing capital assets, and purchases that result in disinvestment in inventories. Turvey has pointed out that the balanced budget theorem does not apply to expenditures for these purposes, and Baumol and Peston have dealt with the value of the balanced budget multiplier when part of the additional expenditure is for purposes other than purchase of newly-produced goods and services.

[12] In order to concentrate on the income effect of taxes, we rule out the possibility of a shift in the consumption function arising from redistribution of income by assuming that all individuals have linear consumption functions with identical marginal propensities to consume.

[13] In this model, and in those considered below, the only behavior relations considered are simple income effects. That is, the dependent variables are made functions either of

Solving for income, we get:

$$Y = \frac{I + G + a - bW}{1 - b} \tag{4}$$

The multiplier relating a change in income to a change in one of the independent variables, investment or government expenditure (or for that matter a parallel shift in the consumption function denoted by the addition of an amount h to the parameter a), takes the familiar form

$$\frac{\Delta Y}{\Delta I} = \frac{\Delta Y}{\Delta G} = \frac{\Delta Y}{h} = \frac{1}{1 - b}. \tag{5}$$

The multiplier relating a change in income to a change in tax receipts is

$$\frac{\Delta Y}{\Delta W} = - \frac{b}{1 - b}. \tag{6}$$

Thus tax changes will have a weaker effect on income, dollar for dollar, than expenditure changes. The ratio of the tax multiplier to the expenditure multiplier is $(-b)$. The effect on income of a change in expenditure accompanied by an equal change in taxes is the algebraic sum of the multipliers (5) and (6):[14]

$$\frac{\Delta Y}{\Delta G} + \frac{\Delta Y}{\Delta W} = 1 \quad \text{when } \Delta G = \Delta W. \tag{7}$$

This is the balanced budget theorem. It means that the increment in income will be equal to the increment in government expenditure and will consist entirely of additional goods and services produced for the government. Consumption will remain unchanged.

The foregoing is familiar ground. Two comments are called for at this point.

1. The values of the expenditure, tax, and balanced budget multipliers follow from the hypothesis in (3) that consumption is a function of disposable income. If instead it had been assumed that taxes were paid entirely out of saving, consumption would be a function of income, Y, and taxes would play no part whatever in income determination. If, on the other hand, it had been assumed that taxes were paid entirely out of consumption, the consumption function would have the form $C = C(Y) - W$, and the effect of taxes

---

aggregate income or of some component of income or expenditure. This treatment excludes the possibility, for example, that changes in marginal tax rates might alter the inducement to invest with unchanged prospective demand, or that government expenditure for a particular purpose might affect private spending for related purposes and thereby shift the consumption function.

[14] It should be noted that the expression ΔY in the left-hand side of (7) refers to the total (or net) change in income resulting from the combined effect of the tax change and the expenditure change, not to that resulting from the expenditure change alone.

on the level of income would be equal and opposite to that of government or investment expenditure. The hypothesis that consumption varies with income after taxes appears most applicable to personal income taxes. Thus the balanced budget theorem applies primarily to these taxes, rather than to indirect taxes or corporate income taxes.[15]

2. The balanced budget theorem can be deduced directly by solving the underlying equations (1), (2), and (3) for disposable income, without going through the intermediate stages of calculating the expenditure multiplier and the tax multiplier. The solution for disposable income is

$$X = \frac{a + I + G - W}{1 - b}. \tag{8}$$

Since a, b, and I are unchanged, and the change in taxes offsets the change in government expenditure, disposable income must be unchanged. Hence the change in income must be equal to the change in the budget.[16] We shall find this short-cut proof useful later in dealing with more complicated models.

III: TAXES A FUNCTION OF INCOME

We shall now consider the case in which taxes less transfers are assumed to be a linear function of income:[17]

$$W = s + tY. \tag{9}$$

Solving for income, we now get

$$Y = \frac{I + G + a - bs}{1 - b(1 - t)}. \tag{10}$$

With a given tax structure, the multiplier for changes in either investment or government expenditure, or for an increment h to the constant term in

---

[15] Somers has considered all three possibilities mentioned above: taxes falling on saving, those falling on consumption, and taxes falling on income that leave the marginal propensity to consume (out of disposable income) unchanged. See Harold M. Somers, "The Impact of Fiscal Policy on National Income," *Canadian Journal of Economics and Political Science*, August, 1942, p. 364, and *Public Finance and National Income* (Philadelphia, 1949), pp. 500–503 and 507–12. E. Cary Brown has analyzed the effect of consumption taxes in "Analysis of Consumption Taxes in Terms of the Theory of Income Determination," *American Economic Review*, Vol. XL (March, 1950), p. 74.

[16] This method of demonstrating the balanced budget theorem is due to Samuelson. See "The Simple Mathematics of Income Determination," *op. cit.*, p. 142.

[17] The reader may, if he finds it convenient, think of this function as representing a proportional income tax levied at rate t, along with a head tax s. Alternatively, he may think of s as a lump-sum transfer payment or tax exemption, in which case its value would be negative. The assumption of linearity rules out consideration of an income tax with rising marginal rates.

consumption, is:

$$\frac{\Delta Y}{\Delta I} = \frac{\Delta Y}{\Delta G} = \frac{\Delta Y}{h} = \frac{1}{1 - b(1 - t)}. \tag{11}$$

It should be noted that changes in any of these variables will alter tax receipts. In particular, an increment in G will not result in an equal change in the budget deficit.

Changes in the tax function may be caused by changes in either of the parameters s or t. The former correspond geometrically to parallel vertical shifts in the tax function, the latter to changes in its slope resulting from rotation around its intercept with the vertical axis. We shall consider first parallel shifts resulting from the addition of an increment, denoted by Δs, to the term s. The multiplier will be:

$$\frac{\Delta Y}{\Delta s} = - \frac{b}{1 - b(1 - t)}. \tag{12}$$

The ratio of the tax multiplier to the expenditure multiplier is still ($-b$), as it was in the first model. The sum of the multipliers, however, which indicates the effect on income of a change in expenditure accompanied by an equal change in the terms of the tax function, is now:

$$\frac{\Delta Y}{\Delta G} = \frac{1 - b}{1 - b(1 - t)} \quad \text{when} \quad \Delta G = \Delta s. \tag{13}$$

This quantity will be less than unity as long as the marginal tax rate t is positive. Consumption, instead of remaining constant, as it does when the marginal tax rate is zero, will decline. A balanced change in expenditure and in tax receipts *at the initial level of income* will not produce an equal change in income.

This, however, is not the whole story. The ultimate change in tax receipts at the new equilibrium level of income (ΔW in our notation) will be greater than Δs, and therefore greater than ΔG. Instead of equal changes in expenditures and taxes, we have an expenditure change accompanied by a somewhat greater change in taxes. The multiplier in (13) can hardly be called a "balanced budget" multiplier.

In order to determine the balanced budget multiplier for this model, we must so adjust the shift in the tax function that, *at the new equilibrium position*, the tax change and the expenditure change are equal. One way to find this multiplier is to set $\Delta W = \Delta G$, solve for the required shift in the tax function Δs, and then for the resulting change in income ΔY. We can proceed more directly, however, by solving for disposable income as in the final paragraph of section II above. Since the solution for disposable income is identical with that developed in section II, equation (8), we know at once that disposable income must remain unchanged if $\Delta G = \Delta W$. Thus the change in income again equals the change in expenditures and the ultimate change in tax receipts. The "balanced budget" multiplier is again unity even when tax receipts are assumed to vary with income, but "balance" in the budget change must be understood to refer to the equality of ΔG with ΔW, the *ultimate* change in tax receipts, rather than Δs, the initial change.[18]

We turn now to the effect of changes in the marginal tax rate t on income.[19] Denoting the original tax rate t' and the new rate t'' and the original level of income Y' and the new equilibrium level Y'', we first solve for the change in income resulting from a change in the marginal tax rate from t' to t''.[20] The result is a fraction, equation (16) in footnote 20, of which the numerator represents the product of the change in tax yield at the *original* level of income and the marginal propensity to consume, while the denominator is the same expression that appeared in the denominators of the multipliers in equations (11) and (12) above, but calculated at the *new* tax rate t''.

Equation (16) is the first case in which the initial level of income Y' appears in the solution for ΔY. By dividing through by Y', we can find the *relative* change in income as a function of the marginal propensity to consume and the new and old tax rates. This result is in accordance with common sense; a given change in tax rates (as opposed to tax receipts) will produce a determinate relative change in income, rather than a determinate absolute change.

The conclusions with respect to the balanced budget theorem are similar to those reached above in the case of parallel shifts in the tax function. When the change in tax receipts at the *original* level of income is set equal to the change in expenditure, i.e., when $(t'' - t')Y' = \Delta G$, the resulting change in income will be less than the change in revenues and expenditures. When,

---

[18] One loose end remains. While we have assumed a vertical shift, Δs, in the tax function just sufficient to insure that $\Delta W = \Delta G$, we have yet to determine how great this shift must be. Since we know that $\Delta Y = \Delta G = \Delta W$, the calculation is simple. Substituting ΔG for both ΔY and ΔW in the tax equation (9), we get

$$\Delta s = \Delta G(1 - t). \tag{14}$$

[19] This case has been considered only in geometric terms, so far as I am aware, except for Turvey's article, *loc. cit.*, p. 285. Geometric treatments include Robert L. Bishop, "Alternative Expansionist Policies: A Diagrammatic Analysis," in *Income, Employment and Public Policy*, p. 317; E. Cary Brown, *loc. cit.*, p. 74, in which the effect of consumption taxes is compared to that of income taxes; and J. G. Gurley, "Fiscal Policy for Full Employment," *Journal of Political Economy*, Vol. LX (December, 1952), p. 525.

[20] From equation (10) we obtain for the change in income the unwieldy expression

$$\Delta Y = Y'' - Y' = \frac{I + G + a - bs}{1 - b(1 - t'')} - \frac{I + G + a - bs}{1 - b(1 - t')} \tag{15}$$

which fortunately simplifies to

$$\Delta Y = -\frac{b(t'' - t')Y'}{1 - b(1 - t'')}. \tag{16}$$

This result corresponds to Turvey's conclusion, *loc. cit.*, p. 285.

however, the *ultimate* change in taxes is set equal to the change in expenditures, i.e., when $\Delta W = \Delta G$, an equal change in income will result. This conclusion can again be derived from inspection of equation (8), the solution for disposable income, which remains unchanged.[21] It might be added that, since the form of tax and consumption functions does not affect equation (8), this conclusion does not depend on the assumption of linear functions.

We have shown that the treatment of taxes as a dependent variable instead of an independent parameter does not alter the value of the balanced budget multiplier. Similar conclusions apply if government expenditure is treated as a dependent variable.

Up to this point, we have been concerned largely with balanced changes in expenditure and taxation. What can we say about the relative effectiveness of tax changes by themselves, as compared with expenditure changes, in inducing changes in income? The first problem is to decide on the appropriate terms for comparison. We might compare the increase in income resulting from a dollar of expenditure with that resulting from a dollar of tax remission (either at the initial or at the new equilibrium level of income). This, however, does not seem an entirely appropriate comparison, because, in the present model, the expenditure will itself induce a change in tax receipts, and the change in the budget surplus or deficit will be less than the additional expenditure. It would appear to be more interesting to compare the increase in income resulting from one dollar of additional *deficit* caused by expenditure with the increase resulting from a dollar of deficit caused by tax remission.

The result of this comparison is that the increase in income per dollar of deficit resulting from increased expenditure bears a ratio to the increase in income per dollar of deficit caused by tax remission of $1/b\,(1-t)$.[22] Since

---

[21] The calculation of the change in the marginal tax rate required to preserve the original state of budgetary balance is somewhat more complicated than before. The change in tax receipts, ΔW, which results from both the change in rates and the change in income, can be expressed as

$$\Delta W = t''Y'' - t'Y'.$$

By assumption $\Delta W = \Delta G = \Delta Y$.

Manipulation of these expressions gives the following result for the required change in rates:

$$t'' - t' = \frac{\Delta G(1 - t')}{\Delta G + Y'}.$$

[22] The increase in income ΔY resulting from an increment of expenditure ΔG is given by equation (11). The rise in tax receipts is $t\Delta Y$, and the change in the deficit (which we may denote as $\Delta G - \Delta W$), is therefore $\Delta G - t\Delta Y$. The ratio of the change in income to the change in the deficit is

$$\frac{\Delta Y}{(\Delta G - \Delta W)} = \frac{1}{(1 - b)(1 - t)} \quad \text{with } s \text{ and } t \text{ constant.} \tag{17}$$

This result agrees with Samuelson, "Simple Mathematics," p. 145, equation (11). The corresponding ratio for changes in the tax function, whether they result from changes in the

the quantity $b(1 - t)$ must be less than unity in a stable system,[23] we can conclude that, per unit of deficit, expenditure has a greater impact on income than tax remission, just as it did in the first model.

IV. ADDITIONAL DEPENDENT VARIABLES INTRODUCED

We have just considered a model in which tax receipts (or expenditures) are considered a function of income, and we have found that the value of the balanced budget multiplier is still unity, provided the "balanced" change in expenditures and taxes is understood to refer to the values of those variables at the new equilibrium position. In this section we shall see what happens to the balanced budget multiplier when new dependent variables (whether leakages like imports or business saving, or expenditures like investment), other than taxes and household saving, are introduced. To anticipate the results, the conclusions will be that (1) the balanced budget multiplier will be unity if the new dependent variables are made functions of disposable income $(Y - W)$ or of private expenditure $(Y - G)$, but not if they are functions of national income (Y); (2) in any event, the balanced budget mutliplier will be greater than zero and may be greater or less than unity.

To simplify the analysis, we shall first consider tax receipts an independent variable, as in section II above. We introduce investment as a new dependent variable, which we shall assume initially to be a linear function of national income:[24]

$$I = u + vY. \tag{19}$$

Solving the new system of equations (1), (2), (3), and (19) for income, we obtain

$$Y = \frac{a + u + G - bW}{1 - b - v}. \tag{20}$$

It is readily seen that the multiplier for changes in government expenditures, assuming all other parameters constant, is

$$\frac{\Delta Y}{\Delta G} = \frac{1}{1 - b - v} \tag{21}$$

---

constant term s or in the marginal tax rate t, is

$$\frac{\Delta Y}{\Delta W} = -\frac{b}{1 - b} \text{ with } G \text{ constant.} \tag{18}$$

The value of the ratio $\Delta Y/\Delta W$ is the same as in the first model considered, in which taxes were an independent variable—see equation (6) above. This equality has been pointed out by Thomas C. Schelling, *National Income Behavior* (New York, 1951), p. 100.

[23] See Schelling, *op. cit.*, p. 85.

[24] Investment has been selected as the new dependent variable because its introduction requires less change in the system of equations than would that of, say, business saving or imports, and it serves equally well to illustrate the propositions with which we are concerned here.

while the multiplier for tax changes alone is

$$\frac{\Delta Y}{\Delta W} = -\frac{b}{1 - b - v}. \tag{22}$$

While the ratio of the tax multiplier to the expenditure multiplier remains $(-b)$, as in the first model considered in section II, the balanced budget multiplier, which is equal to the sum of the separate multipliers, is no longer unity but rather $\left(\dfrac{1-b}{1-b-v}\right)$, which is greater than unity if v is positive.

Why does the introduction of induced investment affect the balanced budget multiplier? While there are differences between investment and consumption which are vital for other purposes, inspection of the system of equations shows that, in the present context, the only difference is that investment is assumed to be a function of national income (Y), while consumption is made a function of disposable income ($Y - W$). Thus, while a balanced change in G and W will initially (i.e., in the "first round") leave disposable income and hence consumption unchanged, it will affect Y, and hence investment, and will set in motion a multiplier process.

If induced investment were assumed to be a function of disposable income instead of national income, equation (20), the investment function, would be exactly similar in form to equation (3), the consumption function, and the balanced budget multiplier would be unity.[25] Alternatively, investment might be assumed, with equal plausibility, to be a function of private expenditure (i.e., of $C + I$ which equals $Y - G$). The balanced budget multiplier would still be unity (although the government expenditure multiplier would now be reduced to $\dfrac{1-v}{1-b-v}$).

More generally, when each of the individual dependent variables is treated as a function of either disposable income ($Y - W$) or private expenditure ($Y - G$), they will be uniquely determined by $G - W$ (assuming the parameters of the behavior equations, such as a, b, v, and u in the present system, and any other independent variables, constant). Since a balanced change in G and W means that $G - W$ remains unchanged, all these dependent variables will also remain constant. Government expenditure will be the only type of expenditure that changes, and ΔY will equal ΔG; the balanced budget multiplier will be unity.

If, however, some dependent variable is not uniquely determined by $Y - W$ or $Y - G$ and, in particular, if it is a function of Y, then it cannot be expressed as a unique function of $G - W$, and it will be affected by balanced changes in G and W.

These conclusions can be readily applied to an open system with foreign

---

[25] Smithies has treated investment in this way in his chapter on "Federal Budgeting and Fiscal Policy," in *A Survey of Contemporary Economics* (Philadelphia, 1948), p. 188.

trade. If, for example, exports are considered an independent variable which remains constant for the present purpose, and imports are made a function of national income (or of total expenditure $C + I + G + E$ where E denotes exports), then the balanced budget multiplier will be less than unity (but greater than zero). If, however, imports were assumed to consist entirely of goods destined for private consumption and investment but not for government use, then the introduction of foreign trade would not affect a balanced budget multiplier which had a value of unity in a closed system.[26]

If business saving is introduced, the "disposable income" available to households is now reduced by the amount of the business saving, and the consumption equation must be adjusted accordingly. Under most conditions, the introduction of business saving reduces the value of the balanced budget multiplier. There is, however, a special case which illustrates the general conclusions stated above. If personal taxes, imports, and investment are all zero or constant, and if business saving is a function of national income less business taxes, then business saving, disposable income, and consumption will all be uniquely determined by national income less taxes. Under these conditions, a change in expenditure fully balanced by a change in business taxes will have a multiplier of unity.

All of the preceding discussion has been based on the assumption that taxes are an independent variable. How are the conclusions altered if taxes are allowed to vary with income? It can be shown that, as in section III above when a tax function was added, the value of the expenditure multiplier will change, but the balanced budget multiplier will not be affected.[27]

---

[26] Disaggregation of imports into components, each of which is treated as a function of the corresponding component of aggregate demand, could alter these conclusions. For example, the balanced budget multiplier would be negative if the marginal imports associated with a unit change in government expenditure were greater than consumers' marginal propensities to save and to import out of disposable income.

[27] The calculation of the value of the balanced budget multiplier when taxes are a function of income, and the balanced budget multiplier is not unity, is rather complex. The difficulty lies in determining how much of a shift in the tax function is required to insure that the change in tax receipts balances the change in expenditure. It will be recalled that in section III above, where taxes were treated as a function of income, we deduced at once by inspection of the equations that the balanced budget multiplier must be unity. Knowing the change in income, we could easily compute the required shift of the tax function. If, however, the value of the balanced budget multiplier cannot be determined by inspection, then it is necessary to calculate the shift in the tax function *before* the change in income can be determined. For example, if a given change in expenditure ΔG is to be balanced by an equal change in taxes ΔW, achieved through a vertical shift in the tax function Δs and the induced change in taxes $t\Delta Y$, but with no change in the marginal tax rate t, the determination of the resulting change in income requires the following steps: (1) calculate the change in income resulting from ΔG alone; (2) calculate the change in the budget surplus resulting from ΔG alone, by applying the marginal tax rate to the change in income calculated in (1), and subtracting the result from ΔG; (3) calculate the change in the parameter s required to offset the change in the deficit resulting from ΔG alone, as found in (2); and finally (4) calculate the change in income resulting from the change in s alone, and add it to that resulting from ΔG alone. The sum is the change in income resulting from the balanced change in expenditures and taxes.

It also remains true that, per dollar of deficit, the income-generating effect of expenditures is higher than that of taxes.

The foregoing conclusions may be compared with Turvey's remark that the balanced budget multiplier will be unity when "household saving is the only leakage; i.e., business saving, marginal rates of government expenditure, all marginal tax rates, and the marginal propensity to import are all zero."[28] In section III above we concluded that marginal rates of government expenditure (on goods and services) and of personal income tax need not be zero if the balanced budget condition is interpreted to refer to the ultimate rather than the initial change in the budget. We can now conclude that the other leakages need not be zero provided the relevant dependent variables are functions of disposable income (or of $Y - G$).[29]

V. CONCLUDING REMARKS

The foregoing analysis suggests the following general conclusions about the income effects of personal income taxes (or transfer payments) and of balanced changes in such taxes and government expenditures on goods and services:[30]

1. Per dollar of additional deficit, an increase in expenditures with unchanged tax rates will have a greater income-generating effect than a dollar of deficit arising from a reduction in tax rates.
2. It follows from (1) that an increase in expenditures fully offset by an equal increase in tax receipts will have *some* income-generating effect. The magnitude of this effect will vary in different models.
3. An increase in expenditure fully offset by an equal increase in tax receipts will generate an equal increase in income in a system in which all the income-determining dependent variables, such as consumption, induced investment, and imports, are functions of disposable income ($Y - W$) or of private expenditure less imports ($Y - G$), but not when they are functions of national income.
4. The foregoing propositions apply even when income taxes (or for that matter government expenditures) are themselves dependent variables, provided it is understood that the relevant changes in expenditures and tax receipts are the *ultimate* changes at the new equilibrium levels of income, rather than the initial or impact effects of shifts in the tax (or expenditure) function at the original income level.

---

[28] *Loc. cit.*, pp. 285–86.

[29] In the particular model used by Turvey, neither imports nor business saving satisfies this condition, but indirect taxes are considered a function of disposable income. For this reason, the balanced budget multiplier will be unity in Turvey's model even if the marginal rate of indirect taxes (which Turvey assumes to fall entirely on consumption) is not zero, as Peston has pointed out. See "A Note on the Balanced Budget Multiplier," *American Economic Review*, Vol. XLIV (March, 1954), p. 129.

[30] These conclusions apply to models of the type considered in this paper, in which all functional relations involve only simple income effects, government expenditures consist entirely of purchases of currently-produced goods and services (transfer payments being treated as negative taxes), taxes are levied on income, consumption is a function of disposable income, and imports are not disaggregated.

The balanced budget theorem, in what we may call its strict form, states that a balanced change in taxes and expenditures has a multiplier of exactly unity. As (3) above indicates, this proposition is valid only under certain conditions. In particular, it applies to simple models in which consumption (and taxes themselves) are the only dependent variables (and the hypothesis about the behavior of consumption is that it varies with income after taxes). Nevertheless, as stated in (2) above, a balanced change in taxes (or transfer payments) and expenditures will always have *some* income-generating effect under the conditions stated in footnote 30; the appropriate multiplier may be greater or less than one, depending on the model. The balanced budget theorem, while only an approximation to the truth (like any statement derived from simplified models), is a better approximation than the view it superseded, that the income-generating effects of taxes (or transfer payments) are equal and opposite to those of expenditures on goods and services, and hence that the balanced budget multiplier is zero.

38

CED's Stabilizing Budget Policy after Ten Years*

By WALTER W. HELLER†

THE YEAR 1957 is an appropriate time to take stock of the prescription of the Committee for Economic Development for the role of federal tax policy in economic stabilization, not only because tenth anniversaries are good occasions for stock-taking, but more important because recent experience in positive monetary and fiscal policy calls into question some of the assumptions and judgments on which CED's "stabilizing budget policy" is based.[1] Recent modifications of the original CED formula, together with CED's current re-examination of its entire monetary-fiscal policy, also suggest that a re-appraisal of the stabilizing budget policy may be timely.[2]

A review of CED's tax policy for economic stability is a review of the dominant theme in postwar fiscal-policy thinking. A dozen years ago, in view of depression and war experience and under the intellectual impact of Keynes, Hansen, and Lerner, it appeared that the discredited dogma of annual budget balancing might be replaced in the affections of most economists— even if not in the halls of Congress and the White House—by a policy of compensatory or functional finance. But instead, by 1949, the doctrine of automatic flexibility largely held sway—a doctrine which confines the role of budget policy in economic stabilization to the contribution it can make within the limits of (1) marginal budget balancing, (*i.e.*, matching of new expenditures

* *American Economic Review*, Vol. XLVII (September, 1957). Reprinted by courtesy of the American Economic Association and the author. The author is indebted to John H. Kareken and Harlan M. Smith for many helpful criticisms. An earlier version of this paper was presented at the April, 1957 meeting of the Midwest Economic Association.

† University of Minnesota and formerly Chairman, Council of Economic Advisers.

[1] The basic document in which the stabilizing budget policy was first enunciated is *Taxes and the Budget: A Program for Prosperity in a Free Economy* (New York, November, 1947). Restatements are available in the 16 national policy statements and other pamphlets on fiscal and/or monetary policy issued by CED since 1947. The latest restatement is in *The Budget, the Economy and Tax Reduction in 1956*, issued June, 1956. The May, 1957 statement, *Tax Reduction and Tax Reform—When and How*, contains no explicit statement or application of the stabilizing budget policy.

[2] Having toiled rewardingly in the CED vineyards as a consultant and technical advisor on budgetary policy, and having been among the worshippers at the shrine of fiscal automaticity, I should perhaps note that this reappraisal has not been entirely unagonizing.

with new tax revenues even though the budget *as a whole* may be unbalanced except at some agreed high level of national income), and (2) the deficits and surpluses automatically generated by fluctuations in the level of national income (augmented by discretionary changes only in "serious" recessions or inflations).

What turned the main stream of economic-policy thinking so strongly towards automation of fiscal policy? Intellectual antecedents are not hard to find in the writings on built-in flexibility of Gunnar Myrdal, A. G. Hart, Alan Sweezy, Beardsley Ruml, and even Alvin Hansen in the late 'thirties and early 'forties.[3] But what pushed their efforts to the center of the policy stage and led to the de-emphasis of discretionary compensatory finance? Among the factors that played a major role were: (1) the expansion of the federal budget to a size which made automatic flexibility quantitatively important; (2) the shift of emphasis from secular stagnation to the problem of cyclical fluctuations, a shift which gave a higher priority to flexibility and reversibility in policy; (3) the disappointing record of the immediate postwar economic forecasts that seemed to undercut the foundation on which discretionary policy must rest; and (4) the attractions of a budgetary policy based on automaticity and marginal budget balancing as a pragmatic middle ground on which a consensus of otherwise widely divergent groups might be reached.[4]

Among professional economists, a remarkable degree of consensus on underlying fiscal strategy was, in fact, reached. After issuance of the basic CED statement in 1947 and important further explorations of built-in flexibility and automatic policy by A. G. Hart, Richard Musgrave and Merton Miller, and Milton Friedman, this trend of thinking culminated in the "Princeton Manifesto" of September, 1949. In it, 16 economists of such widely differing persuasions as Howard Bowen, Howard Ellis, J. K. Galbraith, James K. Hall, Paul Samuelson, Sumner Slichter, Arthur Smithies, and Jacob Viner agreed unanimously on a set of policies centering on built-in flexibility buttressed by more or less automatic supplements. The essence of their recommendations was embodied in the Douglas subcommittee report early in 1950.[5]

---

[3] For a useful survey of this subject, see N. F. Keiser, "The Development of the Concept of 'Automatic Stabilizers'," *Jour. Fin.*, Vol. XI (December, 1956), pp. 422–41. His survey impresses one with the multiplicity of antecedents which provided the raw materials of the CED policy. However, to CED and its present research director, Herbert Stein, must go most of the credit for developing the specific rationale by which fiscal policy could simultaneously serve two masters, *i.e.*, economic stabilization and budgetary discipline.

[4] For an analytical discussion of the background, content, and rationale of CED's policy, see Herbert Stein, "Budget Policy to Maintain Stability," in *Problems in Anti-Recession Policy*, Committee for Economic Development (New York, 1954).

[5] Joint Committee on the Economic Report, *Monetary, Credit and Fiscal Policies*, 81st Cong., 2nd sess., Sen. Doc. No. 129 (Washington, 1950), esp. pp. 11–17. "Federal Expenditure and Revenue Policy for Economic Stability," the statement of the 16 economists who had been convened by the National Planning Association at Princeton (in September, 1949), was published in *Am. Econ. Rev.*, Vol. XXXIX (December, 1949), pp. 1263–68.

It should be noted that the Princeton statement, for all its automation of fiscal policy, fell short of a complete victory of rules over authority. It left considerable room for discretion in the light of "recent events and the outlook for the near future." For example, it provided that under conditions of unemployment and deflation, tax increases to match new expenditure programs should be suspended until they could be put into effect without impeding recovery. In addition, it urged that the possibilities of "formula flexibility" be explored since automatic flexibility was no more than "a first line of defense." The statement also called for "more strenuous fiscal measures" "where there is a definite expectation, justified by events, of serious recession or inflation . . .," a prescription which left considerable latitude for differences of interpretation among the signers. Thus, although the Princeton statement represents the high-water mark of the doctrine of fiscal automaticity (among economists, at least), it did not go as far as CED's original stabilizing budget formula in relying on automatic stabilizers.

I. *The Stabilizing Budget Formula and Philosophy*

The main elements of current CED fiscal doctrine as presented, applied, and modified in a series of policy statements since 1947 may be summarized as follows:

1. *The Balanced Budget Rule.* (a) Tax rates shall be high enough to balance the cash budget at high employment (defined as employment equaling 96 percent of the labor force)—the rule of "high-level balance";[6] and (b) additional expenditure programs shall be matched by additional taxes (in terms of their high-employment yield) to maintain this balance at high employment—the rule of "marginal budget balancing." These rules also require that cash surpluses generated by economic growth be eliminated by tax reduction.

2. *Automatic Flexibility.* Surpluses and deficits generated by inflationary and deflationary deviations from high employment should be welcomed as stabilizing influences, but tax rates should not be altered to magnify these surpluses and deficits as an offset to moderate economic fluctuations.

3. *Nonautomatic Deviations.* Given severe inflation or unemployment, either at hand or clearly in the offing, discretionary changes in tax rates (and, more reluctantly, in expenditure programs) may be made to enlarge the

---

[6] The original 1947 formula called for a $3 billion surplus at the agreed high level of employment, but implicitly in 1952 and 1953 and explicitly in 1954, CED changed its fiscal target to a balanced cash budget at high employment. Since the choice of a surplus, balance, or deficit as the high-employment target is an arbitrary one, a more generalized label such as "a fixed revenue-expenditure relationship at high employment" would be more accurate.

deficits or surpluses beyond the levels generated by built-in flexibility. Recessions or inflations falling short of this "severe" category may call for some adjustments in the effective dates of tax changes designed to maintain high-level balance.

4. *Other Exceptions.* Large, temporary bulges of expenditures need not be covered immediately by tax increases. Surpluses generated by economic growth or expenditure reductions should not be converted into tax reductions until they are large enough and certain enough "to give room for significant tax reform" without danger of creating deficits during prosperity.[7]

5. *Relation to Other Policies.* "The stabilizing budget policy . . . should be regarded as part of an overall financial policy for greater economic stability, in which not only budget policy but also monetary policy, debt management, federal loans and guarantees have important functions."[8]

What assumptions underlie these policy prescriptions? Most basically, CED policy rests on the assumption that human frailties and institutional deficiencies—reflected in imperfections and errors of forecasting, slow-moving executive and legislative processes in taxation, and a tendency of human beings to be timid, unpredictable, and biased towards inflation—make it necessary to utilize automatic rather than discretionary fiscal changes in national stabilization policy. As Herbert Stein put it, "The Committee apparently felt that this plan embodied all that fiscal policy could do—in the existing state of affairs—to maintain stability. While 'stronger' programs could be easily conceived, the Committee argued that these stronger programs are likely to be unstabilizing, because of errors of forecasting, lags, and biases in the decision-making process."[9]

Second, even if human and institutional factors were favorable to counter-cyclical manipulation of tax rates, the desirable "disciplinary effect" of the marginal-budget-balancing rule would still argue for restricting the ordinary scope of fiscal policy to its built-in flexibility. This restriction permits taxes to play their traditional role as a restraint on expenditures.

CED policy appears to reflect two additional articles of faith. The first is that stabilization policy, if forced to choose, should give a relatively strong guarantee of price stability and a relatively weak guarantee of full employment, lest it promote secular inflation.

The second is that heavy reliance on monetary controls for economic stabilization is desirable not only because of their *effectiveness* as a tool for stabilizing aggregate demand (an economic judgment) but also because their *effects* on resource allocation and income distribution are preferred to those of a more aggressive use of fiscal policy, given our present and prospective tax-expenditure structure (a value preference).

---

[7] CED, *The Budget, The Economy and Tax Reduction in 1956* (New York, 1956), p. 7.
[8] *Ibid.*, p. 6.
[9] Stein, *op. cit.*, p. 87.

II. *The Issues of Neutrality and Discretionary Action*

In evaluating the stabilizing budget policy, one should be careful to distinguish between true and false issues. In particular, there may have been some misunderstanding on the question of budget neutrality and the role of discretion in CED's policy.

Neutrality. First, those who espouse high-level balance and marginal budget balancing cannot claim (nor does CED claim) that a balanced cash budget will be neutral in its impact on aggregate demand at high employment nor that balanced-budget increments will be neutral at whatever level of employment they are introduced. It is not surprising that there should be misunderstanding on this point since a policy designed to run a surplus above a "satisfactory high employment" level and a deficit below that level may *seem* to say that the budget is neutral *at* that level. But several considerations quickly make it clear that balance is not at all synonymous with neutrality.

Only a brief reminder of multiplier theory is needed to establish this point. The somewhat battle-scarred "balanced budget theorem" makes clear (1) that matched increments of taxes and factor-purchase expenditures are very likely, if not certain, to have an expansionary effect, and (2) that this effect will vary with consumption propensities and with government expenditure leakages via imports, purchases of capital assets, and the like.[10] Or, turning from marginal to total budgets in terms of high-level balance, we are long since aware that different types of expenditure activity and different types of revenues may have different multipliers. There is no reason to believe that the multiplied income effects of the two sides of the budget will balance each other just because revenues and expenditures happen to be in balance. Neutrality would require attaching a multiplier to each category of taxes and expenditures and then balancing the two sums of the multiplied products.[11]

At a cruder level of budget definition, one encounters significant year-to-year shifts in budget coverage and timing which upset the relationship between the size of the federal cash surplus or deficit and the size of federal subtractions from or additions to private-income flows. For example, a transfer of the financing of certain farm price-support operations from the budget into the banking system via "certificates of interest" reduced recorded federal expenditures and deficits by over $1 billion in fiscal 1954. The "Mills Plan" for

---

[10] For a good bibliography on the subject and for the latest rounds in the controversy on this theorem, see W. J. Baumol and M. H. Peston, "More on the Multiplier Effects of a Balanced Budget," *Am. Econ. Rev.*, Vol. XLV (March, 1955), pp. 140–48, and the "Comment" by Alvin Hansen, together with their "Reply," *Am. Econ. Rev.*, Vol. XLVI (March, 1956), pp. 157–62.

[11] For an interesting attempt to estimate the initial demand effects of various broad classes of federal expenditure and revenues, see Arthur Smithies, "The Impact of the Federal Budget," *Rev. Econ. Stat.*, Vol. XXIX (February, 1947), pp. 28–31. See also A. H. Conrad, "The Multiplier Effects of Redistributive Public Budgets," *Rev. Econ. Stat.*, Vol. XXXVII (May, 1955), pp. 160–73.

speeding up corporate income-tax payments fattened federal receipts by $1 to $2 billion a year for five years without changing corporate-tax liabilities. Year-end manipulations can shift significant amounts of revenues and expenditures from one year to another. For example, the devices of retarding the processing of tax payments and accelerating the payment of certain bills have been used to shift hundreds of millions of dollars of budget surplus from one year into the next. The shifting content of the budget as an economic yardstick of government activity not only interferes with any concept of budget neutrality but poses special problems for the managers of federal fiscal policy. If those managers are tightly tied to a rule of high-level budget balance, they will have less flexibility to adjust tax levels to compensate for these budget vagaries, thereby throwing an added burden on monetary policy as the economic adjuster.

Finally, federal surplus and deficit figures fail to reflect adequately the far-flung federal credit programs, which have an important impact on private income and investment. Budget estimates for 1958 show net expenditures of only $1.4 billion for these programs. Yet total new commitments in the form of loans, investments, guarantees, and insurance will exceed $21.0 billion. Outstanding federal guarantees now cover over $50 billion, or 13 percent, of total private debt.[12] Although largely outside the budget, federal credit programs have a positive role to play in economic stabilization (as CED policy recognizes).

Discretion. A second issue is that of implicit and explicit discretion involved in the stabilizing budget policy. Can this policy, and does it, live by rules alone? Does it draw a defensible line between rules and authority? Samuelson argues persuasively that there is no such thing as a truly automatic mechanism in fiscal policy.[13] Not only is the mechanism established, continued, modified, and abolished by discretion, which rules out any "notion of a genuine difference of kind" but, more than this, "efforts to establish a logically rigorous difference of degree have not met with success." This does not rule out the pragmatic case for pursuing the kind of discretionary action which an automatic mechanism provides, but it does do violence to any concept that a nonautomatic policy is uncertainly managed by fallible men while an automatic fiscal policy is divinely guided by infallible rules.

There are also many explicitly discretionary features in CED's policy. It is left to human judgment to decide when a recession is so moderate that one leaves tax rates completely untouched, when it has reached the point that makes it advisable to suspend the effective dates of tax increases, and when it is "serious" or "severe" enough (CED does not define these terms) to call for

[12] The Budget of the United States Government for the Fiscal Year 1958, *Budget Message of the President and Summary Budget Statements* (Washington, 1957), pp. 1103–5.

[13] P. A. Samuelson, "Principles and Rules in Modern Fiscal Policy: a Neo-Classical Reformulation," in *Money, Trade, and Economic Growth* (New York, 1951), pp. 162–66.

outright compensatory rate changes. There are even more difficult decisions on the inflationary side: when is the revenue surplus clearly a product of economic growth which threatens to retard the rate of further growth, and when is it a welcome contribution (perhaps even too small a one) to the fight against inflation?

CED's fiscal formula provides these general guidelines on a surplus at full employment: if employment does not exceed 96 percent of the labor force, a substantial surplus signals tax reduction, but if employment rises above 96 percent, one should hold the tax line against inflation. But what if 96 percent is just a point on a clearly rising trend of employment, or if it is accompanied by a rising price level? Should one simply project the existing employment and price levels into the future, follow the formula, cut taxes, and leave the rest of the job to monetary policy?[14]

Two considerations suggest that CED's generally affirmative answer is not as doctrinaire as one might infer from overemphasis on the automaticity of the stabilizing budget rule. First, in a current study of the problem of inflation, CED is considering this question: does the economic record of the postwar decade establish reliable clues to the "terms of trade" between the level of unemployment and the rate of increase in the price level? Is 4 percent the magic number that is consistent with a 0 percent price rise? Or are the terms of trade such that insistence on a 3 percent unemployment target will bring about a 1 to 2 percent price rise per annum? Once these terms of trade have been established empirically, of course, one still has to make a choice between the higher level of employment with the greater inflation potential and the lower level with the greater likelihood of price stability.[15]

---

[14] In two recent policy statements (*Tax Policy in 1956*, December, 1955 and *The Budget, The Economy and Tax Reduction in 1956*, June, 1956), CED interpreted its rule in a setting of roughly 4 percent unemployment, rising price levels, and prospective budget surpluses of $3 to $4 billion. It called in effect for elimination of the surplus. In its December, 1955 statement (p. 5), CED said, "Although the actual figure may turn out to be more or less than this, we believe an assumption that taxes can be cut by $3 or $4 billion is a reasonable basis for considering what kind of a tax reduction program is most desirable." The actual cash surplus for fiscal 1956 was $4.5 billion. In the June, 1956 statement (p. 8), CED recommended that decisions on tax cuts (to take effect January 1, 1957) "should be based on a comprehensive, authoritative review of the 1957 budget prospect"; the Budget Bureau's *Mid-Year Budget Review* estimated the fiscal 1957 cash surplus at $3.7 billion. Apparently, tax cuts of this magnitude were felt to be justified even in the face of incipient inflation on grounds (a) that the transition from a non-CED policy to the CED formula required elimination of the budget surplus at 96 percent employment and (b) that additional inflationary pressure generated by moving onto the CED track was to be offset by a tightening of monetary policy, thus combining a less restrictive budget policy with a more restrictive monetary policy. While this was perhaps a correct application of the CED formula (though unemployment figures hovering between 3.2 and 3.7 percent of the labor force in the last half of 1955 raise some doubts on this score about the late-1955 recommendation), one may question whether it was a wise recommendation in the light of the facts available *at that time* (*i.e.*, not just in retrospect).

[15] Note that CED has long since abandoned its initial 1947–48 position of trying to roll prices back to a pre-existing (lower) level. As introduced in 1947 and applied in recommendations to the Senate Finance Committee in 1948, the CED formula used the early-1947

Second, CED has opened the door slightly to further exercise of discretion in its year-to-year applications of the rule. For example, concern over inflation in 1955 apparently influenced CED's choice among alternative budgetary predictions in a direction indicating no tax reduction at that time, and in 1956 led it to suggest that the effective date of proposed tax cuts be deferred to January 1, 1957.

Given this much discretion in the management of its fiscal formula, why does CED stop so far short of full discretion? Is it justified in assigning to fiscal measures an essentially passive role and to monetary measures a decidedly active role in stabilization policy? The search for an answer leads us to consider the forecasting issue, the relative effectiveness and impacts of monetary and fiscal policy, and the expenditure discipline of CED's budget-balancing rule.

III. *Economic Forecasting and Diagnosis in Stabilization Policy*

Deficiencies in our ability to forecast have loomed large in CED's case for automaticity in budget policy coupled with heavy reliance on flexible credit policy.[16] But forecasting is only one element of a broader issue. The question is not merely (a) whether forecasts of future economic conditions are reliable enough to permit discretionary preventive action but (b) whether diagnoses of current business conditions and movements should be used to guide tax and expenditure policies as instruments of discretionary remedial action.[17] CED does not eschew this "comprehensive look" at the economic situation, but, except in severe recession or inflation, it permits only monetary policy to respond to and be guided by the resulting diagnosis.

What conditions would be sufficient to make a defensible case for letting fiscal policy also respond to the "comprehensive look" rather than keeping it on a straight and narrow path with the aid of blinders attached by the CED rule? The first is that information excluded from the decision-making process under the rule would, if granted entry, clearly call for remedial or preventive fiscal action where the CED rule calls for inaction or contrary action. The second is that the information be reasonably complete and reliable.

As suggestive rather than conclusive demonstrations that these conditions

---

price level in its calculations of high-employment national income, federal expenditures, and revenues. But by 1949, it became apparent that a roll-back of prices to 1947 would involve severe tax rates and serious threats to full employment. Starting in 1949, CED has employed the current price level as the basis for its calculations. The effect of this is (1) to accept past inflation as a *fait accompli*, but (2) to assume that future inflation will be prevented by appropriate stabilization policy (or by developments in the private economy).

[16] See, for example, CED's *The Stabilizing Budget Policy* (New York, 1950), pp. 5–6.

[17] In putting the point this way, I am not unaware, first, that remedial action for current economic ills must either be appropriate to future economic circumstances or be quickly reversible and, second, that the discussion here sidesteps for the moment the question of how rapidly tax and expenditure policy can respond to the economic information and diagnosis we put at its disposal.

may be met, the following four sets of situations which seem to find counter-parts in postwar experience may be postulated. All four are presumed to occur in a setting of roughly 96 percent employment and short of the boundary line labeled "serious inflation."

1. One case combines ample capital capacity, gently rising consumer demand, and strong pressures for public, especially state-local, construction; the other combines limited capital capacity, strong consumer demand, and little pressure for public construction. The first case might well call for credit restrictions, a balanced federal-state-local budget, and some federal tax reductions or tax sharing to put more fiscal resources at the disposal of state-local government; the second suggests less monetary restrictions, federal budgetary surpluses, and less transfer of fiscal capacity to state-local government.

2. In one case the 4 percent unemployed group consists of regular members of the labor force pressing for a job, while in the other the group consists largely of people who are only loosely part of the labor force (elderly persons, housewives, etc.), and who less adequately satisfy employer needs. The second case may require more restrictive budgetary policy than the first.

3. In one case, "privately financed deficit spending on government account" (*e.g.*, business borrowing to cover construction and production costs incurred on the basis of military orders) may be large and rising as in 1951–52, in another, small and falling, as in 1956–57.[18] The former situation might call for a larger federal surplus, the latter, a smaller one, than CED's rule.[19]

4. Most cases of inflation will satisfy the traditional assumption (accepted by CED) that with stable tax rates and expenditure programs, the federal surplus will automatically grow and thereby dampen inflationary pressures. But the possibility of a disturbing alternative case has been raised by 1957 experience. In this case, the type (or stage) of inflation may be such as to expand federal expenditures for military procurement, public construction, and government salaries faster than federal revenues expand. The resulting decline in the surplus might be the signal for a tax increase if inflationary pressures were diagnosed as persistent.[20]

---

[18] For a development of this concept and statistical estimates of the magnitudes involved, see A. G. Hart, "Fiscal Policy Implications of Reductions in Appropriations for Fiscal 1958," *Fiscal Policy Implications of the Economic Outlook and Budget Developments: Hearings before the Subcommittee on Fiscal Policy of the Joint Economic Committee* (Washington, 1957), pp. 72–76.

[19] Whether one should consider such induced deficits as a manageable stabilization-policy variable or as part of the complex of developments in the private sector to be counter-balanced, if necessary, by budgetary and monetary policy depends in good part on their controllability. From Hart's analysis one may infer that while they may be controlable by military authorities, they are not likely to be controlable by stabilization authorities.

[20] To test the traditional and alternative assumptions on inflation's budgetary impact calls for analysis and, to the extent possible, measurement of the relative behavior of government resource-using expenditures, transfer payments, and various kinds of taxes under the impact of different types and stages of inflation.

On the recession side, the need for going behind the aggregates as a basis for determining the appropriate fiscal policy can also be illustrated. R. A. Gordon makes a convincing case for early diagnosis of a moderate downturn to determine whether it is (1) a "pure" minor recession calling for reliance on automatic stabilizers, easy money, and perhaps discretionary action to liberalize unemployment payments and accelerate light public works expenditures or (2) an "intermediate" or "hybrid" recession calling for the "fullest scope of the conventional instruments of stabilization policy. . . ."[21]

The foregoing discussion serves to illustrate the case, conceptually, for discretionary adjustment of fiscal policy to take account of a far broader range of information than is admissible under the CED rule. But one should also confront the forecasting issue on CED's own terms as a basis for preferring its rule to a managed compensatory fiscal policy.

First, managing even an "automatic" budgetary policy involves many explicit and implicit forecasts. To calculate revenues and expenditures under existing programs in terms of the "assumed high level of employment" requires assumptions or projections (forecasts?) of price levels, labor force, and productivity. Projection of the current price level into the future involves obvious hazards, and the jerky rate of gain in productivity (*e.g.*, fast in 1955 and slow in 1956) may make reliance on average rates of gain misleading for any given year. Even more vexing is the forecasting of federal expenditure levels, a vexation that no formula can escape.[22] Recent official budget estimates made well along in a particular fiscal year have turned out to be several billions wide of the mark. It may well be that CED's rule denies the fiscal policy-making process access to other economic variables which can be forecast within ranges of tolerance as narrow as, or even narrower than, those which apply to its budgetary forecasts.

Second, is economic forecasting as slender a reed as it appeared to be 10 years ago? No conclusive evidence is available to prove that forecasting techniques are now a thoroughly reliable basis for discretionary stabilization policy. But many new or improved forecasts of important segments of the economy, such as plant and equipment outlays, are now available. The Council of Economic Advisers does not hesitate to invoke "prospective economic conditions" as a basis for discretionary judgments to hold the line

---

[21] R. A. Gordon, "Types of Depressions and How to Combat Them," *Policies to Combat Depression*, National Bureau of Economic Research (Princeton, 1956), pp. 13–16. Gordon's analysis leads him to conclude that "Discretionary action, extending beyond the field of merely monetary policy, is necessary in all except relatively pure minor cycles" (p. 12).

[22] CED's formula involves the additional demanding problem of differentiating among (1) those federal expenditure changes which are not to be matched by tax changes, namely, expenditure responses to fluctuations in the level of income and employment; (2) those which are to be matched, namely, the increases or decreases in government programs and the noncyclical expansions or contractions of open-ended programs; and (3) those which fall under the intermediate heading of "large, temporary bulges of expenditure" no requiring fully matching tax increases.

on federal taxes.[23] Qualified observers judge our short-term forecasting record as having operated "not too unsuccessfully" in recent years.[24] Guarded optimism as to the future of economic forecasting seems justified.

Third, it does not *necessarily* follow that present limitations on our forecasting abilities strengthen the case against flexible, discretionary tax action. It can be argued, on the contrary, that these limitations should lead policy-makers to bend every effort to make tax and expenditure devices more readily adjustable to unfolding economic developments.[25] CED prefers monetary policy on this score because it can be "reconsidered, changed, and, if necessary, reversed at short intervals," while tax action tends to be slow, intermittent, and difficult to reverse.[26] More progress might be made in overcoming these defects of the taxing process if reliance on fiscal automaticity and monetary manipulation did not remove some of the pressure for action.

IV. *The Relative Roles of Fiscal and Monetary Policy*

The presumed operational superiority of monetary over fiscal policy as a flexible stabilization instrument, especially in dealing with inflationary pressure, requires rigorous re-examination in the light of six years of experience with an unleashed monetary policy and the rising tide of informed criticism based on this experience. Since the preference for monetary policy also involves "the diverse values and objectives that move men,"[27] one needs to go beyond questions of effectiveness to questions of effects.

Time Lags.   Automatic fiscal stabilizers gain strong support from their superiority with respect to the three familiar lags in stabilization policy: the recognition lag, the administrative lag, and the operational lag. Income-tax collections, unemployment compensation, and similar built-in stabilizers respond promptly to economic events which may take months for the human eye or electric brain to recognize. No legislative or executive body has to intervene to bring them into play. Automatically, the fiscal stabilizers offset between 35 and 40 percent of a change in gross national product. Yet, while

---

[23] In view of the budgetary outlook and prospective economic conditions, present tax rates should be continued . . .," *Economic Report of the President* (January, 1957), p. 48.

[24] R. A. Gordon, "Stabilization Policy and the Study of Business Cycles," *Am. Econ. Rev.*, Proceedings, Vol. XLVII (May, 1957), esp. p. 121.

[25] A. G. Hart (*op. cit.*, p. 73) strongly urges new efforts to develop speedy and reversible tax measures, including intrayear adjustments of the withholding rate, to cope with the difficulties of forecasting budget magnitudes, let alone developments in the private economy.

[26] CED, *op. cit.*, 1956, pp. 6–7.

[27] "At any given moment, policy must be based not only on known facts about the nature and operation of the economy, but also on guesses and conjecture and on a balance of the diverse values and objectives that move men," National Bureau of Economic Research, *Financial Research and the Problems of Our Day*, 34th Annual Report (New York, 1957), p. 20.

this offset to economic fluctuations is substantial, the effect of automatic stabilizers is more to cushion the shocks of recession and inflation than to set up powerful counterforces. By themselves, they constitute a "tranquilizing budget policy" rather than a truly stabilizing one.

But going beyond these built-in tranquilizers, we promptly come face to face with the issue of the relative behavior of discretionary fiscal and monetary policy in terms of the three lags. This issue, which had in the past been clearly resolved in favor of monetary policy, has been reopened on the basis of new evidence and new thinking. On the recognition lag, both policies suffer the same disability. On the administrative lag, monetary policy clearly carries the day. The basic question is whether its superiority on this score is more than offset by its inferiority in terms of the operational lag, i.e., the length of time between policy action and the effective impact of that action on the economic situation.

In fiscal policy, we are dealing *directly* with income flows, with definitive and direct action to increase or decrease them. But in monetary policy and debt management, we are dealing only *indirectly* with income flows via impacts on liquidity and asset structure. The large cushion of short-term governments in the hands of banks means that the credit reins do not tighten on bank loans until the banks have disgorged these securities over a period of many months after tight-money policies are instituted (and unfortunately for the next period of inflation, experience suggests that the short-term securities flow back to the banks in times of slack loan demand). These and other factors led Warren Smith to conclude that "the operational lag may be considerably longer for monetary than for fiscal policy, at least in many situations."[28]

Further, the administrative lag in taxation need not always be a long one. Under pressure, Congress enacted $5 billion of additional taxes within weeks after the outbreak of war in Korea and rushed through a $1 billion excise tax reduction in one month in 1954. If one were to add to the scheduled federal excise and corporate income tax reductions now on the statute books an individual income tax component, one would have on the shelf three important potential offsets to recession that Congress could put into effect in a matter of days or at most weeks.[29]

---

[28] W. L. Smith, "On the Effectiveness of Monetary Policy," *Am. Econ. Rev.*, Vol. XLVI (September, 1956), pp. 588–606.

[29] The Congress in effect created a "shelf" of tax reductions much like the "public works shelf" often urged as an antidepression measure when it legislated automatic expiration dates for some of the tax increases enacted in 1951 (previously March 31, but beginning in 1958, June 30, a date by which the validity of year-end economic forecasts and the nature of the budget picture are much clearer). The conscious development of a broader program of "on-the-shelf" tax reductions has much to commend it. When inflation threatens, the cuts could be postponed as they were in 1955, 1956, and 1957. But when an economic recession or a slowdown of economic growth faces the country, Congress could pull the tax cuts off the shelf or let them come down on the specified date. This would greatly shorten the lag between an economic downturn and positive tax action to counteract it.

Other Operational Considerations. Without going into detail one may cite other doubts and questions about the effectiveness of monetary policy that have been raised by close students of the subject. Hyman Minsky shows that restrictive central banking measures and rising interest rates generate institutional changes which increase velocity and decrease liquidity and thereby destabilize the money market. He concludes, "The asserted asymmetry of monetary policy (that it is effective in constraining an inflation and ineffective in constraining a depression) is not true; monetary policy is of very limited effectiveness both in constraining an inflation and in counteracting a depression."[30]

Relatively stable tax rates as a favorable factor in business expectations are often cited as one of the important advantages of the stabilizing budget policy. But analyses by Ervin Miller and Alvin Hansen lead to the conclusion that the upsetting expectational effects of the large fluctuations in interest rates and capital values required to stabilize the economy via monetary policy are a high price to pay for more stable tax rates.[31]

Canada's recent experience has revealed distressing limitations to the effectiveness of restrictive monetary policy. As in the United States, these limits resulted partly from sales of government securities by banks and the existence of consumer finance and other credit sources outside of the direct reach of central banking policy. In part, the desire to maintain "orderly conditions in financial markets" played a role.[32]

On recent British experience with monetary restrictions, Warren Smith and Raymond Mikesell conclude that "while some of the weakness of British monetary policy is due to peculiar features of the British economy and its monetary system, the episode is indicative of the general limitations of monetary policy."[33]

The disappointing record of recent monetary restrictionism strongly suggests that monetary policy as a curb on inflation is subject to limitations and side effects to which CED (among many others) did not give sufficient weight in determining its relative reliance on fiscal and monetary measures. If this is true, a reappraisal would logically lead to a shift of emphasis toward discretionary tax and expenditure policy unless it could be demonstrated that the deficiences of monetary policy are more amenable to correction (perhaps by selective credit controls) than those of fiscal policy.

---

[30] H. P. Minsky, "Central Banking and Money Market Changes," *Quart. Jour. Econ.*, Vol. LXX (May, 1957), p. 184.

[31] Ervin Miller, "Monetary Policy in a Changing World," *Quart. Jour. Econ.*, Vol. LXX (February, 1956), pp. 23–43; A. H. Hansen, *The American Economy* (New York, 1957), Ch. 3.

[32] Bank of Canada, *Annual Report of the Governor for the Year 1956* (Ottawa, February, 1957), esp. pp. 23–36.

[33] W. L. Smith and R. P. Mikesell, "The Effectiveness of Monetary Policy: Recent British Experience," *Jour. Pol. Econ.*, Vol. LXV (February, 1957), p. 38.

Value Preferences. Evidence on the inadequacies of monetary policy may or may not dislodge some of its advocates from their existing positions, depending on how strongly they prefer the patterns of resource allocation and income distribution (by income brackets as well as social classes) implicit in monetary controls to those implicit in fiscal controls.

The issue was pointedly drawn by Stein and Samuelson recently.[34] While essentially agreeing that we have it within our fiscal-monetary power to achieve reasonable stabilization together with the capital accumulation rate and distributive objectives we desire, they differed sharply in the uses to which they would put monetary and fiscal tools. Stein would use a "faster or slower growth of the money supply" to expand or restrict total demand, thereby allowing us "to determine both the structure of taxes and the total amount of taxes by considerations other than the desired level of total demand" and, in particular, "to choose the tax structure that imposes the least direct interference to investment without fear that such a tax structure may restrict investment indirectly by causing a deficiency of total demand."[35] In contrast, Samuelson would rely mainly on fiscal policy to control aggregate demand. To achieve the goals of high investment, substantial redistribution, and full employment without inflation, he would (1) make investment funds easy and cheap to get by low interest rates and liberal credit programs; (2) impose progressive taxes, and (3) enact tax increases to produce inflation-curbing surpluses.[36]

The important point here is not to choose between these two alternative approaches, but to make clear that they involve fundamental differences in their impact on the structure of our economy and the distribution of income among different income-size and functional groups. Among the effects of the high-tax low-interest policy, for example, would be (1) to promote government capital formation at the expense of private consumption, (2) to lower the relative rewards for less risky as against more risky uses of money, and (3) to offer a net stimulus to uses (like public construction) which could take advantage of the low interest rates without encountering the high tax rates. The opposite policy, judging by recent experience, tends to pinch particularly hard in the field of state and local construction activities, home building, and small business, without noticeably curbing the business capital-goods boom. This is not to say that one set of effects is "right" and the other "wrong." Rather, it signifies that we have an acute problem of social priorities to resolve before we can come to any consensus on the proper combination of monetary and

---

[34] Herbert Stein, "Stimulation of Consumption or Investment through Tax Policy," pp. 245–49, and P. A. Samuelson, "The New Look in Tax and Fiscal Policy," pp. 229–34, Joint Committee on the Economic Report, *Federal Tax Policy for Economic Growth and Stability*, Papers Submitted by Panelists Appearing Before the Subcommittee on Tax Policy (Washington, November 9, 1955).

[35] *Ibid.*, p. 248.

[36] *Ibid.*, pp. 232–34.

fiscal policy, and consequently, on the basic question of automatic versus discretionary tax and expenditure policy.[37]

V. *Expenditure Restraint*

Finally, the expenditure-restraining effect of the rule that an additional dollar of expenditures must be matched by an additional dollar of taxes (in terms of the agreed high level of employment) has been one of the CED policy's chief attractions to many groups. Even if the forecasting and timing barriers to compensatory fiscal action could be overcome, preservation of this disciplinary effect would involve severely limiting the scope for countercyclical manipulation of tax and expenditure rates. This raises two important questions. First, does the CED rule effectively restrain spending and promote economy in government? Second, is this restraint a good thing, *i.e.*, does it result in wiser public-expenditure decisions and a better allocation of resources between public and private use, than we would have in the absence of a balanced-budget rule?

As to the first question, we should note that the restraint exerts its force not on those who are pressing for the expenditures but on the President and Congress, whose resistance to pressures is presumably strengthened by the unpleasant political consequences of higher taxes. But one can readily perceive a number of loopholes and by-passes to this restraining effect. For many expenditure programs the initial tax consequences, which are the ones that bear most directly on the political decision, may be only a small fraction of the eventual tax requirements (*e.g.*, the "open-end programs" for farm price supports, veterans benefits, and home mortgage purchases and the large resource development programs like the Missouri basin project). Moreover, there is considerable evidence that when the tax shoe pinches, it tends to jeopardize broad but diffused-interest programs of national significance like aids for school construction or foreign economic aids while exerting little restraint on expenditures infused with a strong sectional interest. The raw pork of the annual rivers and harbors bill gets very little exposure to the heat of the tax fire.

The restraining effect of the tax test may also be undermined by sustained economic growth which automatically increases federal tax revenues by about

---

[37] Smith and Mikesell, *op. cit.*, pp. 38–39, state that "if orthodox monetary policy had been successful in checking inflation in Britain in 1955, it probably would have accomplished this result mainly by causing a reduction in the fixed investment expenditures of the private sector. ... There is more than one way to control aggregate demand, and monetary policy is not always the best way, even if it works effectively." For a discussion of distributional effects of different policies, see E. R. Rolph, "Economic Stabilization via Taxation, Debt Management, and Monetary Policy," National Tax Association, *1956 Proceedings* (Sacramento, 1957), pp. 251–57.

$3 billion a year. This "easy money" may be an open invitation to added spending.[38]

The answers to the second question are even less reassuring. Our problem may not be so much that we will fail to count the cost of government expenditures and therefore overexpand government, but that our folkways and fiscal practices tend to discriminate against collective use of resources, even where public use would represent a more efficient resource allocation than private use.[39] Our Puritan insistence on "tax directness" or "tax consciousness" may have had this type of effect. We have failed to distinguish clearly between the two elements of tax consciousness, namely, (1) making the taxpayer aware of his tax payments and (2) making taxes painful to pay. Public goods are not likely to compete on even terms with private goods if taxes are made hard to pay and if taxpayers are made more acutely aware of the tax costs than the service benefits of government.

When economic growth produces slack in the federal budget, the "tax test" does not tell us whether the slack should be taken up by increased federal programs, by increased federal aids to hard-pressed state and local units, by tax reductions to make room for state and local tax increases, or by tax reduction to put money into private pockets. To make these decisions requires a careful balancing of the relative benefits of alternative federal, state-local, or private uses of the funds, not simple reliance on the willingness to bear federal taxes.[40]

Possibly, even if the restraining effect of a balanced-budget rule is weak and often misdirected, the popular devotion to the balanced-budget dogma is so strong that fiscal policy must in some way be accommodated to it. In that case, we might be thoroughly aware of the defects of the rule and yet regard it as a lesser evil than an annually or cyclically balanced-budget rule. But there is a sharp distinction between reluctant acceptance of this rule as a least-evil solution and the implicit suggestion that it represents an optimal solution. And

---

[38] CED's members are not unaware of this problem. A footnote to CED's June, 1956, statement (p. 4) severely criticizes the stabilizing budget policy on this score. Perhaps to meet this criticism, J. Cameron Thomson, Vice-chairman of CED, paraphrased the disciplinary rule under present conditions as follows: ". . . every new expenditure program . . . should be undertaken only after the advantages of a tax reduction of similar magnitude are *explicitly* weighed against the need for the new program." "The Realities of Tight Money," an address by J. Cameron Thomson, Committee for Economic Development (New York, 1956).

[39] For example, while "extra-buyer benefits" as well as the cost criterion strongly support mosquito-control programs (estimates for area control by local governments against individual or small-group control indicate that the per-person cost of the former may be less than one-tenth of the latter), the adoption of such programs is often thwarted by the attached "mill-levy."

[40] CED's May, 1957 statement clearly recognizes this need for developing standards other than the balanced-budget test to determine the worthwhileness of public expenditures. In fact, its discussion of "How to Restrain Expenditures" (*op. cit.*, pp. 8–28) does not base itself on the balanced-budget rule at all, noting that "Even if total expenditures are balanced by receipts, any expenditure is excessive if it costs too much for the national benefit it provides" (p. 8).

in no event should the rule be allowed to serve, or even to appear, as a substitute for a positive and well-reasoned theory of public expenditures.

VI. *Conclusion*

We are all very much indebted to CED for helping to rechannel public thinking about federal fiscal policy along informed and responsible lines, for stimulating professional fiscal-policy thinking in pragmatic terms, for alerting us to the perils of indiscriminate compensatory fiscal action, and for giving us a periodic perceptive analysis of the tax and budget situation. But the foregoing review offers grounds for skepticism concerning the operational assumptions and conclusions which have led CED to assign fiscal measures an inherently passive role via the stabilizing-budget policy, reserving the active role for monetary controls. If the alternative assumptions and conclusions developed in this paper are acceptable, the practical implication for CED's fiscal-monetary policy is simply this: that its operational effectiveness as an instrument of economic stabilization can be materially improved by increasing its reliance on discretionary relative to automatic fiscal controls and its reliance on fiscal relative to monetary policy.

39

Monetary Policy and Its Critics*

By JAMES R. SCHLESINGER†

IN ASSESSING the import of the criticisms of monetary policy which seemingly have flowed in an unending stream during the last three decades, it is wise to recognize at the outset that some people simply do not *like* monetary policy. This antipathy arises from nonlogical policy judgments concerning the *suitability* of monetary restraints, but it is reflected in a continuously evolving set of charges concerning the *operation* of monetary policy. Whenever one argument appears defective, these critics readily turn to another—one which may or may not be consistent with what was previously espoused. It is this underlying emotional response which helps to explain the quality of change-ableness that has characterized the debate over monetary policy.

Much of the antagonism to monetary policy stems from its reliance on the price mechanism. A rationing process that operates through the market seems inhuman to many people, and the results are regarded as unfair or harmful. In addition, the impact of monetary policy on spending decisions is so subtle that many doubt that it is there at all. Influencing total spending by bringing about changes in the value, the volume, or the composition of the financial assets of the community strikes some observers as a mechanism too weak or too indirect to be relied upon. Thus there are doubts about the effectiveness of monetary policy as well as about its appropriateness, and, of course, legitimate doubts along these lines inevitably are seized upon by self-interested groups to attain monetary conditions more satisfactory from their point of view. Still, the genuine misgivings do raise certain issues of public policy which ought to be considered explicitly.

A substantial portion of the recent debate has been concerned not with the monetary mechanism itself but with a particular monetary policy. For example, it has been argued that the level of demand consistent with a stable price level is somewhat lower than that necessary to achieve full employment. Much of the present criticism of Federal Reserve policies consists of assertions that the System has chosen the wrong monetary goal—preventing cost inflation—

* *Journal of Political Economy*, Vol. LXVIII (December, 1960). Reprinted by courtesy of the *Journal of Political Economy*, the University of Chicago Press, and the author. Copyright 1960 by the University of Chicago.
† The RAND Corporation.

and that its attempt to influence aggregate supply conditions through its control over the money stock is foolhardy. Such criticisms do not imply that the critic necessarily distrusts or disapproves of the use of monetary controls; they are simply disagreements over details of monetary policy. To cite one prominent example, Sumner Slichter was a vigorous critic of Federal Reserve policies, yet nowhere in his writings is there any indication that he felt any doubt that some degree of monetary restraint is necessary for the proper functioning of the economy. Other observers, especially quantity theorists, have argued that the Federal Reserve is at fault for permitting rises in the price level. By the very nature of their position, such critics cannot be taken to believe that monetary controls are either unnecessary or inappropriate.

In this paper we shall not be concerned with such surface disputes over goals but with the much more fundamental criticisms of those who argue that monetary policy is, for one reason or another, *inherently defective*. Put into three general categories, these charges maintain that monetary policy is (1) ineffective, (2) discriminatory, and (3) contrary to sound social policy. Each will be considered in turn.

I. THE QUESTION OF EFFECTIVENESS

Although it is almost a truism that to question the effectiveness of monetary policy is potentially the most devastating of the criticisms, the neoclassical economists never appeared to entertain such doubts. From Wicksell to Keynes (of the *Treatise*) it was generally believed that monetary policy, by lowering interest rates and, concurrently, the supply prices of capital goods, could induce investment demand sufficient to maintain the constancy of the price level or, to stress a more modern consideration, sufficient to achieve the utilization of all factors of production. Conversely, it was. believed that a rise in interest rates would serve to deter enough marginal borrowers to contain total spending within the limits of total supply at the prevailing price level. The investment-demand schedule was assumed to be sufficiently elastic so that correct monetary policy, in the long run if not in the business cycle, would insure the absorption of full-employment savings. Yet this Age of Faith was soon to be followed by an Age of Despair.

(*a*) *The 1930's.* The deep and seemingly unshakable depression of the thirties simultaneously dragged monetary policy down from the position of honor that it had occupied and raised doubts as to whether it had any influence on spending at all. Skeptics questioned whether so minor an item in the total cost picture as a small rise in the interest rate was sufficient to alter the spending decisions of borrowers. For short-lived investments such as those in machinery and equipment, the period of investment was too brief for changes in the interest rate to have any substantial influence on costs. (Such considerations were reinforced by corporate rules of thumb which required every piece of machinery to pay for itself in some arbitrary time period.) On the other hand, it was argued that, for long-lived investments, where it is obvious that even a small change in the rate of interest will have a substantial impact on costs, the risk allowance was so large that variations in the cost of borrowing would be swallowed up by the allowance for risk. Consequently, investment demand could be considered insensitive to interest-rate variation. Of course, the abler critics, such as the late Sir Hubert Henderson, who was the guiding figure in the iconoclastic Oxford studies of the price mechanism, did recognize that there were certain long-lived, relatively riskless investments—in housing, public utilities, and public investments—which were extremely sensitive to interest-rate changes. They argued, however, that population growth in most Western nations had either slowed down or ceased entirely and that it was toward population growth that the interest-sensitive categories of long-lived investment were oriented.[1] The fact that this area of investment activity had shrunk further reduced the impact of interest-rate changes.

Empirical studies during the period tended to confirm this skeptical appraisal of monetary policy. Investigators,[2] using either questionnaires or case studies, reached the conclusion that perhaps half the firms studied paid no attention whatsoever to interest rates and that only a small minority considered them to be significant. Of course, it is necessary to make allowance for the period in which these studies were made; nevertheless, the number of relevant issues which the investigators *failed* to consider is noteworthy:

1. Since the bulk of investment activity is concentrated in the largest firms, is not the percentage-of-firms criterion misleading? Were the minority of firms that borrowed heavily and invested heavily the ones that were sensitive to interest-rate changes, as seems likely?
2. Does not the responsiveness of firms to monetary policy vary with the time and the economic climate? Consequently, will conclusions drawn in a depressed period characterized by excess capacity be applicable under other conditions—particularly periods of expansion?
3. If interest rates do not control the investment decision, do they influence the *timing* of the expenditures which follow from that decision?
4. Do interest rates affect corporate dividend policy (that is, corporate savings), thus providing non-credit sources of expenditures?
5. Are expenditures influenced by credit conditions other than interest rates or by the general tone of the money market of which the interest rate is simply a symptom?
6. Are businessmen actually able to appraise the determinants of their own decisions; is it not likely that they are constitutionally far more alert to positive inducements such as sales than to (negative) inhibitors like interest rates?

---

[1] H. D. Henderson, "The Significance of the Rate of Interest," *Oxford Economic Papers*, No. 1 (January, 1938), reprinted in T. Wilson and P. W. S. Andrews (eds.), *Oxford Studies in the Price Mechanism* (New York: Oxford University Press, 1951), pp. 20–22.

[2] See the articles by J. E. Meade and P. W. S. Andrews reprinted in *Oxford Studies in the Price Mechanism*, pp. 27–30, 51–66; also J. F. Ebersole, "The Influence of Interest Rates upon Entrepreneurial Decisions in Business—a Case Study," *Harvard Business Review*, Vol. XVII, No. 1 (Autumn, 1938), pp. 35–39.

7. Finally—and perhaps most important of all—do not investigations of this sort, which make inquiries of individual businessmen and then argue from the specific to the general, ignore the *indirect* influence of interest rates on spending decisions? Cannot an all-round process of expansion be generated from slender beginnings? If even a few businesses are induced by cheaper credit to expand outlays, may not other concerns also be persuaded to increase expenditures as their sales rise?

To raise questions of this sort is to underscore the conceptual defects of the empirical investigations. Nevertheless, at the time, these studies did tend to confirm the new analytical presupposition that investment decisions were insensitive to changes in the interest rate. Moreover, difficulties posed by the inelasticity of the investment-demand schedule were compounded by the Keynesian view of liquidity preference, which hinted that monetary policy had little effect on interest rates anyway. Even with limited demand for investment funds, the long-term interest rate, it was believed, would not fall below some positive level, say 2 percent, because the threat of capital loss at lower interest rates was so great that the public would absorb in cash balances more and more money without bidding up bond prices or lowering interest rates. Buttressed by such conceptions, dominant opinion in the late thirties in the government and in academic circles held that monetary policy was ineffective.

Nevertheless, it remains a distinct possibility that the sensitivity of invest-ment to interest-rate changes and the strength of liquidity preference may vary substantially with changes in the over-all economic climate. If we recall the influences bearing on the effectiveness of monetary policy, it seems plausible to argue that the observers of the thirties erred in generalizing from conditions prevailing in the deepest depression ever experienced. When national income has at one point fallen by almost 50 percent, when many industries are operating at 20–30 percent of capacity, when new investment is deterred by excess capacity, when no new markets are foreseen and business confidence has ebbed, low interest rates are unlikely to have much stimulative effect, no matter how low they fall. Such conditions may well be described by an inelastic investment-demand schedule.

In addition, consider the strong desire for liquidity then prevailing, the willingness of the public and the banks to hoard rather than to commit funds (the theory of credit expansion precludes excess reserves). In the period after 1929 there was a run to liquidity. By 1933 the banking system had reached a state of collapse. Many banks were forced to shut their doors because of illiquidity at the same time that the financial community was still being blamed for the speculative excesses of the twenties. Is it surprising that both the public and the banking community exhibited under these conditions a strong liquidity preference, reflected in excess reserves and in the astonishing gap between long-term and short-term interest rates?

Moreover, the economic difficulties were reinforced by political conditions that were hardly conducive to business confidence. Monetary policy attempts to influence business decisions at the margin; yet such considerations become insignificant when the social system appears to be in chaos. Labor conditions were unsettled. Businessmen, who were widely used as scapegoats, were apprehensive. Neither the path to an effective monetary policy nor the path to recovery lies in the direction of alarming those who make investment decisions. Plainly, it would be unwise to regard monetary policy as *generally ineffective* on the basis either of the analysis or of the conditions of the thirties.

(b) *The 1940's.* Financial developments of the forties provided an institutional rationalization for the skepticism concerning monetary policy, yet at the same time gave rise to the inflationary pressures which eventually were to strike the wartime chains from monetary policy. At the end of World War II, however, the heritage of control, associated with fear of the consequences of the use of traditional weapons provoked by the enormously expanded public debt, reinforced the antimonetary attitudes of the thirties.[3] Rising interest rates, it was argued, would not inhibit spending, yet would increase the cost of debt service to the taxpayer—failure to reckon the costs of inflation, of course, tended to lead to undue stress on the cost of debt service. Perhaps more important was the belief that the bulk of the debt was infirmly held and that rising interest rates would provoke a panic, in the course of which a substantial part of the debt, perhaps including even savings bonds, would be jettisoned. If, eventually, the Federal Reserve were forced to intervene to pick up the pieces, why not prevent such a cataclysm by an initial policy of support to the government securities market? Periodic Treasury refunding operations which would require Federal Reserve support were held to reinforce such considerations. These arguments were so widely accepted that for a time even the Federal Reserve System readily acquiesced in its own Babylonian captivity.[4]

In vew of the excess liquidity which characterized the postwar period, it is certainly arguable that monetary controls would have had little immediate effect, even though, as a general proposition, monetary policy is more effective in coping with inflationary pressures than with depression. There may always be an interest high enough or monetary pressure severe enough to check

---

[3] Cf. Lawrence H. Seltzer, "Is a Rise in Interest Rates Desirable or Inevitable?" *American Economic Review*, Vol. XXXV, No. 5 (December, 1945). One interesting aspect of Seltzer's article is that it contains an early expression of the belief that monetary policy remains utterly useless up to the point that it becomes potentially disastrous and that there are no intermediate effects. This view has been modified by more recent writers, but (for other reasons) it is still with us. Today it is argued that sizable interest-rate changes may precipitate a depression, but that, up to the point that it becomes dangerous, monetary policy is ineffective. Based on the presupposition that even a small rise in the interest rate would provoke a panic in the government securities market, Seltzer's formulation was far more coherent than the more recent one.

[4] See the 32d, 33d, 34th, 35th, and 36th *Annual Report of the Board of Governors of the Federal Reserve System* (1945–49).

investment demand, but, in conditions already characterized by monetary redundancy, it may not be practicable to bring this about. When anything that is bought can be sold, when inflation will justify any investment, when markets appear overwhelmingly promising, money expenditures will rise as the circulation of money increases, even though the supply be held constant. Some inflation is inevitable as a phase of the process of reducing excess liquidity. Yet, even if monetary restraint could not have dissipated the inflation potential in 1945–46, there is clearly no long-run case against monetary control. Moreover, events have demonstrated that fears of the collapse of the government securities market, understandable as they may have been in light of our lack of experience in handling so large a debt, have been excessive. The market for governments is normally stable in the sense that when some holders wish to sell securities, purchasers other than the central bank stand ready to buy. There is no *cumulative unloading* of securities but rather a *transfer* of securities among holders without the intervention of the Federal Reserve system. Nevertheless, the "loose-cargo" argument did cling curiously to life. As the years passed, the Federal Reserve System became increasingly restive under conditions such that its open-market operations accentuated, first, the inflation of 1946–48, then the recession of 1949, and then the renewed inflation of 1950–51. Yet down to the Accord of 1951 and later, a substantial body of academic opinion regarded monetary restraint as unnecessary, monetary policy as ineffective, and general credit controls as obsolete.[5]

(*c*) *The 1950's.* With the revival of monetary policy, far greater stress was placed upon the *availability* of credit as opposed to its *cost* than would have been deemed appropriate in neoclassical thought. But interest rates move sluggishly. Debt instruments are imperfect substitutes for each other. Save in the open market, lenders are subject to a sense of restraint. Consequently, it seems clear that it is more than the price of credit itself that limits borrowing. The willingness of lenders to lend is an important consideration; lenders may prefer to curtail requests for credit without increasing rates.[6] Borrowers

---

[5] Consider the comments of the various contributors to the "Symposium on Monetary Policy," *Review of Economics and Statistics,* Vol. XXXIII, No. 3 (August, 1951), at the time of the revival of monetary policy in this country and also those of the contributors to "Monetary Policy: A Symposium," *Bulletin of the Oxford University Institute of Statistics* Vol. XIV, Nos. 4, 5, and 8 (April, May, and August, 1952), when British monetary policy was revived.

[6] The new emphasis on the lender as opposed to the borrower was stressed by Robert V. Roosa as a part of what came to be called "the availability doctrine" (see "Interest Rates and the Central Bank," in *Money, Trade, and Economic Growth: In Honor of John Henry Williams* [New York: Macmillan Co., 1951]; also I. O. Scott, Jr., "The Availability Doctrine: Development and Implications," *Canadian Journal of Economics and Political Science,* Vol. XXIII, No. 4 [November, 1957]). One aspect of the doctrine upon which Roosa laid some stress was the belief that a small rise in the rate of interest might bring about a curtailment of lending on the part of conservative financial institutions. Such a rise might generate

themselves may become reluctant to borrow when they do not feel assured about their long-run liquidity position, even if they are undeterred by the cost of borrowing *per se*. It is the availability of credit that is most important, and rising interest rates may merely be symptomatic of the several forces at work during periods of monetary stringency.

In response to the renewed emphasis upon monetary policy, a third type of criticism has developed, drawing on the older arguments, yet transposing or inverting the elements contained therein.[7] Basically, it is contended that the nation's financial machinery, through the lubricating medium of the government debt, can effectively and automatically mobilize idle balances to maintain monetary expenditures whenever pressure is applied. Rising interest rates, which are a consequence of monetary restraint, supply the incentive and the mechanism through which such idle balances are mobilized. During boom periods, banks are subjected to pressure to expand business loans. As they attempt to sell bonds, interest rates rise, and this increase induces those who held idle or excessive balances at lower interest rates to purchase securities. The sale of securities by the banks frees reserves and permits the expansion of business loans. This process of replacing investments by business loans is considered to be inflationary, even though the liabilities side of the banks' balance sheets is left unaffected. The exchange of assets permits the activation of the money supply. As velocity increases, so do monetary expenditures, even though the money stock is held constant. Thus "mere" control of the money supply will not seriously limit expenditures in the short run; monetary policy is ineffective.

It is interesting to compare the ingredients of the current critique with those of the older arguments. First, it is believed that rising interest rates in themselves have little deterrent effect on expenditures—this is, of course, a necessary element in any questioning of the effectiveness of monetary policy. Second, Keynes's notion of liquidity preference has, more or less, been turned on its head. Initially designed to demonstrate that increases in the money stock would not serve to lower interest rates in depression and therefore were

---

caution in disposing of liquid assets like bills and at the same time lock these institutions into their portfolios of long-term governments on account of the reluctance to take capital losses. From the vantage point of the late fifties, it appears that this restraining influence was a phase of the transition from the kept markets of the forties to the free markets of the fifties. In recent years, financial institutions have not been at all reluctant to dispose of government securities in the face of rising interest rates.

[7] The most vigorous exponent is W. L. Smith. See his "On the Effectiveness of Monetary Policy," *American Economic Review*, Vol. XLVI, No. 4 (September, 1956); his "Monetary Policy and the Structure of Markets," in *The Relationship of Prices to Economic Stability and Growth: Compendium of Papers Submitted by Panelists Appearing before the Joint Economic Committee* (Washington, D.C., 1958), pp. 493–98; and his "Some Unsettled Issues in Monetary Policy," in *United States Monetary Policy* (Durham, N.C.: American Assembly, Duke University, 1959), pp. 14–30; see also W. W. Heller, "CED's Stabilizing Budget Policy after Ten Years," *American Economic Review*, Vol. XLVII, No. 3 (September, 1957), pp. 646–49; and L. S. Ritter, "Income Velocity and Monetary Policy," *American Economic Review*, Vol. XLIX, No. 1 (March, 1959).

an ineffective stimulus, it is now used to demonstrate that rising interest rates are the means through which monetary hoards are mobilized and consequently that control over the monetary stock in inflation is an ineffective restraint. Third, the government debt is seen not as an incubus making interest-rate variation risky but as the lubricating element in the financial structure. It is a point of historical irony that some of those who support the new criticism previously held the "loose-cargo" view of the government debt. Nevertheless, it would be folly—despite some rather abrupt changes in the positions of the critics—not to recognize that the new indictment is the most profound criticism of monetary policy yet devised, not at all dependent on the peculiarities of deep depression or the vagaries of wartime finance. There is, no doubt, some element of truth in the argument. Increasing velocity, by activating idle balances, does reduce the *immediate* effectiveness of monetary policy. But there is some limit to the increase of velocity, so that in the intermediate period,[8] at least, monetary restraint does imply the ability to limit money expenditures. The problem is how rapidly. If there is a *substantial* lag before monetary restraints take hold, then, by their nature, monetary controls may be a weak tool to *rely* upon in dealing with *short-run* fluctuations.

Even in the short run, one should recognize the limits of the argument. First, investment demand is probably more sensitive to interest rates than the critics admit, and the declining liquidity associated with the growing pressure for bank loans undoubtedly plays some role in deterring expenditures. Second, the possibility of *substantial* loan expansion through the sale of securities may have been in part a temporary manifestation associated with the high proportion of governments in commercial bank portfolios after the war. The higher the ratio of loans to total bank credit becomes, the more limited is the possibility of further expansion through exchange. Third, the effect of the long-term decline in the securities ratio on the willingness of banks to dispose of investments may be reinforced by a debt-management policy which during recession (unlike the Treasury policy in 1954) prevents the excessive accumulation of highly liquid, short-term items which serve as the basis of loan expansion on the return of prosperity. Finally, it can be argued that increasing velocity is a part of the mechanism of restraint.[9] The Federal Reserve does

---

[8] In the short run, velocity might rise because of the activation of idle balances. In the long run, in principle at least, velocity might rise because of an adjustment in the community's methods of completing financial transactions (frequency of receipts and expenditures, etc.); this is particularly pertinent in the age of the credit card. It is an intermediate period that monetary controls can take hold, that is, after idle balances have been exhausted but before the habits of the community have time to change.

[9] Since velocity is regarded as a constant, increases in velocity could not be expected to be *part* of the mechanism of restraint in a rudimentary quantity theory such as the one based on the Fisherine equation. Milton Friedman has argued, however, that in a more sophisticated version of the quantity theory one would not expect velocity to be a constant but rather to vary with interest rates (*Studies in the Quantity Theory of Money* [Chicago: University of Chicago Press, 1956], pp. 12–13). Without considering one's self a quantity theorist, one can surely accept this position with regard to the effect of restraint on velocity.

not wish to close off spending from borrowed sums but merely to encourage reconsideration of spending decisions. Unless velocity is perfectly elastic in its response to monetary pressure, some restraint will occur. Although the argument based on loan expansion and variable velocity is the most reasonable of the criticisms of the effectiveness of monetary policy, it should be emphasized that the argument does not imply any doubt concerning the necessity for monetary control; it asserts only that monetary policy should not be *exclusively* relied upon for dealing with short-term fluctuations. This position is perfectly consistent with advocating monetary restraint in boom times for the purpose of alarming potential spenders about their future liquidity positions. Monetary policy, although it should be employed, may not be *sufficiently* effective by itself; therefore, it should be strengthened and supplemented by other devices.

II. THE QUESTION OF DISCRIMINATION

The broad charge of discrimination implies that monetary restraint is unfair because of its disproportionate impact on certain categories of borrowers who either lose access to funds or else become subject to *exceptionally* onerous terms of borrowing.[10] The ordinary indictment implies that monetary restraint affects the *allocation of resources* in a way that drastically and inappropriately affects the interests of certain categories of borrowers and at the same time is potentially damaging to the national economy. Plainly, this charge is wholly inconsistent with the preceding argument, for if monetary policy can affect the allocation of resources and the volume of expenditures, it cannot at the same time be *ineffective*. Yet resource allocation is inextricably meshed with the *distribution of income*, so that sometimes the charge becomes the assertion that monetary restraint unfairly alters the income distribution. This is a traditional political refrain among legislators whose constituents include large numbers of farmers or small businessmen—the charge having overtones of "the people" versus "the interests." It is essentially a protest against higher interest rates which ignores both the change in the demand for borrowed funds and the possible costs of inflation. To be valid, it has to be assumed that those who need borrowed funds are somehow more deserving than those who supply them. Some of the current cries of discrimination do involve such a notion—consumer credit is almost a pure case in

---

[10] The most prominent proponent of this position is Leon H. Keyserling, see, *inter alia*, his statement, *January 1957 Economic Report of the President: Hearings before the Joint Economic Committee* (Washington: Government Printing Office, 1957). It has also been indorsed by J. K. Galbraith and S. E. Harris, see Galbraith's statement, *January 1958 Economic Report of the President: Hearings before the Joint Economic Committee* (Washington: Government Printing Office, 1958), and the joint communication, "The Failure of Monetary Policy," which is included. This position has also been reiterated perenially by countless representatives of affected groups.

point—yet, for the most part, charges of discrimination are concerned with the effect on resource allocation.

It must be recognized at the outset that monetary policy cannot fail to affect different citizens differently. Since it affects the availability of credit, the impact of monetary policy must be "disproportionate" in that it is asymmetrical in its consequences. Such inherent asymmetry may be traced to two causes: (1) Some institutions are more dependent on borrowed funds than are others; of those dependent on borrowed funds, some are especially dependent on bank credit, whereas others have access to other sources—that is, security markets. (2) Within the camp of borrowers, the strength of the demand will vary among the several groups. Those whose demand is not so inelastic will be unwilling to pay as high a price as will others, and consequently as interest rates rise, their share of the funds will fall. Now surely it would be trivial if those who charge discrimination had these kinds of disparities in mind. It is hardly logical to charge discrimination simply because the cost of borrowing has risen, even though those who are forced to pay higher rates are likely to be resentful. Nor would it appear logical to charge discrimination because those who use borrowed funds more than others are more damaged by increased competition (that is, demand) for such funds or a reduction in supply. (Is it contended that the available funds be allotted by some sort of parity system based on historical norms?) Nor would it appear logical to charge discrimination when those whose demand is less intense receive a smaller share of the available funds.[11] (Would it then be fairer or less discriminatory for those whose demand is less intense to share equally with those whose demand is more intense?)

Plainly, those who argue that monetary policy is discriminatory must have something more than these banalities in mind. After all, in a market *not characterized by discrimination*, one may anticipate that, with the tightening of credit, interest rates will rise most and borrowings fall least in money submarkets in which demand is most inelastic and that interest rates will rise least but borrowings will fall most in money submarkets in which demand is most elastic.[12] Any results other than these would constitute a prima facie case of discrimination. Critics of monetary policy, however, must have in mind situations in which the market does not behave in this normal way— that is, situations in which some borrowers are faced with a more-than-to-be-anticipated increase in rates or decrease in funds. Complaints of this type are put forward by, or on behalf of, five categories of borrowers—homebuilders,

---

[11] If this were not so, the charge of discrimination could be raised in behalf of any and all borrowers. When money becomes tight, some borrowers will pay substantially higher rates; all others will discover substantial reductions in their volume of borrowings. Since all pay higher rates or suffer from a reduction in funds, all may charge discrimination, according to the above logic.

[12] Those categories of borrowers who are unwilling to pay higher rates will probably not have their borrowings fall to zero because of the desire for the diversification of holdings on the part of lenders.

municipalities and state governments, small businesses, consumer borrowers, and affected industries. Each type of complaint will be examined in turn.[13]

(a) *Homebuilding.* In periods of tight money, new housing starts sometimes show an extraordinary rapid decline. For example, from 1955 to 1957— years of intensifying boom and rising interest rates—housing starts actually dropped from 1.3 million to 1.0 million per year, although housing starts had risen by some 20 percent in the preceding period of recession. Such changes may in large degree reflect the elasticity of demand for housing credit— housing is a long-lived asset, so that a small rise in the interest rate means a sharp rise in the supply price. Nevertheless, other factors may help to account for the decline—in particular, the entire fall may be attributed to the decrease in Veterans Administration and Federal Housing Authority mortgages. While government-underwritten new housing starts fell by 400 thousand units, those with conventional mortgages rose moderately by some 70 thousand.[14] Congress has set a maximum rate on mortgages, beyond which the Veterans Administration and Federal Housing Authority cannot insure. Is the sharp drop in government-underwritten mortgages a type of discrimination attributable to monetary policy? When credit grows tight, what other result could be expected than that those who are restrained by legal restrictions from bidding emphatically will be eliminated from the market? Clearly, it is the law that discriminates, implying that homebuilders should not be encouraged in an unwise inclination to sign a mortgage bearing (at that time) more than $4\frac{3}{4}$ percent interest. In any event, the charge that it is monetary restraint which is discriminatory should be dropped.

(b) *Local Government Borrowing.* During the boom, 1955–57, complaints were heard from both municipalities and state governments that they were unable to raise the funds that they needed. Despite rising demand for funds, new-security issues of state and municipal governments fell from $7.0 billion in 1954 to $5.4 billion in 1956. Yet, during the mid-fifties, interest rates rose proportionally more rapidly for municipal bonds than for corporate bonds or for United States government bonds. To put the issue another way, the

---

[13] In the discussion which follows I am very much indebted to the investigations of Harmon H. Haymes ("An Investigation of the Alleged Discriminatory Impact of General Credit Controls in Periods of Monetary Stringency" [unpublished Ph.D. dissertation, University of Virginia, 1959]).

[14] The *Federal Reserve Bulletin* provides the following data on new housing starts:

	New Housing Starts (Thousands)	Mortgages Gov't- Underwritten	Conventional
1955	1,329	670	659
1957	1,042	313	729

Since the value of construction as opposed to the number of starts fell relatively little, it may be argued that the effect of the law was to encourage the building of fewer but bigger houses.

premium which municipals had previously enjoyed over competing bonds disappeared during the same period. Is this not a case of discrimination, with both volume falling and interest rates rising sharply? The fall in volume is largely explicable in terms of the attitudes of local governments. Many municipalities have ordinances prohibiting the paying of more than, say, 4 percent on debt issues; when market rates rise, they are unable to borrow and are eliminated from the market. The same results follow in other munici- palities because of the unwillingness of officials to pay more than some stipulated rate. Apparently, the citizens in the localities have examined the intensity of their demand for local improvements and their willingness to pay taxes and have correspondingly limited their bids for funds. Consequently, during periods of tight money, the volume of borrowing falls. The reluctance to pay higher taxes may be shortsighted, to be sure, but the fall in volume cannot be charged to the discriminatory impact of monetary policy.[15]

The proportionally more rapid rise of interest rates on municipal bonds may be attributed to another structural characteristic of the market—the response to the tax-exemption privilege. As long as demand is small enough to be satisfied by the supply of funds from those who benefit sufficiently to pay a premium for tax-exempt returns, interest rates will remain low. When, however, the demand rises (as it has in the fifties) or the supply of funds from those willing to pay a premium drops, interest rates will rise suddenly to a competitive level, since the municipalities will have to pay enough at the margin to fulfil their requirements. Such results can hardly be charged to the discriminatory impact of monetary policy but rather to the evaporation of a tax feature designed to aid (discriminate in favor of) local governments.[16]

(*c*) *Small Business.*   During periods of credit restraint the accusation is invariably made that tight money discriminates against small business vis-à-vis large business. Of all the charges of discrimination, it is here that the evidence seems best to substantiate the charge. "True" discrimination—a failure of ordinary market forces—occurs when certain categories of borrowers lose access to credit, although they are willing to pay competitive rates. Large business concerns usually maintain substantial lines of credit which may normally be unused. In boom periods they will draw upon these lines of credit; so that banks may be forced to reject loan requests by small businesses willing to pay market rates or higher. In the main this appears to be a problem

---

[15] The niggardliness of local governments has come in for considerable criticism lately. The underlying notion that the citizen-consumer is foolish or misguided, although difficult to express publicly, is really somewhat different from the charge that there has been discrimina- tion.

[16] This does not eliminate the equity problem posed by the fact that certain well-to-do people have been obtaining high tax-free returns while the municipalities have not been obtaining any compensating advantage in the terms of borrowing. The justification that municipalities could get cheaper financing without dispensing much in the way of ill-gotten gains seems to have worn thin in recent years.

of small businesses located in larger communities where banks are likely to have "big business" customers. Of course, during boom periods small businesses can and do turn to other sources of credit—open-book accounts, factors, etc. Such substitutes are inferior to bank credit and frequently far more costly. Much bank credit is siphoned to small business through the accounts receivable of large business borrowers. Small businesses do get by, but this does not solve the problem posed by the fact that our financial system discourages small business, while it is public policy to encourage it. Action by the Small Business Administration and the recently formed investment companies under the Small Business Investment Act seems desirable in counteracting such tendencies.

(*d*) *Consumer Credit.* Sometimes it is argued that tight money discriminates against users of consumer credit. In fact, consumer credit rises rapidly during periods of boom (tight money) and tends to contract mildly in periods of recession, so that the charge of discrimination must relate to its allegedly unfair impact on income distribution rather than resource allocation. A leading congressional critic is fond of rhetorically informing Federal Reserve officials that they are forcing the ordinary man to pay more for his house, for his car, and for any other purchase on time. With respect to consumer credit, at least, this charge seems to be inaccurate. Interest rates on consumer credit are normally very high and rigid, some of them pressing against state maximums; the demand for this credit is highly inelastic. Thus, during prosperity, rates rise little, if at all. Because of the relatively high rates, lenders, including banks, are always ready to satisfy any demand for consumer credit. In prosperity the rise of other rates reduces the relative attractiveness of consumer credit, but not enough to divert funds to other uses. In a market in which tight money barely affects the volume of funds lent and has only a slight effect on interest rates, the charge of discrimination would appear to be at its wildest.

(*e*) *Affected Industries.* As might easily be anticipated, industries especially sensitive to monetary restraint are likely to see themselves as victims of discrimination. This is especially true of the construction and railroad industries. The late Robert R. Young, for example, was one of industry's most persistent, if not most perceptive, critics of tight money, ready to explain to interested congressional committees how many more box-cars the New York Central could have bought, had interest rates not been so unwarrantedly high.[17] On occasion similar criticisms are heard from the electric-power,

---

[17] In his statement (*Monetary Policy: 1955–56: Hearings before the Subcommittee on Economic Stabilization of the Joint Economic Committee* [Washington: Government Printing Office, 1957], p. 54), he comments: "We have slowed down the scheduling of our building of boxcars just because we cannot afford to pay $5\frac{1}{2}$ percent for money when the Interstate Commerce Commission gives us a 3-percent return. It is just that simple. . . . If the figures

natural-gas-transmission, and automobile industries as—for other reasons—
from the farming and small-business sectors of the economy. Most of such
complaints use the word "discrimination" in the sense that a general control
bears down more heavily on those sectors of the economy which are sensitive
to it than on those sections which are not, rather than that there are discriminatory standards for the several industries. It should be understood that such
complaints do bring to the surface grave policy issues. How fair is it, for
example, to help stabilize the general economy by forcing a particular industry
like housing through wider fluctuations, using monetary policy reinforced by
Veterans Administration and Federal Housing Authority controls? But, for
the most part, the policy issues raised by the affected industries verge upon the
third general criticism of monetary policy—that its results are contrary to
sound social policy.

III. THE QUESTION OF SOCIAL POLICY

Even if monetary policy is effective, even if it is non-discriminatory, it
may be argued that its consquences are in conflict with either long-run welfare
considerations or the national interest. In particular, restrictive monetary
policy operates by cutting down on investment activity and thus militates
against economic growth.[18] Monetary policy may be all too effective in
reducing what may be referred to as "social investment" and for this reason
may be less attractive than certain forms of fiscal policy. By its nature,
monetary policy is particularly effective in deterring the long-lived, relatively
riskless investment that can be considered especially conducive to progress
(business investment in plant, electric-power production, transportation,
including pipelines, and educational facilities) or conducive to social health
(housing, municipal and other public services). Even if monetary policy is not
discriminatory in the technical sense, it works by curtailing those expenditures
which are in the public interest. The affected categories of borrowers (in effect,
those charging discrimination) do not have to be protected against discrimination; they should nevertheless be encouraged in the long-run interests of the
society.

---

were reversed, we would start building; if we paid 3 percent for money and we were allowed
to earn 5 percent, we would cure the boxcar shortage overnight."

Young was, no doubt, correct in his last assessment. The problems of the regulated
industries, in which investment tends to be long-lived and riskless, cannot simply be laid at
the door of monetary policy, however.

[18] Keyserling and others have argued in these terms but have failed to recognize the
implications of the argument, in that some alternative restraint on spending must be
employed. Of those economists concerned with the growth issue, Arthur Smithies has been
most forthright and consistent in urging not only fiscal restraints but the use of selective
controls to restrict consumption (see his "Uses of Selective Credit Controls," *United States
Monetary Policy* [New York: American Assembly, Columbia University, 1958], esp.
pp. 73–81).

Reliance on monetary policy, so the argument runs, means that national resources are wasted on additional consumption goods or on "silly" investment in neon lighting and amusement parks rather than being devoted to "worthwhile" purposes. This view of consumer expenditures as superfluous is plainly at the opposite pole from the one maintaining that the defect of monetary policy is that it discriminates against the poor man who must use consumer credit to lift his standard of living, since the chief defect alleged in this case is that credit resources are "wasted" on consumption goods and other fripperies. It may readily be understood how the appeal of an argument stating that our social values are wrong and that we are not sacrificing enough for economic growth has been reinforced by concern over the menacing posture of the Soviet Union.

It is difficult not to have some immediate sympathy for this position. Our scale of social priorities may indeed be askew. Many are affronted by the current "boom psychology" and its accompanying orgy of materialism. Surely we ought not to permit credit to be wasted on consumer goods when it might be used to create additional productive capacity. Still, if this orgy of materialism is so vicious, what is the purpose of additional economic progress? Why should consumers not buy automobiles now, so that plants may be built to produce more automobiles in the future? Why should resources be diverted from washing machines to electric-power facilities at the present time, so that future generations of consumers have electric power for their washing machines? Viewed in this way, the criterion of more investment for more rapid growth becomes somewhat less compelling. Even in regard to social services, particularly those provided by municipalities, it seems perfectly apparent that the higher interest costs of new schools, new sewerage systems, and the like could be met without inducing a lower interest rate, if citizens saw a compelling social reason. The taxpayers have decided, rightly or wrongly, that they do not wish to bear the cost. Stern Galbraithian denunciations of "the unseemly economics of opulence" notwithstanding, the American people seem to like more, shiny, tasteless consumer goods. In monetary policy as elsewhere, responsibility for unsound social standards should be placed where it belongs and not attributed to the conventional wisdom of economists.[19]

Still, it may be that our scale of social priorities is distorted and that reliance on monetary policy tends to aggravate such perversions. Assuming that the American people could be converted to this way of thinking, what kinds of alternative policies seem appropriate? What remedies can be suggested by

---

[19] Economists as a group can no more be accused of discouraging the public from paying for public services than they can of urging the public to litter the national parks. (Despite the entreaties of billboards and broadcasts, the public seems to regard littering as a constitutional right, not to be compromised by the penalty of paying for the picking-up of the beer cans they have been unwilling to refrain from discarding. "The fault, dear Brutus, lies not in our stars but in ourselves that we are underlings.") Cf. J. K. Galbraith, *The Affluent Society* (New York: Houghton Mifflin Co., 1958), p. 253.

those who argue that restrictive monetary policy is inconsistent with a desirable level of social investment? Disregarding those who explicitly or implicitly argue that there are no limits to the nation's resources and all that need be done to increase production is to increase demand, it seems plain that if restrictive monetary policies are de-emphasized, some substitute method of restricting total expenditures must be employed. The likeliest choice is a more restrictive fiscal policy. If the protests against the social implications of restrictive monetary policy are to be anything more than the futile whine that it is unpleasant to have the nation's aspirations limited by its resources, those who make such criticisms must in all consistency demand more rigorous fiscal restraints, particularly those which bear down heavily on consumption. Failing in this, if the argument is to make any sense at all, it represents a plea for direct controls over investment activities (and other activities?), and, until now, the American people have given no indication that they would permit such powers to be exercised in peacetime. If one abandons general controls, there is no alternative save direct controls to rapid inflation. Selective controls, particularly on consumer spending, may ease the problem somewhat, but selective controls have in the past revealed administrative, political, and economic weaknesses that have inevitably led to their breakdown. If the argument that monetary restraint leads to undesirable social consequences is accepted, the nation must be assured that some alternative form of control will, in fact, be substituted for such restraint before it can be abandoned.

IV. IMPLICATIONS FOR MONETARY CONTROL

It should be clear that the various strands of criticism cannot be woven to-gether to form a well-meshed case against monetary policy. Each line of argument is discrete, and sometimes inconsistent with other lines. Plainly, if monetary policy is ineffective, if it has no impact on total expenditures and resource allocation, then it cannot be undesirable because it brings about an allocation of resources which is contrary to sound social policy or because it squeezes particular sectors of the economy in a discriminatory manner. Monetary policy can hardly be defective *both* because it discriminates against consumer credit *and* because it permits credit that could be used "productively" to be diverted into frivolous consumption. Much of the criticism of monetary policy reflects the desire of the critic to substitute his own judgment for what he regards to be the defective results of the market process. Since individual judgments vary widely, clearly the critics are likely to disapprove as vehemently of each other's diagnoses and prescriptions as they are of monetary restraint itself.

Any single criticism may quite reasonably be defended. Most of the more perceptive critics do confine themselves to one line of attack—that is, in-effectiveness or discrimination. Others, with much less logic, attempt simul-taneously to maintain several contradictory lines of criticism. Such attitudes can only be ascribed to the emotional, rather than the critical, faculties. Some of the inconsistencies may be attributed to the fact that the defects of monetary policy have varied with economic circumstances over the last three decades. Since the arguments have emerged fortuitously, they could not be expected to form a logical whole.[20] At one time monetary policy might be ineffective, at another it might be effective but discriminatory, etc. Nevertheless, the simultaneous employment of contradictory arguments can hardly be defended, and the rapidity with which new arguments emerged as the debate shifted over the years can be attributed to the antagonism felt by many professional and lay observers toward monetary policy.

Monetary policy is surviving the debate, albeit somewhat scarred in places. Plainly, the Arcadian view of monetary policy of the twenties has departed. Various institutional changes—the rise of liquidity, the declining importance of bank credit in the spending decisions of large corporations, the problems of debt management, and the removal of certain spending decisions from the market—have reduced somewhat the immediate effectiveness of monetary policy. But the major attacks on monetary policy have also been blunted. The technical charge of discrimination is, for the most part, fallacious, save in the case of small versus large businesses, and even here the importance should not be exaggerated. With regard to effectiveness, the extreme, depression-born doubts that monetary policy could have little influence on spending decisions have disappeared, along with the war-born refusal to use credit policy for any purpose other than maintenance of the interest-rate pattern on the government debt. What remains is a reasoned critique of monetary

---

[20] The views of Seymour E. Harris, who has frequently been a penetrating critic of monetary policy, may be one example. Over the years they have undergone various metamorphoses. In *Twenty Years of Federal Reserve Policy* (Cambridge, Mass.: Harvard University Press, 1933), he argued that monetary policy failed in the twenties because the Federal Reserve officials invariably were timid in the face of political pressure. To this theme he returned after a Keynesian interlude (*The New Economics* [New York: Alfred A. Knopf, 1948], pp. 50–51) in his comments in the "Symposium on Monetary Policy" (*op. cit.*, pp. 179–84, 198–200), arguing that it is the lack of courage on the part of the central bank rather than the weakness of its weapons that frustrates monetary policy. At various points in the argument he makes the following observations: "The problem [of monetary policy] has certainly not been one of impotency of weapons. . . . The Federal Reserve . . . is surely in a position to deny the economy the money without which a large inflation could not be carried on" (p. 183), and "monetary restraints are the easiest approach to inflation control—much less painful than more taxes or less public expenditures. . . . [T]heir atrophy is the result not of ignorance, but of the determination not to fight inflation which prevails in the country" (p. 180). In the *January 1959 Economic Report of the President: Hearings before the Joint Economic Committee* (Washington: Government Printing Office, 1959), he readily admits, though with mixed feelings, that this generation of Federal Reserve officials has not yielded to political pressure and has in his view been altogether too courageous in defending its convictions. All this is understandable. But in the communication with Galbraith ("The Failure of Monetary Policy," *loc. cit.*), he argues that monetary policy simultaneously is ineffective, discriminatory, and dangerous. How the view that tight money is ineffective can be reconciled with his views of 1951 is not made clear, nor is it explained to the reader how monetary policy can be so ineffective in dealing with inflationary pressure, yet curtail demand sufficiently to bring on a depression.

restraint, not so much a case *against* monetary control as a case *for* recognizing its limitations and its defects and for searching for alternative policies and tools. This critique consists of two parts:

1. In boom periods, monetary controls may "take hold" only after an operational lag of substantial duration. The integration of the financial community in association with the widespread holding of government securities permits rapid mobilization of idle balances during periods of pressure. A restructuring of the assets of the banking system may permit rising money expenditures through rising velocity, though the money supply is held constant. But this *does not imply that monetary control is unnecessary.* Control over the money stock is essential in the long run. Even in the short run, rising interest rates, rising velocity, and falling liquidity are all parts of the mechanism of restraint. Even if it operates slowly, monetary control operates in the right direction. At worst, all that this argument implies is that the nation should not rely upon monetary restraint as its sole instrument for combating short-term fluctuations. Monetary control cannot be dispensed with, but the search should continue for other instruments of general control.

2. Monetary restraint, as it becomes effective, may lead to results which we would not prefer on other grounds—national interests, economic progress, welfare considerations, etc. But this does not imply that monetary restraint in itself is undesirable, it merely hints that the results of alternative policies might be better. It imposes upon the critics the obligation of proposing and of obtaining public acceptance of alternative instruments of control. The use of alternative instruments may permit the alleviation of monetary restraint; it will never permit dispensing with monetary control.

From the standpoint of the more dramatic charges, the above critique is very modest indeed, representing a plea for de-emphasizing monetary pol'cy, while accepting the necessity of monetary control. Needless to say, it would not be accepted by all economists, particularly those who feel that maximum welfare is invariably obtained through the market process. For the latter, monetary policy has additional advantages in that it reflects the current savings decisions by individuals in a way that fiscal restraints cannot. Yet, supposing the critique is accepted, it is clear even then that there is a residue of monetary policy which must be used. Until such time that fiscal restraints and other alternative controls have been perfected to the point that over-all demand can be precisely controlled, there will be minimal need for monetary policy at the fringes. To argue to the contrary is to imply that fiscal policy is more flexible, less crude, than we have experienced it to be in fact—a Beveridge Plan type of utopianism. In democracies, particularly those in which authority is divided, fiscal controls have proved to be incapable of achieving a delicate adjustment of demand. Since a free economy is prone to periodic surges of spending, inevitably, in the quest for stability, a minimal use of monetary policy cannot be avoided.

Much of the public criticism of monetary policy arises from restlessness under any form of restraint, a restlessness that reflects a natural and inevitable human distress at the fact that resources are limited. Economists should try to counteract such tendencies. In order to achieve maximum impact on public policy, it is necessary that economists occasionally coalesce on fundamentals. With the exception of a few ultra-moderns,[21] virtually all economists do agree that monetary policy must be used to some extent in the attempt to stabilize the economy. True, under some conditions monetary policy may not be effective, particularly in the short run; in any given case, however, the only way to learn how effective it is, is to use it. In discussing the need for co-ordinating monetary policy and fiscal policy, economists have come to recognize that neither of these instruments is necessarily either immediately or precisely effective; that is the nature of instruments which seek to influence *voluntary* spending decisions on the part of the public. But both instruments have their roles to play; neither can be disregarded.

---

[21] It is somewhat ironical that the recent arguments that monetary policy is ineffective in the short run but potentially dangerous in the long run *because of the existence of lags* (as in the Galbraith-Harris communication cited in nn. 11 and 20) run exactly parallel to criticisms directed against discretionary fiscal policy (see Milton Friedman, "A Monetary and Fiscal Framework for Economic Stability," *American Economic Review*, Vol. XXXVIII, No. 3 [June, 1948], esp. pp. 254–58). Friedman has consistently adhered to the logically impeccable position that lags constitute an argument against all forms of discretionary authority. But many of those who currently criticize monetary policy on the basis of lags can hardly be described as skeptics about discretionary *fiscal* policy. To me, it appears true that lags do complicate the work of using either the fiscal or the monetary instrument and place limits on the effectiveness of both. This represents, however, an argument for greater flexibility rather than the abandonment of either instrument. That is tantamount to throwing out the baby with the bath water.